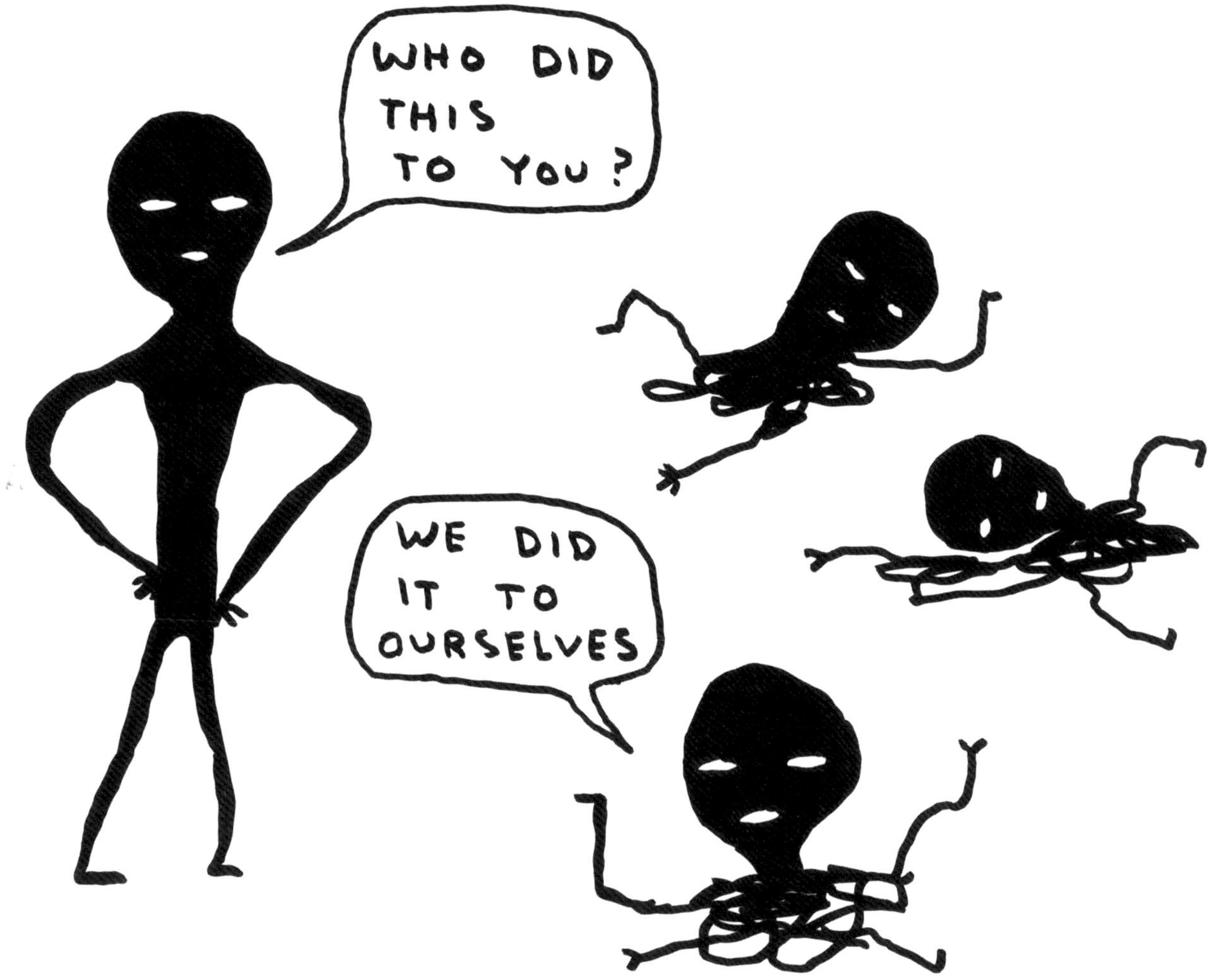

David Shrigley, Untitled (Who did this to you?), 2019

LEAVE TO REMAIN

A SNAPSHOT OF BREXIT

Noni Stacey

LUND HUMPHRIES

First published in 2023 by Lund Humphries

Lund Humphries
Huckletree Shoreditch
Alphabeta Building
18 Finsbury Square
London EC2A 1AH
UK

www.lundhumphries.com

ISBN: 978–1–84822–589–3

A Cataloguing-in-Publication record for this book is available from the British Library.

Cover: Led By Donkeys

Copy edited by Pamela Bertram
Designed by Jacqui Cornish
Proofread by Patrick Cole
Cover design by Mark Thomson
Set in Circular and Unica77
Printed in Bosnia and Herzegovina

MIX
Paper | Supporting responsible forestry
FSC® C118234

Contents

Chapter 1

Dissent, protest and resistance amid the 'sunlit uplands'

This is a work of personal protest. I'm not shouting in the street, so I am not liable to arrest under the new law outlawing protest in the UK.[1] The research for this book involved gazing at the entrails of Brexit: it was in part insalubrious, occasionally funny, sometimes fantastical, quite often mildly depressing. If the tone seems temperate, that is because the combined wealth and might of those involved precludes me from being more forthright. I am minded to avoid scorching missives from top law firms and evade the clutches of reputation managers acting for non-domiciled, right-wing press barons. These men – citizens of everywhere, who do not live permanently in the UK – promoted Brexit. It was at times difficult to keep despair and anger at bay. This much I know – that with Brexit now baring its rotten teeth all the while, the rupture with our European neighbours and partners cannot endure.

In the dog days of summer 2022, during the Conservative Party leadership campaign, Rishi Sunak said he would embolden the Prevent programme, a component of the government's counter-terrorism strategy, to include those who 'vilify' the UK. This would now include any dissenter who is not a fledgling terrorist, but who holds up an anti-monarchy sign.[2] As I write this, a woman who held up such a sign in Edinburgh during the Accession Proclamation for the new king has been charged with a criminal offence.[3] This is one measure of the authoritarian turn crouching on the back of Brexit from those who turn to the law to stifle protest and then, conversely, show a blatant disregard for the law and human rights in other ways. And it is extraordinary that those who champion sovereignty have, on occasion, evaded the ruling and scrutiny of parliament and parliamentary committees by not turning up. Dominic Raab and Priti Patel pulled out of committee hearings in July 2022.[4]

In June 2022, a UK parliamentary committee warned of this turn to the right:

> New policing powers risk creating a hostile environment for peaceful protestors, the Joint Committee on Human Rights warns in a report published following legislative scrutiny of the public order bill. Designed to combat disruptive protests, the draft legislation would instead have a 'chilling effect' on the right to peaceful protest, putting fundamental democratic rights at risk.[5]

So, this work is in part a manifesto, a call for a return to working relations and trade with our closest neighbours, and a survey of some of the artistic statements of protest and resistance around the Leave and Remain campaigns. To the sound of crunching gears as Brexit stalls, these documents – these interviews and these works of art and protest – constitute an archive of resistance.

In 2021 Professor Alexander Stubb, director of the School of Transnational Governance at the European University Institute in Florence, Italy, and former prime minister of Finland, wrote in a tweet: 'Really sad to see what #Brexit is doing to a country that used to be great. Brexit is the biggest mistake a modern nation has inflicted on itself in recent history. Hope to see an end to this mess.'[6] This statement is a starting point and, as such, is a challenge to the omertà that has smothered debate around Brexit since the EU referendum on 23 June 2016. With the exception of the Scottish National

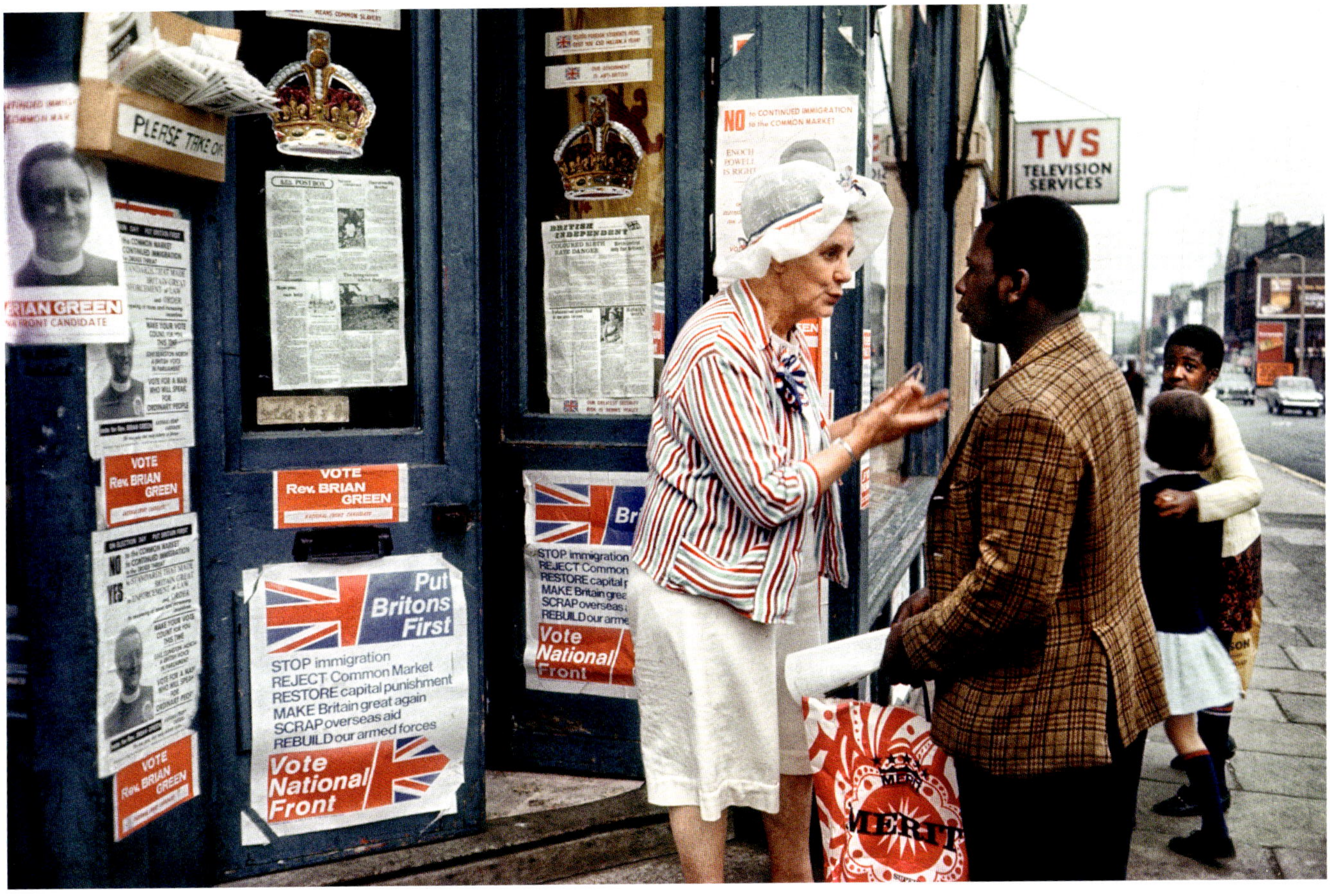

1 Romano Cagnoni, National Front office and campaigner (on left), London, 1971

The National Front was formed in 1967 as a result of the merger of three far-right groups – the League of Empire Loyalists, the British National Party and the Racial Preservation Society.

Party, the avoidance of debate has been evident across the political spectrum, much of broadcasting and some parts of the press. So omniscient is the fear that the political base for the populist Brexit will be enraged that it must now not be mentioned, and so pervasive is the concern among broadcasters that the government will muzzle them in some way, that avoidance has become a strategy. In summer 2022, broadcasters who had shied away from attributing to Brexit any detrimental effects on trade, travel and more, began, somewhat gingerly, to speak out. But even as criticisms of Brexit began to creep into the news agenda in a way that they had not before, suggestions that the British government was planning to open negotiations with the EU brought forth a volley of denials from hard-line Eurosceptics.[7]

This is in keeping with a Tory government that abhors scrutiny. It seems absurd, given the catastrophic economic consequences for the economy, and the instability and encroaching uncertainty experienced by Europeans who have made their lives in Britain. In a democracy, every political decision may be overturned, every vote challenged. The referendum was a chimera in that the Leave campaigns were rooted in lies. Brexit has not been 'done' and there is no endpoint in sight. So, it is refreshing to hear Stubb navigate the complexities of European politics cogently and in the spirit of collaboration and debate. It is also affirming to hear European politicians talking about the EU, free of the hysteria of Brexiters regarding 'sovereignty'. And, for me and many others who have left the UK, it is a relief to be in Europe with

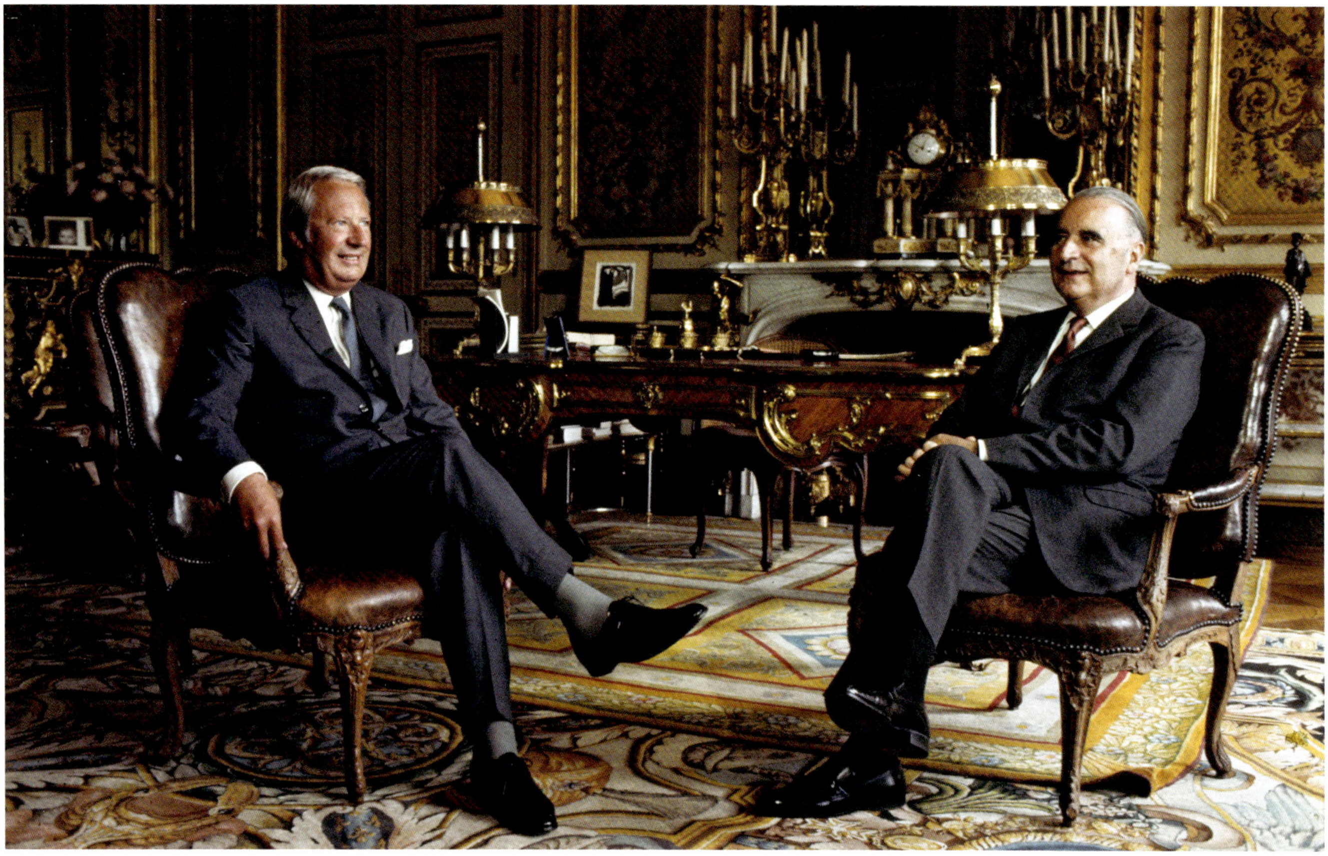

2 Prime Minister Edward Heath and President Pompidou at their press conference after their meeting at the Elysée Palace in Paris in May 1971. © Keystone-France/GAMMA RAPHO

> together succeed in the negotiations now begun 'then as Sir Winston Churchill said there will be no limit to the happiness, to the prosperity and glory which Europe's people will enjoy'.[18]

This archival research has revealed an uncanny sense of things not changing: whether it be the articulation of concern about the USSR and China, as threats both to each other and everyone else; mounting anxiety about the depletion and supplies of natural resources in oil and gas; food security; and on the local front, housing, transport and strikes by workers seeking to preserve their jobs or improve their poor working conditions.

A contemporary take on sovereignty comes from Sylvie Bermann, who was French ambassador to London from 2014 to 2017. In her book *Au Revoir Britannia*, Bermann concludes that Brexit has been catastrophic for Britain. Given the silences over Brexit, it is refreshing to hear someone speak truth to power from a position of knowledge and experience and without fear or favour.[19] On sovereignty alone she is adamant: France is sovereign, Germany is sovereign, but EU countries work together. *Au Revoir Britannia* eviscerates a Leave campaign built on lies (for example, the claim plastered on the Leave campaign bus: 'We send the EU £350 million a week, let's fund our NHS instead').

Simon Kuper's book, *Chums: How a Tiny Caste of Oxford Tories Took Over the UK*, outlines the conditions for Brexit and shows how the linchpins of the campaign emanated from the arcane institutions of the University of Oxford and its debating society, the Oxford Union, before making their frictionless entry into the House of Commons (fig.3).[20] Having previously not known how the Oxford Union worked as a feeder for parliament, or much about the pivotal Leave campaigners and players, Boris Johnson,

Daniel Hannan, Patrick Robertson, Michael Gove and Dominic Cummings, this vexed me. It seemed to me that the campaign represented little more than a game, one in which Britain must engage in battle with the EU, while few outside the group knew the rules. As Kuper shows, all were schooled in the skill of rhetoric, which privileged steering debate over facts. This singular path of education imbued a sense of overarching confidence while constructing the architecture of Brexit. Facts were deemed inessential, and opponents could be derided and diminished.

Kuper cites Margaret Thatcher's speech to the College of Europe – 'The Bruges Speech' – of 20 September 1988 as a point of divergence from formerly Euro-positive views. Thatcher was responding to Jacques Delors, the president of the European Commission, who urged Britain's labour unions to adopt a 'uniquely European model of society', replete with 'guaranteed social rights'. She said: 'We have not successfully rolled back the frontiers of the state in Britain, only to see them reimposed at European level, with a European super-state exercising a new dominance from Brussels.'[21]

Thatcher's speech triggered the swaggering Oxford Tories who would later give birth to Brexit. Kuper writes:

> Her speech spooked the Oxford Tories. Ruling Britain was the prerogative of their caste. They didn't want outsiders in Brussels muscling in. Tory 'Euroscepticism' began in part as a jobs protection scheme, much like taxi drivers fighting back against Uber. And to some degree, Oxford public schoolboys had come to think of the country they ruled as their own caste writ large. Nobody told Britain – even postwar Britain – what to do.[22]

The French journalist and broadcaster Agnès Poirier, in her review of Kuper's book, said that France is not immune to elite institutions: it is just that they have a different tenor and operate in a different register, characterised by seriousness and hard work as opposed to the banter and cavorting of these Oxford students.[23] It is not possible to reproduce the original photograph of the Bullingdon Club at Oxford University that shows Boris Johnson and David Cameron as members. The Oxford portrait photographers Gillman & Soame, which holds the copyright, withdrew permission to republish it shortly after it first appeared in the *Mail on Sunday* (2007). Gillman & Soame responded to my reproduction request as follows: 'Unfortunately we are unable to approve this without the approval of those featured in the photograph. We do not make our photographs available in this way unless featuring and requested by the author.'[24] When the then BBC *Newsnight* journalist Michael Crick had come up against this problem, he commissioned an artist to paint the photograph (fig.4).[25]

Rona Marsden was the Oxford-based painter and gallerist commissioned by Crick. She completed the painting in 24 hours, and it was taken to the studio for the programme while the canvas was still wet. How does she feel about the Bullingdon Club? 'I think that university clubs are fine, but this particular club was elitist and behaved very badly.

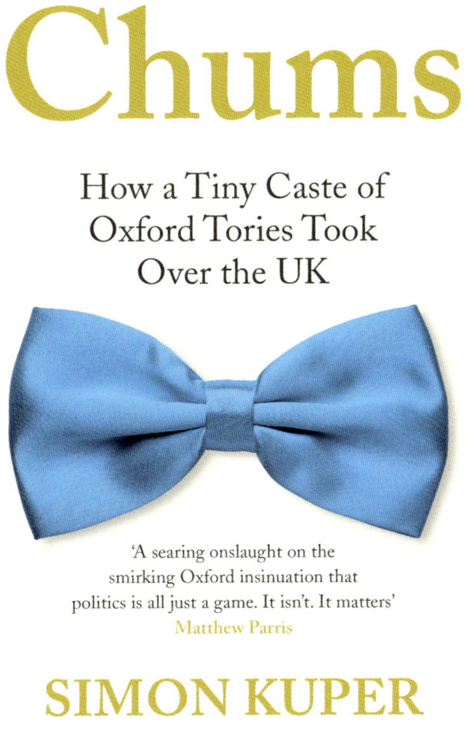

3 Simon Kuper, in *Chums*, illustrates how Oxford University, and the friendships and worldviews it created, have shaped modern Britain. Published by Profile Books, 2022

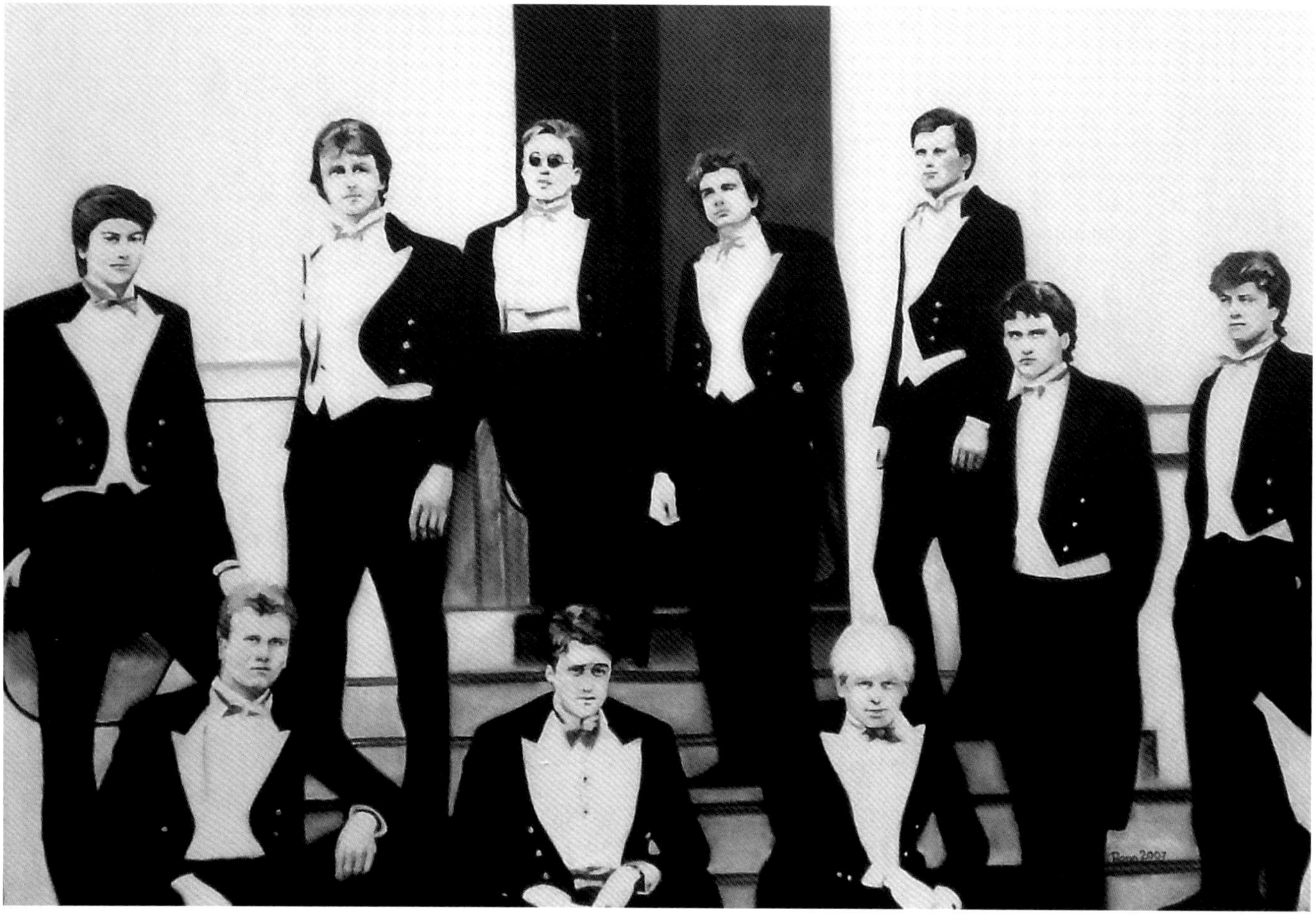

4 Rona Marsden, *Bullingdon Club*, 2007, oil on canvas

BBC Newsnight *commissioned this painting to evade copyright restrictions on the reproduction of a photograph of the Bullingdon Club.*

The significance of this image is that two people in the photo [Cameron and Johnson] were prime ministers from this privileged class.'[26]

In June 2022, Daniel Hannan, both a Leave campaign organiser and a British MEP for 16 years, voiced regret about the UK leaving the EU single market, complaining that the 'total freedom' promised by Brexit has not been realised, among other things.[27] He reiterates the line that it would be 'madness' for Britain to return to the EU single market, and rebuffs any responsibility for anything not going well, because Brexit opportunities have been thrown by the wayside, and the 'complete autonomy' – note the freedom mantra again – has not been enjoyed. 'Brexit could have created a freer, more prosperous and more global Britain. Instead, we are pursuing semi-socialist economic policies, which poll well in the short-term, but condemn us to long-term poverty.'[28] Daniel Hannan is now in the House of Lords, elevated there by Boris Johnson in 2020, despite previously calling the members of the House of Lords 'inconsequential nobodies'.[29]

In a response to Kuper's book, Mike Savage, professor of sociology at the London School of Economics, said his research data showed that Oxford University's Brexit cohort could not easily be reproduced now, given that there is now a greater percentage of state-educated students at Oxford and a much larger intake of international students.[30] In this way, the elite universities have become international universities, he said. Jane Gingrich, professor of comparative political economy at Oxford University, articulated a changed and changing world at the university where students work harder, show an interest in the social implications of their studies and slackers are barred. So, the mores of the Oxford Union in the 1980s are no longer supported. The antics of the Bullingdon Club, of which Johnson, Cameron and former chancellor George Osborne were keen members, would no longer be tolerated: yet Johnson behaved in Number 10 for all the world like a person whose [mis]behaviour had no consequences. He continued to be evasive with the truth and avoid answering questions in the House of Commons, and his capacity for dismissive banter remained undiminished.

In one respect, Oxford has not changed that much – it is still a city with marked social and economic inequality. To my mind, the elite who forged Brexit will never relinquish their grip on power through Britain's institutions; power will be taken from them gradually through evolving entry requirements to universities, lower costs and greater accessibility. Wealth is the driver that opens doors everywhere (think oligarchs), so cultural and economic capital will buoy these elites in whichever country they live.

Patrick Robertson, founder of the Bruges Group, and ardent supporter of Brexit through his WorldPR company, founded Sock!t, a technological platform for people to 'express their binary choices on any topic accurately' and which his bio on WorldPR calls an 'invaluable tool to help address the growing challenge of flawed or contradictory datasets'.[31] The slogan from Brexiters about the money that would flow to the NHS after Brexit – with the sum of £350 million that was plastered on the side of the bus – escaped the forensic examination of Robertson's invaluable tool. One campaign that he champions is Global Britain, brimful of the promises of Brexit: 'Leaving the EU and shedding the weight of many of its restrictions will help unleash a new tiger economy no longer trapped in the regulatory orbit of the European Commission. Global Britain is already spreading its wings by forging closer economic and security links with traditional allies such as the US, Canada, Australia and New Zealand.' And so it goes on, in the language of victimhood entwined with calls for victory that is adopted by Brexiters whenever referring to the EU. This extraordinary belief that the EU has kept Britain in chains is explored in *Britannia Unchained: Global Lessons for Growth and Prosperity* (2012), another key text that framed the debate around Brexit. In this book, Elizabeth Truss, Kwasi Kwarteng, Dominic Raab, Priti Patel and Chris Skidmore bemoan lazy workers in Britain and display an admiration for Libertarian regimes. All but one of the writers were members of Boris Johnson's cabinet in 2019. Chris Skidmore attended cabinet. This is not one of the books Skidmore mentions writing on his web page.[32] And we know how it went with former prime minister Truss and former chancellor Kwarteng and the 'mini budget'. In contrast, Margaret Thatcher had a respect for parliament and the legal system and an eye for detail that distinguishes her from some of her admirers; she espoused Europe and even sported an EEC-inspired sweater during the 1975 campaign to remain in the EEC (fig.5).

President Pompidou shed light on unease between France and the UK and Germany in the EEC. In November 1973 he travelled in a car with Edward Heath from Heathrow Airport, London, to Chequers, the country house of the prime minister, and mentioned a poll published in *Le Figaro* about French and British attitudes to Europe. The Minutes of the Meeting record:

> He [Pompidou] had been struck in particular by a response to a question asking which member country of the Community was considered to be the most determined to protect its own national interest. A substantial majority of those polled in France had replied 'Britain': and an equally substantial majority polled in Britain had replied 'France'. This seemed to him to illustrate the national attitudes in each country towards each other. The prime minister [Heath] commented that it perhaps exemplified the respect which the people of each country had for the other. M. Pompidou added that Germany was not far behind in the opinion of those polled.[33]

Here follows a snapshot of the London School of Economic's Brexit Collection: a selection of campaigning leaflets from the 1975 and 2016 referendums (figs 7–15). This collection shows that the earlier literature is wordier, albeit with very basic graphic design (this was the era of cut-and-

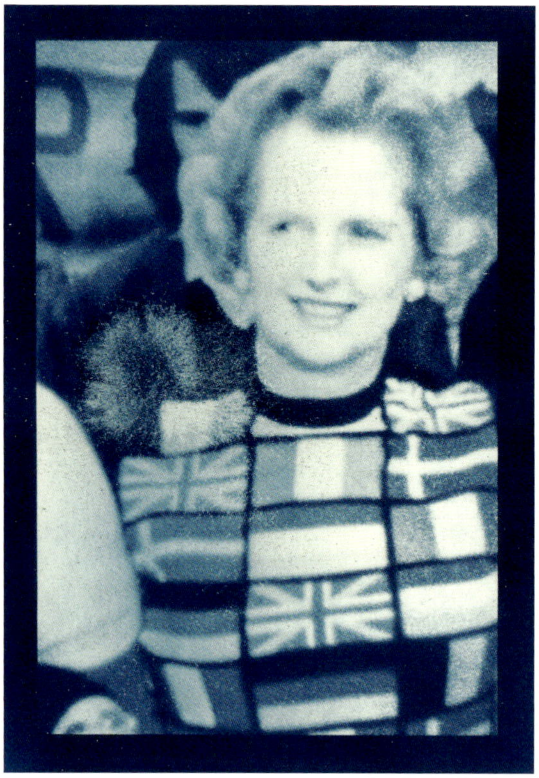

5 Norman Behrendt, 'Margaret Thatcher sports a pro-Europe jumper which bears the flags of European nations during her "Yes to Europe" campaign in the 1975 referendum', from *Blueprint 2017–2020*, Kult Books, 2021

paste and typewriters), while the 2016 material is sharper, slick with slogans and promises. The 1975 campaign literature shows it was big on statements, trammelled allegations and, in some cases, explicit racism. And in 1975, the Federation of Conservative Students rooted to stay in the EEC in a poster proclaiming that 'Europe helps the world', with a photograph of a clearly identifiable young child of colour being examined by a white doctor or nurse. Photography ethics preclude the republication of this image, which shows no regard for the privacy of this child during a medical examination.

The anti-European racism continues and was evident following delays at Dover in the summer of 2022, with anti-French remonstrations pouring from media outlets – mostly from right-wing newspapers, broadcasters and commentators.

Catherine Fieschi's book *Populocracy, The Tyranny of Authenticity and the Rise of Populism*, looks at the phenomenon that drove Brexit and other populist movements. Fieschi's research started with a PhD, and her interviewees included, among others, Jean-Marie Le Pen, leader of the far-right populist movement Front National in France. In the summer of 1996, Fieschi interviewed Le Pen at the European Parliament, where he occupied a bare desk as an MEP, and 'where no one wanted anything to do with him'. During her first encounter, he would 'sing, dance, laugh and flirt. And lie.' This lying became a constant whenever she met him: it was a strategy for him, as it would become for others:

> The lies which he instinctively told, his manner of recounting a story in ways in which fact, half-fact and fiction collided, would become the modus operandi of a whole generation of populist politicians. Over time, his successors in liberal democracies would grow to develop a fine line in this sort of behaviour, in contexts and with citizens who would be increasingly ready to forgive them and even to reward them for it.[34]

We may recall Sarah Palin, vice presidential candidate to John McCain's Republican nominee in America, and Italy's president, Silvio Berlusconi, who most surely put the party into Italian politics. On the whole, these figures engendered simultaneous amusement and horror, and their appearance on the public stage was viewed as an aberration rather than an incipient threat to democracy. This changed, however, with Donald Trump and his colleagues and supporters (who sought to usurp the 2020 presidential elections), Brazil's Jair Bolsonaro and Viktor Orbán in Hungary, and Johnson and the Leave campaigners. Anger and fear have supplanted derision around these figures who would go on to bend democratic electoral processes to breaking point.

Fieschi's analysis shows that populism feeds off a complex interaction of economic and cultural deficits – markets crashing, globalisation and immigration – which is in turn stoked by social media, simplistic slogans and distrust of elites.

Fieschi calls for an integrated policy to tackle ingrained inequality and those undercut by economic slumps, deindustrialisation and austerity:

> It is time to reconcile the cultural and economic explanations – each only makes sense in the context of the other. Privileging one explanation over the other leads to unrealistic expectations: that full employment will be enough to make people feel valued, or that curtailing immigration will be enough to restore their sense of belonging. Neither of them ever works on its own. And while governments address one, populist parties instrumentalise the other.[35]

This toggling between the two has always been evident in the run-up to and aftermath of Brexit, the topic of immigration and a concomitant effect on employment and jobs holding the front page of right-wing newspapers. Yet it has played out in a different way as EU workers who had found a place in Britain's economy packed up and went home. Immigration and migration, often couched in racist terms, runs through the political posters and pamphlets in the LSE archive. It is interesting to note that in both referendums, major trade unions voted to stay out of the EEC and later the EU.[36]

So, populism means different things to different people but feeds off discontent and a sense of disenfranchisement and a refusal of democratic norms. What is evident is the theme of superannuated national pride that runs through the afterlife of Brexit. Flags were evident before but now they are ubiquitous, like dictators with their accompanying floozies. The UK government has issued a directive:

> Flags are a very British way of expressing joy and pride – they are emotive symbols which can boost local and national identities, strengthen community cohesion and mark civic pride.
>
> The government wants to see more flags flown, particularly the Union Flag, the flag of the United Kingdom. It is a symbol of national unity and pride. The government has recently issued guidance encouraging the flying of the Union Flag on all UK government buildings throughout the year, alongside other national and local flags. We are keen for local authorities and other local organisations to follow suit. We have made it easier for the Union Flag to be flown alongside other flags, so organisations can highlight their local identities, as well as their national identities, and celebrate special days or events which champion civic pride.[37]

The repeated use of the words 'pride' and 'identity' makes me wonder how people survived before this surfeit of flag-waving and in what ways they felt deprived, and whether someone who chooses not to display a flag as directed will automatically be categorised as unpatriotic. It also reminds me that the word 'pride' means different things to different people.

In the Netherlands the impact of Brexit in terms of trade and culture has been huge. British companies have been relocating to the Netherlands so that they can continue to trade

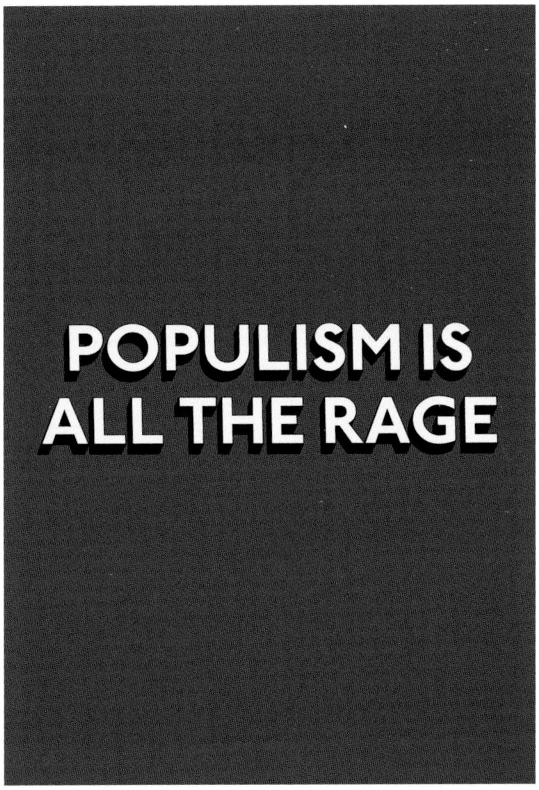

6 Tim Fishlock, *Populism*, 2019

Fishlock's work is reductive and true. It strikes at the heart of populism, with its fusion of rage, political ambition and a refusal of democratic norms.

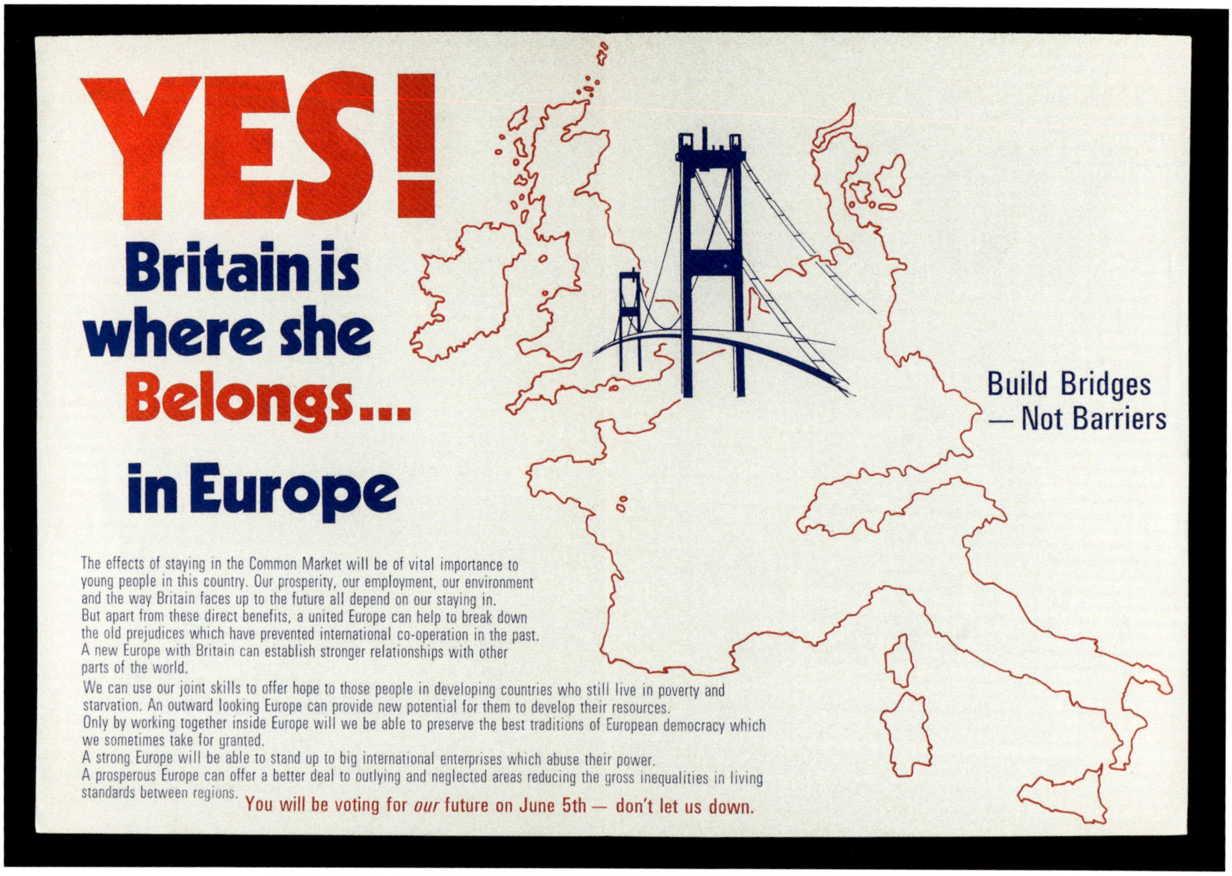
YES!
Britain is where she Belongs...
in Europe
Build Bridges
— Not Barriers
The effects of staying in the Common Market will be of vital importance to young people in this country. Our prosperity, our employment, our environment and the way Britain faces up to the future all depend on our staying in.
But apart from these direct benefits, a united Europe can help to break down the old prejudices which have prevented international co-operation in the past.
A new Europe with Britain can establish stronger relationships with other parts of the world.
We can use our joint skills to offer hope to those people in developing countries who still live in poverty and starvation. An outward looking Europe can provide new potential for them to develop their resources.
Only by working together inside Europe will we be able to preserve the best traditions of European democracy which we sometimes take for granted.
A strong Europe will be able to stand up to big international enterprises which abuse their power.
A prosperous Europe can offer a better deal to outlying and neglected areas reducing the gross inequalities in living standards between regions.
You will be voting for *our* future on June 5th — don't let us down.

7

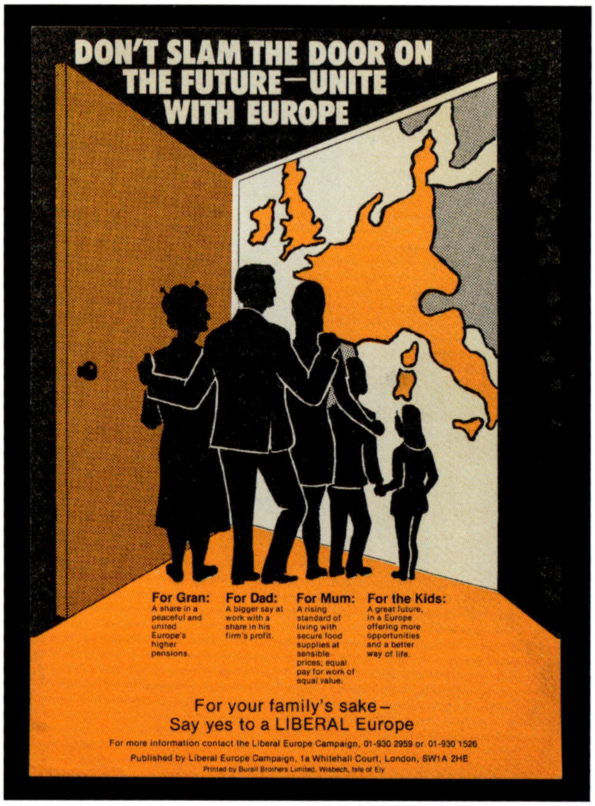
DON'T SLAM THE DOOR ON THE FUTURE—UNITE WITH EUROPE
For Gran: A share in a peaceful and united Europe's higher pensions.
For Dad: A bigger say at work with a share in his firm's profit.
For Mum: A rising standard of living with secure food supplies at sensible prices; equal pay for work of equal value.
For the Kids: A great future, in a Europe offering more opportunities and a better way of life.
For your family's sake –
Say yes to a LIBERAL Europe
For more information contact the Liberal Europe Campaign, 01-930 2959 or 01-930 1526
Published by Liberal Europe Campaign, 1a Whitehall Court, London, SW1A 2HE
Printed by Burall Brothers Limited, Wisbech, Isle of Ely

8

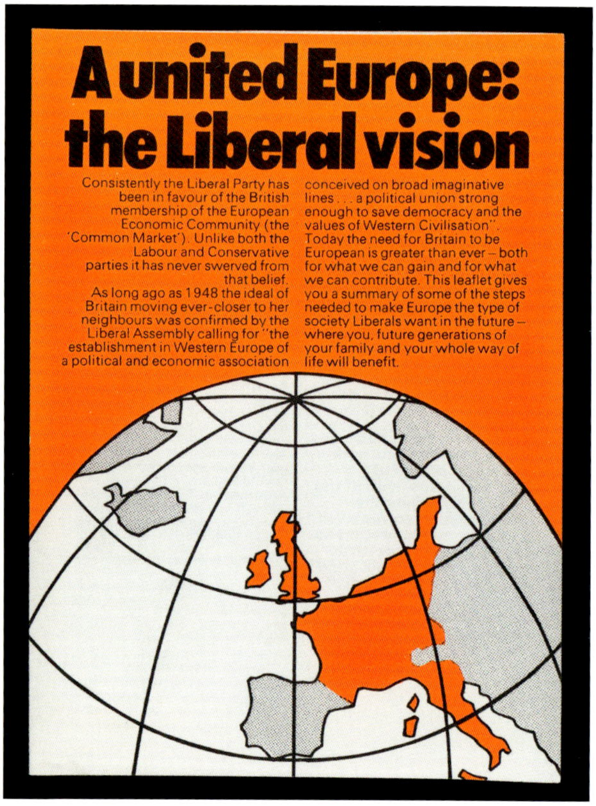
A united Europe: the Liberal vision
Consistently the Liberal Party has been in favour of the British membership of the European Economic Community (the 'Common Market'). Unlike both the Labour and Conservative parties it has never swerved from that belief.
As long ago as 1948 the ideal of Britain moving ever-closer to her neighbours was confirmed by the Liberal Assembly calling for "the establishment in Western Europe of a political and economic association conceived on broad imaginative lines . . . a political union strong enough to save democracy and the values of Western Civilisation".
Today the need for Britain to be European is greater than ever – both for what we can gain and for what we can contribute. This leaflet gives you a summary of some of the steps needed to make Europe the type of society Liberals want in the future – where you, future generations of your family and your whole way of life will benefit.

9

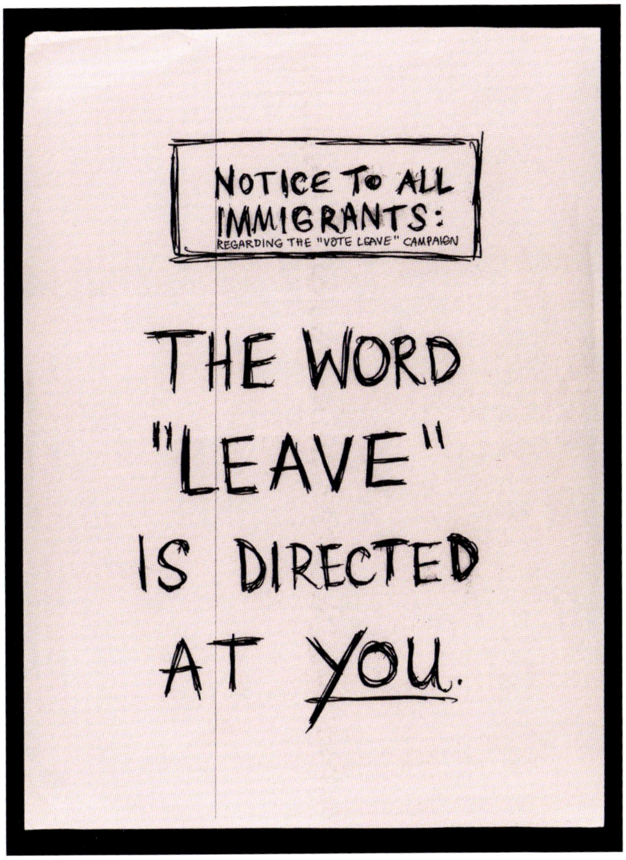

10

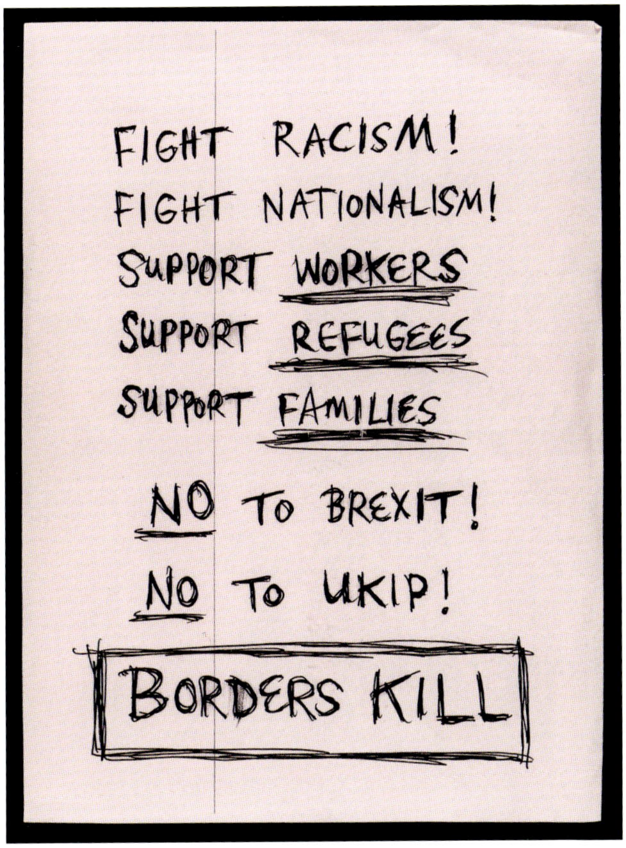

11

pages 16–19

7–15 A collection of campaigning leaflets from the 1975 and 2016 referendums on the UK's membership of the Common Market and European Union; the leaflets are from a variety of individuals, political parties and organisations active during both campaigns.

GUNS OR BUTTER

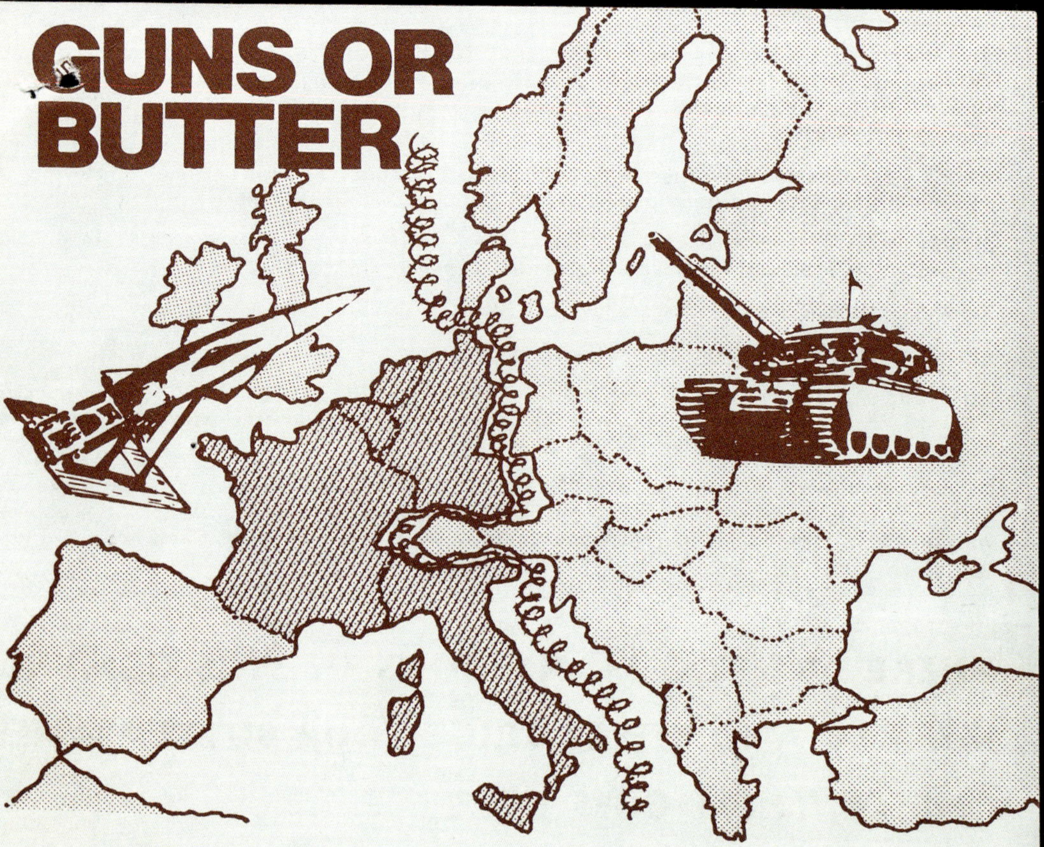

HAVE YOU DONE YOUR MARKET RESEARCH?

The Debate You have heard and read a lot about the advantages and disadvantages for trade, for prices and employment; about butter, fish, sugar, all matters of importance to the life of every family, to the farmer, fisherman and industrial worker in far-off lands as well as in Britain.

But . . . the far-reaching and more dangerous military and political consequences of Britain remaining in the Common Market are not discussed. Yet these will affect our future and the future not only of Western Europe, not only the whole of Europe, but the future of world peace, a great deal more seriously than the price of consumer goods or the standard of life in Britain.

LABOUR, LIBERAL OR CONSERVATIVE GOVERNMENT—it will make no difference. . . . "common policies and common action, not only in economic affairs but also in foreign policy . . ." are to be the rule between the member countries. Western Europe intends . . . "to re-establish collective defence arrangements against threats from outside . . . to prevent future wars. . . ."

DIVIDE AND RULE This method, an old British favourite, has been tried again and again throughout our history. In the end it has always failed. *NOW, THE PLAN IS TO DIVIDE EUROPE INTO TWO, EVEN MORE DECISIVELY THAN AFTER THE LAST WORLD WAR.* As each frontier goes down a stronger one is raised between East and West. A power bloc is created, tensions increase, and the East European countries will be threatened. The armaments race will increase the fears and the real dangers of war.

This involves a common foreign policy, a common trade policy and a common military policy. To this, Britain signs on for life. Government becomes increasingly remote from the man in the street and more and more decisions will be taken out of the hands of your own Member of Parliament.

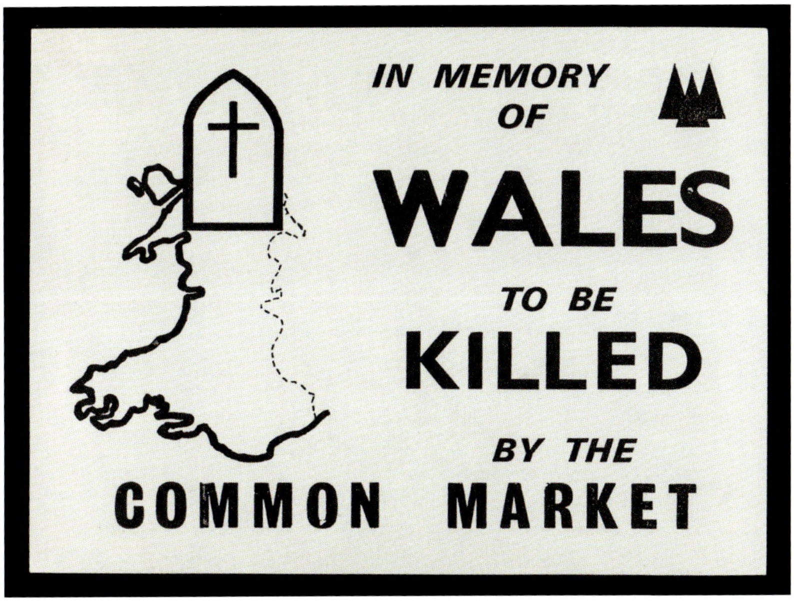
IN MEMORY
OF
WALES
TO BE
KILLED
BY THE
COMMON MARKET

13

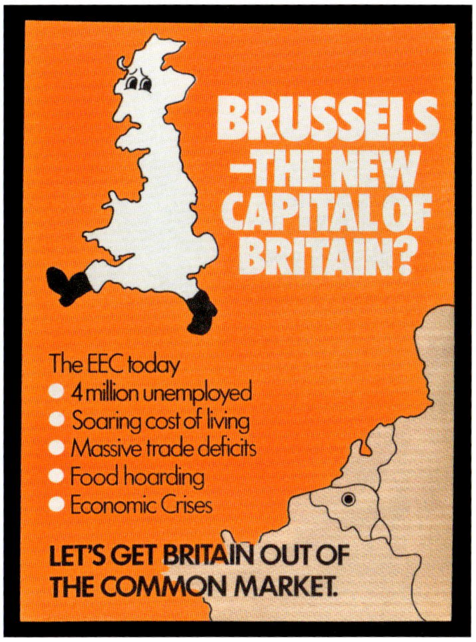
BRUSSELS
–THE NEW
CAPITAL OF
BRITAIN?
The EEC today
4 million unemployed
Soaring cost of living
Massive trade deficits
Food hoarding
Economic Crises
LET'S GET BRITAIN OUT OF
THE COMMON MARKET.

15

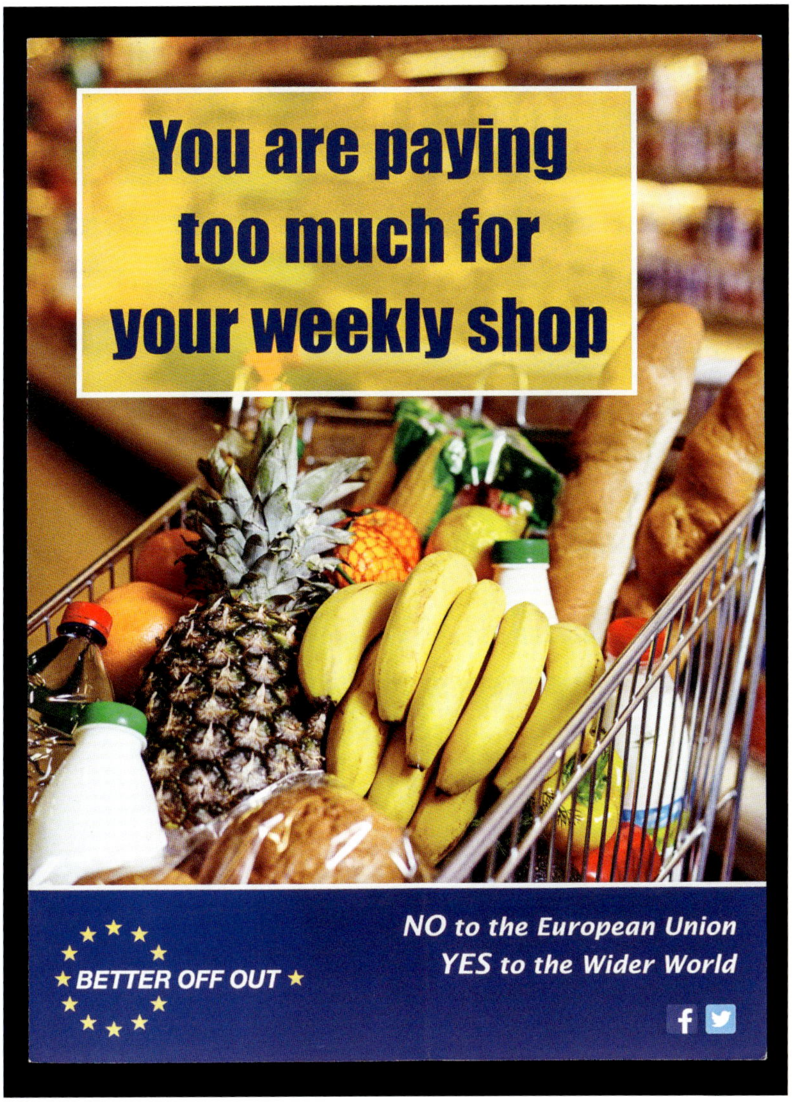
You are paying
too much for
your weekly shop
BETTER OFF OUT
NO to the European Union
YES to the Wider World

14

in a frictionless way throughout the EU. British culture has been damaged because art and touring exhibitions will no longer be selected as they used to be, because of the cost and hassle of traversing the border.

In 2018, Sjoerd Feitsma was alderman for culture in the city of Leeuwarden in Friesland, in the north of the Netherlands, when the city was European Capital of Culture. He took the decision in 2020 to replace the Union Jack with the Scottish saltire among the 28 EU member state flags. The saltire still hangs outside the railway station there.[38] Feitsma was inspired by the close co-operation on arts and culture between Leeuwarden and Edinburgh, and Scotland and the Netherlands in general. While on a visit to Scotland – and enjoying the Burns Night festival – Feitsma heard of the decision to fly the EU flag across the road from the Scottish Parliament: 'This came after a whole weekend of conversations with people who felt devastated, specifically in Scotland, because of leaving the European Union, and [who were] also very worried about the cultural ties with the rest of the continent.'[39]

In fact, there had been a fractious debate in the Scottish Parliament about whether to keep the EU flag flying – the SNP won the vote with the support of the Scottish Greens – reversing a previous decision to lower the flag at 23.00 on 31 January 2020, when the UK officially left the EU.[40] There is a tipping point at which the number and visibility of Union Jacks looks like a nationalist statement. Whereas previously flags were flown at major public buildings, now they are to be seen in children's playgrounds.

Feitsma tells of the disappointment when Leeds was unable to pursue its bid to be a European Capital of Culture. All these decisions loosen cultural ties, and although there is now a network called Eurocities – with 16 British cities signed up for membership – it does not make up for the loss of ties that stemmed from Brexit, and should one of the 16 British cities seek to collaborate on a project with a city outside the UK, it leads to funding difficulties.[41]

Simon Tubb was born in Britain and has now become a Dutch citizen.[42] He is one of many people I came across while writing this book who has left Britain because of Brexit and become a citizen of an EU country. He used to work for Eurocities in Brussels and now works in the educational sector in Friesland, and is the international co-ordinator at Oerol Festival, a landscape arts festival that takes place every June on the island of Terschelling, off the northern coast. Tubb's work in this sector depends on European funding and the maintenance of close ties with other festivals and organisations around Europe. While alliances remain strong with a number of British festivals, and some pre-Brexit funding streams still underwrite some collaborations, problems begin in getting over the border.

The Oerol Festival has worked hand-in-hand with the Inside Out festival in Dorset, as both focus on art and ecology, with collaboration between scientific organisations, environmental groups and the arts. Oerol has submitted a Creative Europe project proposal with Inside Out, in which the Dorset-based organisation is the subcontractor for the training element of the project. Tubb says:

> It's for festivals and organisations that programme work in protected natural landscapes, which involves a lot of collaboration, which is a really cool project . . . in the case of Oerol, we work very closely with the Dutch Forestry Commission, because it owns the island. And so, wherever we programme work, there's been months of preparation, working with the forest rangers to ensure that that's been done in a way that it's not going to have an ecological impact. And that way of working is becoming more widespread, luckily. And so that's what that project is about. They [Inside Out] in the UK, actually run training for all of the areas of outstanding natural beauty, on how to work with arts organisations.

Oerol is open to looking at other ways to include British organisations. There was a symposium this year for Dutch and British festivals funded by the Dutch Performing Arts Fund. 'The overwhelming feeling from the British organisations that are invited was just gratitude to have been invited to something,' Tubb says. The irony is that the UK was an exemplar in local, collaborative cultural and social activities in neighbourhoods, Feitsma points out. 'It's been the case for years because these activities have been around in the UK since the 1970s and they only started here about 10 years ago,' he says. So, Britain is losing a leadership role in this sector, as well as being outside the circle. No freedom of movement, the costs of touring, paperwork, visas, all of this damages Britain's standing in the arts. Feitsma says: 'It's really painful, especially for people working in the arts and cultural sector, because they were sort of leading in international connections and collaborations – and were probably not pro-Brexit.'

One of artist Cornelia Parker's recent works, *FLAG* (2022), a film about a factory in Cardiff that makes Union Jacks, reverses the manufacturing process, working from finished product back to cutting the cloth, to the soundtrack of the hymn 'Jerusalem' (figs 16 and 17). It is one of several of Parker's works that focus on British identity and commemoration, another being her installation reflecting on Remembrance poppies, *War Room* (2015).[43] It is unusual to see flag-making explored through the prism of labour, but the state of the union, of the United Kingdom, preoccupies Parker in her film:

> The thing that's most under threat is the union. The film I made, FLAG, was (perhaps a premonition) pointing to how we're sleepwalking into something that we mostly don't intend. David Cameron didn't seem to realise that the breakup of the union could be the unforeseen consequence when he proposed the referendum. If Scotland leaves, they'll want to rejoin the EU. Southern Ireland is still in the EU, but will there be a united Ireland? Will it trigger a return to the Troubles? And Wales, I'm sure, will be wanting to be in the EU if Scotland and Ireland are. The only people who don't want to be in the EU seem to be in England, and what does that mean? We're diminishing ourselves on the world stage in every possible way. I have friends from all over the world and they live in London because they love it. But they've had a horrendous time over the last few years, with residencies [and] feeling like they are not wanted. And we've benefited hugely from them, from people from all over the world. Pulling up the drawbridge at this point in history is not really helping anything.[44]

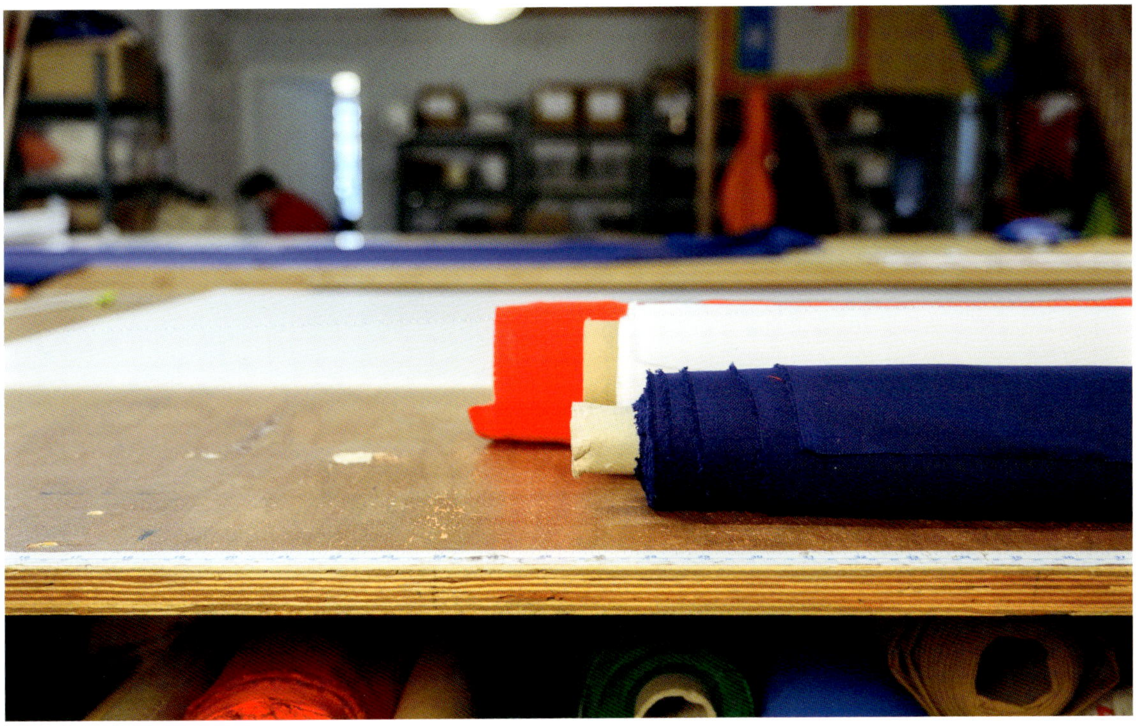

16 and 17 (*overleaf*) Cornelia Parker, *FLAG*, 2022, video. Parker's film, with its distinctive soundtrack, begins with a flag and rewinds through the production process to disconcerting effect

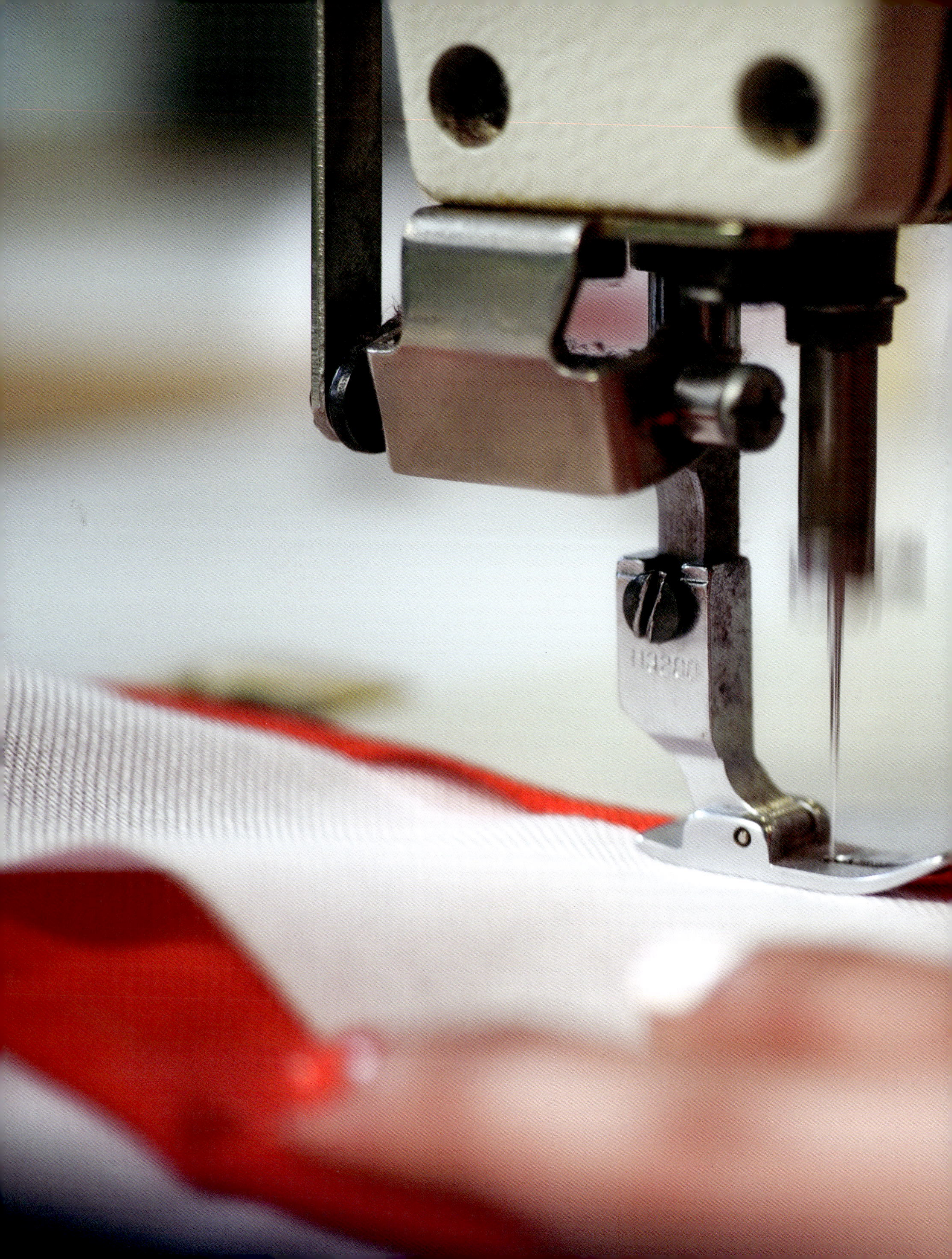

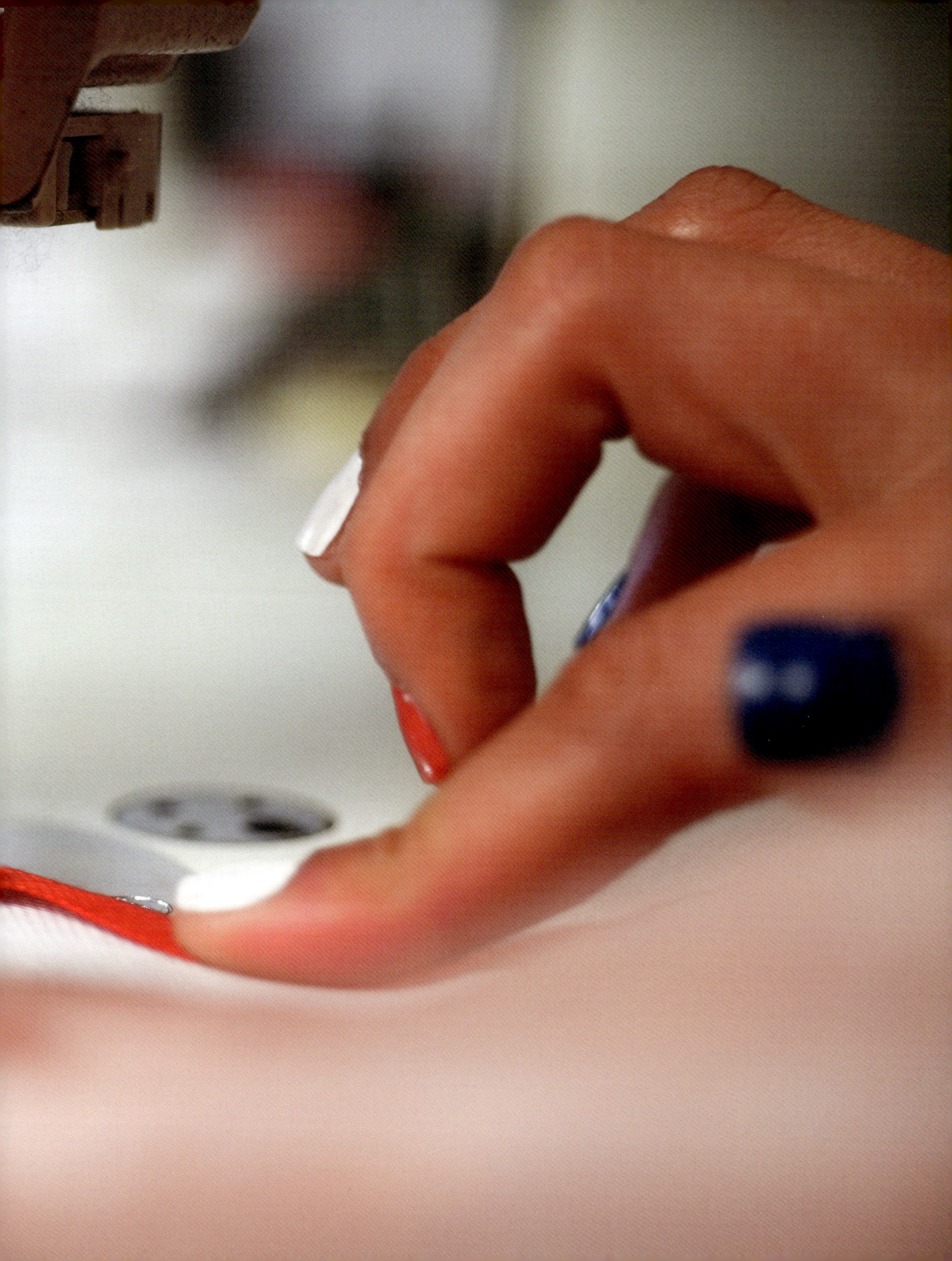

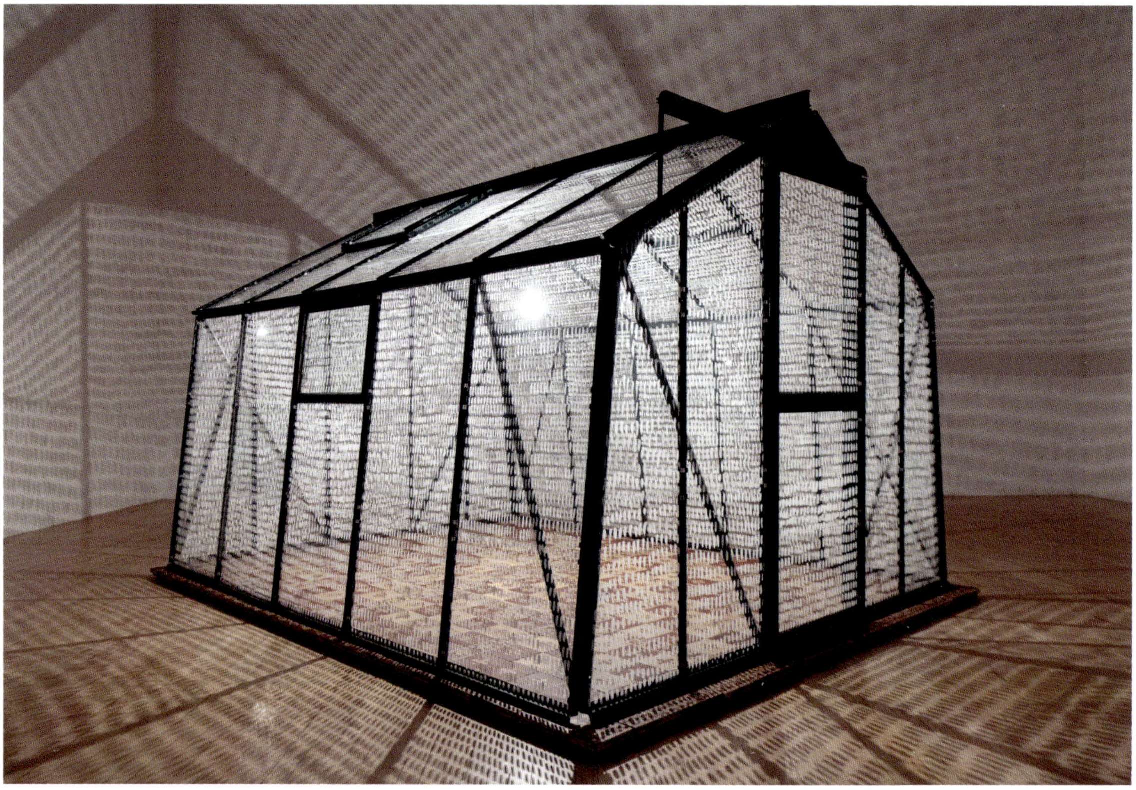

18 Cornelia Parker, *Island*, 2022, installation view at Tate Britain, domestic greenhouse, pigment made from chalk from cliffs at Dover, storm light, 2440 × 3050 × 1980 cm (960 ⅝ × 1200 13⁄16 × 799 ½ in)

This installation, with its flashing beacon, summons and unnerves. The chalk smudges daubed on the structure resemble the marks of incarceration by a prisoner in a cell, counting the days.

Wales voted to leave, but Parker secured access to shoot her film in Wales as the woman who runs the factory liked the idea:

> The woman who ran it was [a] very intelligent woman and she liked what the idea was. There was an English flag factory that kind of wavered and thought perhaps it wouldn't be a good thing to be part of, so they opted out. So we went to Wales, happily, and she said yes, that the Union Jack flying in Wales is not always a welcome thing. They don't believe in it the same way we do in England. So, there was quite a bit of politics going down when I made the piece with them. It was great, it was really wonderful.
>
> I [had] wanted to make this film ever since Brexit, this idea of the taking apart of the union flag. And then we use some kind of stock music of 'Jerusalem'. We had the Queen's brass band, but they didn't want to be part of something that was about dismembering the union flag. So even though it's a cautionary tale, I think the film, even when you think things are moving forward, they're not, they are moving backwards.
>
> I deliberately wanted it to feel like you didn't really know that the Union Jack is coming apart or being fabricated. It's only at the end when all the red, white and blue pieces get put back on

their separate rolls you think, 'Oh, shit. It's gone. Poof.' And it all could go very quickly, very easily. It's a beautiful flag, actually it's a shame that it's got such nationalist overtones. One of the world's most beautiful flags is in such jeopardy.

For Parker, as with other artists I interviewed, the central thread of issues of identity, nationality and the iconography of Brexit run throughout her work. Her retrospective at Tate Britain (19 May–16 October 2022) illustrated the aesthetic sense with which she imbues her subject matter, bringing political debate and skirmish into the gallery, and therefore the continuing discussion around these painful subjects. *Island* (2022), which she created for the retrospective, is a greenhouse 'sitting on a raft of floor tiles from the House of Commons', and which looks adrift in a gallery (fig.18).

Nothing grows here and the space functions like a cell. A storm light shines within, but this is an empty, uninviting place. Parker has daubed chalk marks on the glass – with pigment made from chalk from the white cliffs of Dover – and these soft white marks, at once decoration and pattern, resemble the lines prisoners draw on the walls of their cells to mark the length of their sentence. Parker described the genesis of the work to Andrea Schlieker, director of exhibitions and displays at Tate Britain:

So, the glasshouse becomes enclosed, inward looking, a vulnerable domain, a Little England with a cliff-face veil. In our time of Brexit, alienated from France and Ireland, Britain is emptied out of Europeans just when we need them most. The spectre of climate crisis is looming large: with crumbling coastlines and rising sea levels, things seem very precarious. And with Scotland wanting to leave the Union and Ireland not far behind, the idea of Albion feels uncertain too.

The greenhouse appears to be adrift. It's like a lighthouse lantern with the lights going on and off and signalling danger. It is painted with chalk marks from the white cliffs, as if it's chalking up time. The raft of tiles, recycled from the Houses of Parliament, represents the magic carpet of government – not! It was something a little bit ominous because we really don't know where we are going as a nation post-Brexit.[45]

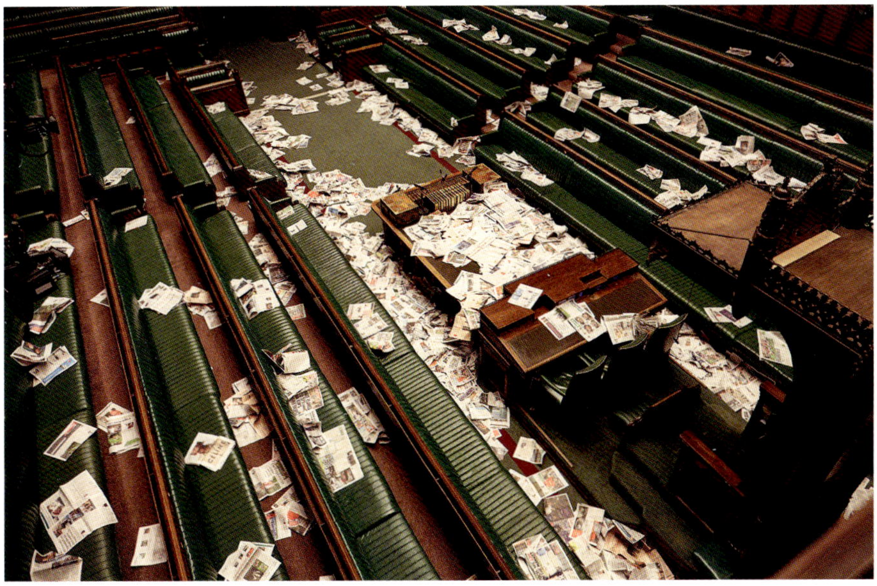

19 Cornelia Parker, *Left Right & Centre*, 2017, film still

As official election artist in 2017 and the first woman to take this position, Parker sought and gained unprecedented access to the chamber of the House of Commons. This was the first time drones have been flown in this space, and the image shows newspapers from across the political spectrum scattered around.

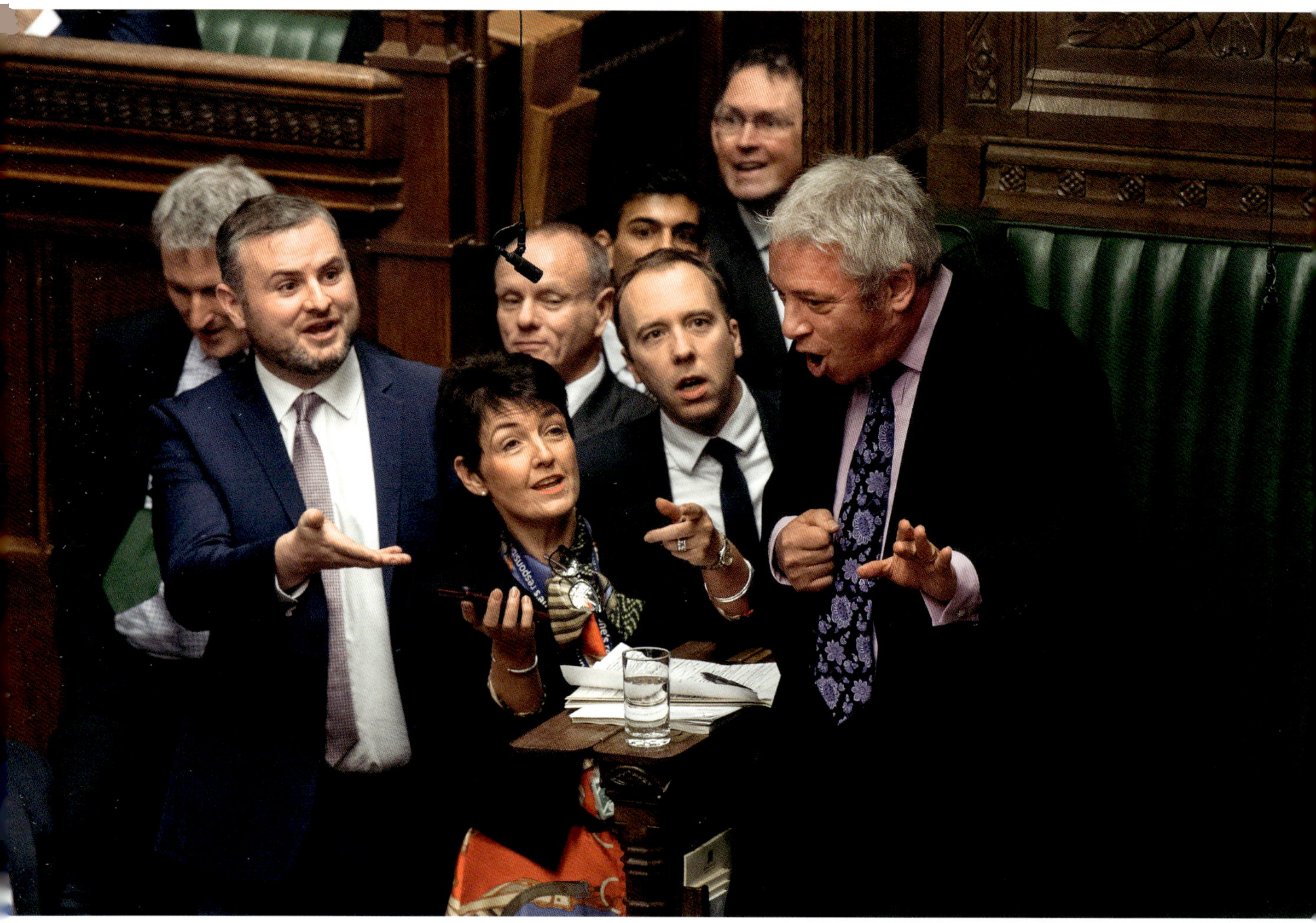

20 Mark Duffy, the House of Commons, 19 December 2018

Parker has long been making work with chalk – she photographed Einstein's equations on his blackboard through a microscope, in *Einstein's Abstracts* (1999):

> If you looked at them through an electron microscope, you might find that they're made up of the shells of tiny marine animals, nature and culture colliding. I've starched bedsheets with the chalk from the white cliffs of Dover, *Inhaled Cliffs* (1996). I've used charcoal from burned churches to make drawings. Chalk and charcoal are also traditional drawing materials, black and white. I like their polarity. White cliff chalk just seems like a perfect material which I return to.[46]

Parker is staunchly against Brexit. She is half-German (her mother was German) and considers the repercussions of Britain leaving the EU all the time, not least because there are consequences for her daughter's future. Parker is applying for German citizenship.[47] She did not feel well represented by Jeremy Corbyn (Leader of the Opposition and Leader of the Labour Party, 2015–2020) in the referendum campaign, and talks about the possibility of interference in the referendum from other countries, such as Russia, which 'were really invested in Britain leaving the EU'. The government report on Russian interference in the referendum showed a lackadaisical attitude to this possibility from the UK government and the security services; and reports of Russian money flowing into Tory coffers are legion.[48]

Left Right & Centre, the film Parker made when she was the official artist for the UK's 2017 general election, brings art and the business of newspapers into the chamber of the House of Commons (fig.19). This film – and the access secured to make it – is unprecedented. Parker negotiated the use of a drone, which hovered above the green leather benches, producing a downdraft that scattered Britain's newspapers all around. And the chamber is empty of politicians. The vociferous chatter of MPs has grown much louder since Brexit as opposition parties challenge the government on lies, sleaze, lockdown parties and its muted migrant itinerary. For me, *Left Right & Centre* and the flurry of newsprint draws attention specifically to the press and its role in Brexit, and references the continuation of the chaos. For Parker, it was born of a request by those who commissioned her to be 'apolitical':

> I took on the job of election artist because I wanted to have access to that. And I thought the only way I can do it is if I'm in some way in some more official capacity. The access we managed to get was amazing, but it was very hard to pull off. I was told that I wasn't allowed to be party political, to not show my political colours. So, I thought: 'Oh, OK, this is really fun.' So that's where the ideas in *Left Right & Centre* originated.[49]

The Irish artist and photographer Mark Duffy was in situ as an official House of Commons photographer during the Brexit negotiations. His photographs of the chamber bring back to me the visceral battles after the referendum. Duffy's experiences of working in the House of Commons were fractious and include – along with thinly veiled racism – disputes over the copyright of images and where and how they would be circulated, and a manifestly absurd visit

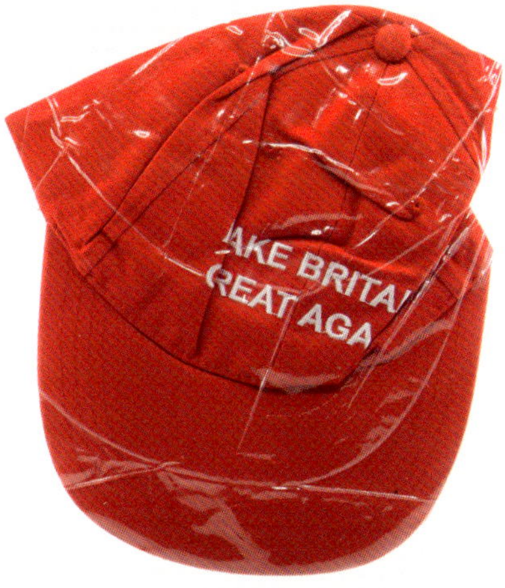

21 A *Make Britain Great Again* hat, an example of Brexit merchandise, photo by Mark Duffy, 2019

from the police after he had left concerning items that had been reported as stolen from the House. Duffy forged a path for photography in the chamber: his photograph of MPs around the Speaker's chair is an extraordinary record of that time, and his photographs were published on the front pages of newspapers (fig.20). In October 2017, Duffy exhibited his Brexit archive in his home, including his photographs and his archive of Brexit ephemera: the beermats, the keyrings, the mugs – and worse, the Trump-inspired, shouty 'Make Britain Great Again' hats (fig.21).

It is an odd place, the Houses of Parliament, where the struggle to get Brexit 'done' has been played out. Unlike the calm and airiness within the Scottish Parliament, the House of Commons is a rabbit warren of corridors, committee rooms, plush carpets, ornate Pugin wallpaper and dark wood panelling. Duffy's account of working there in 2015–19 describes incidents and bullying, and not a little racism.[50]

Chapter 2

Border force[d] + identity

The history of Britain and its borders is the focus of dispute and throws up a series of questions about who comes to the country and how. The government has recently debated how those seeking refuge will be expelled if they are refused entry. This touches on recent historical research and the reassessment of Britain's history and heritage stemming from colonialism, which has provoked ire from conservatives. Some groups are enraged by protests around statues and refuse to engage in debates on cultural restitution or studies that trace the tentacles of colonialism. There is also the question of nostalgia, which carries a range of connotations, from warm to cold, and truth to wishful thinking. There is no doubt in my mind that a core element of Brexit was a looking back to a Britain that never existed.

The debates reverberate in the public sphere, ricocheting around social media with scant regard to verifiable facts. On the subject of statues, why would a country *not* reconsider the position of public monuments to controversial colonialists? Who are the gatekeepers of Britain, given that it has never been a whiter-than-white nation? The consequences of colonialism are evident all around us in the built environment. These debates have provoked uproar from those who resist findings based on historical research, or who contest multiculturalism while slinging allegations of 'wokeism' at all concerned. This invocation of 'wokeism' is in line with Trump's culture wars in the US and is a vehicle for permanent disruption from this populist elite in government: their wealth, education, property portfolios, economic and cultural capital mark them out as an elite, even before they hit the 'speech' circuit, pocketing vast amounts simply to espouse their views.

BLACK 'N' BLUE

The passport document was integral to the campaigns around Brexit. When, in March 2020, the new, 'old-style blue' British passport appeared, the then home secretary, Priti Patel, said it would 'once again be entwined with our national identity'.[1] The conversation around this passport arouses passions. In 2016, a BBC *Newsnight* report featured an archival piece in which the programme's then presenter (in 1995), Jeremy Paxman, celebrated the British passport while casting aspersions on its EU counterpart:

> The British passport wasn't so much something you presented for inspection by some grubby little border policeman, but an icon you brandished proudly. It demanded admission.
>
> It [the blue one] was solid, sturdy, and understated, like the front door of No 10 [Downing Street], the radiator grille of a Rolls-Royce or the buildings of Whitehall. These days people still want to travel in style, but they have to do so on something smaller and flimsier [shows Jaguar car] and looking like a passbook of the Nuneaton Building Society.[2]

The Sun newspaper, which is owned by the fervent Leave campaigner Rupert Murdoch (a US citizen), had long called for a return of the blue passport, as did the long-term Member of the European Parliament, Nigel Farage. The EU passport had been 'enforced on the nation in 1988', *The Sun* bleated, in the language of domination and victimhood that characterised the Leave campaign. The old blue passport had been introduced in 1921 and the burgundy EU passport in 1988. 'Britain resisted strongly until 1988. We were the last of the then EU nations to go burgundy,' *The Sun* wrote, with a cheer for the notion of British exceptionalism that underpinned Brexit. Back to Paxman's report, in which a man (unidentified), lounging in one of London's iconic black cabs, remarks:

> This document's a very flimsy and rather sort of bureaucratic-looking thing. Your name isn't written in ink. You have a sort of laser printout thing on it, which makes you like a packet of biscuits in a supermarket. It's lost some of the imperial standing that the old document used to have.[3]

Coincidentally, Rolls-Royce Motor Cars is now owned by the German group BMW (Bayerische Motoren Werke AG). The new 'blue' UK passport was designed by a Franco-Dutch company, Gemalto, at its site in Tczew, Poland, and, in 2019, the French, Paris-based, aerospace and defence electronics multinational Thales swallowed up Gemalto.[4] I say 'blue' because I referred to the Pigment Colour Index. The Passport Index tracks these facts and offers a dashboard and passport rankings, although the colour on the UK passport in the colour rankings bears no relation to the real thing, which is closer to black, in my view.[5] The Home Office said it was a return to the 'iconic blue' – and identified the colour in the Pantone® classification as '5395 C'. Stephen Westland, professor of colour science and technology at the University of Leeds, told the BBC that it is more black than blue, and Craig Burston, a design academic at London College of Communication, University of the Arts London, said: 'It's as black as blue gets. You'd be hard pushed to get something that is darker that would be defined as blue.'[6]

And while Paxman disparaged the EU passport for resembling a Nuneaton Building Society passbook, Nuneaton was deeply dissatisfied with the EU, voting strongly for Leave.[7] As for the central government policy of 'levelling up', Nuneaton has four foodbanks that I could count at the time of writing, including one set up by the Trussell Trust. This charity runs the largest network of foodbanks in the UK: in July 2020, there were more than 1,400 Trussell Trust food banks in the UK, in addition to at least 1,172 independent food banks.[8] David Stanier, chairman of Nuneaton Foodbank, reported dismal news in June 2022:

> Sadly the cost of living crisis has had a massive impact locally, and the numbers of people being referred to the foodbank by professional agencies has increased since April to today by 72.5 per cent for the same period last year. The number of children [relying on] food parcels has increased by 70.5 per cent for the same period last year. Since 1 January this year the numbers have increased by 48.3 per cent with the number of children [relying on] food parcels increased by 47 per cent.

There had also been a significant reduction in the amount of food being donated, he said.[9] These numbers will have increased exponentially by the time this book is published.

THIS ENGLAND, THAT NATIONALISM

Brexit is wrapped in nationalism, specifically English nationalism. Scotland and Northern Ireland did not vote Leave; Wales and England did, though recent polls show that, over time, many people have changed their minds and increasing numbers of people feel that, with hindsight, it was a mistake to leave the EU.[10] Leave was, in the main, an English phenomenon, and it is interesting to look at the visual and other components for Englishness.

Professor Catherine Clarke, director of the Centre for the History of People, Place and Community at the Institute of Historical Research (University of London), considers the long view of Britain's borders and the formation of national identity.[11] Set against the background of queues at Dover and clogged airports, Clarke cites the importance to Britain's identity of being an island, with a continuing ambivalence towards its borders. These exalted notions of the island nation thread through history, she argues, from John of Gaunt's speech in Shakespeare's *Richard II* – 'this other Eden', and 'this fortress built by nature for herself' – to the 8th-century historian Tiberius Bede, with his imaginary turn around Britain as a land of plenty with an abundance of grain, trees, fish, hot springs, seals, dolphins and all manner of metals and minerals. It is a bounteous land, with its valleys, rivers, vines and castles and this has tempted people, such as the Picts and Romans, to voyage to its shores in order to both explore and plunder. Clarke outlines the relevance of the literary works that rest on Britain's sense of its own exceptionalism and its self-appointed right to roam the world; this touches on the current debate and its inbuilt conflict:

> The emblematic island valorises borders, enclosure and exclusion: the nation as Shakespeare's moated castle, or heir to the fortress city of Troy. Yet, simultaneously, the maritime edges of the island are a symbol of global connectedness – and have been used, over centuries of history, to assert the rights of the English to travel freely and to assume a uniquely powerful status on the world stage. In the aftermath of Brexit, and in the traffic jams in Kent, we see these two different inflections of our island imaginary in seemingly irreconcilable conflict.[12]

British artists incorporate this gash of a coastline in their work, not least because there is a concentration of them living on the south coast. But primarily, this is the gateway to Britain for travellers of leisure and for refugees and asylum seekers who approach this coastline with trepidation and often in dangerous circumstances in search of safety, a home, work, or a better life.

Mandy Williams, an artist who works in photography and film, creates work around the chalk cliffs of Dover. Her film *Chalk* (2021) is redolent of art that is inspired by this landscape and history with its eerie 'landscape as language' circling the mystical chalk markings left by tribes on hillsides across the south of England. The Bronze Age Uffington White Horse, on the chalk downs of Oxfordshire, is one of these, a huge beast, measuring 111 metres from the tip of its tail to its ear. Every seven years, from about 1677 until the late-18th century, local people would tidy the outline of the horse before settling down to a celebratory feast within the hillfort known as Uffington Castle.[13] Today, these places are managed by the National Trust on behalf of English Heritage.

The Uffington White Horse is a crux of history and English identity, with the Manger valley and its steep, ridged sides – or 'giant's steps' – on its left, and below Dragon Hill. This circular hillock, about 10 metres high, is said to be where St George slayed a 'fire-breathing' dragon.[14] St George is the patron saint of England, yet he was not English. He was born in Turkey and is thought to have died in Lydda (Israel), and it is likely that he never visited England, but his mythical status reflecting 'virtue and holiness' took root in the public imagination across Europe over the centuries. British monarchs in particular called on his name, and Edward I (1272–1307) flew banners of St George's emblem, a red cross on a white background.

In Williams's *Chalk*, the White Horse is imbued with hope for some, false hope for others: 'The story says if you stand on its eye and turn three times, your wish comes true.' These horses and diagrams on England's hillsides, the voice-over suggests, pitch towards 'propaganda, headlines on vast green billboards shaping the imagination', and it is this inflexion towards message that characterises these works around chalk. The images, the otherworldly voice-over and the gnashing and discordant echo of the soundtrack all amplify the uncomfortable nature of this poetic film. The 'bone white' paths are tethered in folklore and history, and here Buddhist monks, walking on a day out, gamely agreed to appear in the film (fig.22). Another of Williams's projects is a free newspaper, *England* (fig.23), and a video, *Inward Isle*, that speak to this heritage, preserved and shaped by heritage organisations such as the National Trust. The National Trust has come under attack from some conservatives who have been incensed by its attempts to explore its links to colonial history.

For these artists, making these works is an act of resistance. Williams says of her decision to use landscape as a metaphor for nostalgia and memory:

> I lived away from England for 12 years. I went to Canada on a five-month visa to spend time with somebody I'd met the year before and I ended up staying. As I had not planned to move away, I was frequently homesick. I missed family and friends, and thought of England in an idealistic, nostalgic way – that it was a diverse and progressive country. It was really London that I was missing, but I also missed the English countryside; the archetypal rolling green hills, and chalk paths of the south coast. The landscape was approachable, whereas the Canadian landscape was very different. It was

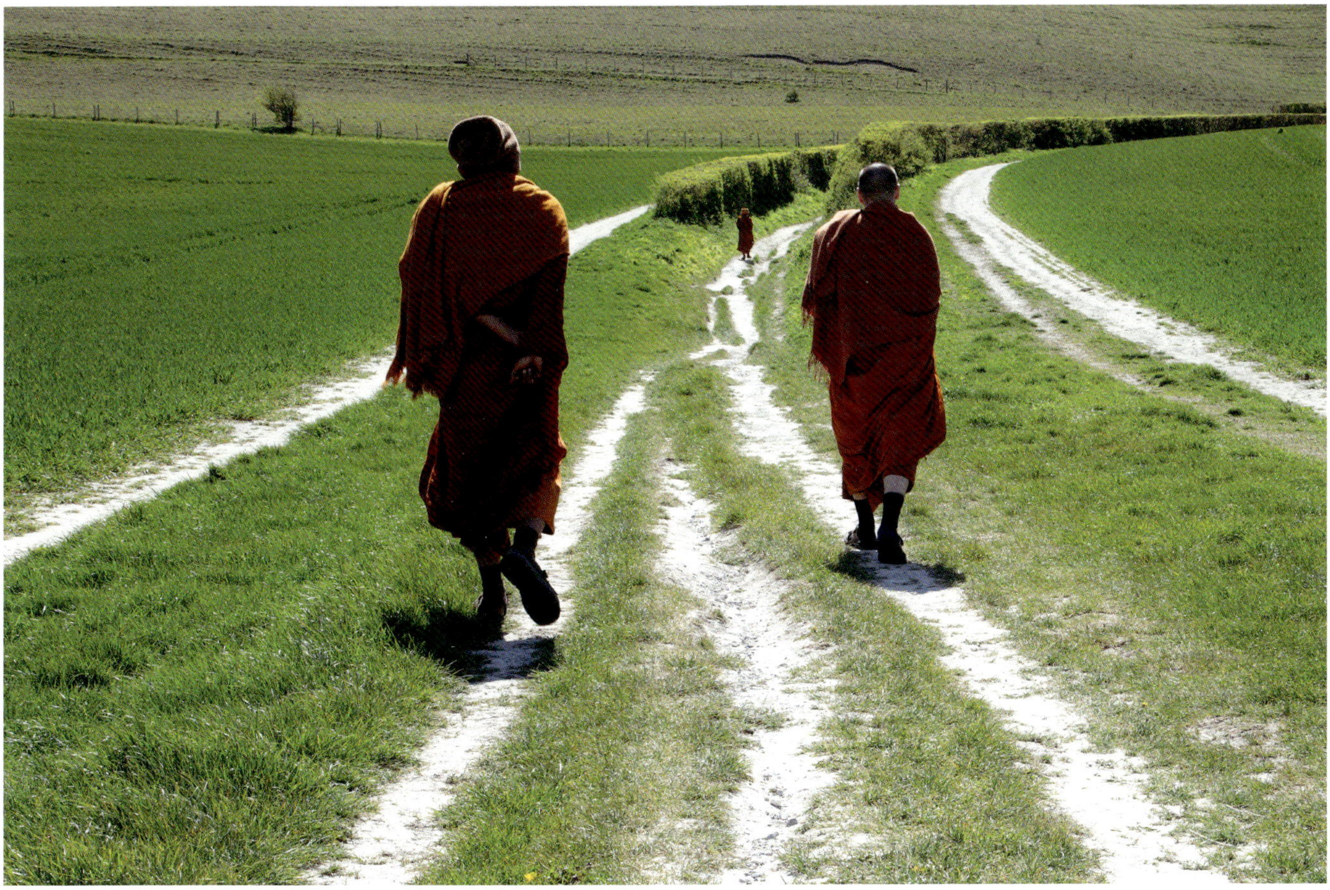

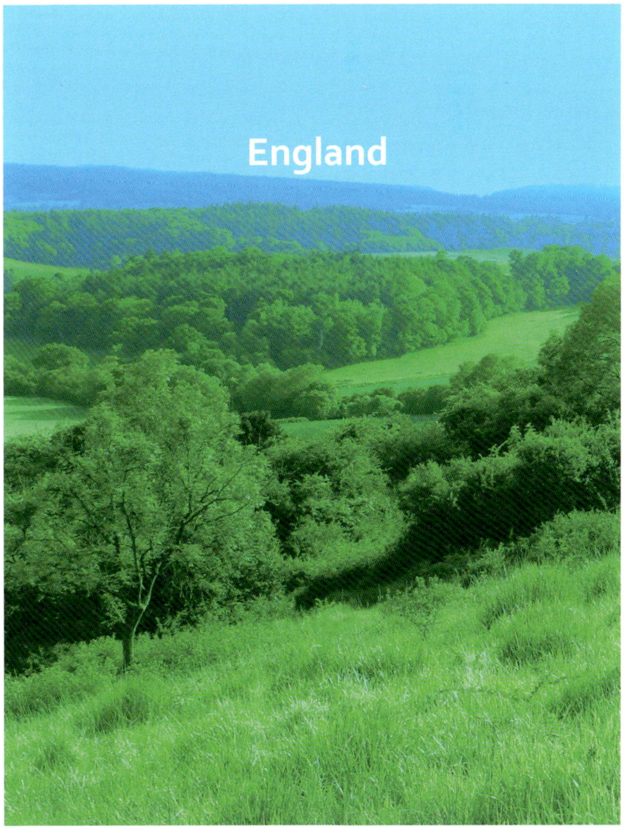

above

22 Mandy Williams, *Chalk*, 2021, video

In this experimental film Williams explores all aspects of chalk, from landscape to language, and how it is used to communicate ideas, and is tied to myth, English tradition, history and ideas of English national identity.

right

23 Mandy Williams, *England* newspaper, 2020

This image is taken from Williams's MA project at the London College of Communication, University of the Arts London, which explores the exclusionary politics of contemporary England through the metaphor of landscape and included a video, Inward Island, 7 Disrupted Landscapes *photographs, and a free newspaper.*

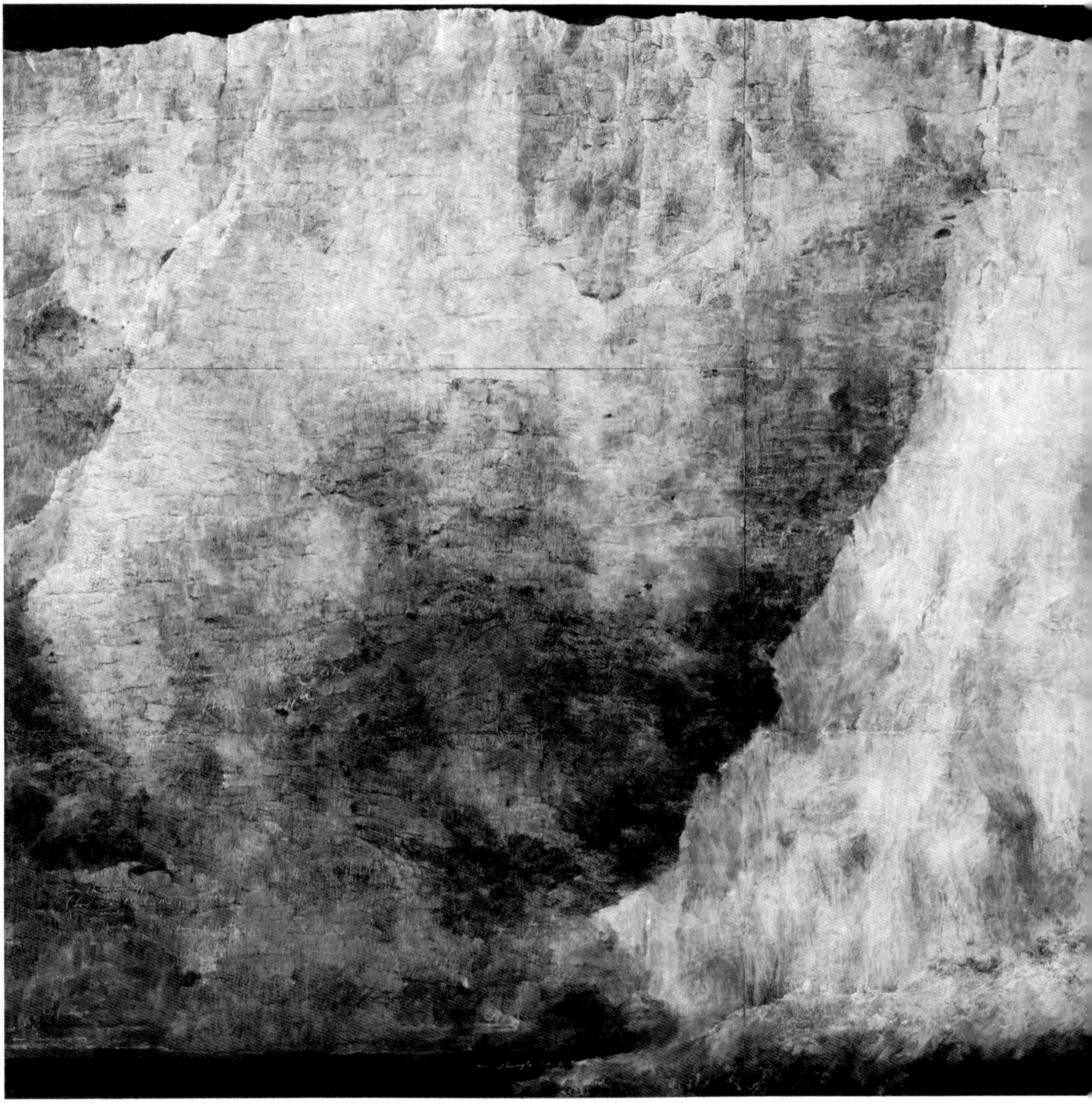

24 Tacita Dean, *Chalk Fall*, 2018, Chalk on blackboard, 366 × 732 cm

In its depiction of crumbling chalk cliffs, Dean's work marries subject matter with the medium she has used to create the work.

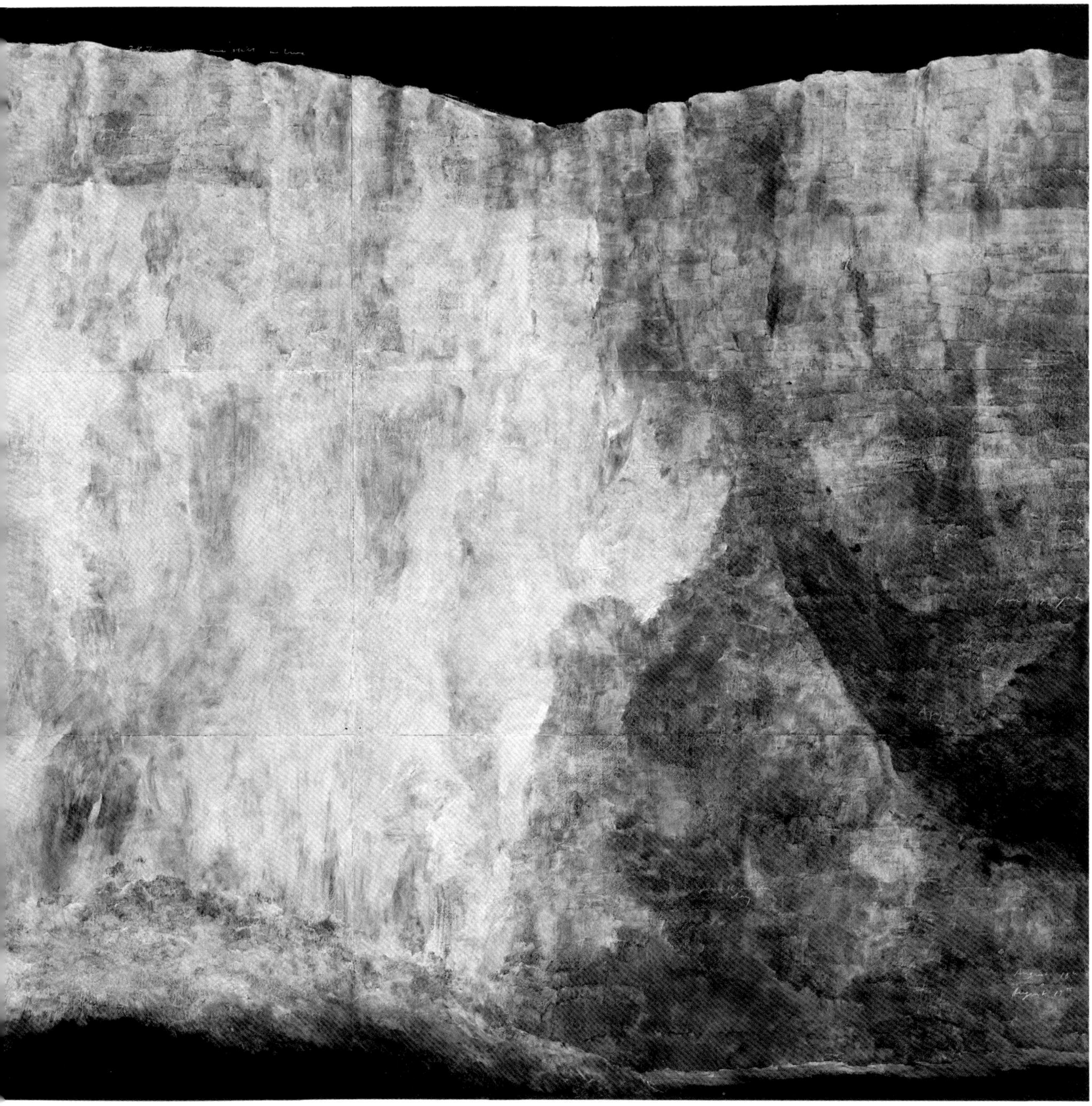

extremely beautiful, but it didn't emotionally affect me in the same way. It didn't represent home. So, landscape was an important part of my nostalgia and memory of England.

I came back in 2002 and my view of England has changed over the past 10 years because of the government's hostile policies, the racist Brexit campaign, and the division in the country since the referendum. England has felt less like home and one way to reflect this dislocation has been to create work using the English landscape that had once been an integral part of my sense of belonging.[15]

Turner Prize nominee Tacita Dean says her work *The Montafon Letter* (2017), which depicts a snowy mountain landscape, is in some ways a metaphor for the extraordinary parliamentary wrangling around Brexit legislation. The work consists of nine blackboards joined together. The tragic tale of Montafon itself twists and turns around a sequence of avalanches in 17th-century Austria 'that buried some people, then buried the priest who went to officiate at the site of the burial, then – finally – unburied the priest, still alive', which would lend itself to tragicomedy, if it were not true.[16] Dean says the angst around the avalanches was matched by the pitch and fall of the hope for a second referendum on Brexit – and 'hope that the last avalanche will uncover us', as Thelma Pott recounts in the exhibition catalogue for Dean's 2018 *Landscape* exhibition at the Royal Academy.[17]

The cliffs of Dean's beautiful and daunting landscape, *Chalk Fall* (2018), a similarly vast chalk drawing, depicts, she says, 'what could be the white cliffs of Dover and a moment when the chalk collapses' (fig.24). The inspiration for the work, which was made in Los Angeles and is now in the collection of the Queensland Art Gallery in Australia, stemmed from a preoccupation with the growing obsolescence of film, as well as the illness and death of a close friend and the disjuncture of Brexit:

This resonates with two things . . . I am always fighting for the preservation of my mediums, film and photography, photochemical film and photography, so this became an analogy [with] the collapse of the medium because it is made of chalk, and it depicts a chalk cliff collapsing. And the second thing, of course, in 2018 and before the whole debate and agony of Brexit was raging. The collapse of the white cliffs of Dover somehow has also resonated with the historic collapse of reason that happened in the United Kingdom and I literally worked from the top to the bottom of that drawing.

As I was working, this very, very close friend of mine, whose name was Keith Collins, was diagnosed with a brain tumour and very, very rapidly declined . . . every day I would write the date of the drawing . . . and so the drawing is also built up with the sedimentation of time, as is chalk. *Chalk* is about sedimentation. Before I went back to England, I was in intense correspondence with Keith and then, by the time I came back, I couldn't communicate with him anymore, so it was about waiting and knowing he was still alive, just notching time on the drawing as I descended down, so for me it's a very, very emotional drawing . . .[18]

Anyone who grew up in the days of school blackboards and chalk will recall the soundtrack and scent of these tactile materials – the sharp snap of the chalk as it broke, the ear-splitting screech if chalk – or worse, fingernails – scratched the surface of the blackboard, and the muffled thumps as the teacher cleaned the board with a wooden block with a cloth pad on one side, which dispersed rather than erased the chalk. Picking a piece of chalk from the uneven chards nestled in the dusty shelf running along the bottom of the blackboard elicited a satisfying rustle of clicks. And it is difficult to write clearly on a blackboard – and doubly so to draw. Dean's painstaking work stands alongside photographic darkrooms in its particularity and its hues, in which are embedded traces of dates, names, places and events that impinge as she makes the work.

On a personal level, the result of the 2016 referendum pushed Dean and her family up against an uncomfortable deadline. Dean is British but was living in Germany. The referendum took place while she and her family were away from their home in Berlin on an artist's residency in Los Angeles, where she has a studio. They arrived in LA as Europeans

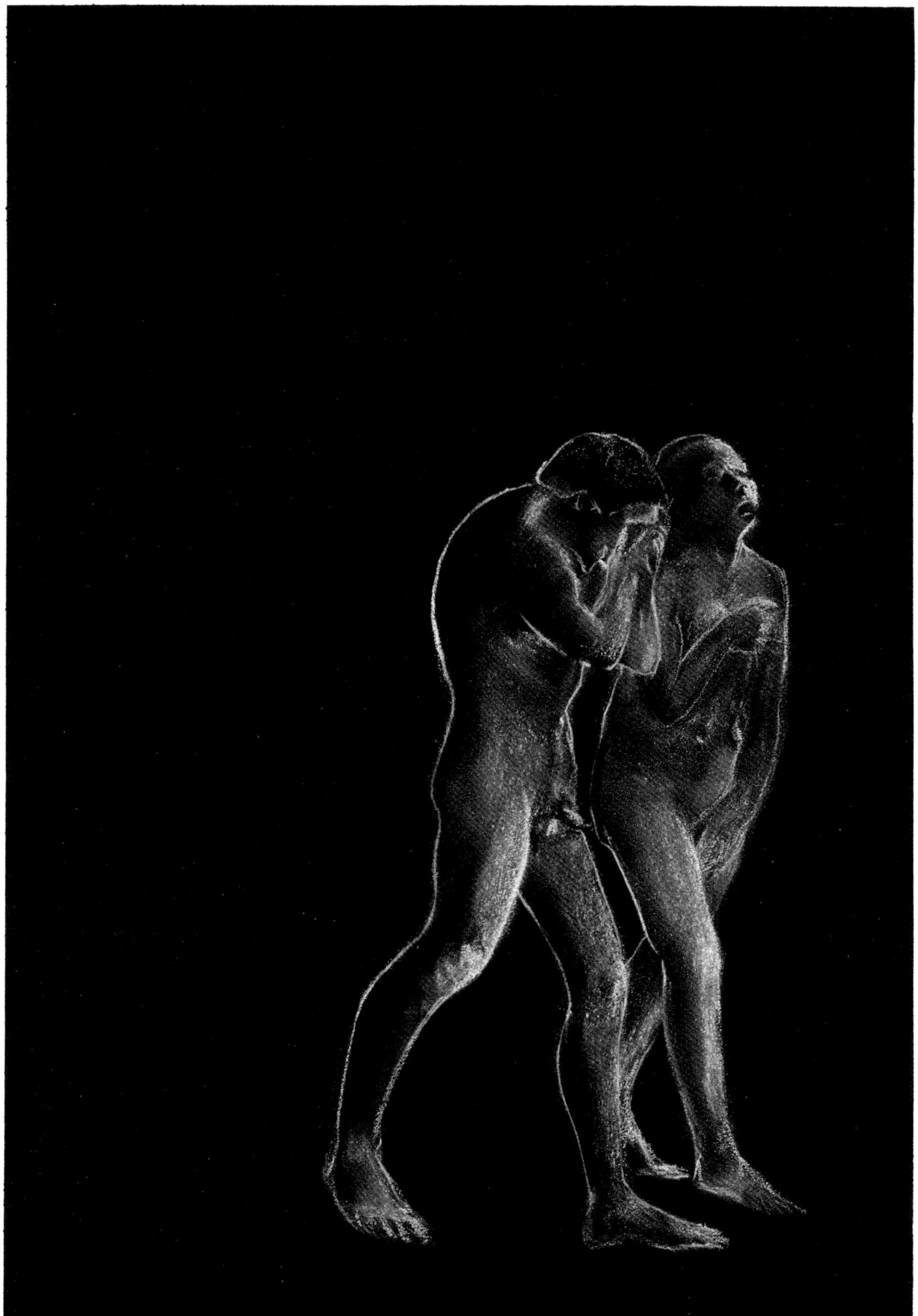

25 Tacita Dean, *Expulsion*, 2019, Chalk on blackboard paint on paper, 29.6 × 42 cm, after Masaccio's (b.1401, San Giovanni Altura, d.1428, Rome) fresco in the Brancacci Chapel in Florence, depicts Adam and Eve's expulsion from Eden. Commissioned in 2019 by the *Süddeutsche Zeitung Magazin*, the drawing was made in response to Britain's exit from the EU

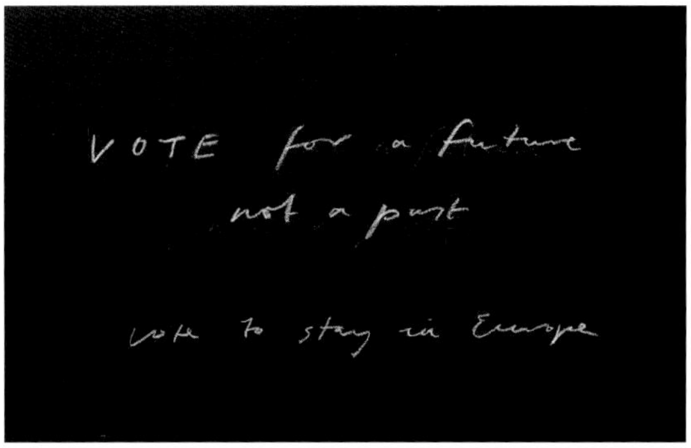

26 Tacita Dean, 'Statement on Brexit. VOTE for a future not a past', 2016

Tacita Dean campaigned for Remain; she is a German citizen and lives and works in Berlin and Los Angeles.

and after the referendum they were British, but had the possibility of becoming German citizens. Dean and her family had to decide whether to uproot themselves from the US – her son was 12 at the time – and return to Germany. EU resident status means that those who have lived in an EU country for at least five years may apply to become a resident. In the event, Dean and her family returned to Germany and became German citizens (fig.25).[19] Dean speaks of the incomprehension in Germany at the Brexit result, which raised questions about leaving a trading agreement. In sharp contrast to the UK, Germans 'understand what the EU is, and it's been explained to them properly. It's a trading arrangement and with the freedom to travel that goes along with that.'

As I have said, there is an elephant in the room in the UK concerning Brexit. The European press describe its catastrophic consequences, and those who have left Britain see it, but in Britain in late 2022 there is a silence around the issues. At the time of the referendum, Dean sensed a lack of conviction on the part of British art institutions in opposing the campaign to leave the EU. And there was a complacency among those who supported Remain, a belief that Britain would not vote to leave (fig.26). Putting aside the lies on which the Leave campaign rested, Dean says there was an underestimation of support for leaving:

> I had a text correspondence with a friend who said: 'It's not going to happen; it's not going to happen.' But my mother comes from Ashford in Kent. There wasn't a single person she knew who wasn't voting for Brexit. And I had a friend in Cornwall, and he said: 'Everyone is voting for Brexit.' And I was thinking, well, I was really, really worried.[20]

Dean makes the point that the radical energy of the 1970s – about which I wrote in my previous book, *Photography of Protest and Community: The Radical Collectives of the 1970s* – when photographers and artists worked to mitigate punishing economic policies using a range of strategies, is now funnelled into right-wing politics.

The right-wing populism that is cropping up across Britain and Europe is fuelled by rage, with a vituperative focus on the movement of people. The German photographer Wolfgang Tillmans edited the multidisciplinary book, *What Is Different?* (2018), in which he asks scientists, publicists, politicians and experts to talk about the conditions for the 'backfire effect'.[21]

> The theory argues that people who are entirely convinced by a statement, regardless of how incorrect it might be, cannot be persuaded to change their minds by facts and proofs to the contrary; quite the opposite, such evidence reinforces their belief in the fallacy. The backfire effect plays a particularly powerful role in matters involving emotional questions that have an impact on our identity and political beliefs.[22]

Tillmans has been preoccupied with the circulation of truth and mistruth in the public discourse for some time (figs 27–30). In 2005, he exhibited an installation entitled *Truth Study Centre* in London, spurred on by misinformation and statements about diverse subjects:

pages 37–9

27–30 Wolfgang Tillmans, 2016, posters from pro-EU/anti-Brexit campaign

Tillmans studied in Britain and made London his home for many years, before returning to live in Berlin in 2011.

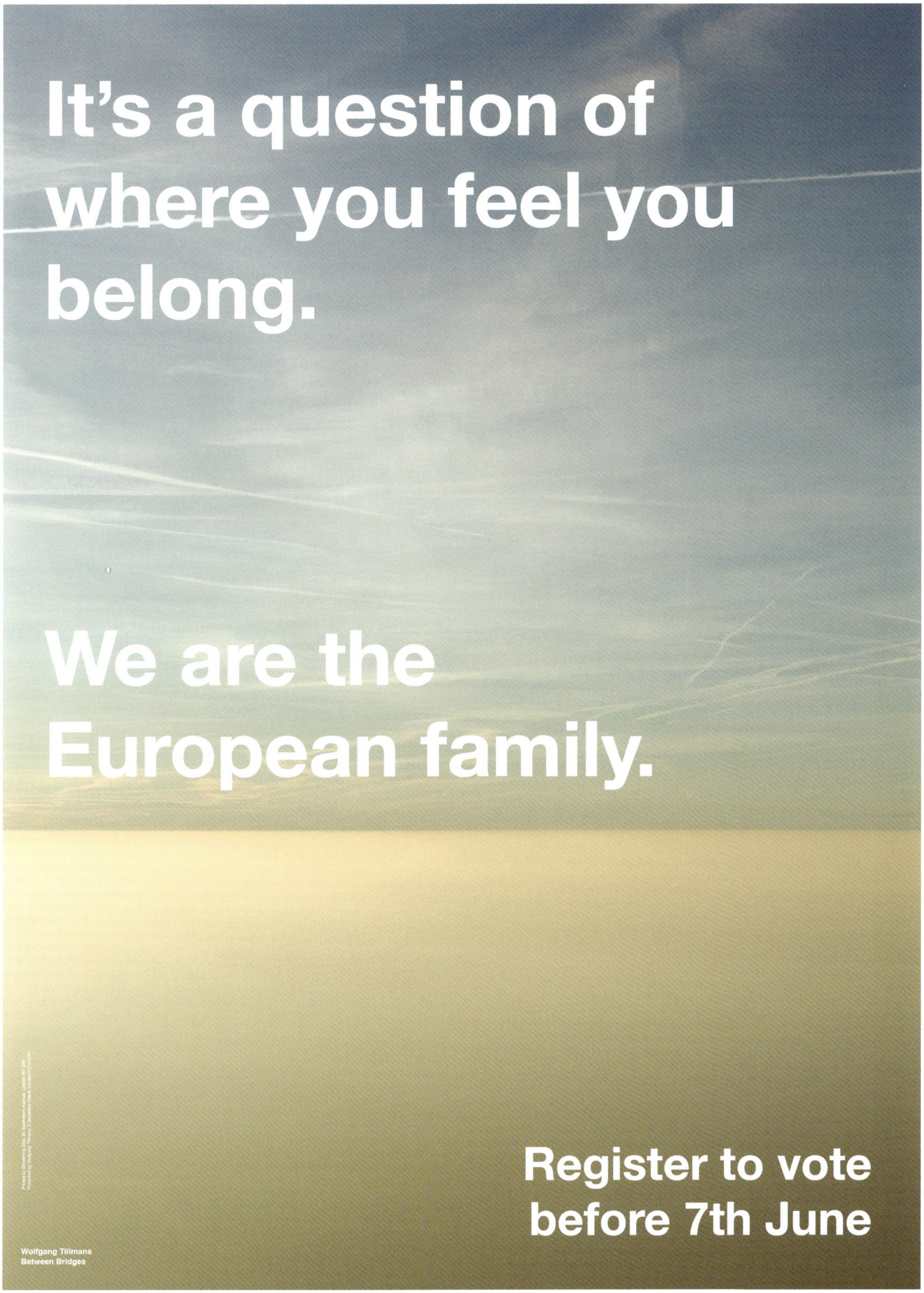
It’s a question of
where you feel you
belong.
We are the
European family.
Register to vote
before 7th June
Wolfgang Tillmans
Between Bridges

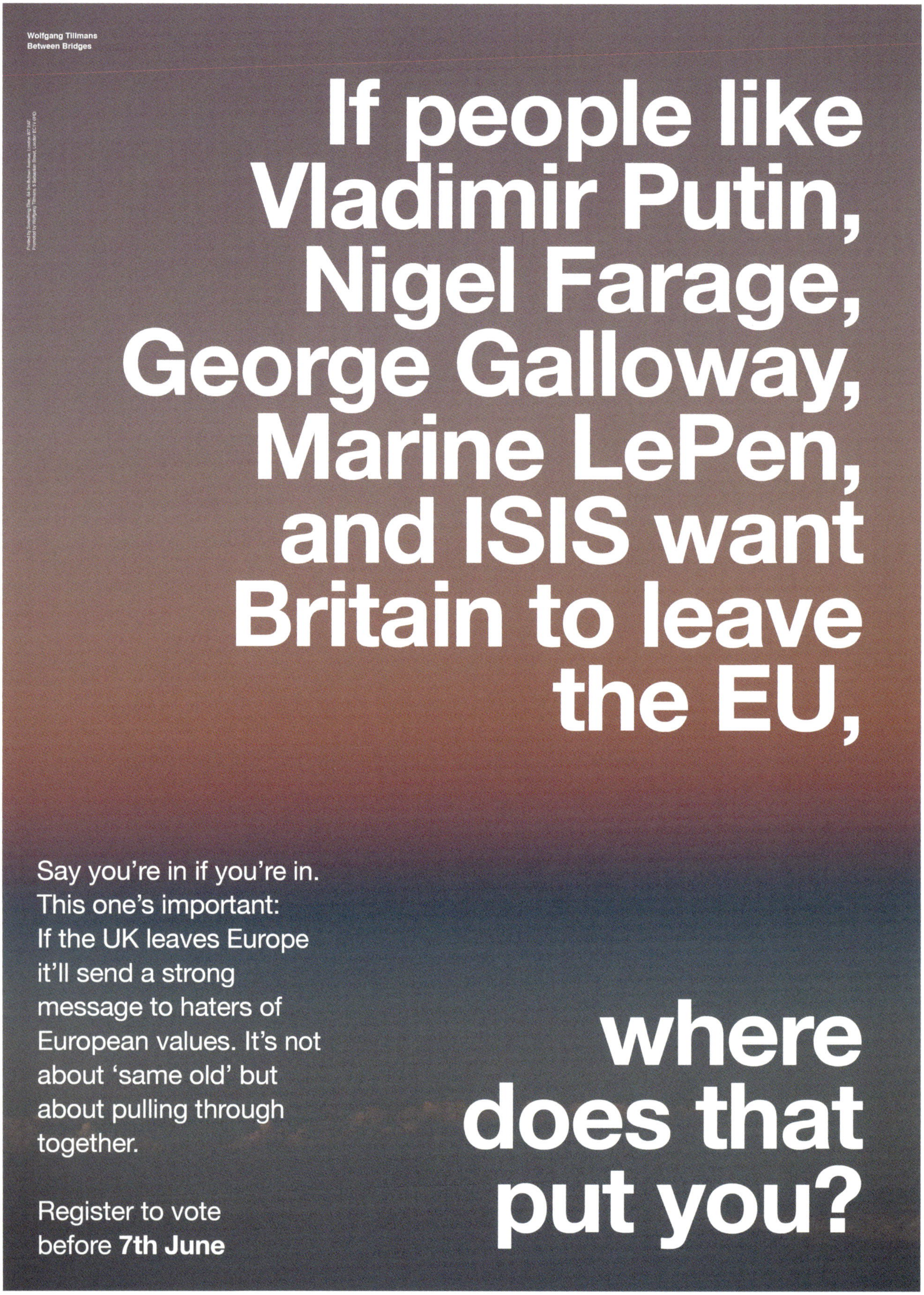
Wolfgang Tillmans
Between Bridges
If people like Vladimir Putin, Nigel Farage, George Galloway, Marine LePen, and ISIS want Britain to leave the EU,
Say you're in if you're in. This one's important: If the UK leaves Europe it'll send a strong message to haters of European values. It's not about 'same old' but about pulling through together.
Register to vote before 7th June
where does that put you?

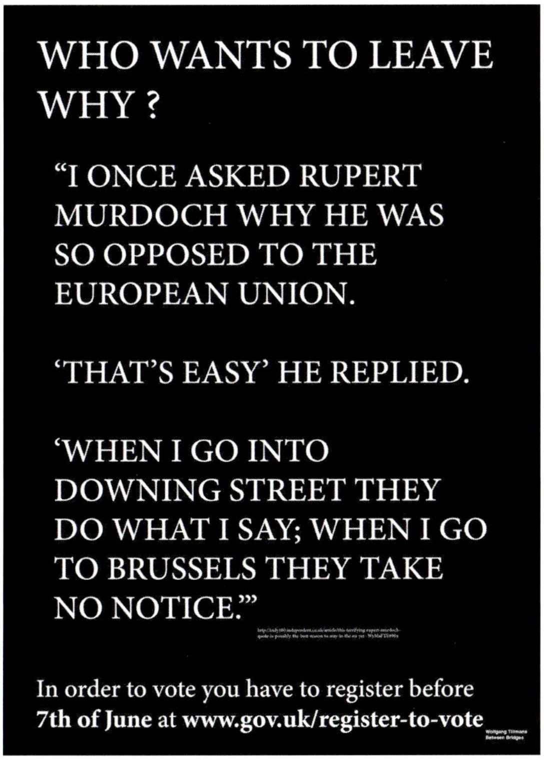

29

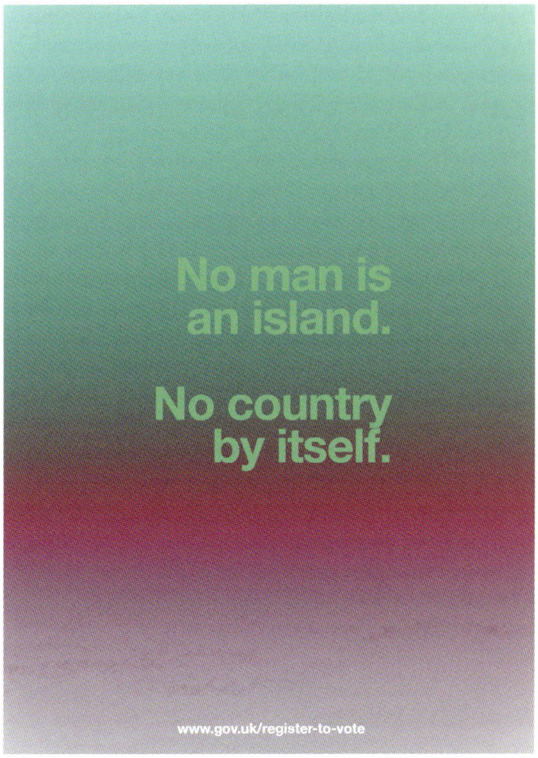

30

> I was driven by the realisation that many of the problems of our age result from claims of absolute truth: the claim of absolute truth made by Islamists, for example, whose propaganda I would read on stickers posted around the neighbourhood of my London studio, or the claim by the then South African health minister that HIV was not the cause of AIDS. Or the claim made shortly afterward that Saddam Hussein was in some way involved with al-Qaida and, furthermore, had access to weapons of mass destruction.

Joe Keohane, a journalist writing in *What Is Different?*, identifies the 'backfire effect' as being the difficulty people experience in rowing back from a political decision – even when facts are laid out clearly. The amount of information hurtling round the internet and social media means that anyone can find information to back up their beliefs. And therein lies the nub, Keohane explains:

> In reality, we often base our opinions on our beliefs, which can have an uneasy relationship with facts. And rather than facts driving beliefs, our beliefs can dictate the facts we chose to accept. They can cause us to twist facts so they fit better with our preconceived notions. Worst of all, they can lead us to uncritically accept bad information just because it reinforces our beliefs. This reinforcement makes us more confident we're right, and even less likely to listen to any new information. And then we vote.[23]

The abrasive tone of the post-Brexit government manoeuvres on the Northern Ireland Protocol has activated fears that a return to a hard border

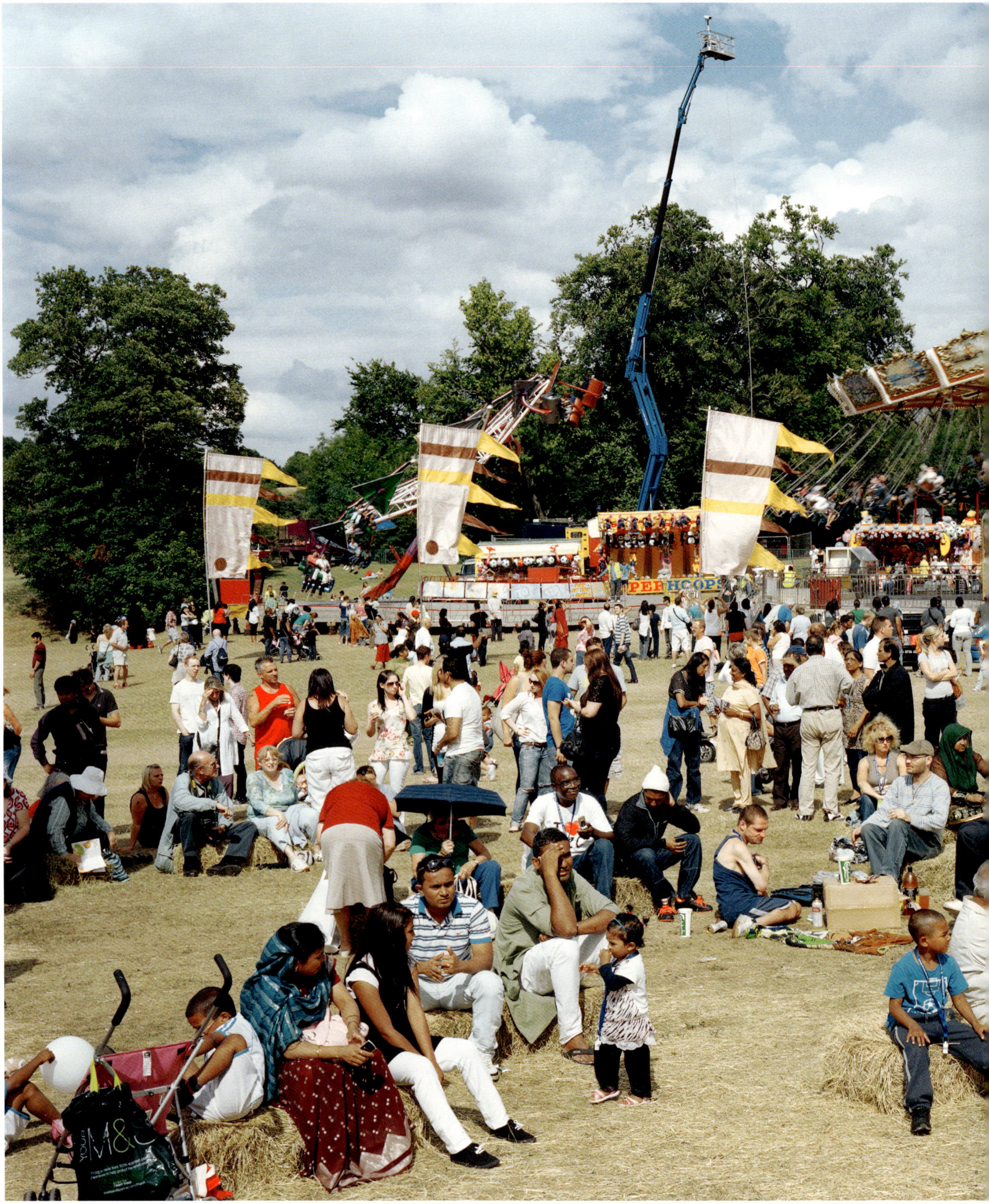
HOOPS

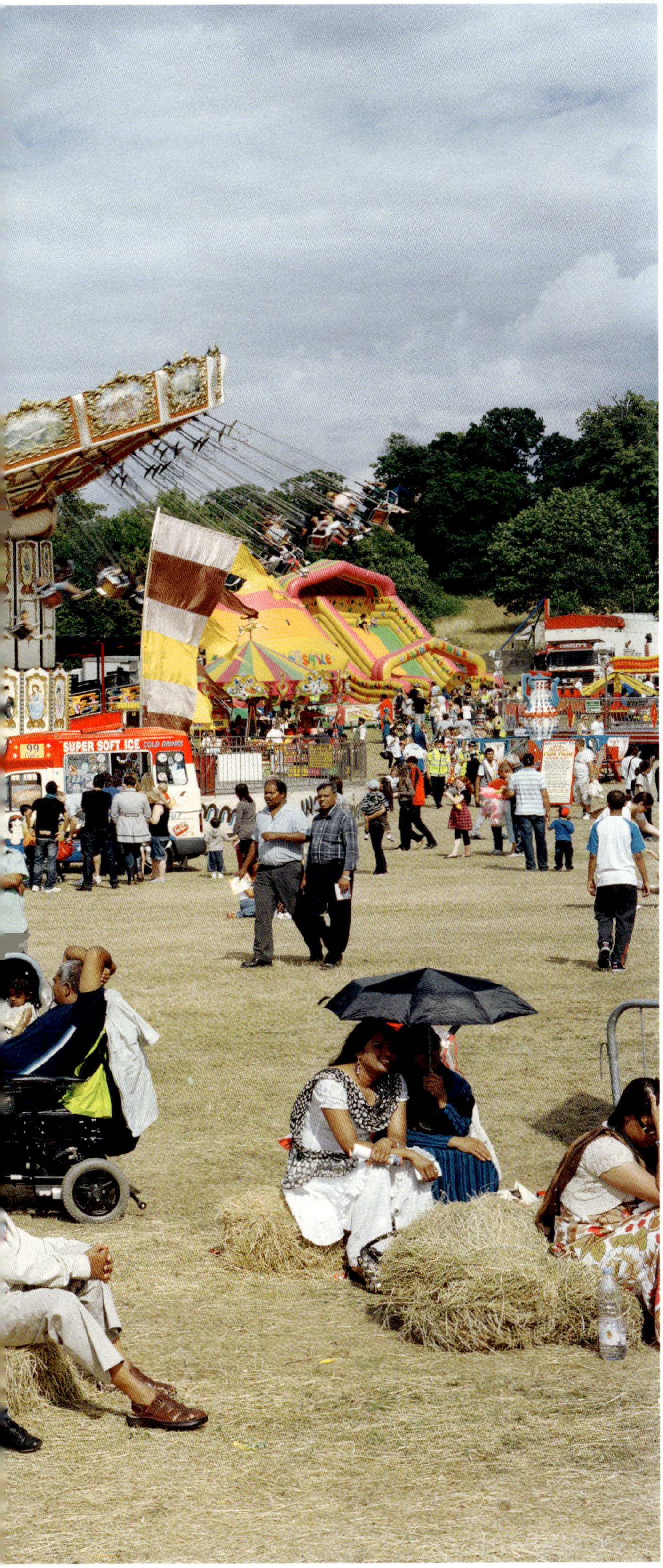

32 Simon Roberts, 'The World Party and Croydon Mela, Lloyd Park, Surrey, 1 August 2010', *Merrie Albion – Landscape Studies of a Small Island, 2007–2017*

Roberts's photographs, taken with a large format camera, reflect on acts of unity and community across a divided country.

these themes are represented and reflected in the landscape'. Roberts, who studied cultural geography at Sheffield University before becoming a photographer, focuses on the sometimes arcane or idiosyncratic groupings and community-oriented leisure pursuits that bind people together within these parameters (figs 31–33).

In my view, Brexit casts its shadow over this work. Looking through the book and talking about the decisions behind the photographs, Roberts reflects that, in retrospect, his generation of photographers [in Britain] were looking elsewhere while the conditions for Brexit were taking root. In the areas of the country already blighted by deindustrialisation, the financial meltdown of 2007–9 and the subsequent hollowing out by the austerity programme following the crash, blunted opportunity and ramped up inequality. Local government was denuded, and a layer of vital scrutiny over local government provisions and decisions hitherto provided by local newspapers disappeared when large newspaper groups snapped up the local press. Oxfam's 2013 report 'The True Cost of Austerity and Inequality' tells how poverty became endemic and public services were slashed in line with the Tory mantra to cut the size of the state.[35]

When I asked Roberts what impact he thought Brexit would have on him and other artists, he said he thinks that one of the consequences of Brexit is that more photographers will necessarily consider climate change, and work on long-term projects in Britain:

> On this point, we are all now thinking about how we make our practices more sustainable. What is my carbon footprint? What exhibitions do I ship abroad? What flights should I take for a commission? The idea that I can't just head over on the Eurostar and work with European partners as easily as I once could is a great shame, and vice versa . . . I believe we have to find ways around it,

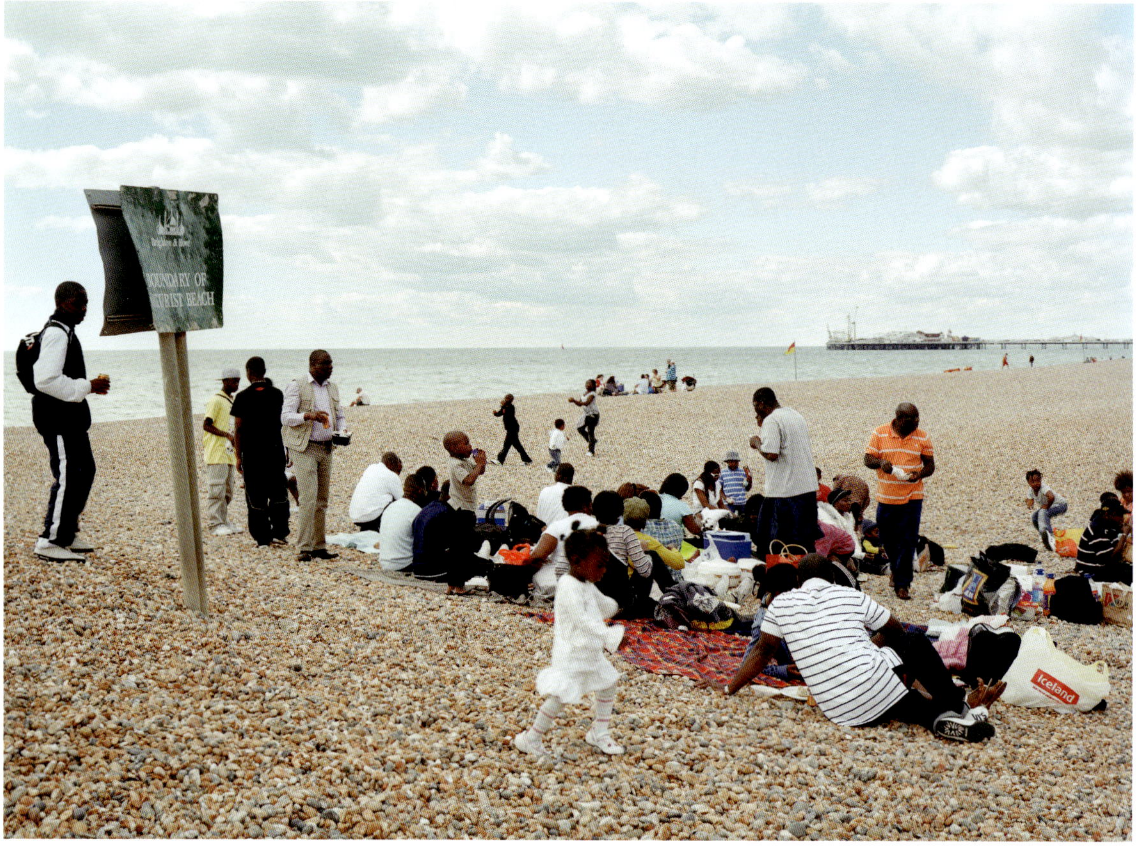

33 Simon Roberts, 'Edmonton Church of Christ Bank Holiday Picnic, Brighton, East Sussex, 30 August 2010', *Merrie Albion – Landscape Studies of a Small Island*, 2007–2017

> whether that means that we become more British-centric, regional or local in the work we make, which to some extent isn't necessarily a bad thing, in that I do feel one of the motivations for making my *Merrie Albion* series was the fact that a lot of my generation travelled abroad to make work and there was very little introspection; there was very little work really considering what was going on at home.
>
> Perhaps that is why few in the cultural sector saw Brexit coming, because we weren't in those local communities – or very few of us at least – making work on the ground, in the same way that our forebears in the 1970s were. That was a generation very much motivated by making work that interrogated political decisions and ramifications of post-industrial Britain, and so there is certainly an argument now that says that we need to take closer stock on exploring and questioning and pushing the boundaries of how we comment on our own country, and question what is going on socially, economically, and culturally.[36]

The artist, who is based in Hove, talks of the repercussions of the referendum for artists, and the wider environmental factors that now impact on the art world. All the artists and photographers I have spoken to talk of the personal impact Brexit has had on their lives through the loss of opportunities, such as the Erasmus student exchange programme, fellowships and artist residencies.[37] This is quite apart from the barriers to touring exhibitions or the possibility of moving to Europe for full- or part-time work. These avenues for artistic collaboration, growth and exploration are blocked to varying degrees. And then there is the impact and implications of Brexit and climate change on art moving around the world (see Chapter 4.)

For Roberts, Brexit meant the cancellation, in September 2020, of a two-year residency in Antwerp:

> I had the funding – and the project was going to be about new borders and would be looking at the changing relationship between Britain and Europe but concentrating on the coastal regions. After months of trying, the Academy couldn't find a way of employing me because they can't get a visa and there was no way around paying me unless I was a resident or an EU citizen. I had to kiss goodbye to two years of funding, and I can't really do the project without their support. It's not the sort of thing the Arts Council would fund so I'm in a position where I have spent nine months researching something and it stopped overnight.
>
> I suppose that when people say, 'What has been the impact of Brexit?', well, I think now we're starting to see the ramifications for artists and the cultural sector. There was a lot of discussion and talk for two or three years about suggested ideas about what it might be like, but now the reality is starting to set in. Another thing is that I was supposed to have an Erasmus student [come to work with me]. I've always had a student come to work with me for two or three months from the Netherlands and we are no longer in their programme – and that was a great experience for me, but also for them working with a professional photographer, experiencing another city and it's a great shame.[38]

Ewan Macbeth, a Scottish artist living and working in Rotterdam, had benefited from the Erasmus programme when he was at Glasgow School of Art.[39] He chose Leipzig:

> I've always been drawn to the alternative cities – not the capitals. The alternative cities are usually a bit more underground to live in, which is nice, but I can't really remember the logic of it. I had read a book which mentioned Leipzig, called *Stasiland* by Anna Funder, with stories from behind the wall, and it's really just about people and their experience with the East German Stasi.[40]

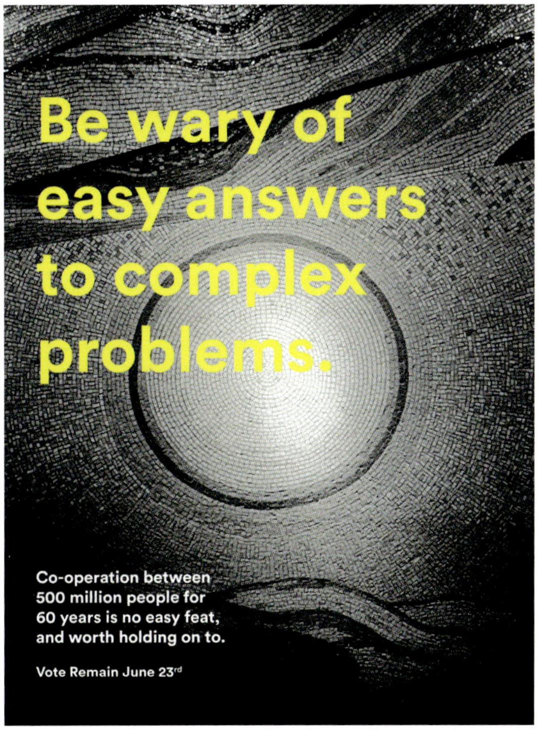

34 Ewan Macbeth, 2016, poster produced at the time of the referendum, published in *The Guardian* newspaper

It was an eye-opening experience for Macbeth – not least because the classes were in German – yet Erasmus offered new insights into art and photography, with some classes being taught by Joachim Brohm who is seen by some as the 'German Eggleston'. The American photographer William Eggleston's singular, visceral colour portraits of the American South found a place for colour photography at a time when black-and-white images held sway in art and documentary.[41] The point is that studying in a different country opens up possibilities and augments study programmes offered in the home country. Because of Brexit Macbeth left the UK to do an MA degree in lens-based media at the Piet Zwart Institute in Rotterdam. As one of a generation who grew up while the UK was at war in Iraq and Tony Blair's Labour Party marched with George Bush's Republican might, Macbeth's work explores the corrosive nature of corruption on politicians and political networks (fig.34). His short film *Divided Together* (2018) is 'based on the behaviour and lies of coalition leaders at the start of the so-called "war on terror"', and his film *Prison With Songbirds* (2022) blends documentary with fiction to unsettling effect.

The cliffs at Dover hold an iconic status, not just in the British imagination but also for visitors. Vera Lynn's much-loved song 'The White Cliffs of Dover', full of promise and longing, bolstered morale during the Second World War.

> There'll be bluebirds over
> The white cliffs of Dover
> Tomorrow, just you wait and see
>
> There'll be love and laughter
> And peace ever after
> Tomorrow, when the world is free
>
> The shepherd will tend his sheep
> The valley will bloom again
> And Jimmy will go to sleep
> In his own little room again
>
> There'll be bluebirds over
> The white cliffs of Dover
> Tomorrow, just you wait and see
>
> The shepherd will tend his sheep
> The valley will bloom again
> And Jimmy will go to sleep
> In his own little room again
>
> There'll be bluebirds over
> The white cliffs of Dover
> Tomorrow, just you wait and see

'The White Cliffs of Dover'
Words and Music by Walter Kent and Nat Burton

The shepherd tending his flock and the sense of care, security and safety that thread through the song, which was released in 1942, became locked in the English imagination. I have always wondered about the bluebirds, which are nowhere to be found in Britain. The songwriters were American, and they had never been to Britain. Peter Wilby, writing in the *New Statesman*, suggested there may have been more to these birds:

> Why didn't somebody insert blackbirds or swallows instead? Well, swallows look quite blue and RAF uniforms were blue. But the most likely explanation, to my mind, is that, with continued US involvement in the war still uncertain, the British thought bluebirds would persuade Americans to keep fighting alongside us.[42]

People often mistake the chalk cliffs at the Seven Sisters near Eastbourne in Sussex for the white cliffs of Dover in Kent, says Roberts. He was drawn to the daunting coastline of the Seven Sisters as, in March 2017, nine months after the UK voted to leave, the then prime minister Theresa May signed Article 50,[43] activating the official mechanism that would set this departure in motion. Article 50 of the Lisbon Treaty came into law in 2009 and set out for the first time how a country could leave the EU. For those who view Britain as part of Europe, 28 March 2017 was a bleak day. Roberts adapted an image from *Merrie Albion*. This image of people walking along the clifftop was for *Between the Acts*, Part 1, an artist poster commissioned by flyingleaps and accompanied by a quote from Virginia Woolf's novel *Between the Acts*: 'They looked at the view; they looked at what they knew, to see if what they knew might perhaps be different today. Most days it was the same.'[44]

> Of course, I had no idea that that's how it would end, but that became a position where I thought, this is such a significant political moment in recent history, in 50 years really, that it seemed to be an important moment to end this particular way of looking at the British landscape. How could I mark this particular moment in time? And because, of course, I was looking at the landscape, I was thinking, what would be the landscape that represents ideas of British-ness,

right

35 Simon Roberts, *Between the Acts*, Part 1, #1, 2018

Between the Acts *(2018) is an artist poster commissioned by flyingleaps and created in response to the Brexit negotiations.*

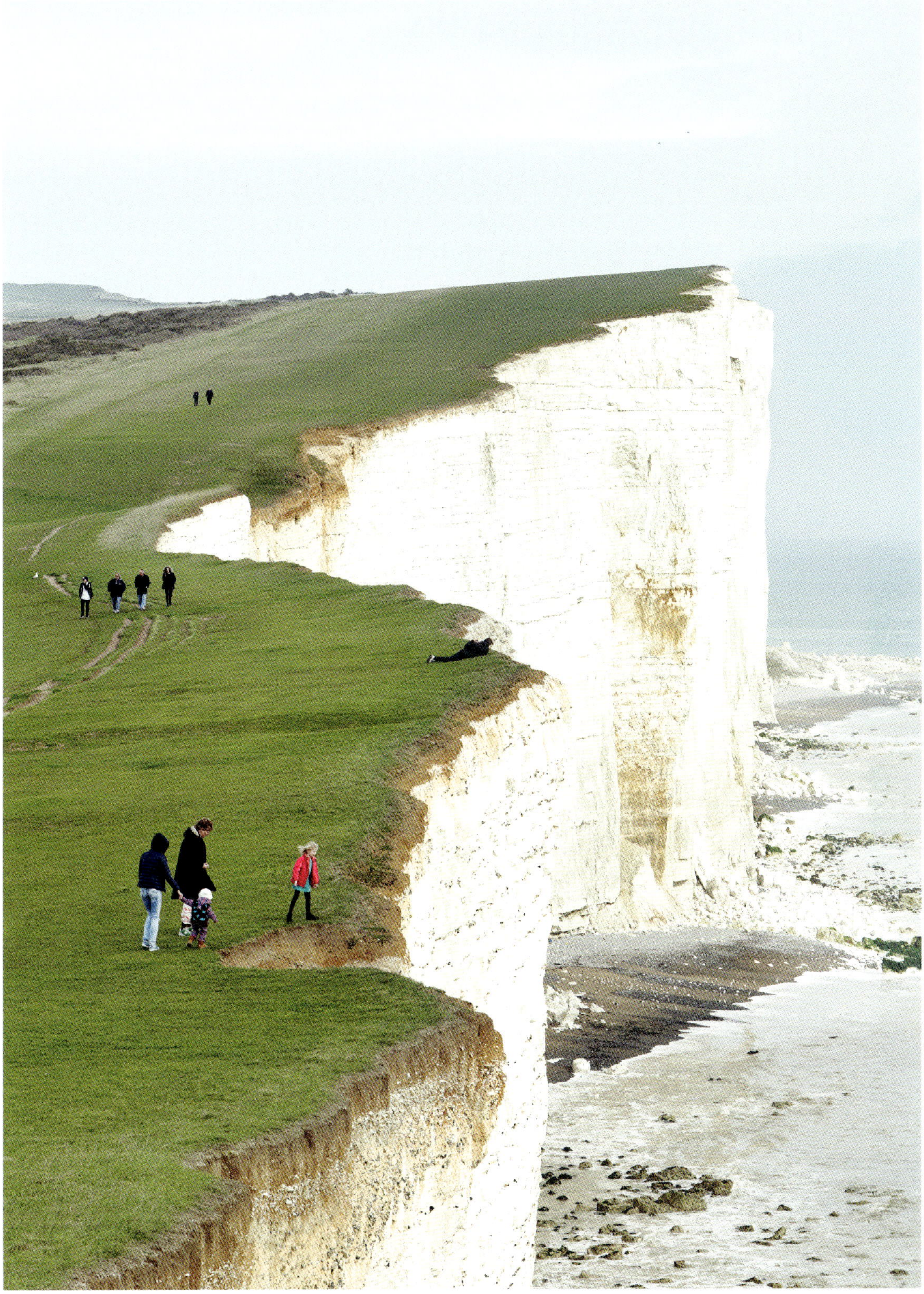

“THEY LOOKED AT THE VIEW; THEY LOOKED AT WHAT THEY KNEW, TO SEE IF WHAT THEY KNEW MIGHT PERHAPS BE DIFFERENT TODAY. MOST DAYS IT WAS THE SAME.”

VIRGINIA WOOLF (1941)

Between the Acts, 2018
SIMON ROBERTS

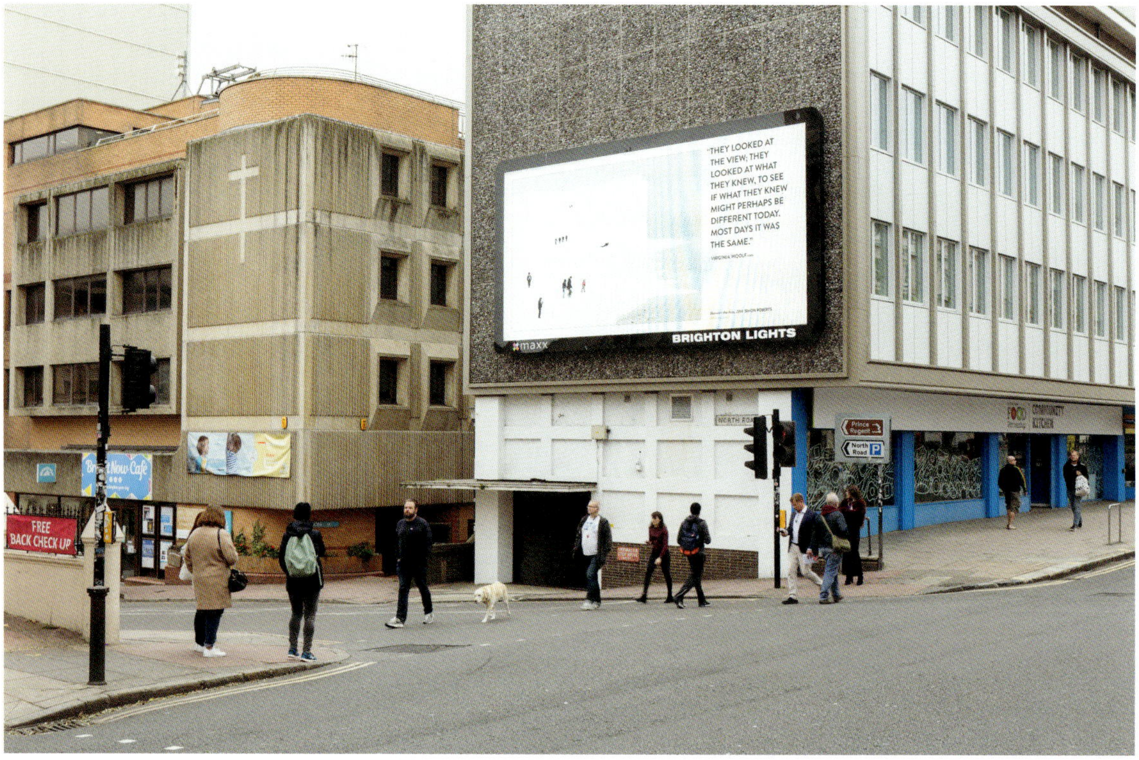

36 Simon Roberts, *Between the Acts*, Part 1, #2, Brighton, October 2018

Roberts created an abstract version of the image of the cliffs in response to an intervention on public safety from Brighton and Hove City Council, who felt the image of a local landmark, associated with suicide and accidental deaths was inappropriate.

> and of course, one of the major ones for me would be the white cliffs.
>
> It seemed a pertinent way of thinking and looking at this current moment in time. When faced with an abyss – whether natural or man-made – it's difficult to resist staring into it. And by displaying the poster in the public realm, the aim was to create an unexpected, thought-provoking contribution to the urban spectacle, turning the street into a platform to challenge ideas and attitudes towards Brexit.

These cliffs instil fear in me. Some people go there to take their own lives, others fall by accident: yet there are no barriers as there are further along by Beachy Head. It is certainly a stark metaphor for a turning away from Europe. The poster was originally pasted on billboards across the country, in Bristol, Glasgow, London and Manchester early in 2018, but when the posters were then displayed across Brighton as part of the 2018 Photo Fringe, Brighton and Hove City Council removed several of them (fig.35).

The image of the local landmark, which is associated with suicides and accidental deaths, was deemed inappropriate by some residents, who suggested it could encourage people to kill themselves. Roberts reworked the posters (fig.36) – leaving white space where the cliffs had been – and thereby opening up a broader debate about art in the public space:

> I took them at their word and removed the cliff in Photoshop and put the new image up on exactly the same billboard spaces in an attempt to open up a wider conversation about civic power and censorship. It was interesting to watch how the public reacted with this new iteration of the poster with its liminal space and somewhat ghostly appearance. People tended to spend more time looking at this new version, possibly because we're quite immune to seeing so much blank space on advertising billboards, which are usually so bold and garish.[45]

Uta Kögelsberger, who was born and raised in Brussels to German parents and is now professor of history of art at Newcastle University, surveys the scene of Brexit from these vantage points. Living and working in the north-east of England, which voted overwhelmingly to leave the EU, meant that the artist was at odds with many around her:

> The morning the referendum result was announced I took the metro from Tynemouth to Newcastle town centre. The outskirts of Newcastle had heavily voted Leave. I remember looking around the train packed with commuters and thinking: '54 per cent of you would rather I wasn't here.' It was an absolutely gutting feeling. I moved to the UK in 1989, so many of the people I was looking at were younger than me and probably were born after I moved here. They had a right to vote in this election and they had a right to vote on whether I would stay or not, and that felt really wrong. All of my adult working life has been spent working here, and over these years all my resources have fed back into this culture, both as an artist and as a lecturer at Newcastle University. Many of my European friends, me included, felt like we had been 'dumped'. The kind of relationship breakdown where someone leaves you without even trying to work at it or without having a discussion.[46]

Kögelsberger came to the UK, inspired by the Young British Artists, and in awe of the feeling of London:

> There was such a buzz, and I was in awe of its multiculturalism. It just felt like such a free, independent and wild hotchpotch of people who seemed to live together in a live and let live attitude. You are talking about your multiculturalism. Growing up in a foreign country makes you kind of homeless – you don't really belong anywhere properly. Homeless is a bit of an exaggeration, but there's a different sense of the relationship to the place that you are living if you are not a national.

Kögelsberger's visceral response to the referendum produced a fusion of formal artistic considerations, a pump of activism and a desire to place photographs of those affected by Brexit in the public domain. The portrait series *Uncertain Subjects I*, *II*, *III* and *IV* has evolved through different iterations, starting in 2017 as *Mail Art: Uncertain Subjects Part 1*. These were postcards that were posted out: it was up to the recipient whether to archive, jettison or send on the postcard. *Uncertain Subjects* moved into the public sphere with billboard-sized portraits, posted up in the street and on the side of shipping containers. This continuing project was configured as a response to the insecurity that Brexit introduced for the three million Europeans in the UK. It is a pithy retort to those who would ask of people who had made Britain their home and contributed substantially to the cultural, intellectual and financial capital of Britain pre-2016, and who called into question their right to remain: Why are you here? Where do you come from? When are you going home?

Kögelsberger initiated the project in this way as a counterpoint to the rupture of Brexit. The bare-shouldered portraits in *Uncertain Subjects* exude a sense of vulnerability and authenticity. Initially, the artist photographed only men as a study in masculine vulnerability. The impetus for this study came from a head-and-shoulders shot that she took of her husband one morning to focus her camera, so that *he* could take a photograph of *her* for Yale radio. But this image of him was raw and striking: 'He looked like he'd just come out of an egg with egg yolk still stuck to him. I knew I wanted to do something with this kind of portrait.'

The shedding of clothes and signifiers of habitat and class brings these people together in the same space. Their direct gaze counters the command of Brexit. The aesthetic considerations in the portraits align with activism, Kögelsberger says:

> *Uncertain Subjects* may be activist, but there are many formal and aesthetic decisions that have gone into making this work. I think form and content are inseparable from one another when making work. That is what makes *Uncertain Subjects* both artistic practice, document and activism. Or in other words, *Uncertain Subjects*' activism is as much a part of the work as are the formal decisions about how the subjects are photographed: with bare shoulders, engaging the viewer through a gaze directly into the camera as if they were looking at the viewer and in their home environments, as a metaphor for how unstable their situation has become. The way the work was materialised first as postcards and then later as billboard performances is as much a part of the message as it is a formal decision.

The political came to the fore – and Kögelsberger's response stemmed in part from childhood memories of exclusion as a German growing up in Belgium:

> Brexit really changed the way I think about making work. My work was always political, but never as directly as it has become since. After the referendum result, it felt no longer OK to make work that 'just' makes you think. It needed to engage people more directly.
>
> Growing up in Belgium as a German in the '70s and '80s, I was often confronted with the question why so many Germans stood by when they witnessed the rise of nationalism. So, when this hugely flawed election process, based on the fabrication of misinformation carefully crafted to trigger fears led to the Leave vote, to me, it felt like my civic responsibility to directly engage with the situation. As an artist and academic, I have a public platform. There are channels that I can use to make myself and others heard, and it felt critical to start using these channels.

The consecutive iterations of *Uncertain Subjects, Parts II*, *III* and *IV,* are termed 'Action Photographs', and took the project into different areas of the public sphere, from Art Night in London to the Brighton Photo Biennial and lastly to Grainger Market in Newcastle (figs 37–41). This synthesis of photograph and political activism builds on the action photography of the 1970s. This was the term given to photographic strategies within collectives and community darkrooms, as photographers sought to effect social and political change and take these politicised exhibitions into the public sphere.[47] As Lisa Le Feuvre, a curator, writer and editor, outlines in her discussion with Kögelsberger, the artist creates the conditions for looking at the world in a different way. And this is something that the art projects around and subsequent to the referendum seek to do, to reshape disappointment or despair, and direct enquiry through a contemplation of landscape and portraiture. And this functions as a reclaiming.[48]

Le Feuvre speaks of the iterations of *Uncertain Subjects* as a 'billboard performance' and the portraits – on the side of shipping containers, and on huge billboards, which incorporate the labour of pasting them up and pasting over them, as one image erases the other – as a metaphor for the shifting plates of Brexit. Kögelsberger describes the process:

> The billboards are made of 12 sheets, that tile one after the other. Maybe the most compelling part is that moment when one person's face starts to be covered up by the next: often the images join up in unexpected ways to break down and reconstruct a coherent image. It starts acting like a metaphor for the loss of identity or belonging that was triggered by the process of Brexit. By the end of a performance, you have 30 or 40 people that have been billboarded on top of each other. It's also like an erasure of voices, an erasure of positions, like one voice that gets drowned out by the next, that I think is very

right

37 Uta Kögelsberger, *Uncertain Subjects Part IV*: Grainger Market, Newcastle Upon Tyne, 2019

overleaf

38 Uta Kögelsberger, *Uncertain Subjects Part V* (ongoing)

In 2019, stills from the previous Uncertain Subjects *performances were installed on the Great Eastern Wall, East London, as a long term display.*

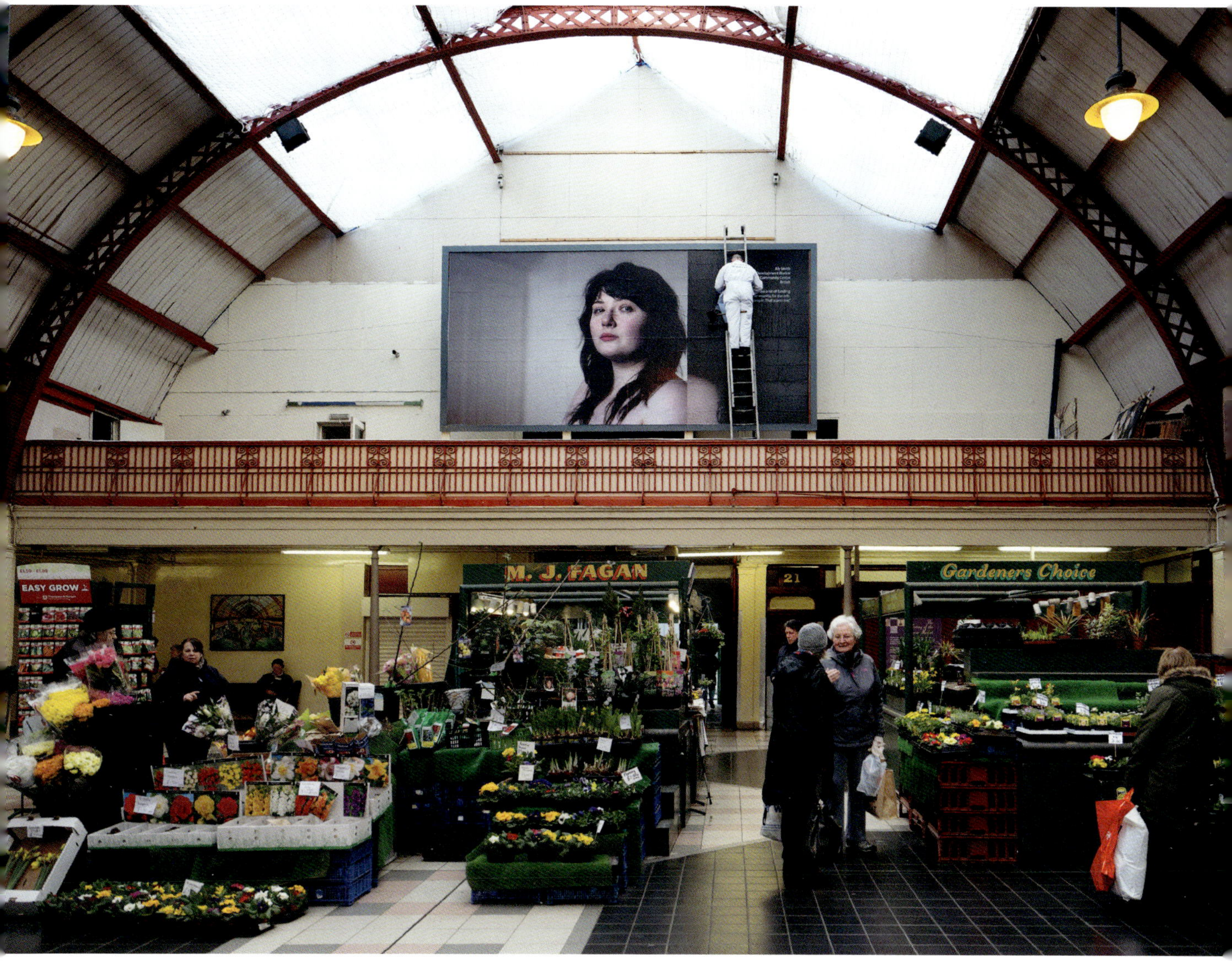

“I fear we are going to lose a lot of funding around here, for the community, for the arts and the young people. That scares me.”

ALY SMITH,
COMMUNITY DEVELOPMENT WORKER,
BYKER COMMUNITY CENTRE

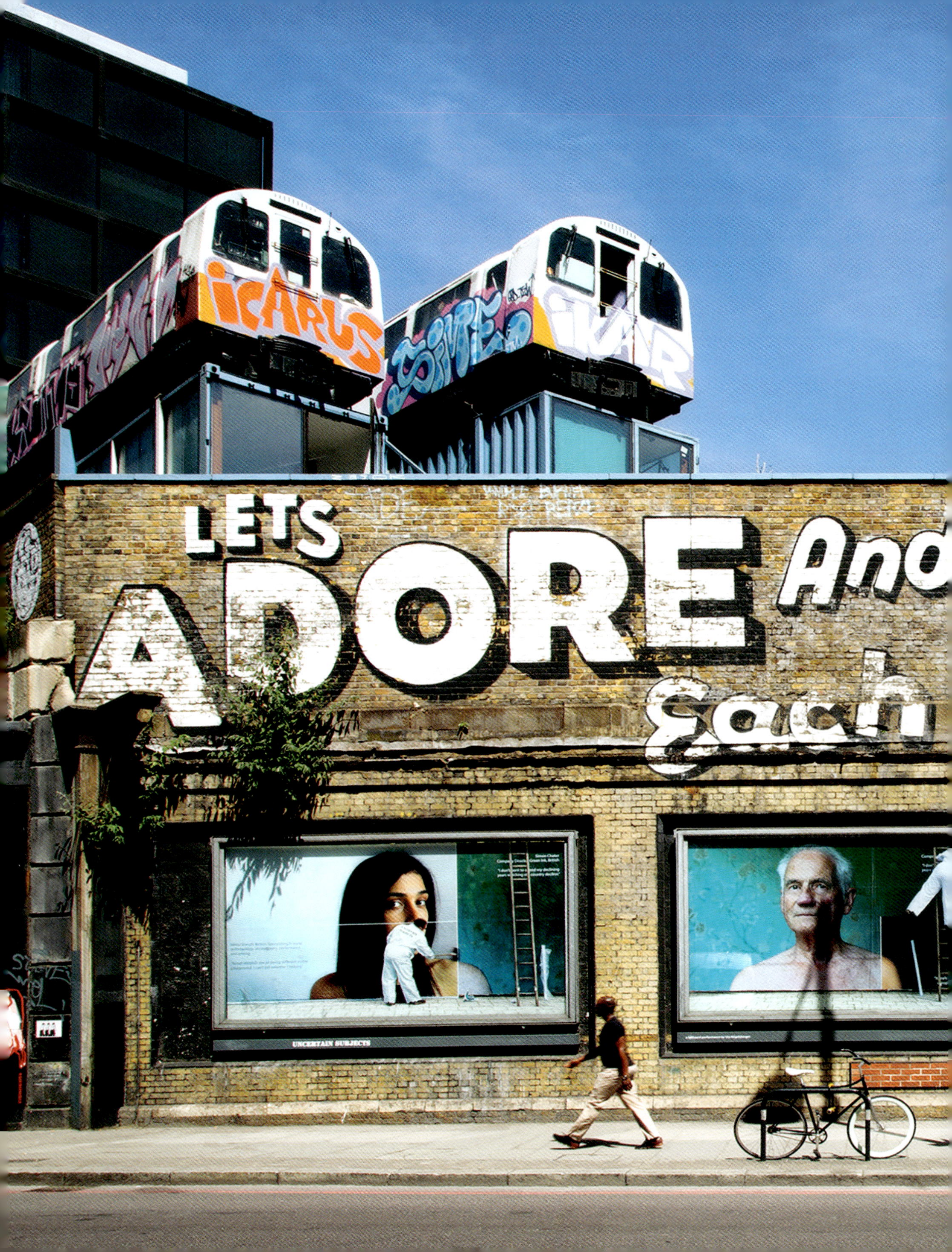

LETS
ADORE And
Each
UNCERTAIN SUBJECTS

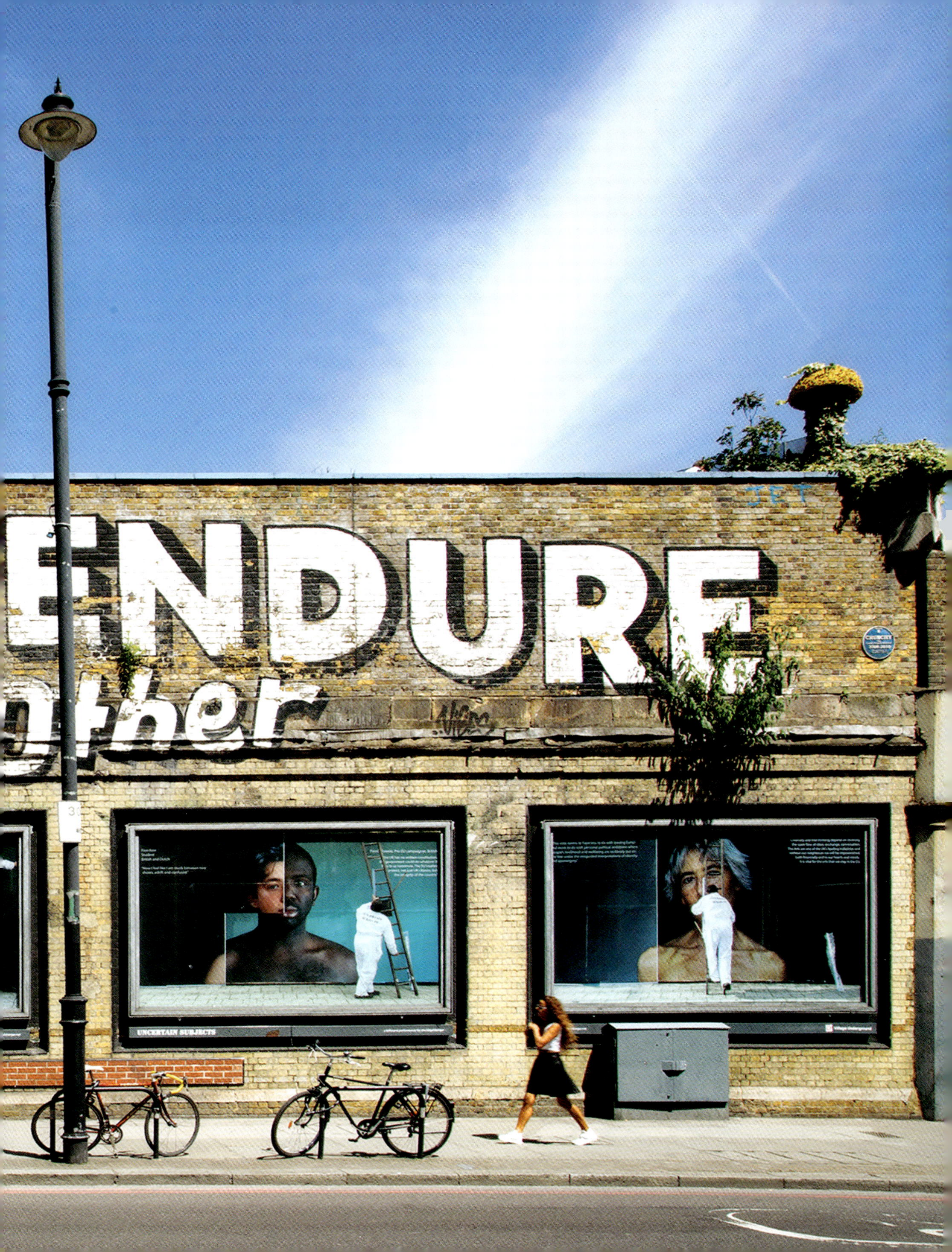
ENDURE
UNCERTAIN SUBJECTS

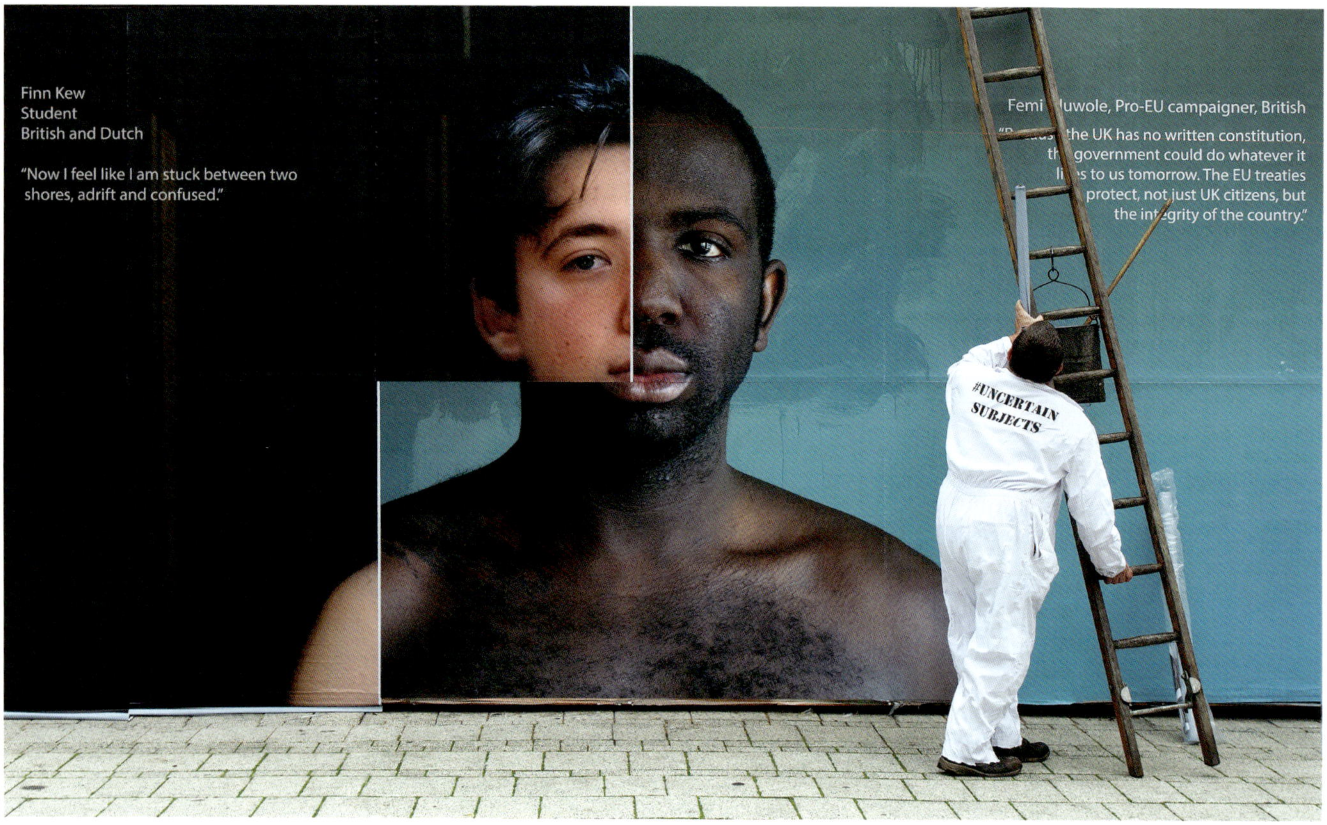

left

"Now I feel like I am stuck between two shores, adrift and confused."

FINN KEW, STUDENT, BRITISH AND DUTCH

right

"Because the UK has no written constitution, the government could do whatever it likes to us tomorrow. The EU treaties protect, not just UK citizens, but the integrity of the country."

FEMI OLUWOLE, PRO EU CAMPAIGNER, BRITISH

39 Uta Kögelsberger, *Uncertain Subjects Part III*: Brighton Photo Biennial, 2018

> representative of what was happening in the run-up to Brexit and is being continued with the ongoing wider populist agenda – recently, the government cut 50 per cent of funding to the arts in higher education. That, to me, represents a very intentional move of crushing independent thinking – the current government knows that we are not likely to vote for them.

Over the course of *Uncertain Subjects*, the cohort within the portraits has widened to include British citizens who felt that they did not have a voice after the referendum. But the artist found that although every portrait showed someone who voted Remain, the audience, whether watching the performance at Brighton Photo Biennial or at Grainger Market, made their views clear:

> There was a lot of discussion during these performances about Brexit, in Brighton in particular, maybe because of the way the work was set up on the side of a container, in a central square in front of the library. On the very first day when we started [the] performance, after an hour one person sat down and broke down in tears because they were so horrified about what was happening in the UK. A couple of hours later a person came up to me and he was so angry – he was shaking from anger. Most of the people in the billboards were against Brexit. So, the public reactions to the work differed greatly depending on people's position.
>
> It was also interesting to understand who was willing to be photographed. By the time I developed the work for Art Night, the work had moved on from the initial postcard series, which had focused on EU citizens, and had started to include British citizens who felt like they had no representation in parliament after the referendum. It was such a crazy time. It felt like half the country had lost its voice. By the time I

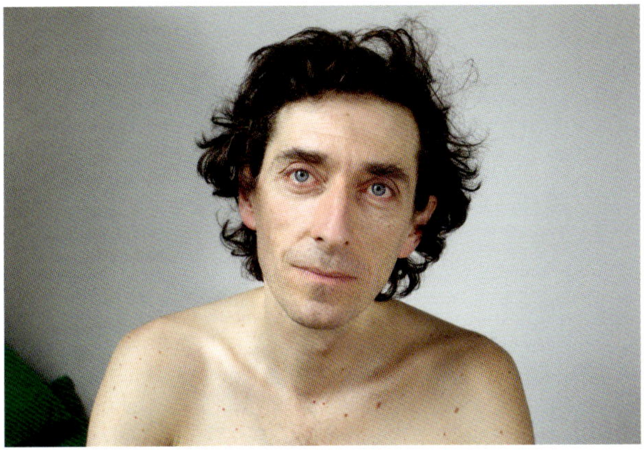

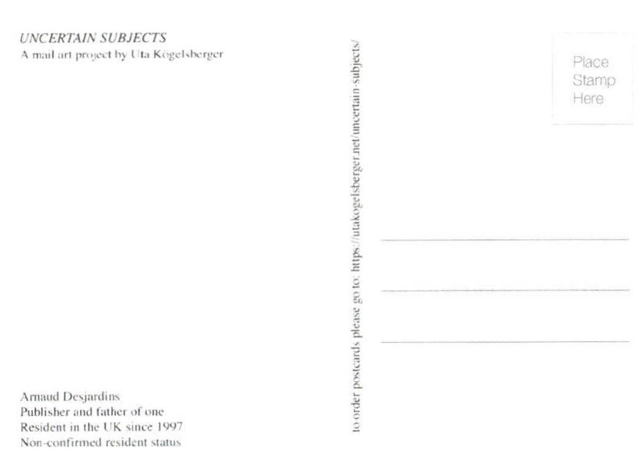
UNCERTAIN SUBJECTS
A mail art project by Uta Kögelsberger

Place
Stamp
Here

to order postcards please go to: https://utakogelsberger.net/uncertain-subjects/

Arnaud Desjardins
Publisher and father of one
Resident in the UK since 1997
Non-confirmed resident status

'I feel betrayed and the object of political manipulations – not a human being – not a citizen. Fuck nationalism."

ARNAUD DESJARDINS
PUBLISHER AND FATHER OF ONE
RESIDENT IN THE UK SINCE 1997
NON-CONFIRMED RESIDENT STATUS

40 Uta Kögelsberger, *Mail Art: Uncertain Subjects Part I*, 2017

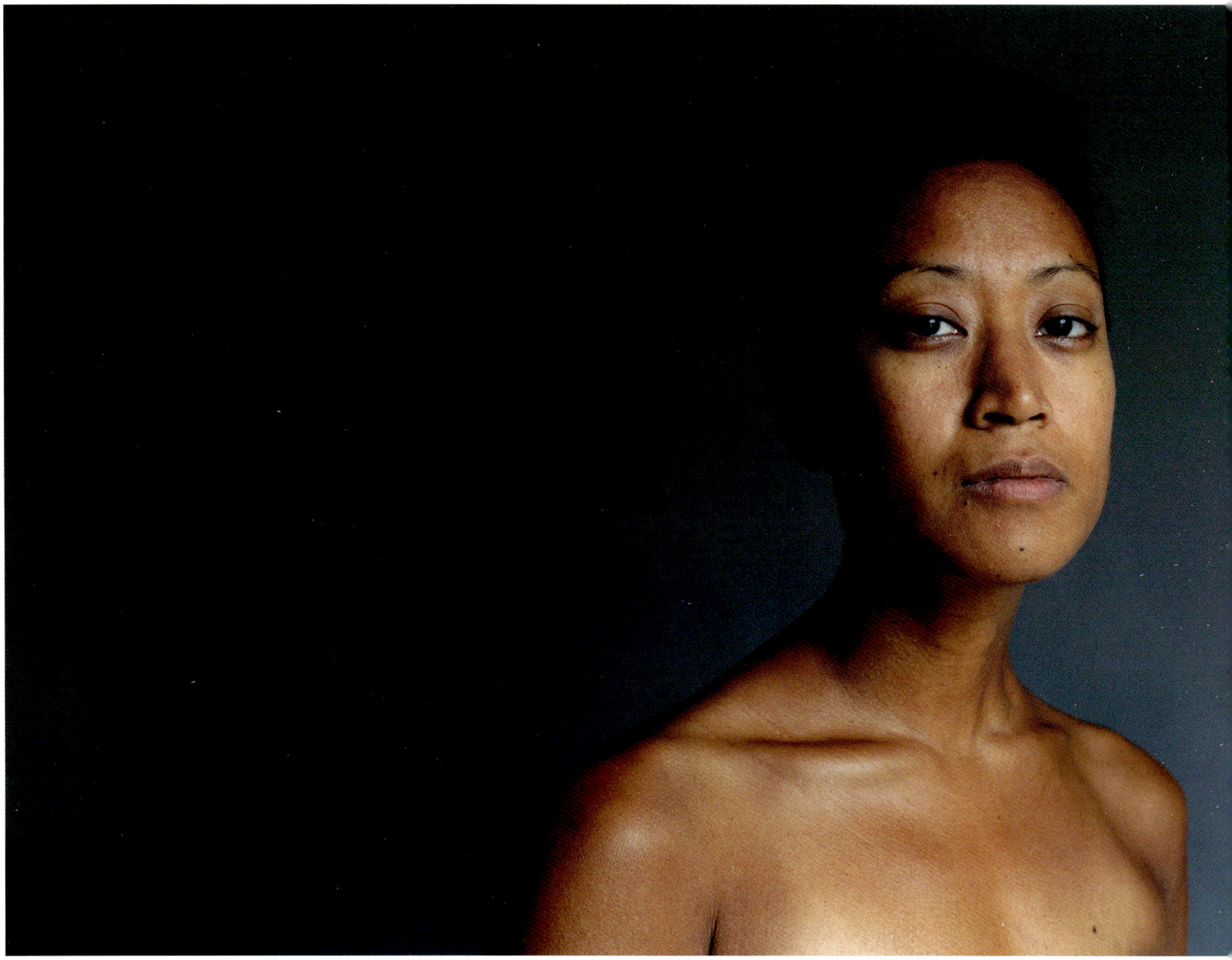

developed the performance for Brighton, I was really looking very hard to include people who had voted Leave and had changed to Remain since then.

The portraits are accompanied by statements: on the upheaval to people's lives, dashed hopes, and a fragmented identity. There is doubt where there was once a sense of belonging: when someone has built a life in Britain and contemplates moving away, applying for British citizenship, or remaining in the UK on *different* terms.

Kögelsberger placed portraits in Newcastle at the Grainger Indoor Market, which was built in 1835 and is home to a huge range of small and independent traders. In a gallery or museum, there is a critical space. It is expected that visitors will engage with the art and form opinions on the work, but not intervene with it publicly, although art in galleries is currently the site of protest for climate change activists. Art in the street invites intervention: there is no mediation and rebuttal may be swift, as Kögelsberger found when billboards were installed in the street in Newcastle at night but had been torn down by morning.

In 2021, *Division/Revision*, a billboard exhibition curated by Kögelsberger, displayed 16 artworks across the UK on 16 billboards which changed

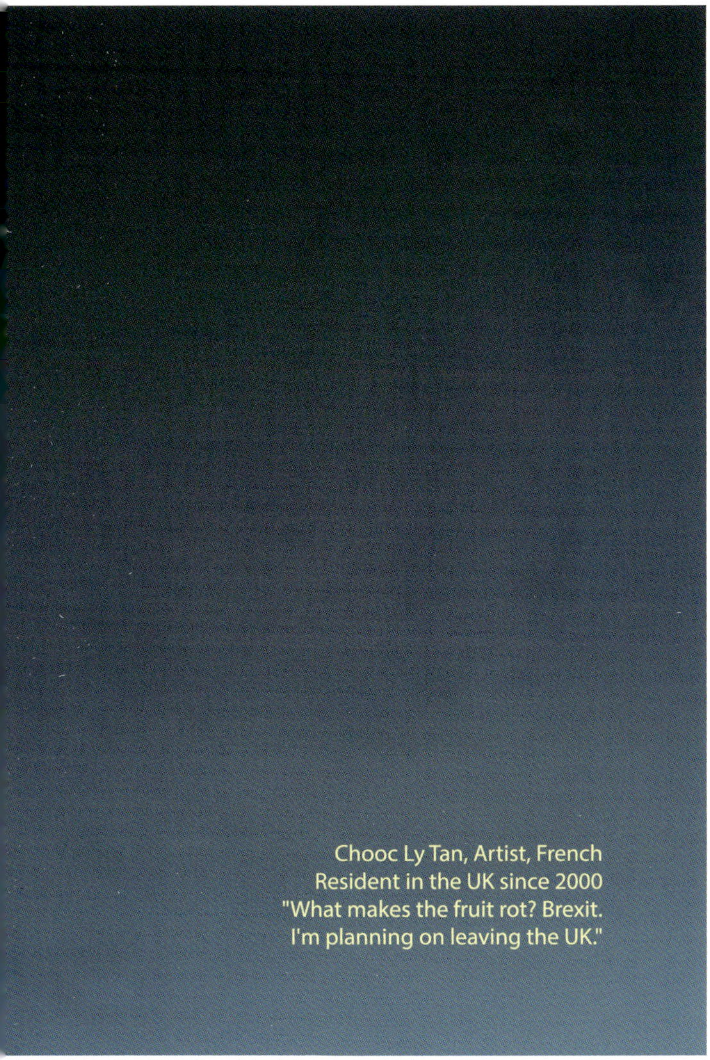

"What makes the fruit rot? Brexit. I'm planning on leaving the UK."

CHOOC LY TAN, ARTIST, FRENCH, RESIDENT IN THE UK SINCE 2000

41 Uta Kögelsberger, *Uncertain Subjects: The Subjects* (2017–ongoing), 2018

daily for 16 consecutive days.[49] This is another example of the exuberance of street art in response to social and political turmoil – in this case, the desire to reflect on what brings us together and what pushes us apart. The billboard exhibition, supported by Buildhollywood with its 'Your Space Or Mine' agenda, included Kögelsberger's *Together/Apart* (2021).

This push for public art and political retort is evident in the work of flyingleaps, an initiative launched by Adrian Burnham with the artist/activist duo Peter Kennard and Cat Phillipps (known as kennardphillipps) on the day of the Brexit referendum, 23 June 2016.[50] This rebel grouping glues protest and provocation in the public sphere by placing posters in the street in 'an index of political, economic and civic power' (figs 6, 42, 43, 44 and 45). This is particularly important with Brexit, with its leaders and campaigners plucked in part from an elite, who claim to speak directly for 'the people', in the way that populist leaders describe this undifferentiated block of voters. Over egg sandwiches at a cafe in north London, Burnham talks of his previous job as a commercial fly poster: 'I did art projects as well. But, basically, I earned my money in the '80s and '90s doing that, so I know a lot of people who do still put posters up. In 1995, I moved from working

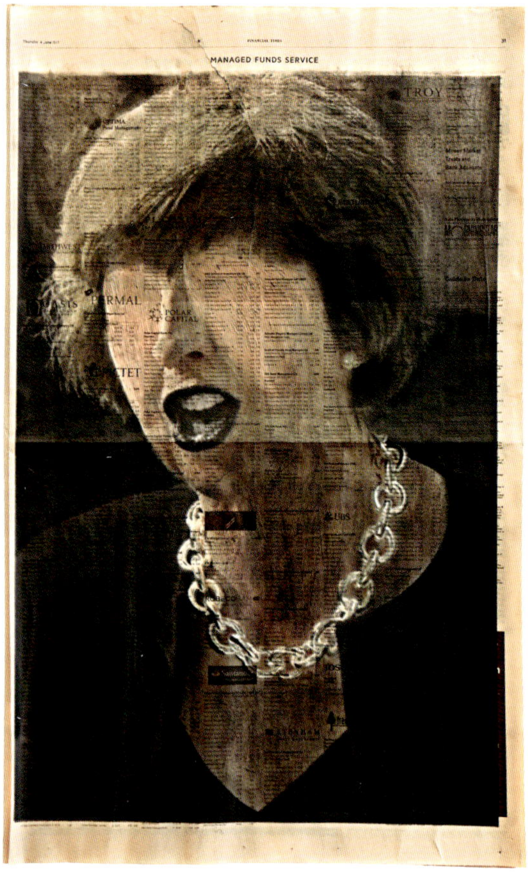

42 kennardphillips, *Profit*, 2017

Conservative leader, Theresa May, blind to the destruction her party has wreaked on the country and void of imagination of how to address the chaos. Her photographic portrait, damaged by paint, is printed on a Market Data page of the Financial Times. *The chain around her neck is her own but in this work becomes a symbol of greed manifest in the Conservatives' drive for austerity, kennardphillipps write.*

on the street flyposting, into an office organising art projects and billboards and various other special builds.'[51]

Burnham moved into teaching, and by 2007 he was running the art and design foundation course at Hackney Community College. This was at a time when further education was being cut back, budgets were slashed and the staff became caught in a merry-go-round of redundancy and rehire (or 'fire and rehire', as it was termed when, in March 2021, P&O Ferries laid off 800 British seafarers and replaced them with agency staff.)[52] The final redundancy at Hackney took place in 2015 and Burnham was able to enlist the support of artists Bob and Roberta Smith and Jeremy Deller for the new project.

kennardphillipps's poster of the then prime minister, David Cameron, against the background of the *Financial Times* was a starting point, Burnham says: '[I think] Cameron's motivation was money and that has come out subsequently since he left the premiership and they [kennardphillipps] jokingly refer to themselves as "prophets of the resistance" and often their images seem to work both currently and also going forward. They have just come up with some great stuff.' This, and Deller's *Strong and Stable My Arse*, have been topical since the inception of flyingleaps. Burnham has to persuade artists to include their work in the collection: some veer towards the gallery and there's a sort of 'hierarchy of ambition' that he navigates. This public-facing work is allied with other groups that stage and explore interventions in the street, such as NuArt, an annual festival of street art held in Stavanger, Norway, and the Spanish artist Ampparito, who makes 'research interventions' across Europe, 'testing out our awareness on multiple levels'.[53] The tone of the work is key, Burnham says:

> There is a problem, though, in that you can't just call people stupid and that's something that I have been aware of with the posters. A lot of people send me stuff and it doesn't have . . . I mean, you could say that Jeremy Deller's *Strong and Stable My Arse* doesn't have much nuance, but it kind of had so many social references. Obviously, it was lampooning Theresa May's

right

43 kennardphillipps, *Study for a Head IV*, 2012

The image of David Cameron is printed on a Market Data page of the Financial Times. *His smooth, empty features are blanked out and filled by the profits data of the financial markets, ripped through to reveal a corporate skyscraper lurking behind the void that is his face, kennardphillipps write.*

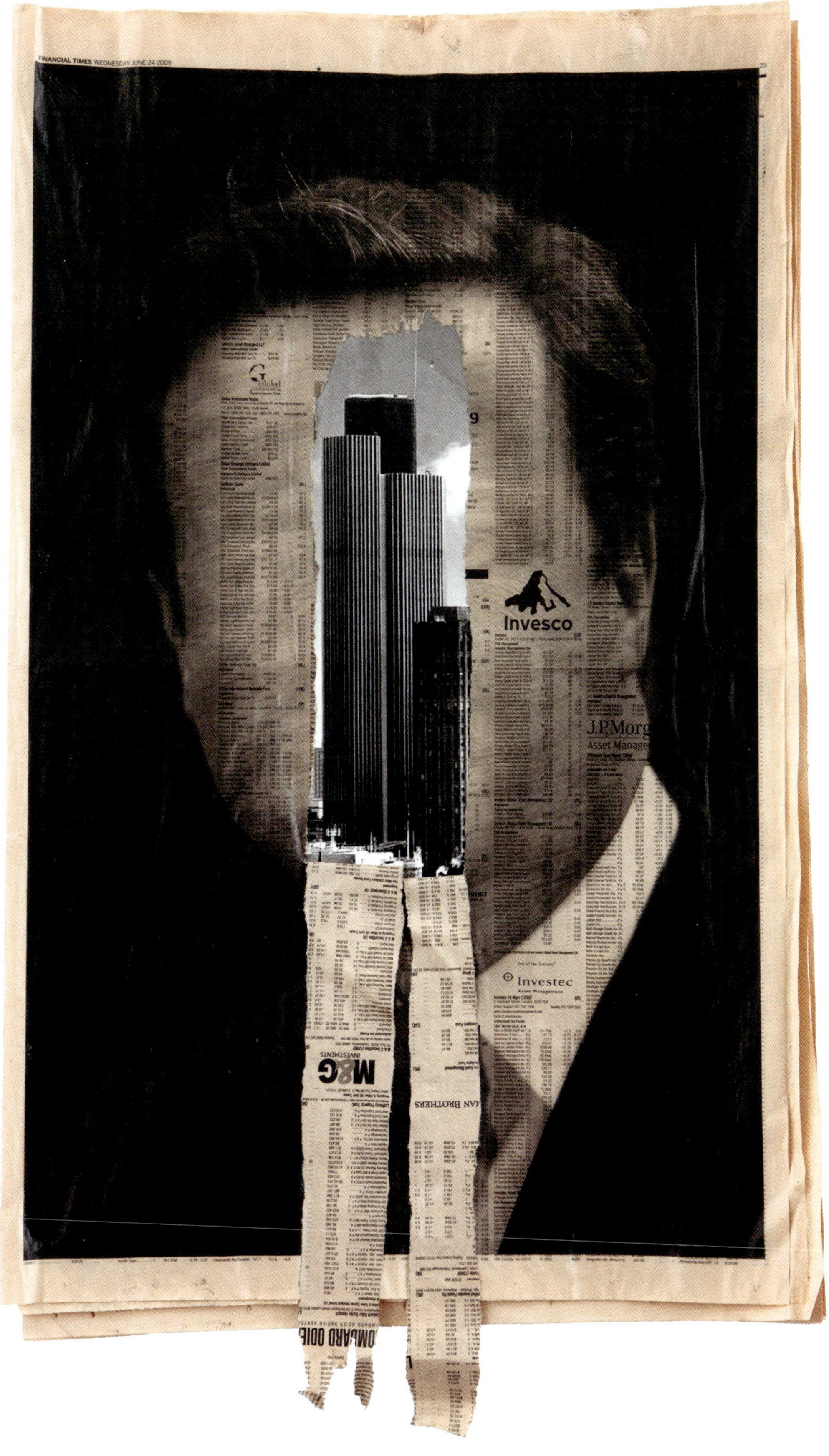
FINANCIAL TIMES WEDNESDAY JUNE 24 2009
Global
Invesco
J.P.Morg
Asset Manage
Investec
Asset Management
M&G
INVESTMENTS
AN BROTHERS
OMBARD ODIE

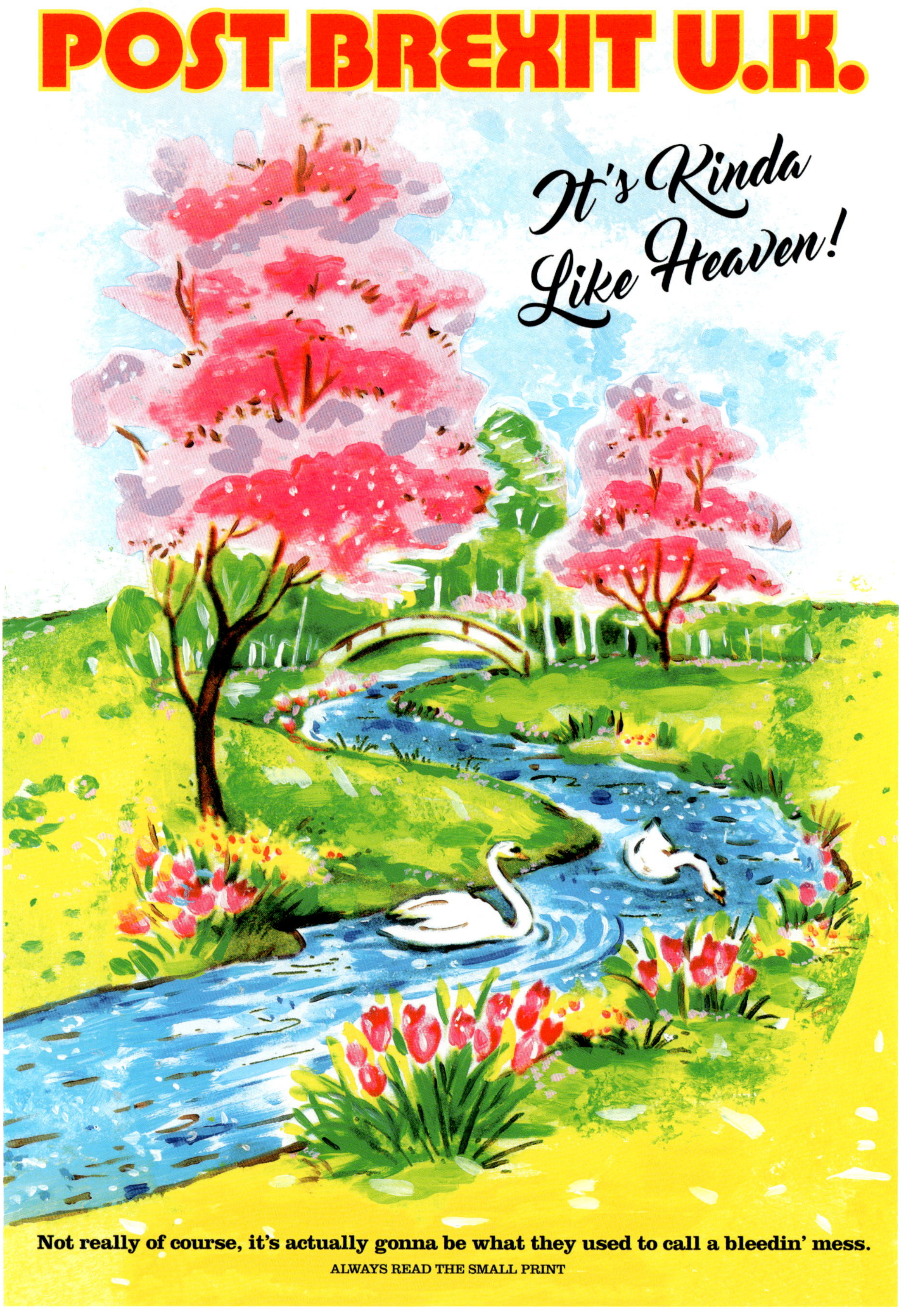
POST BREXIT U.K.
It's Kinda Like Heaven!
Not really of course, it's actually gonna be what they used to call a bleedin' mess.
ALWAYS READ THE SMALL PRINT

> claims about 'Strong, stable government'. But it also brings to mind the character Jim Royle from the sitcom *The Royle Family*, who used the phrase 'my arse' after anything he thought questionable or pretentious. It fell into that sort of comical, critical, ironic vein.[54]

Deller's highly topical poster has sold well, partly because it is affordable for people who cannot afford a piece of his art, and also because Burnham's contacts in the flyposting world saw it 'splattered' around Soho in London where it was spotted by journalists and 'media types' who 'spread the message further' through social media. Burnham does not describe himself as a 'political beast', but says he appreciates 'people who can make thoughtful interventions and humorous interventions'. At one point he worked for the outdoor advertising agency Buildhollywood, which works with Kögelsberger in this ad hoc, effective network of social and political public happenings.

Jeremy Deller was shocked but not surprised at the outcome of the referendum.[55] The London-based artist welcomes the possibility of putting work in the streets, rather than on people's phones, and, as he says, work soon travels from the street to social media, amplifying the message, but the circulation of art, whether in the gallery, street, publication or social media, depends on the project in question:

> You have a decent idea, and within a week it could be up in the streets, which is brilliant. It's very helpful and quite thrilling to see something you've done up on the streets so quickly, in real life rather than just on a phone.

> When you are making work for the streets and it's meant to be almost propaganda, then yes, of course it's much more obvious when it's a poster with a text on it – it's so clear.

On whether this is the 'most comfortable' space for him, he says:

> Most comfortable? It depends on the work and what I'm doing, but I like the street. I like being in the open and making work for the public in that respect. Sometimes, you know, a museum or a gallery are very good places to present work as well that wouldn't be able to exist on the street. They're a very good way of gathering work together to see a retrospective or something. Each space has its own best use, in a sense, or best context. I try and navigate myself around all these different spaces as best

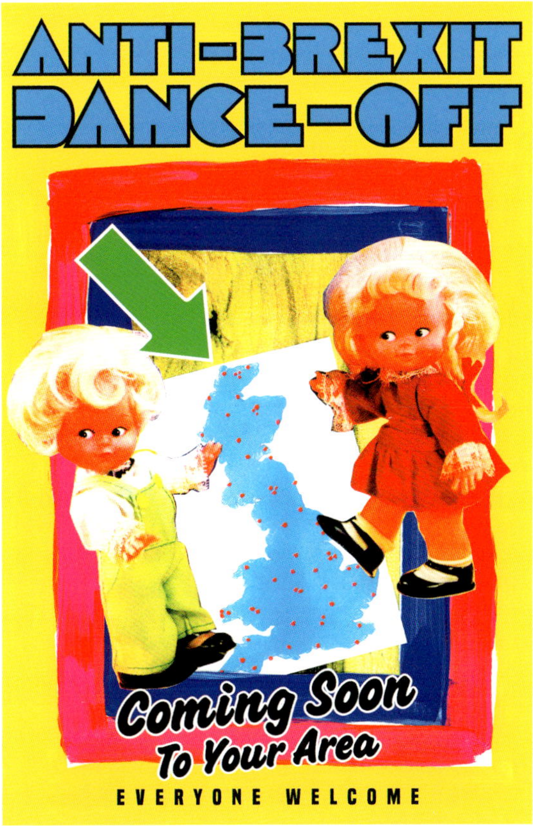

left

44 Magda Archer, *Post Brexit*, 2017

right

45 Magda Archer, *Anti-Brexit Dance-Off*, 2017

Archer's work is included in the flyingleaps group of artists whose art and politics commentary shocks and delights, whether in the street or in the gallery.

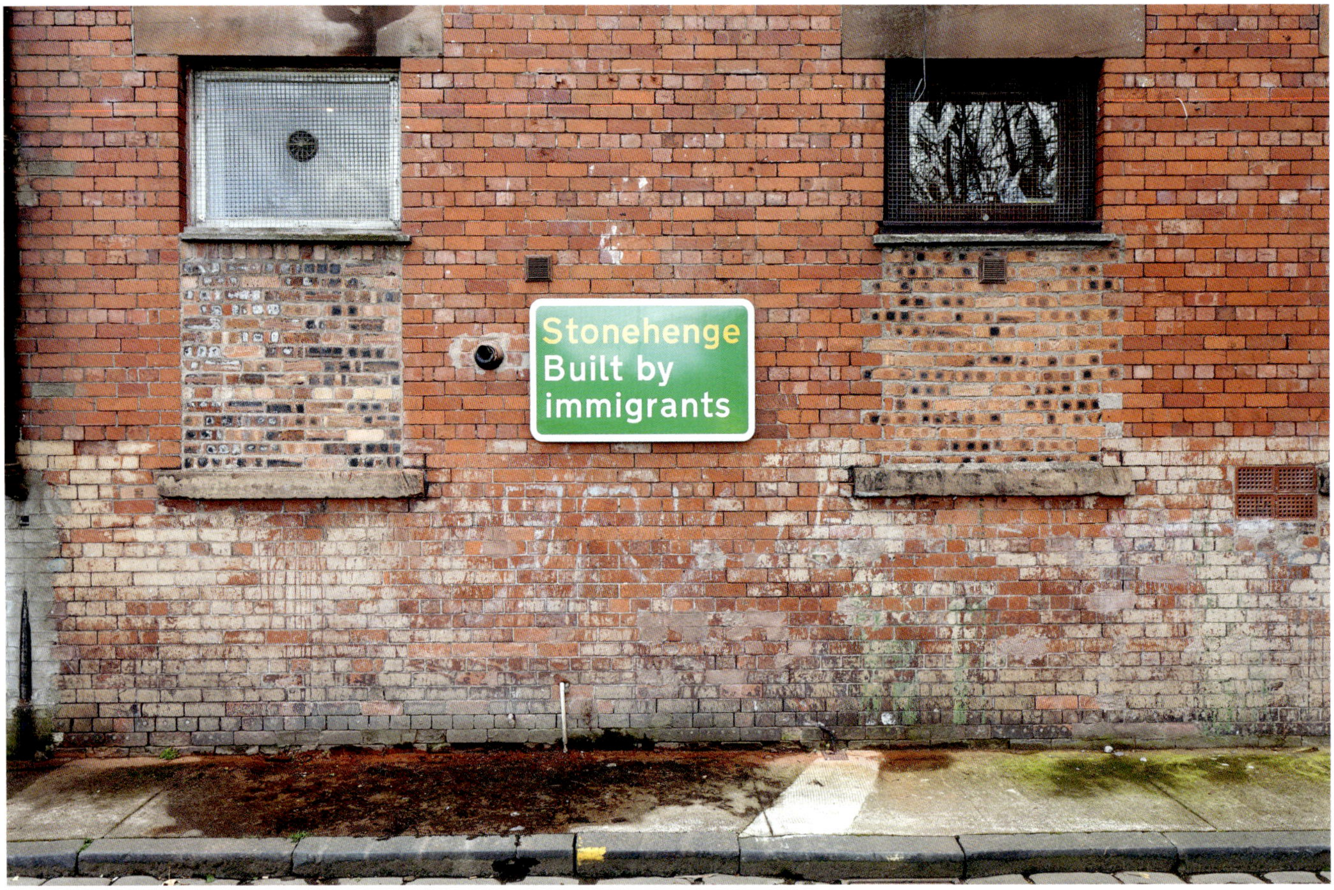

think people, instinctively . . . maybe it was an opportunity to be emotional about Britain in a way that wasn't about Brexit. But it actually was [about Brexit].[59]

As I crossed London on my way home that day, I encountered groups of the soldier volunteers at Waterloo station, standing silently and holding everyone's attention, and I felt a lump in my throat.

In 2021–22, the exhibition, *Warning Graphic Content* (fig.47–49), which brought together all Deller's prints and posters from the last 30 years, was shown concurrently at the Modern Institute in Glasgow and Galerie Art Concept in Paris. The works, although produced between 1993 and 2021, speak to the chaotic and self-serving nature of British governance since Brexit. 'Cronyism is English for Corruption' reads a billboard-sized poster, and again, this intervention rouses the sound of protest and the chorus of dismay in the crowd at demonstrations – of the tapping of keyboards as journalists painstakingly research and document the network of contracts handed out during the COVID-19 pandemic by the government to individuals, some of whom are, coincidentally, Conservative Party donors, or friends of government ministers. But as Deller told *The Art Newspaper*, the statement about cronyism now sits in a broader context: 'That was made at a specific moment about how people were awarded contracts for Covid. But it just keeps going on and on, the corruption. It's a poster that keeps being relevant. Not that you'd want it to be, but it just is because of what's going on.'[60]

Looking at these works in this space activates a political dialogue, and as a whole the exhibition resembles a manifesto: not so much a manifesto of demands, rather an articulation of discontent and resistance – against the naysaying of migrants that runs throughout Brexit and subsequent government policy, government corruption and a fistful of lies.

left

48 Jeremy Deller, *Built by Immigrants*, 2019, 79.5 × 123.5 × 1.7 cm (31 5⁄16 × 48 5⁄8 × 11⁄16 in), edition of 1 plus 1 artist's proof

DNA studies have shown migrants who arrived in Britain around 6,000 years ago constructed the world's most famous prehistoric monument. Some of these migrants arrived in small boats.

below

49 Jeremy Deller, *Warning Graphic Content*, 1993–2021, print works, wall painting, dimensions variable, edition of 2, installation view, The Modern Institute, Aird's Lane, Glasgow, 5 November 2021–22 January 2022

Deller reflects on the political discourse with humour, bite and not a little anger – or as he would have it: 'Welcome to the Shitshow'.

CRISS-CROSSING THE CHANNEL

The French artist Chrystel Lebas's *La traversée* (The Crossing) series of large-format photographs are a personal study of journeys that she has made since 2013, criss-crossing the Channel by ferry, to work as an artist and educator in London and returning to Europe on a regular basis to see friends and family. These works begin at the border of Britain and build a bridge with France (figs 50 and 51).

> Since 2013, I have been photographing each one of my Channel crossings, looking towards France from South Foreland then looking towards the UK from Cap Gris-Nez. Longing to be on the other side.
>
> I started the series in an attempt to deal with my mum's progressive sight loss, and with the years passing, each crossing [became] charged with other significant political, geographical, historical events and personal stories, layers upon layers shaping each one of the photographs taken on my journey. The photographs show approximately the same view but with the sea changing colour, according to the day, time of day, low or high tides, seasons, weather and exposure times; it's never the same. The series is ongoing and will be accompanied with commentaries, writings, and stories collected that refer to the dates of the crossings.

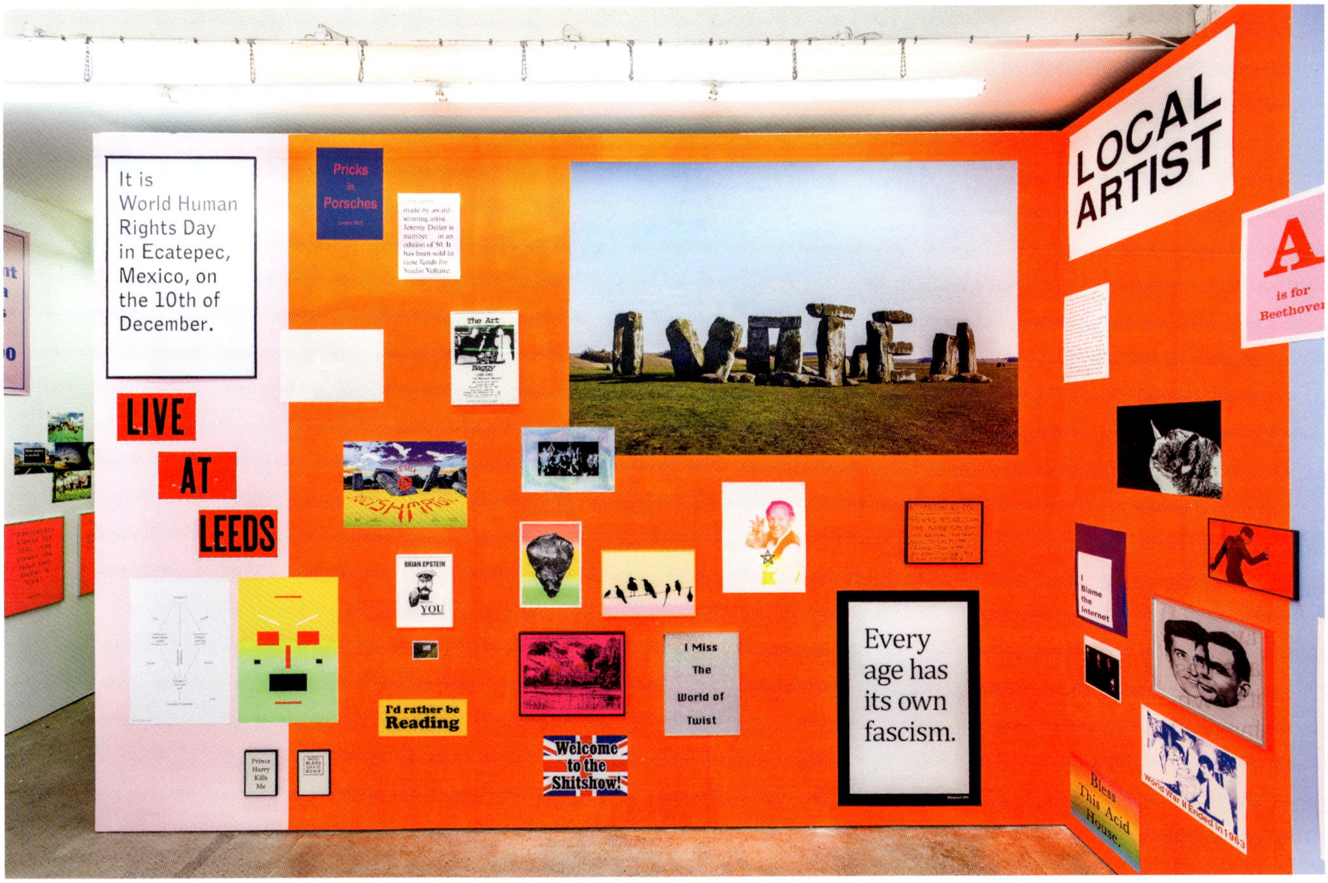

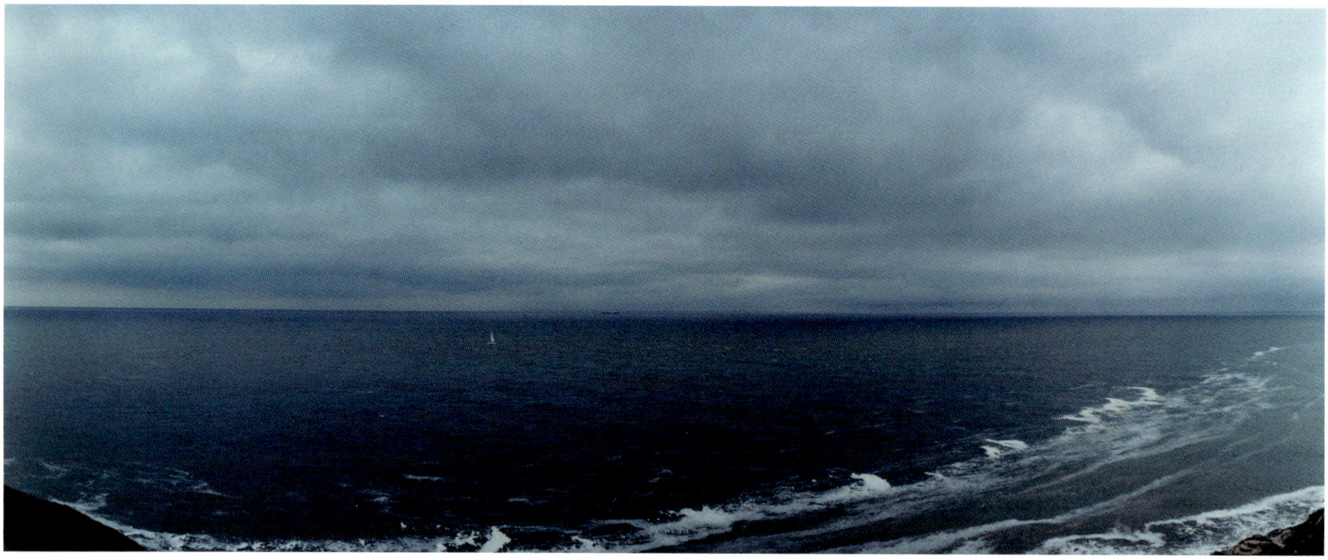

50 Chrystel Lebas, *La traversée* (The Crossing), Cap Gris-Nez, 17 May 2013, 18h30

> If I [used to long] to be on the other side of the Channel, always wondering when the next crossing [would] be, now the psychological and physical drift is becoming even wider.[61]

Lebas started this long-term and hitherto unseen photographic project before Brexit, so it traverses political and social upheaval, as well as making a pair of photographs every time she left Britain for France, and vice versa – always from the same place and reflecting the shortest distance between the two countries. Speaking to me in her studio in a south London mews, alongside the studios of an assortment of artists, designers, ceramicists and picture-framers, Lebas describes her working method, writing notes about her journeys, marking the time she makes each photograph and charting these details. We are used to seeing photographs of people by the seaside, all jolly, ice-cream in hand, building sandcastles, walking their dogs, or sunbathing, but Lebas's images are notable for the absence of people in this liminal space between her two lives. One of the features of *La traversée* is that the French side, Cap Gris-Nez, looks so different from South Foreland:

> In Cap Gris-Nez on the French side, they have a platform they've built for people [who are] looking. It's interesting because the location is very different to the English side. So, on the French side, there's a platform and there is a noticeboard that tells you what's happened in the Channel – and the battles . . . there lots of concrete constructions – bunkers – so the story is kind of related to that, to the war and also the shipping, how the Channel is used by shipping companies, and travelling and all of that, but on the English side it is wild.

There is no mention that the strait between these two places is the shortest distance between France and Britain. There is a lighthouse nearby, managed by the National Trust. Lebas positions her tripod in the same spot. Looking at the series of photographs in Lebas's studio, some showing lights on either coast, here and there a boat, or the light trail of a boat at night, I find it quite difficult to root myself in the images although I am drawn in, as with Lebas's alluring and disconcerting photographs taken in forests, which are sumptuous in their foliage and hues.[62]

51 Chrystel Lebas, *La traversée* (The Crossing), South Foreland, 27 May 2013, 19h40

'It's quite eerie, yes. There's still an element of, you don't know what you are looking at,' she says. It was a conscious decision to avoid including tourists or other people in the images: there are simply traces of people. Lebas has started to make voice recordings to augment the detailed journey crossings and conditions for her photographs, 'because otherwise I was taking written notes, a bit like a shipping forecast, of these first years . . . and so this is something that is going to be embedded in the work as well. I want to have a bit more text, a bit more consistency on what was happening when I was actually shooting.'

When we spoke, Lebas said that visits from friends and family had fallen off since Brexit, because of the hassle of passports and visas, but also because of the psychological barrier of visiting a country whose government and Leave-voting constituents rail against the EU and France. The other factor is that the cost of crossing the Channel – by train, ferry or air – has risen sharply. Lebas sees *La traversée* as a way of 'giving away' the landscape: 'I'm totally giving it away and not really appropriating it. I am appropriating it within the frame. I decided on the frame, on the view, on what we are looking at and when. Even so, this is not really up to me to decide because it's always due to my journey when I arrive.' The political charge of these images stems from the people who gaze at Britain from the French side, where barriers now exist to this short crossing, but also importantly for the migrants who try to cross: 'We witnessed some boats of migrants trying to cross as well and some Medway boats trying to stop them. So, there's all of those layers. People trying to cross, the ongoing issues around migration, which is really so painful.'

Journeys from Calais are fraught as migrants at the port cross the roads and appear from behind trucks, so that drivers have to remain vigilant. Lebas does not envisage a settling between Britain and France, and points to press reports in France and Germany, which are markedly different from those appearing in the mainly right-wing UK press and which function as an alternative source of information. Lebas reflects on the demonstrations in France in support of rights and protest, and sees no match for this, either in the demonstrations against Brexit, which have dwindled, or a rekindling of protest around pro-re-join sentiment.

Lebas reflects on how good her life has been in England in terms of education, opportunities, work and friendships – now all curtailed. As a fellow artist said to her, it is as though artists are captive in the UK. Relations between the UK and France have deteriorated since Brexit, with anti-French invective gushing from the mouth of government. Who could forget Liz Truss, the former foreign secretary and short-lived prime minister, saying 'the jury is still out', when asked during her bid to become PM whether the French president, Emmanuel Macron, was 'friend or foe'.[63] The Conservative press feasted on this nationalistic fervour and did not waste a moment in vilifying France.[64]

In Lebas's images, there is the sense and stillness of contemplation and the unknown. Her artistic practice and her education, like that of so many others in this book, has taken place across different countries, and she often travels by ferry to Germany and the Netherlands, as well as France. With her family history in mind, Brexit seems like a regression, she says:

> My grandmother was Polish, so they migrated to France in the 1930s and hence that whole kind of [sense of] nationalities and understanding, about how living in the eastern bloc prevented you from moving, from doing anything and actually now it feels like here we are [going] backwards, to what I was experiencing when I was young in the eastern bloc. OK, in the eastern bloc, they also had the political issues as well, which was really difficult.
>
> I lived, after my art studies, in Paris, and I applied for a scholarship to go to live in Krakow. So, I lived for two years in Krakow, and I documented it, actually, it was more . . . my past work was more, kind of, portraiture, documenting. I documented all the society that was, kind of lost – the aristocrats, the Jewish community.[65]

This was a fraught time to be setting up in Krakow, Poland – in 1989 and against the background of the collapse of communism and the fall of the Berlin Wall. Lebas created work in Poland but found the political turmoil 'hardcore for a 20-year-old', so rather than learning Polish, she learned English. On her return to France, she exhibited her work at the Palais de Tokyo (at that time the Museum of Photography), then applied to go to FAMU, the film and photography school in Prague, following which she attended the Royal College of Art in London. This was at a time when it was much simpler to pitch up in Britain:

> Oh my God, [it was] so much more open . . . I moved to the UK – [and] just to say, now you couldn't do that because of Brexit – so, as a French person, I moved to the UK. I got my national insurance card, no questions asked, because I worked in telemarketing while doing my two-year MA at the Royal College of Art.

Living in London, Lebas encountered the odd anti-French sentiment, but nothing much, until Brexit, which horrified her:

> I cried . . . because I just didn't really understand what was going on for me, it was really a broken, broken state. I think it was really broken, like, ties and connections and now, I mean, I knew what was going to happen because it was just brewing . . .

So *La traversée* resonates with the exploration of cultural identity before Brexit and in the aftermath. Lebas has encountered problems in taking work across borders, ordering supplies and working with her long-term printer in the Netherlands – but there is a wider and more malign consequence for art in Britain, she says, as European curators are now overlooking Britain when organising exhibitions. This is partly because of the expense and bother of the paperwork in moving art around, but also because the constant stream of anti-European invective from those who supported Brexit and successive Tory governments has soured relations with European cultural producers.

The experiences of migrants to Britain are woven throughout this book. Adam Broomberg was born in South Africa. His family history illustrates how political events, and specifically right-wing and fascist movements, push people from country to country. Broomberg felt uneasy well before the referendum:

> Coming from South Africa, I felt an ominous atmosphere that was blowing in. And I was very worried. I was really, really worried. I think the referendum was the kind of culmination of a number of things that were in the air before. I think to call this whole thing Brexit is also slightly problematic, because it simplifies it down to one thing, whereas if you expand it out, and you trace it backwards, a number of things led towards that thing. And if you think about it, a referendum is such a clumsy way of dealing with a very intricate web of scary – like climactic – conditions, and I think it could be quite interesting to think about, what was the atmosphere before? How did Gordon Brown collapse? Who took over?
>
> And I think about what was going on around the world at the same time. And the various kinds of political movements that were more or less established in different countries in Europe . . . and in America a certain kind of language was emerging. So I think it's really important for me to have seen it as predating that specific day, because it was already a feeling . . . there were very worrying trends that were really palpable for me. And I think that manifesto, it was a bit like your chances of winning in a casino, are, I don't know, 30 per cent or whatever they are, but the manifesto meant we had entered the casino . . . it literally was a roll of the dice . . . I mean, nobody knew what the outcome would be. And the point is something that got us to that place, that toxic place.[66]

Broomberg, working with his then long-time art partner, Oliver Chanarin, galvanised support for Remain among artists working in art, photography and film, and galleries and cultural producers.[67] They produced a T-shirt – 'Baby, it's cold outside, vote Remain' – before the referendum, and photographs of people wearing this spun across social media. Broomberg and Chanarin also conscripted artists such as Jeremy Deller and Laure Prouvost to make posters, while remaining in the background themselves:

> But my feelings on the morning after, well, first of all, my former work partner and I attempted a campaign, a kind of quite populist one using kind of fashion magazines and celebrities to try and push back against this kind of populist drive.
>
> But the morning after has now – if you think about it – it's how many of those mornings have we had now? You know, November 2016, it was Trump. I mean, over and over again, the last one was last week with Israel, but they're all the same thing. And, you know, if you look at that horrific documentary about [Steve Bannon] the former head of Breitbart . . .[68]

After the referendum, Broomberg mobilised artists to stand against the rise of right-wing populism in *Hands Off Our Revolution*, with its manifesto seeking to harness the 'radical nature of art': 'We believe that art can help counter the rising rhetoric of right-wing populism, fascism and the increasingly stark expressions of xenophobia, racism, sexism, homophobia and unapologetic intolerance.'[69] More than 200 artists signed up.

Broomberg's response to the referendum was immediate and life-changing: his family moved to Berlin shortly afterwards. It is the latest in a series of moves made by his family when in peril, or jeopardy:

> My grandmother moved in the 1930s from Lithuania and escaped the Holocaust. I'm of Jewish background, born into an apartheid South Africa, and I left just because I was called up – there was still military conscription – I moved to London then to Italy, watched the rise of Berlusconi there, moved back to England and then watched this kind of very slow-moving tsunami called Brexit come in, and then moved here [Berlin].

Berlusconi, as I have mentioned before, was a frontrunner for right-wing populism, and his ownership of large swathes of the Italian media facilitated his rise and rise. This diminishment of media as a source of information and news was evident to Broomberg when he lived in Italy:

> You could actually watch the culture change on television – it just degraded until you had these revolting, kind of misogynistic hideous

series of posters and distribute them as they saw fit. In the poster, Tillmans pays tribute to the gains that the EU has made – and points out that EU laws account for just 10 per cent of laws made in the UK. The importance of this quota is that it encompasses workers' rights, such as four weeks' paid holiday, health and safety, and more. Tillmans acknowledges that there are flaws in the EU and points out that this is unsurprising given that 28 (before the UK left) member states are in constant negotiation, navigating compromise and shared decision-making throughout all areas of government: health, defence, education, environment, and so on. For instance, the EU provided an environmental standard on water: 'Water pollution doesn't respect borders, and here, especially, Brits benefit from rules that span the continent.'[4] In this respect Tillmans was prescient: the failure to maintain these standards is tangible as sewage ebbs and flows along Britain's shoreline and waterways.[5] A 2017 report in the House of Commons library warned of the dangers of British water resuming its 'dirty' reputation of the 1970s.[6]

There was also a strong whiff of British 'exceptionalism' in the Leave campaigns. The Irish writer and journalist Fintan O'Toole has written in his book, *Heroic Failure: Brexit and the Politics of Pain* (2018) about the fusion between 'the strange sense of imaginary oppression that underlies Brexit' with the notion of exceptionalism:

> Self-pity thus combines two things that may seem incompatible: a deep sense of grievance and a high sense of superiority. It is this doubleness that makes it so important to the understanding of Brexit, a political phenomenon that is driven by ideas that would not otherwise combine. Crudely, passionate nationalism has taken two antagonistic forms. There is an imperial nationalism and an anti-imperial nationalism; one sets out to dominate the world, the other to throw off such dominance. The incoherence of the new English nationalism that lies behind Brexit is that it wants to be both simultaneously. On the one hand, Brexit is fuelled by fantasies of 'Empire 2.0', a reconstructed global mercantilist trading empire in which the old white colonies will be reconnected to the mother country. On the other, it is an insurgency and therefore needs to imagine that it is a revolt against intolerable oppression. It therefore requires both a sense of superiority and a sense of grievance. Self-pity is the only emotion that can bring them together.[7]

Norman Behrendt, a German artist, came to the University of Westminster to complete an MA in photography in 2017. Behrendt met with the full force of Brexit fervour, which played out in the streets and across media platforms in a bewildering way. *Blueprint 2017–2020*, his unusual and incisive book, came out of his end of MA exhibition and is realised in cyanotype blue. The book stands as a visual record of a plethora of characters and narratives in the period after the referendum. It took some time for the now Berlin-based artist to devise a strategy for what he saw around him: 'This is for me a project where I left a lot of my comfort zones in my own artistic practice. We always have certain ways that we work or how we approach things, and we know they work, but I had no idea if this was going to work out. So, it was very liberating.'[8]

Behrendt, born and raised in Berlin, knew the benefits of moving around as a photographer, getting to know various cities that would stimulate ideas for photographic projects. London was no different. The irony is that he went there in search of a revitalised and re-energised practice through the much-respected MA in photography at the University of Westminster and to expand his horizons professionally, just as Britain's border was closing. But this worked in his favour. *Blueprint* brings together a swathe of cut and cropped images – taken from the internet, television and the press – from coverage of the whirling dervish that was the prolonged Brexit negotiations (figs 52–54).[9] In common with Wolfgang Tillmans, Norman Behrendt completes this project in an interdisciplinary way by including key speeches

right

52 A grid of assorted images selected from Norman Behrendt's *Blueprint 2017–2020*. Behrendt photographed online content on Brexit, and coverage in newspapers and magazines and in rearranging these visual accounts the artist created a new narrative

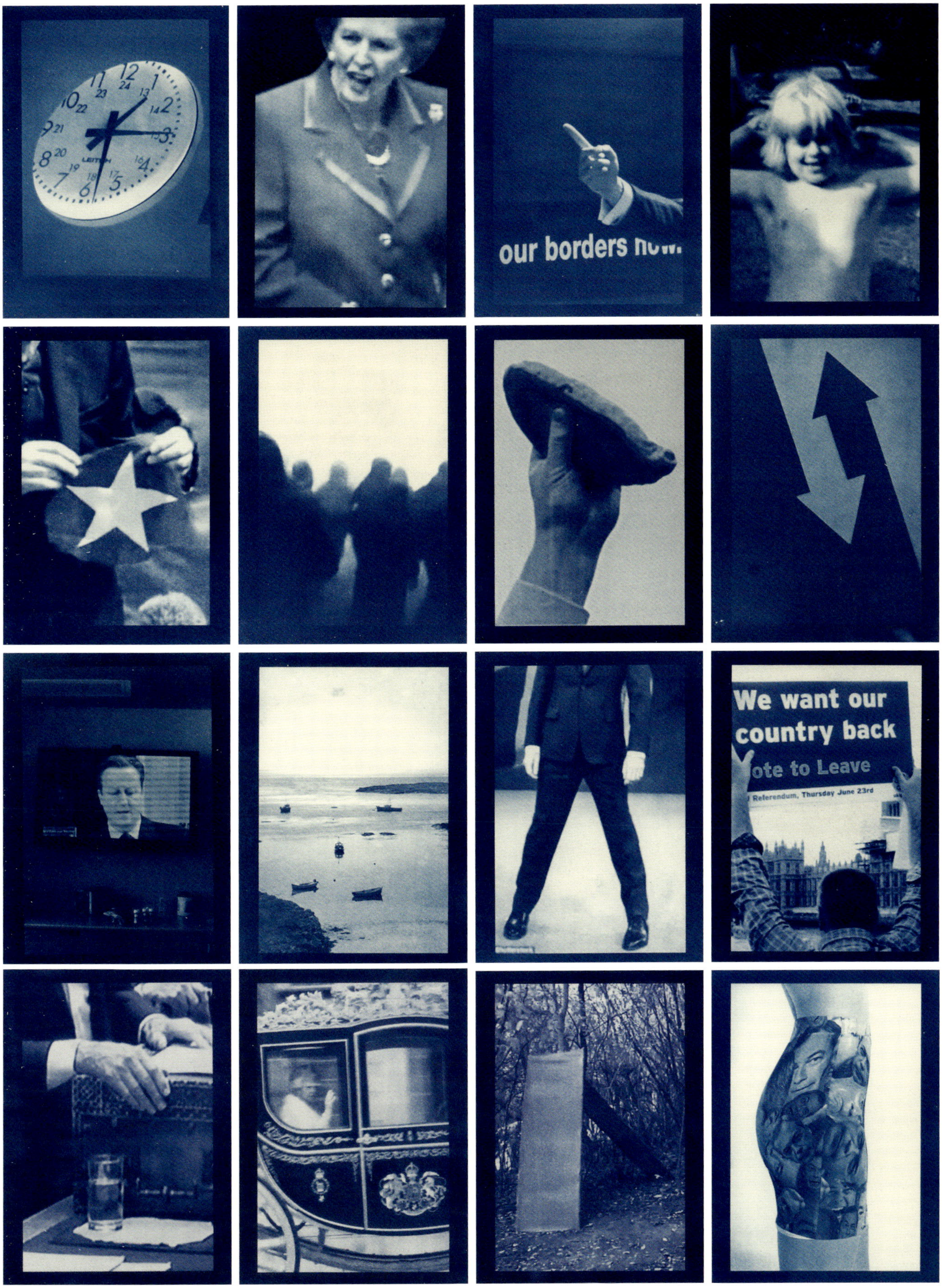
our borders
We want our
country back
ote to Leave
Referendum, Thursday June 23rd

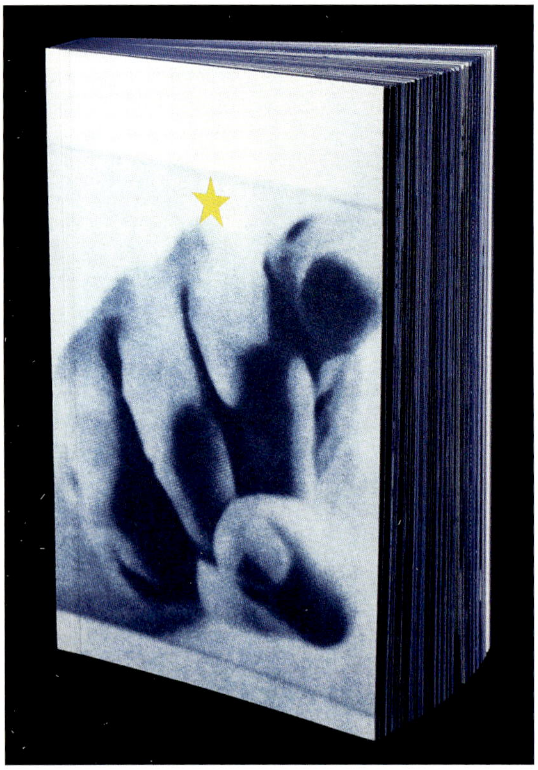

53 Norman Behrendt's visual exploration of Brexit Britain through images across TV, print and social media, *Blueprint 2017–2020*, Kult Books, 2021

and turning points of Britain's relations with Europe. This essential collection of the political appends the image section of the book.

Lucy Soutter, artist and writer, and the course leader of the photography arts masters' course at the University of Westminster, wrote an afterword to *Blueprint*. This encapsulates the conditions for Brexit amid the rise in populism in the US with Trump, the razor-sharp teeth of the Tory Party austerity policy and constant pictures on TV screens and in newspapers of migrants at Calais, a place migrants dubbed the 'jungle'.[10] Soutter writes of how the Leave campaign and its catchphrase, 'take back control', encapsulated this moment in Britain, but also derived legitimacy in the slippery channels of social media, even though the campaign's messaging veered away from truth:

> While the official debate took place in slogans, speeches and statistics, personal decisions played out on a symbolic level, across memories, emotions and symbolic attachments. In the old days, political campaigns unfolded on a public stage, through live events and shared mass media outlets. Historians can look over past elections with a level of certainty about which moments were decisive, which errors fatal. The Brexit referendum marked a new era of political campaigning, far more fragmented, decentralised and open to rogue operators. We will never know how much it mattered that social media advertising for leave was used to micro-target specific voters based on personal data reaped without their consent. It will never be possible to quantify the impact of thousands of Russia-baked fake social media accounts used to generate and propagate pro-Brexit messaging.[11]

So, the aesthetic decision of cyanotype married well with Behrendt's visual research methods, in the combing of media for faces, signs and motifs, and scattered among here the faces of the ringmasters staring back at us: Farage, Johnson, Gove, etc. This use of colour provides a synthesis:

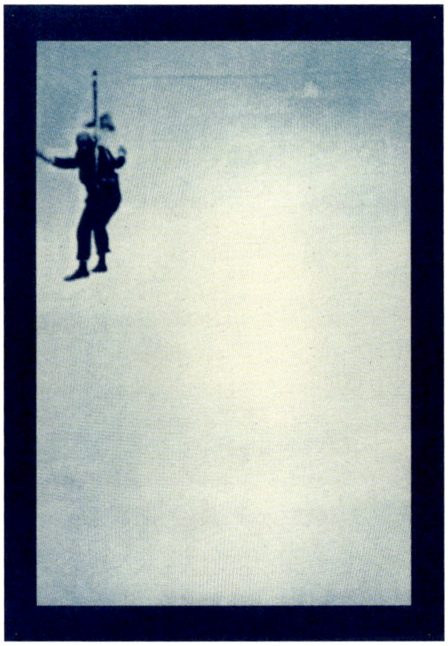

54 Norman Behrendt, 'Boris Johnson MP gets stuck on a zipwire at the Olympic Games in London in 2012', from *Blueprint, 2017–2020*

it melds together this batch of images and binds them to Conservative Party blue. This blue, this phantasmagoria, functions as a conveyor belt of right-wing populists, politicians, opponents and hapless bystanders.

Behrendt's decision to include historical texts and key political speeches in his book reflects the gestation period for Brexit. He says he wanted to show that Brexit was just the tip of the iceberg:

> So, it's not that all the decisions were taken at that point and that's it. It's a long-term relationship, nearly 50 years, that we are talking about, a relationship of two very different characters. And it was always contested – a back and forth. There were always discussions going on.[12]

This work raises questions about how artists intervene in political debates, especially right-wing populism, where arguments are reduced to simplistic terms and where scapegoating abounds, and all woven into social media platforms. The advent of Trump shocked Behrendt – who was then living at a distance in Germany – but Brexit was much closer to home:

> I guess we are all political beings unless we live in a bubble. It's hard to say that I am a political artist because I don't see myself like this, but on the other hand, I am, of course, very interested in politics, and I am very interested in what's going on in general in the world and I am not always looking positively at the things that are going on around us. I see populism as a risk and as a complex phenomenon that we do not really understand because there are not so many markers and buoys that lead our way to transparency or to understanding. So, I feel a responsibility to look myself into these subjects in order to speak about it.[13]

At the root of democracy is the need to safeguard our institutions and parliamentary procedures. Populist leaders seek to throw a wrench into this process. Two ways in which they do this are through constant attacks on the media and by sneering and deriding anyone who seeks to scrutinise them. In this way, with the media denigrated and derided, the populist leader seeks to draw a line connecting 'the people' and themselves: this blocks the scrutiny of investigative media coverage and keeps journalists out of the conversation. Donald Trump, the former US president, achieved this by besmirching journalists, and by employing a rallying call to 'drain the swamp' in Washington, DC, thereby casting doubt on any political opponent by association.

Language is key here. Simon Roberts found a way to encapsulate the lexicon of Brexit, as he had done with the economic crash of 2007, by compiling all the language around Brexit. Entitled *The Brexshit Machine*, this work performs well in the exhibition space, which sees a newsreader reading from a teleprompt all the new words that entered the British language using 'Brex' as a prefix. Roberts also turned the teleprompt into an artist's book, which unfolds to 30 feet (Fig.55). And what a great deal of language there was around Brexit.

With language came lies and obfuscations. Peter Oborne, a former colleague of Boris Johnson, has compiled a rap sheet of the latter's evasions of the truth on a website and in a book, *The Assault on Truth: Boris Johnson, Donald Trump and the Emergence of a New Moral Barbarism*.[14] One of the main points of interest, apart from a useful mapping and timeline of Johnson's lies, is the extent to which a photograph has become implicated in Brexit. Leave.EU's red battle bus, emblazoned with the words 'We send the EU £350 million a week, let's fund our NHS instead. Let's take back control', has winged its way round the world by now and become the epicentre of Brexit lies. It took a letter to Johnson, then foreign secretary, from Sir David Norgrove, chair of the UK Statistics Authority, to set the record straight:

> I am surprised and disappointed that you have chosen to repeat the figure of £350m per week, in connection with the amount that might be available for extra public spending when we leave the European Union. This confuses gross and net contributions. It also assumes that payments currently made to the UK by the EU, including for example for the support of agriculture and scientific research, will not be paid by the UK government when we leave. It is a clear misuse of official statistics.[15]

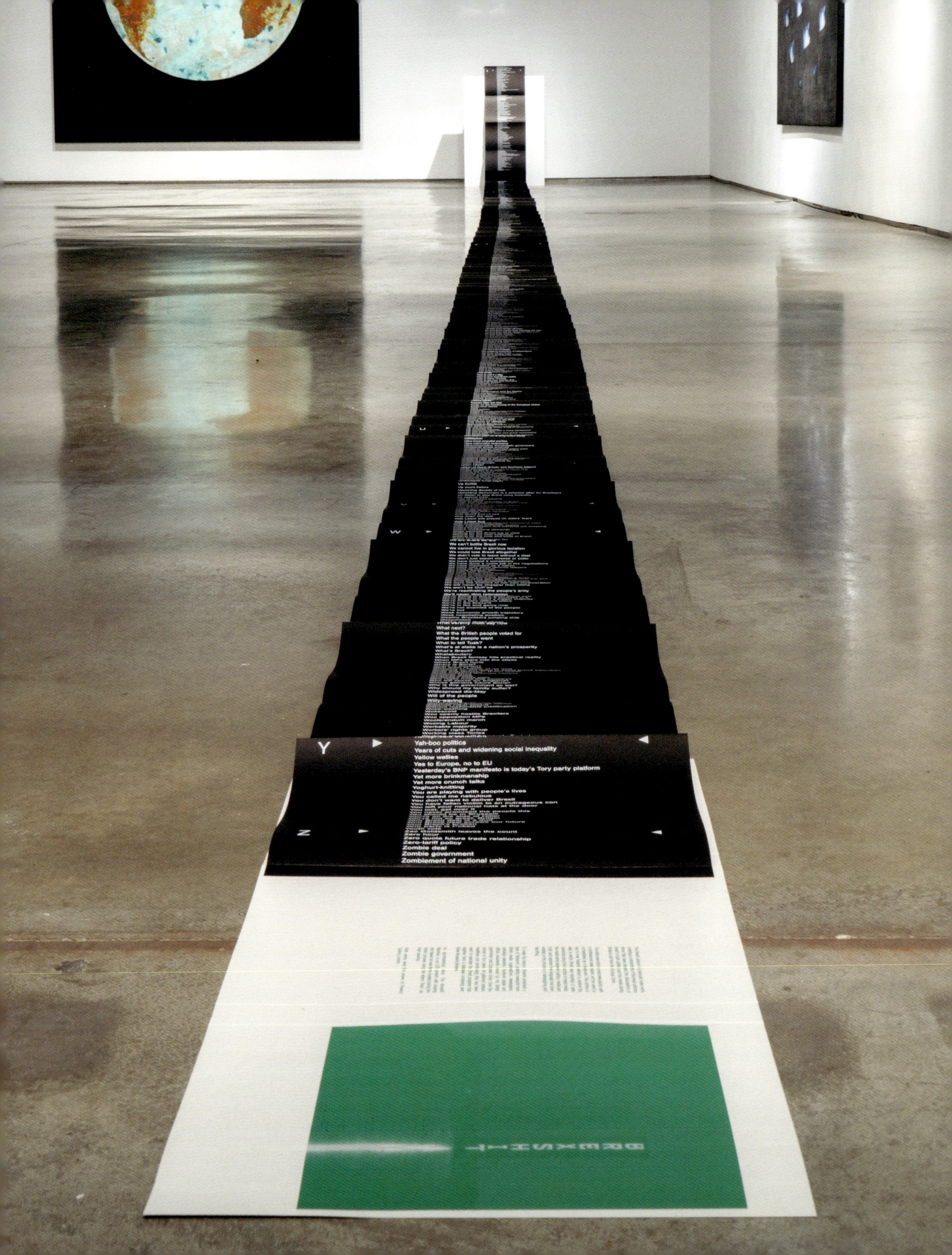
Y
Yah-boo politics
Years of cuts and widening social inequality
Yellow wellies
Yes to Europe, no to EU
Yesterday's BNP manifesto is today's Tory party platform
Yet more brinkmanship
Yet more crunch talks
Yoghurt-knitting
You are playing with people's lives
You called me nebulous
You don't want to deliver Brexit
You have fallen victim to an outrageous con
Z
Zac Goldsmith leaves the count
Zero hour
Zero quota future trade relationship
Zero-tariff policy
Zombie deal
Zombie government
Zombiement of national unity
BREXIT

left

55 Simon Roberts, *The Brexit Lexicon*, Flowers Gallery, London, 2020

Roberts collated the notable headlines and terminology that was used to describe the Brexit journey in a database containing over 5,000 individual words.

The fact that nobody has retracted these comments, or apologised, exemplifies the assumed British exceptionalism that Fintan O'Toole refers to.[16]

Political cartoons of Boris Johnson tend to focus on his mendacity, but this is to draw a line between Johnson and Carlo Collodi's famous literary character Pinocchio, whose legacy stretches across the world (fig.56). Collodi is the Tuscan town where the writer, whose real name was Carlo Lorenzini, spent much of his childhood. A new annotated translation of *The Adventures of Pinocchio* delves into the social and political strands of the story.[17] Collodi himself was public-spirited, generous and learned. In his youth, he founded a satirical newspaper called *Il Lampione* (The Streetlamp) – which the Grand Duchy of Tuscany suppressed – and then founded a second one, *La Scaramuccia* (The Controversy).[18] Slowly, the continuities and discontinuities between Pinocchio and facets of British politics become clear and begin to make more sense.

Collodi was acutely concerned about hunger in Italy in the late 19th century. When he first wrote up the stories which were serialised between 1881 and 1883 in *Giornale per I bambini* [Children's Newspaper], Italy had become a unified nation. Before this, the country had been a patchwork of republics, kingdoms, city states and duchies; there was no unified education system. At the time of unification in 1861, for which Collodi fought twice, a quarter of the population were literate, but by 1880 this had risen to 40 per cent with the advent of free, compulsory schooling. Literacy was a cause close to Collodi's heart – he wrote the stories for children, but inflected them towards adults – and in his open letter of 1884, *Pane e libri* [Bread and Books], he signals his concern about child hunger.[19] During 2020, here in the UK, it was the footballer Marcus

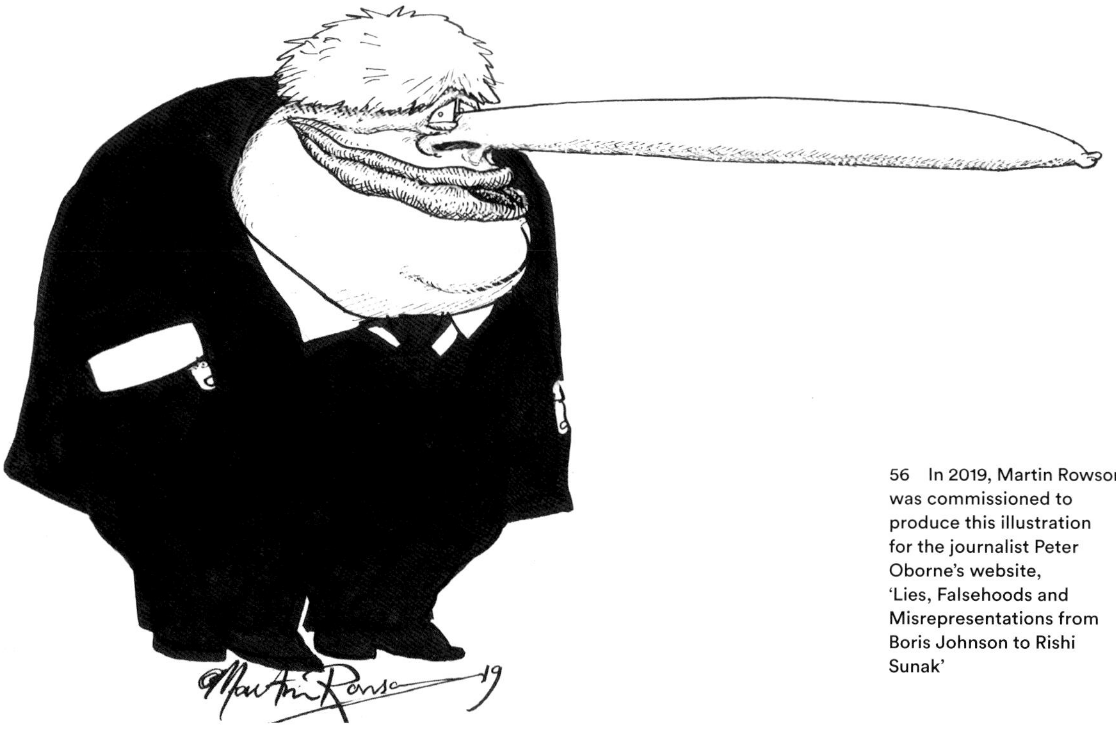

56 In 2019, Martin Rowson was commissioned to produce this illustration for the journalist Peter Oborne's website, 'Lies, Falsehoods and Misrepresentations from Boris Johnson to Rishi Sunak'

> commission and then going straight to a prison visit in the morning. I approached my line manager and confessed to this secret life I'd been living. Up until that point I had remained anonymous online, not for any mysterious 'Banksy'-type reasons, it was just that I didn't want to get the sack from Probation [service]. I was classed as a civil servant and as such had to follow the Civil Service Code of not publicly professing political allegiances either way. The fact that I was relentlessly attacking the government on a daily basis would have been difficult to defend. I have to say that I didn't know a single probation worker who didn't share my views, however. The service had been decimated by the ill-judged privatisation under Chris Grayling. The impact and consequences of the government's cruel austerity measures were seen first-hand in probation officers' increasingly growing caseloads.[25]

Spencer created 'Cold War Steve' and his Twitter account in 2016. At first, he placed images of the *Eastenders* character Phil Mitchell alongside Cold War leaders, such as the Soviet Union's Leonid Brezhnev and Mikhail Gorbachev, or the former US president, Ronald Reagan. His work started out as a 'joke of incongruity', but with Brexit, everything changed:

> I was utterly distraught and began channelling my despair into my artwork – a decent platform for which I had established with my Phil Mitchell Twitter account. I have therefore been tracking the architects of Brexit since then and evolved my compositions over time, to keep up with their corruption and depravity. I am therefore well accustomed to the endless bullshit sleaze, which makes it easier to satirise the 'beyond-satire' behaviour of them.

Brexit would have been a 'dark spiral' for Spencer, who has spoken of his sometime struggle with mental health issues and the use of alcohol as a 'coping mechanism', but Cold War Steve saved the day: 'The Brexit result alone would have sent me down a very dark spiral, but I now had something in place, where I could channel the despair and anger into something positive.' He knows he creates his images for the millions of people who have been 'vocal on the utter travesty of Brexit. It's extremely frustrating that, even now, when it is palpably obvious that it's the fucking disaster we all said it would be, that it still isn't being called out more.' He attributes this to the power of the right-wing press:

> Unfortunately, whilst vast swathes of the country continue to be groomed by right-wing, non-dom billionaire newspaper tycoons, we don't stand a chance. With regard to Labour, well, Starmer's just scared shitless of upsetting potential 'red-wall' voters.

Spencer consumes news and comment – mostly through radio. His collage images, alive with the political characters strolling in and out of Downing Street and the news, depict politicians peddling their wares – and bake the consequences of their policies into a visual landscape, sometimes inspired by or borrowed from the photographs of Martin Parr or other works of art, quite often from William Hogarth (figs 58–60, and fig.75). The photoshopped satire spins across social media and publishing. The rotten politicians are in plain sight, stripped of the trappings of office, and often bundled in with 'the people': those who bear the consequences of political machinations, from sending older people back to care homes from hospital without testing them for COVID-19, to those turning to food banks.

It remains to be seen to what extent the sharp rise in mortgage payments and huge household bills will show in rent arrears, repossessions and an increase in homelessness. Spencer shows his work on social media and does commissions for magazines and newspapers. His book, *Cold War Steve Presents . . . The Festival of Brexit*, is both a joy and horror to behold.[26] The journalist Jon Savage prescribes a dose of satire:

> These images are at once very funny and very cruel. They are designed to be. When organised politics is in chaos – indeed, when politicians are purposefully working to harm the population who have elected them – then the only response is a scalding rage which, to avoid its turning inwards, must be transmuted into activism or

> artistic activity. It's time to send in the satirists, and Cold War Steve is the leading satirist of Benighted Blightonia – the ostentatiously Anglophilic breakdown that is Brexit.[27]

Savage is right in now locating satire across the muddle of media – and that includes 'social' (or is it 'antisocial') media (Elon the 'Musketeer') – where once it was broadcast on television. I remember the puppets of *Spitting Image* genuflecting before Margaret Thatcher when she played the dominatrix surrounded by her cabinet floozies.[28] Spencer's art echoes outrage and paints it large. The speed of political turnover since Brexit has sucked the breath out of our lungs, quite literally for those who have died of COVID-19 in the UK – more than 210,000 by the first week of December 2022.[29] Thousands perished amid government mismanagement, while those in government partied. Those who sought Brexit are always in the picture, 'stripped of their privilege', both soiled and soiling by association. Slumped in a wasteland – Jacob Rees-Mogg, Michael Gove, any of them really; Boris Johnson clutching Union Jacks suspended in his 'baby bouncer' from a zipwire.

As for Led By Donkeys, Spencer wanted people to see his work other than on their mobile phones, and the artists collaborated at Glastonbury in 2020. Spencer was 'blown away by seeing my work on a huge billboard'. The COVID-19 pandemic arrived, Twitter became

58

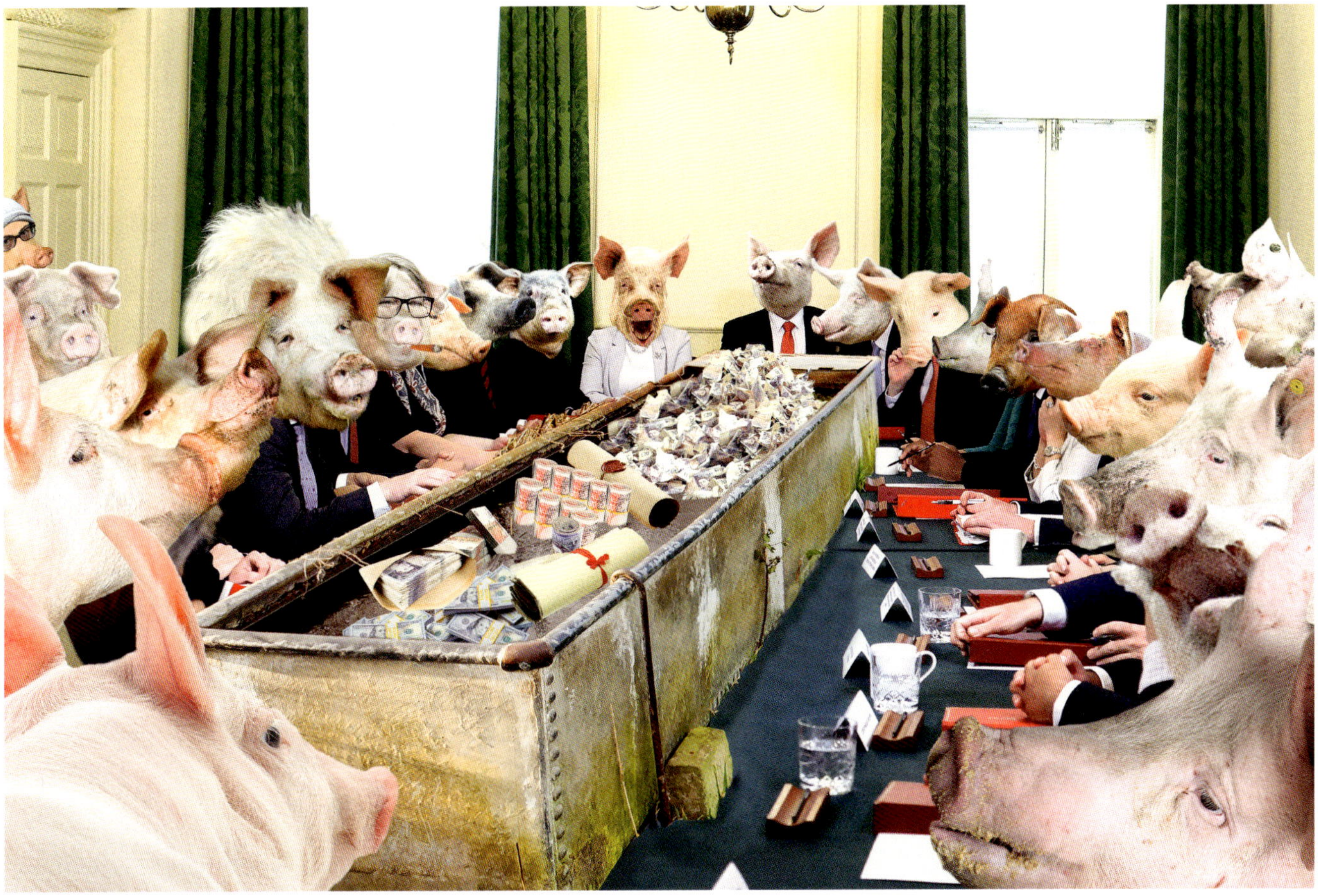

Pages 81, 82–3, 84–5 and 114–15

58–60 and 75 Cold War Steve borrows from art history, snatches characters from politics, and welds them together in Photoshop to deliver a satirical bite

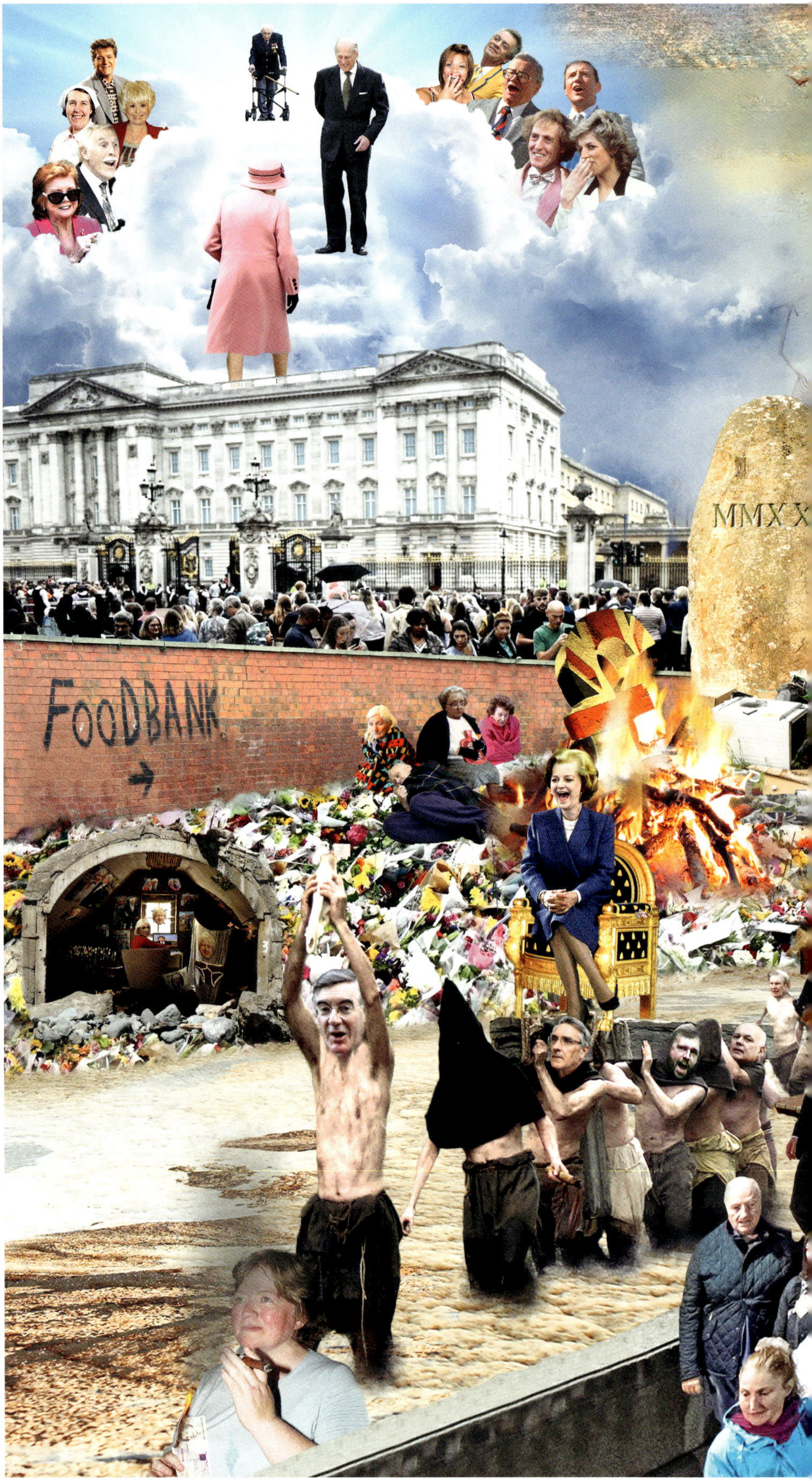
MMXX
FOODBANK

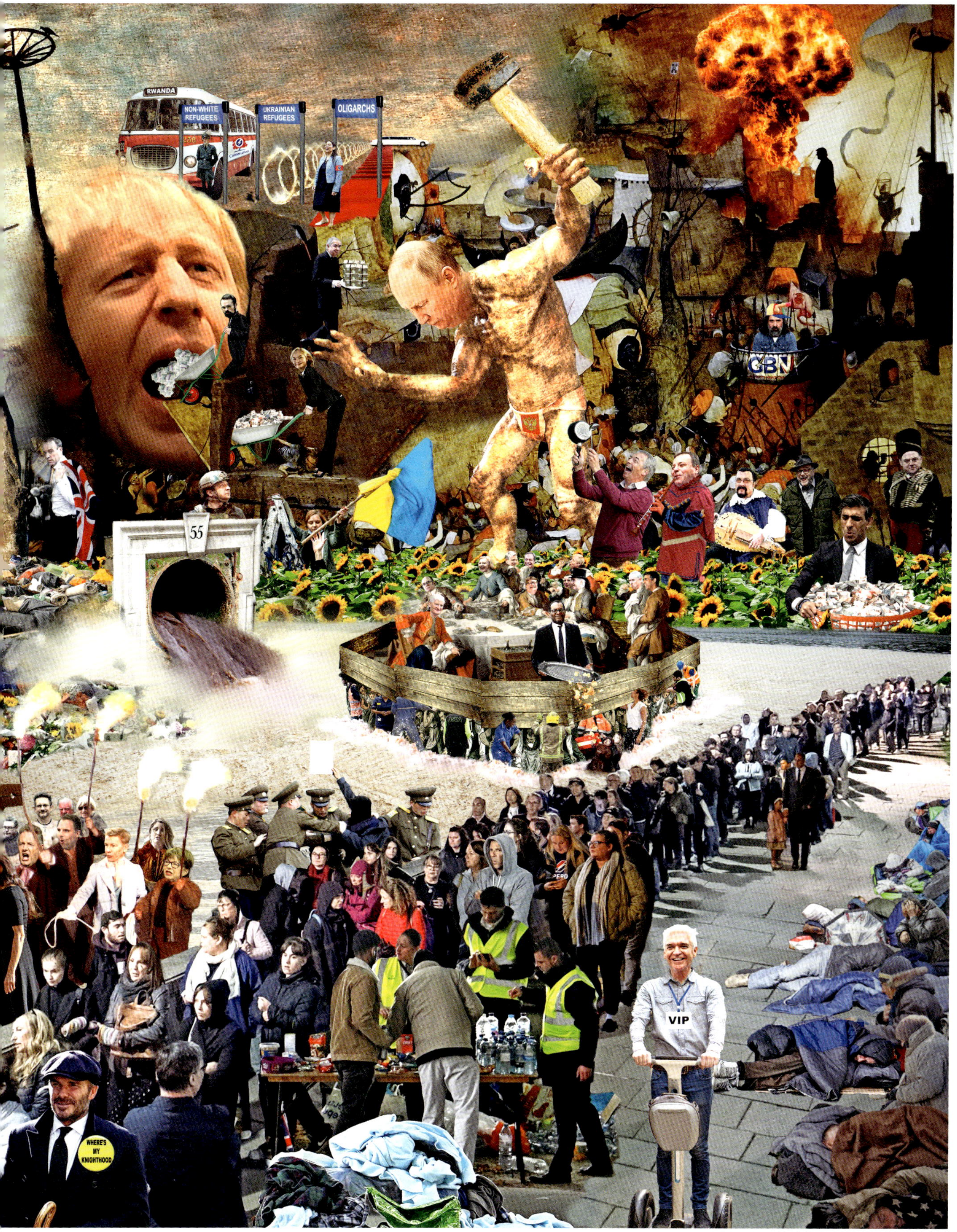

RWANDA
NON-WHITE REFUGEES
UKRAINIAN REFUGEES
OLIGARCHS
GBN
55
VIP
WHERE'S MY KNIGHTHOOD

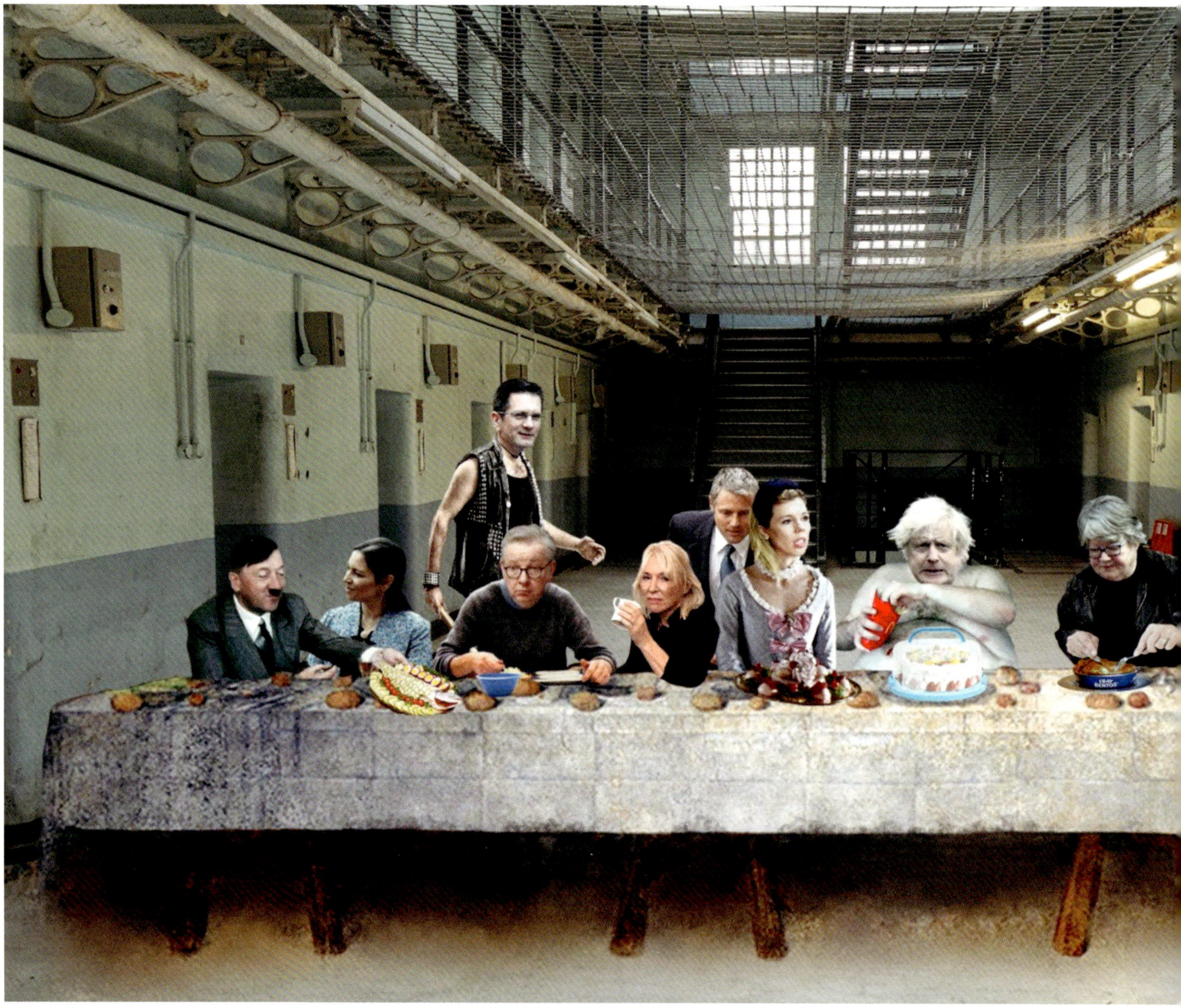

his 'spiritual home', and it suffices for now (it remains to be seen in which direction owner Elon Musk takes the company). Spencer has set up an account on Mastodon, a social media site, but it is not quite the same: 'I am also conscious that people have been using Mastodon for ages, then I suddenly turn up, barging into the room with my snarky visceral images of serial killers and miscreants.'

Led By Donkeys was formed by Oliver Knowles and Ben Stewart, both employees of Greenpeace, and James Sadri and Will Rose, who had previously worked with the environmental campaign group: they all voted Remain. Their

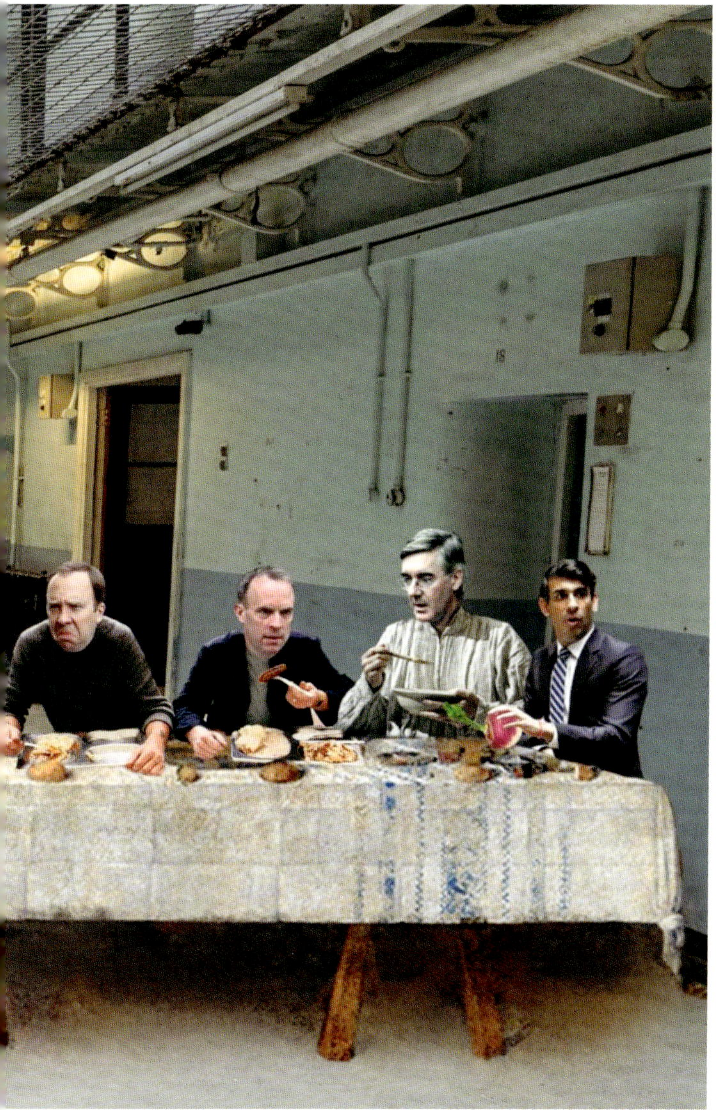

work has been unfaltering in shining a light, quite literally, on the tweets and lies of Leave campaigners – and then pasting them on billboards, or a much larger canvas, such as the House of Commons, the Home Office or the white cliffs of Dover (figs 61–3). Their book, *Led By Donkeys: How Four Friends With a Ladder Took on Brexit*, is a tale of ingenuity and of much more risk-taking than I had imagined (fig.64).[30] The book provides a manual on how to erect billboards – it is not as easy as it looks. What could go wrong? What could go right? Picture huge sheets of paper flapping in the wind or crinkling with glue. There's also an episode involving a dog and its excrement, on the street, on the ladder and finally in the glue. Read the book as a manual for protest. All this, and yet at the beginning Led By Donkeys did not have permission to post on some of the sites. Fast forward, and every architect of Brexit, along with their lies or promises, has been pasted up on billboards round the country. They are then rapidly circulated on social media. Led By Donkeys emailed me about their ethos:

> We are at heart an accountability project. We want to ask the questions not being asked by much of the media and fill a gap in our politics. For us, success is increasing awareness of the broken promises made and accountability for populist politicians who for too long have escaped it.

This countering of mistruth in the public realm, in common with Cold War Steve, was timely and their protest has gained a huge following:

> It's one of the main objectives of the project. Without a shared understanding of the facts, it's very hard for a society to operate (as we're discovering on both sides of the Atlantic). We're a small team, but we aim to have an outsized influence on the national conversation, bringing some accountability when politicians lie and dissemble.

This protest – these loud voices against Brexit – have been a contributory factor to the turn of the tide. People are now discussing Brexit in a way that they weren't just a few months ago:

> It does feel like the omertà is ending. Economic reality is biting, and people are evaluating the promises made against the lives we're not living. An important indicator is the increasing willingness of media figures to ask direct questions to the Brexiters, demanding to know

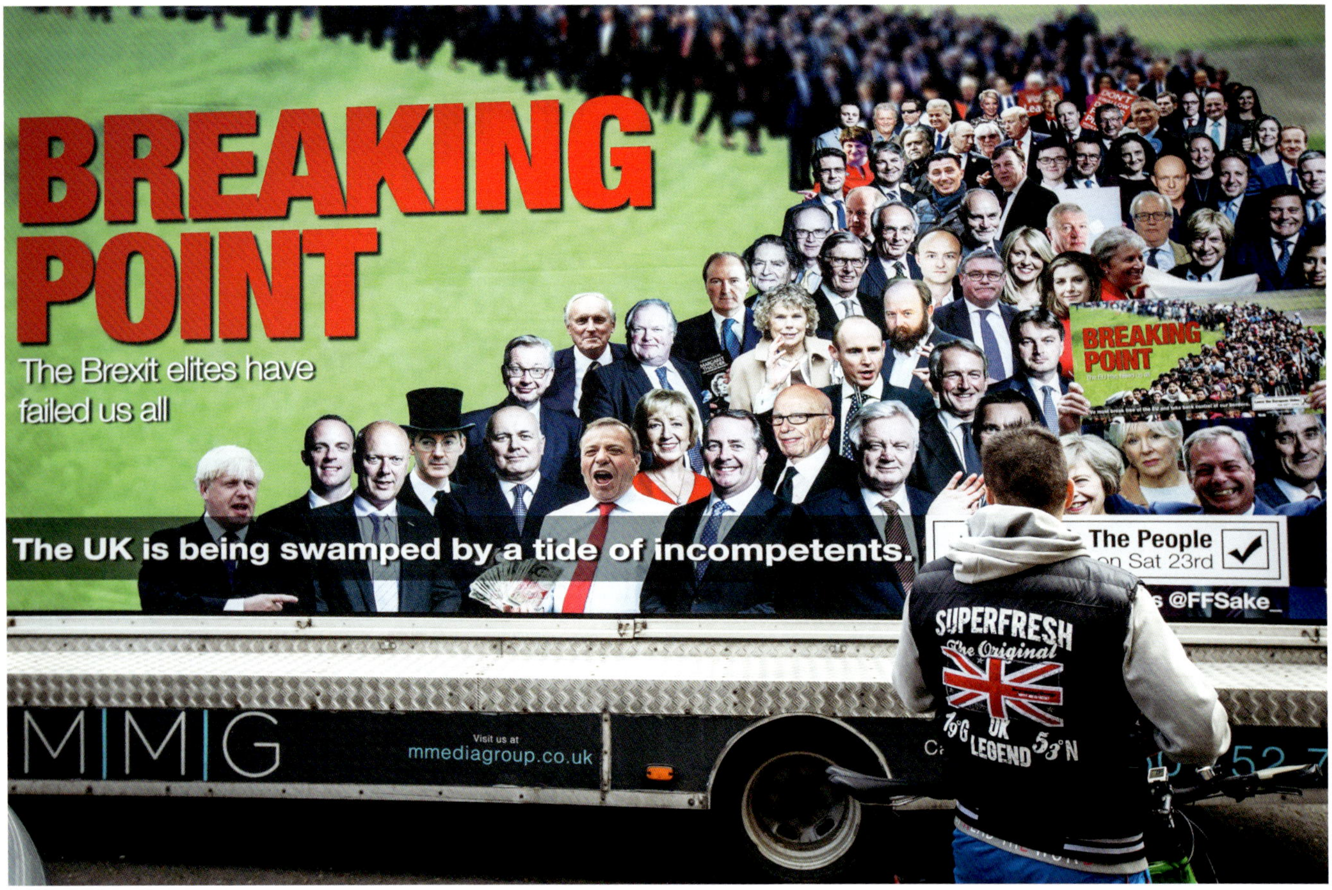

61 Led By Donkeys redesigned Nigel Farage's Breaking Point poster, 'replacing asylum seekers with a swarm of Brexiters swamping Britain with their incompetence', 2019

> where the benefits are. For years the Brexit crew 'played the ref' – pressured the media not to ask difficult questions and accused them of bias when they did. It feels like that strategy has less juice now.[31]

Emily Maitlis, a former BBC journalist and *Newsnight* presenter, is now co-host, along with Jon Sopel and Lewis Goodall, of *The News Agents*, a daily podcast from the British media company Global. This podcast has garnered huge support and, alongside Alastair Campbell and Rory Stewart's *The Rest Is Politics*, provides a much-needed expansion of the political debate. Maitlis talked of the difficulties in reporting on politics in *On Point*, a public radio programme in the US, hosted by Meghna Chakrabarti with news analyst Jack Beatty. This account was a searing indictment of the constraints on journalists and the way in which populist politicians attack them and peddle lies in a constant cycle of disruption.[32]

This is important because, if populist leaders disparage reporters and news outlets, it is because they then feel that they have a direct line to 'the people' – and create the feeling that they are in the same boat together. They are not, however. Donald Trump lives in ornate splendour in the resort of Mar-a-Lago in Florida; Boris Johnson received £276,130.00 plus expenses, for delivering a speech to insurance agents in Colorado Springs, and he popped in on Rupert Murdoch in Montana. Johnson has raked in close to £5 million in earnings since leaving office.[33]

Maitlis argues cogently for a recognition of the strategies that buoy populists, with their denigration of media and law, corruption and the constant carping that all institutions around them are rotten. It is the insidious nature of the method – and the populist ideology that propels it – that has a corrosive effect on scrutiny within a democracy:

> It is playbook stuff. And what I mean by that is that as soon as you step back and stop treating sort of every intervention or every critique as a kind of, 'what have I done?' moment, you suddenly realise that it fits a pattern. And the pattern it fits is one of populist rhetoric. It's very easy to sell populist rhetoric at home, as it is in America. Because you create divides . . . Tom Newton Dunn, as you've said, he works for Rupert Murdoch. He works on Talk TV. Before that, he was political editor of *The Sun*.
>
> *The Sun* is very much a staple of the right-wing media, nearly always supports the government on the right or the government of the day. And yet here was Liz Truss basically telling Tom Newton Dunn that there was a certain way that he should or shouldn't ask questions and trying to create this divide. And essentially what that does is it says 'I, your populist politician, I'm connected to the people, the populists. And you, the journalist, are getting in the way of that relationship.' And there are a whole host of ways that that manifests itself.And it sort of has been dawning on me for a long time.[34]

62 Led By Donkeys projected Dominic Raab's confession of ignorance (November 2018) onto the White Cliffs of Dover, 2019

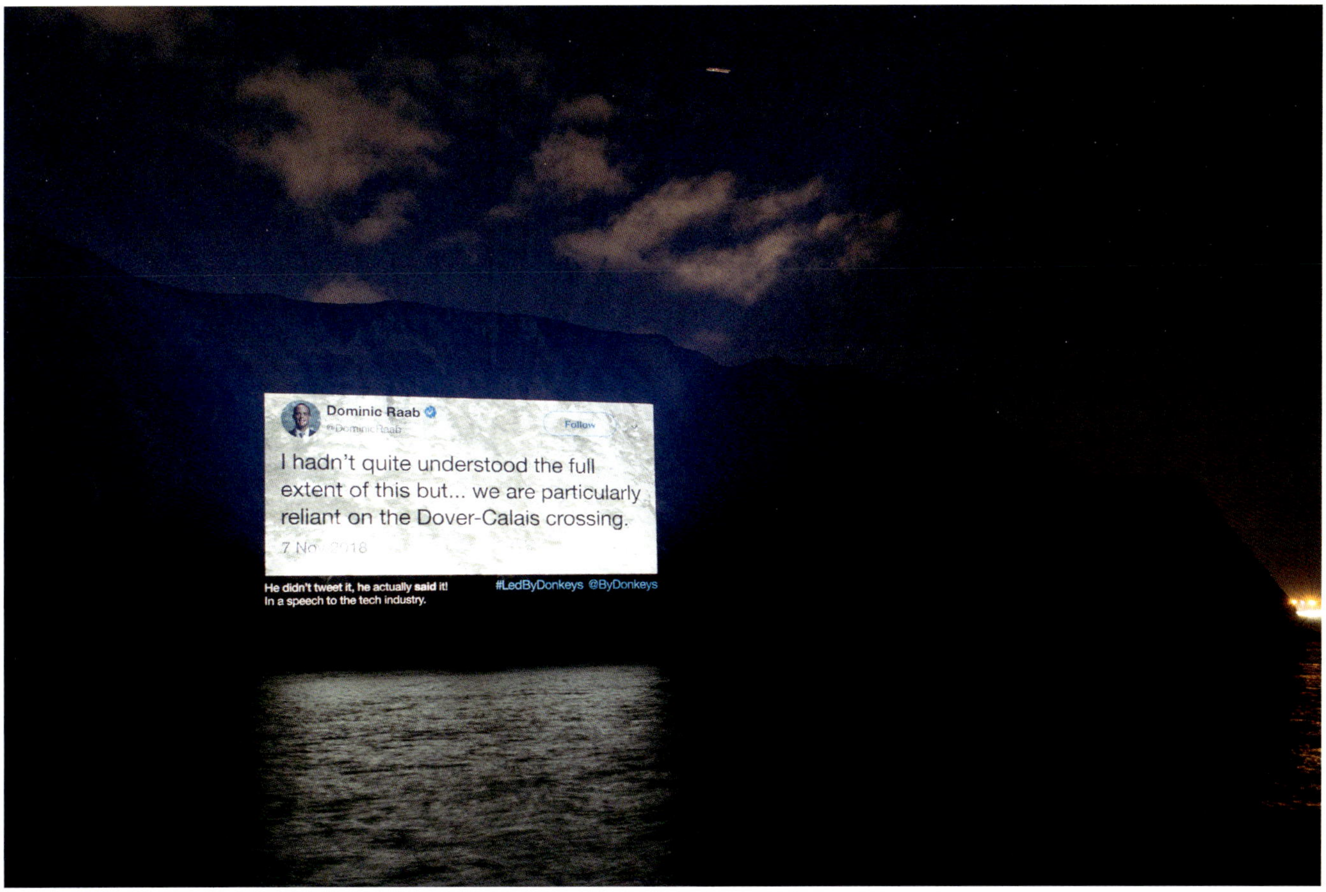

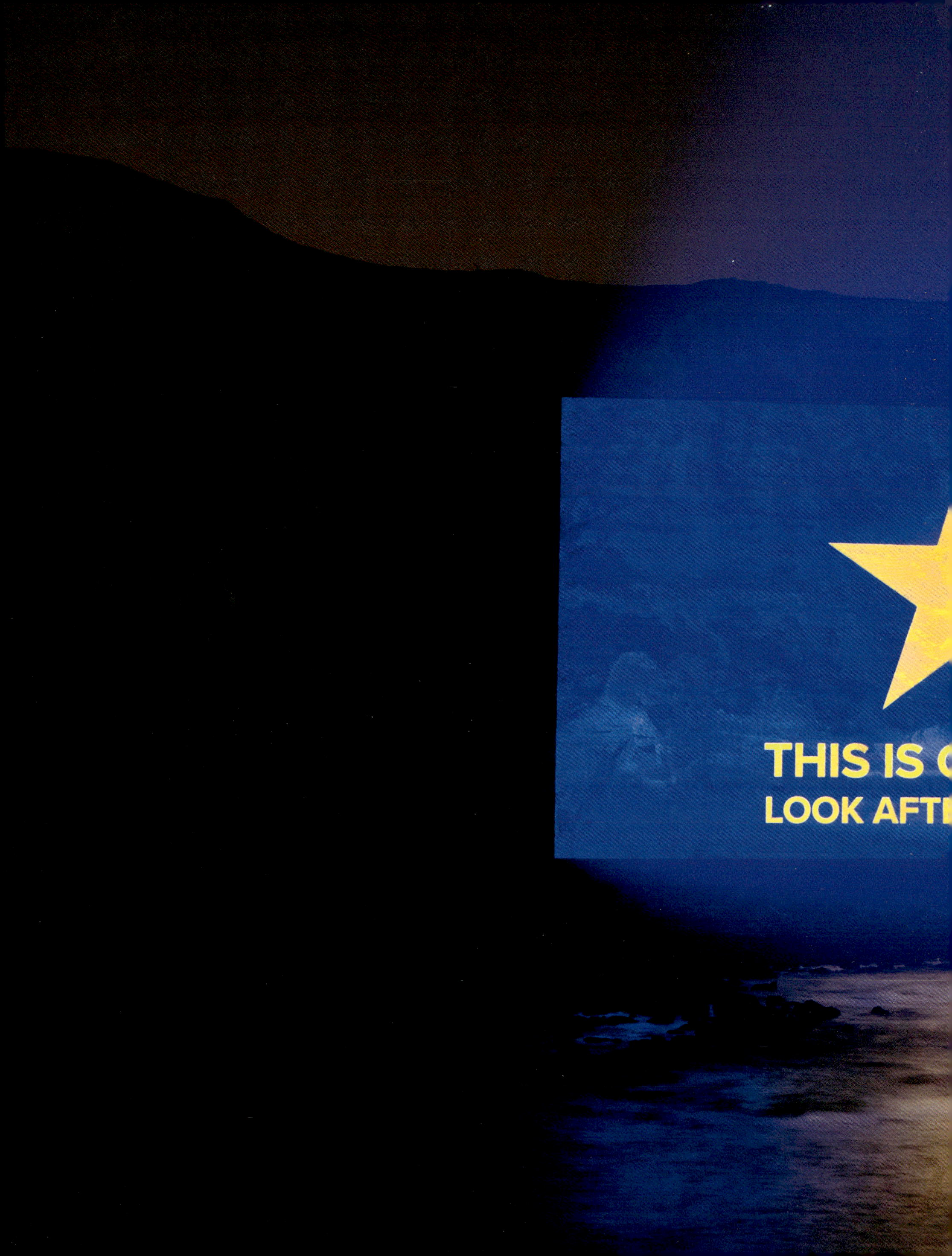
THIS IS
LOOK

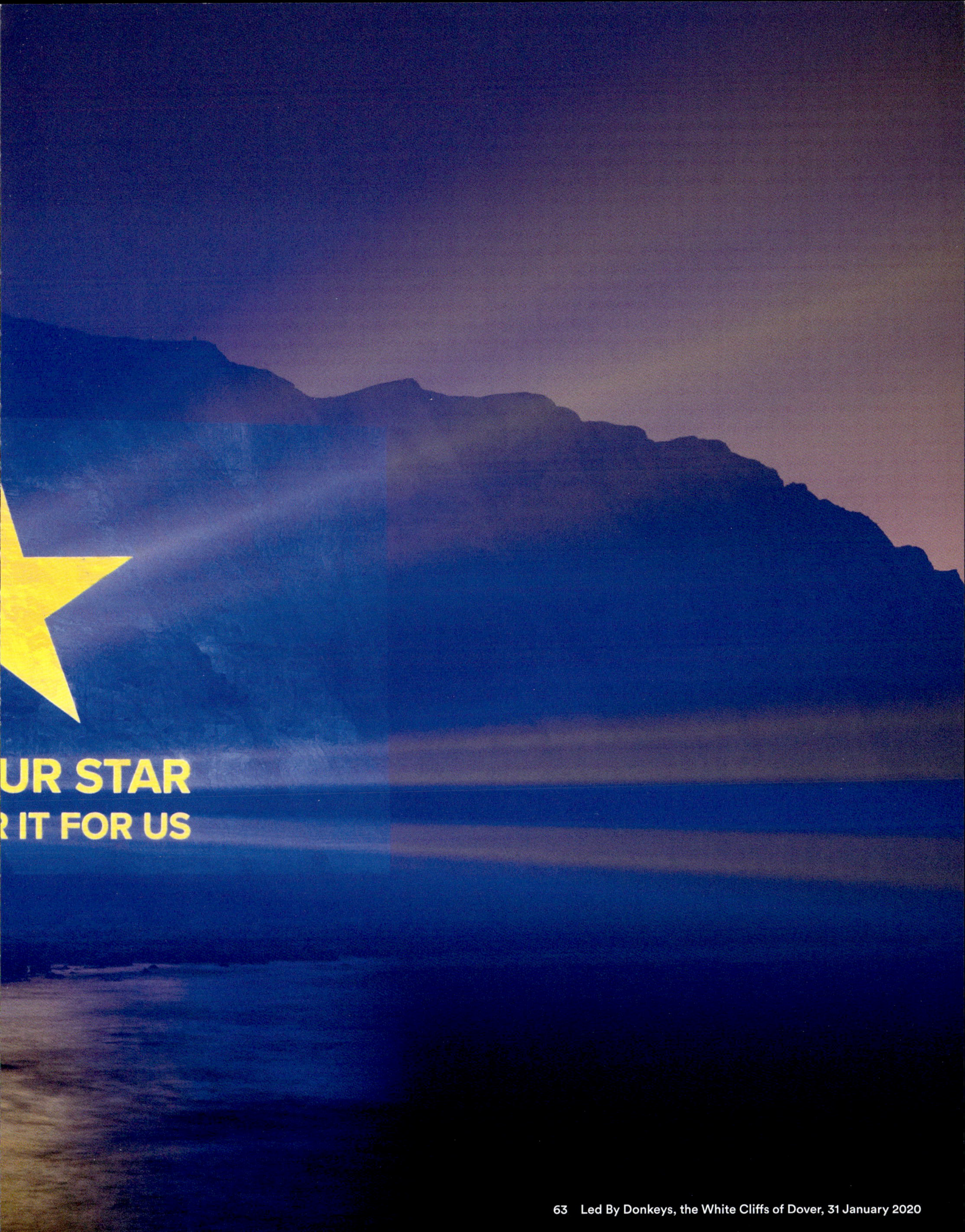

 Led By Donkeys, the White Cliffs of Dover, 31 January 2020

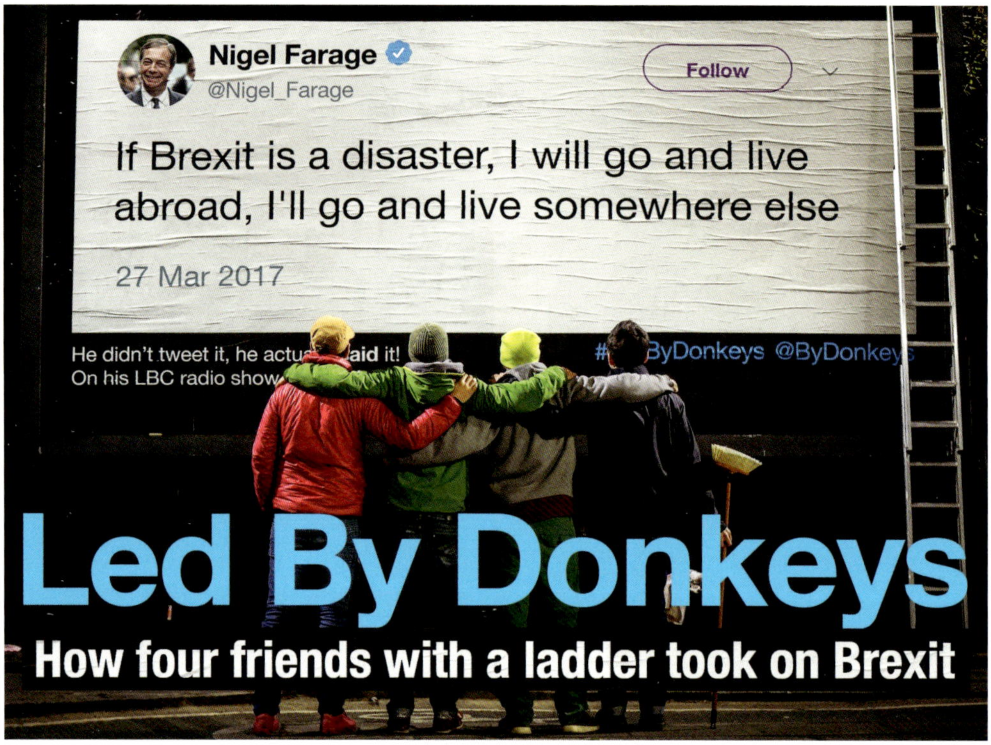

64 Cover of Led By Donkeys's story of how they have held politicians to account on billboards and through social media, published by Atlantic Books, 2019

Chapter 4

Building bridges

Nowhere is it more apparent that Brexit is nothing but a feeling and a yearning than with the incipient threat to the Good Friday Agreement (Belfast Agreement, 10 April 1998) and the border between Ireland, a European country, and Northern Ireland, which voted to remain in the EU. Nowhere is it clearer that Brexit is a catastrophic error, which never needed to happen.

My focus is on the art around the border. In 2021 Kate Nolan, a Dublin-based artist, was commissioned by the then Gallery of Photography Ireland (now Photo Museum Ireland) to make a short film, in collaboration with the composer Irene Buckley. This was part of her series LACUNA, 'a multi-disciplinary project considering the contemporary experience, physical and psychological impact of the partition

65 Kate Nolan, *Having Regard*, 2021, film still, 8 minutes, single channel monochrome and colour video with sound. Composer: Irene Buckley; Voiceover Artist: Annabelle Leddy – 13-year-old from Warrenpoint, Co. Down. Installation: *Having Regard* is projected directly onto a wall in a dark space and shown as a loop

Nolan is a filmmaker and artist who grew up in America. Her long-term project LACUNA (2015–21) was first exhibited at Gallery of Photography Ireland (now Photo Museum Ireland) in 2017. Nolan describes LACUNA as an 'audio visual work that considers the physical and psychological impact of partition on young people of the Irish borderlands'.

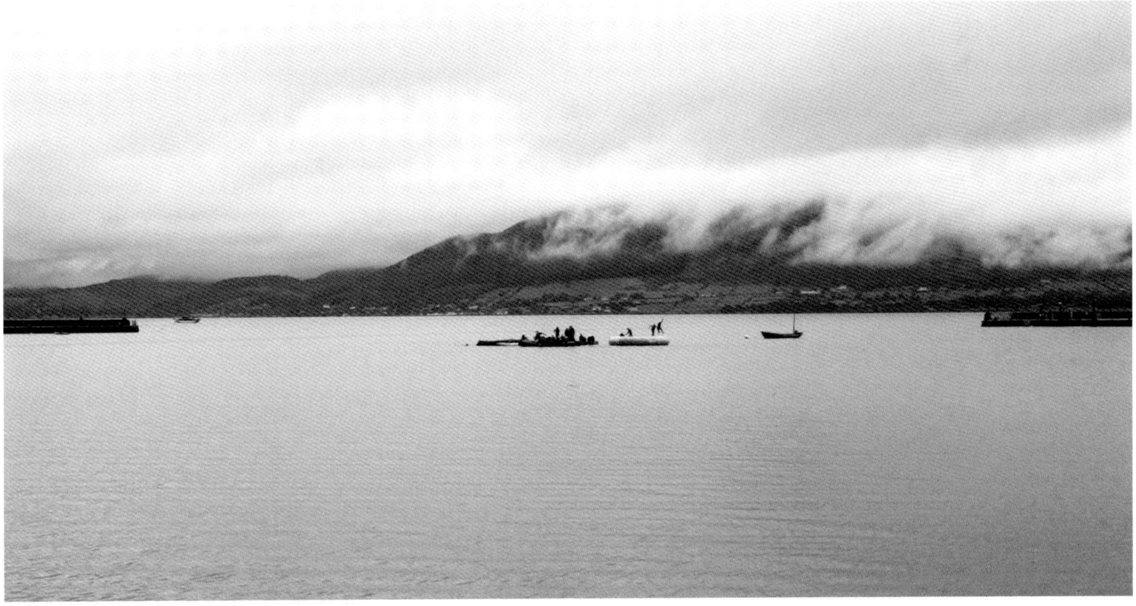

on the children of the borderlands'.[1] This is part of the Photo Museum Ireland's 'Reframing the Border' programme.[2] The way in which history, memory, trauma and colonisation are framed and realised throughout these projects is a testament to the enduring desire for peace in Ireland. These works of art show how artists worry at the edges of political and social issues to provoke clarity and contemplation.

Nolan's elegiac film, entitled *Having Regard* (fig.65), sets a lexicon of the language circulating truth and reconciliation and international treaties to moving images of people milling about between boats and rafts in the middle of a lake, assembling and reassembling. Nolan holds this image as the lexicon of words on the left of the frame scroll down: *Having Regard, Recalling, Recognising, Affirming . . . Having Agreed Upon . . .* This is the language of the Northern Ireland protocol. The film ends with statements that include these words and phrases, this language of international legal, binding agreements. The film is shot in black and white. The soundtrack amplifies the message with echoing sounds and organs fusing and repeating plaintive chords and phrases.

NORTHERN IRELAND PROTOCOL

The Northern Ireland Protocol came about because of this agreement between the UK and the EU as part of the Withdrawal Agreement:

> Since very early on in the Withdrawal Agreement negotiations, both the United Kingdom and the EU acknowledged the unique circumstances on the island of Ireland. They recognised the necessity of safeguarding the 1998 Good Friday (Belfast) agreement, avoiding a hard border on the island of Ireland and protecting North-South cooperation.
>
> This solution was found in the form of the protocol on Ireland and Northern Ireland, which:
>
> - Avoids a hard border between Ireland and Northern Ireland, thereby enabling the smooth functioning of the all-island economy and safeguarding the Good Friday (Belfast) agreement in all its dimensions.
> - Ensures the integrity of the EU's single market for goods, along with all the guarantees it offers in terms of consumer protection, public and animal health protection, and combatting fraud and trafficking.
> - The protocol on Ireland and Northern Ireland was conceived as a stable and lasting solution, and will apply alongside any agreement on the future partnership.[3]

Not a 'stable and lasting solution' for the Conservative Party, which at the time of writing placed possible revisions to the Northern Ireland protocol in the hands of Brexiter zealots, MPs Michael Gove and Steve Baker, the latter being a stalwart of the European Research Group (ERG), a charity that boasts the membership of fellow MPs Jacob Rees-Mogg and Suella Braverman. It is worth watching a Channel 4 news report on the ERG, as Braverman stumbles and stutters on being asked who is in the ERG.[4]

'Reframing the Border' ran from 2017 to 2021, 'exploring the diverse geographical, social and psychological and imagined spaces of the borderlands in Ireland'.[5] A small selection of these images is shown here, by the artists Anthony Haughey, Kate Nolan and Seán Hillen. Haughey's film, *Blind Spot* (2019), tracks the surveillance with a drone: the detritus of the state and military presence during the Troubles is a scar on the landscape. A broken bridge is left behind alongside the skeletons of commercial activity (figs 66 and 67).

right, top

66 Anthony Haughey, *Blind Spot*, *Field Notes from the Border*, 2019, film still

Blind Spot *is filmed in various border crossings from Carlingford to Donegal where most of the border infrastructure was dismantled following the Good Friday Agreement (1998). This was a political agreement designed to bring an end to 30 years of violent conflict in Northern Ireland, known as the Troubles.*

right, bottom

67 Anthony Haughey, *Bridge Cavan-Fermanagh Border*, *Field Notes from the Border*, 2019

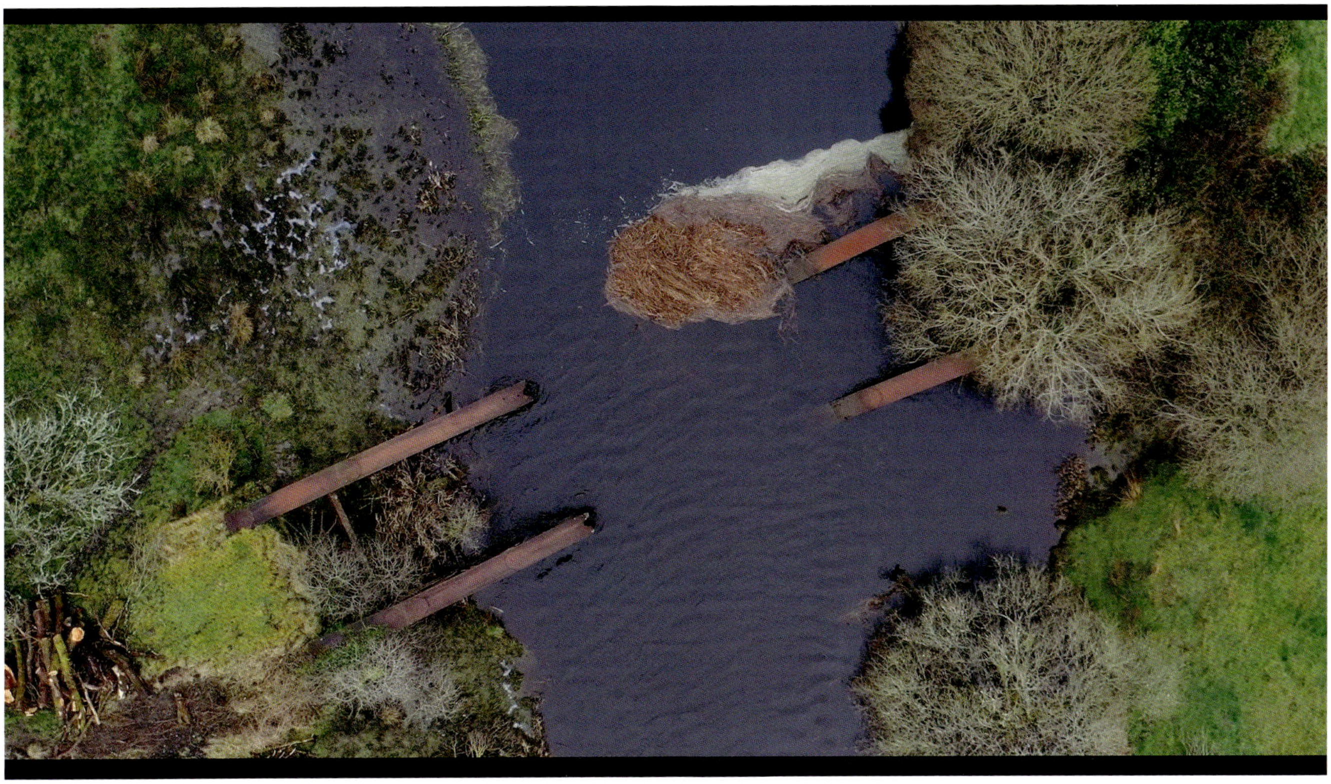

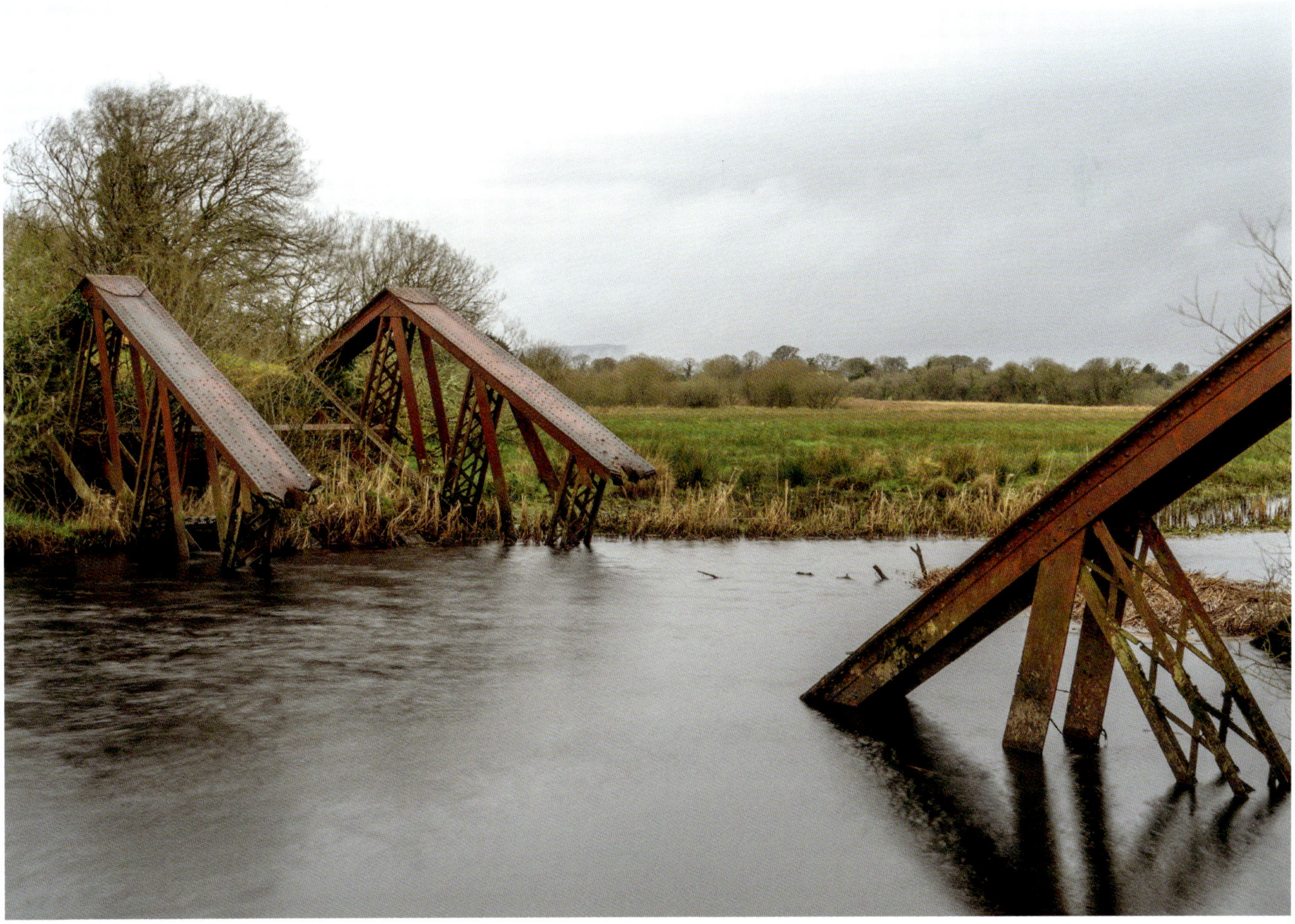

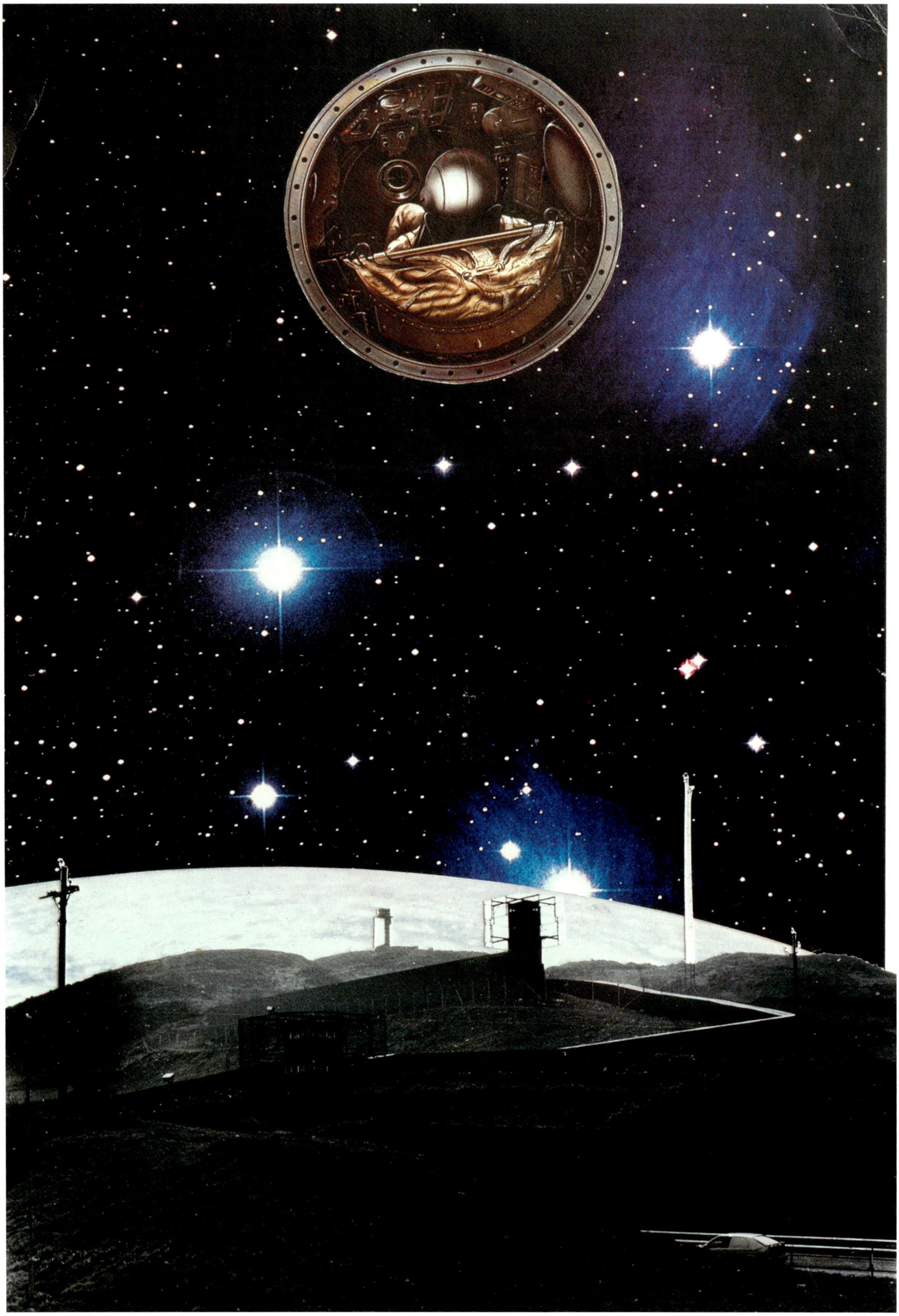

left

68 Seán Hillen, *Newry Gagarin Crosses the Border*, 1993, collage, 498 × 400 mm (196 1⁄16 × 157 ½ in)

below

69 Ciarán Dunbar, 'Ballynahattin', from his self-published artist book, *Diesel*, 2022

'Diesel traces the illegal dumping of toxic waste material, commonly referred to as "sludge", by diesel launderers at sites along the Irish border between Counties Louth, Armagh and Down', Dunbar writes. This 'laundering' refers to the removal of the dye colour that distinguished it from automotive diesel.

As Haughey notes, this surveillance is ubiquitous now through the business of social media.[6] Hillen's otherworldly take on the encampments of the British military, *Newry Gagarin Crosses the Border*, intrigues with its fusion of collage and colour, and the night sky. With the reference to the Russian cosmonaut Yuri Gagarin, the first man in space, this 'politically engaged' collage looks to and beyond the Troubles (fig.68).[7]

Ciarán Dunbar's book *Diesel* maps the places of resistance along the border for the 'laundering' of fuel – that is, extracting the dye from commercial stuff (cheaper than regular car diesel) so that it could be sold for use in ordinary vehicles without detection (fig.69).[8] There were myriad ways in which the porous border became a conduit for goods and a line of resistance after the Partition of Ireland in May 1921. Marcel Krueger writes in his afterword of smuggling in the period before the beginning of the conflict in the north in the late 1960s: of women secreting pats of butter in their underwear, or pigs being given a splash of Guinness so that they would trot quietly cross the border. During the Troubles the routes were closed by the British military.[9]

Trish Lambe, artistic director of the Photo Museum Ireland, Dublin, grew up on the border and wanted to bring the art being made around this

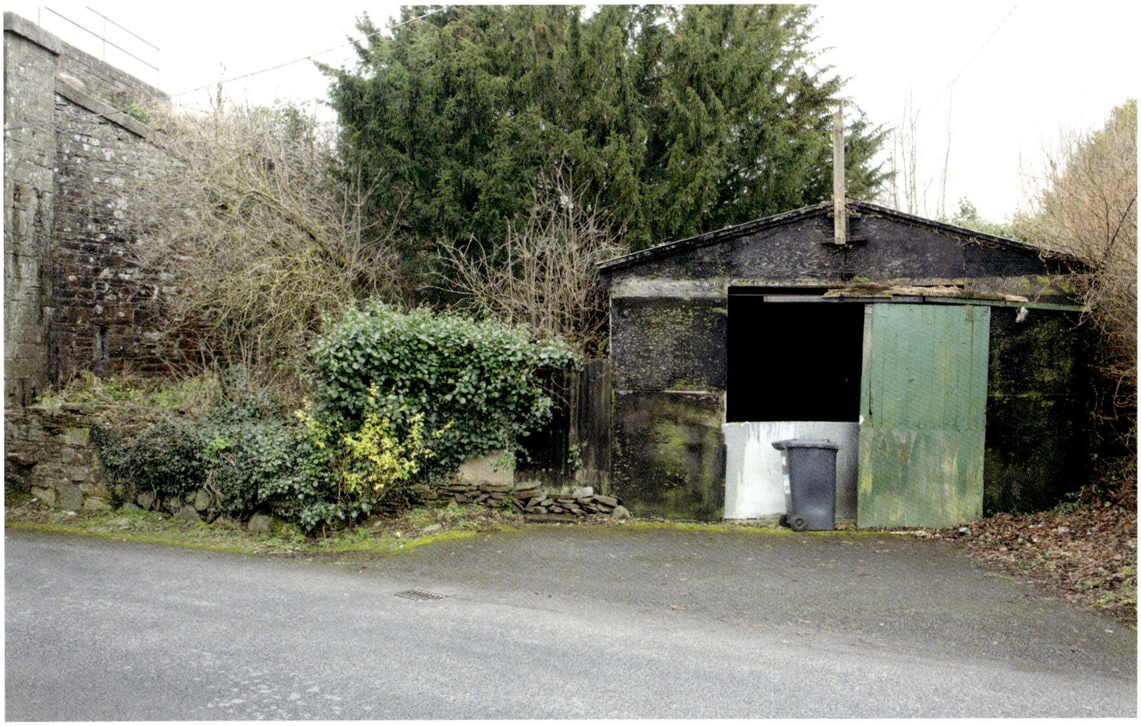

and media. His films, *Sleaford Mods: Invisible Britain* (2015), *Dispossession* (2017), *Social Housing, Social Cleansing* (2018) and *Poly Styrene: I Am a Cliche* (2021), the last co-directed with Celeste Bell, have garnered awards and facilitated Sng's move between filmmaking and the world of photography and exhibition. He has also edited two books, *Invisible Britain: Portraits of Hope and Resilience* (2018) and *This Separated Isle: Invisible Britain* (2021), published by Policy Press. The former is a searing indictment of austerity Britain; the latter features portraits of people across Britain and 'explores how concepts of "Britishness" reveal an inclusive range of opinions and understandings about our national character'.[19]

As I write this, the word 'austerity' is ringing in our ears again, trumpeted by the government as a must-do policy in the wake of the 'mini-budget' of 23 September 2022, devised by the then prime minister Liz Truss and her chancellor, Kwasi Kwarteng. The politicians who usher in austerity are immune to its consequences, with their property portfolios and personal interests in capital investment.

This Separated Isle includes Jim Mortram's portrait of Simon Tyson, whose testimony speaks of inequality in contemporary Britain: 'Not much has changed in my lifetime. It's just got shittier. The cost of living just gets worse.'[20] The Norfolk-based Mortram photographs the world in his immediate vicinity. As a carer he is not able to move far: his longterm social documentary study, *Small Town Inertia*, shows the effects of a hollowed-out social welfare system on the people he gets to know around the town of Dereham.[21] Kit de Waal, in her introduction to *This Separated Isle*, probes the difficulties that people encounter when others would categorise and stigmatise them, and calls for an acceptance of a 'multiplicity of identities':

> *This Separated Isle* is personal stuff. It's not only the subject that is examined but we, the readers, are being looked at and addressed. Black Lives Matter, climate change, Windrush, antisemitism, land access, gentrification, immigration, racism – it's impossible to read these narratives and not be moved to sorrow and anger and to ask ourselves what we are thinking, what we are doing.
>
> While Britain talks up the Brexit emperor's new clothes, we have the opportunity to call out its colonial and imperialistic legacy, its suicidal adherence to class constructs and notions of who can and who cannot belong here. We can be the child with 20:20 vision who points and says: 'But look! You are naked.'[22]

Sng was used to the power and responsibility of being a documentary filmmaker, in telling people's stories and making sure that their voices were heard, and framed, with care. He wanted to work in a different but collaborative way with those in the photographs, to give them agency. So, a photographer took a single portrait, and Sng and others did interviews, which were each turned into 700-word stories and returned to the subject to give them the opportunity to make edits. Sng says:

> I was interested in exploring how deindustrialisation austerity and cuts to public services have affected people, hearing from a range of people who had experienced difficult times and shown some form of resilience.
>
> And so, I thought about a narrative documentary photography book, where a single image would be accompanied by the person's story, told in their own words using text from an interview with them. And the rules were that once it was transcribed, we would edit together a story with up to 700 words about a particular subject or a particular theme. And once that story has been edited, we send it back to them for their approval and sign off.[23]

Since Sng started working on the two books, the whole world has changed. Sng wanted to mark this time with these projects, and plans for a third, to complete the trilogy, in another 10 years. It has been a tumultuous time to arrange these portraits of a country:

> The last few years that we've gone through have seen Brexit, COVID, Black Lives Matter and any number of issues divide our society. I wanted to take the pulse of the country really and, although it's a very divided society, explore the ties that bind people together. And what unites us – not in a clichéd way along the lines of 'we have more in common than we do not', because

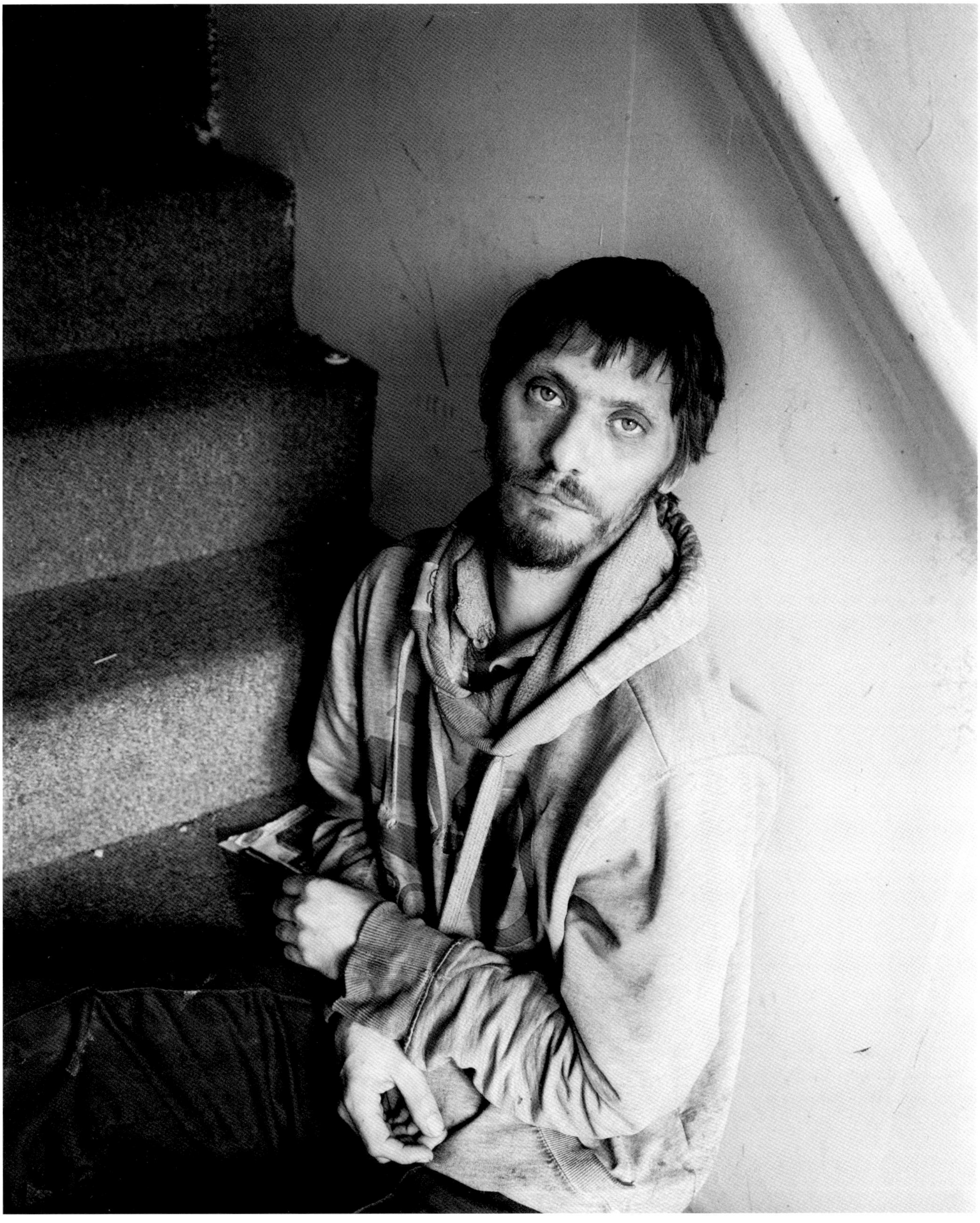

71 Jim Mortram, *Simon Tyson, Dereham, Norfolk*, May 2018. Mortram continues to work on his longform stories, and this portrait will be included in his forthcoming *Small Town Inertia 3*

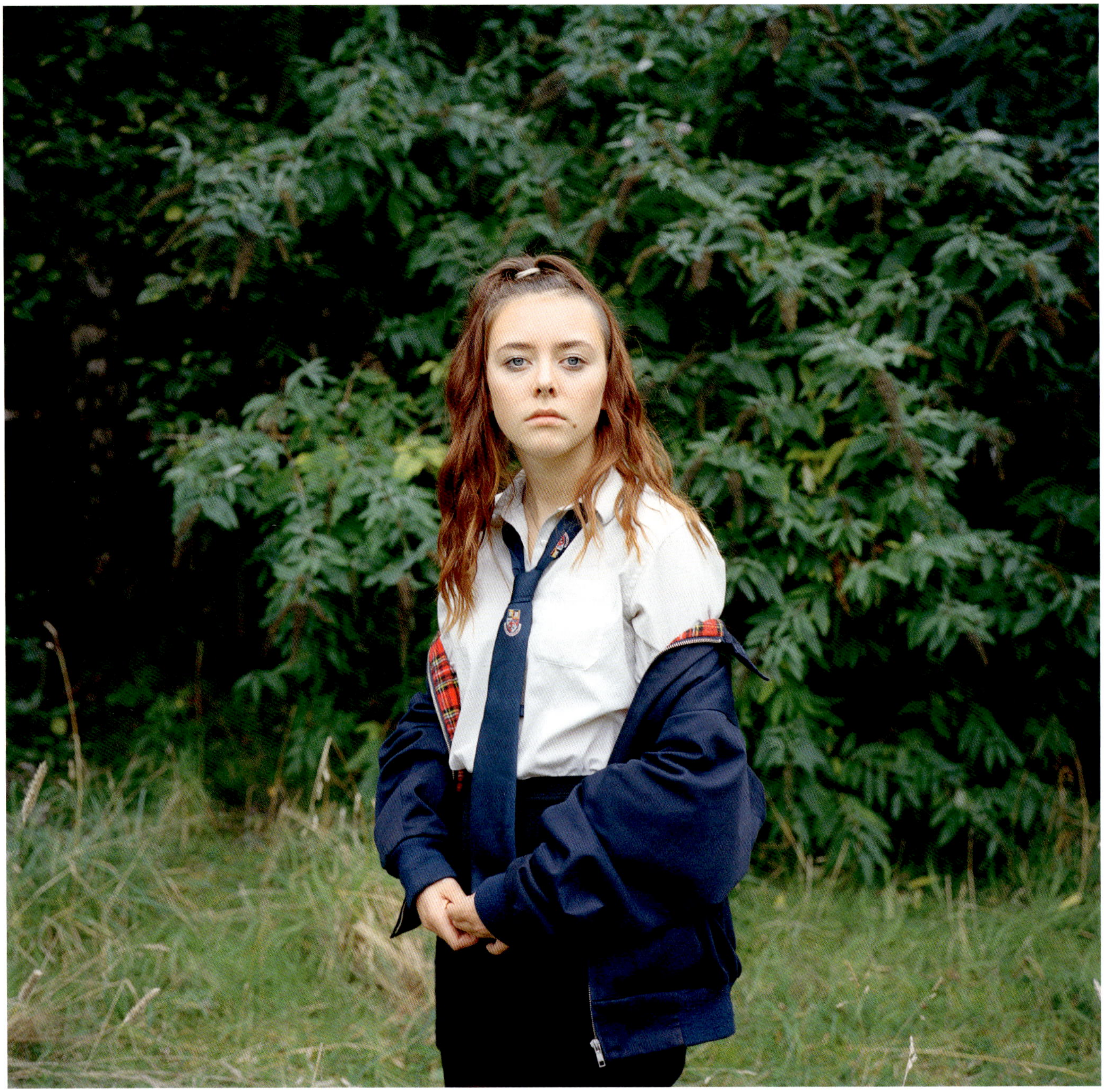

72 Margaret Mitchell, *Stina in the Children's Wood*, 2019

Stina Fisher lives in Scotland. She is half-German – and she is contemplating her future following the rupture of Brexit. Scotland voted to remain.

> I think there's nothing wrong with having differences. I think it's about respecting them. And there's one word that gets thrown around in these debates, which I really detest, which is the word 'tolerance': 'We should tolerate people who are different from us.' I think it's a dreadful word; people who are different don't want to be tolerated. They want to be understood, accepted, respected . . .

Sng does not think it is possible to revisit the referendum, despite the lies told during the Leave campaign. I do not understand myself why this vote cannot be revisited; every political decision may be revised, whether or not it is a referendum. But it is fine to disagree, and there is much that we agree on, such as the Leave vote was not simply a white, working-class vote. In the book *Rule Britannia*, co-written by Danny Dorling and Sally Tomlinson, they show that most Leave voters lived in the south of England. Dorling writes: 'This was surprising, as it was where only a minority of the UK electorate lived. But it was where the Tory and UKIP voters who most wanted to leave resided in the greatest numbers.'[24]

One of the portraits in Sng's *This Separated Isle* that resonates strongly with me is *Stina in the Children's Wood*, by the Glasgow-based artist Margaret Mitchell (fig.72). It is a poignant photograph, not least because Stina Fisher is half-German and is considering her options in the wake of Brexit. But also because Mitchell's husband, Professor Klaas Wijnne, chair of chemical physics at the University of Glasgow, is Dutch. Their son, Guus Wijnne, was 10 when the referendum took place. The result filled Guus with an 'awful dread':

> In the days after, I remember asking myself 'How?' It felt as if my connection to my Dutch roots had been severed by a vote I had no say in. It really felt like a regression of all the progress made in the UK; some people had made bigotry and intolerance win, and they were celebrating it.

For Mitchell and her family, who lived happily between Scotland and the Netherlands for many years, Brexit has been, and continues to be, a huge shock. Mitchell's background is key to this:

> I was completely blindsided by the referendum results. I woke up on the morning following the vote, looked at the news, and was speechless. I really thought it was all just a nonsense and that there was no way it would succeed. I mean, who would want to create barriers and intolerance instead of alliances? As a teenager, my dad fought in the Second World War and, after that terribly tragic time, it was so clear that European countries should come together to avoid that in the future.

Wijnne has worked in Scotland for more than 27 years.[25] His response, and the way in which Brexit has impacted on his scientific research, is redolent of so many stories of those who have worked in Britain. I did not edit these statements:

> The day after the Brexit referendum, I woke up at 4am, looked at my phone, saw the news, and actually cried . . . What affected me most was not so much the leaving of the EU in and of itself: I suppose a reasonably well-argued case could have been made, for example, for taking on a position more like Switzerland or Norway. The heartbreaking thing for me was that the referendum outcome was mostly caused by blatant lies, deception and xenophobia. Worst of all, Europeans living in the UK for decades, such as me, weren't even allowed to vote. At least in Scotland, the first minister, Nicola Sturgeon, immediately went out of her way to state the importance of EU citizens to the country. I have not personally experienced any xenophobic attitudes towards me. However, scientists in England reported being told to 'go home' and some did indeed leave. Lies and deception have been central to politics ever since the Brexit vote in 2016. Johnson's 2019 election win was predicated on the greatest lie of all: that you can have your cake and eat it, be outside of the EU yet have all the benefits it brings. Ever since, things have been gradually unravelling with more lies and the blaming of others, a fifth column of EU-lovers who supposedly undermined the Brexit project.
>
> As I have lived in Scotland for 27 years and always been employed, it wasn't hard to get

'settled status', which allowed me to stay. However, with the lack of physical evidence and with the mood in England being so xenophobic, I decided to take on UK citizenship in addition to my Dutch one, if only to avoid getting harassed at the border. The Life in the UK test you have to sit is preposterous: you have to remember all the English kings and queens from time immemorial, arcane cultural titbits, and some practical things. The citizenship ceremony in Glasgow was a very low-key affair and there was lots of annoyed murmuring at the point where we had to pledge allegiance to Her Majesty the Queen and all her descendants.

In the year just before the actual Brexit, I managed to secure a substantial research grant from the European Research Council, and I did consider if I should try and move to a university in the EU. However, I love this place: Glasgow has a big city feel yet is so close to wild nature, you can't really beat that. And, of course, my son is a Glaswegian, he was born here, this is his home, as indeed it is mine and my spouse's. The effect of Brexit for work has been, for example, that the Erasmus programme has been abandoned, so we get far fewer students from the EU. UK-based scientists can no longer apply for EU research grants due to the stubbornness of the UK government. There has not been a sudden dramatic change, people have not suddenly left in droves. It's just that UK universities have become a lot less attractive to students and staff, and that will lead to a slow decline, people declining offers and going elsewhere, a drip, drip loss of experience, diversity, and excellence.[26]

For Mitchell, her work as an artist has been affected by the difficulty of getting copies of her book, *Passage*, to Europe:

When my book came out, I had a lot of interest from the continent, but the copies I sold personally were delayed, often for weeks, at customs and with import costs added for the recipient. Small trade by artists has become more difficult if you are not part of a wider worldwide network that can distribute work.

So, in this scenario, it is individuals and small businesses that are disadvantaged. I also think that some of the effects we will never be aware of, that opportunities might not be offered as before as part of the wider cultural exchange and collaboration within Europe. Any difficulty at organisation level would obviously trickle down to individual artists.

Mitchell had lived and worked in Europe, as so many in this account have. Her life has been affected in many ways:

My husband was so concerned that a country he's made his home for over 27 years might no longer welcome him that he applied for UK citizenship. We had issues sending our usual gift at Christmas last year to the Netherlands where the recipients had to pay charges to receive it. This sounds like a small, rather trivial example, but it represents how relationships and connections have been made more difficult. Obviously, I have to queue in a different lane at airports and I feel deep shame that I may be judged as wanting to leave Europe when nothing could be further from the truth.

In my late teens, I worked in various jobs in Belgium for four years. The ability to do that broadened my outlook immeasurably and influenced how I saw my future. I cannot understand why the UK has decided to return to a situation where this is limited. I cannot even begin to comprehend why it was a votable matter in the first place. All it does is encourage the general feeling of xenophobia and the ills that can come from that. I feel my son is one of the lucky ones – being a dual national, he is still part of Europe. Whether he can retain that going into the future I am not sure. But what about others who no longer can or for whom it is just much more difficult to study, travel or live as Europeans as we previously did. Really, what use was Brexit for? It was driven by propaganda and lies and now we are left with it. Moreover, what I think Brexit did was create an environment where some people seemed to think it is acceptable to verbally abuse people from other countries.

Guus, who is 16 now, looks to the future:

> I don't feel Brexit hasn't had a noticeable effect on my daily life as a teenager. I'm very fortunate to go to a school where there are students of many ethnicities speaking multiple languages, so I don't feel as if any xenophobia due to Brexit has seeped in. I'm a dual national as well, so my future access to living and working in Europe is different to many of my peers, which is an incredible loss of opportunity for them. The only real effect I sense from Brexit is my utter loss of faith in the British system. My homeland, Scotland, I now believe, is being kept hostage by England and is forced to languish in a backwards, xenophobic, country run by the rich for the rich. I completely refuse to designate myself as British and it feels as if we have become the laughing stock of the world, the bumbling buffoons of the Isles. In a couple of years, I hope to study politics at university and contribute to a better future, a European future.

With music and the business of art, the repercussions of the referendum have been stark. Phil Young has his own conservation business and works on 'very high-value paintings', many of which exist in tax-free environments (bonds), either in freeports in Switzerland and Luxembourg, or in 'bonded' premises in Europe and the UK. When paintings move from their place of 'bond', their movement is facilitated by an import scheme known as Temporary Admission (TA). These TA accounts are a conduit for dealers, auction houses and galleries – and import VAT is temporarily suspended 'under certain conditions'. While these works may be shown, examined, sold or transported under such schemes, conservators are not able to work on artworks under bond or under TA. In order to do work, the conservator must apply for 'inward processing relief' (IPR) – and the conservator becomes the importer. HMRC categorises conservation work as 'modification', putting it in the same bag as foodstuffs and engineering parts. Young writes of the consequences:

> Their fear is that modification changes the nature of the object, or that the object disappears into a subsequent assembly, clearly ridiculous and not valid for artworks, which require maintenance and conservation.
>
> All bond, TA and IPR paperwork and regulations are extremely complicated: few people entirely understand them, and the room for error is significant. HMRC is ruthless in pursuing any errors or discrepancies. We have to employ consultants to administer the paperwork.

He continues:

> I have had IPR for some years; we used to take the occasional work from the US or Asia, and we used to be able to work on paintings in bonded warehouses. Now, with Brexit, everything is an import. We cannot work in bonded premises anymore. There has been no change in regulations to allow us to export our skills in this way; indeed, HMRC has become stricter and hardened the rules. I have fallen foul three times. Once, I had a VAT bill for £800,000, with threats to close my business over paperwork errors. This took two years and cost me £70,000 to resolve. My MP then stepped in and I was cleared and refunded. I have had two scares since. I have now decided I cannot risk my entire business and career every time I import a painting for small amounts of work. Other conservators feel the same.
>
> I have been working for 40 years, but I cannot now be available for international clients or work on important paintings – this market has closed for me. I have specialist skills with modern paintings in demand from around the world. Brexit has killed my international work. HMRC has to look at this and recognise that not only does this sector in the UK have world-renowned specialists, being regularly treated as tax criminals, but that artworks require maintenance and their own rules for import tax relief.[27]

Young acknowledges that the situation stems from wealthy owners who don't pay tax, but the burden now rests on the professionals who work on these artworks.

In 1995, Karen Sanig founded Art Law at Mishcon de Reya in London. Her clients across the world include artists and their estates, collectors, dealers, art foundations and charities, auction houses, galleries, museums and governments. She has a bird's eye view of Brexit and its effect on the art world. Sanig studied in France, learnt French and is married to a Frenchman. While she knows that her children will benefit from EU citizenship in terms of opportunities, she recognises that the opportunities have been curtailed for those not in possession of an EU passport:

> Thanks to the foresight of Professor Emeritus of Comparative Law, L. Neville Brown, who created one of the first law and French courses over 40 years ago, of which I was a graduate, I inadvertently Brexit-proofed myself and my family by studying and working in France and importing a French husband to the UK. He helped to found a French school in London and our children were educated there with many other children of pan-European parents. This is all very fortuitous and the children's future with free movement for work, life experience and cultural exchange is as good as mine was, thanks to their French passports.
>
> This is now not the case for many other young people who will not benefit from the incredible opportunities for European study, exchange and work. No longer can au pair jobs or other temporary work to perfect language skills be easily obtained. Educational establishments will have to be as inventive as Professor Neville Brown and devise new and affordable schemes to ensure that English students continue to benefit from educational versatility.[28]

Sanig describes the consequences of the rupture with the EU as mixed. She points to the robust nature of the art market and the invigoration of online markets:

> It is going to be even tougher to attract the leading sales to auction in the UK, to retain the burgeoning UK artistic talent, and encourage European neighbours to live, work and study here. However, it is not impossible. Despite the lack of inward investment in the creative industries by the UK Government (not new or the result of Brexit) there is an enthusiasm and determination to maintain the stronghold the UK has built over the past decades, as one of the most important world centres for the art market. This is more of a hiatus than a rupture. We are already au fait with the detail of the workings of post-Brexit transactions. Online art sales and digital art itself are revolutionising the way art business is transacted which makes the art market less about the specific rules and regulations of one jurisdiction. There are many brilliant art online businesses in development in the UK and these will definitely help bridge gaps caused by Brexit.
>
> It's not all bad news either; the antiquities market is able to trade in the UK more easily than in the rest of Europe. Post-Brexit, the UK was free to reject EU trade regulations requiring licensing and registration on the import of artefacts more than 250 years old which originate outside the EU.
>
> UK institutions are also looking more closely at how to remedy the misdemeanours of Britain's colonial past plundering of cultural heritage artefacts. A new law enabling UK national institutions to release and return cultural heritage artefacts in their collections to other countries in certain circumstances is in process although not yet in force. The art market, like art itself, is always changing and will adapt.

As regards her work at Mishcon de Reya, the complications arising from Brexit have been felt across the board:

> The end of free movement of art and art market specialists within Europe has created a plethora of new legal issues. Our international art market clients rushed to move collections out of London homes shortly before the end of the transition period but inevitably there were those who were caught. Buying and selling art suddenly became even more complicated owing to the new documentation required for import and export. Sometimes clients felt they were paying

> tax to the UK twice. For example, an important work which had attracted import duty from outside Europe moved to the UK shortly before Brexit and then to a different European location, then faced import duty again at 5 per cent when returning to the UK just after the end of the transition period. There has been more to advise on, but fewer well predisposed clients in such circumstances.
>
> On the other hand, the falling pound has brought great opportunities for foreign buyers in the UK from the USA and south-east Asia particularly. We have been increasingly advising collectors, dealers and galleries how to navigate the sometimes choppy waters of the post-Brexit export licencing and new AML rules applicable to the art market. Speaking fluent French and understanding the workings of continental Europe's civil law, in addition to English common law, has been a bonus as cross-border complications multiply.
>
> Unfortunately, however, we have been less able to welcome young European lawyers keen to gain experience in art law with us. There is plenty of home-grown talent but it has always been really beneficial for everyone to have the benefit of cross-cultural influence in the team. Art is always on the move and the laws that apply to it do not operate in isolation or in one jurisdiction alone.

For music and musicians, the situation is possibly even bleaker, as musicians need to play to audiences. This is especially important for bands and musicians who are starting out, and it is disastrous for them if the only place in the world they are able to play is the UK. They need to gain experience by touring and building a following – and this stands for classical musicians as well as contemporary bands. Andrew Trendell, writing in the *NME*, quotes Naomi Smith, CEO of the campaign Best for Britain, which is working for closer ties with Europe: 'Arguably, music is Britain's most famous export, so it's just insanity that the government is refusing to improve the Brexit deal for UK musicians and are strangling that next generation of talent in the cradle.'[29]

Professor Linda Merrick, Principal of the Royal Northern College of Music and chair of Conservatoires UK, has outlined the many ways in which Britain's conservatoires have suffered since Brexit, with the loss of EU applicants, the barriers to British students working in Europe, EU tutors leaving and funding opportunities lost. It is a long list of negatives. The Turing Scheme, which the government promotes as a substitute for Erasmus, does not match up.[30] The latter impacts in many ways, says Merrick:

> All of this is disadvantageous for us from numerous perspectives – profile, partnership, international relations, financial, recruitment etc. In short, our focus will inevitably shift now to other overseas non-EU markets. This has some benefits, of course, in a global landscape and international profession, but has increased competition significantly for both home and overseas non-EU students and staff. It has also increased our costs and development efforts at a time when finances are extremely tight.
>
> In summary, our fear is that we become increasingly isolated from the EU, which damages not only us, but the future of the UK music profession as a whole. Whilst some of the issues above will no doubt be addressed over time, time is not on our side and some of the damage will be irreversible.

Beth Taylor, a mezzo-soprano, was born and raised in Glasgow.[31] She attended the Royal Conservatoire of Scotland (2012–18), and she has been dealing with paperwork and visa issues since Brexit. Opera singers depend on the European circuit to build their career through work with a variety of opera companies and venues, and most importantly, to learn the opera repertoire. Since graduating, Taylor has worked in France, Germany, Spain, Switzerland, Luxembourg, Italy, the Netherlands and Belgium. Following Brexit, she has experienced some anti-British sentiment – which she had not previously encountered, especially as a Scottish artist: 'It's becoming more of a resentment because of the paperwork I now bring along with me in the weeks leading up to a contract.' In the past, younger artists often

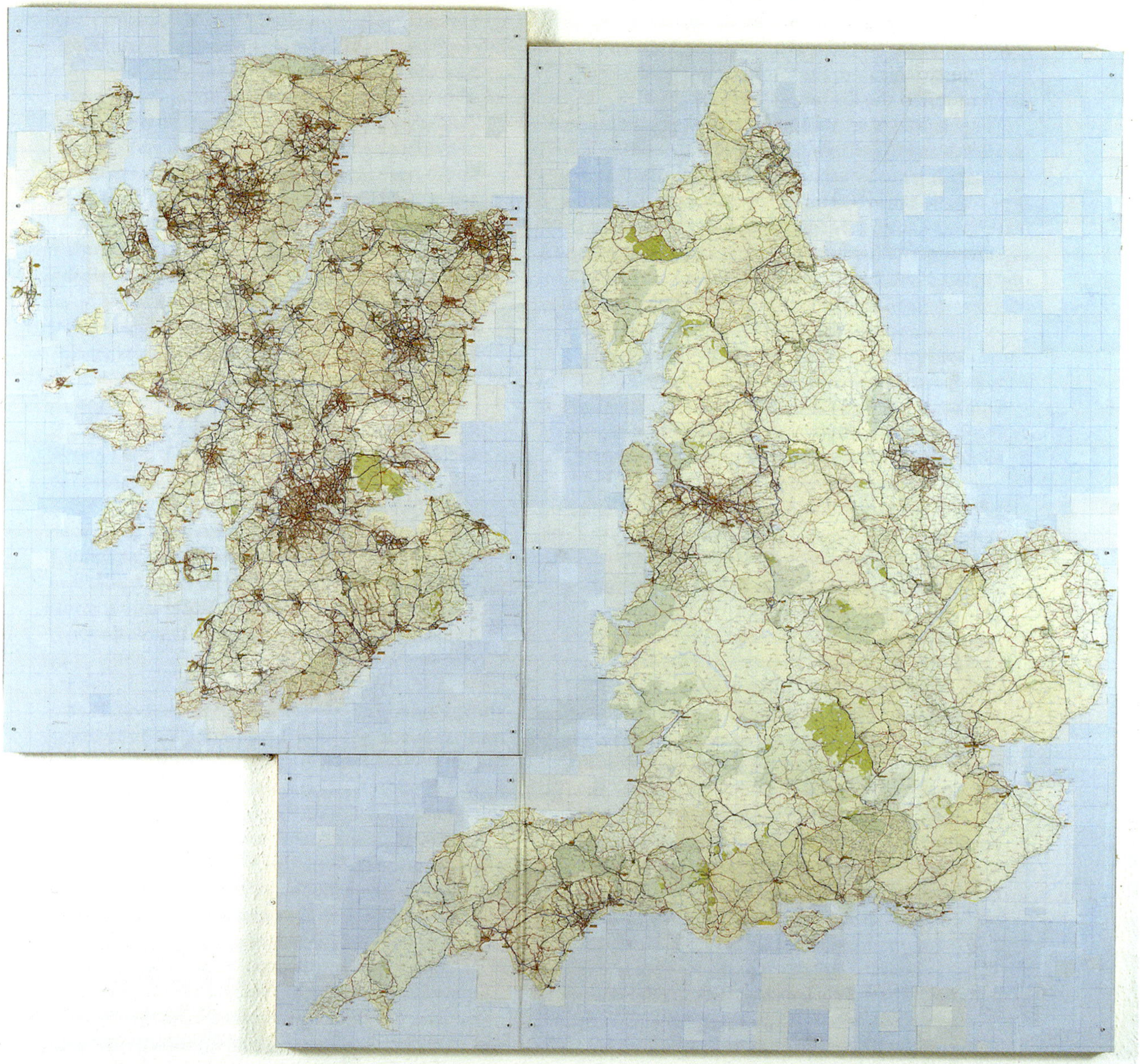

73 Layla Curtis, *United Kingdom*, 1999, two lithographs on paper mounted onto foam core on hardboard, Tate (purchased 2000)

The map became the conduit for her art in her prescient *United European Union* series, which she started in 2000, 'way ahead of Brexit'. This work continues to this day. Curtis views this work as a 'celebration of the European Union', though she did not attach this label at the time and was 'shocked to the core' when Brexit happened.

Like other parents, Curtis considers the impact Brexit will have on her child's life. There will be no freedom of movement, and the loss of the Erasmus scheme means it will be harder for Curtis's daughter to follow a similar trajectory to her in terms of studying abroad and the sort of carefree, visa-free travel that all Britons used to enjoy. Curtis's recent works, *United Kingdom + United European Union*, disturb the boundaries once more.

Ordnance Survey, which has mapped every inch of the UK, was founded in 1791 and produced its first map in 1801. This map of Kent was created in response to a perceived threat of invasion from France, as the Ordnance Survey's chief geospatial officer, David Henderson, points out:

> Ordnance Survey's original purpose was to create a map that would help our military to defend and protect a nation. England's most south-easterly county, Kent, was the area most vulnerable to French invasion, so that was our subject – highlighting the county's communication routes and including elaborate hill-shading to interpret the landscape precisely for those men at arms.[38]

It was during the First World War that Ordnance Survey maps, with their attention to detail, became indispensable to Britain's armed forces: OS published 33,000,000 maps; in the Second World War, 342,000,000. As Britain's 'national mapping agency', Ordnance Survey is a 100 per cent 'government owned company and is accountable to the Secretary of State for Business, Energy and Industrial Strategy'. It represents government and addresses the thirst for data, the raw material of information on which government and commercial decisions are based in the property, land and corporate logistics areas. OS has also produced a map of Mars, which should be of use to the technology, social media and transport behemoths as they seek to colonise space.[39]

Economic data and trade figures reveal the damage done by Brexit, and Chris Grey's Brexit blog is an indispensable source of information.[40] Naomi Smith, of Best for Britain, said of the recent slew of opinion polls that show a majority in favour of rejoining the EU:

> These polls reflect the undeniable reality that Brexit has been an unmitigated political and economic catastrophe for the UK, and that voters see through the Vote Leave falsehoods which are still parroted by the government.
>
> The economic turmoil caused by the Tories' political circus has voters demanding a sea change in policy at home and abroad, which requires a general election and a government that pursues a better political and economic relationship with the EU.[41]

Artists, photographers, filmmakers, cultural producers, conservators, publishers, auction houses, galleries, the fishing industry, farmers, scientists, NHS workers, academics, traders, importers and exporters, cultural groups, museums, musicians and truckers/hauliers continue to grapple with the inherent impossibility of a hard border, the end of the free movement of people, and the reality of friction-heavy, rather than frictionless, trade with 27 potential trading partners in the EU. The only way to achieve the latter, to borrow a phrase from the government's *Benefits of Brexit* report, is to go 'further, faster and forward' towards the EU. Opinion polls chart the increasing number of people who would vote to rejoin the EU. This is not over, not by a long chalk.

I marvel at the praise lavished on the Windsor Framework (27 February 2023), a new deal to change trade rules for Northern Ireland, by the UK prime minister and Brexiter Rishi Sunak at a Q&A in Belfast: 'Northern Ireland is in the unbelievably special position, unique in the entire world, European continent – in having privileged access, not just to the UK home market, which is enormous, but also the European Union single market.' He added: 'That's like the world's most exciting economic zone!' Downing Street officials dismissed the idea that access to both markets would benefit the UK, although these trading opportunities match the pre-Brexit trading framework.[42]

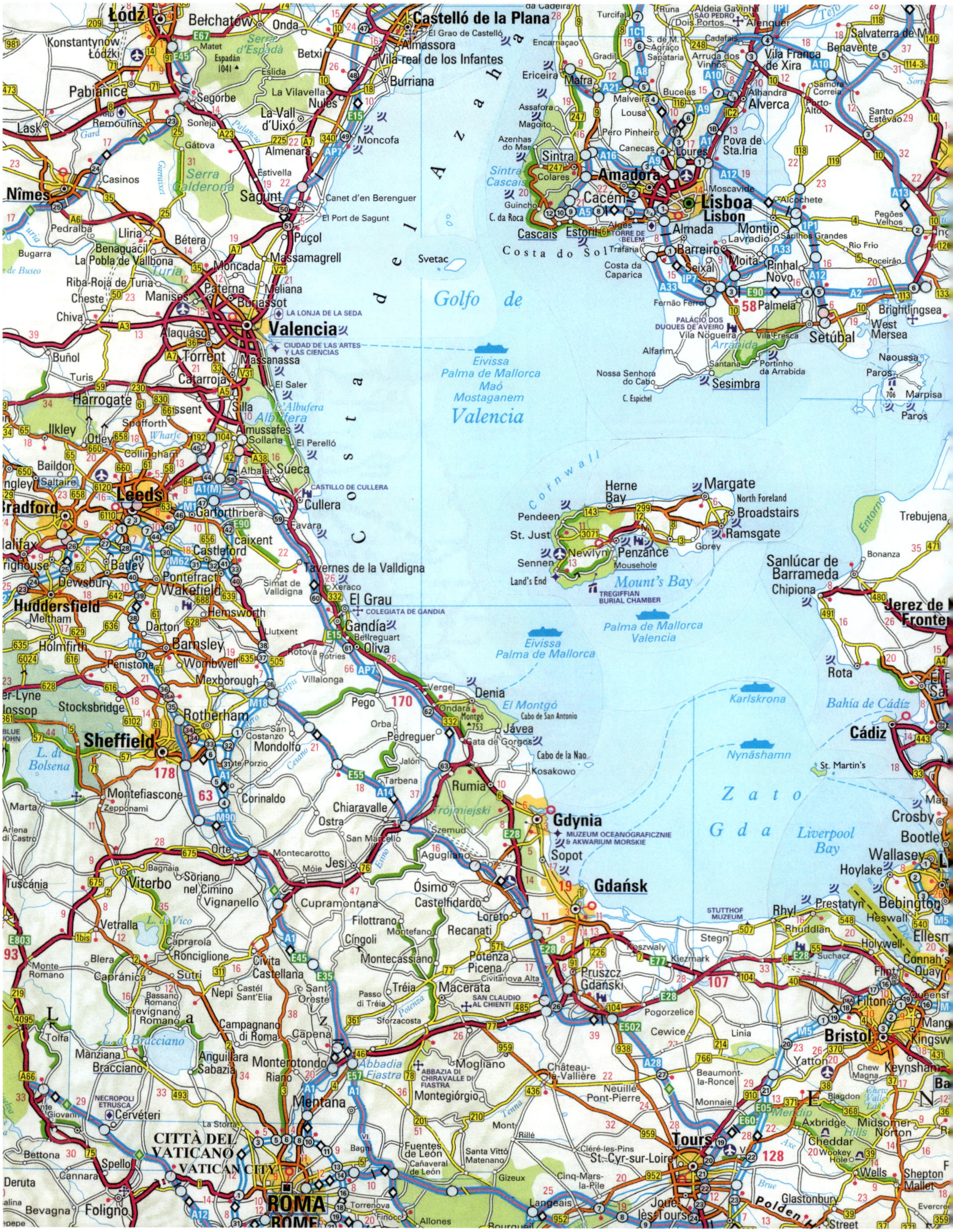

Łódź
Bełchatów
Konstantynów Łódzki
Pabianice
Łask
Castelló de la Plana
Almassora
Vila-real de los Infantes
Burriana
Nules
La Vall d'Uixó
Moncofa
Segorbe
Almenara
Sagunt
Canet d'en Berenguer
El Port de Sagunt
Puçol
Massamagrell
Moncada
Paterna
Burjassot
Meliana
Valencia
LA LONJA DE LA SEDA
CIUDAD DE LAS ARTES Y LAS CIENCIAS
Alaquàs
Torrent
Massanassa
Catarroja
El Saler
Silla
L'Albufera
Almussafes
Sollana
El Perelló
Sueca
Cullera
CASTILLO DE CULLERA
Favara
Tavernes de la Valldigna
Xeraco
El Grau
COLEGIATA DE GANDIA
Gandía
Bellreguart
Oliva
Pego
Denia
El Montgó
Jávea
Cabo de la Nao
Costa del Azahar
Golfo de Valencia
Eivissa
Palma de Mallorca
Maó
Mostaganem
Valencia
Nîmes
Casinos
Pedralba
Lliria
Bétera
Benaguacil
La Pobla de Vallbona
Turia
Riba-Roja de Turia
Cheste
Manises
Chiva
Buñol
Turis
Serra Calderona
Serra d'Espadà
Lisboa
Lisbon
Amadora
Sintra
Cacém
Cascais
Estoril
Loures
Almada
Barreiro
Moita
Seixal
Montijo
Alcochete
Pinhal Novo
Palmela
Setúbal
Sesimbra
Costa do Sol
Costa da Caparica
Trafaria
Mafra
Ericeira
Vila Franca de Xira
Alverca
Benavente
Salvaterra de Magos
Alfarim
Arrábida
Fernão Ferro
C. da Roca
C. Espichel
Nossa Senhora do Cabo
PALÁCIO DOS DUQUES DE AVEIRO
Vila Nogueira
Brightlingsea
West Mersea
Harrogate
Ilkley
Otley
Leeds
Bradford
Baildon
Saltaire
Garforth
Castleford
Batley
Dewsbury
Pontefract
Wakefield
Huddersfield
Holmfirth
Barnsley
Penistone
Wombwell
Mexborough
Rotherham
Sheffield
Stocksbridge
Hemsworth
Darton
Meltham
Herne Bay
Margate
North Foreland
Broadstairs
Ramsgate
Pendeen
St. Just
Sennen
Land's End
Newlyn
Penzance
Mousehole
Mount's Bay
TREGIFFIAN BURIAL CHAMBER
Cornwall
Sanlúcar de Barrameda
Chipiona
Jerez de la Frontera
Rota
Bahía de Cádiz
Cádiz
Trebujena
Bonanza
Karlskrona
Nynäshamn
Gdynia
MUZEUM OCEANOGRAFICZNIE & AKWARIUM MORSKIE
Sopot
Gdańsk
Zatoka Gdańska
Pruszcz Gdański
Trójmiejski
STUTTHOF MUZEUM
Liverpool Bay
Crosby
Bootle
Wallasey
Hoylake
Bebington
Heswall
Ellesmere Port
Rhyl
Prestatyn
Rhuddlan
Holywell
Connah's Quay
Flint
Bristol
Keynsham
Filton
Yatton
Cheddar
Axbridge
Wells
Shepton Mallet
Glastonbury
Midsomer Norton
Tours
St.-Cyr-sur-Loire
Joué-lès-Tours
Château-la-Vallière
Neuillé-Pont-Pierre
Langeais
Beaumont-la-Ronce
Monnaie
Montefiascone
L. di Bolsena
Viterbo
Soriano nel Cimino
Vignanello
Vetralla
Caprarola
Ronciglione
Civita Castellana
Nepi
Sutri
Capránica
Bracciano
L. di Bracciano
Anguillara Sabazia
Campagnano di Roma
Monterotondo
Mentana
Cervéteri
NECROPOLI ETRUSCA
CITTÀ DEL VATICANO
VATICAN CITY
ROMA
ROME
Tolfa
Tuscánia
Orte
Corinaldo
Chiaravalle
Jesi
Ancona
Ósimo
Castelfidardo
Loreto
Recanati
Potenza Picena
Macerata
Filottrano
Cingoli
Montecassiano
Tréia
Mogliano
Montegiórgio
ABBADIA DI CHIARAVALLE DI FIASTRA
SAN CLAUDIO AL CHIENTI
Foligno
Spello
Bevagna
Mondolfo
Rumia
Tarbena
Jalón
Pedreguer
Orba
Villalonga

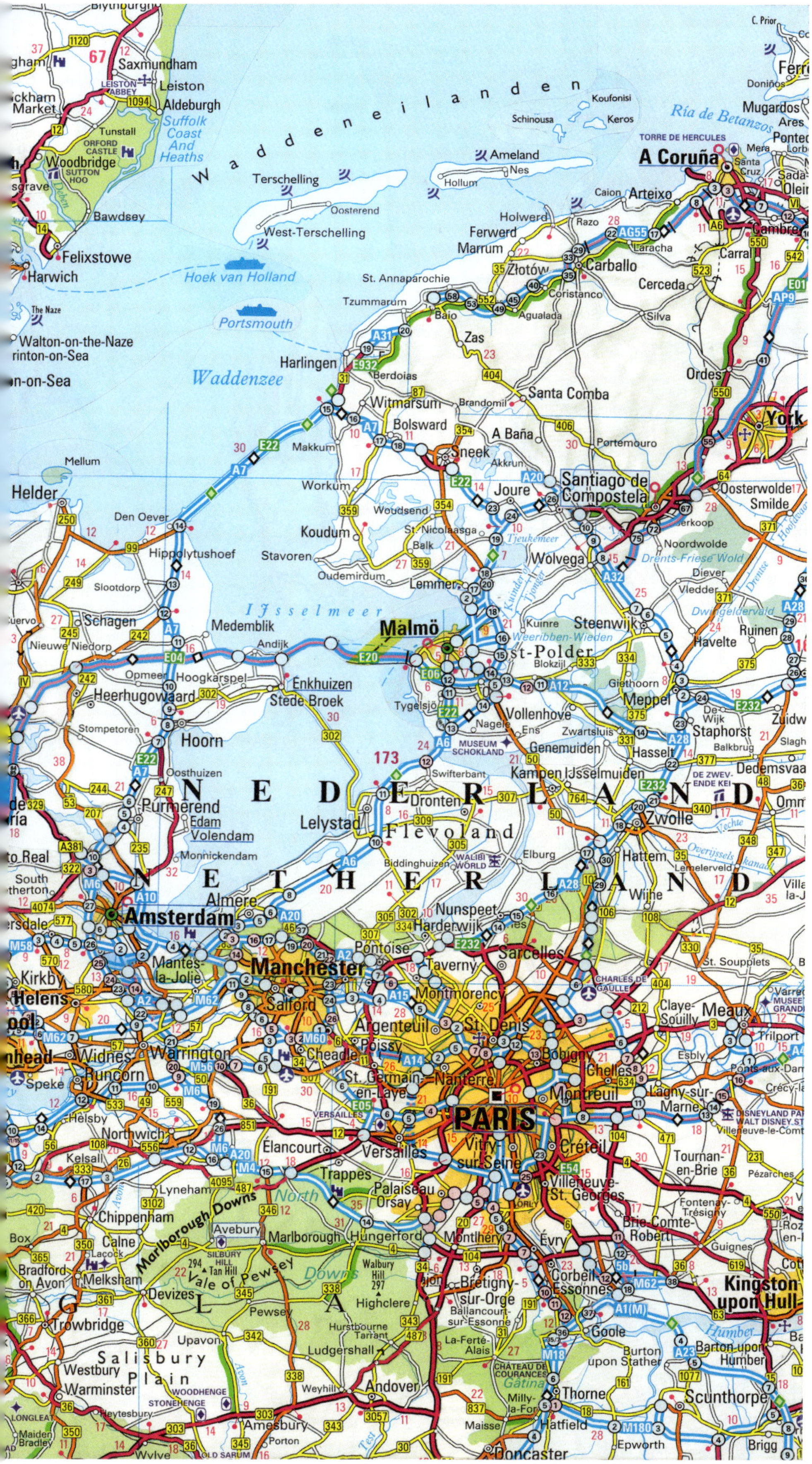

74 Layla Curtis, *United Kingdom + European Union*, 2021, collaged road maps on board, 305 × 407 mm (120 1⁄16 × 160 ¼ in)

Curtis creates original collages from fragments of EU member state road maps combined with fragments of UK road maps.

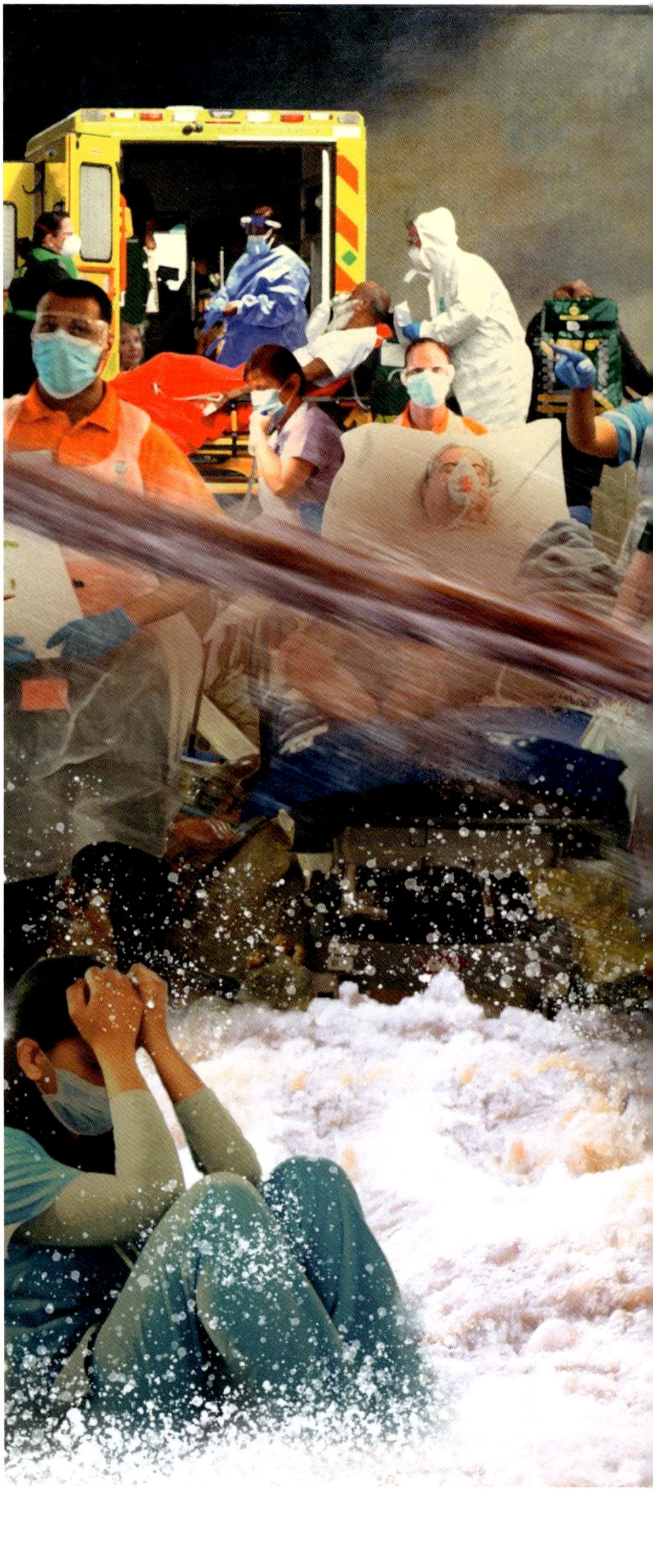

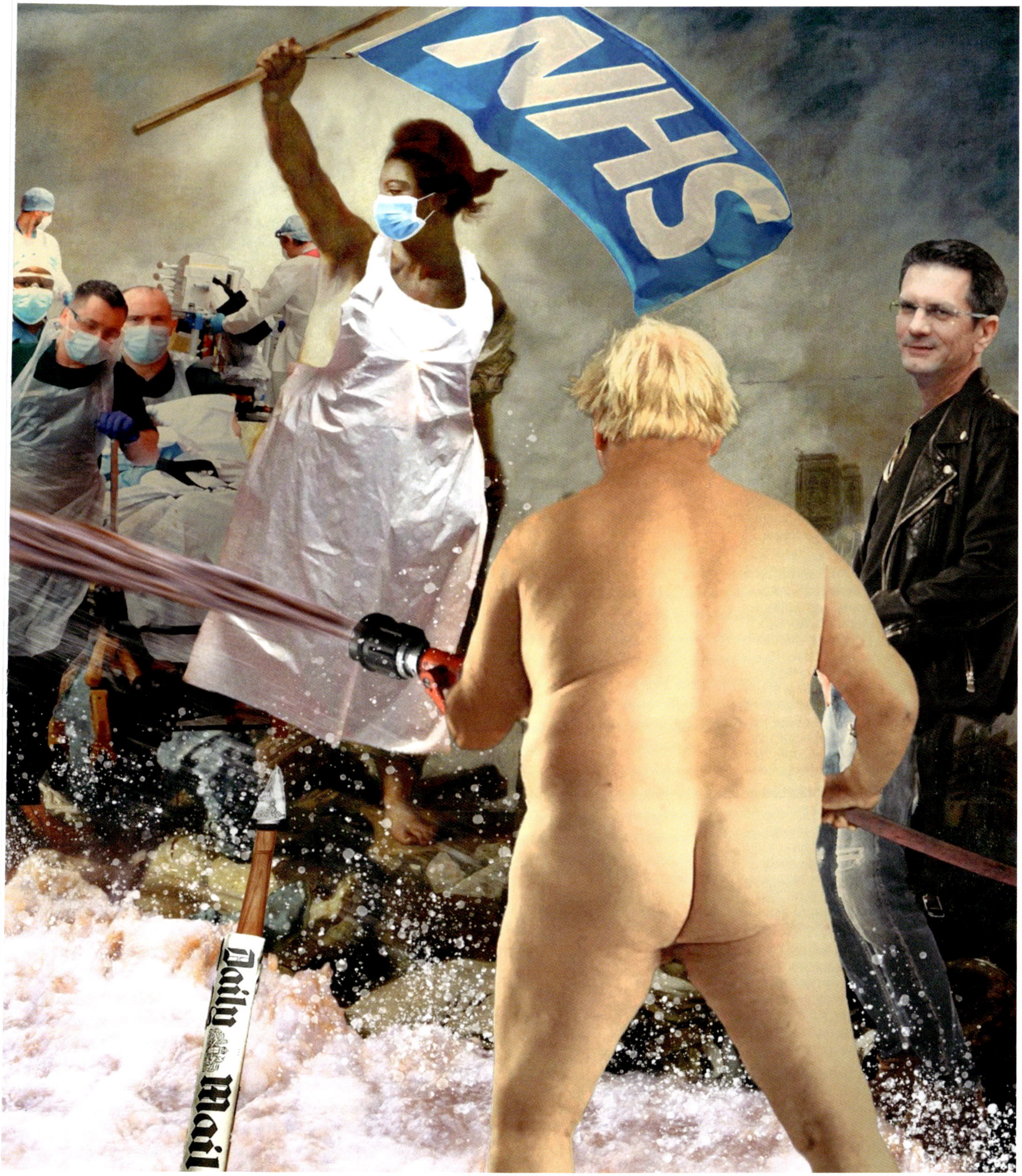
NHS
Daily Mail

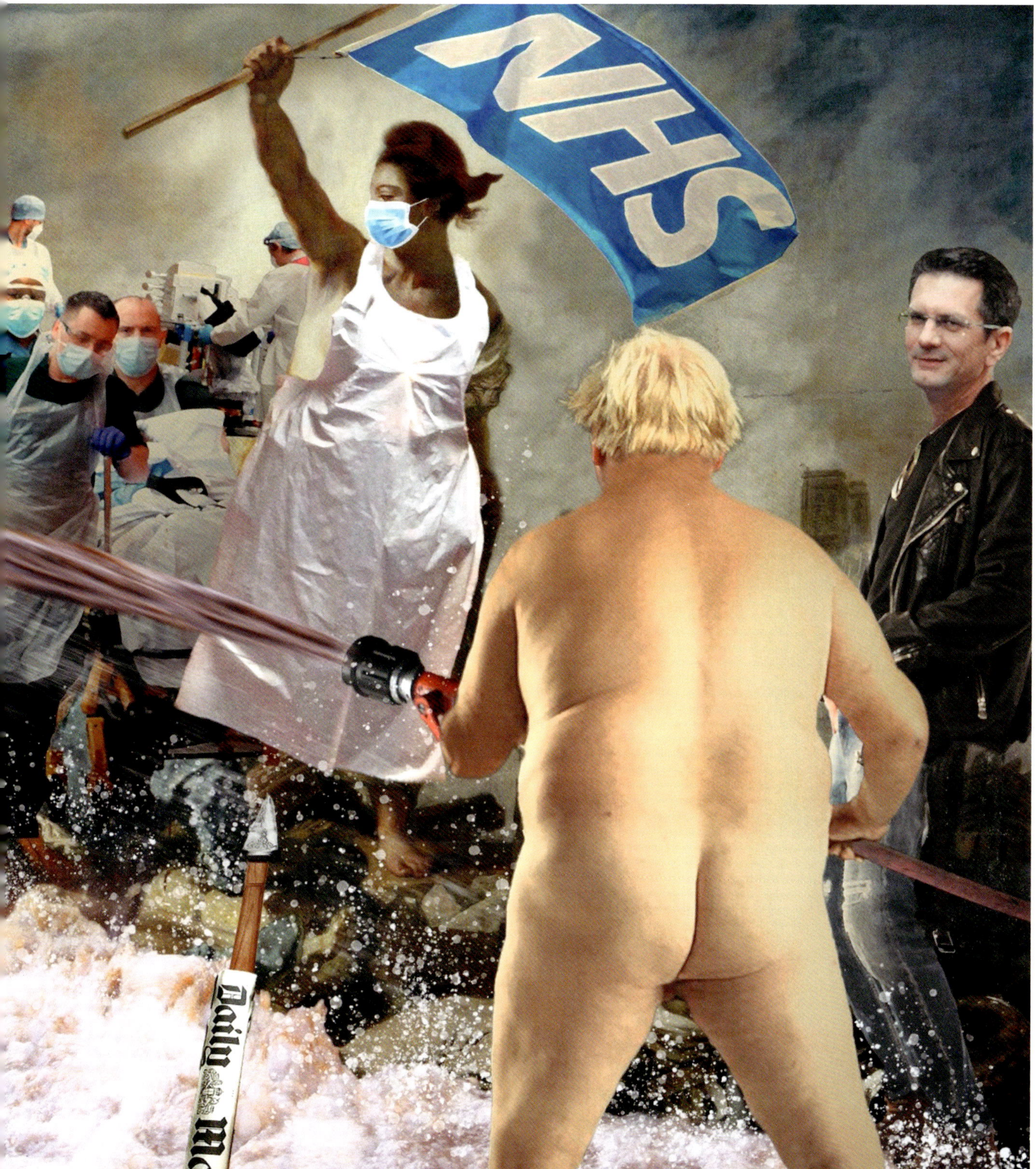
NHS
Daily Mail

Notes

1 Dissent, protest and resistance amid the 'sunlit uplands'

1 'Government creating hostile environment for peaceful protest, report finds', UK Parliament, Committees, 17 June 2022. See https://committees.parliament.uk/committee/93/human-rights-joint-committee/news/171503.

2 Miqdaad Versi, 'Sunak wants to punish those who "vilify the UK". That's wrong – and he's chosen the wrong target', *The Guardian*, 3 August 2022, www.theguardian.com/commentisfree/2022/aug/03/rishi-sunak-prevent-strategy-conservative-leadership.

3 Bill Chappell, 'Anti-royal protesters are being arrested in the U.K. as the "Not My King" tag grows', *NPR*, 12 September 2022, www.npr.org/2022/09/12/1122379162/uk-anti-royal-arrests; Emily Clark, Tim Leslie and James Glenday, 'As the UK mourns the Queen, police treatment of "Not my King" protesters is sparking freedom of speech fears', *ABC*, News, 13 September 2022, www.abc.net.au/news/2022-09-14/uk-anti-monarchy-protesters-arrested-raising-free-speech-fears/101436854.

4 Peter Walker and Rob Davies, 'Anger at absent ministers grows as Raab pulls out of bill of rights session', *The Guardian*, 14 July 2022, www.theguardian.com/politics/2022/jul/14/dominic-raab-priti-patel-absent-ministers-bill-of-rights.

5 'Government creating hostile environment for peaceful protest, report finds', UK Parliament, Committees, 17 June 2022, https://committees.parliament.uk/committee/93/human-rights-joint-committee/news/171503.

6 Alexander Stubb (@alexstubb), 'Reading news about petrol shortages', Twitter, 25 September 2021, 6.28 pm, https://twitter.com/alexstubb/status/1441816802837901312.

7 Andrew Macaskill, 'UK Eurosceptics warn British government against Swiss-style ties with EU', 20 November 2022, www.reuters.com/world/uk/uk-minister-does-not-recognise-report-government-wants-swiss-style-ties-with-eu-2022-11-20/.

8 Hannah Rose Woods, *Rule, Nostalgia: A Backwards History of Britain*, W.H. Allen, London, 2022, p.35.

9 David Olusoga, *Black and British: A Forgotten History*, Pan Macmillan, London, 2016.

10 Sathnam Sanghera, *Empireland: How Imperialism Has Shaped Modern Britain*, Penguin Books, Harmondsworth, 2021, pp 337–9; Sathnam Sanghera, Channel 4 documentary, 'The Massacre That Shook the Empire'; Emine Saner, 'The Massacre That Shook the Empire review – brutal truth of colonial India', *The Guardian*, 13 April 2019, www.theguardian.com/tv-and-radio/2019/apr/13/amritsar-massacre-that-shook-the-empire-channel-4.

11 Saner, 'The Massacre That Shook the Empire review'.

12 Dan Hicks, *The Brutish Museums: The Benin Bronzes, Colonial Violence and Cultural Restitution*, Pluto Press, London, 2020.

13 Barnaby Phillips, 'Can Digital Benin Reconnect Future Nigerians with Their History?', Opinion, *Art Review*, 16 November 2022, https://artreview.com/can-digital-benin-reconnect-future-nigerians-with-their-history/; Digital Benin, Explore Digital Benin, https://digitalbenin.org/; Simon Stephens, 'Digital Benin project unveils online platform', News, Benin Bronzes, 15 November 2022, www.museumsassociation.org/museums-journal/news/2022/11/digital-benin-project-unveils-online-platform/#.

14 See https://www.europarl.europa.eu/factsheets/en/sheet/1/the-first-treaties.

15 Background from EEC Debate: The National Archives, PREM 15/381, 'FCO Brief No. 34: Sovereignty', 16 July 1971, enclosure with Nield to Armstrong, 16 July 1971.

16 Background from EEC Debate: The National Archives, PREM 15/381, 'FCO Brief No. 34: Sovereignty', 16 July 1971.

17 The National Archives: The Cabinet Papers, 'The EEC and Britain's late entry', www.nationalarchives.gov.uk/cabinetpapers/themes/eec-britains-late-entry.htm. For background on this, see Jon Henley, '"Lying is no longer a sin": former French ambassador on Brexit and Boris Johnson', interview, *The Guardian*, 26 February 2021, www.theguardian.com/politics/2021/feb/26/lying-is-no-longer-a-sin-sylvie-bermann-on-brexit-and-boris-johnson.

18 'Membership of the European Communities: Opening Statement for 30 June 1970'. Note by the Secretary of State for Foreign and Commonwealth Affairs, The National Archives: TNA CAB 129/50/2.

19 Sylvie Bermann, *Au Revoir Britannia*, translated by Colin McIntosh, Luath Press, Edinburgh, 2022.

20 Simon Kuper, *Chums: How a Tiny Caste of Oxford Tories Took Over the UK*, Profile Books, London, 2022.

21 David Willetts, 'How Thatcher's Bruges speech put Britain on the road to Brexit', *Financial Times*, 31 August 2018; Laurence Peter, 'Thatcher's Bruges speech "not anti-EU" – former aide', *BBC News*, 27 September 2013, www.bbc.com/news/world-europe-24301837.

22 Kuper, *Chums*, p.100.

23 Agnès Poirier, 'Chums by Simon Kuper – the Oxford breed of

political bluff', *Financial Times*, 20 May 2022.

24 Email from Gillman & Soame, 1 September 2022.

25 Mark Brown, 'Bullingdon Club portrait of Cameron and Johnson in tails to go on sale', *The Guardian*, 10 November 2016, www.theguardian.com/politics/2016/nov/10/bullingdon-club-portrait-cameron-johnson-sale-oil-painting-oxford.

26 Rona Marsden, email to author, 26 September 2022.

27 Allan Preston, 'Prominent Brexiteer Daniel Hannan admits staying in the single market would have saved us "a lot of trouble"', *Belfast Telegraph*, 5 June 2022, www.belfasttelegraph.co.uk/news/northern-ireland/prominent-brexiteer-daniel-hannan-admits-staying-in-single-market-would-have-saved-us-a-lot-of-trouble-41722813.html.

28 Preston, 'Prominent Brexiteer Daniel Hannan admits'.

29 Andrew Woodcock, 'Boris Johnson gives peerage to ex-MEP who branded lords "inconsequential nobodies"', *Independent*, 22 November 2020, www.independent.co.uk/news/uk/politics/boris-johnson-peerages-daniel-hannan-b1777767.html.

30 'Power, Privilege, Parties: the shaping of modern Britain', International Inequalities Institute, London School of Economics, 26 May 2022: https://www.lse.ac.uk/Events/2022/05/202205261830/power.

31 WorldPR, Patrick Robertson, Founder and CEO, https://www.worldpr.org/patrick-robertson/.

32 Conservatives, 'About Chris', www.chrisskidmore.com/about-chris.

33 'Record of a Conversation Between the Prime Minister and the President of the French Republic in the Car Between London Airport and Chequers at 10.50 a.m. on Friday 16 November 1973', Margaret Thatcher Foundation, 'Newly declassified British Government archives from 1973–74 and 1984–85', https://www.margaretthatcher.org/archive/1974-tna-releases; 'Prime Minister's Meeting with President Pompidou, 16–17 November 1973', http://09b37156ee7ea2a93a5e-6db7349bced3b64202e14ff100a12173.r35.cf1.rackcdn.com/Arcdocs/731116%201.pdf.

34 Catherine Fieschi, *Populocracy, The Tyranny of Authenticity and the Rise of Populism*, Agenda Publishing, Newcastle upon Tyne, 2019, pp 1–5.

35 Fieschi, *Populocracy*, pp 19–20.

36 See The Brexit Collection, LSE Digital Library: https://digital.library.lse.ac.uk/collections/brexit.

37 Gov.UK, Guidance, 'Flying flags: a plain English guide', updated 20 July 2021, www.gov.uk/government/publications/flying-flags-a-plain-english-guide/flying-flags-a-plain-english-guide.

38 Anna Koslerova, 'Why is there a Scottish Saltire hanging in the Dutch city of Leeuwarden?', *The Scotsman*, 5 March 2020; Dutch News.nl, 'Leeuwarden replaces Union Jack with Scottish saltire after Brexit', 3 February 2020, www.dutchnews.nl/news/2020/02/leeuwarden-replaces-union-jack-with-scottish-saltire-after-brexit/.

39 Sjoerd Feitsma, interview with author, Leeuwarden, Netherlands, 26 August 2022.

40 Libby Brooks, 'Scottish government wins vote to keep EU flag flying over Holyrood', *The Guardian*, 29 January 2020, www.theguardian.com/uk-news/2020/jan/29/scottish-government-wins-vote-to-keep-eu-flag-flying-over-holyrood.

41 See, https://eurocities.eu/.

42 Simon Tubb, interview with author, Leeuwarden, Netherlands, 26 August 2022.

43 Eleanor Mills, 'Cornelia Parker's poppies at the Whitworth', *RA Magazine*, 26 February 2015, www.royalacademy.org.uk/article/cornelia-parker-poppies; see The University of Manchester and the Whitworth website, Cornelia Parker, *Double Negative*, 2015, www.whitworth.manchester.ac.uk/visit/shop/limitededitionprints/corneliaparker/.

44 Cornelia Parker, interview with author, via Zoom, 28 November 2022.

45 Cornelia Parker in conversation with Andrea Schlieker, 'Matter and What It Means', in *Cornelia Parker*, exh. cat., edited by Andrea Schlieker, Tate Enterprises Ltd, London, 2022.

46 Science Museum Group, Collection, Cornelia Parker, 'Einstein's Abstracts [1]', 2000, https://collection.sciencemuseumgroup.org.uk/objects/co8658691/einsteins-abstracts-1-photomicrograph.

47 Nadia Khomami, interview, 'I don't want to be a little Englander – Cornelia Parker on BP, bombs and becoming a German', *The Guardian*, 10 May 2022, www.theguardian.com/artanddesign/2022/may/10/cornelia-parker-bp-bombs-becoming-a-german-little-englander.

48 See Elizabeth Piper and William James, 'UK government failed to find out whether Russia meddled in Brexit vote: report', *Reuters*, 21 July 2020, www.reuters.com/article/us-britain-russia-idUSKCN24M15I; Dan Sabbagh, Luke Harding and Andrew Roth, 'Russia report reveals UK government failed to investigate Kremlin interference', *The Guardian*, 21 July 2020, www.theguardian.com/world/2020/jul/21/russia-report-reveals-uk-government-failed-to-address-kremlin-interference-scottish-referendum-brexit; Jane Bradley, 'Major Donation of U.K. Conservative Party Was Flagged Over Russia Concerns', *New York Times*, 12 May 2022.

49 Parker, interview with author, 28 November 2022.

50 Mark Duffy, interview with author, Newcastle, 16 November 2021; see also the photographer's website at https://www.markduffyphotographer.com; Colin Pantall, 'Photography in the Time of Brexit: The Curious Case of Mark Duffy', *Witness*, 17 March 2020, https://witness.worldpressphoto.org/photography-in-the-time-of-brexit-the-curious-case-of-mark-duffy-9979e312fe39.

2 Border force[d] + identity

1 *BBC News*, 'New blue British passport rollout to begin in March',

22 February 2020, www.bbc.com/news/uk-51585018; GOV.UK, News story, 'Iconic blue passports return next month', 22 February 2020, www.gov.uk/government/news/iconic-blue-passports-return-next-month.

2 BBC *Newsnight*, 'Brexit . . . Should the UK bring back the blue passport?', 3 August 2016, YouTube video, www.youtube.com/watch?v=XpiGsF0G25U.

3 BBC *Newsnight*, 'Paxman on the new EU passport' (Newsnight archives 1995), YouTube video, www.youtube.com/watch?v=QBp-KPrJjSc.

4 *Reuters*, 'French group Thales completes 4.8 billion euro takeover of Gemalto', 2 April 2019, www.reuters.com/article/us-gemalto-m-a-thales-idUSKCN1RE0BH; Warwick Ashford, 'Thales completes acquisition of Gemalto', *Computerweekly.com*, 2 April 2019, www.computerweekly.com/news/252460813/Thales-completes-acquisition-of-Gemalto.

5 Passport Index, www.passportindex.org/byColor.php.

6 Sean Coughlan, 'Is the new passport really blue or black?', *BBC News*, 5 March 2020, www.bbc.com/news/education-51737116.

7 *Reuters*, 'Brexit vote – Parliamentary bellwether Nuneaton votes strongly for Leave', 24 June 2016, www.reuters.com/article/britain-eu-nuneaton-idUKU8N19F03H.

8 Research briefing, 'Food Banks in the UK', House of Commons Library, 14 July 2022.

9 Claire Harrison, '"Massive" impact of cost-of-living crisis sees demand on Nuneaton's foodbank rise more than 70 per cent in just two months', *Coventry Telegraph*, 14 June 2022, www.coventrytelegraph.net/news/cost-of-living/massive-impact-cost-living-crisis-24209671.

10 See YouGov, Brexit, Articles, https://yougov.co.uk/topics/politics/explore/issue/Brexit?content=articles; Ipsos, Public sector, 30 June 2022, www.ipsos.com/en-uk/almost-half-britons-say-brexit-has-made-their-daily-life-worse-1-3-say-it-has-made-little; Statista, 26 January 2023, www.statista.com/statistics/987347/brexit-opinion-poll/.

11 Professor Catherine Clarke, 'How to Be an Island: A Long-View Look at Britain's Borders and National Identity', History and Policy, www.historyandpolicy.org/opinion-articles/articles/how-to-be-an-island-a-long-view-look-at-britains-borders-and-national-identity, 10 August 2022.

12 Catherine Clarke, 'How to Be an Island'.

13 For background, see www.english-heritage.org.uk/visit/places/uffington-castle-white-horse-and-dragon-hill/history/.

14 For background on St George, see www.english-heritage.org.uk/visit/whats-on/st-georges-day/9-things-you-didnt-know-about-st-george/; https://www.nationaltrust.org.uk/white-horse-hill/features/did-saint-george-slay-the-dragon-on-dragon-hill.

15 Mandy Williams, email correspondence with author, 24 September 2022.

16 Jonathan Griffin, 'Tacita Dean: "I don't care about the long run. I care about now"', 21 March 2018, www.royalacademy.org.uk/article/magazine-tacita-dean; Aesthetica, 'Multi-layered Narratives', https://aestheticamagazine.com/multi-layered-narratives/.

17 Thelma Pott, 'Tacita Dean "Landscape"', exh.cat., Royal Academy of Arts, London, UK, 2018, www.thelmapott.com/exhibitiontexts-tacitadean.

18 QAGOMA (Queensland Art Gallery | Gallery of Modern Art), 'Tacita Dean discusses "Chalk Fall"', 22 June 2022, YouTube video, www.youtube.com/watch?v=T6yniwuIDGU; Tacita Dean, 'Keith Collins obituary', *The Guardian*, 2 September 2018, www.theguardian.com/film/2018/sep/02/keith-collins-obituary.

19 Tacita Dean, interview with author via Zoom, 4 October 2022.

20 Dean, interview with author, 4 October 2022.

21 Wolfgang Tillmans (ed.), *What Is Different?* Jahresring 64, Sternberg Press, London, 2018.

22 Quotations from Wolfgang Tillmans, 'Introduction', in *What Is Different?*, p.8.

23 Joe Keohane, 'How Facts Backfire', in *What Is Different?*, p.14.

24 Social Science Space, 'A Social Scientist Looks at the Irish Border and Its Future', 7 August 2021, www.socialsciencespace.com/2021/07/a-social-scientist-looks-at-the-irish-border-and-its-future/?utm_source=dlvr.it&utm_medium=twitter.

25 Social Science Space, 'A Social Scientist Looks at the Irish Border'.

26 Robert Schertzer and Eric Taylor Woods, 'English Nationalism and the Campaign for Brexit', in *The New Nationalism in America and Beyond: The Deep Roots of Ethnic Nationalism in the Digital Age*, Oxford Academic, (online), 21 April 2022.

27 Schertzer and Taylor Woods, 'English Nationalism and the Campaign for Brexit'.

28 Colin Grant, 'The Story of Windrush', English Heritage, n.d., www.english-heritage.org.uk/visit/inspire-me/the-story-of-windrush/; and background from *BBC News*, 'Windrush generation: Who are they and why are they facing problems?', 24 November 2021, www.bbc.com/news/uk-43782241.

29 Amelia Gentleman, 'Windrush: only one in four applicants have received compensation', *The Guardian*, 22 June 2022, www.theguardian.com/uk-news/2022/jun/22/windrush-one-in-four-applicants-received-compensation-home-office; Home Affairs Committee Report, 'The Windrush Compensation Scheme: Government Response to the Committee's Fifth Report', 7 February 2022, https://publications.parliament.uk/pa/cm5802/cmselect/cmhaff/1098/report.html.

30 Amelia Gentleman, 'Windrush compensation scheme beset by slow repayments to victims', *The Guardian*, 28 October 2022, www.theguardian.com/uk-news/2022/oct/28/windrush-compensation-scheme-beset-by-slow-repayments-to-victims.

31 Home Affairs Committee Report, 'The Windrush Compensation Scheme'.

32 'Windrush Scandal Explained', The Joint Council for the Welfare of Immigrants, https://www.jcwi.org.uk/windrush-scandal-explained; 'The story of the Windrush', Royal Museums Greenwich, https://www.rmg.co.uk/stories/windrush-histories/story-of-windrush-ship; Theresa May interview, *The Telegraph*, 25 May 2012; Melanie Griffiths and Colin Yeo, 'The UK's hostile environment: Deputising immigration control', *Critical Social Policy*, vol.41, no.4 (2021), pp 521–44, https://doi.org/10.1177/0261018320980653; BBC documentary, *The Unwanted: The Secret Windrush Files* (2019), YouTube video, https://www.youtube.com/watch?v=f_rzJTNZSLM&t=27s; 'Windrush Stories', British Library, https://www.bl.uk/windrush; 'Selfies and Stories from Hackney's Windrush Generation' (2021), Hackney Council, London, The Real Selfie Project, Autograph ABP, https://autograph.org.uk/exhibitions/selfies-and-stories-from-hackneys-windrush-generation; https://www.bbc.com/news/uk-64414451.

33 Schertzer and Taylor Woods, 'English Nationalism and the Campaign for Brexit'.

34 Simon Roberts, *Merrie Albion: Landscape Studies of a Small Island*, Dewi Lewis Publishing, Stockport, 2017.

35 Oxfam.org, Case Study, 'The True Cost of Austerity and Inequality', September 2013, www-cdn.oxfam.org/s3fs-public/file_attachments/cs-true-cost-austerity-inequality-uk-120913-en_0.pdf.

36 Simon Roberts, interview with author, Hove, England, 5 February 2022.

37 European Commission, Erasmus+, https://erasmus-plus.ec.europa.eu/; Erasmus+ is the EU's current programme to support education, training, youth and sport in Europe, with a budget of €26.2 billion (2021–27).

38 Roberts, interview with author, Hove, England, 5 February 2022.

39 See https://ewanmacbeth.com/; Ewan Macbeth, interview with author, Rotterdam, 23 November 2021.

40 Anna Funder, *Stasiland*, Granta, London, 2003; see www.annafunder.com/stasiland/.

41 See Eggleston Foundation, https://egglestonartfoundation.org/; Joachim Brohm, see www.joachimbrohm.com/.

42 Peter Wilby, 'First Thoughts: Trade deals after Brexit, Vera Lynn's bluebirds, and the know-nothing right', *The New Statesman*, 24 June 2020, www.newstatesman.com/politics/2020/06/first-thoughts-trade-deals-after-brexit-vera-lynn-s-bluebirds-and-know-nothing-right.

43 *BBC News*, 'Article 50: UK set to formally trigger Brexit process', 29 March 2017, www.bbc.com/news/uk-politics-39422353.

44 Simon Roberts, *Merrie Albion*; see also www.simoncroberts.com/work/between-the-acts/; Virginia Woolf, *Between the Acts*, Hogarth Press, London, 1941.

45 Roberts, interview with author, 5 February 2022.

46 Uta Kögelsberger, interview with author, Hackney, London, 16 May 2022. See https://utakogelsberger.uk/.

47 For background on this, and the touring of laminated exhibitions, see Noni Stacey, *Photography of Protest and Community: The Radical Collectives of the 1970s*, Lund Humphries, London, 2020.

48 *Uncertain Subjects*, interview with Lisa Le Feuvre and Uta Kögelsberger, 17 October 2020, https://vimeo.com/483576064. Lisa Le Feuvre, executive director, Holt-Smithson Foundation, Sante Fe, New Mexico, https://holtsmithsonfoundation.org/.

49 Buildhollywood, www.buildhollywood.co.uk/work/uta-kogelsberger-division-revision/.

50 flyingsleaps, www.flyingleaps.co.uk/.

51 Quotations and background from Adrian Burnham, interview with author, London, 20 April 2022.

52 *The Maritime Executive*, 'P&O Ferries Draws More Fire for Mass Layoffs in UK', 21 March 2022, https://maritime-executive.com/article/p-o-ferries-draws-fire-for-mass-layoffs-in-uk.

53 http://www.nuartfestival.no/home; http://www.ampparito.com/murals; https://streetartcities.com/artists/ampparito.

54 Quotations from Burnham, interview with author, London, 20 April 2022.

55 Background and quotations from, Jeremy Deller, interview with author, London, 1 February 2022. See: https://www.jeremydeller.org/.

56 Jeremy Deller (dir.), *Putin's Happy* (2019), YouTube video, www.youtube.com/watch?v=KTh8mETQ6RA; Museum of London, 'Putin's Happy: Museum of London acquires Jeremy Deller film revealing divided country and a city full of protest', 23 June 2022, www.museumoflondon.org.uk/news-room/press-releases/putins-happy-museum-london-acquires-jeremy-deller-film-2016-brexit-referendum; https://www.studiointernational.com/jeremy-deller-putins-happy-review-hannah-barry-gallery-london.

57 Carole Cadwalladr, 'Arron Banks almost crushed me in court. Instead my quest for the facts was vindicated', *The Observer*, 19 June 2022, www.theguardian.com/uk-news/commentisfree/2022/jun/19/arron-banks-set-out-to-crush-me-in-court-instead-my-quest-for-the-facts-was-vindicated; David D. Kirkpatrick, 'Signs of Russian Meddling in Brexit Referendum', *The New York Times*, 15 November 2017.

58 See Artangel, *The Battle of Orgreave*, www.artangel.org.uk/artwork/the-battle-of-orgreave/; Jeremy Deller, *we're here because we're here*, 2016, www.tate.org.uk/art/artworks/deller-were-here-because-were-here-p82019; 14–18 NOW, WW1 Centenary Art Commissions, https://becausewearehere.co.uk/.

59 Deller, interview with author, 1 February 2022.

60 Lee Cheshire, 'Content warning: Jeremy Deller brings together 30 years of prints and poster', *The Art*

Newspaper, 5 November 2021, www.theartnewspaper.com/2021/11/05/content-warning-jeremy-deller-brings-together-30-years-of-prints-and-posters.

61 Chrystel Lebas, note to author via email, 16 July 2022; Chrystel Lebas, interview with author, Camberwell, London, 4 February 2022.

62 See: http://www.chrystellebas.com/.

63 *BBC News*, 'Tory leadership: Truss criticised for Macron "jury is out" remark', 26 August, https://www.bbc.com/news/uk-politics-62682448.

64 Alessandra Scotto di Santolo, '"Jury is out!" Even Remainers back Liz Truss' comments on Emmanuel Macron – exclusive poll', *Express*, 3 September 2022, www.express.co.uk/news/politics/1663839/liz-truss-Emmanuel-macron-jury-is-out-remainers-brexit-uk-poll.

65 Quotations from Lebas, interview with author, 4 February 2022; email to author, 21 July 2022. See http://www.chrystellebas.com/.

66 Adam Broomberg, interview with author via Zoom, 28 November 2022.

67 Adam Broomberg: https://adambroomberg.com/?authors=adam-broomberg; https://www.kabk.nl/docenten/adam-broomberg; Oliver Chanarin: https://www.chanarin.com/; http://www.broombergchanarin.com/.

68 Frontline, 'Bannon's War', 23 May 2017, https://www.pbs.org/wgbh/frontline/documentary/bannons-war/.

69 Lorena Muñoz-Alonso, 'Anish Kapoor Among 200 Leading Artists Launching Movement Against Right-Wing Populism', *artnet*, 16 February 2017, https://news.artnet.com/art-world/artists-launch-global-movement-hands-off-our-revolution-862955; https://adambroomberg.com/?projects=hands-off-our-revolution.

3 Fairy tales, oligarchs and billionaires

1 Rupert Booth and Jane Martinson, 'Rupert Murdoch: "I've never asked any prime minister for anything"', *The Guardian*, 19 December 2016. Rupert Murdoch owns *The Times*, *The Sunday Times*, *The Sun*, *The Washington Post*, *Fox News*, and much more besides. He is an American citizen and spends much of his time in Beverly Hills and New York City.

2 Wolfgang Tillmans, interview with author, 26 October 2022.

3 Wolfgang Tillmans, 'Statement for pro-EU/anti-Brexit campaign', 26 May 2016, in Roxana Marcoci and Phil Taylor (eds), *Wolfgang Tillmans: A Reader*, The Museum of Modern Art, New York, 2021, p.236.

4 Tillmans, 'Statement', p.236.

5 Katharine Swindells, 'How does the UK's beach water quality compare with Europe?', *New Statesman,* 22 August 2022, www.newstatesman.com/chart-of-the-day/2022/08/uk-dirty-beach-water-quality-compare-europe; European Commission, Environment, 'Bathing water quality', 3 June 2022, https://ec.europa.eu/environment/water/water-bathing/index_en.html.

6 See UK Parliament, Insight Report, 'What does Brexit mean for the UK's beaches?', 7 September 2017, https://commonslibrary.parliament.uk/what-does-brexit-mean-for-the-uks-beaches/; India Bourke, '"We're staring down the gun barrel": singer Feargal Sharkey on Britain's polluted rivers', *New Statesman*, 2 June 2022, www.newstatesman.com/the-environment-interview/2022/06/feargal-sharkey-britains-river-pollution.

7 Fintan O'Toole, *Heroic Failure: Brexit and the Politics of Pain*, Apollo, London, 2018, pp 2–3.

8 Norman Behrendt, interview with author, Berlin, 13 February 2022.

9 Norman Behrendt, *Blueprint 2017–2020*, Kult Books, Stockholm, 2021.

10 Lucy Soutter, 'Reading the Signs', in Norman Behrendt, *Blueprint 2017–2020*, n.p.

11 Soutter, 'Reading the Signs', in Behrendt, *Blueprint 2017–2020*.

12 Behrendt, interview with author, 13 February 2022.

13 Behrendt, interview with author, 13 February 2022.

14 Peter Oborne, *The Assault on Truth: Boris Johnson, Donald Trump and the Emergence of a New Moral Barbarism*, Simon & Schuster, London, 2021. See Tim Adams, 'The Assault on Truth by Peter Oborne review – how Boris Johnson played the press', *The Guardian*, 7 February 2021, www.theguardian.com/books/2021/feb/07/the-assault-on-truth-by-peter-oborne-review-how-boris-johnson-played-the-press.

15 Sir David Norgrove, Chair of the UK Statistics Authority, Letter to Boris Johnson, 17 September 2017.

16 O'Toole, *Heroic Failure.*

17 John Hooper and Anna Kraczyna (translators), *Carlo Collodi, The Adventures of Pinocchio*, Penguin Classics, London, 2021.

18 For background, see Perri Klass, 'The Real Story of Pinocchio Tells No Lies', *Smithsonian Magazine*, The Smithsonian Institution, Washington DC, June 2022, www.smithsonianmag.com/travel/the-real-pinocchio-180980027/.

19 Carlo Collodi, *Pane e libri* (Bread and Books), *La Vedetta. Gazzetta del popolo*, 1884; see Andrea Pagani, 'Beyond Pinocchio: Italian National Identity in Carlo Collodi's Works for Primary Schools (1877–1890)', Monash University, Melbourne, PhD thesis, 2021, https://doi.org/10.26180/16437861.v3.

20 'Let's end child food poverty together', https://endchildfoodpoverty.org/.

21 Hooper and Kraczyna, *Carlo Collodi*, p.xiii.

22 Hooper and Kraczyna, p.xiii.

23 Roberto Vezzani, Fondazione Nazionale Carlo Collodi, email to the author, 10 November 2022; see also C. Collodi, *Le avventure di Pinocchio: storia di un burattino*, Edizione Nazionale delle Opere di Carlo Lorenzini, vol.III, edited by R. Randaccio, with an Introduction by D. Marcheschi and Preface by M.V. Llosa, original illustrations by E. Mazzanti, Fondazione Nazionale Carlo Collodi/Giunti, 2012 (see here the Introduction by Professor Marcheschi, especially

pp. 42–3); D. Marcheschi, *Il naso corto: una rilettura delle Avventure di Pinocchio*, EDB, Bologna, 2016 – see, especially, pp 14–19.

24 Mandy Williams, email correspondence with the author, 24 September 2022.

25 Cold War Steve, aka Christopher Spencer, email to the author, 29 November 2022.

26 Christopher Spencer, *Cold War Steve Presents . . . The Festival of Brexit*, Thames & Hudson, London, 2019.

27 Jon Savage, 'Introduction', in *Cold War Steve Presents . . . The Festival of Brexit*, Thames & Hudson, London, 2019, p.7.

28 Classic British Comedy, 'Margaret Thatcher on Spitting Image', YouTube video, www.youtube.com/watch?v=omC3xeCZBX0.

29 GOV.UK, 'Deaths in the United Kingdom', https://coronavirus.data.gov.uk/details/deaths.

30 Led By Donkeys, *Led By Donkeys: How Four Friends with a Ladder Took on Brexit*, Atlantic Books, London, 2019.

31 Quotations from Led By Donkeys, email to the author, 25 November 2022.

32 Edinburgh TV Festival, The James MacTaggart Lecture 2022, Emily Maitlis, YouTube video, www.youtube.com/watch?v=e0dRBtSAvLM.

33 Francesca Gillett, *BBC News*, 'Rupert Murdoch pays £11,000 for Boris Johnson to visit', 17 November 2022, https://www.bbc.com/news/uk-63668626; Paul Seddon, *BBC News*, 'Boris Johnson nears £5m in earnings since leaving office', 8 February 2021, https://www.bbc.com/news/uk-politics-64569598.

34 John Ringer and Meghna Chakrabarti, 'Modern conservatism and its discontents in Britain', WBUR, *On Point*, 28 October 2022, interview with Emily Maitlis, hosted by Meghna Chakrabarti, video, www.wbur.org/onpoint/2022/10/28/modern-conservatism-and-its-discontents-in-britain.

4 Building bridges

1 Kate Nolan, https://www.katenolan.ie/.

2 Photo Museum Ireland, https://photomuseumireland.ie/; 'Reframing the Border: Responses to the Border in Ireland', https://photomuseumireland.ie/reframing-the-border.

3 See: 'The EU–UK Withdrawal Agreement, https://ec.europa.eu/info/strategy/relations-non-eu-countries/relations-united-kingdom/eu-uk-withdrawal-agreement_en; European Commission, 'Protocol on Ireland and Northern Ireland', https://ec.europa.eu/info/strategy/relations-non-eu-countries/relations-united-kingdom/eu-uk-withdrawal-agreement/protocol-ireland-and-northern-ireland_en.

4 Krishnan Guru-Murthy, interview, 'Conservative MP Suella Fernandes [Braverman] warns Theresa May not to keep Britain in the Single Market', 7 September 2017, www.channel4.com/news/conservative-mp-suella-fernandes-warns-theresa-may-not-to-keep-britain-in-single-market.

5 Photo Museum Ireland, 'Reframing the Border', https://photomuseumireland.ie/reframing-the-border.

6 Anthony Haughey, *Field Notes from the Border*, http://anthonyhaughey.com/projects/field-notes-from-the-border/.

7 Seán Hillen, https://seanhillen.com/; '"Troubles" era photomontages 1983–1993', https://www.flickr.com/photos/seanhillen/albums/72157650596902587.

8 Artists' websites: Kate Nolan, https://www.katenolan.ie/; Anthony Haughey, http://anthonyhaughey.com/; https://seanhillen.com/; https://ciarandunbar.com/home.

9 Ciarán Dunbar, *Diesel*, 2022, https://ciarandunbar.com/home. Marcel Krueger, 'Smuggling along the Border', afterword to *Diesel*; see also Marcel Krueger, 'King of Pain', author website, http://marcel-krueger.squarespace.com/; James Connor Patterson (ed.), *The New Frontier: Reflections From the Irish Border*, New Island Books, Dublin, 2021.

10 Quotations from Trish Lambe, artistic director of Photo Museum Ireland, Dublin, interview with author via Zoom, 30 October 2022.

11 Pauline Vermare, *PROTEST! Photography, Activism and Social Change in Ireland*, Photo Museum Ireland, Dublin, 21 April – 11 June 2022, https://photomuseumireland.ie/protest-photography-activism-and-social-change-in-ireland; https://photomuseumireland.ie/pauline-vermare-protest.

12 Irish Photo Network website, www.irishphotonetwork.com/.

13 Trish Lambe, artistic director of Photo Museum Ireland, Dublin, and Deirdre Robb, chief executive of *Belfast Exposed*, Street Level Photoworks, Glasgow, 20 October 2022; Street Level Photoworks, 'Irish Photography Now', panel session with Trish Lambe and Deirdre Robb, www.streetlevelphotoworks.org/event/irish-photography-now; Street Level Photoworks, Frank McElhinney, *Flight*, https://www.streetlevelphotoworks.org/event/flight-exhibition.

14 Calum Colvin and Robert Crawford, *Brexit Tears*, Kettillonia, Angus, 2020.

15 Uta Kögelsberger, interview with author, Hackney, London, 16 May 2022.

16 Wolfgang Tillmans, interview with author via Zoom, 26 October 2022.

17 Robbie Shilliam, 'Enoch Powell: Britain's First Neoliberal Politician', *New Political Economy*, vol.26, no.2, pp 239–49.

18 Shilliam, 'Enoch Powell', p.246.

19 Paul Sng (ed.), *Invisible Britain: Portraits of Hope and Resilience*, Policy Press, Bristol, 2018; Paul Sng (ed.), *This Separated Isle: Invisible Britain*, Policy Press, Bristol, 2021, exhibition website, www.streetlevelphotoworks.org/event/this-separated-isle; see also Paul Sng, Velvet Joy Productions, https://www.velvetjoyproductions.com/.

20 Jim Mortram, 'Simon Tyson, Dereham', portrait, *This Separated Isle*, p.62.

21 Jim Mortram, *Small Town Inertia*, Bluecoat Press, Shrewsbury, 2017; 'Small Town Inertia: Documentary and Portraits', https://smalltowninertia.co.uk/market-town-tilney1-watching-a-plane-fall-from-the-sky-aflame/; *British Journal of Photography*, Diane Smyth, 'Q&A: J.A. Mortram on his ten-year project Small Town Inertia', https://www.1854.photography/2019/01/qa-j-a-mortram-on-his-ten-year-project-small-town-inertia/; 'Small Town Inertia: Portraits of a nation in need', *The Guardian*, 19 February 2014, https://www.theguardian.com/artanddesign/gallery/2014/feb/19/jim-mortram-small-town-inertia-in-pictures; Photofusion Photography Centre, exhibition, 'J.A. Mortram, Small Town Inertia', www.photofusion.org/exhibitions/j-a-mortram-l-small-town-inertia/.

22 Kit de Waal, 'Introduction', in Sng, *This Separated Isle*; Kit de Waal, website, https://www.kitdewaal.com/about.

23 Background and quotations from Paul Sng, interview with author, Portobello, Scotland, 11 July 2022.

24 Danny Dorling and Sally Tomlinson, *Rule Britannia: Brexit and the End of Empire*, Biteback Publishing, Hull, 2019; Danny Dorling, 'The Geography and Demography of Brexit', Mutiny Blog, 6 January 2020, www.dannydorling.org/wp-content/files/dannydorling_publication_id7587.pdf.

25 Margaret Mitchell, artist website, https://margaretmitchell.co.uk/; Margaret Mitchell, *Passage*, Bluecoat Press, Shrewsbury, 2021; Klaas Wijnne, Chemical Photonics, University of Glasgow, https://www.wijnne.com/.

26 Margaret Mitchell, Klaas Wijnne and Guus Wijnne, email correspondence with author, 5 November 2022.

27 Phil Young, email to author, 17 July 2022.

28 Karen Sanig, email to author, 12 December 2022; Karen Sanig, personal profile, www.mishcon.com/people/karen-sanig; Obituary, 'Professor Neville Brown', *The Times*, 9 August 2018.

29 Andrew Trendell, 'Brexit is "strangling the next generation of UK talent in the cradle" in returning summer of touring', *NME*, 12 August 2022, www.nme.com/news/music/brexit-touring-europe-strangling-talent-carnets-visa-merch-crew-government-response-summer-2022-3288735.

30 Professor Linda Merrick, email to author, 29 August 2022; Isabella Jewell, *Euronews*, 'Turing Scheme: How does the UK's Erasmus replacement work and has it been a success?', 13 September 2022, www.euronews.com/my-europe/2022/09/01/turing-scheme-how-does-the-uks-erasmus-replacement-work-and-has-it-been-a-success.

31 Beth Taylor, artist/performer's website, https://bethmtaylor.com/; quotations from Beth Taylor, interview with author, Cluny, France, 5 July 2021.

32 Stuart McGurk, 'How the Government's £120m "Festival of Brexit" Went Rogue', *The House*, 31 August 2022, https://longreads.politicshome.com/carnival-of-brexit; UK Parliament, Committees, 'National Audit Office to investigate management of Unboxed Festival', 11 October 2022, https://committees.parliament.uk/committee/378/digital-culture-media-and-sport-committee/news/173454/national-audit-office-to-investigate-management-of-unboxed-festival/.

33 Saskia Solomon, 'Britain's "Brexit Festival" is Under Investigation', *New York Times*, 12 October 2022.

34 HM Government, *The Benefits of Brexit: How the UK is Taking Advantage of Leaving the EU*, January 2022, https://assets.publishing.service.gov.uk/government/uploads/system/uploads/attachment_data/file/1054643/beneits-of-brexit.pdf.

35 'NI Protocol: White House warns again against unilateral action', *BBC News*, 7 September 2022, www.bbc.com/news/uk-northern-ireland-62818906; Rajeev Syal, 'Suella Braverman speaks out against likely UK trade deal with India', *The Guardian*, 6 October 2022, www.theguardian.com/politics/2022/oct/06/suella-braverman-speaks-out-against-likely-uk-trade-deal-with-india; Jon Craig, 'George Eustice brands Australia free trade deal a "failure" in brutal swipe at Liz Truss', *Sky News*, 14 November 2022, https://news.sky.com/story/george-eustice-brands-australia-free-trade-deal-a-failure-in-brutal-swipe-at-liz-truss-12747723.

36 Matt Murphy, *BBC News*, 'Viktor Orban: Hungary "autocracy" verdict from EU correct, say activists', 16 September 2022, www.bbc.com/news/world-europe-62925460.

37 Layla Curtis, interview with author, Hackney, London, 10 March 2022; http://laylacurtis.com/; https://www.tate.org.uk/art/artworks/curtis-united-kingdom-t07596.

38 David Henderson, Ordnance Survey, 'Top 10 mapping moments in OS history', 28 June 2016, www.ordnancesurvey.co.uk/newsroom/blog/top-10-mapping-moments-in-the-history-of-os; W.A. Seymour (ed.), *A History of the Ordnance Survey*, Wm Dawson & Sons, Folkestone, 1980, https://www.ordnancesurvey.co.uk/documents/resources/os-history.pdf.

39 Ordnance Survey, 'OS maps go off the planet', 15 February 2016, www.ordnancesurvey.co.uk/newsroom/blog/21157; Isobel Asher Hamilton, *Business Insider NL*, 17 August 2019, 'Here are some of the gaping holes in Elon Musk and Jeff Bezos' plans to conquer space', www.businessinsider.nl/gaping-holes-elon-musk-and-jeff-bezos-space-plans-2019-7?international=true&r=US.

40 Chris Grey, 'Brexit and Beyond', https://chrisgreybrexitblog.blogspot.com/.

41 Naomi Smith, 'New polling: 57% would vote to rejoin EU', 28 October 2022, https://www.bestforbritain.org/new_polling_57_would_vote_to_rejoin_eu.

42 'Number 10 denies Sunak seeks single market access after hailing NI's opportunities, the Irish Times, 28 February 2023: https://www.irishtimes.com/ireland/2023/02/28/windsor-framework-deal-will-make-positivedifference-to-people-in-northern-ireland-sunak-says/.

Index

Note: *italic* page numbers indicate figures.

Acknowledgements

Thank you to all those artists, photographers and those in the cultural sector who took the time to give me interviews for this book and generously shared their art and archives with me. A huge thank you to my editor at Lund Humphries, Val Rose, for supporting this idea from the start in 2021 and the group around Lund Humphries who supported and worked with me on the edit and design of the book. For John Farrell, Robin Silas Christian and Monica Takvam, who contributed work on the images for this book, assisted with transcripts and offered advice along the way, thank you. Andrew Lewis, a specialist archive researcher, dashed to the National Archives at Kew, London, to pin down references when I was unable to travel from the Netherlands.

Thank you to those artists who suggested other artists to talk with, and to Frith Street Gallery, London, Studio Tacita Dean, Studio Wolfgang Tillmans, the Modern Institute, Glasgow, and Adrian Burnham at flyingleaps.co.uk for taking time to work with me on image selection. A special thanks to Faber Music for permission to reproduce the lyrics to 'The White Cliffs of Dover', and to Daniel Payne, Curator for Politics and International Relations at the London School of Economics, for permission to reproduce material from the Brexit Collection at LSE. Ralf Zimmermann at *Süddeutsche Zeitung Magazin* readily made available images from the magazine's 2019 Brexit issue, and Lucy Conticello at *Le Monde*'s *M* magazine offered vital last-minute assistance in finding the photograph I sought of Edward Heath and Georges Pompidou. I am grateful that David Shrigley and the Design and Artists Copyright Society (DACS) agreed to the reproduction of his illustration as a frontispiece, and thank you to Led By Donkeys and Cold War Steve for permission to reproduce their art of activism.

For those who supported me throughout the writing of this book in many different ways, thank you to Linda Coffey, Malcolm Dickson, Trish Lambe, Roberta McGrath, Juan Peces, Lucy Soutter, Mark Curran, Jane Garrett, Chris Clarke, Marcia Hadjimarkos, Janet Matthews, Sara MacVane. Thanks, too, to Kim Knoppers, in whose book-lined Amsterdam apartment I wrote part of this book and who pointed me towards a residency in Phlox, Folkert van der Hoek's beautifully restored schoolhouse in Friesland. I researched and wrote there in the sizzling hot summer of 2022, where I came across the artists Margaretha Posthumus and Pieter Dirk Torensma who welcomed me and told me tales of the land amid the entrancing cloudscapes in that northernmost tip of the Netherlands. And lastly to Frans Pijnenburg and Victor Wiener, who were a steady source of humour, support and astute advice throughout the writing of this book.

This book is a snapshot and as such it is a contribution to a debate. I wrote it so that it would be accessible to all those who are watching the bonfire that is Brexit. In researching this book, I sought references that are readily available to all. I stand by every word.

Picture credits

Frontispiece © David Shrigley. All Rights Reserved, DACS/ Artimage 2022, Courtesy the artist; 1 Courtesy, Fondazione Romano Cagnoni; 2 Keystone-France/GAMMA RAPHO; 3 Courtesy Profile Books; 4 Photo courtesy Rona Marsden; 5 Courtesy the artist; 6 Courtesy the artist, flyingleaps (www.flyingleaps.co.uk); 7, 8, 9, 10, 11, 12, 13, 14 and 15 Courtesy, The Brexit Collection, London School of Economics; 16 and 17 Photo: Harry Dwyer, Courtesy the artist and Frith Street Gallery, London; 18 © Cornelia Parker/Photo © Tate (Oli Cowling); 19 Courtesy the artist; 20 and 21 Courtesy of the artist; 22 and 23 Courtesy the artist; 24 Photo: Studio Fredrik Nilsen, courtesy the artist; Frith Street Gallery, London and Marian Goodman Gallery New York/Paris; 25 Courtesy the artist; Frith Street Gallery, London and Marian Goodman Gallery New York/Paris; 26 Courtesy the artist; 27, 28, 29 and 30 Courtesy Wolfgang Tillmans; 31, 32 and 33 Courtesy the artist; 34 Courtesy the artist; 35 and 36 Courtesy the artist; 37, 38, 39, 40 and 41 Courtesy the artist; 42 and 43 Courtesy kennardphillipps; 44 and 45 Courtesy the artist, flyingleaps (www.flyingleaps.co.uk); 46 https://www.youtube.com/watch?v=KTh8mETQ6RA; 47 Courtesy of the Artist, The Modern Institute/Toby Webster Ltd, Glasgow and Art: Concept, Paris. Photo: Patrick Jameson; 48 Courtesy of the Artist and The Modern Institute/Toby Webster Ltd, Glasgow. Photo: Patrick Jameson; 49 Courtesy of the Artist, Art: Concept, Paris and The Modern Institute/Toby Webster Ltd, Glasgow. Photo: Patrick Jameson; 50 and 51 Courtesy the artist; 52, 53 and 54 Courtesy the artist; 55 Courtesy the artist; 56 Courtesy the artist; 57 Courtesy the artist; 58, 59 and 60 Courtesy the artist; 61, 62 and 63 Courtesy LBD; 64 Courtesy Atlantic Books; 65 Excerpt: https://vimeo.com/682824107/6fe4ee4244. Courtesy the artist; 66 and 67 Courtesy the artist; 68 Courtesy the artist; 69 Courtesy the artist; 70 Courtesy the artists; 71 Courtesy the artist; 72 Courtesy the artist; 73 and 74 © Layla Curtis; 75 Courtesy the artist

BIOLOGY: UNIFORMITY & DIVERSITY

The Open University

PLANTS

EDITED BY IRENE RIDGE

Photos on Cover

① ②

③ ④ ⑤

① Genetically engineered seedlings

View of a pipette dropping nutrient fluid onto genetically engineered seedlings. The seedlings are being grown in petri dishes. The aim of genetic engineering is to alter the plant's DNA (deoxyribonucleic acid) and thus its repertoire of functional genes which may change the plant's characteristics to include protection against cold, parasites and disease. It can also make the crop more resistant to spoilage after it has been harvested. Courtesy of TEK IMAGE/Science Photo Library.

② Ragweed pollen

Coloured scanning electron micrograph of pollen grains on the stigma of a ragweed plant *Ambrosia* sp. The surface of the grains of pollen (yellow) have a spiked appearance. The multi-lobed stigma is green. *Ambrosia* is a daisy-like flower that grows in bare and waste ground. Its pollen is windborne and released in great quantities for cross-pollination. It can act as an allergen causing hay fever in allergic individuals. Courtesy of Biophoto Associates/Science Photo Library.

③ Sea horse

X-ray (in false colours) of a sea horse, *Hippocampus* sp. A sea horse is a type of teleost fish. Sea horses swim slowly using fins (not seen here) and can use their tails to attach to seaweed or coral. The male sea horse incubates the fertilized eggs in a brood pouch on his abdomen. Courtesy of D. Roberts/Science Photo Library.

④ Sunflowers

A group of blooming sunflowers, *Helianthus* sp., against the sky. The plant produces composite flowers: the small, true flowers are clustered into a compact, round head which resembles a single flower. The plant is widely cultivated for its seeds which are used to make cooking oil and as food for livestock. Courtesy of David Nunuk/Science Photo Library.

⑤ Viruses

Illustration based on a transmission electron micrograph of human immunodeficiency viruses (HIV) (shown in yellow) budding out of a human T cell. HIV causes AIDS (Acquired Immune Deficiency Syndrome) by damaging T cells — the white blood cells that play a crucial role in the immune system. Courtesy of Chris Bjornberg/Science Photo Library.

The Open University, Walton Hall, Milton Keynes, MK7 6AA

First published 2001

Edited, designed and typeset by The Open University.

Printed in the United Kingdom by The Alden Group, Oxford.

ISBN 0 7492 97514

This publication forms part of an Open University course, S204 *Biology: Uniformity and Diversity*. The complete list of texts which make up this course can be found at the back. Details of this and other Open University courses can be obtained from the Call Centre, PO Box 724, The Open University, Milton Keynes MK7 6ZS, United Kingdom: tel. +44 (0)1908 653231, e-mail ces-gen@open.ac.uk

Alternatively, you may visit the Open University website at http://www.open.ac.uk where you can learn more about the wide range of courses and packs offered at all levels by The Open University.

To purchase this publication or other components of Open University courses, contact Open University Worldwide Ltd, The Berrill Building, Walton Hall, Milton Keynes MK7 6AA, United Kingdom: tel. +44 (0)1908 858785; fax +44 (0)1908 858787; e-mail ouwenq@open.ac.uk; website http://www.ouw.co.uk

1.1

s204book 5i1.1

The S204 Course Team

Course Team Chair
Hilary MacQueen

Academic Editor
Caroline Pond

Course Managers
Vivien Bacigalupo
Chris Edwards
Christine Gorman

Course Secretary
Dawn Partner

Authors
Mary Bell (Book 5)
Eric Bowers (Book 6)
John Burnett (Book 4)
Alan Cann (Book 4)
Mel Clements (Book 3)
Basiro Davey (Book 2)
Hilary Denny (Book 5)
Sue Downs (Book 5)
Mandy Dyson (Books 2 and 6)
Anna Furth (Books 3 and 4)
Mike Gillman (Book 2)
Tim Halliday (Book 2)
Jane Loughlin (Book 3)
David Male (Book 4)
Hilary MacQueen (Book 4)
Judith Metcalfe (Book 3)
Phil Parker (Book 5)
Caroline Pond (Books 1, 2 and 6)
Irene Ridge (Books 1, 4 and 5)
Jerry Roberts (Book 5)
David Robinson (Book 6)
Jill Saffrey (Book 3)
Robert Saunders (Book 6)
Ayona Silva-Fletcher (Book 3)
Valda Stevens (Book 2)
Margaret Swithenby (Books 3 and 4)
Colin Walker ((Books 3 and 4)

GLO Editor
Peggy Varley

Editors
Ian Nuttall
Gillian Riley
Bina Sharma
Margaret Swithenby
Peter Twomey

OU Graphic Design
Ruth Drage
Pam Owen
Howard Twiner
Andrew Whitehead
Liz Yeomans

Library
Lydia Eaton
Judy Thomas

Picture Research
Lydia Eaton

Book assessors
Giovanni Novarino (Book 1)
Aubrey Manning (Book 2)
Karl Swann and David Harris (Book 3)
Peter White (Book 4)
David Clarkson and Rachel Leech (Book 5)
John Currey and Brian James (Book 6)

External course assessor
Professor Sir David Smith

Consultants
Patricia Ash
Sue Downs
Christine Gorman
Jean MacQueen
Terry Whatson

Skills
Patricia Ash
Hilary Denny

CD-ROM AND VIDEO PRODUCTION

Mary Bell
Gail Block
Jacki Brown
Phil Butcher
Hilary Denny
Mike Dodd
Anna Furth
Phil Gauron
Michael Gillman
Tim Halliday
Nicky Heath
Caryl Hooper
G. D. Jayalakshmi
Juliet Kauffmann
Martin Kemp
Hilary MacQueen
Derek Martin
Mark Murphy
Phil Parker
Caroline Pond
Irene Ridge
Jerry Roberts
David Robinson
Jill Saffrey
Liz Sugden
Andrew Sutton
Margaret Swithenby
Gary Tucknott
Verina Waights
Darren Wycherley

CONTENTS

PLANT EVOLUTION AND STRUCTURE

1

1.1 INTRODUCTION

An essential background to the study of plants is knowledge of their evolutionary history, life cycles and structure, which are the subjects of this chapter. Later chapters consider how plants function, grow and interact with microbes, concentrating mainly on flowering plants (angiosperms or Anthophyta), but this chapter takes in the full range of plant phyla from bryophytes to angiosperms.

Despite their aquatic origins, plants evolved on land (Ridge, 2001[A]). The focus here is on the increasing specialization of plants to life on land, which illustrates some of the important evolutionary trends in the plant kingdom. These trends are apparent in plant life cycles (Sections 1.1 to 1.4), and in the morphology and anatomy of plant cells and organs, especially those related to transport and support mechanisms (Sections 1.5 and 1.6). Morphology and anatomy provide clear indications of evolutionary processes, but they also link directly to the rest of this book, and form an essential background to studies of plant physiology and development.

1.1.1 THE PROBLEMS OF LIFE ON LAND

What are the important trends in plant evolution? The available evidence (including molecular phylogeny) suggests that plants evolved from freshwater green algae (Chlorophyta, Protoctista), and emerged onto land to live on mud banks, and the sides of lakes and streams. Most green algae reproduce by means of motile gametes; so the development of *reproductive mechanisms that are independent of water* has been absolutely essential to the complete and successful adaptation of plants to the land environment.

The first land plants were almost certainly prostrate, overgrowing each other in their relatively damp habitats. Light absorption would necessarily have been limited because of this habit, and so competition for light may have provided a selective force favouring the evolution of upright shoots in vascular plants and bryophytes. Fossil evidence suggests that these earliest upright plants of the mid-Silurian Period (425 Ma ago) branched dichotomously (Figure 1.1); that is, pairs of branches arising at the same junction were of equal importance. Similar evidence also suggests that shoots were naked and leaves had not evolved. However, specialized support cells that helped to keep plants upright were already present in tissues by the late Silurian.

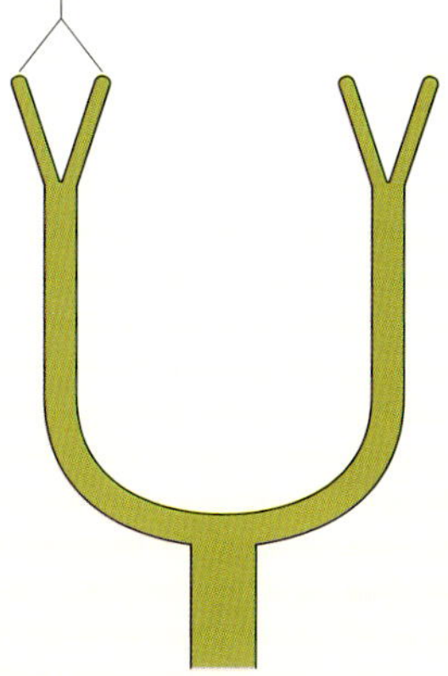

Figure 1.1 Dichotomous branching. Note that in this condition neither branch becomes a leader; instead both develop equally and both have the potential to branch again.

The necessity to absorb light more effectively, and also to limit the loss of water from cells must, almost certainly, have led to evolution of expanded leaves and waterproofing of external cells. As leaves became larger and more effective as photosynthetic surfaces, the need to prevent evaporation losses would have grown, not diminished. Absorption of CO_2 and retention of water make competing demands on the design of leaves, so a more effective mechanism for waterproofing the aerial surface, pores to allow access for CO_2, and systems for absorption and transport of water would have promoted survival.

Early plants were anchored to soil by simple **rhizoids** (see Figure 1.4), which have only a limited capacity for absorption. Roots absorb water much more effectively, and are found in nearly all the later-evolved vascular plants that diversified during the late Devonian and the Carboniferous Periods (370–270 Ma ago). They are not found in bryophytes, which evolved and diversified earlier than vascular plants. Similarly, more efficient water-conducting tissues occur in the roots and shoots of later vascular plants, but are not found in more primitive plant groups, including bryophytes.

Increasing size is also an important issue, because it requires more strengthening and water-transporting tissues. Overall, therefore, the adaptation of plants to land involved major changes in life cycles, cell structure, morphology and physiology. Some general aspects of life cycles are considered in Section 1.2 before we examine in detail examples from different plant phyla.

1.2 ALTERNATION OF GENERATIONS

A key difference between animals and plants is the occurrence of multicellular haploid and diploid stages — that is, the *alternation of generations* — in the plant life cycle (Ridge, 2001[B]).

❍ Name these two generations in Figure 1.2 by filling in the two empty boxes.

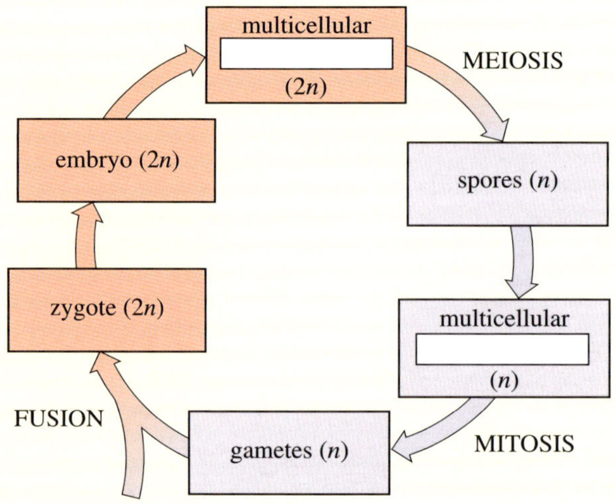

Figure 1.2 Simplified diagram showing a typical plant life cycle. Two gametes from the same or different individuals fuse to form a zygote.

● The multicellular diploid generation (pink box) is the **sporophyte** (note that it produces haploid *spores* after meiosis); the multicellular haploid generation (mauve box) is the **gametophyte** (note that it produces *gametes* by mitosis).

Most algae (Protoctista) also show alternation of generations and, unlike plants, the two generations are often indistinguishable except that one produces gametes and the other spores. The green seaweed *Ulva lactuca* (sea lettuce) has such a life cycle with **isomorphic** (*iso*, Greek meaning 'equal', *morphe* meaning 'form') alternation of generations (Ridge, 2001[B]). Even in the algae, however, some species are **heteromorphic**; that is, they have morphologically different forms of gametophyte and sporophyte. In the red alga, *Porphyra* (Rhodophyta), for example, the two generations are so different that they were not even recognized as belonging to the same organism until relatively recently. Heteromorphic species are considered to be more advanced (i.e. later evolved) than isomorphic types, and all living plants are heteromorphic.

A feature of heteromorphism is that one generation may dominate, being of larger size or surviving longer than the other.

❍ What is the dominant generation (i.e. sporophyte or gametophyte) of the following plant groups: bryophytes, club mosses, whisk ferns, ferns, cycads, conifers and flowering plants? (See Figure 1.3 for the relationship between these groups.)

● For all phyla except bryophytes, the dominant generation is the sporophyte.

The phylogenetic tree (Figure 1.3, see overleaf) will need to be referred to at intervals from now on.

Early, and now extinct, land plants may have shown isomorphic alternation of generations, but the evidence is circumstantial and inconclusive. The problem for palaeontologists is that it is often difficult to establish that fossil material really represents two generations of the same plant — that is, definite sporophyte and gametophyte generations that are still attached to each other, and, therefore, definitely belonging to the same species. Such ideal material has not been found. However, circumstantial evidence can sometimes be convincing or at least suggestive. For instance, the two fossils *Sciadophyton* (a gametophyte form bearing gametes in *gametangia*) and *Rhynia* (a sporophyte form bearing spores in sporangia; Figure 1.4) may possibly be different phases of the life cycle of the same species, as they are morphologically identical and are found in the same fossiliferous location.

Because of this uncertainty there are two theories about the way in which the sporophyte generation of the vascular plants may have originated. The **transformation theory** assumes isomorphic alternation of generations to be the primitive state, and that differential development of one generation or another followed. The alternative idea is that a sporophyte generation did not exist in ancestral forms of higher plants, which would have been purely gametophytic with no alternation of generations. This **interpolation theory** proposes that the sporophytic generation could have been the consequence of delayed meiosis in zygotes that previously would have undergone meiosis as the first step after fertilization. The early sporophytes would presumably have been small and relatively undifferentiated.

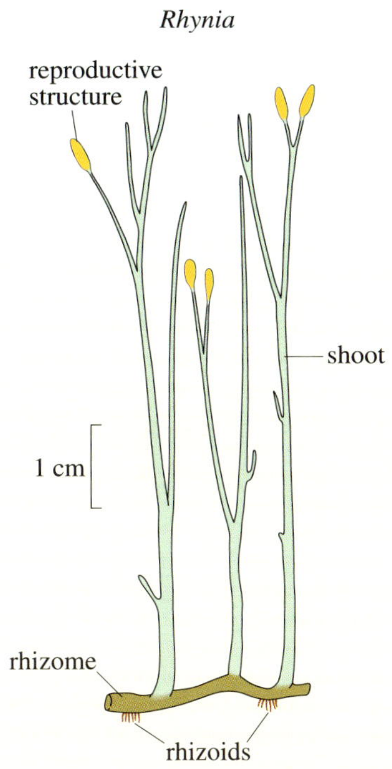

Figure 1.4 *Rhynia*, an extinct early plant (from about 400 Ma ago), which may be the isomorphic sporophyte generation of another fossil genus, *Sciadophyton* (a gametophyte), because the two fossils occur together in the same fossil beds.

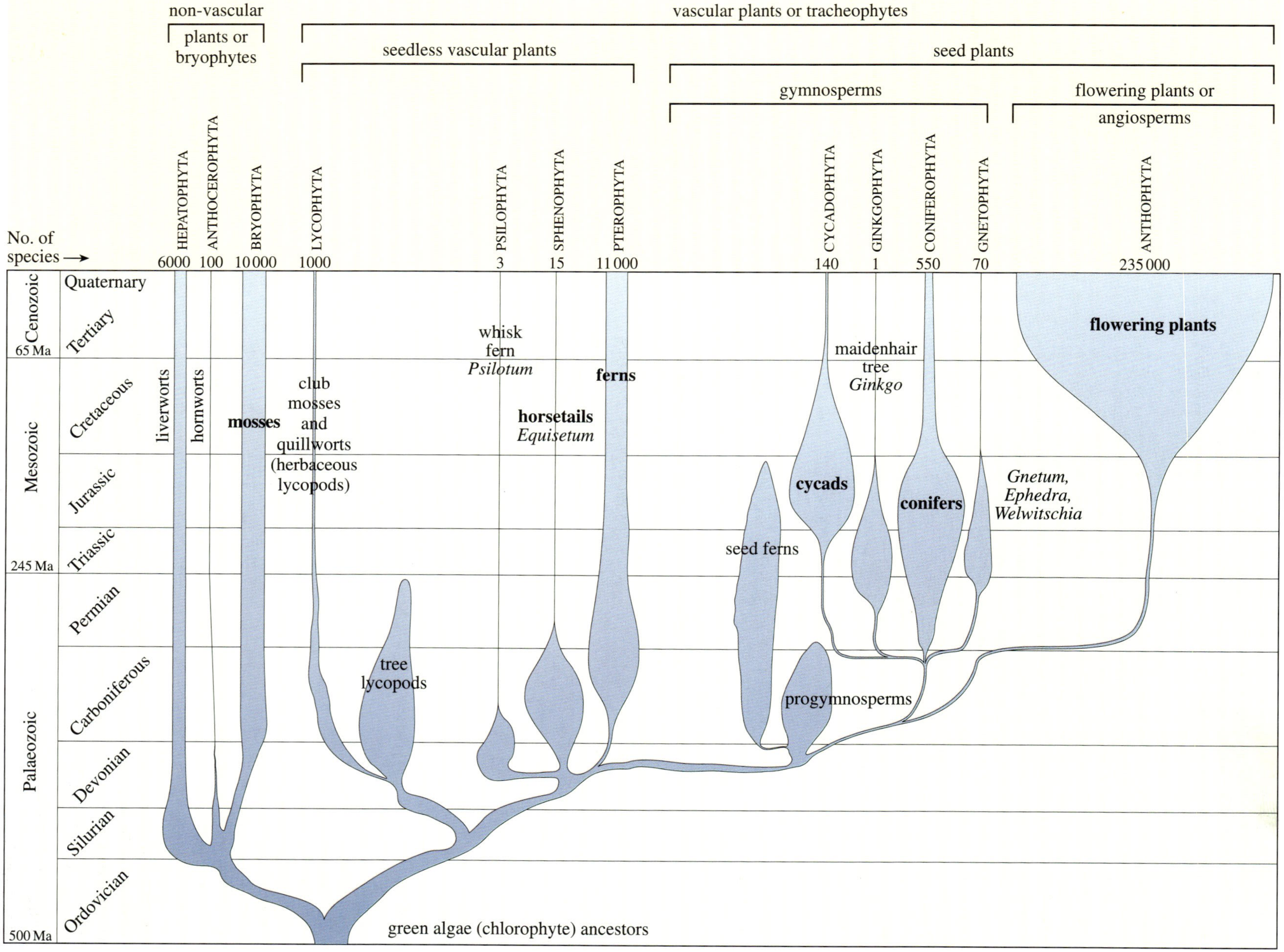

Figure 1.3 Outline of plant phylogeny, showing the probable relationship between bryophytes and tracheophytes. The vertical axis represents time, and the width of different lineages indicates relative abundance. Names of phyla are shown in capital letters, with estimated numbers of living species given for each. Names in lower case are either the common name for the phylum (e.g. ferns) or the name of a representative genus, with the best-known ones in bold.

Heteromorphy, with clear anatomical distinction between gametophyte and sporophyte 'plants', is only one of the features of plant life cycles which is important in classification of the major groups. Other features that are particularly significant include:

- whether male and female gametes are produced by the same or by different gametophytes;
- the degree to which the gametophyte generation is independent of water in the environment, especially for gamete transfer;
- the degree to which the sporophyte and gametophyte exist independently of each other;
- the degree to which the sporophyte embryo is enclosed and protected, the ultimate in protection being a seed.

SUMMARY OF SECTIONS 1.1 AND 1.2

1 Plants evolved from freshwater green algae; the earliest plants were prostrate in habit, but later developed upright shoots with leaves.

2 Other developments that were important adaptations to life on land include: reduced dependence on water for sexual reproduction; waterproof coverings for shoots; roots; specialized cells for strengthening and for internal transport of water and nutrients; increased size.

3 The relative dominance of gametophyte and sporophyte generations is used in plant classification.

4 The concepts of isomorphic and heteromorphic alternation of generations were revised and two theories — transformation and interpolation — were described which could explain the way in which a dominant sporophyte lifestyle may have originated.

5 Finally a number of other characteristics of life cycles were listed as an introduction to more detailed study of ferns, mosses, club mosses and flowering plants.

1.3 LIFE CYCLES OF MOSSES AND FERNS

Bryophytes have long been regarded as the least modified descendants of the earliest plants, a view that is now confirmed by molecular studies. So in this section we compare the life cycle of a **moss** (phylum Bryophyta, Figure 1.3), a type of bryophyte which is probably familiar to you, with that of a fern. Bryophytes are non-vascular plants, whereas ferns (phylum Pterophyta) are vascular plants, and these seedless vascular plants will probably be familiar to most of you.

Figures 1.5 and 1.6 give overviews of the life cycles of typical mosses and ferns. If you quickly compare these two figures, you can immediately confirm that both demonstrate heteromorphic alternation of generations, and that different phases of the life cycle are dominant in the two groups.

Before drawing attention to the important differences between these cycles, we describe each of the life cycles in some detail; you should try to relate the descriptions to Figures 1.5 and 1.6.

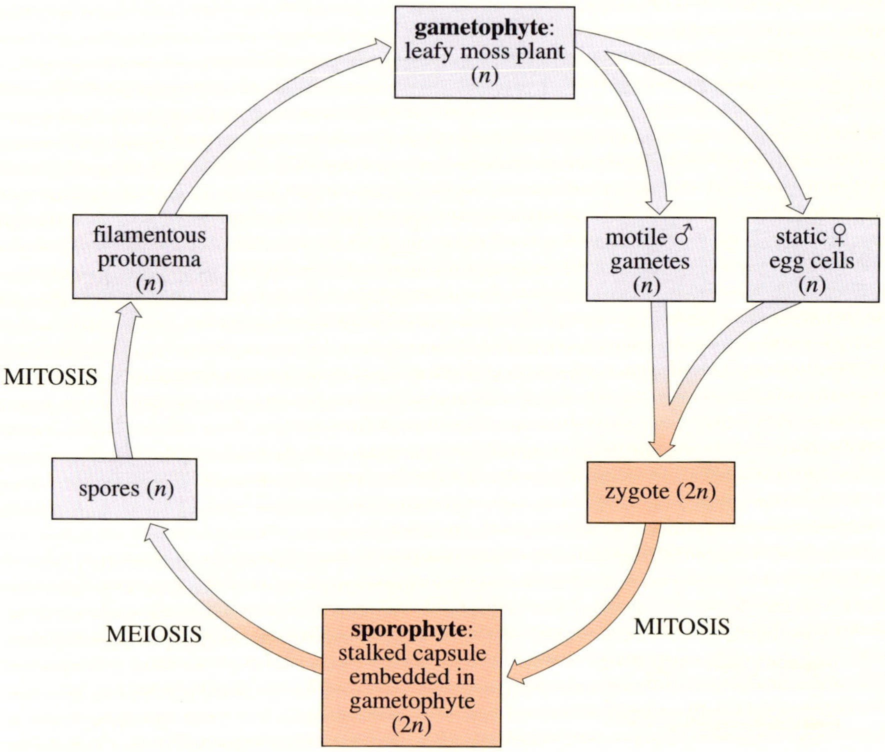

Figure 1.5 An outline life cycle of a typical moss (*Polytrichum* sp.).

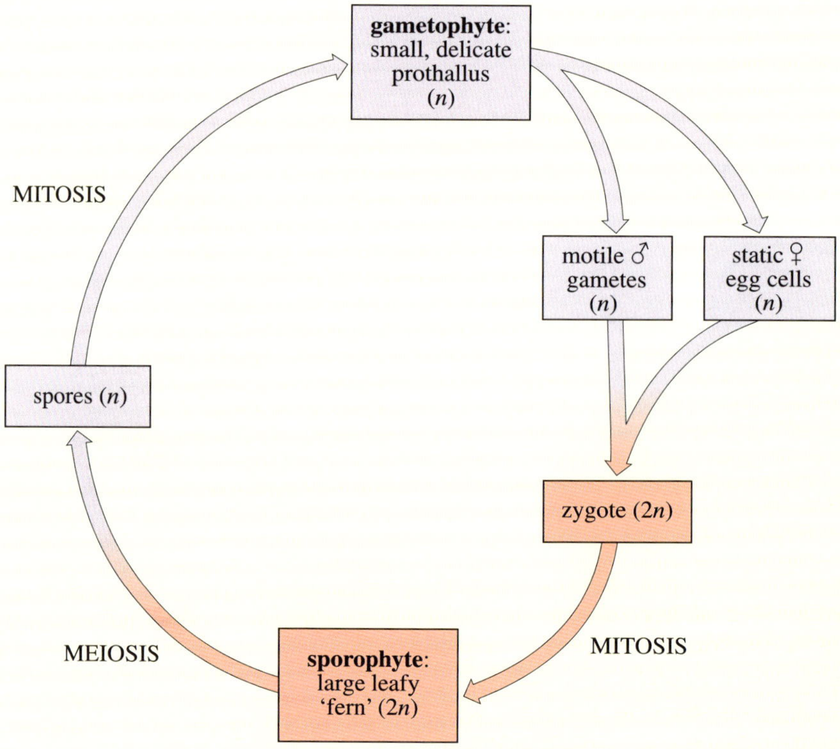

Figure 1.6 An outline life cycle of a typical fern (the male fern, *Dryopteris filix-mas*).

1.3.1 GAMETOPHYTE-DOMINATED MOSSES AND OTHER BRYOPHYTES

Partially completed diagrams in the following sections are designed to help you summarize mitotic and meiotic events in both the gametophyte and sporophyte generations as you read the text relating to the four main life cycles described in Sections 1.3 and 1.4.

Moss plants are gametophytes. Types you have almost certainly seen — even if you could not identify them — may include the low-growing flattish clumps typical of genera like *Funaria*, *Grimmia* and *Tortula*, which are common on dry stone walls; the larger *Sphagnum* and *Polytrichum* species, which occur in wetter, boggy habitats; and flattened dark green sheets of *Hypnum*, frequently found around the base of trees (Figure 1.7). In every case these plants have relatively short stems which carry three rows of small (sometimes very small) leaves, often

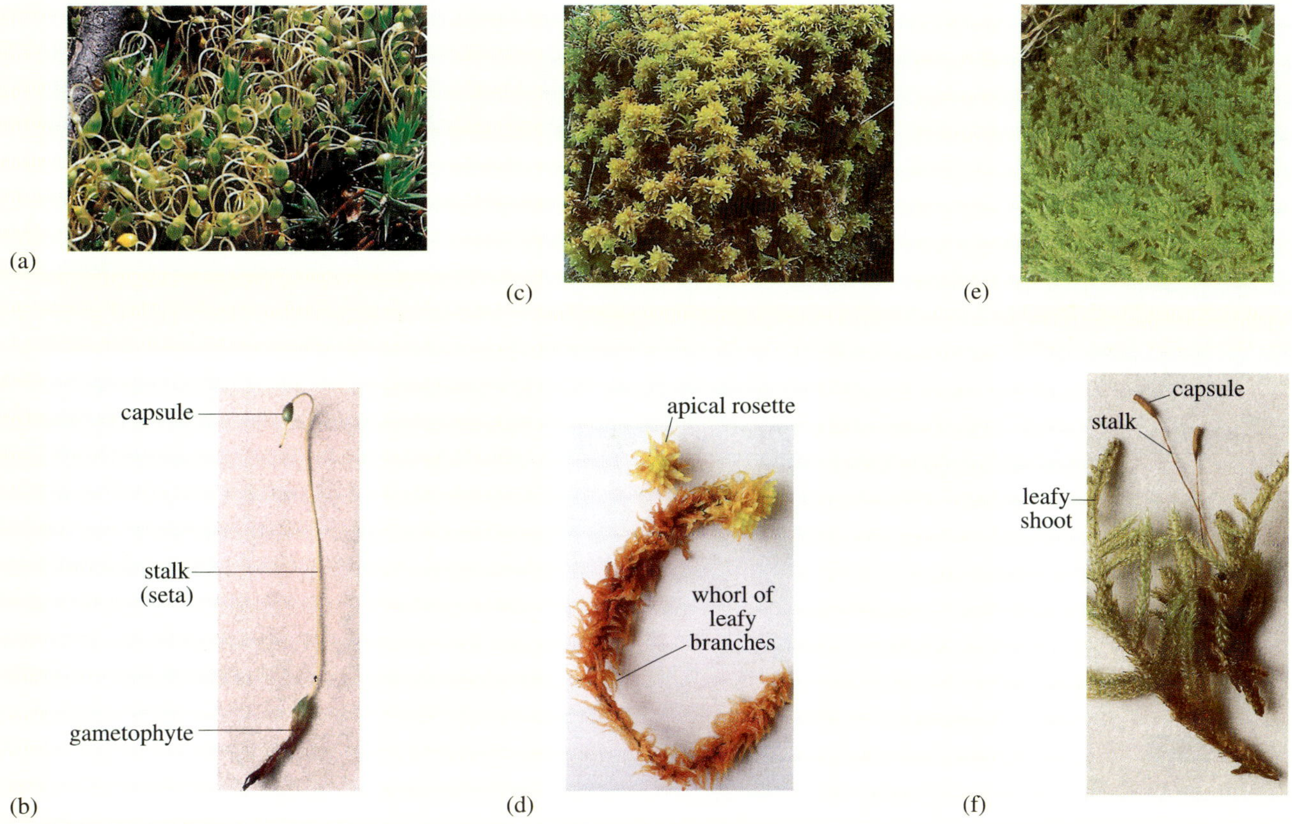

Figure 1.7 The growth habits of some common moss species (a) *Funaria hygrometrica*, which forms small cushions on rocks and disturbed ground, including bonfire sites, and is especially common on the surface of plant pots. Plants are about 1.5 cm tall with very distinct leaves, and produce capsules (b) on curved stalks in autumn and winter. (c) *Sphagnum papillosum* is commonly found in acid wet conditions at the base of hummocks in bogs. Plants are up to 25 cm tall with short blunt branches forming apical rosettes (d); they form large tussocks, and fruiting capsules are not common. (e) *Hypnum cupressiforme* occurs at the base of trees, on walls, and on wood and soil, forming dense mats with small, overlapping pointed leaves on branched stems. Fruiting capsules (f) are frequently seen in autumn.

lying close to the stem, a positioning referred to as *adpressed*. Shoots have rhizoids either at the stem base, or along the stem on procumbent species, which help to anchor the plant. However, they are not important in the absorption of nutrients or water, which are taken in over all surfaces of the plant. Moss plants are generally not waterproof, and there is no true conducting (vascular) tissue. Most species, however, have the potential to dry out and then rehydrate and revive when re-wetted.

In many species, fertile areas occur on the top of shoots in a flattened ring of leaflets (Figure 1.8a). These areas carry male, female, or a mixture of male and female gamete-producing organs (i.e. **gametangia**, singular **gametangium**). In other species, gametangia occur in the axils of leaves up the stem. Both male and female gamete-bearing structures are stalked, and have walls which are one cell thick.

Male gametangia, called **antheridia** (singular = **antheridium**), are club shaped (Figure 1.8b′); female gametangia, called **archegonia** (singular = **archegonium,** pronounced ark-ee-gon`-i-um), are stalked, flask-shaped structures with a long hollow neck (Figure 1.8b). Cells formed by mitosis within the antheridium differentiate to form motile biflagellate sperm (Figure 1.8b′). The archegonium contains a single egg cell, again a product of mitosis, which is retained in the central chamber.

When an antheridium matures, it breaks open and sperm are extruded, after which they are splashed onwards in rain drops, or swim in water films to an archegonium. Here they penetrate the neck, swim down the canal and once in the chamber, one of the sperm will fuse with the large egg cell (Figure 1.8c). As antheridia do not break open in dry weather, transport of the male gametes (sperm) is assured.

❍ What are the advantages to the plant of this *anisogamy* (unequal size) of gametes?

● Conservation of resource. Many small motile sperm are more likely to ensure that fertilization actually takes place. Fewer but large egg cells result in conservation of resources to support the zygote.

❍ What environmental condition is essential to ensure fertilization in mosses?

● Moisture: either rain or a film of moisture over the gametophyte to enable sperm to swim to the archegonium.

Figure 1.8 The life cycle of a moss, *Polytrichum* sp., showing the gametophyte (a and a′) and sporophyte (f) structures, and other features that are important in reproduction. These include antheridia and sperm (b′), archegonia (b and c), zygote (d) and the developing sporophyte (e). (g) shows a germinating spore, and (h) a young gametophyte or protonema.

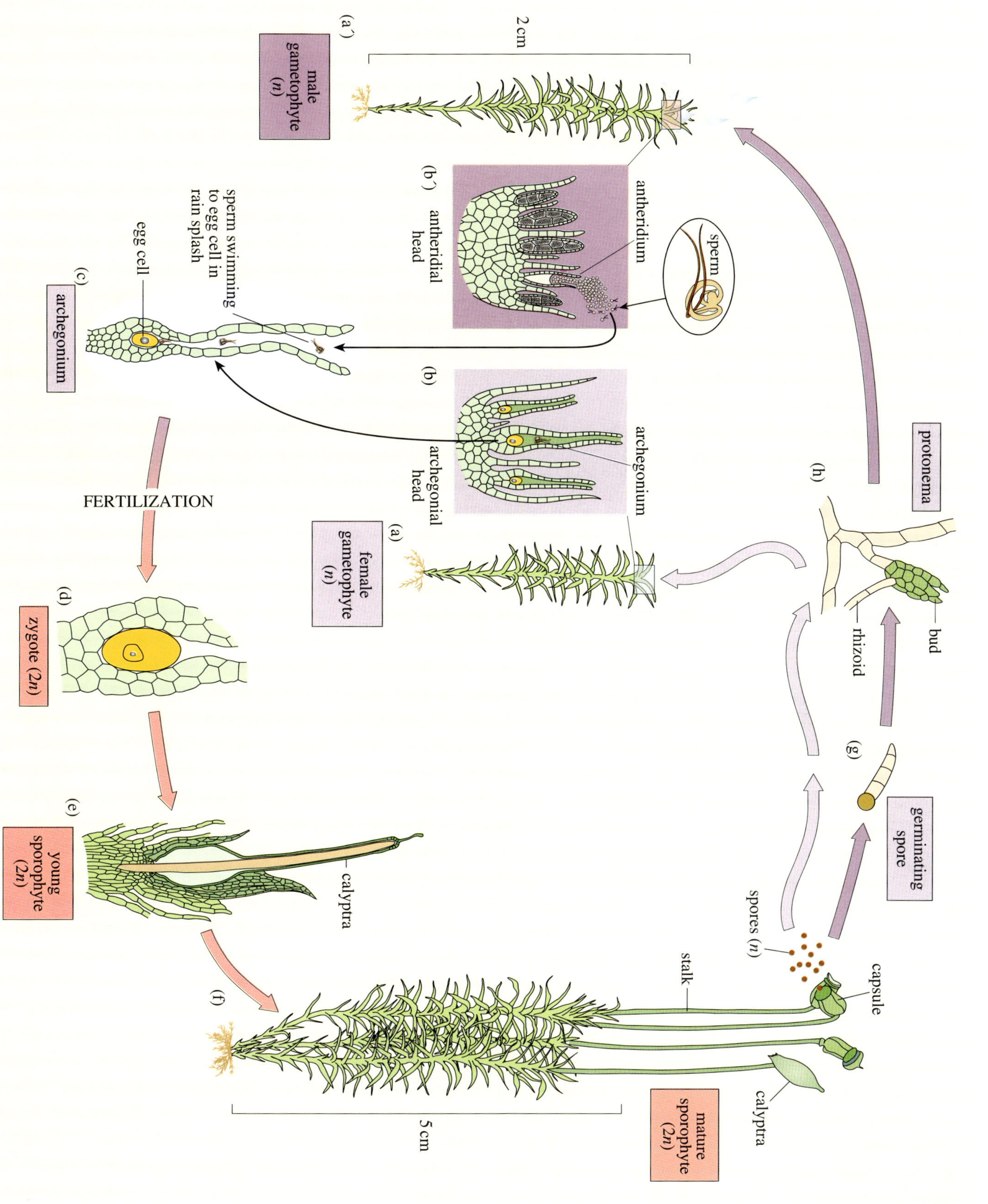
(a′)
male gametophyte (n)
2 cm
(b′) antheridial head
antheridium
sperm
sperm swimming to egg cell in rain splash
egg cell
(c)
archegonium
(b) archegonial head
archegonium
(a)
female gametophyte (n)
FERTILIZATION
(d)
zygote (2n)
(e)
young sporophyte (2n)
calyptra
(f)
5 cm
mature sporophyte (2n)
calyptra
stalk
capsule
spores (n)
germinating spore
(g)
rhizoid
bud
(h)
protonema

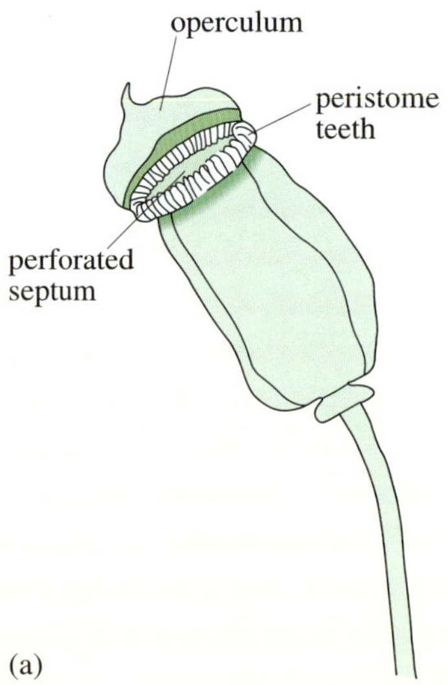

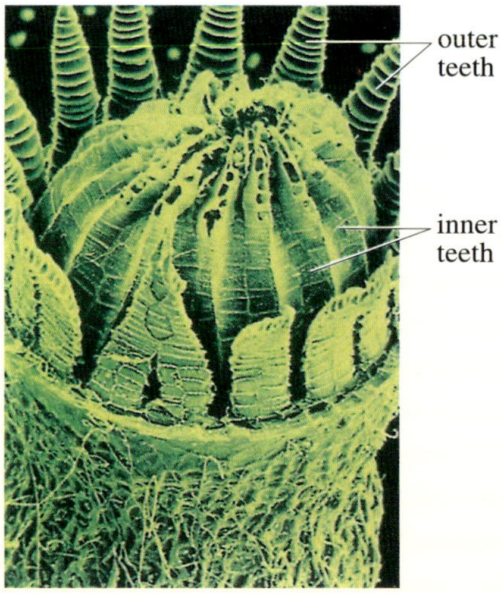

Figure 1.9 (a) The capsule from the sporophyte of the moss *Polytrichum*; spores are released through the perforated septum. (b) Scanning electron micrograph of the capsule apex of a moss with two rows of peristome teeth, which curl back in dry weather to release spores.

The resultant diploid cell, the zygote (Figure 1.8d), divides *mitotically* to form an embryo and eventually a sporophyte, which consists of a stalk (seta) and an apical **capsule** (see Figure 1.9). The sporophyte is attached to its parent gametophyte by a rooting base throughout life (Figure 1.8e), and is thus never wholly independent of the gametophyte, even if some tissue is green and able to photosynthesize.

Usually, there are pores (stomata) on the surface, which can open and close, a feature also found in the sporophytes of vascular plants. Meiosis occurs in the capsule, each parent cell ultimately producing four haploid spores. When immature, the capsule is often covered by a thin, protective cap, the *calyptra*, which is lost as the capsule reaches maturity revealing a closed lid (the *operculum*, Figure 1.9), which splits from the rest of the capsule to reveal a ring of teeth (the *peristome*). In *Polytrichum*, the teeth are fused to form a perforated septum like a pepper pot, through which spores are released. In other mosses, teeth are free to pick up and lose water (i.e. they are hygroscopic), bending outwards in dry conditions and inwards when it is wet, so closing the capsule (Figure 1.9b). Spores are consequently ejected when the peristome is open — that is, in dry conditions — and are then carried away from the parent capsule in wind currents. Most mosses, therefore, require dry conditions for spore dispersal, and spores are well protected by a decay-resistant, waterproof wall.

On germination, moss spores give rise initially to a filamentous and branched green **protonema** (pronounced pro-to-nee`-ma; plural **protonemata**, pronounced proto-nem-a`-ta; Figure 1.8h). This algal-like, juvenile stage is unique to mosses and some liverworts. Eventually, protonemata produce bud-like structures, from which gametophytes develop (Figure 1.8a and a′).

- ❍ Which stage of the moss life cycle — mature gametophyte, sporophyte or protonema — would you expect to be most vulnerable to desiccation?
- ● The protonema because of its thread-like structure.

❍ Now complete Figure 1.10 by filling in the blank boxes A–C. (Answers are on p. 52.)

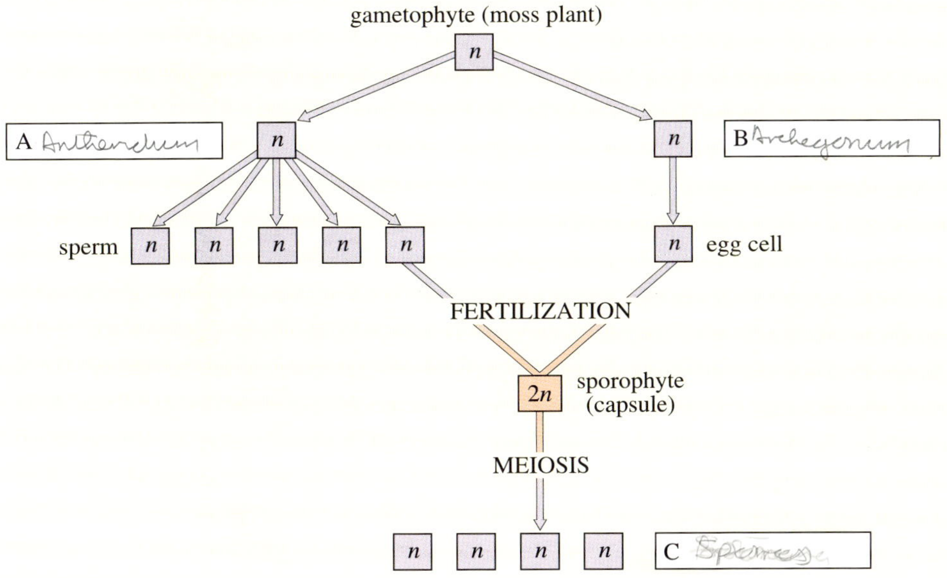

Figure 1.10 Summary of mitotic events in the male and female moss gametangia, and of meiotic events in capsules of the sporophyte generation.

OTHER BRYOPHYTES: LIVERWORTS AND HORNWORTS

Liverworts (phylum Hepatophyta) are often regarded as an earlier-evolved and more 'primitive' group than mosses. They tend to be more restricted to very damp or sheltered habitats. Their gametophytes have two basic growth forms.

❍ From Figure 1.11a and b, and before reading the caption, describe these two growth forms.

● There is a flat form (a **thallus**, plural **thalli**), and a leafy form which resembles that of mosses.

Marchantia sp. is a thalloid liverwort, which may be familiar because it often grows on the surface of plant pots. Its gametophytes are unisexual, and bear antheridia and archegonia on disc-like structures (antheridiophores and archegoniophores) held on stalks (Figure 1.11c). *Marchantia* depends on rain splash to transfer sperm to archegonia. In most other liverworts the sex organs are grouped close to the thallus or leafy shoot, as in mosses, and life cycles resemble closely those of mosses.

There are some notable differences between the sporophytes of mosses and liverworts, however. For example, those of liverworts are never photosynthetic; capsules (Figure 1.11d) have no operculum or peristome and simply split open or develop slits in the side walls; and spore dispersal is aided by unique cells called *elaters* (Figure 1.11e and f).

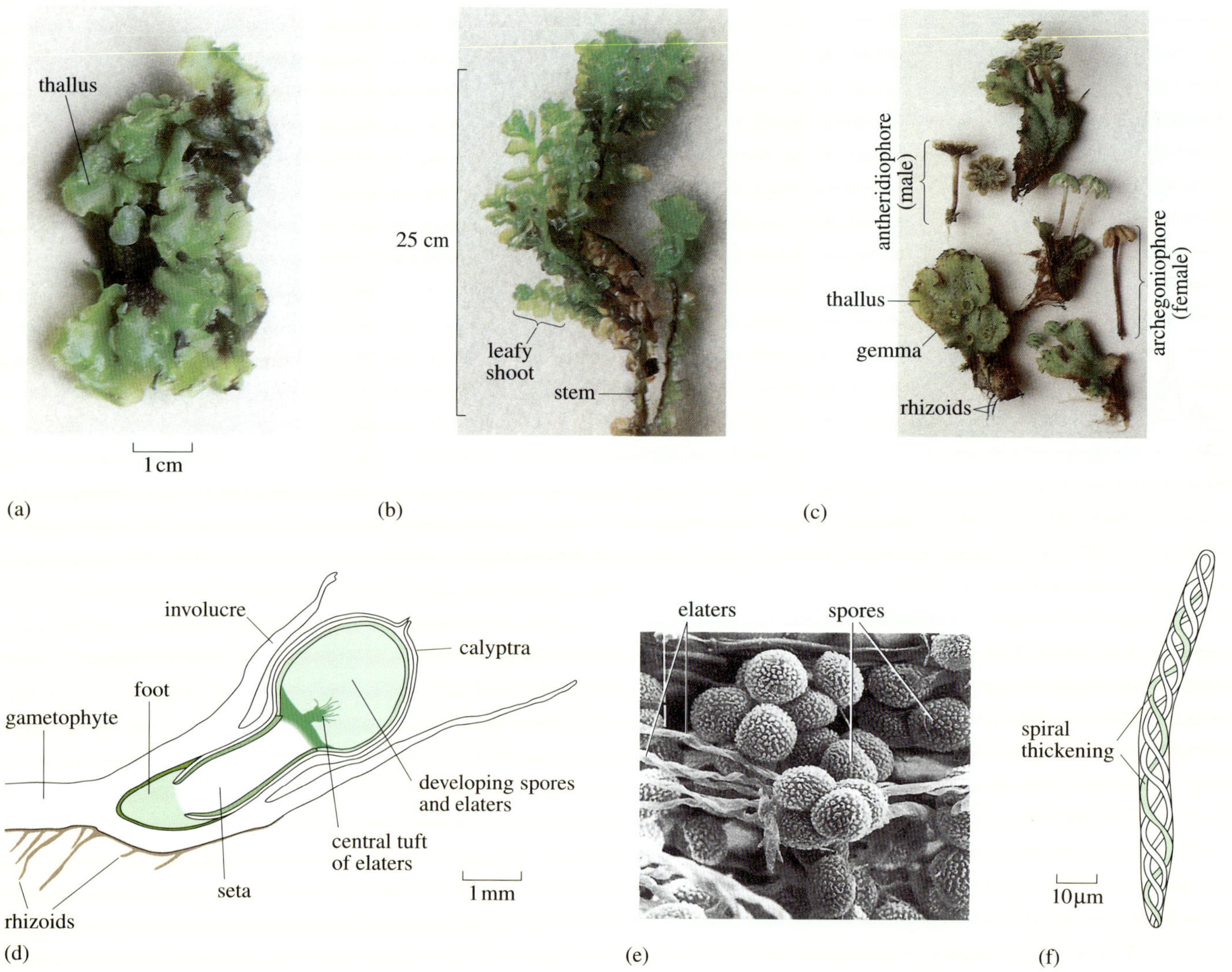

Figure 1.11 Features of liverworts: (a) *Pellia epiphylla*, a thalloid gametophyte form, and (b) *Tritomeria* sp., a leafy, moss-like form. (c) The gametophyte of *Marchantia polymorpha*, bearing antheridia on stalked structures called antheridiophores and archegoniophores; a 'gemma' is an asexual propagule. (d) The capsule (sporophyte) of *Pellia epiphylla*. (e) An electron micrograph of spores and elaters within a capsule of *Haplometrium hookeri*. (f) A spirally thickened elater.

❍ From Figure 1.11f, how do you think the structure of elaters enables them to promote spore dispersal?

● The spirally thickened wall (which is also hygroscopic) means that elaters dry out unevenly, and hence twist about, causing spores to be flung into the air.

Hornworts (Anthocerophyta) are much less diverse than the other bryophyte phyla; and it is unclear if they are more 'primitive' or more 'advanced' than mosses or liverworts. In some characteristics they resemble green algae (e.g. cells with only a single chloroplast containing a special region where starch is synthesized); in others they resemble later-evolved mosses and

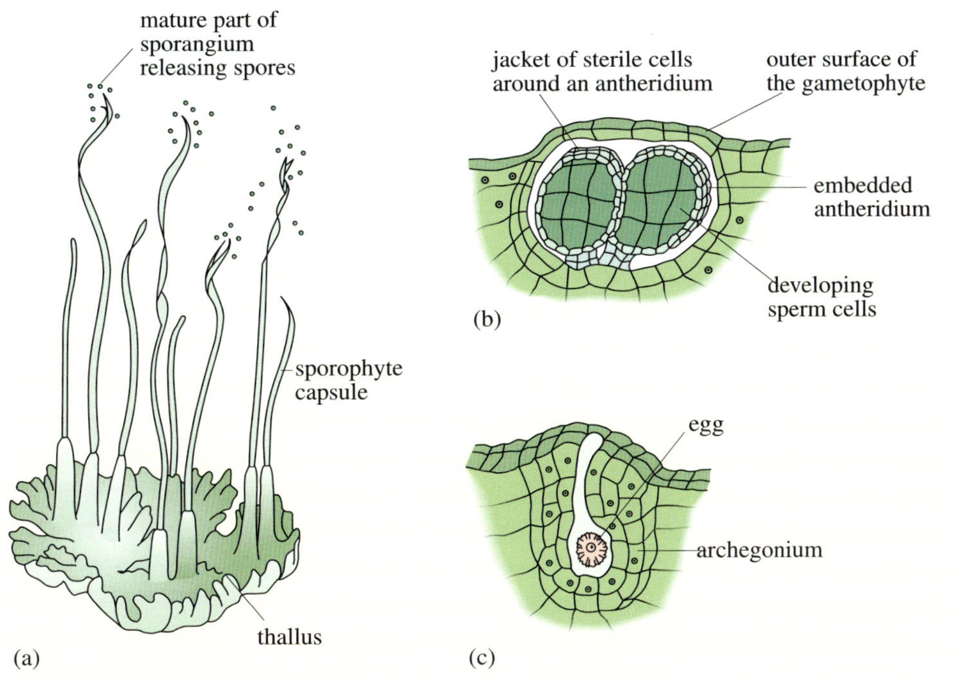

Figure 1.12 Characteristics of hornworts: (a) general features of *Anthoceros*, which shows the gametophyte thallus bearing several sporophytes. Sections through gametophytes, showing the location and anatomy of (b) an antheridium and (c) an archegonium.

vascular plants (e.g. the presence of *stomata* (pores) on the sporophyte). Superficially, hornworts look like small thalloid liverworts (Figure 1.12a), but unlike liverworts or mosses they are short-lived annuals, growing mainly in winter.

❍ From Figure 1.12 how do the sporophyte and gametangia of *Anthoceros* differ from those of mosses or liverworts?

● The sporophyte shows no division into seta and capsule; the whole structure seems to act like a capsule or sporangium, and twists and splits as it matures and releases spores. The gametangia (antheridia and archegonia) are embedded rather than protruding from the surface of the gametophyte (cf. Figure 1.8b and b′).

In fact, cells are produced continuously at the base of the hornwort capsule, which grows throughout life and is attached to the gametophyte by an absorptive foot region. It is the 'horn'-like shape of the sporophyte that gives the phylum its name.

Despite the similarity of their life cycles, there are sufficient differences between mosses, liverworts and hornworts to justify separating them into distinct phyla, although the precise relationship between the three groups remains obscure. One reason is that fossil remains of bryophytes are very rare, so there has been little material for palaeobotanists and taxonomists to work with. Although often referred to as 'lower plants', bryophytes are globally abundant and especially diverse in rainforests; one moss genus, *Sphagnum*, is dominant in bogs which cover one per cent of the Earth's surface.

1.3.2 Sporophyte-dominated ferns

Ferns (phylum Pterophyta) are the most diverse and abundant of the seedless vascular plants alive today (Figure 1.3). They originated in the Devonian Period, reaching their zenith in the late Carboniferous Period (about 300 Ma ago), which is often called the 'age of ferns' because the vegetation was dominated by ferns, including large tree ferns. Extant species like bracken (*Pteridium aquilinum*), which is found on moors and in woods, and male fern (*Dryopteris filix-mas*) and hart's tongue (*Asplenium scolopendrium*), which are woodland species (Figure 1.13a, b and c) are common, large and noticeable, so they may be known to you already. Others are small and less obvious — yet still very common — for instance, wall rue, *Asplenium ruta-muraria* (Figure 1.13d), which occurs in cracks (alongside wall mosses) on limestone walls throughout

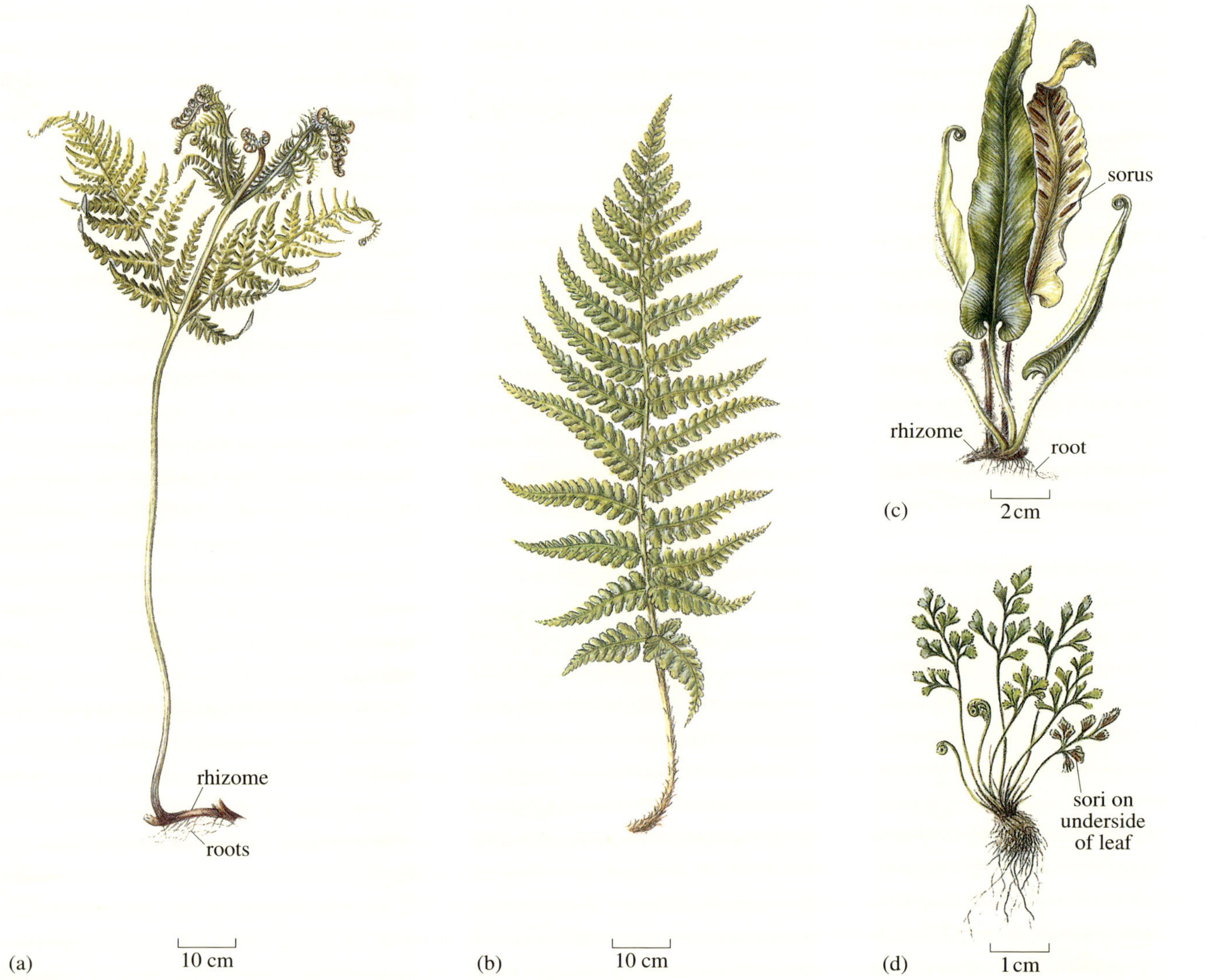

Figure 1.13 The growth forms of some rare and common ferns: (a) tall branched fronds of bracken, *Pteridium aquilinum;* (b) unbranched fronds of male fern *Dryopteris filix-mas*; (c) tongue-like hart's tongue, *Asplenium scolopendrium*; (d) small flattened fronds of wall rue *Asplenium ruta-muraria.*

the UK. Most fern leaves (fronds) are relatively resistant to drying out because they have a waterproof cuticle over their surface, which limits water loss (Section 1.5). However, ferns are often more common in shady habitats. There are also a number of rarer, more delicate native species, like the filmy fern, *Hymenophyllum tunbridgense* (Figure 1.15c), which is limited to damp rocks in south-eastern England, and is very susceptible to drying out. These ferns, which are so different in size and form, are all examples of the sporophyte generation.

In contrast to mosses the gametophyte of a typical fern is a small thin, strap or heart-shaped, short-lived **prothallus** (pronounced pro-thall`-us, plural **prothalli**, Figure 1.14a, overleaf). It grows on, or close to, damp ground attached by single-celled rhizoids, which arise from the lower surface. Prothalli usually contain chloroplasts, but most have little protection against water loss and so they develop and survive only in habitats that remain moist. In some species, gametophytes are subterranean and non-photosynthetic, obtaining energy from symbiotic fungal partners.

Unlike in mosses, the antheridia and archegonia of ferns are formed deep in the prothallial tissue rather than at the surface (Figures 1.14b–d). They are located on the underside and difficult to find, even with a microscope, as they often develop among the rhizoids. However, they are similar in shape and form to those of mosses, and the formation of sperm and egg cells and the process of fertilization are virtually identical (Figures 1.14b and c).

When the fertilized egg — that is, a diploid zygote — germinates, it is dependent on the prothallus until it forms both aerial shoots and young roots (Figure 1.14e), and becomes self-sustaining when the prothallus dies. At maturity the sporophyte generation consists of leaves and a rooting stem or rhizome, which is usually underground (Figure 1.14f). Simple or compound, small or large leaves arise from nodes on the rhizome. The whole structure is generally both larger and tougher than the leafy shoots of mosses, and altogether better suited to life on land. For example, the leaf surface is covered by a waterproof cuticle bearing stomata; there is an extensive vascular system which transports water and mineral nutrients between roots and shoots, and contains woody cells that provide support.

Fern spores are produced by meiosis within **sporangia**, which are usually grouped into structures called **sori** (pronounced 'saw-ri', singular **sorus**, Figure 1.14g and h). Different patterns of distribution and variations in shapes of leaf sori are typical of specific families and genera, and are used in their classification. Some examples are shown in Figure 1.15. Notice how whole portions of leaves are modified as fertile spore-producing organs in moonwort (*Botrychium lunaria)* and royal fern (*Osmunda regalis*) (Figure 1.15a and b, respectively), whereas in the male fern the sori are borne on the undersides of normal leaves and are covered with a protective scale or *indusium* (Figure 1.14h). You may have noticed sori as brown or black patches or lines on fern leaves.

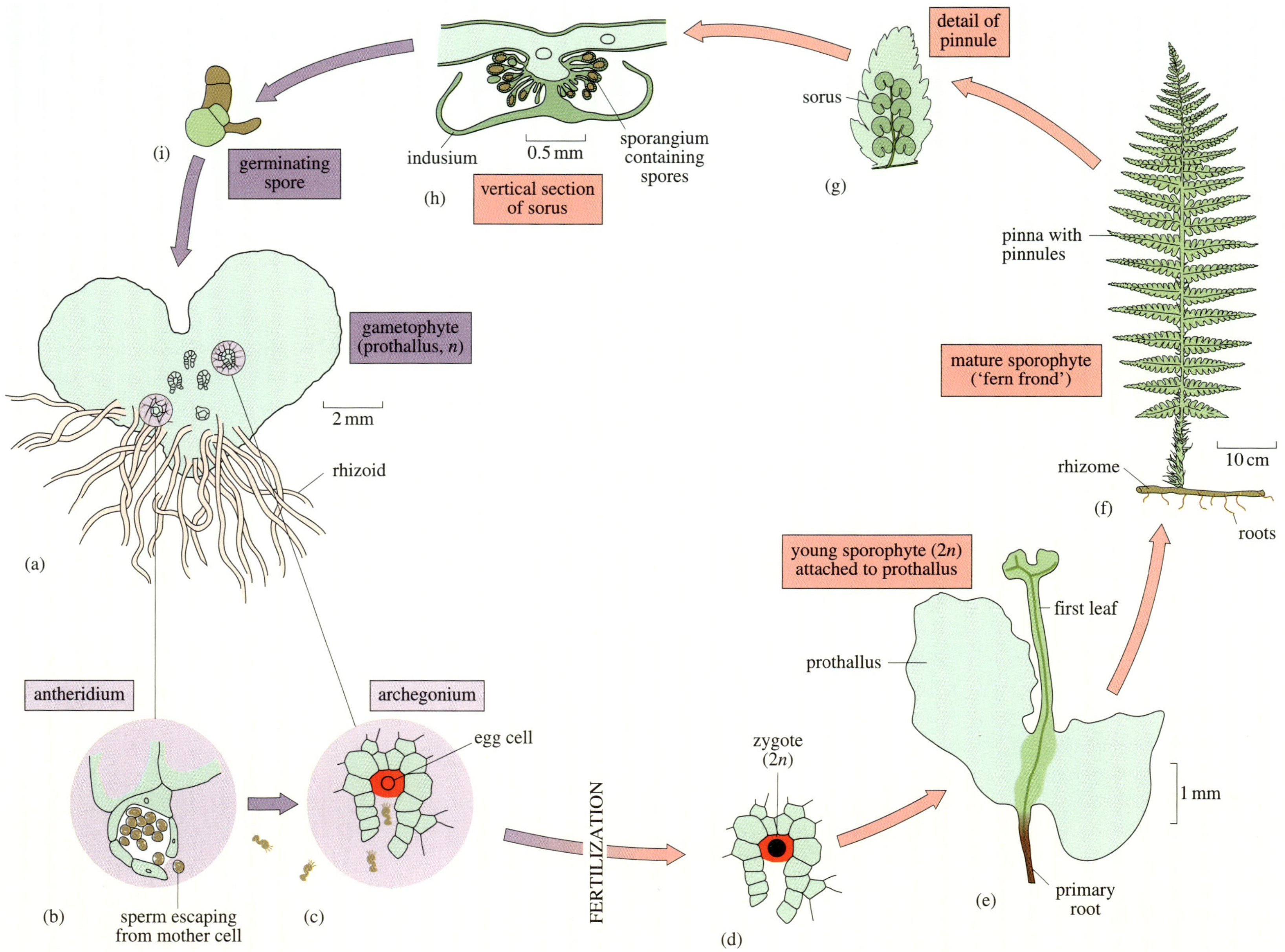

Figure 1.14 Life cycle of the male fern, *Dryopteris filix-mas*: (a) the gametophyte (prothallus); (b) antheridium deep in the prothallus; (c) an archegonium; (d) a zygote within an archegonium; (e) a young sporophyte attached to a prothallus; (f) a fully grown sporophyte plant with rhizome, roots and leafy frond; (g) sori (spore-producing structures) on the underside of a frond, seen in vertical section in (h); (i) germinataing spore.

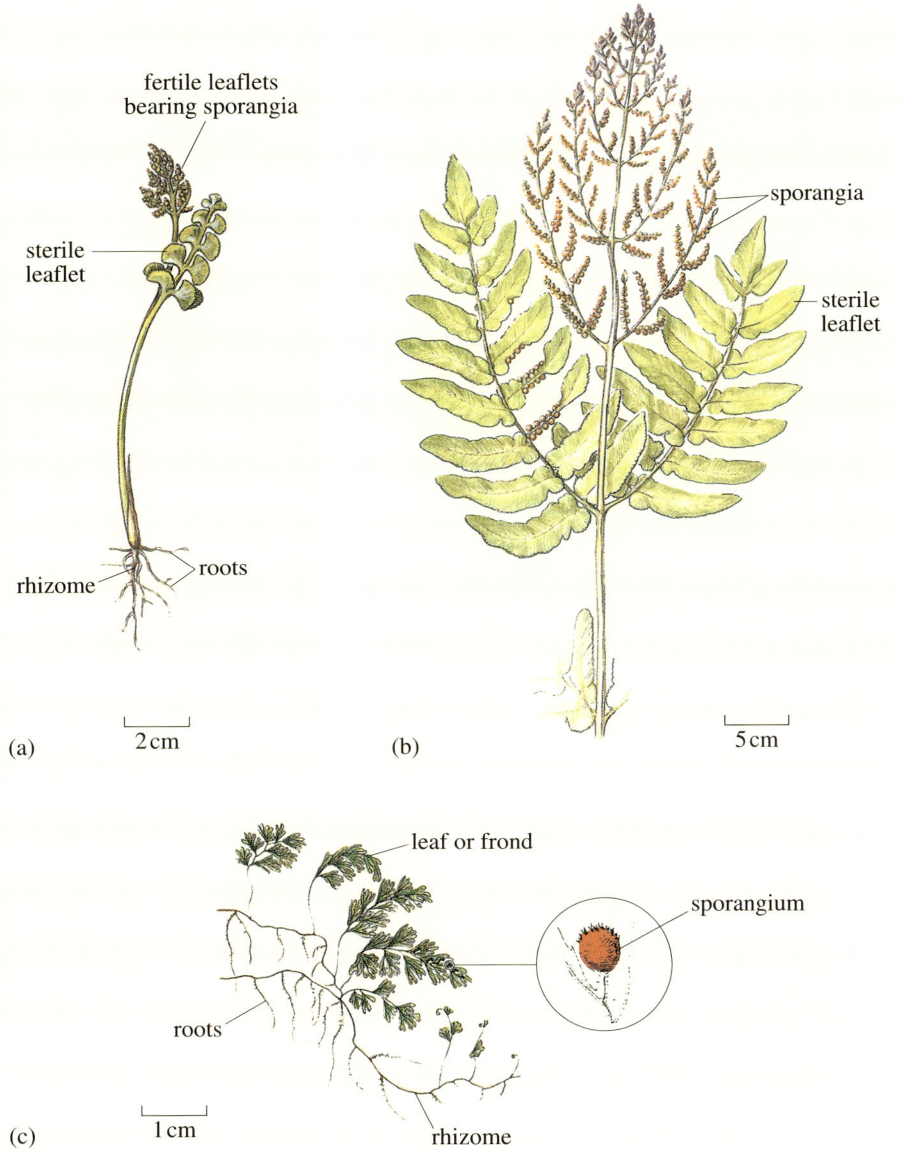

Figure 1.15 Spore-bearing structures in ferns: (a) moonwort (*Botrychium lunaria*), where sporangia develop on a special part of the leaf; (b) royal fern (*Osmunda regalis*), with sporangia on special leaflets; (c) Tunbridge filmy fern (*Hymenophyllum tunbridgense*), a delicate species with sporangia on the edges of fronds.

The thick-walled fern spores are resistant to desiccation, and are usually released violently into dry air as illustrated in Figure 1.16b and c. When spores germinate, an apical cell cuts off new cells on three sides (unlike a moss protonema) so that a three-dimensional prothallus is formed immediately.

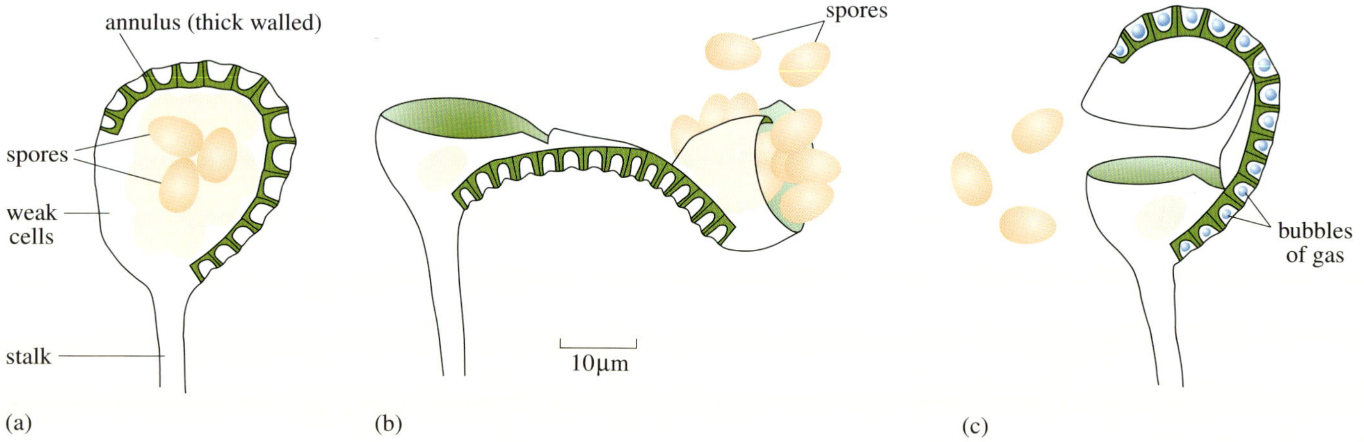

Figure 1.16 Spore release from the sporangium of a fern such as *Dryopteris*. (a) Immature sporangium containing spores; the outer ring of cells has unevenly thickened walls (the annulus). (b) As the annulus dries out, it creates tension across the sporangium, causing it to split at an unthickened region and straighten out the annulus, causing some spores to be flung out. (c) The remaining spores are discharged when tension in the annulus reaches a critical point and gas bubbles form; this releases tension so that the upper part of the sporangium flips back to its original position.

❍ Now check your understanding of the fern life cycle by filling in the blank boxes A–C in Figure 1.17. (Answers are on p. 52.)

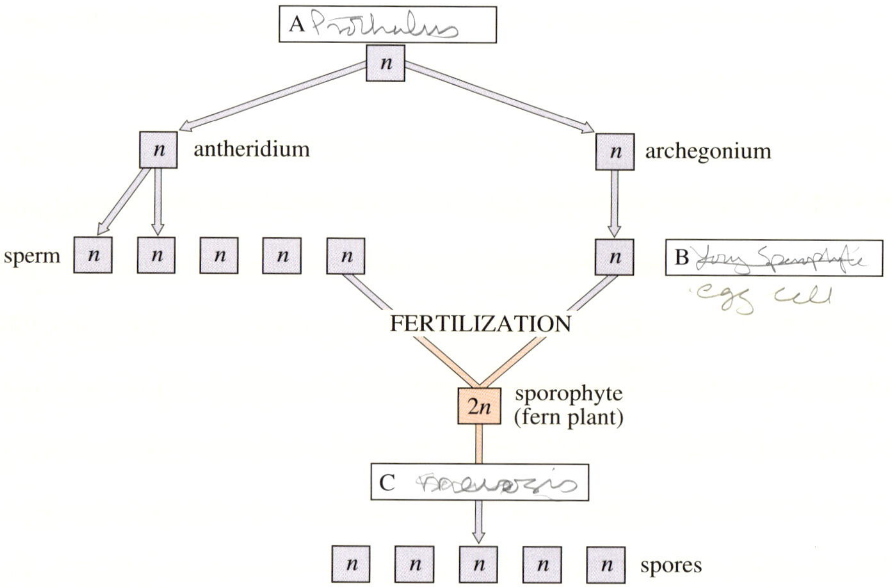

Figure 1.17 Summary of mitotic events (in antheridia and archegonia) and meiotic events (in sporangia) of ferns.

Many fern sporophytes grow and reproduce in dry habitats. But films of dew or rainwater are necessary to facilitate sperm transfer at the stage when antheridia are mature and releasing male gametes. Not surprisingly then, many temperate-zone ferns produce their sporangia in late summer, whereas the prothallus is a winter phase which is more likely to survive and so reproduce, despite its relative delicacy, in cooler, wetter winter conditions. Nevertheless, there is much wastage, as a considerable density of prothalli and sperm is necessary to ensure adequate fertilization of the available archegonia and consequent development of sporophytes.

One last issue: it is a moot point why mosses, which have been around for a very long time, have not diversified to produce large and complex forms. A possible reason is that a diploid genome can act as a buffer against unhelpful mutations, which nevertheless remain in the gene pool, and may consequently be available. When further modified in a different environment, they may produce a beneficial product. A haploid genome might be unable to retain a less favourable allele, as seems to be the case in bacteria. An alternative, and probably more plausible, explanation is that small and simple plants like mosses, whether haploid or diploid, may always have had a great selective advantage in certain micro-habitats.

1.3.3 Comparing life cycles of ferns and mosses

Although both mosses and ferns show alternation of generations, the most striking difference in their life cycles is that the dominant 'plant' generation of mosses is a leafy gametophyte, whereas for the ferns it is a leafy sporophyte. Here is the prime reason why bryophytes (mosses, liverworts and hornworts) are separated from vascular plants (the rest of the plant kingdom).

The gametophyte generations of mosses and ferns may look different but they bear similar-looking antheridia and archegonia, which produce similar products — that is, motile sperm and static egg cells. Moss and fern sporophytes also look very different, and have different survival mechanisms, but again the sporangial apparatus (capsules versus sori), though distinctly different morphologically, produces haploid spores following meiosis. To some extent, both groups are dependent on moisture (more precisely lack of it) for spore dispersal, although the more robust and thicker-walled spores of ferns can survive longer than moss spores in dry conditions.

In addition to these life-cycle strategies, the clumped growth habit of moss gametophytes conserves water, and mosses are usually able to revive after drying out. The thin texture of most fern gametophytes and their inability to survive drying out makes them more vulnerable, so they tend to establish and reproduce in moister habitats. Moss sporophytes are dependent on the gametophyte generation throughout their life, and due to the reduced amount of tissue and the presence of a rudimentary cuticle, they are not highly vulnerable in dry conditions. By contrast, fern sporophytes are dependent on the gametophyte for a very short time; they are often relatively massive and leafy but, because leaves have a waxy cuticle, tissue water loss is even less of a problem. Nevertheless, many ferns grow optimally in shady habitats where spores, once released, can give rise to gametophytes in less stressful conditions.

The details of the life cycles of typical mosses and ferns have introduced a series of new scientific terms. However, the most critical outcome of studying these cycles is not remembering the exact detail of the reproductive structures, but understanding why particular features of the cycle may have led to success in colonizing the terrestrial environment.

1.3.4 HETEROSPORY: THE NEXT STEP

In all the bryophytes and ferns considered so far, the spores look identical: the plants are described as **homosporous** and show **homospory** (Greek *homos*, same). However, in two orders of ferns and two families of **lycophytes** (phylum Lycophyta) there are two different kinds of spores; that is, they are **heterosporous** (Greek *heteros*, other, different). **Heterospory** evolved independently in ferns and lycophytes, and also in seed plants, all of which show this character. It is regarded as a crucial step in the evolution of a life cycle that is independent of free water. We describe here a heterosporous life cycle in a lycophyte, the **club moss** *Selaginella*, because it helps in understanding the more extreme form of heterospory found in seed plants (Section 1.4).

A club moss life cycle has been chosen to illustrate heterospory because, paradoxically, the heterosporous ferns (Marsileales and Salviniales) are all aquatic. Pillwort (*Pilularia globulifera*, Marsileales) is a rare British fern found in and round the edges of acid lakes, and the water ferns *Azolla* and *Salvinia* (Salviniales) are floating, sub-tropical species, sometimes grown on garden ponds (Figure 1.18). Heterospory in these ferns seems to have evolved as an adaptation to aquatic life and there are special features of the life cycles related to this habitat. In *Selaginella* and seed plants, by contrast, heterospory is seen as an adaptation to life on land.

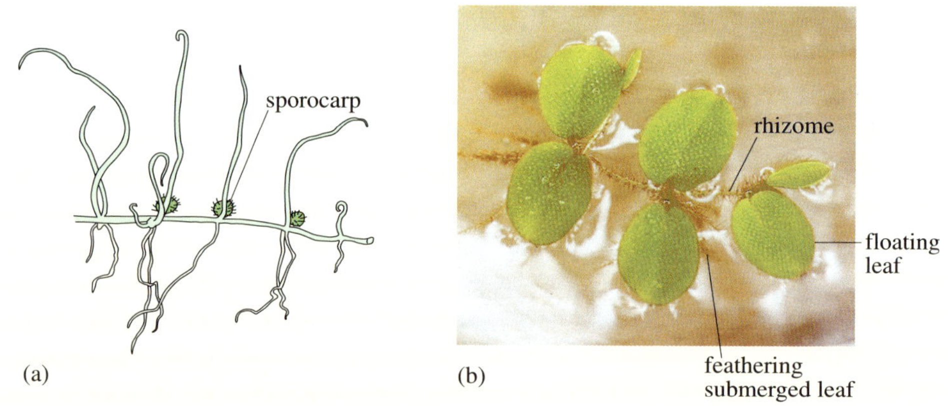

Figure 1.18 Aquatic, heterosporous ferns: (a) *Pilularia* sp. (pillwort); (b) *Salvinia*.

From Figure 1.3 you can see that lycophytes are thought to have evolved in parallel with ferns, and are related to the tree lycopods, which were much more diverse and frequent in the Carboniferous and Permian Periods more than 250 Ma ago. As in ferns, the sporophyte generation of lycophytes is dominant.

Selaginella spp. grow mainly in the tropics but *Selaginella selaginoides* (lesser club moss, Figure 1.19a) is a native British species found in damp mountain grasslands. It looks like a rather stout moss, and produces spores in cones or *strobili* (singular, *strobilus*) in the bases of leaves. The two types of spore are produced in separate sporangia on the same cone: many small **microspores** in microsporangia, and, depending on species, between one and twelve, very large (up to 1 mm) **megaspores** in megasporangia (Figure 1.19b). Spores are shed at the same time and close to the parent plant, so there is a good chance that microspores and megaspores land close together. The gametophytes start to develop *within the spore walls* even before spores are shed.

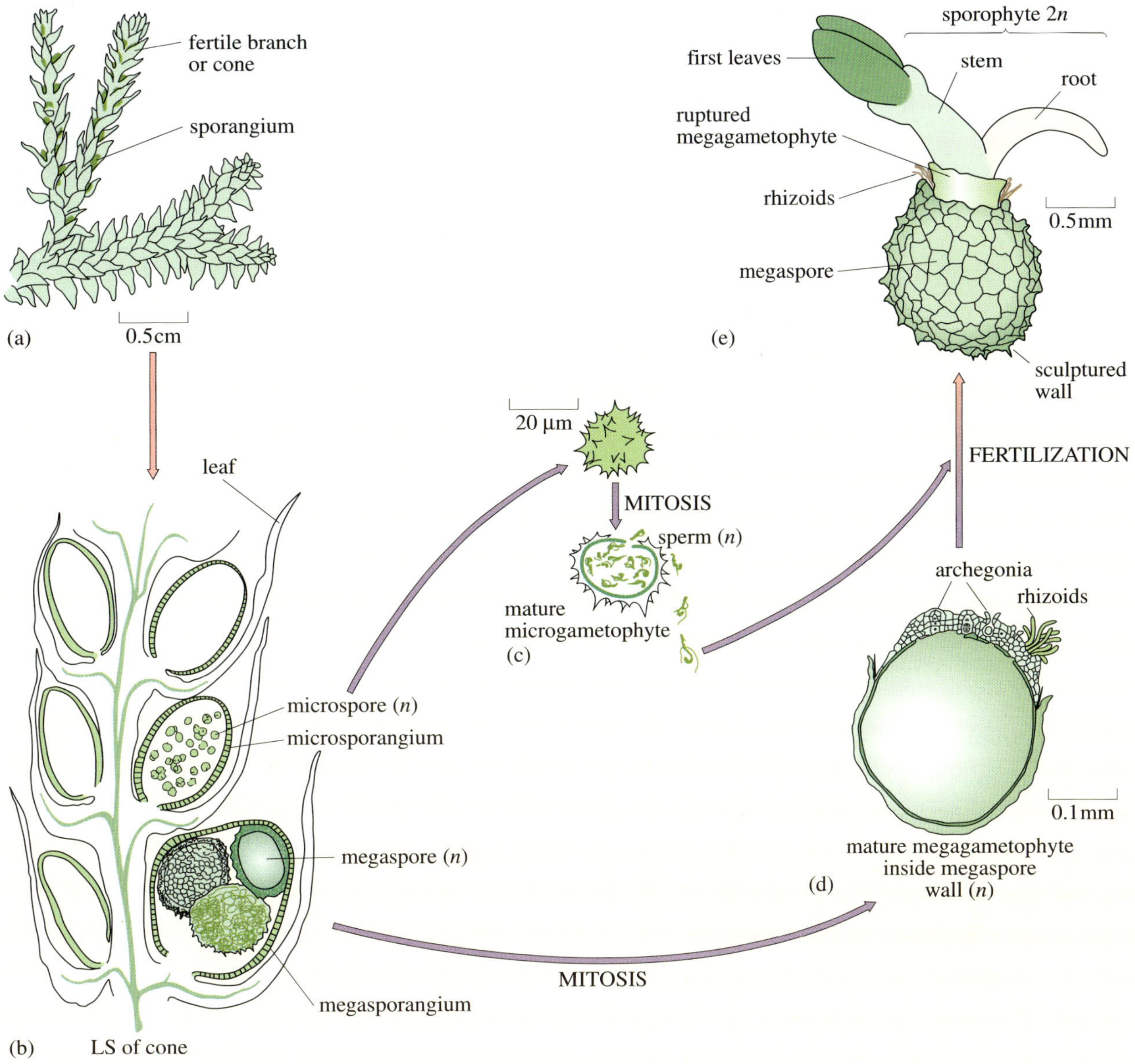

Figure 1.19 Life cycle of a typical *Selaginella*. (a) Mature sporophyte bearing fertile branches or cones. (b) Vertical section through a cone (enlarged) showing micro- and megasporangia containing microspores and megaspores, respectively. (c) A microspore and its development within the ruptured microspore wall to a microgametophyte, which releases sperm. (d) LS of a multicelled megagametophyte protruding from the ruptured megaspore wall within which it has developed. (e) A young sporophyte growing from the megagametophyte still within the megaspore wall.

❍ From Figure 1.19d, describe what happens to the megaspore.

● Cell division occurs within the thick spore wall, which eventually splits so that the megagametophyte protrudes. There are archegonia (containing egg cells), and rhizoids on the protruding surface. (The rest of the megagametophyte comprises food storage tissue, which may be only partially divided up into cells, the rest being acellular.)

The mature microgametophyte (Figure 1.19c) formed within microspores consists of only a single vegetative cell and the antheridium, which produces many motile male gametes. These sperm require a film of water to swim towards female gametophytes. After fertilization, the diploid sporophyte embryo develops within the megagametophyte, still within the megaspore wall and dependent on stored food reserves (Figure 1.19e).

In *Selaginella*, therefore, free water is still required for sperm to reach egg cells, but neither the 'female' megagametophyte nor the 'male' microgametophyte is ever truly independent: they are always retained within spore walls and depend on food reserves in the spores. You will see (Section 1.4) that in seed plants the female megaspores are never actually released from the megasporangium, and the male microgametophytes release gametes so close to the egg cell that no free water is required for fertilization.

❍ Why is a free-living gametophyte potentially wasteful?

● Because many do not survive to form gametes which can unite to form zygotes that develop into the next diploid generation.

Retaining the food-storing megaspores on the parent plant minimizes this waste. In the same way the massive number of male gametes which need to be produced to ensure fertilization of the available egg cells is wasteful. But the modified fertilization mechanisms of seed plants reduce even this wastage.

SUMMARY OF SECTION 1.3

1 In bryophytes the dominant generation is the haploid gametophyte, whereas in ferns and all other vascular plants it is the diploid sporophyte.

2 In mosses, flask-like archegonia and club-shaped antheridia on the leafy gametophyte produce, respectively, egg cells and motile sperm. After fertilization, the zygote develops into a sporophyte, which remains attached to, and dependent on, the gametophyte; it consists of a rooting base, stem and capsule. Meiosis in the capsule results in formation of haploid spores, which are released into the air and germinate to give a flat, delicate protonema (with cell division in only one plane) from which the gametophyte develops (with cell division in two planes).

3 In most ferns, similar archegonia and antheridia, with egg cells and motile sperm, are formed within a delicate green prothallus, from which the sporophyte develops after fertilization. The sporophyte is soon independent. Spores are produced within sporangia grouped into sori on leaves, and after release develop into prothalli.

4 Some ferns (all aquatic types) and some lycophytes (e.g. *Selaginella*) are heterosporous, and the gametophyte generation is reduced. Separate micro- (male) and mega- (female) gametophytes develop within, respectively, micro- and megaspores, which are released from, respectively, micro- and megasporangia. When spore walls rupture, the minute male gametophyte, comprising a vegetative cell and an antheridium, releases sperm, which swim to the archegonia exposed on the relatively massive, food-storing female gametophyte.

5 Bryophytes, ferns and all other seedless vascular plants depend on free water for fertilization in the gametophyte, but air currents plus gravity disperse the haploid spores. Water loss from specialized cells is the trigger for spore release in mosses and ferns.

6 Fern sporophytes are better adapted to life on land than mosses, by virtue of their waterproof cuticle, vascular tissue and roots. The clumping habit of many mosses contributes to water retention, and mosses may also be revived after drying out.

1.4 Life cycles in seed plants

The most complete adaptation to life on land is found among **seed plants** — gymnosperms and flowering plants (or angiosperms, which first appear in the fossil records of the early Cretaceous Period, that is 120–40 Ma ago). Like ferns the 'plant' in both these groups is a sporophyte. However, unlike modern ferns, the sporophyte of seed plants may develop into a massive woody structure (trees), and is always heterosporous. Furthermore, the sporangia that produce male (micro-) and female (mega-) spores are borne in separate structures and are different in appearance. The male spores, within which a microgametophyte develops, are released as **pollen** grains, but the female spores are *retained on the parent sporophyte*, a key difference from seedless vascular plants. How this difference removes the need for free water for fertilization and leads to the evolution of seeds — structures in which the embryo is protected and dispersed — is described here for flowering plants (Section 1.4.1); comparisons with gymnosperm life cycles are discussed briefly in Section 1.4.2.

1.4.1 Angiosperms

The flowering plants, or **angiosperms**, are by far the most taxonomically diverse and widespread of all plant phyla. They include almost all our important food plants, have a worldwide distribution and, in addition, show enormous diversity of form and habitat. Their structure and physiology have undoubtedly contributed to this evolutionary success, and are discussed later in this and other chapters, but their life cycle, our main concern here, has also been an important factor. The sporophyte structure that produces the spores in which gametophytes and gametes develop is the **flower**.

Flower structure

Angiosperm flowers, which are often located at the tips of shoots, typically consist of four whorls of modified leaves (Figure 1.20a): outer **sepals** (usually greenish), which protect the flower in bud; **petals** (which may be brightly coloured); **stamens**, collectively called the *androecium* (meaning 'house of man'), which contain microsporangia in which pollen develops; and **carpels**, which are often fused and collectively called the **gynoecium** (meaning 'house of woman), which contain the megasporangia (Figure 1.20a). In effect, the flower is equivalent to a greatly modified cone of *Selaginella* (Figure 1.19b).

Stamens usually consist of a stalk, called a *filament,* and a terminal swollen **anther** (Figure 1.20a), which, when ripe, holds pollen. Pollen is one of the main causes of 'hay fever', an allergic reaction. The two carpels are partially fused in the

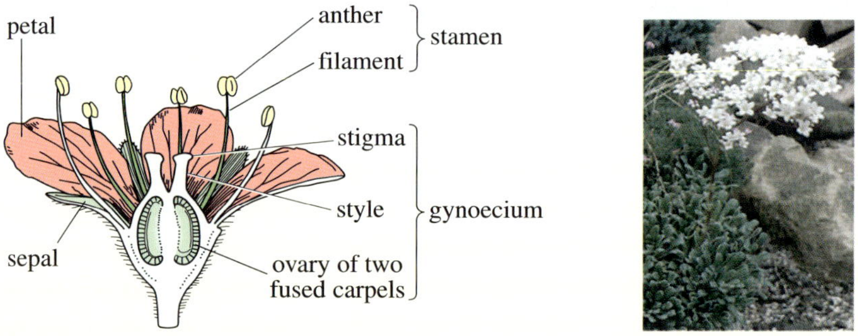

(a) (b)

Figure 1.20 (a) The anatomy of a bisexual saxifrage flower, *Saxifraga* sp. in median longitudinal section; (b) group of white saxifrage flowers.

gynoecium, and there are two receptive surfaces, the **stigmas**, each of which receives pollen and is attached by a stalk (the **style**) to the single **ovary**. Inside the ovary are the **ovules**, within which megaspores form, and a single megaspore in each ovule develops into a female gametophyte within which is a single egg cell. Details of this development are described later, but note that at no stage are megaspores released from the parent sporophyte. There is great variation in gynoecium structure, depending on the degree of fusion between carpels; they range from many free carpels, each with an ovary, style and stigma, to ones where ovaries are fused but styles and stigmas remain separate (as in Figure 1.20a), to those where fusion is complete and the only indication of carpel number is the number of chambers in the ovary. Such differences, together with differences in the numbers of sepals, petals and stamens are important in the classification of angiosperms.

To effect fertilization, pollen must be deposited on a stigma. After its release from anthers, pollen is dispersed by diverse mechanisms: wind, insects, birds, bats or water.

❍ What purpose do highly coloured and/or scented flower parts serve, and how and why have they evolved?

● They attract insects and other animals, which transfer pollen from anthers to stigma, often between flowers on different plants. The organs and mechanisms have coevolved with the animals that feed on flowers (Dyson, 2001).

❍ What other attractant features are there?

● Production of nectar and the presence of guides, leading to the nectaries.

Not surprisingly, most wind-pollinated plants have relatively small green-coloured floral parts, and rarely produce scent; grasses (Poaceae) are an obvious example. The majority of flowering plants are *bisexual*, however, and no matter what the pollinating mechanism, there is always some possibility that pollen will be deposited on the stigma of the same flower (or of a flower on the same plant); that is, there will be self-fertilization and hence inbreeding can occur. A great many mechanisms have evolved that regulate the degree of inbreeding. For example, plants may be **monoecious**; that is, the flowers are single sex (unisexual), but both male and female flowers occur on the same plant and usually mature at different times.

❍ Going one step further, what kind of system would completely rule out self-pollination and inbreeding?

● Having unisexual flowers on *different* plants.

Such plants are described as **dioecious**, and are fairly common in certain families, including willows (Salicaceae, Figure 1.21), the spring woodlander dog's mercury (*Mercurialis perennis*, Euphorbiaceae) and hops (*Humulus lupulus*, Cannabiaceae).

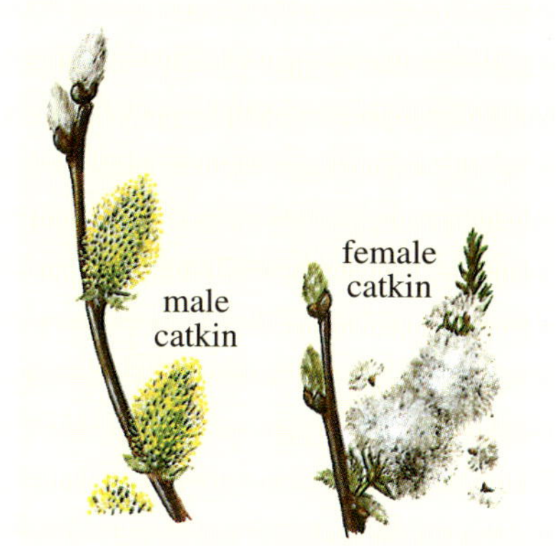

Figure 1.21 Unisexual groups of flowers (catkins) with either male (left) or female (right) flowers of goat willow (*Salix caprea*), Salicaceae, a family in which all species are dioecious.

THE DEVELOPMENT OF POLLEN AND EGG CELLS

So far, you know that in flowering plants the egg cells derive from ovules, and the male gametes from pollen, but the steps leading to the formation of these gametes are drastically condensed and telescoped compared with the process in heterosporous *Selaginella*. Different names are given to the structures involved, but remembering their names is less important than understanding their function, and how the structures contribute to a form of sexual reproduction that is much better suited to life on land than is that of non-seed plants.

Figure 1.22 summarizes the process of pollen formation and maturation. Within anthers (Figure 1.22a), four pollen sacs develop (Figure 1.22b), each equivalent to a microsporangium (cf. Figure 1.19b). The mother cells in each pollen sac

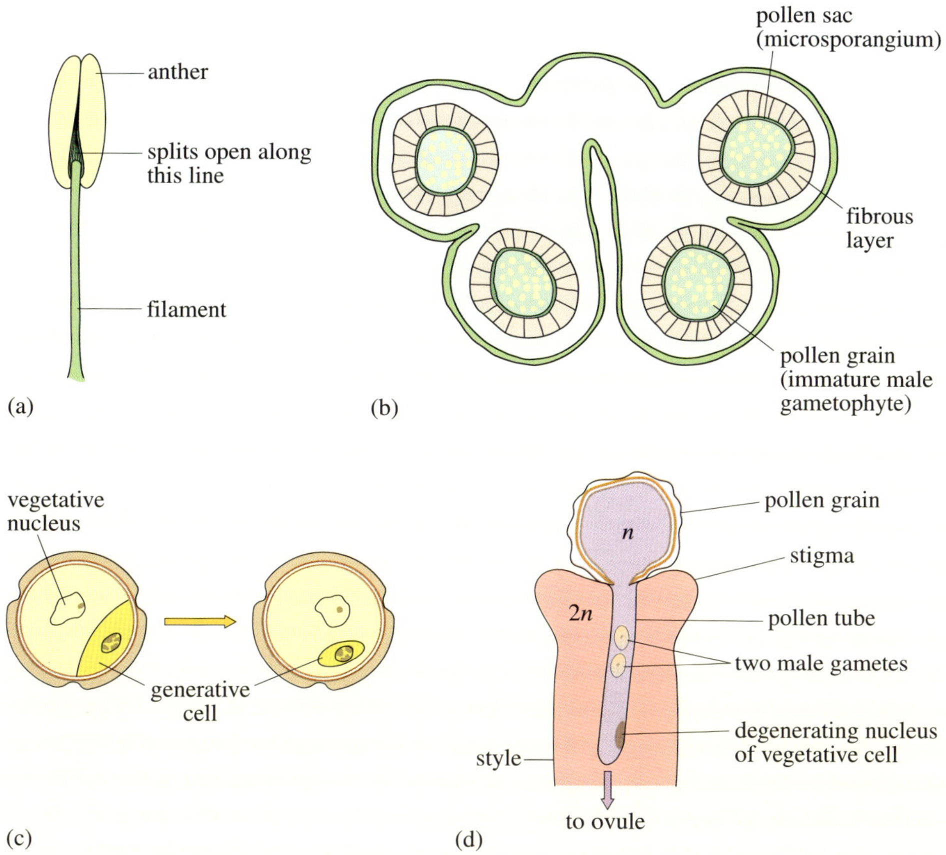

Figure 1.22 Male floral organs and pollen: (a) anther on filament; (b) section through an anther showing four pollen sacs; (c) maturing pollen grains showing progressing development of vegetative and generative cells within a thick wall; (d) germinating pollen grain (haploid) on a stigma (diploid).

divide by meiosis, forming tetrads of microspores, each of which matures to form a pollen grain. A pollen grain develops a thick, two-layered wall, and its nucleus divides giving a large vegetative cell and a smaller generative cell (Figure 1.22c); pollen grains are usually shed in this state.

- ❍ So what *is* a pollen grain when shed?
- ● Because cell division has occurred (albeit inside the spore wall), it is a gametophyte; but since gametes have not formed, pollen is best described as an immature gametophyte.

Once pollen lands on a receptive and compatible stigma, it germinates, producing a pollen tube, which penetrates the stigma and grows down the style (Figure 1.22d). At this stage the vegetative and generative cells of the pollen grain migrate into the pollen tube, and the latter divides to give two 'sperm cells' — two male gametes — each consisting only of nucleus and cytoplasm; the vegetative cell then degenerates. The three cells of a germinated pollen grain are equivalent to the mature male gametophyte whose growth requirements are supplied from the style.

Development of the mature egg cell and surrounding nutritive and protective tissues is fairly complex (Figure 1.23). Initially, part of the ovule called the *nucellus* becomes surrounded by two protective cell layers 'the integuments', and is equivalent to a megasporangium (cf. Figure 1.19b). One large cell in the nucellus divides by meiosis to give four cells (megaspores), three of which abort. The remaining megaspore then undergoes further nuclear divisions and enlarges to form the female gametophyte, which is called the **embryo sac**.

The embryo sac nucleus divides three times producing first two, then four and eight nuclei, four at each end.

Two nuclei migrate to the centre and become surrounded by a membrane to form a binucleate cell. Membranes also form round the other nuclei, and the three that lie adjacent to the micropyle (a hole in the wall at one end of the nucellus) become the egg cell and two 'accessory cells' (Figure 1.23 right).

- ❍ Describe the embryo sac at this last stage.
- ● It is a mature female gametophyte comprising seven cells, one of them the egg cell, and eight nuclei.

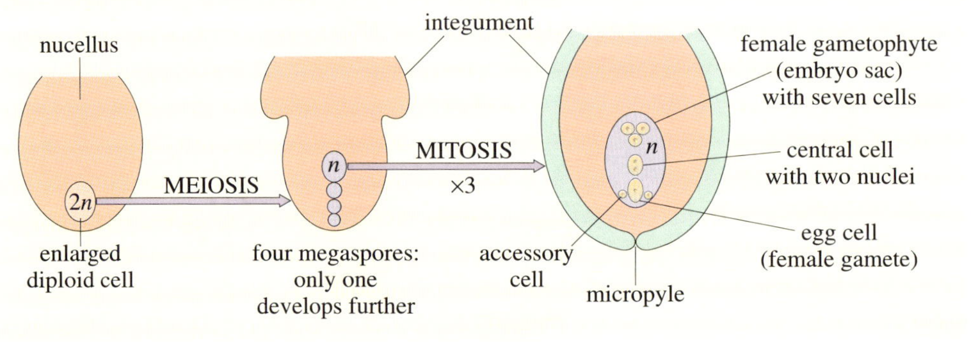

Figure 1.23 Development of the ovule. Part of the ovule (nucellus) containing the megaspore mother cell (left). Formation of four megaspores after meiosis and growth of protective layers or integuments (middle). After three nuclear divisions in one megaspore, a mature embryo sac forms (right), with seven cells and eight nuclei and surrounded by the nucellus and integuments.

FERTILIZATION AND SEED DEVELOPMENT

After the pollen tube grows down the style (Figure 1.22d), it enters the ovule via the micropyle, and then penetrates the embryo sac. Finally, after entering one of the accessory cells, the tip of the pollen tube disintegrates releasing the sperm cells. One sperm cell migrates to the egg cell, losing its plasma membrane and cytoplasm on the way, and the nuclei of sperm and egg cell fuse. The second sperm cell then migrates from the accessory cell (Figure 1.24a) and fuses with the binucleate central cell to form a triploid ($3n$) cell (Figure 1.24b), which divides repeatedly without forming cell walls (Figure 1.24c). Walls are laid down once nuclear division is complete, and the tissue formed (**endosperm**) stores food, which is later used as a nutritional resource for the developing embryo. In some plants, for example grasses, which include all cereal crops, food-storing endosperm is retained in the mature seed, and supports early seedling growth. Because both sperm nuclei are involved in fusion, the whole process is described as **double fertilization**; it is a distinctive feature of angiosperms.

The zygote divides many times forming both the embryo and a stalk-like suspensor, whose growth pushes the embryo deep into the endosperm (Figure 1.24c and d). The embryo has a rudimentary root, shoot and one or two seed leaves (**cotyledons**), which may store food (Figure 1.24e). The ovule develops into a **seed**, which protects and accumulates food stores for the embryo. The two thin integument layers expand and toughen to form a seed coat or **testa** (Figure 1.24f), and the ovary wall develops into a **fruit**, usually enclosing several seeds and often modified to aid in seed dispersal.

Figure 1.24 Seed development starting (a) with double fertilization, and showing endosperm formation and three stages of seed development (globular, heart- and torpedo-shape stages) until a mature seed is formed (f).

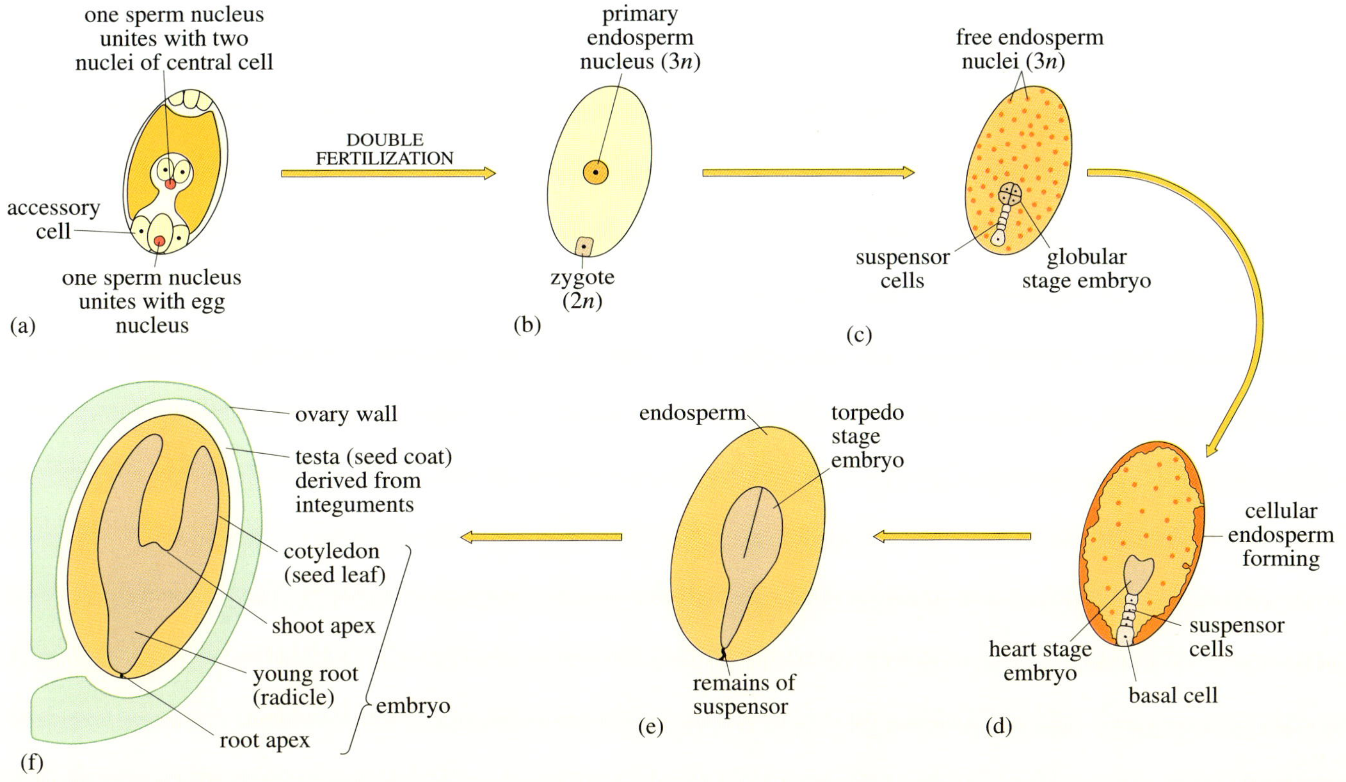

❍ To check your understanding of the angiosperm life cycle and the links with simple heterosporous cycles (as in *Selaginella*), complete Table 1.1. (Answers on p. 52.)

Table 1.1 Checklist of structures involved in sexual reproduction in angiosperms and their equivalent in *Selaginella* (a heterosporous non-seed plant). Complete the blank cells.

	Angiosperms	Equivalent in *Selaginella**
Male	pollen sac	
	products of meiosis in pollen sac	
	pollen when shed	
	germinating pollen	
	products of division of the generative cell	
Female	ovule	
	nucellus	
	embryo sac	
	seed	

* If no equivalent, give a definition of the angiosperm structure.

1.4.2 Comparisons with gymnosperms: why are angiosperms so successful?

Although they are also seed plants, gymnosperms are far less abundant and diverse than angiosperms (Figure 1.3). Here we analyse some of the reasons for the evolutionary success of angiosperms by comparing the two groups.

Firstly, although they have pollen and ovules, gymnosperms *do not form flowers*. Instead they have male and female cones with no petals or sepals, and pollination is nearly always by wind (possible exceptions being cycads, Cycadophyta, and some gnetophytes, where insects are thought to transfer some pollen). Pollination is usually less ‘chancy’ in angiosperms when it involves animal vectors rather than wind currents.

❍ Why are flowers essential for animal (mostly insect) pollination?

● Flowers attract vectors by their scent, colour and rewards in the form of nectar or pollen (Section 1.4.1).

The coevolution of flowers and their pollen vectors has also led to much specialization, so that only certain types of vector are attracted; some examples are shown in Figure 1.25. Such specialization has meant that angiosperms are able to conserve resources by producing relatively less pollen. So the evolution of flowers, and increasingly close links with specialized pollinators, are part of the explanation for angiosperm success.

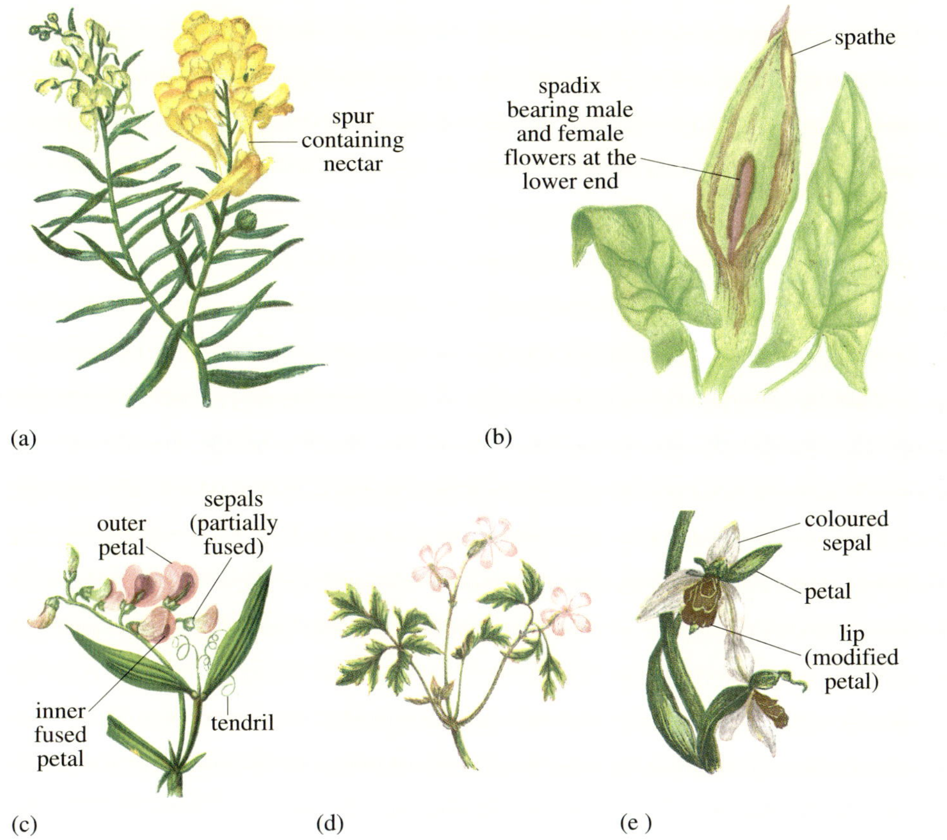

Figure 1.25 Flower structures associated with specialized pollination mechanisms. (a) Toadflax, *Linaria vulgaris*. (b) Wild arum, *Arum maculatum*, which is pollinated by small flies attracted by a smell of rotting carrion; flies crawl into the lower part of the flower, where they pollinate female flowers borne on the central axis or *spadix* and remain, trapped by down-pointing hairs, until pollen ripens in male flowers; flies are released after being dusted with pollen. (c) A wild pea, *Lathyrus* sp. (d) Herb Robert, *Geranium robertianum*, an open flower in which coloured petals have insect guide lines. (e) Bee orchid, *Ophrys apifera*, which, in some parts of Europe is pollinated by male bees that attempt to copulate with the bee-like flower; in the UK self-pollination is the norm.

Another difference between angiosperms and gymnosperms arises during *fertilization and seed development*. Only one nuclear fusion occurs in most gymnosperms (i.e. they do not have double fertilization), so triploid endosperm tissue does not form, and the developing embryo depends for nutrients on the female gametophyte. Furthermore, the gymnosperm seed is not protected within an ovary, but lies on a special scale leaf (gymnosperm means 'naked seed'), and there is no equivalent of the angiosperm fruit.

Seed dispersal mechanisms for angiosperms are also more diverse than for gymnosperms, and may lead to wider dispersion away from the parent plant. Wind dispersal in gymnosperms nearly always involves simple, winged seeds (as in *Pinus sylvestris*, Scots pine), but, in angiosperms, more complex wings and parachutes occur (as in dandelions, *Taraxacum* spp.). Some gymnosperm seeds are surrounded by fleshy scales (e.g. juniper *Juniperus* spp.) and carried off by animals, but angiosperms have a greater variety of mechanisms that aid animal dispersal, including burrs and other sticky appendages which attach seeds to the coats of passing animals. Dispersal by water is another mechanism available to angiosperms; even if seeds are heavy (e.g. coconuts, *Cocos nucifera*), they are always buoyant.

In sum, the success of angiosperms depends not only on the evolution of reproductive mechanisms which are independent of water but also on their more effective strategies that not only increase the chance of fertilization, but also protect, nourish and disperse seeds. However, reproductive strategies do not provide the whole explanation for successful colonization of the land habitat; the anatomical structure of organs and tissues and their physiology is equally important. The former is examined in the rest of this chapter, and the latter in later chapters of this book.

SUMMARY OF SECTION 1.4

1. The reproductive systems of seed plants, especially flowering plants, are the most perfectly adapted of all vascular plants to life on land. Adaptations include retention and reduction of the gametophyte generation, more effective fertilization mechanisms, the evolution of seeds, and also mechanisms and structures assisting in seed dispersal.
2. Angiosperm flowers include a number of structures (sepals, petals, stamens and one or more carpels, which collectively form a gynoecium), some of which may be highly coloured and which originate from modified leaves.
3. The anthers of male stamens produce pollen after meiosis. The nucleus of an initial microspore divides giving a generative and a vegetative cell (immature male gametophyte). Pollen is dispersed at this stage. It matures and germinates on a receptive stigma, producing a pollen tube, which grows down the style, where the generative cell divides to give two male gametes.
4. The female structure (ovule) develops within an ovary in the nucellus tissue. One cell undergoes meiosis to give four megaspores, three of which abort. The remaining megaspore becomes the embryo sac (female gametophyte), within whose wall eight nuclei are produced by mitosis and seven weakly defined cells form — three at each end and two as a binucleate cell in the centre. The central cell of the three, located at the entrance — micropylar end — of the embryo sac, is the egg cell.
5. Double fertilization occurs after the pollen tube penetrates the embryo sac and releases the male gametes. One male gamete fuses with the egg cell, and the zygote develops into an embryo. The second male gamete fuses with the central cell, and the resulting triploid cell divides to give nutritive endosperm tissue.
6. The ovule matures to give a seed, which contains the embryo, food stores and a protective wall (seed coat) formed from the integuments of the ovule. The ovary matures to form a fruit.

7 Flower characteristics such as colour, scent and nectar have arisen by co-evolution with animal (especially insect) pollinators. Wind-pollinated flowers lack these features.

8 Bisexual flowers are the norm but unisexual flowers on the same or different plants occur; the latter (dioecious plants) ensures cross-pollination and outbreeding.

9 The greater diversity and evolutionary success of angiosperms compared with gymnosperms can be related to the following factors: flowers using animal pollinators; double fertilization and endosperm formation; better protected seeds and methods of seed dispersal; greater diversity of morphology (habit) and differences in anatomy.

1.5 Cell structure and function

Green algae (Chlorophyta) — the ancestors of plants — are supported by the buoyancy of a watery environment. Consequently, they do not need additional strengthening materials to keep them afloat in order to maximize the light that they intercept. Water-borne nutrients bathe the tissue, and are absorbed over the surface, so there is no need for specialist absorptive or conducting tissue, even for large multicellular algae like *Chara* (Figure 1.26).

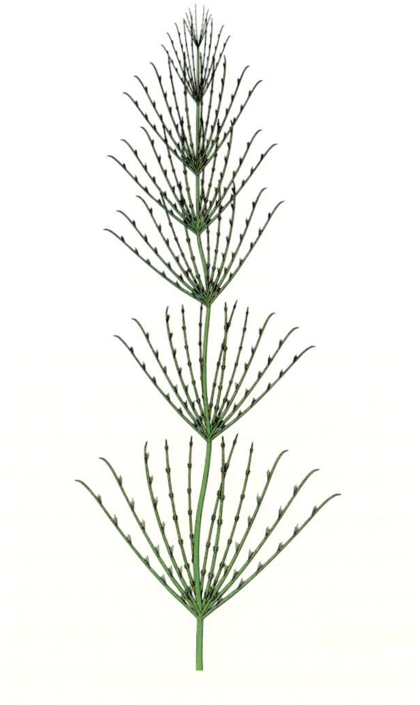

Figure 1.26 *Chara* sp., a multi-cellular green alga found in fresh water.

The sporophytes of all vascular plants (tracheophytes) also have a multicellular three-dimensional structure, which originates in the embryo where terminal cells cut off new cells on several sides. In young cells the walls are usually thin, and they expand in size as a result of water uptake and stretching; this is followed by laying down of additional wall materials.

In Section 1.1 it was suggested that early land plants lay prostrate, colonizing mud banks and the edges of lakes. Furthermore, it is thought that competition for light may have been an important impetus to the evolution of cell types capable of maintaining a beneficial upward growth habit. For very small plants such as mosses, cell turgor (i.e. stiffness; a result of water-filled cells swelling like balloons) and clumping of individuals together may have been adequate to support upright growth, but this mechanism could not have been effective for plants growing to larger sizes. More structural support would have been, and is, necessary. Larger size and upright growth of the **shoot** implies partitioning of metabolic activities to take advantage of local resources, for example nutrients and water from the soil, and light and CO_2 from the atmosphere. Within this context, plant cell types and tissue organization have evolved that provide support, utilize the resources available, and, where necessary, transport both raw materials and products around the plant. So it is clearly not possible to understand plant form and function without knowing something about cell and tissue types and their functions. Specialized cells and tissues have developed in parallel to reproductive strategies for life on land.

However, despite specialization, one type of cell predominates as the basic structural element of all plant tissues; parenchyma (pronounced 'par-en`-ki-ma') cells.

1.5.1 PARENCHYMA

Parenchyma cells, which are illustrated in different views in Figure 1.27a and b, are quite variable in size and shape. The common features are that they are living, so have nuclei and cytoplasm, tend to be orthorhombic to polyhedral in shape, and have thin cellulose walls. Thinness of the cell wall is one reason why they can be deformed by pressure from adjoining tissue (Figure 1.27c). Adjacent cells are linked by pores through the wall called **plasmodesmata** (singular **plasmodesma**; Figure 1.27d), which are lined by a plasma membrane and have a strand of cytoplasm and a tubule of endoplasmic reticulum in the middle. Small molecules usually pass freely through these pores, so their number and disposition can play a key role in cell-to-cell transport and communication. Many parenchymatous cells retain these basic characteristics throughout life. They function partly as ground tissue — that is, for filling or packing — partly for support in non-woody tissue by virtue of their internal pressure (turgor), which provides stiffness, and sometimes as a reservoir of storage materials, for instance starch in potato tubers.

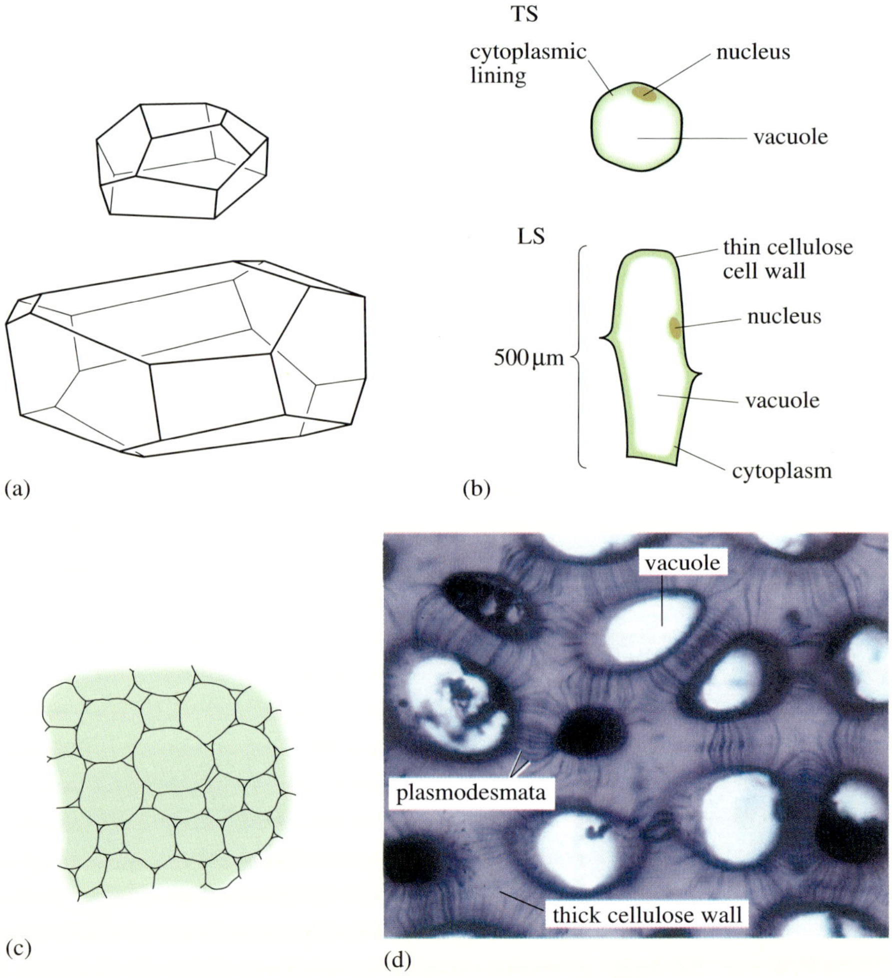

Figure 1.27 (a) Three-dimensional views of different shapes of parenchyma cells; (b) transverse and longitudinal section of a parenchyma cell; (c) TS of parenchyma cells packed together in a tissue; (d) thick-walled parenchyma cells from endosperm tissue, showing plasmodesmata linking adjacent cells.

Cells that can be classified as parenchyma are found in all plants; they form the internal tissues in the gametophyte and sporophyte tissues of bryophytes, for example. However, as you can see from Figure 1.28, the outermost four or five layers of a moss gametophyte stem (and also the seta of sporophytes) may have some extra cellulose wall material.

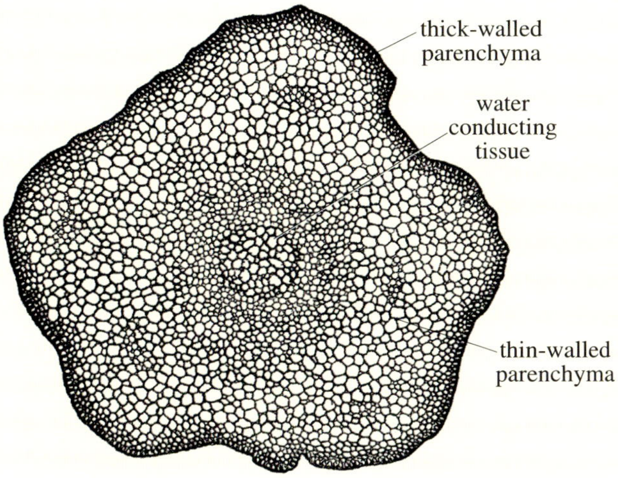

Figure 1.28 Transverse section of the stem of a moss gametophyte (*Polytrichum* sp.), showing peripheral thickened walls as well as unthickened parenchyma internally.

1.5.2 Specialization of living plant cells

Cells with unthickened walls

Four very important examples of cell types where the cell is modified in some way but the cell wall is not are: *storage parenchyma*, *palisade cells*, *phloem* and *transfer cells*.

Storage parenchyma may be packed with reserves such as starch, which forms **starch grains** within chloroplasts or non-green plastids (Figure 1.29).

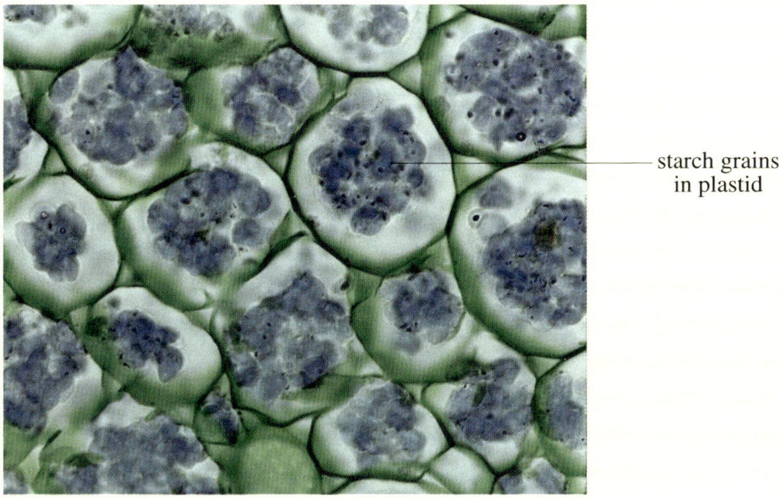

Figure 1.29 Parenchyma cells from potato tubers filled with eccentrically growing starch grains (stained with iodine), which lie within plastids (the organelle that can develop into a chloroplast in the light).

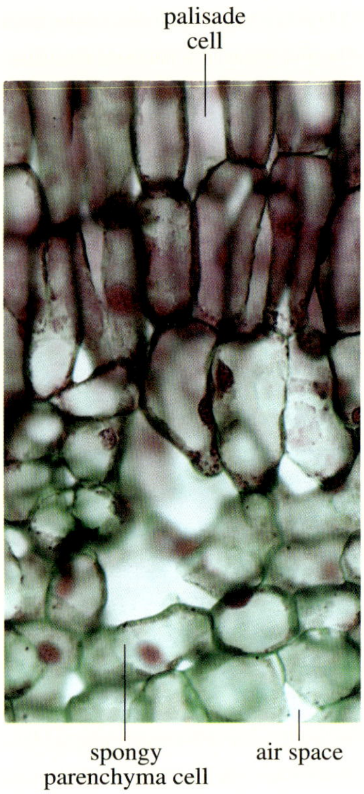

Figure 1.30 Palisade cells from leaves of *Prunus* sp. in vertical section. Note that these cells are thin walled, and approximately four times as long as they are broad.

Palisade cells are found as rows of 'paling-like' cells under the upper surface of angiosperm leaves. These cells are orientated with their long axis at right-angles to the external layer of cells (Figure 1.30), and are densely packed with chloroplasts. They are a major site of photosynthesis (Chapter 2).

Phloem transports photosynthetic products around the plant and is part of the vascular system. It is a tissue rather than a cell type, as it always includes three types of cells, namely standard packing parenchyma, **sieve-tube elements** and **companion cells**, and sometimes fibres (Figure 1.31a). In angiosperms, sieve-

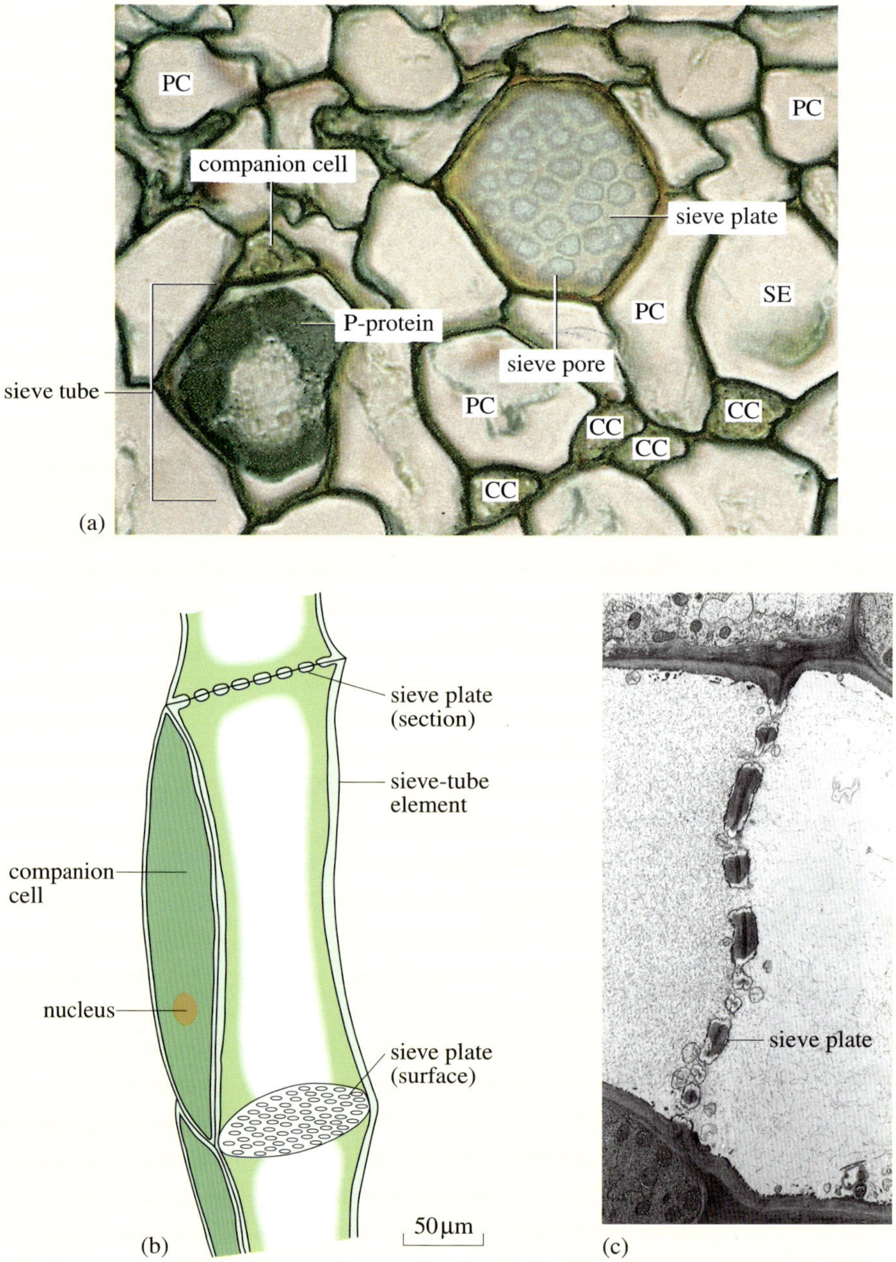

Figure 1.31 (a) Transverse section (light micrograph) of phloem tissue: PC, phloem parenchyma; CC, companion cell; SE, sieve-tube element); (b) longitudinal section (line drawing) of a sieve-tube element and a companion cell. (c) An electron micrograph of a sieve tube in LS at the junction between two sieve-tube elements showing the sieve plate.

tube elements are arranged end to end to form **sieve tubes** and are the actual conduction elements. They do not contain nuclei or organelles at maturity, but the cytoplasm contains large amounts of fibrous P-protein (Chapter 3). The end walls, and sometimes also areas of longitudinal walls separating adjoining sieve tubes, contain clusters of pores through which cytoplasm passes, so giving continuity from cell to cell. These pore zones are referred to as **sieve plates** (Figure 1.31b and c). Companion cells provide the energy requirements of sieve tubes, so it is not surprising that they are rich in mitochondria. They are formed by longitudinal division of a sieve mother cell and are closely aligned to the wall of the relevant sieve tube.

Transfer cells (Figure 1.32) may look like ordinary parenchyma cells under the light microscope. They have an absorptive function, and companion cells are sometimes specialized to function as transfer cells.

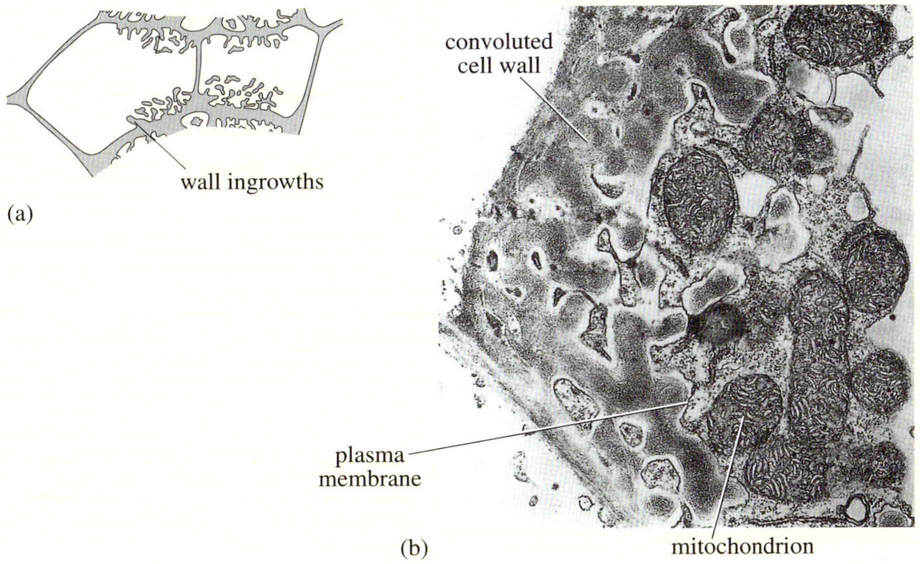

Figure 1.32 (a) Typical transfer cells, showing the convoluted wall ingrowths. (b) An electron micrograph showing a typical convoluted cell wall and plasma membrane of a transfer cell; note the numerous mitochondria.

- From Figure 1.32, what characteristics of transfer cells indicate that they have an absorptive function?

- They have a convoluted wall and plasma membrane, which increases the absorptive surface of the cell (Ridge, 2001[B]).

The functions and operation of phloem and transfer cells are described in detail in Chapter 3.

DIVIDING CELLS: CAMBIUM

Cambium cells (Figure 1.33a and b) look like young small-sized parenchyma, being rectangular in both longitudinal and cross-section. They have thin walls and often look regularly arranged in tiers (Figure 1.33b). These cells are capable of dividing, and are classified as either a primary or secondary meristem. **Apical** and **primary meristems** are located at growing points, and hence are mainly associated with longitudinal growth at root and shoot tips, or at the bases of some leaves (Figure 1.33c and d). Such meristems are formed close behind the apex, and give rise to the first-formed specialized tissues such as parenchyma. **Secondary meristems** are associated with the development of secondary tissue, for instance when a plant organ is expanding in width or forming new protective outer layers such as bark or at the site of wounds. In a transverse section of plant tissue you would normally expect to find a secondary meristem inside the phloem, where new cells are cut off to both the inside and outside of the tissue, and also in the outer cortex, the site of the *cork cambium* (Figure 1.33e). Cell division in the cork cambium give parenchyma cells to the inside and dead, thick-walled **cork** cells to the outside, which give rise to bark. Cork cambium and the cells it produces are collectively called **periderm**. Bark may be interrupted in areas known as lenticels, which act like pores, and have thin-walled, loosely packed cells, which allow air to pass into the tissue.

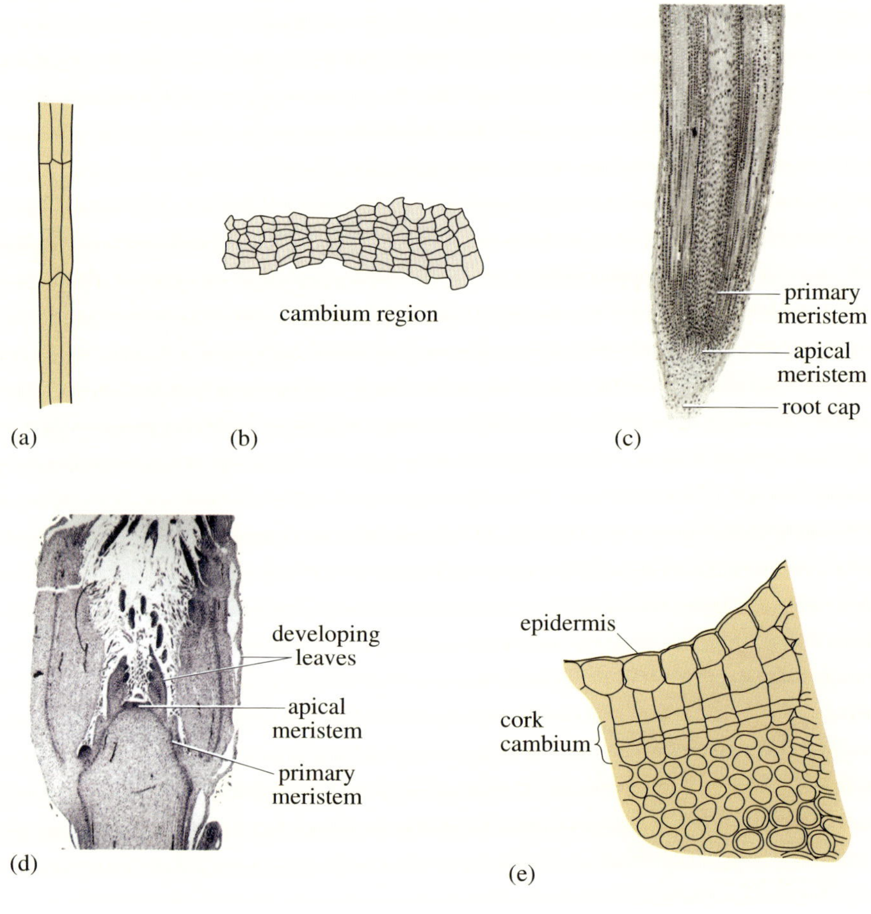

Figure 1.33 Cambium cells in (a) longitudinal and (b) cross-section. (c) Longitudinal section of a root tip, showing the location of the primary and apical meristems. (d) Longitudinal section through a shoot tip, showing the site of the primary meristem. (e) TS through a woody stem, showing the location of the cork cambium just below the epidermis and cutting off cork cells to the outside and thick-walled parenchyma to the inside.

LIVING CELLS WITH THICKENED WALLS

A significant number of cells become specialized by losing their thin-walled parenchymatous characteristics. As in the external layers of mosses (Figure 1.28), cell walls may become thickened with additional **cellulose**. They may also be partially covered with waterproofing substances such as cutin or suberin or by microscopic plates of waxy material. Such cells include *epidermal*, *endodermal* and *hypodermal* (or *exodermal*) cells.

Epidermal cells (Figure 1.34a and b) lie on the outside of roots and shoots in a layer known as the **epidermis**. The outer cell wall is thicker; in shoots, it is covered by a layer of *cutin* forming the **cuticle** (Figure 1.34b and c). Most plants also secrete waxes, which are deposited within and over the shoot cuticle, making it even more waterproof and also giving better protection against insect herbivores (Figure 1.34d).

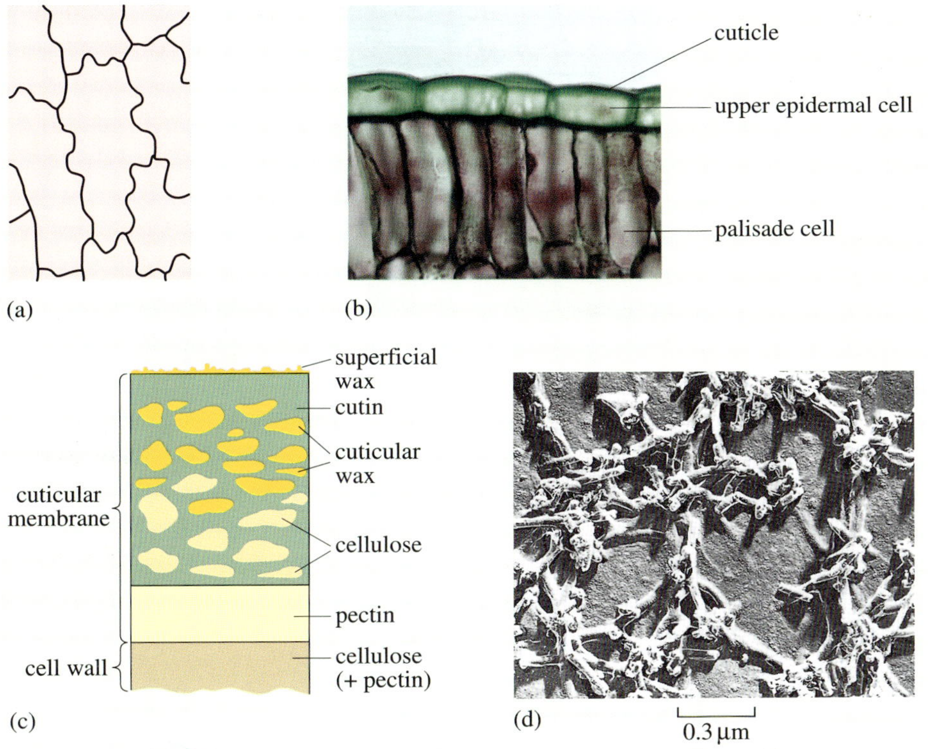

Figure 1.34 Epidermal cells of leaves (a) in surface view; (b) in vertical section; (c) diagrammatic vertical section, showing the complex structure of waxes and cellulose in a cutin matrix of plant cuticles; (d) scanning electron micrograph of a leaf surface showing wax deposits.

The main reason why bryophytes tend to dry out so easily (Section 1.2) is that they lack a well-developed cuticle. **Cutin**, which forms the main waterproofing layer in above-ground organs, is a fatty substance. Formation of cutin does not involve any complex, enzyme-catalysed reactions, as many polyunsaturated fatty acids polymerize spontaneously in an oxygen-rich environment; if such fatty acids are secreted by cells, cutin forms. So it is not surprising that cutin is found in most plant groups, even though rarely in mosses.

Collenchyma (pronounced 'coll-en`-kyma') cells (Figure 1.35) often encircle inner tissues and have additional layers of cellulose in the wall, while leaving the interstices between cells empty. They give strength without rigidity. Collenchyma cells occur mainly in young, growing organs; they are living cells, which continue to elongate.

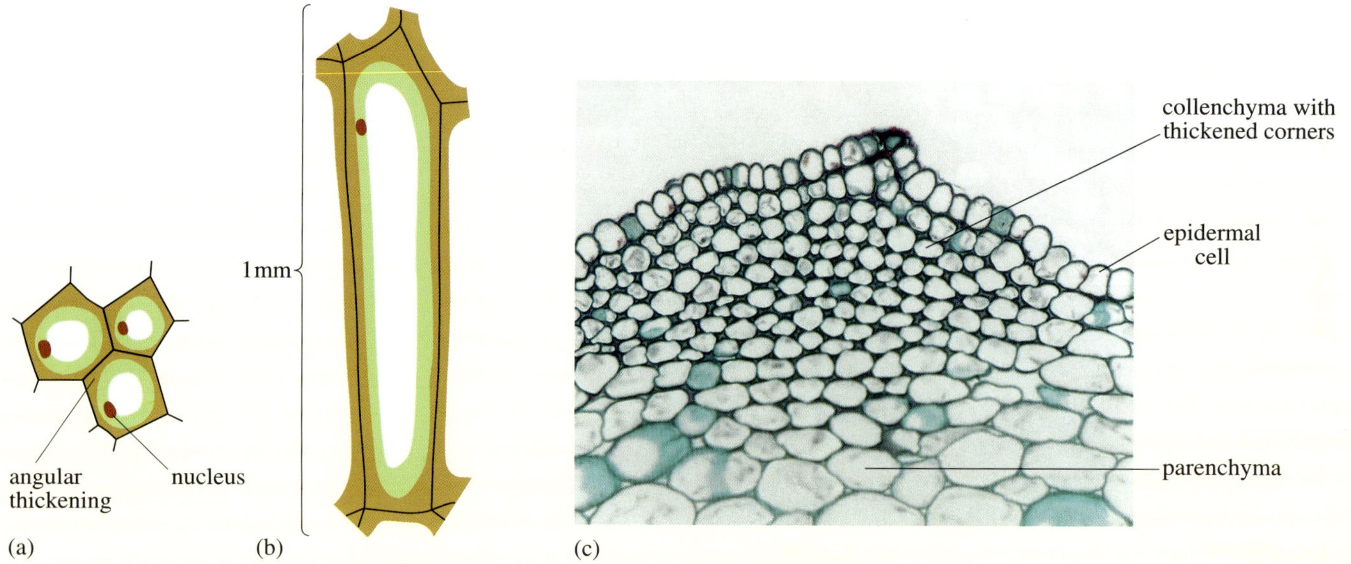

Figure 1.35 Collenchyma cells in (a) transverse and (b) longitudinal sections. Note the shape and uneven thickening of the walls. (c) Cross-section through a stem ridge, showing a cluster of collenchyma cells.

Endodermal cells form a discrete single layer of cells (known as the **endodermis**), which encircle the conducting tissues in roots and demarcates the stele (Section 1.6.3). When these cells are young, a band of ligno-suberin (a complex of the strengthening wall polymer **lignin** and the fat, suberin) is laid down in the radial and longitudinal walls so as to form a continuous band, the **Casparian strip** (Figure 1.36a and b), which greatly reduces passive transport of water and ions through the endodermal walls. Initially, the movement of water and ions is inhibited solely because the pores in the cellulose wall become blocked by lignin and suberin. However, later the wall becomes more generally thickened as plates of cellulose and suberin are laid down internally, giving the walls a layered structure. In monocotyledons, but not dicotyledons, the inner wall may be further thickened so that it looks U-shaped (Figure 1.36c). There are occasional thin-walled cells within the endodermis, which are referred to as 'passage cells'. A true endodermis is not found in stems.

Layers of thickened **hypodermal cells**, forming a **hypodermis** (Figure 1.37), are often found just inside the epidermis of roots as they age; hence this layer is known as the hypodermis. If the wall becomes thickened as in endodermis, the layer of cells is often described as an **exodermis**. As with endodermal cells, thickening is initiated with the formation of a Casparian strip, which is later enhanced by deposition of suberin and cellulose inside the primary wall. The epidermis is gradually eroded as the root grows and passes between soil particles. The exodermis then functions to limit water and ion movements into and out of the plant in older roots.

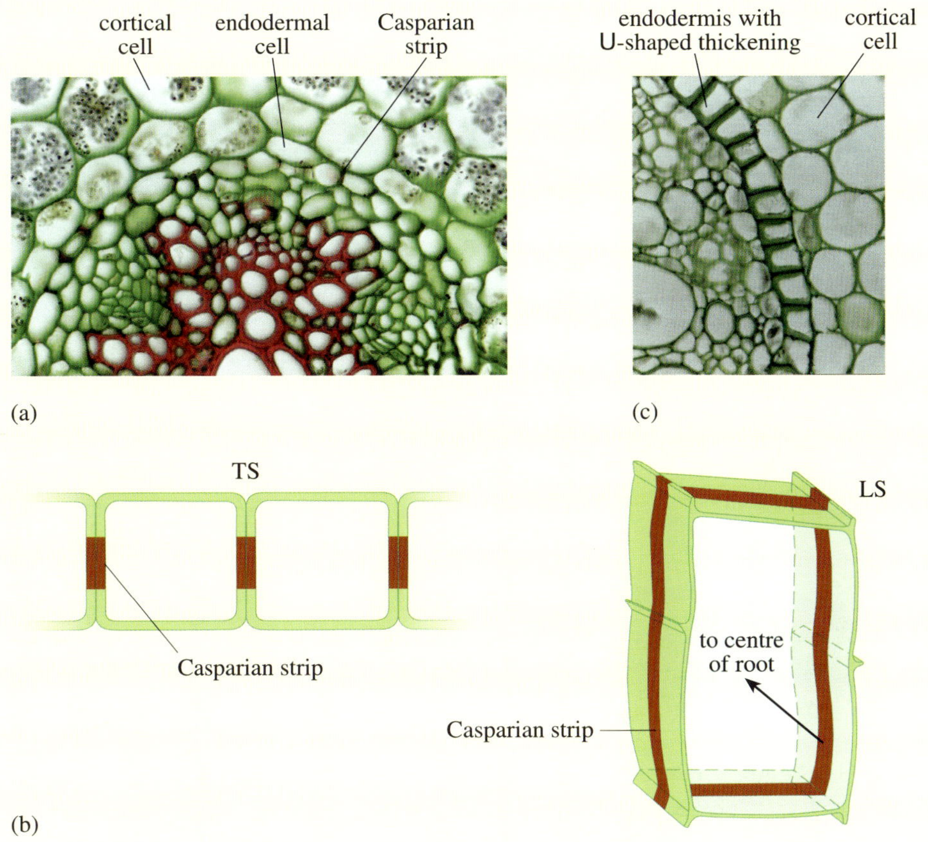

Figure 1.36 Root endodermal cells. (a) TS of young root of a dicotyledon, showing the Casparian strip on radial walls of the endodermis; (b) diagrams of endodermal cells in transverse and longitudinal section; (c) TS of a monocotyledon root showing U-shaped thickenings in the endodermis.

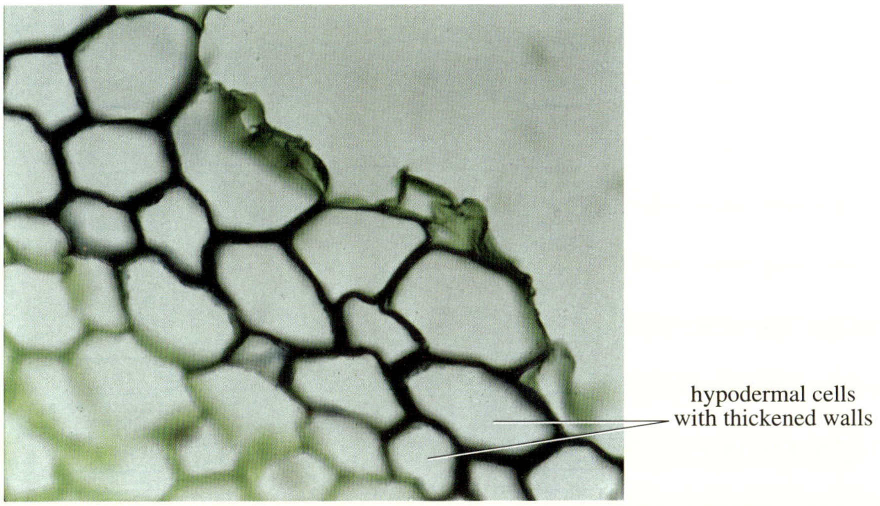

Figure 1.37 Transverse section of a root, showing thickened hypodermal cells. Note that the cells tend to be somewhat irregular in shape.

1.5.3 'DEAD' CELLS

A second group of cells have walls that are thickened with water-impermeable lignin. This complex polymer is laid down in cell walls and inter-layered with cellulose. Once lignified, cells die — an example of programmed cell death or *apoptosis*. Lignified cells are very strong and so are of value in supporting tissue. The presence of lignin in tissues is a defining feature of vascular plants; it is not found in bryophytes. Lignin-rich cells and tissues include *xylem* and *sclerenchyma*.

Xylem (pronounced zy`-lem), like phloem, is a tissue and comprises *vessels*, *tracheids* (pronounced 'tray-keeds') and *fibres* (see below), as well as unthickened **xylem parenchyma**. Vessels and tracheids (Figure 1.38a) both conduct water up the plant and give tissue support, whereas fibres are limited to a support role. The parenchyma may have a packing or storage function. **Tracheids** are frequently long and thin in outline with tapered end walls; in cross-section the cell wall is seen to be very thick, whereas the empty cell interior (*lumen*) is narrow. In contrast, **vessel elements** or cells are broad, and are often quite short with a wider lumen. They are arranged in columns, in which the end walls between individual cells break down to form long tubes — the **vessels**. Vessels are particularly important in rapid water transport from roots to shoots, because relatively little resistance to water flow is offered by their broad lumen. Side walls of parenchyma, tracheids and vessels have thinner areas known as **pits** linking adjoining cells. These may be simple pits (Figure 1.38b) or (especially in vessels and tracheids) bordered pits (Figure 1.38c), the type of pitting found being determined by the degree of wall thickening and the pattern in which it is laid down (Figure 1.38d). Phloem, xylem and (when present) cambium are collectively referred to as **vascular tissue**, or, when forming isolated groups, as **vascular bundles.** Chapter 3 describes the functioning of xylem in more detail.

Lignin is initially laid down within the cellulose cell wall of tracheids and vessels (Figure 1.38d) in bands (*annular thickening*), but this pattern is soon superseded as more lignin is deposited forming spirals (*spiral thickening*). The first-formed xylem of plant organs (protoxylem) is thickened in this way, and such patterns allow cells to continue elongating. Tracheids and vessels of later-formed tissues (metaxylem) become more heavily thickened, giving the spirals a ladder-like look (*scalariform thickening*), and eventually the entire inner surface is thickened except for gaps around pits, forming net-like or *reticulate thickening*. Such thickening occurs only when cells have stopped elongating.

Tracheids are first found in psilophyte fossils from the Devonian Period but also occur in all plant groups that have appeared since. Tracheids en masse provide enough strength to support tall trees, including early tree ferns and also conifers, which can reach a height of 90 m. In contrast, vessels are a feature of ferns and angiosperms, though they are also found in some lycophytes and horsetails; this resemblance is not thought to be evidence for a close relationship between these groups but another example of convergent evolution.

Sclerenchyma (pronounced 'skler-en`-kima') cells and sclereids (pronounced 'skler`-eeds'; Figure 1.39) function purely in support. Sclerenchyma cells are also known as fibres, particularly when they occur as part of another tissue such as xylem. However, when they are present as discrete strands outside the xylem (often a feature of relatively pliant short-lived tissues), they are normally referred to as sclerenchyma fibres. The dried fibres of some plants are of considerable economic importance, for example as flax or hemp. Fibre cells are very long and

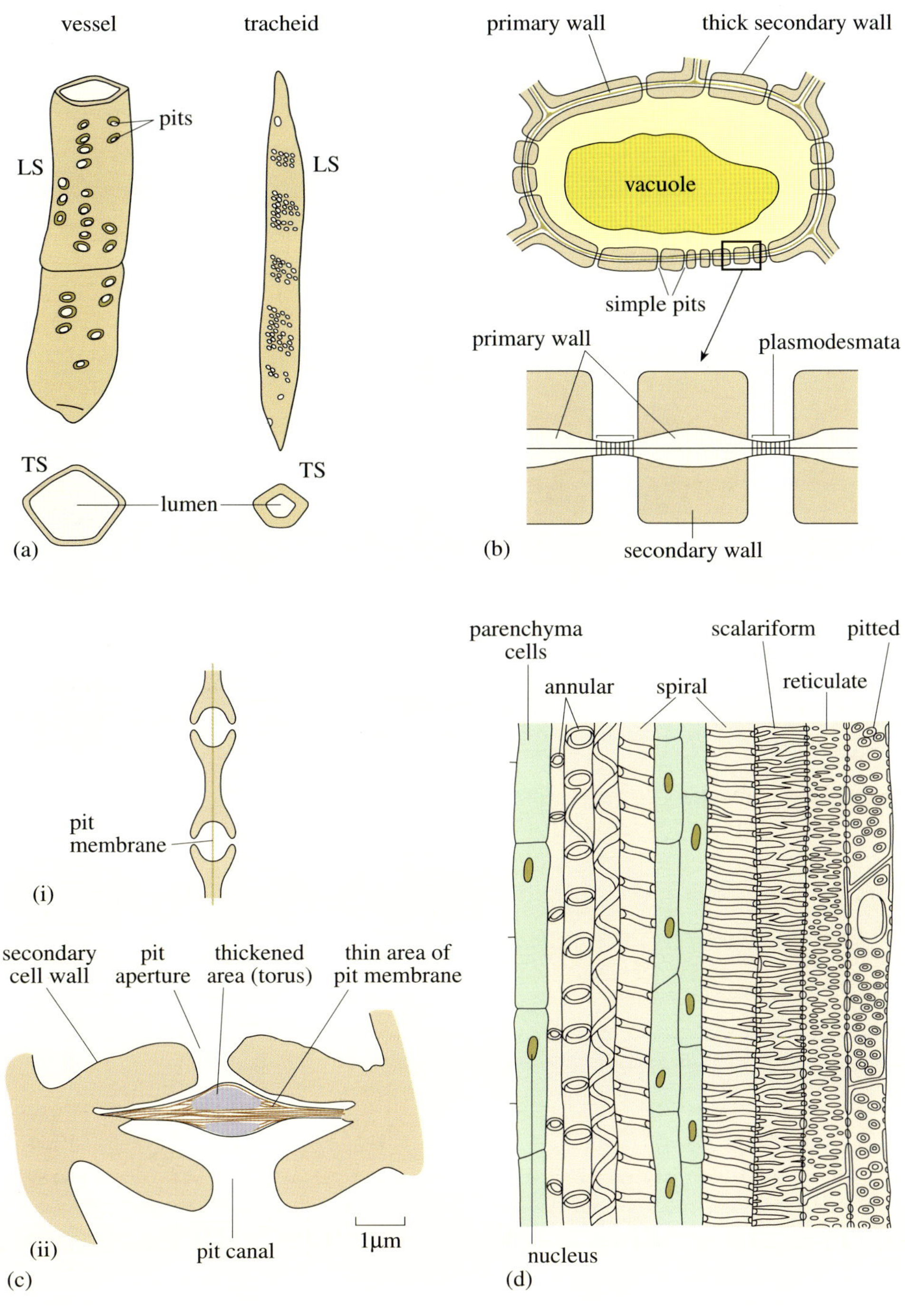

Figure 1.38 (a) Vessel and tracheid in transverse and longitudinal section. Note that tracheids are much longer and thinner than individual vessel elements, and that the walls are thickened so that the cell lumen is narrow. (b) Simple pits in xylem parenchyma cells. Note that the secondary wall is not deposited in the pit areas, where numerous plasmodesmata cross the primary wall. (c) Bordered pits where the wall arches over the pit (i) in a dicot vessel and (ii) in a conifer tracheid. Note that the remains of the primary wall here forms a pit membrane. If air bubbles form, the thickened torus in the conifer tracheid can plug the pit aperture. (d) LS of types of lignified thickening: annular, spiral, scalariform and reticulate.

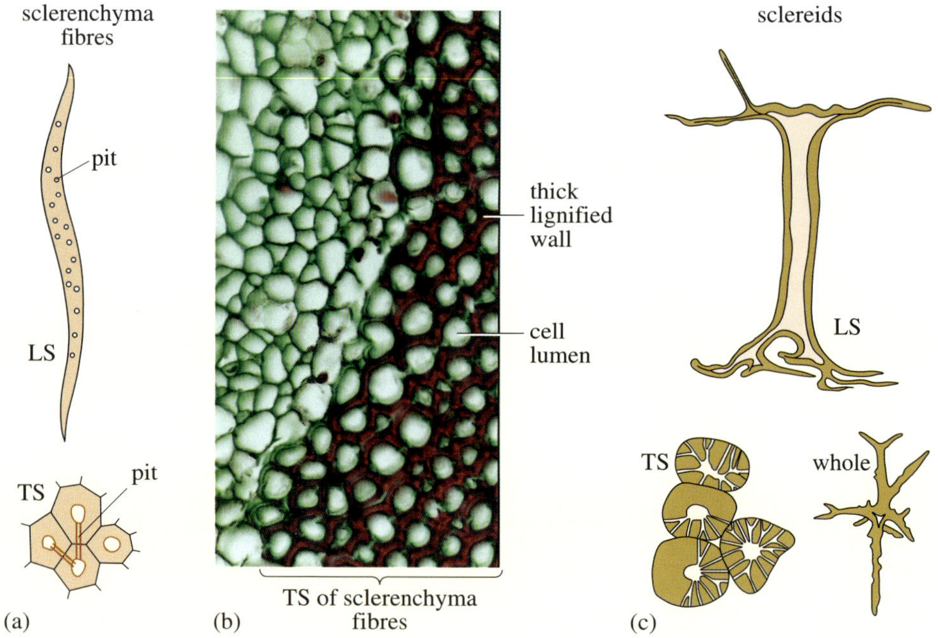

Figure 1.39 Sclerenchyma cells: (a) diagrams of fibres in LS and TS; (b) micrograph showing a bundle of fibres in TS; note the greatly thickened cell walls and very small cell lumen; (c) diagrams of sclereids in LS and TS, and a whole cell.

thin, with very thick walls and simple pits between adjacent cells. In transverse section, all the cells seem to fit closely together at the angular corners, so giving more rigidity than collenchyma, but less than vessels and tracheids. Sclereids are equally thick walled, but solitary, and can take strange shapes; for instance they may have long-armed projections. They may also be called 'stone cells' and it is this type of cell which gives some ripe fruits, for instance pears, their gritty texture.

The evolution of sclerenchyma and collenchyma, which occur generally as support in soft and short-lived tissue, is often associated with the initiation of the herbaceous habit. The earliest angiosperms were probably woody perennials, similar to woody members of the magnoliids, the angiosperms with primitive features which are now classified as a separate group from eudicots and monocots (Ridge, 2001[A]).

Summary of Section 1.5

1 The basic strengthening elements in plant cell walls are cellulose in living cells, and cellulose and lignin and/or suberin in dead cells.

2 Parenchyma is the basic cell type. Other living cells adapted to specific functions are: storage parenchyma; palisade cells, which are rich in chloroplasts, and important sites of photosynthesis; phloem sieve tubes and companion cells, which carry the products of photosynthesis; transfer cells.

3 Living cells with thickened walls include: epidermal cells, which may additionally have an external cuticle plus waxes; collenchyma, which have a support function in outer tissues of young and short-lived organs; endodermal cells, where the wall thickening allows only selective water and ion movement into internal tissues, hypodermal cells and exodermal cells on the outside of older roots.

4 Increase in size (length or width) of plant tissue takes place in primary or secondary meristems. The cells of these tissues are small and rectangular, and have thin walls. The cells of secondary meristems (cambium) are arranged as tiers, with cell walls showing the lineage of the oldest cells of the tissue. Cork cambium produces cork cells to the outside, which gives rise to bark.

5 Dead cells acting as support include sclerenchyma and sclereids, xylem fibres, tracheids and vessels. Tracheids and vessels also conduct water and minerals from roots to the aerial parts of plants.

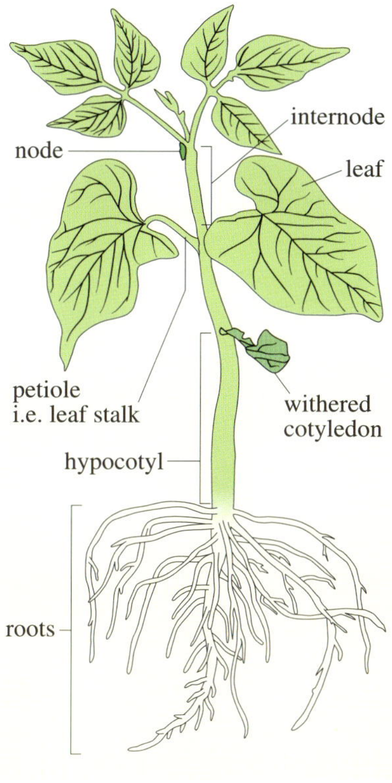

Figure 1.40 Generalized anatomy of a plant.

1.6 IMPORTANT INNOVATIONS

In addition to the print component of this chapter, the CD-ROM *Digital Microscope* provides you with an opportunity to look at plant cells and tissues. These exercises are best studied before Section 1.6.

The basic features of a shoot are illustrated in Figure 1.40. Individual details will be discussed later in this section.

1.6.1 SUPPORT

You should now be aware that cells with thickened walls (such as clusters of collenchyma and sclerenchyma) have a support role even when located external to vascular tissue. You should also recognize that they are a feature of young tissues and short-lived organs. Collenchyma, for example, is frequently located as a ring of tissue just inside the epidermis of stems and leaf stalks; it also occurs as a strengthener of corners or ridges in herbaceous stems, and bordering the veins in dicot leaves. In general, only angiosperms, especially dicots, have well-developed collenchyma.

Sclerenchyma fibres also occur mainly in angiosperms, often as discrete strands in the cortex of non-woody stems. In tough fibrous stems and in leaves | of many grasses, sedges and desert plants such as agaves, sclerenchyma forms strengthening 'girders' outside the vascular bundles; the toughness of such organs also acts as a deterrent to grazers. However, bands of sclerenchyma fibres can sometimes be found (as in lime, *Tilia*, Figure 1.41) within phloem, a tissue with soft-walled cells, which might collapse under pressure from internal and external tissue if not supported. Other structures that add to the rigidity of tissue include spicules and spines of the epidermis, where they also have a protective role, and sclereids within the cortical region. Woody seed coats, including the shells of nuts, are made up largely of sclereids.

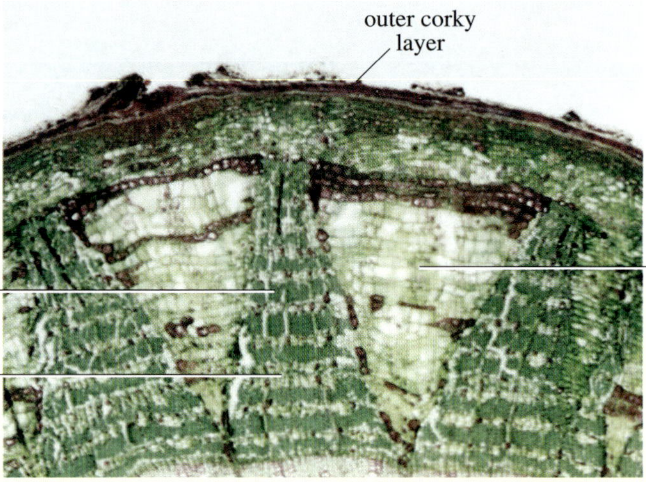

Figure 1.41 Transverse section of part of a three-year old *Tilia* stem, showing groups of cells in the phloem tissue — alternating bands of sclerenchyma (darkly stained) and active phloem cells (sieve-tube cells and companion cells).

The support provided by collenchyma and sclerenchyma in young or short-lived organs contrasts with that provided by xylem. Xylem fibres, tracheids and vessels offer both short- and long-term support in the central cylinder of both roots and stems and in leaf veins. In herbaceous (i.e. non-woody) organs, the role of tracheids and, especially, vessels in water transport (Section 1.5.3) is probably more important than their support role. However, in woody seed plants, where secondary thickening has occurred, the central mass of xylem no longer transports water, and functions only for support: it is what keeps trees upright. Interestingly, modern tree ferns (Pterophyta) and the fossil tree lycopods (Lycophyta, Figure 1.3) do not depend on xylem for support but on lignified cells in the outer cortex.

It seems likely, therefore, that xylem and its sister vascular tissue, phloem, first evolved because of the need for a transport system, the support role of xylem evolving later. Both tissues have a long fossil record; tracheids and phloem are found in early fossil whisk ferns and in *Psilotum* (Psilophyta) — that is, among the earliest-evolved tracheophytes — where they appear as a central strand, but not organized as in angiosperms. It is difficult to imagine how the special functions of root, stem and leaf could have evolved in the absence of vascular tissue.

1.6.2 Roots

Roots have two different functions in terrestrial plants: they anchor the plant in the soil, and they absorb water and mineral nutrients. The ancient plant groups, however, are not wholly dependent on roots as anchorage: like some angiosperms, they have underground stems (*rhizomes*), which subtend fine roots (think of irises). Roots that arise from any part of a shoot are described as *adventitious* (Figure 1.42a). Rhizomes are perennial and usually lie just under the soil (Figure 1.42c). The earliest-known rhizomes are those of fossil psilophytes, so only bryophytes lack roots.

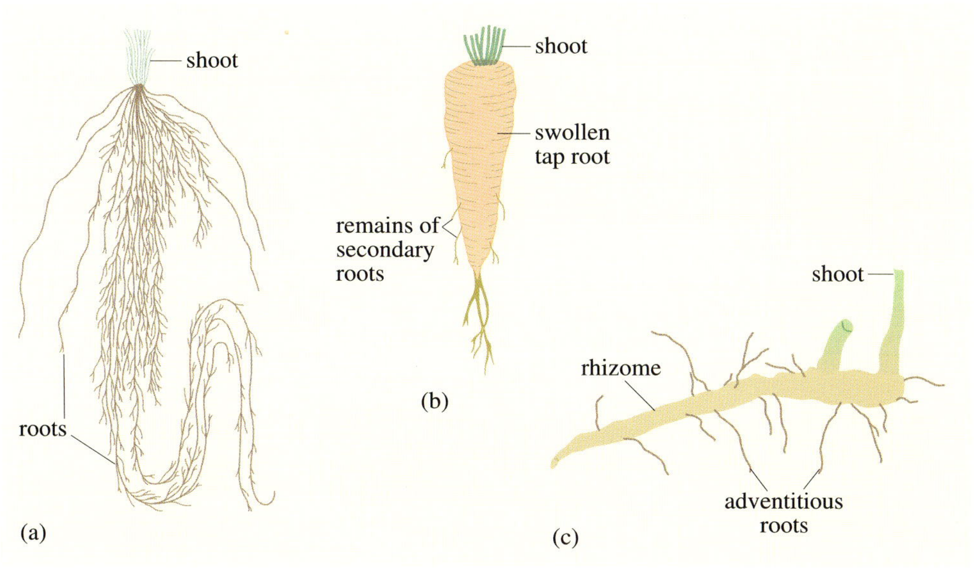

Figure 1.42 (a) Adventitious roots of wheat (*Triticum aestivum*), forming a fibrous root system. (b) Food-storing tap root of carrot (*Daucus carota*). (c) Bracken (*Pteridium aquilinum*) rhizome with adventitious roots.

In general, non-adventitious roots — that is, continuations of the stem base which are present in the embryo — are confined to gymnosperms and angiosperms, where they can take the form of deeply penetrating and massive tap roots, such as those of many deciduous trees, and may also store nutrients (Figure 1.42b). Alternatively they may be finer and well distributed as a branching net in surface soil. Most dicots have such branched, non-adventitious root systems, but in monocots, most of which are relatively low growing, herbaceous, and short-lived, the first root is soon replaced by numerous adventitious roots arising from the shoot (Figure 1.42a). All roots have **root hairs**, which are located immediately behind the root tip and are major sites of absorption of water and essential mineral nutrients (Chapter 3).

The characteristic root endodermis (Section 1.5.2) seems to have evolved in parallel to xylem tissue, and may have been a consequence of the need to ensure some degree of selectivity for water and minerals entering or leaving the central stele.

1.6.3 STELES

All tissue internal to the cortex of roots and stems is known as the **stele** (pronounced 'steel'), which includes all vascular tissue. Different stelar structures have evolved in different organs and different groups of plants. For instance, a solid central cylinder of xylem is a feature of roots and most tree stems, and an incomplete ring of vascular tissue is a feature of young dicot stems like sunflower (*Helianthus*); vascular tissues are dispersed throughout the stele in monocots.

A solid cylinder of thickened cells, referred to as a *protostele* (Figure 1.43a), is a valuable structural device where compression is the major stress (as in roots), but such a system is less effective where there is a need for elasticity, for instance when stems bend in wind. Greater elasticity is possible when thickened cells are

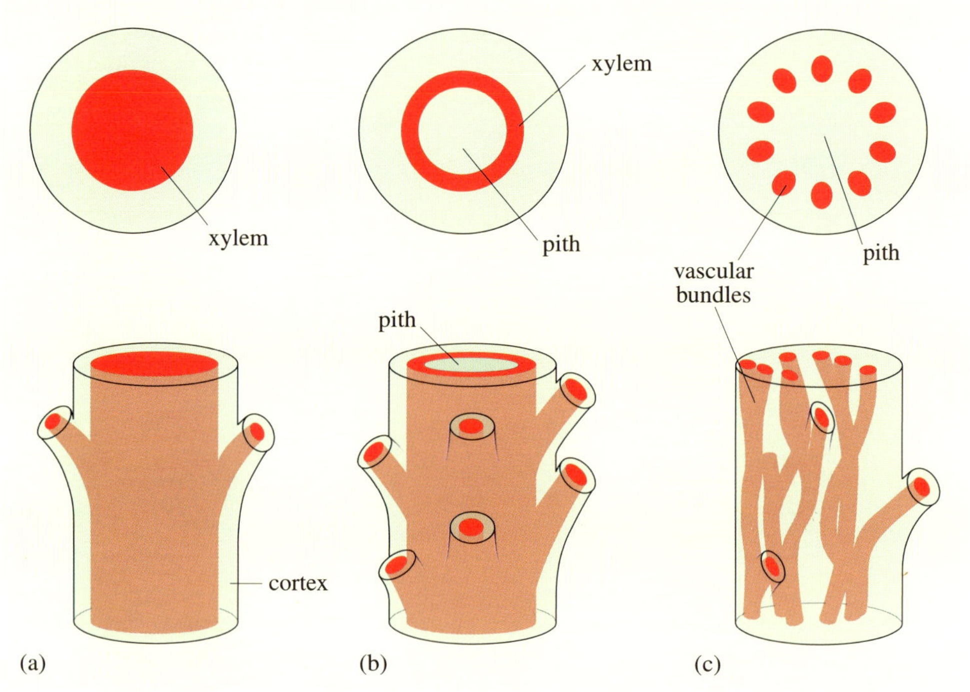

Figure 1.43 Diagrams showing the arrangement of vascular tissues in steles in TS (above) and in 3-D (below): (a) a typical protostele; (b) a hollow cylinder; (c) dissected cylinder, showing vascular bundles.

arranged as a hollow cylinder, which may be filled with pith parenchyma (Figure 1.43b); these are found in, for instance, still-pliable, one-year-old lime (*Tilia*) or older stems of herbaceous dicots. Finally, if the cylinder is broken to form a ring of longitudinal 'girders' (a dissected cylinder, Figure 1.43c), as in dead nettle (*Lamium*) or in many climbing plants such as cucumber (*Cucurbita*), stems have even greater flexibility. These girders are known as **vascular bundles**.

In general, young stems of seed plants have a dissected stele (this feature is not so obvious in their roots, where the individual bundles are very close together and fill the central tissue). As they grow larger and especially when perennial (e.g. trees), the secondary meristem produces new vascular tissue converting the stele into either a hollow or solid cylinder. In perennials, the tree-like form is thought to pre-date the herbaceous habit in which the dissected stele persists.

Secondary growth resulting in increases in width of organs is partly a result of the formation of additional stele material.

❍ Recall which cell type is responsible for growth in width.

● Cambial cells of the secondary meristems (the cambium, Section 1.5.2).

❍ Where does the secondary meristem which produces new vascular tissue lie?

● Between the phloem and the xylem.

In dicot stems, the first-formed cambium is found only in the primary vascular bundles (it is called 'fascicular cambium'); following mitosis, new cells, which differentiate into phloem and xylem, are formed (Figure 1.44a). Gradually, however, a layer of parenchyma cells in the tissue between the bundles starts to divide, and entirely new bundles are laid down (Figure 1.44b). In time, the bundles girdle the stem in both solid and hollow stele types. In stems with a dissected cylinder a proportion of the newly formed cells differentiate as parenchyma, which then lie between the bundles.

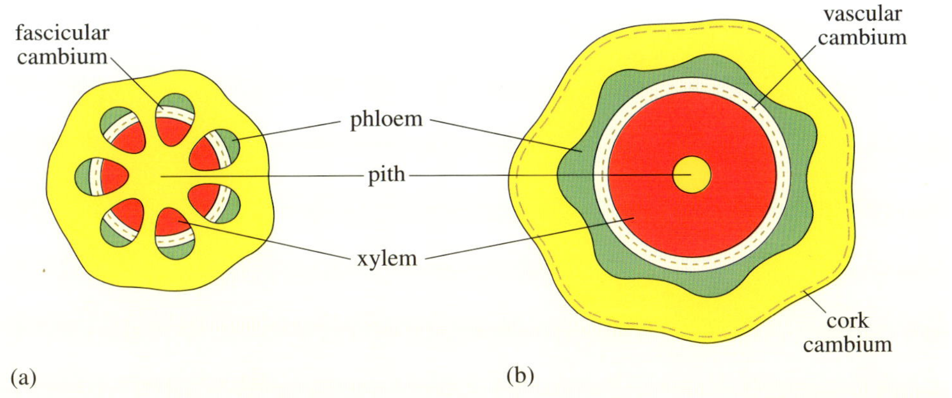

Figure 1.44 Secondary thickening in stems: (a) initial location of cambium (called fascicular cambium) in primary bundles; (b) vascular cambium has extended right round the shoot, forming new xylem and phloem, and cork cambium has formed at the periphery of the shoot.

In roots the process of secondary growth is exactly the same but, as the number of bundles in roots is rarely more than five, and as phloem lies between, not directly outside the xylem, the line of newly active cambial cells initially forms a series of arcs, and later weaves inside the phloem and outside the xylem (Figure 1.45a and b). In time, especially in larger woody roots and as a consequence of more cells being formed to the inside rather than to the outside, the wavy line becomes a ring of active cambium.

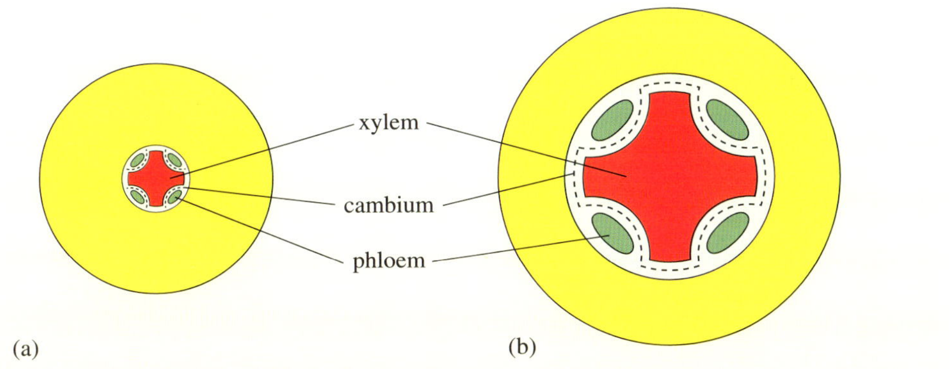

Figure 1.45 Secondary thickening in roots: (a) location of the first-formed cambium between the xylem and phloem; (b) cambium extending right round the root and forming new xylem and phloem.

1.6.4 Leaves

How did leaves evolve? The earliest land plants, like present-day whisk ferns, *Psilotum* (Figure 1.3) may have had dichotomously branched, upright shoots with a simple protostele. These shoots, again like the whisk ferns, probably bore scales which were simple outgrowths of photosynthetic stems called **microphylls** (small leaves). These are recognized to be the simplest leaf form, having only a single vein, and the first of two major lines of leaf evolution in vascular plants. The microphyll lineage culminated in the lycophytes, some of whose fossil genera had microphylls up to 60 cm long (Figure 1.46a). Today, only lycophytes and psilophytes have microphylls.

The alternative leaf form is a **megaphyll** (large leaf), which is also thought to have been derived from dichotomously branching naked shoots like those of the whisk ferns. In this case, however, branches have become fused. Possible evolutionary steps could have involved first one main branch overtopping the other half of the dichotomy (Figure 1.46b), then *planation* (that is, flattening off) of the penultimate tips with subsequent outgrowths of parenchymatous webs between these branches. In megaphylls, several vascular bundles would have been *in situ* from the earliest stages in leaf evolution. An expanded leaf area is obviously of benefit to the photosynthetic potential of plants, and megaphylls occur in all later-evolved plant phyla.

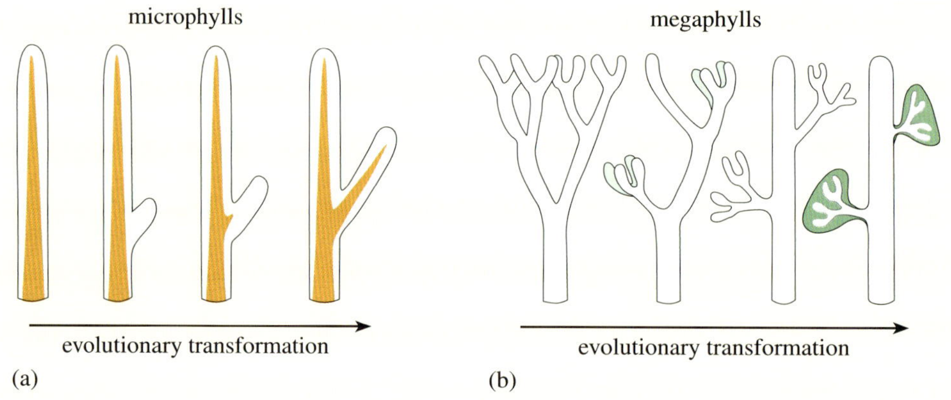

Figure 1.46 (a) A possible sequence of events in the evolution of microphylls; (b) a possible sequence for the evolution of megaphylls.

From *Digital Microscope* studies, you are already familiar with the structure of typical dicot and monocot leaves. But such megaphylls, especially those of dicots, show enormous variation in form and structure; considerable variation also occurs in the leaves of ferns and gymnosperms. Leaf form is very varied according to particular growing conditions. Leaves may be modified to form spines or tendrils; some (for example, grasses and certain ferns) have meristematic regions at ground level (which explains why lawns keep growing after mowing); and special hinge cells allow some leaves to fold or roll up during drought, in response to touch, or at night.

1.6.5 Shoot systems and gas exchange

Water constantly evaporates into the atmosphere at the leaf surface (a process known as **transpiration**) and if plants are to limit water loss, the shoot surface needs some form of protection.

- ❍ Recall the name of the waterproofing layer on the outside of shoots.

- ● The cuticle, especially when impregnated or covered by wax, is the major waterproofing layer (Figure 1.34).

Since a few bryophytes have a rudimentary cuticle over the upper surface of the leaf or flat thallus, this feature is thought to have evolved at a very early period in plant evolution on dry land. Not surprisingly the cuticle is often thin or missing from surfaces that are less affected by airflow over the surface, such as the underside of leaves, and from the surfaces of plants that do not suffer water stress, such as those growing under water. Many plant surfaces bear simple or branched hairs that trap air in the surface layer around the plant; this may also help to reduce water loss.

Study of leaf sections among your *Digital Microscope* slides should have made you aware that leaves are not closed systems but have pores known as **stomata** (singular **stoma**) in the epidermis (Figure 1.47), which open and close, thereby facilitating gas exchange. Closure of stomata greatly reduces water loss.

However, gas exchange is essential for photosynthesis: CO_2 must be able to enter leaves and O_2 to leave. In addition, some water loss is necessary to power the transpiration stream that carries water and mineral nutrients from roots to leaves in xylem. So a balancing mechanism is necessary which limits water loss but allows adequate gas exchange. The stomata occur most frequently on the lower sides of leaves and in other protected areas such as infoldings of stem surfaces. They are bounded by **guard cells**, which change shape in response to internal and external stimuli, so opening and closing the pore, and regulating gas exchange and water loss. Stomata do not occur in the gametophytes of bryophytes, though they are occasionally present in the capsules of sporophytes. They are present in the sporophytes of all vascular plants.

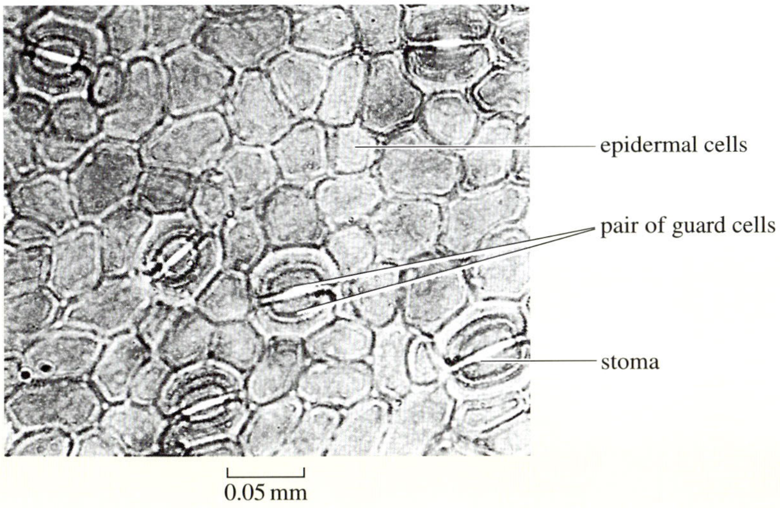

Figure 1.47 Surface view of a leaf epidermis showing stomata, each with a pair of guard cells.

SUMMARY OF POINTS RAISED IN STUDY OF DIGITAL MICROSCOPE SLIDES AND SECTION 1.6

1 Cells are arranged in tissues (epidermis, cortex, endodermis, vascular tissue and pith) of varying dimensions specific to particular organs and species; for example, a wide cortex is typical of dicot roots, whereas herbaceous dicot stems (for example, sunflower, *Helianthus*), have a broad pith and narrow cortex.

2 The arrangement of these tissues in monocot stems and roots differs from that in dicots. In monocot stems, e.g. maize (*Zea mays*), vascular bundles are dispersed through the stele but in maize roots the bundles are arranged in a tight circle towards the outside of the root. In both cases the cortex is relatively narrow.

3 Leaves are relatively thin structures with an external epidermis surrounding a cortex made up of photosynthetic palisade tissue and spongy mesophyll. Vascular bundles are found embedded in the cortex with a single central large bundle; other smaller bundles (not necessarily in the same plane) are the defining structures of dicot leaves, many equal-sized bundles in the same plane being diagnostic of monocots.

4 Tissues for support and the conduction of materials around the plant are essential for the survival of land plants with an upright growth habit.

5 The degree of development of tissues is related to both tissue function and species habit.

6 Vascular tissue, in particular vessels, tracheids and phloem, has a long evolutionary history, but is best developed in ferns and flowering plants. Gymnosperms have tracheids but not vessels.

7 An even more recent development is the herbaceous perennial habit typified by the presence of collenchyma and sclerenchyma in cortical stem tissues and leaves.

8 Roots are essential both as anchorage and for the uptake and initial transport of water and minerals from the soil. They may be adventitious (arising along a stem) or may develop from the embryo root as an extension from the stem base.

9 The central stele of phloem, xylem, fibres and pith takes three major forms, each having a particular support function. Solid protosteles, characteristic of roots and woody long-lived trees, are rigid and withstand compression well; hollow cylinders are more pliable; and dissected cylinders are even more flexible. Both the hollow and dissected forms of stele give adequate support where lateral and bending forces prevail.

10 In dicot stems and roots, division of secondary meristem cells (cambium) increases the width of the stele. Cambium forms mainly xylem to the inside and phloem to the outside; it is present initially as an interrupted ring but eventually encircles the organ.

11 The leaves of plants have evolved in two ways — the micro- and megaphyll lines. The former occur in psilophytes and lycophytes, whereas the latter occur in all other vascular plants.

12 Leaves and stems are the sites of photosynthesis, and much of the gas and water exchange with the atmosphere. Controlling water loss while allowing exchange of gases is essential. The anatomical answer typically involves both the development of a waterproof cuticle and regulation of the opening of stomata in the epidermis, which are the main channels of exchange.

CONCLUSION

To sort out the evolutionary relationships of plant phyla, we need to consider evidence from both life cycles and plant structure. For instance, the gametophytic nature of the 'plant' suggests that bryophytes are not closely related to the sporophytic vascular plants. But there is also useful evidence from fossils and comparative anatomy to justify accepting that the bryophytes are a separate group. Considering all the evidence available from morphology and anatomy, there are also reasonable grounds for accepting the major vascular plant groupings and their origins as shown in Figure 1.3 — for example, the way the plant is branched, the structure of the vascular bundle and kinds of xylem cells present, and the presence of microphyllous or megaphyllous leaves. Such evidence is rarely conclusive, however, and Figure 1.3 is partly based on molecular evidence, which has resulted in the re-evaluation of relationships between some phyla. New evidence might in time lead to a further re-evaluation of this classification. Evolutionary analysis is rarely easy to interpret, and new studies frequently introduce new conundrums!

Even though new molecular data may still alter the way in which plant phyla are grouped, a clear trend from bryophytes to flowering plants is discernible. It is characterized by increasing independence of water and a wide range of specializations for life on land.

REFERENCES

Dyson, M. (2001) Reproduction. In *Generating Diversity*, M. Gillman (ed.), The Open University, Milton Keynes, pp. 111–50.

Ridge, I. (2001[A]) Ordering Diversity. In *Introduction to Diversity*, I. Ridge and C. M. Pond (eds), The Open University, Milton Keynes, pp. 1–54.

Ridge, I. (2001[B]) Diversity in Protoctists. In *Introduction to Diversity*, I. Ridge and C. M. Pond (eds), The Open University, Milton Keynes, pp. 55–92.

FURTHER READING

Bell, P. R. (1992) *Green Plants — their Origin and Diversity* (10th edn), CUP [An excellent, clearly written textbook, available in paperback.]

Bowes, B. G. (1997) *A Colour Atlas of Plant Structure*, Manson Publishing. [A useful and extensive collection of annotated photomicrographs, with short summary chapters about plant organs.]

Mauseth, J. D. (1998) *Botany: an Introduction to Plant Biology* (multimedia enhanced edition), Jones & Bartlett. [A standard textbook, well illustrated with material relevant to this and later chapters of this book.]

Raven, P. H., Evert, R. F., and Eichorn, S. E. (1999) *Biology of Plants* (6th edn), Freeman–Worth. [A standard textbook, beautifully illustrated, and containing material relevant to this and later chapters in this book.]

Rudall, P. (1987) *Anatomy of Flowering Plants*, Edward Arnold. [A slim book, which deals specifically with plant anatomy and development.]

ANSWERS TO TEXT QUESTIONS

1 (p. 11) Box A, antheridia; box B, archegonia; box C, spores.

2 (p. 18) Box A, gametophyte or prothallus; box B, egg cell; box C, meiosis.

Table 1.1 (completed) Checklist of structures involved in sexual reproduction in angiosperms and their equivalent in *Selaginella* (a heterosporous non-seed plant).

	Angiosperms	Equivalent in *Selaginella*
Male	pollen sac	microsporangium
	products of meiosis in pollen sac	microspores
	pollen when shed	immature male gametophyte
	germinating pollen	mature male gametophyte
	products of division of the generative cell	sperm cells or male gametes (flagellated in *Selaginella* but not in angiosperms)
Female	ovule	no equivalent: it is the structure that contains the megasporangium within which all stages up to embryo formation occur; an ovule eventually becomes a seed
	nucellus	megasporangium
	embryo sac	initially a megaspore, but eventually develops into a female gametophyte with 8 nuclei and 7 cells
	seed	no equivalent: it is formed from the ovule following fertilization and comprises the sporophyte embryo, food stores and a tough seed coat

PHOTOSYNTHESIS

2

2.1 INTRODUCTION

Green plants obtain all their energy by photosynthesis, the process in which light is converted to chemical energy. The light reactions are the 'photo' part of photosynthesis, while the so-called 'dark' reactions constitute the 'synthesis' part of the process, which is also called carbon fixation. The light and dark reactions are intimately linked and are summarized by the left-to-right reaction in Equation 2.1, the overall equation for photosynthesis in plants, algae and cyanobacteria.

Note that $[CH_2O]$ denotes carbohydrate.

$$CO_2 + H_2O \underset{\text{RESPIRATION (in light and dark)}}{\overset{\text{PHOTOSYNTHESIS (in light)}}{\rightleftharpoons}} [CH_2O] + O_2 \qquad (2.1)$$

The right-to-left reaction in Equation 2.1 emphasizes that, like all other aerobic organisms, plants carry out respiration which, in summary, is the reverse of photosynthesis. This simple fact has profound implications when measuring rates of photosynthesis, depending on the level at which the process is being studied. Photosynthesis (like respiration) can be studied at the molecular level, but there are two other levels at which the process is studied and explained (see Table 2.1).

Table 2.1 Levels at which photosynthesis is studied and explained in different biological material using different experimental systems and time-scales.

Level of explanation	Subject area	Material studied	Common types of measurement	Measurement time-scale
level 1: molecules, organelles and cells	biochemistry	isolated chloroplasts, single -celled green algae or purified enzymes	O_2 release, CO_2 uptake, enzyme activity, chlorophyll fluorescence*	seconds (or below) to minutes
level 2: whole plants or leaves	plant physiology	single plants or leaves in controlled conditions	O_2 release, CO_2 uptake	minutes to hours
level 3: communities or crops	ecology or crop physiology (agronomy)	(i) groups of plants growing outside in the field.	gain in dry weight	weeks to months or years
		(ii) phytoplankton in open water	O_2 release, CO_2 uptake	minutes to hours

* Fluorescence is discussed in Box 2.1.

- ❍ Bearing in mind Equation 2.1, how might respiration affect measurements of the rate of photosynthesis at level 2 (whole plants or leaves)?

- ● Respiration reduces the apparent (measured) rate of photosynthesis because some of the CO_2 uptake (or O_2 release) is balanced by CO_2 release (or O_2 uptake) in respiration.

At level 2, what is measured is called **net photosynthesis (*NP*)**, which is total or **gross photosynthesis (*GP*)** minus respiration (*R*). In symbols:

$$NP = GP - R \tag{2.2}$$

- ❍ Does respiration affect measurement of photosynthesis at levels 1 and 3, i.e. do these measurements relate to gross or net photosynthesis?

- ● For level 1, there is no effect of respiration: measurements with isolated chloroplasts inevitably relate to gross photosynthesis because respiratory organelles (mitochondria) are absent and, even with whole algal or plant cells, the very short time-scales of measurement mean that respiration can be ignored. For level 3, yes, respiration does have an effect: *net* gain in dry weight is measured and corresponds to net photosynthesis (carbon fixed) plus assimilation of all the other elements (nitrogen, phosphorus, etc.) that make up organic matter. Over long periods of time, a substantial loss of fixed carbon occurs through respiration.

The above case is a simple example of how the level of measurement or study affects interpretation of experimental results. Whenever you see data about the rate of photosynthesis, think about whether gross or net photosynthesis is implied.

This chapter is concerned mainly with levels 1 and 2 and tries to do three things:

(i) Consolidate (for the light reactions of photosynthesis) and introduce (for carbon fixation) the basic biochemical mechanisms that are common to all green plants.

(ii) Illustrate how these molecular processes are controlled and how environmental factors such as temperature and light intensity influence photosynthesis at both the molecular level and the whole-plant level.

(iii) Show how plants have adapted to different environments by modifications at both levels. For example, some plants can grow in deep shade below other plants and the mechanisms that enable them to do this include changes in leaf structure (level 2) coupled with molecular changes in the light-trapping systems and their control (level 1, discussed in Section 2.2). Variation in photosynthetic systems is one factor (among many) that contributes to plant diversity.

We begin (Section 2.2) with the light reactions, including their control, coordination and protection. Absorbing high intensity light, for example, is potentially dangerous because it can generate free radicals and cause oxidative damage, so elaborate protective mechanisms have evolved (Section 2.2.3).

Section 2.3 then describes the basic dark reactions of carbon fixation, the *C3* or *Calvin cycle* (Section 2.3.1). In green plants (and many autotrophic bacteria) this pathway alone gives a *net* fixation of CO_2. The first step in the pathway, in which CO_2 reacts, in a *carboxylase* reaction, is catalysed by a huge enzyme complex, *Rubisco* (whose name is explained in Section 2.3.2), which plays a key regulatory role. The active site for CO_2 on Rubisco also binds O_2 and catalyses an *oxidase* reaction. So oxygen acts as a competitive inhibitor of carbon fixation in the C3 cycle, and the product of the oxidase reaction is the substrate of an 'anti'-photosynthetic pathway known as the *C2 cycle* or *photorespiration* (Section 2.4). The overall reaction of the C2 cycle is the same as for respiration, i.e. O_2 uptake and CO_2 release, but unlike true respiration, no ATP is generated. Although it might seem paradoxical, the C2 cycle is now regarded as an integral and probably essential part of photosynthetic carbon metabolism.

In Sections 2.5 and 2.6 we focus more on whole plants and the ways in which environmental factors affect the rate of photosynthesis. Certain environmental conditions, notably high light intensity, high temperature and low availability of CO_2, strongly favour the oxidase reaction of Rubisco over the carboxylase reaction, resulting in a reduction of net photosynthesis and plant growth. However, some plants have evolved mechanisms that circumvent this problem by effectively concentrating CO_2 at the site of Rubisco action, so that CO_2 out-competes O_2. The mechanisms, involving both additional biochemical pathways and structural changes in green tissues, are found in so-called C4 and CAM plants (Sections 2.5.2 and 2.5.3) and are an important aspect of the diversification of plants and their adaptation to a wide range of environments.

The control of photosynthesis and what determines its overall rate are prominent themes in this chapter and are of more than academic interest, because photosynthesis in crop plants equates broadly with plant growth and food production. There is much controversy, for example, as to whether rising levels of atmospheric CO_2 might have the beneficial effect of increasing crop growth and this question is one we ask you to think about again after reading the chapter. Another question we consider is whether photosynthetic performance might be improved by introducing new or modified genes using the techniques of genetic engineering.

2.2 PHOTOSYNTHETIC LIGHT REACTIONS: CONTROL AND PROTECTION

2.2.1 CHLOROPLASTS AND THE STUDY OF THE LIGHT REACTIONS

You will already be familiar with the biochemistry of the light reactions. In this chapter, we consider the reactions more from the plants' perspective but, since you need to be completely familiar with the basic light reactions and with chloroplast structure, Figures 2.1 and 2.2 are included for easy reference.

❍ (i) *Before* looking at the legend to Figure 2.1, give the full names of all the components whose names are abbreviated (PSII, etc.). (ii) Using Figure 2.2b as a guide (if necessary), name the structures or regions labelled A–D in Figure 2.2a.

● (i) See the legend to Figure 2.1. (ii) A, double outer membrane or envelope (the outer and inner membranes are labelled separately in Figure 2.2b); B, stroma (the aqueous matrix); C, stroma lamellae; D, granum composed of a stack of membranous vesicles called thylakoids.

Some additional information about the antenna systems (antennae) is relevant to this chapter. First, they contain two other types of pigment in addition to chlorophyll *a*: chlorophyll *b* and carotenoids (the pigments that give carrots their orange colour and contribute to autumn leaf colours). These **accessory pigments** absorb light of shorter (i.e. higher energy) wavelengths than does chlorophyll *a*, so they increase the width of the spectrum available for photosynthesis. Energy transfer occurs in the sequence: carotenoids → chlorophyll *b* → chlorophyll *a* →

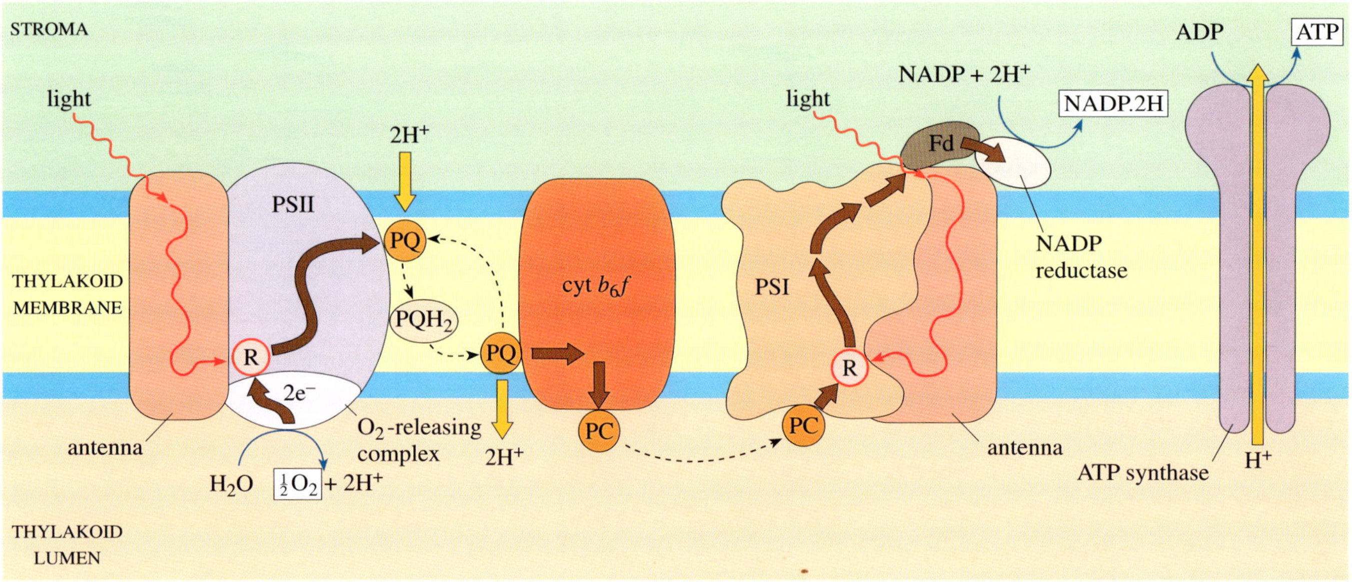

Figure 2.1 The components and pathway of non-cyclic photosynthetic electron transport and photophosphorylation in green plants. Light absorbed by groups of pigment molecules (**antennae**) is funnelled to the reaction centre (R), initially of **photosystem II (PSII)**. For each photon absorbed, an excited or energized electron is transferred to an electron acceptor in PSII and is replaced by electron donation from water via the oxygen-releasing complex. Two electrons are transferred per molecule of water oxidized and four electrons per molecule of oxygen released. Electrons from PSII pass via the mobile carrier plastoquinone (PQ) to the complex of cytochrome b_6 and cytochrome *f* (cyt b_6f) and thence to the mobile carrier plastocyanin (PC). PC donates electrons to photosystem I (PSI) after it has absorbed light and emitted excited electrons, which pass via the carrier ferredoxin (Fd) to NADP reductase. This last enzyme reduces NADP, generating reducing power, as NADP.2H. The proton gradient generated during electron transport (with protons accumulating in the interior or lumen of thylakoids) is discharged via the ATP synthase and used to power ATP synthesis. The brown arrows denote electron transfer.

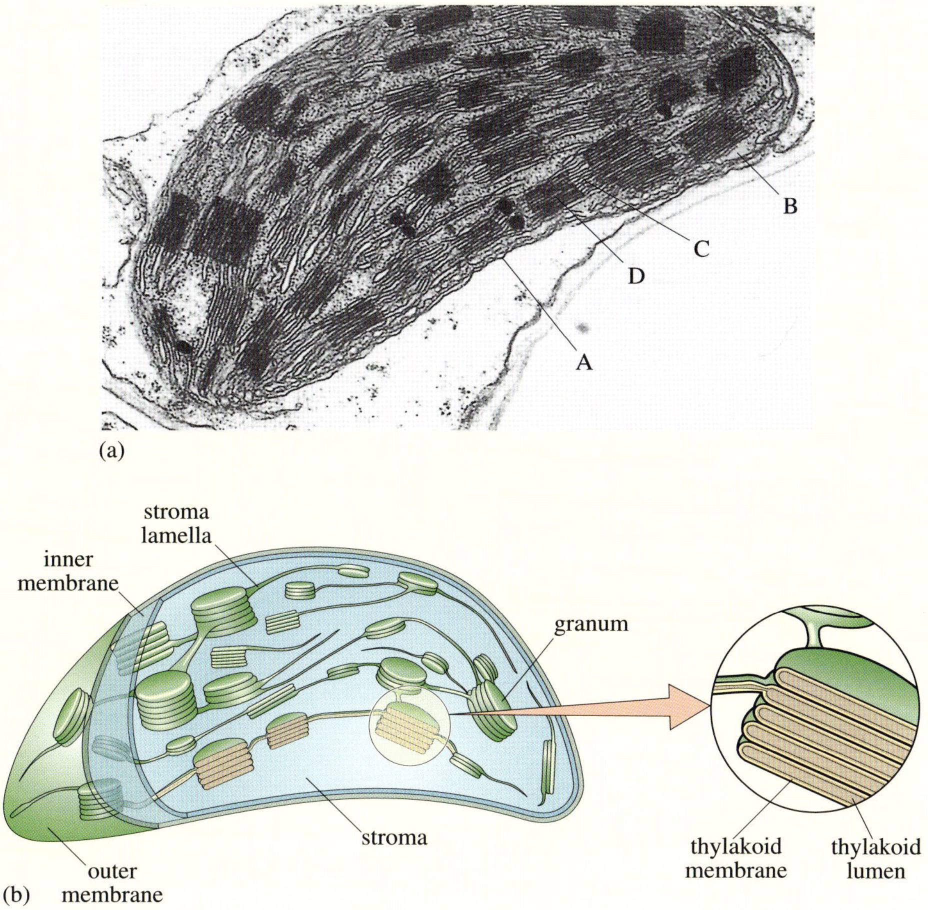

Figure 2.2 (a) Electron micrograph of a chloroplast. For labels A–D, see the answer to the text question on the previous page. (b) Schematic diagram of chloroplast structure.

reaction centre, with the whole antenna acting like a funnel, channelling the energy of absorbed quanta to the reaction centre. Different accessory pigments occur in other photosynthetic organisms; for example, red algae and cyanobacteria contain chlorophyll *d*, carotenoids and phycobiliproteins (which absorb green wavelengths).

❍ Three pigments from plant chloroplasts absorb maximally light of wavelengths (i) 540 nm, (ii) 670 nm and (iii) 650 nm; identify these pigments as either chlorophyll *a*, chlorophyll *b* or carotenoid.

● (i) is carotenoid (because it absorbs maximally the shortest wavelength), (ii) is chlorophyll *a* and (iii) is chlorophyll *b*.

In addition to pigments, antennae also contain structural proteins, which are different for photosystems I and II and play an important protective role (Section 2.2.2): the terms *light-harvesting complexes I and II* (LHCI and LHCII) are often used to describe the pigment–protein complexes associated with PSI and PSII respectively.

Photosynthetic electron transport and photophosphorylation occur on the membranes or lamellae (singular lamella) in chloroplasts, but the molecular components (Figure 2.1) are not arranged randomly, as you can see in Figure 2.3. This non-random arrangement is significant for control and coordination of the light reactions, so it is worth examining closely.

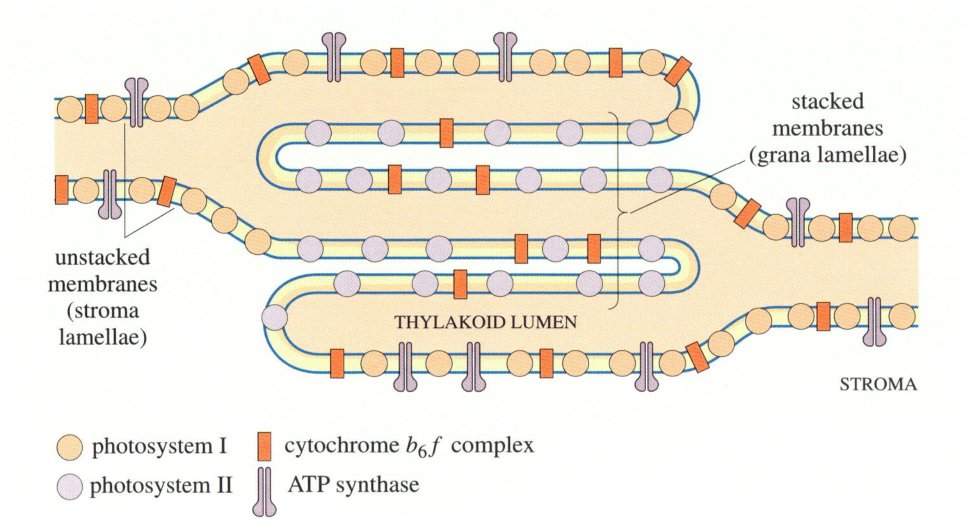

Figure 2.3 The location of molecular complexes on grana and stroma lamellae.

Notice first that one molecular complex is restricted mainly to the inner membranes (lamellae) of grana where they lie close together and are described as appressed membranes.

- ❍ Which complex is localized in this way?

- ● PSII.

Two other complexes, PSI and ATP synthase, are restricted to the unstacked stroma lamellae (Figure 2.2), which link grana across the chloroplast stroma, and to the outermost lamellae of grana; and the cytochrome b_6f complex occurs on all lamellae. So most of PSII is relatively far from PSI. Bearing in mind the pathway of non-cyclic electron transport (PSII → cytochrome b_6f → PSI, Figure 2.1), consider the functional implications of this structural arrangement. It must involve some remarkable long-distance shuttling by the mobile electron carriers plastoquinone (PQ) and plastocyanin (PC), so why should there be such a wide separation of PSI and PSII?

One possibility is that spatial separation of the photosystems is necessary in order to regulate and balance light input so that each photosystem receives the same number of quanta during non-cyclic electron flow; the molecular machinery can be damaged if light input is unbalanced (see Section 2.2.2). Another possibility is that physical separation facilitates *cyclic electron flow*, which is purely as an ATP-producing system and generates no reducing power (NADP.2H).

- ❍ What are the components and pathway of cyclic electron flow in chloroplasts?

- Cyclic electron flow involves absorption of light by PSI and transfer of excited electrons via ferredoxin to plastoquinone, cytochrome b_6f and then, via the mobile carrier plastocyanin, back to PSI. No NADP.2H is produced, but the coupled proton pumping can be used for ATP synthesis.

This cyclic flow operates mainly in the stroma lamellae and provides a flexible way of generating ATP in situations where there is a need for ATP but relatively less demand for reducing power. At present, however, there is no *completely* satisfactory explanation for the wide separation of the two photosystems in chloroplast lamellae. The arrangement is strikingly different from that in mitochondria, where electron carriers are all packed closely together.

You might wonder how information was obtained about the location of molecular complexes on chloroplast membranes. Box 2.1 describes three approaches and now would be a suitable time to study it. The rest of this section is concerned with how plants can grow over a huge range of light intensities.

BOX 2.1 STUDYING CHLOROPLAST MEMBRANES

MEMBRANE FRACTIONATION

In order to locate molecular complexes, chloroplast membranes must first be separated into stroma and grana lamellae. A rough separation can be obtained by exposing isolated chloroplasts to high-frequency sound waves (sonication) and/or high pressure, followed by differential centrifugation to separate the dense grana membranes from the less dense stroma membranes. A more refined method is illustrated in Figure 2.4. Membranes are fragmented under very high pressure and the membrane fragments then re-seal to form vesicles. Vesicles from stroma lamellae and the outer thylakoids of grana re-seal so that the originally outside surface remains outside (normal or right-side-out vesicles). Vesicles from the inner, appressed grana lamellae re-seal so that the original outer surface is now inside (inverted or inside-out vesicles). The two types of vesicle, which differ in surface charge, can be separated in solutions of polymers of different molecular mass, as shown here.

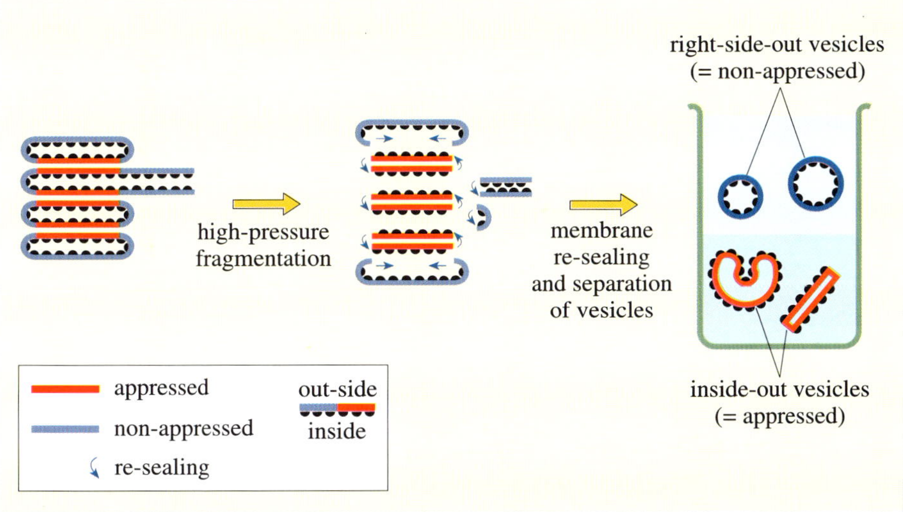

Figure 2.4 Diagram to illustrate how normal (right-side-out) and inverted (inside-out) vesicles are formed from different chloroplast membranes and then separated.

IDENTIFYING MOLECULAR COMPLEXES

The location of molecular complexes on membrane fractions can be demonstrated using three main methods:

1 *Immunohistochemistry* The molecular complexes can be visualized (and hence located) by raising antibodies to them, labelling the antibodies with a suitable marker (e.g. a fluorescent tag), and exposing chloroplast membranes to a labelled antibody.

2 *Freeze-etch/freeze fracture electron microscopy of photosynthetic mutants* If photosynthetic membranes are rapidly frozen and surface water evaporated under vacuum, molecular complexes which protrude from the membrane surface become visible in electron micrographs as characteristic knobs. Parts of complexes that are embedded in the membrane can be made visible by cleaving the lipid bilayer (freeze fracture). Using these techniques, the distribution of knobs on inside-out vesicles derived from grana was compared between normal plants and mutants known to be deficient in PSII or PSI. The results indicated that PSI mutants are deficient in knobs characteristic of stroma vesicles whereas PSII mutants are deficient in knobs characteristic of grana vesicles.

3 *Low-temperature fluorescence emission spectroscopy* A chlorophyll molecule excited by absorption of a photon of light may get rid of this energy either by transferring it to another molecule (the route to photosynthetic electron transport) or by releasing the energy partly as heat and partly by emission of a photon of light of lower energy (and hence longer wavelength) than that of the absorbed photon. Such emission is called **fluorescence**. The two photosystems fluoresce at different wavelengths when illuminated at very low temperature (77 K or −196 °C): the fluorescence emission maximum for PSII is 685 nm and that for PSI is 735 nm. Hence by comparing fluorescence emission spectra of different chloroplast membrane fractions, the locations of the photosystems can be deduced.

❍ Figure 2.5 shows the low-temperature fluorescence emission spectra of two chloroplast membrane fractions, one derived from internal grana membranes (inside-out vesicles) and the other from stroma membranes (right-side out vesicles). Knowing the distribution of PSI and PSII, identify the source (grana or stroma) of membrane fractions 1 and 2 in Figure 2.5.

● Membrane fraction 1 derives from internal grana membranes because the maximum fluorescence emission occurs at 685 nm, characteristic of PSII, which is located mainly on these membranes (Figure 2.3). Membrane fraction 2 derives from stroma membranes, which contain only PSI.

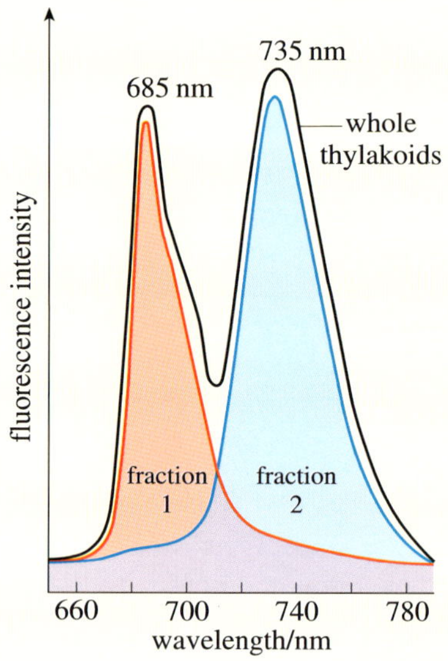

Figure 2.5 Low-temperature fluorescence emission spectra of isolated chloroplast membranes derived from internal grana or stroma.

2.2.2 ADAPTATIONS TO DIFFERENT LIGHT ENVIRONMENTS

The difference in light intensity, or 'strength', between a deeply shaded forest floor and midday tropical sun in the open is about 160-fold, i.e. from 15–2400 μmol m^{-2} s^{-1} of light quanta of wavelengths 400–700 nm (the **photosynthetic photon flux density** or **PPFD**), yet plants flourish over this whole range of light conditions. Some species are genetically adapted to permanent shade, others to full sun and yet others tolerate or adapt physiologically to a wide range of light intensities. Such physiological adaptation is properly described as **acclimation**. We examine first some of the structural and biochemical mechanisms that allow plants to survive and grow in shady habitats.

In addition to low average light intensity, shady habitats — which nearly always occur beneath a plant canopy — have two other characteristics that affect plants:

(i) The quality of light, or spectral composition (i.e. the relative numbers of quanta of different wavelengths) is changed because of selective absorption by the canopy.

❍ From Figure 2.6, describe how the light beneath a canopy differs from that above it.

● Compared to full sun, shade light contains proportionately fewer quanta in the range 400–680 nm, but proportionately more quanta above 680 nm, especially in the far-red and infrared.

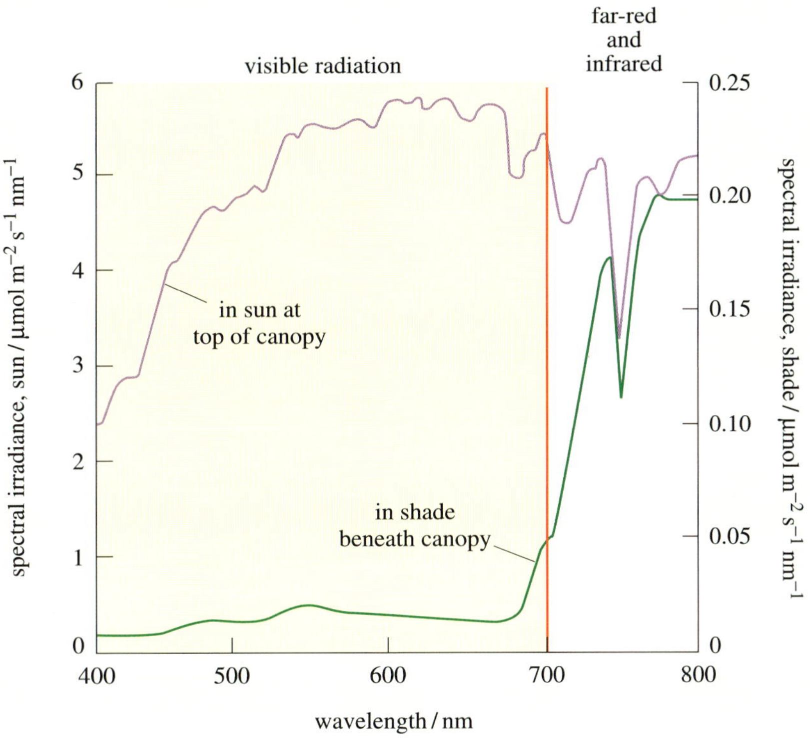

Figure 2.6 The spectral distribution of sunlight at the top of a plant canopy and under the canopy. The units of photosynthetic photon flux density are μmol m^{-2} s^{-1} nm^{-1} (i.e. μmoles of light quanta per square metre of leaf surface per second per unit wavelength).

(ii) Light conditions may change abruptly during the day. For example, discontinuities in the canopy mean that sunbeams occasionally pass right down to ground level, producing **sunflecks**. Quite suddenly and lasting for only a few minutes, deeply shaded leaves may receive a tenfold increase in light flux from sunflecks.

Shade plants have a range of adaptations to their environment, which may be determined genetically or result from acclimation. For example, they have very low rates of respiration (discussed further in Section 2.6.1). Here, however, we consider the adaptations that allow them to harvest light very efficiently when it is available at low average intensity, is relatively enriched in longer wavelengths compared with sunlight and may show brief periods of high intensity during sunflecks.

The first type of adaptation is at the level of whole leaves and is illustrated in Figure 2.7. Compared with a leaf that developed in the open (sun leaf), a leaf that developed in shade is much thinner overall and, in particular, has a very shallow layer of palisade mesophyll (Chapter 1) and patchy spongy mesophyll with more air spaces. It takes energy and resources to construct and maintain thick leaves, so this minimal structure of shade leaves is an efficient way in which to harvest the meagre supply of light normally available.

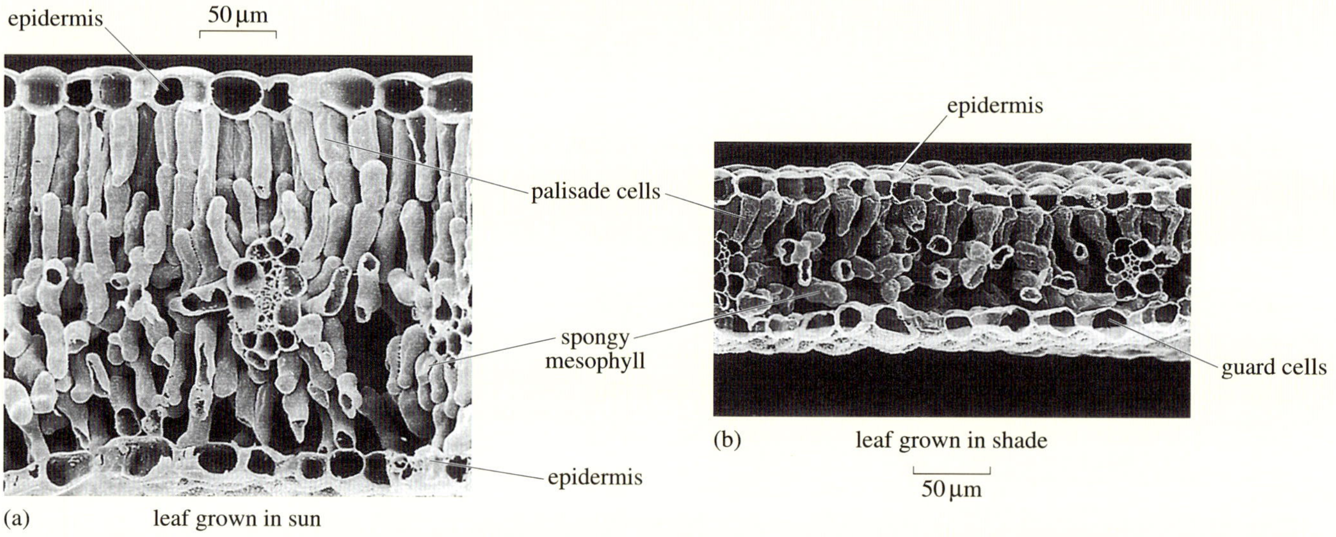

Figure 2.7 Scanning electron micrograph of vertical sections of *Impatiens parviflora* leaves that developed in (a) strong light (a sun leaf) and (b) low light (a shade leaf).

Other types of adaptation occur at a biochemical level within chloroplasts. For example, shade leaves have more chlorophyll molecules in the antenna systems that collect and feed light energy to each reaction centre. In addition, there is much greater proportion of PSII relative to PSI, which is often reflected in the presence of wide grana containing large numbers of stacked thylakoids, giving a ratio of appressed to non-appressed lamellae up to five times greater than in sun leaves.

- Why should this arrangement increase the ratio of PSII to PSI?
- PSII is located mainly on the appressed lamellae of grana and PSI on the non-appressed lamellae on the outside of grana or in the stroma (Figure 2.3).

The increase in PSII in shade plants relates to the far-red enrichment of shade light. The reaction centre of PSII shows maximum light absorption at a slightly shorter wavelength (680 nm) compared with the reaction centre of PSI (700 nm) — hence the names of the reaction centres, P680 and P700 respectively, where P stands for 'pigment'. This difference in absorption properties means that in far-red-enriched light, PSI is relatively more excited (emitting energized electrons at a faster rate) than PSII. But the smooth operation of non-cyclic electron transport requires that the two photosystems are excited *equally*, hence the requirement in shady habitats for increased absorption by PSII, by either increasing the number of reaction centres or the size of the pigment funnels channelling energy to each PSII reaction centre.

Finally, there is the question of sunflecks which, for leaves in deep shade, may provide nearly half the daily light income, but which are potentially damaging for shade leaves. Damage may arise because sunflecks are not far-red-enriched and hence over-excitation of PSII can occur. Such over-excitation — literally, funnelling more energy to PSII reaction centres than they can deal with or, alternatively, having too small a pool of electron acceptors to cope with the flow of excited electrons from reaction centres — leads to a form of reversible inhibition of photosynthesis called **photoinhibition**. This phenomenon is widespread in plants and is not restricted to shade plants exposed to sunflecks, so in Section 2.2.3 we discuss the general nature of photoinhibition and plant defences against it. Other adaptations that are necessary for the efficient use of precious sunfleck light do not involve the light reactions *per se* but rather:

- an ability to increase rapidly the rate of carbon fixation, i.e. make use of the increased supply of NADP.2H and ATP (discussed in Section 2.3.3);
- an ability to tolerate abrupt increases in leaf temperature (as much as 20 °C during prolonged, bright sunflecks), which increase water loss and may cause wilting; there is evidence that plants growing in moderately shaded habitats where sunflecks are relatively prolonged or abundant have larger root systems, which facilitate water uptake compared with plants adapted to more deeply shaded sites.

So adaptation of individual leaves or whole plants to variable light conditions (i.e. sunflecks) involves many aspects of their physiology. We explore these physiological adaptations further in later chapters.

Not all sunflecks are intense enough to cause photoinhibition, however, and in shade leaves, redistribution of light energy from PSII to PSI must occur so that both photosystems are again equally excited. **Energy redistribution** is thought to occur frequently in shade leaves, as the spectral composition of incident light shifts at different times of day or with different atmospheric conditions. It is a short-term, fine tuning of the photosynthetic light reactions, which allows light to be used with maximum efficiency. Figure 2.8 illustrates the mechanism of energy redistribution which was unravelled by research in the 1980s and 90s. PSII is now thought to exist as a huge dimeric complex with two reaction centres plus associated proteins and two pigment–protein funnels or light-harvesting complexes (LHCII).

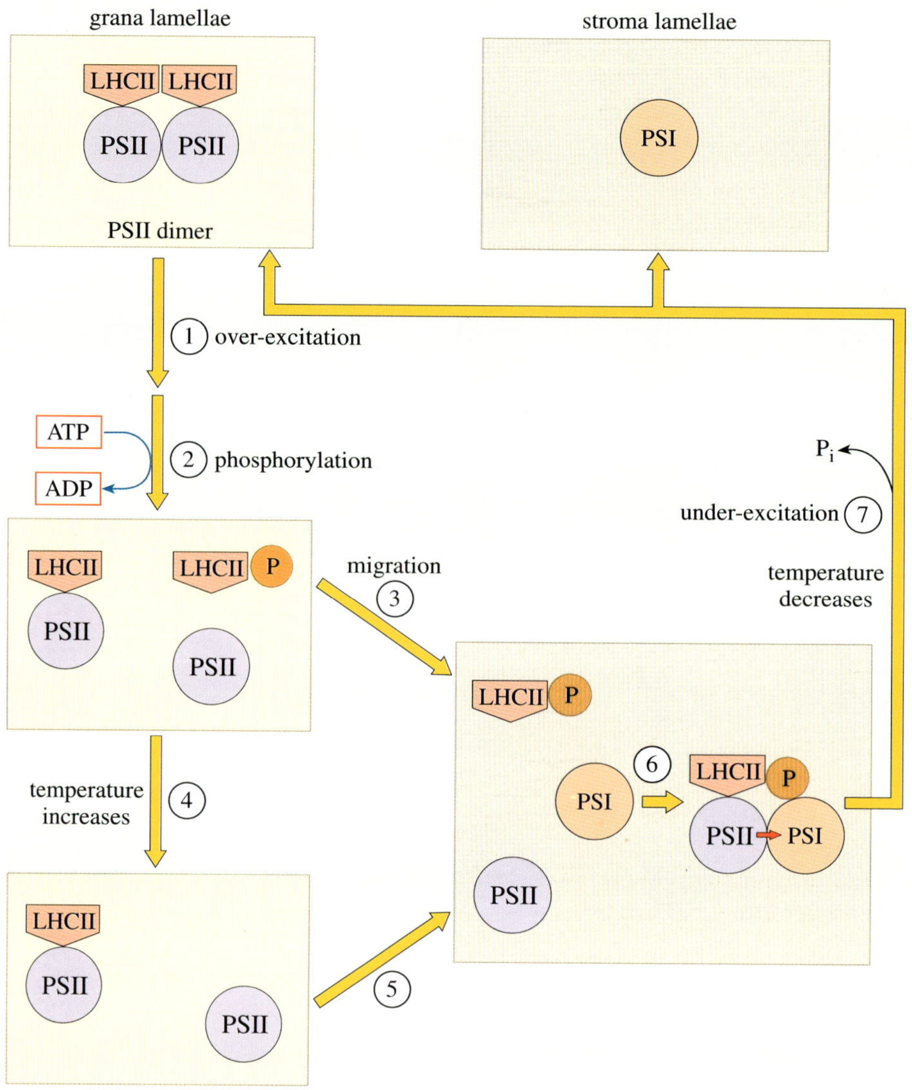

Figure 2.8 Energy redistribution after over-excitation of photosystem II, and its reversal. Numbered steps are described in the text. The small red arrow indicates energy transfer to PSI during step 6.

Over-excitation of PSII (step 1) has two consequences:

(a) A kinase enzyme is activated and this enzyme then phosphorylates a protein in one of the two LHCII complexes in the dimer (step 2). This change alters the electrical charge of the LHCII, reducing the adhesion between stacked lamellae and causing the dimer to split and then the phosphorylated LHCII to separate from its PSII and migrate into the non-appressed stroma region (step 3).

(b) Temperature increases (step 4) because some of the excess light energy entering PSII is dissipated as heat, which causes isolated PSII complexes to migrate into the stroma lamellae (step 5).

Reassembly of phosphorylated LHCII, PSII and PSI in the stroma lamellae (step 6) effectively channels more energy into PSI. The whole process can proceed in reverse (step 7) if PSII becomes under-excited (dephosphorylation of LHCII, fall in temperature and reverse migrations of the PSII and LHCII components).

This process is a good example illustrating how covalent modification of a protein (phosphorylation of the LHCII complex) can alter its properties. Energy redistribution is one of the mechanisms that helps plants to survive in low light conditions when light quality and quantity vary erratically.

2.2.3 PROTECTION AGAINST TOO MUCH LIGHT: PHOTOINHIBITION AND PHOTO-OXIDATION

As explained above, excess light can be harmful and plants have evolved a wide variety of mechanisms that prevent or minimize this harm, with the minimum 'cost' in terms of energy and resources. A first line of defence operates at the level of leaf behaviour and structure and involves decreased light absorption. Some plants adjust the orientation of leaf blades so that they lie parallel to the Sun's rays and thus minimize light interception. The shade plant *Oxalis oregana* (redwood sorrel), for example, grows in the redwood forests of North America and is often exposed to sunflecks lasting 20 minutes or more. Within a few minutes of sunfleck exposure, this species folds down its leaves. Table 2.2 shows the consequences of this behaviour for photosynthesis compared with those when leaves were artificially prevented from folding.

Table 2.2 The effects on photosynthesis in *Oxalis oregana* of leaf folding during exposure to sunflecks. The efficiency of the light reactions was estimated by measuring fluorescence characteristics which are proportional to quantum efficiency (the number of light quanta absorbed per molecule of O_2 evolved). Data from Powles and Björkman (1981).

Conditions during sunfleck exposure	% reduction in efficiency of light reactions during sunfleck	% reduction in rate of CO_2 uptake in low light following sunfleck
leaves allowed to fold down	9	0
leaves prevented from folding down	47	30

- From Table 2.2, suggest two reasons why leaf folding during sunflecks appears advantageous to *O. oregana*.

- Leaf folding (compared with not folding) results in: (1) greater efficiency of the light reactions, i.e. less photoinhibition, during sunflecks; and (2) no inhibition of photosynthesis after the sunfleck. Post-sunfleck inhibition in non-folding leaves results from damage, which takes time (and energy) to repair.

Some plants from open habitats show similar leaf movements, but it is not a common response to excess light. More common in high-light environments are longer-term adaptations such as the development of a thick waxy layer on the leaf surface. Such layers may perform several functions, including protection from insect or fungal attack and reduction of water loss, but they also reflect light very effectively. Experimental removal of surface wax from the succulent plant *Cotyledon orbiculata*, for example, increased light absorption by 50% and greatly increased photoinhibition in strong light.

The other lines of defence against excess light all involve molecular mechanisms that are universal among plants but are developed to different degrees in different habitats. Before describing these mechanisms, we need to examine more closely *why* light may cause damage. The basic cause is the formation of highly dangerous forms of oxygen, known as **reactive oxygen species** (**ROS**), which include the superoxide anion radical, $O_2{\bullet}^-$ (essentially an oxygen molecule with an extra electron). ROS are all free radicals and are especially harmful to membranes. During the photosynthetic light reactions, ROS may form either by energy transfer from excited chlorophyll molecules to O_2 (when reaction centres are too few to accept all the absorbed energy), or by transfer of electrons to O_2 from carriers such as ferredoxin (when there are too few suitable electron acceptors).

Molecular protective mechanisms

Molecular protective mechanisms against light-induced ROS operate at three levels:

1. Prevention of ROS formation by dissipating as heat the excess light energy absorbed by pigments. Heat dissipation is mediated by a pigment called zeaxanthin, a type of carotenoid pigment (Section 2.2.1) belonging to a group called the xanthophylls. As light levels increase, zeaxanthin is synthesized enzymically from another, precursor xanthophyll and accumulates in chloroplasts. The reverse occurs as light levels fall, i.e. conversion of zeaxanthin to its precursor, so that a **xanthophyll cycle**, finely tuned to prevailing light conditions, operates to protect leaves from light through thermal energy dissipation.
2. Rapid destruction of any ROS that form. The enzyme superoxide dismutase (SOD), for example, converts $O_2{\bullet}^-$ very efficiently to hydrogen peroxide, H_2O_2, which is then disposed of by other enzymes because its bleaching action is also potentially damaging.
3. If ROS start to build up, damage occurs first to PSII, culminating in the destruction of a particular protein, named D1, which acts as a weak link within the PSII complex. D1 has a very rapid turnover rate, with a half-life of about 2 h, so it can be replaced within hours or days. So, by breaking the electron transport chain at one easily repaired link, damage to the rest of the photosynthetic machinery is minimized.

- Suppose that you wish to carry out experiments to test the hypothesis that repair of photoinhibitory damage at level 3 involves the synthesis of new D1 protein. The first need is to establish that protein synthesis is required in order to recover from level 3 photoinhibition. For this investigation (Experiment 1), you are provided with: leafy plants that had experienced strong photoinhibition at level 3; an inhibitor of protein synthesis which is taken up by leaves; a suitable incubation medium; and apparatus to measure the rate of photosynthesis by O_2 evolution.

  (a) Describe (i) how you would carry out Experiment 1 with an appropriate control; and (ii) the result that would support the hypothesis.

  Assuming that Experiment 1 supported the hypothesis, a second experiment is needed to establish that more D1 protein is synthesized in leaves recovering from photoinhibition than in controls. To carry out Experiment 2 you are provided with: leaves from photoinhibited plants and from similar plants that had not experienced photoinhibition; radiolabelled amino acids; incubation medium; equipment to isolate chloroplasts and to extract chloroplast proteins and separate them by electrophoresis; information about the location of D1 after electrophoresis; and equipment to measure the amount of labelled D1 protein present.

  (b) Describe (i) how you would carry out Experiment 2 with an appropriate control; (ii) the result that would support the hypothesis.

- (a) (i) For Experiment 1, incubate photoinhibited leaves in the incubation medium under low light conditions (which would allow recovery from photoinhibition) and with and without (controls) the protein synthesis inhibitor. At the same time, monitor rates of photosynthesis (O_2 release). (ii) An increase in the rate of photosynthesis in controls but not in leaves incubated with the inhibitor would support the hypothesis, i.e. protein synthesis is necessary for recovery from level 3 photoinhibition.

  (b) (i) For Experiment 2, incubate photoinhibited and non-inhibited (control) leaves in the presence of radiolabelled amino acids (which are incorporated into newly synthesized proteins). Isolate chloroplasts and then extract chloroplast proteins from these leaves and separate the proteins by electrophoresis. Measure the amount of radioactivity associated with separated D1 protein. (ii) If D1 from previously photoinhibited leaves was much more heavily labelled with radioactivity than that from control leaves, this result would suggest that more D1 was synthesized during recovery from photoinhibition, which is consistent with and supports the hypothesis.

If, despite all the protective measures, ROS continue to accumulate, then irreversible damage occurs, a process described as **photo-oxidation**. Bleached leaves are a common sign of photo-oxidative damage preceding leaf death. Figure 2.9a illustrates the different stages as a leaf passes from relatively low light through increasing light fluxes when different protective mechanisms come into play up to the stage of photo-oxidation. The green area represents an environment where light limits the rate of photosynthesis and not only do the light reactions cope fully with all the harvested light but, equally important, the carbon fixation reactions utilize all of the ATP and NADP.2H as fast as these products are made, hence the label 'utilization' for this stage.

Figure 2.9b shows, for three different kinds of leaf, the relative magnitude of the utilization, protection and damage stages in a light gradient. Study this Figure carefully and look back at the descriptions of sun and shade leaves in Section 2.2.1.

❍ (a) Why do shade leaves (Figure 2.9b, top) have such a narrow window of light utilization and enter the photoprotection stages at such a low light flux? (b) Why do they enter the damage stage at such a low light flux compared with sun leaves?

● (a) Shade leaves are adapted to low light conditions and they have a high ratio of light-harvesting pigments to reaction centres. Reaction centres are rapidly over-excited as light levels rise and, in addition, carbon fixation cannot keep pace with the light reactions. Hence photoprotection becomes necessary at low light fluxes. (b) The only explanation is that protection at levels 1 and 2 (p. 66) is weak.

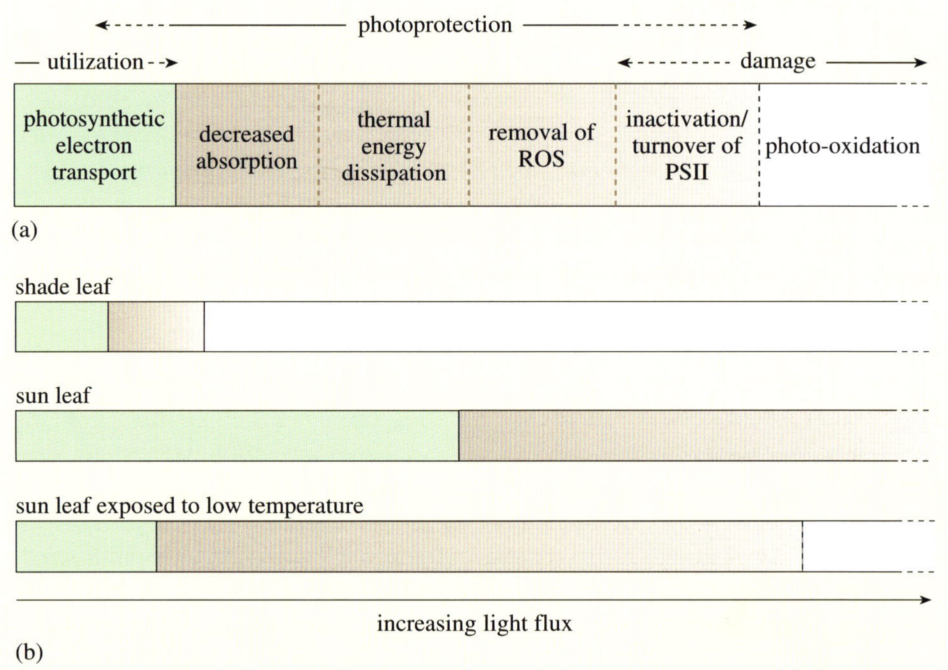

Figure 2.9 (a) The response of leaves to increasing fluxes of light from the utilization stage when all or most of the light absorbed is translated into photosynthetic electron transport (green), through the various, easily reversible photoprotection stages (brown) to the damage stages, which take much longer to reverse or are irreversible (photo-oxidation, white). (b) The relative magnitude of the stages shown in (a) for three kinds of leaves.

Shade leaves have only limited capacity to form zeaxanthin and contain low levels of protective enzymes such as SOD. The interesting point to notice about sun leaves in Figure 2.9b (middle) is that they never enter the damage stage at all! Sun leaves have very large pools of xanthophyll pigments and may dissipate harmlessly as heat over 50% of the light energy absorbed by these pigments. They also have high levels of photoprotective enzymes, so that even in the strongest sunlight only slight photoinhibition occurs. If raised in strong light, some shade plants can adapt physiologically (i.e. acclimate) to these conditions, performing almost as effectively as true sun plants. Such acclimation is an example of **phenotypic plasticity** (the production of different phenotypes in different environments by organisms with the same genotype) and contrasts with the genetically determined adaptations of obligate shade plants, which cannot acclimate to high light and are confined to shaded habitats.

Finally there is the situation illustrated in Figure 2.9b (bottom): that of sun leaves exposed to low temperature. In laboratory experiments, these leaves often show strong photoinhibition at light fluxes equivalent to only half full sunlight and may show photo-oxidative damage at higher fluxes. This is why house-plants of tropical origin, exposed to strong light in a cool room (around 10 °C), commonly grow poorly and may be permanently damaged. To explain this phenomenon, you need to bear in mind that photochemical reactions are insensitive to temperature but that the rates of enzyme-catalysed reactions and electron transport are reduced at low temperatures.

❍ Given this information, suggest an explanation for the altered behaviour of sun leaves at low temperatures.

● Firstly, the utilization of absorbed light is greatly slowed down; rates of photosynthetic electron transport and carbon fixation do not keep pace with photochemical reactions as light levels increase. Secondly, protection by the xanthophyll cycle and SOD is less effective at low temperatures because both processes involve enzyme-catalysed reactions.

Strong light on cold days can have detrimental effects on both crops and wild plants. Crop plants such as maize (*Zea mays*), for example, showed photoinhibition of up to 45% when sunny conditions coincided with morning temperatures of 10 °C or less, with recovery requiring 2–3 days of warm dull weather. Crops such as winter rape (*Brassica napus*) and evergreen trees such as holly (*Ilex aquifolium*) and Scots pine (*Pinus sylvestris*) likewise show increased photoinhibition on sunny winter days. In fact, any stress that reduces the rate of carbon fixation — such as shortage of water, high or low temperatures or shortage of mineral nutrients — tends to exacerbate photoinhibition by reducing the magnitude of the utilization stage. There is a delicate and closely regulated balance between the light and dark reactions of photosynthesis. The next section looks in more detail at the latter, i.e. the process of carbon fixation.

SUMMARY OF SECTION 2.2

1. The molecular components of photosynthetic light reactions are arranged on chloroplast membranes such that PSII is largely confined to appressed lamellae inside grana and PSI to the non-appressed stroma lamellae.
2. Information about molecular arrangements on chloroplast membranes can be obtained using low-temperature fluorescence emission spectra, immunohistochemistry and freeze-etch/freeze fracture electron microscopy of particular membrane fractions.

3 Shade plants are genetically or physiologically adapted to conditions of low light, rich in far-red wavelengths, and to exposure to sunflecks. They harvest light efficiently under these conditions and minimize damage due to over-excitation of PSII.

4 Shade-plant characteristics include thin leaves, low rates of leaf respiration, large antenna (or light-harvesting) systems and a high ratio of PSII to PSI. Protection during sunflecks is achieved by physiological and molecular mechanisms (energy redistribution involving covalent modification and migration of PSII components).

5 Strong light (high PPFD) can damage leaves through the production of free radicals (ROS). General protection against ROS may be through leaf movements and a range of molecular mechanisms, which include the xanthophyll cycle (preventing formation of ROS), enzymatic destruction of ROS, and rapid destruction and repair of D1 protein in PSII.

6 Damage due to strong light which is reversible (by repair mechanisms) is called photoinhibition. Irreversible damage is called photo-oxidation. Shade leaves have only very limited capacity for damage repair and are easily photo-oxidized, whereas sun leaves have a high repair capacity (unless stressed, e.g. by low temperatures) and do not usually become photo-oxidized.

2.3 Carbon fixation: the C3 cycle

Carbon fixation, the conversion of inorganic carbon (CO_2 or hydrogen carbonate, HCO_3^-) to organic compounds, is usually taken as the defining metabolic activity of autotrophs and, from cyanobacteria to eukaryotic algae to the plant kingdom, only one series of reactions achieves *net* carbon fixation: the **C3** or **Calvin cycle**. Other processes in both plants and animals may fix CO_2, but for every molecule of CO_2 fixed, a molecule is released later in the process, so there is no net carbon fixation. There are also other pathways that achieve net carbon fixation among the anaerobic photosynthetic bacteria and chemosynthetic archaeons but, on a global scale, the C3 cycle dominates. Here we begin by describing what the reactions of the C3 cycle are and some aspects of product synthesis (Section 2.3.1); then we examine Rubisco, the most important enzyme in the cycle (Section 2.3.2); and finally, we look at how the cycle is controlled and coordinated with the light reactions (Section 2.3.3).

2.3.1 Reactions of the C3 cycle

In the C3 cycle, CO_2 and water combine with a 5-carbon acceptor molecule and the products are converted to sugars (using reducing power (NADP.2H) and ATP from the light reactions) with regeneration of the acceptor. The cycle occurs in the chloroplast stroma (Section 2.2.1) and involves many small steps, but it can be divided into three main stages. They are illustrated in Figure 2.10a, with more detail provided in Figure 2.10b.

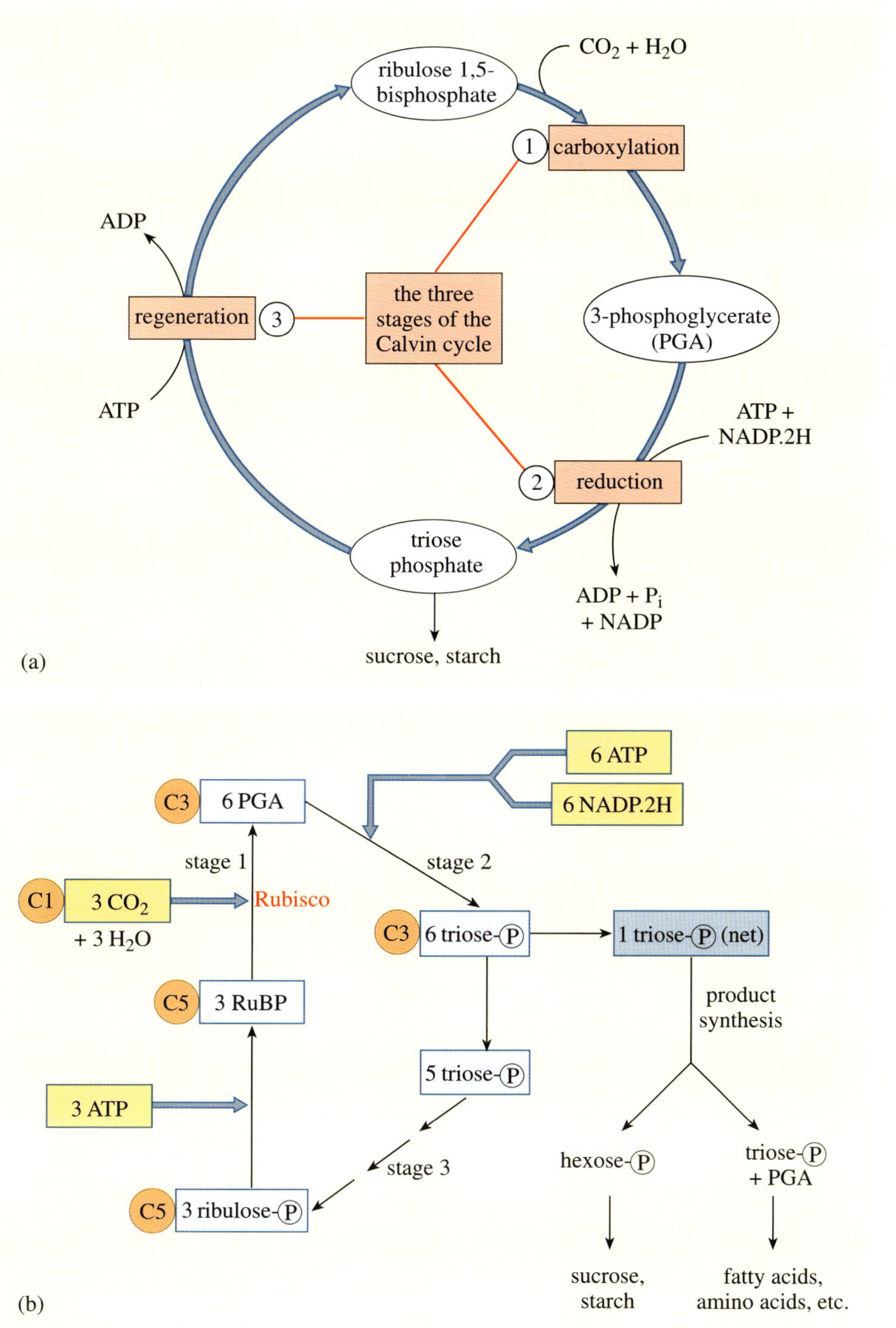

Figure 2.10 (a) A simplified version of the C3 or Calvin cycle showing the three stages. (b) A quantitative version of the Calvin cycle. 'C1', 'C2', etc. on orange circles beside intermediates denote the number of carbon atoms present. RuBP = ribulose 1,5-bisphosphate.

Stage 1: *Carboxylation* The acceptor ribulose bisphosphate (a 5-carbon sugar with two phosphate groups, which is commonly abbreviated to RuBP) is carboxylated by combining with CO_2 and the product splits to give two molecules of a 3-carbon intermediate, 3-phosphoglycerate (PGA).

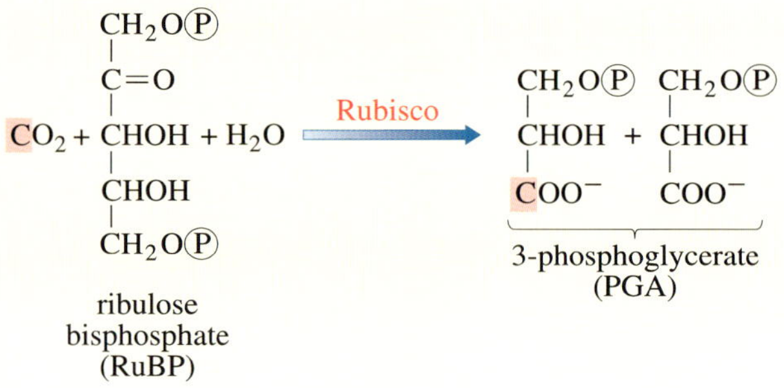

(2.3)

The enzyme that catalyses this key reaction has a long name (explained in Section 2.3.2), which is shortened to **Rubisco**. It is because the first stable product of the Calvin cycle is a 3-carbon compound that the alternative name, C3 cycle, is used.

Stage 2: *Reduction* The reduction of PGA to a 3-carbon sugar (i.e. triose) phosphate called glyceraldehyde 3-phosphate is the exact reverse of one of the central, energy-releasing reaction in glycolysis. Not surprisingly, this reaction requires a large input of energy in the C3 cycle: one molecule of ATP and one of NADP.2H for each molecule of PGA reduced.

Stage 3: *Regeneration* From the pool of triose phosphate molecules, five-sixths are used to regenerate the acceptor, ribulose bisphosphate. The remaining one-sixth is available for synthesizing useful end-products, which include not only 6-carbon sugars (hexoses), such as glucose, from which sucrose and storage and structural carbohydrates (e.g. starch and cellulose, respectively) are synthesized, but also fatty acids and amino acids. We shall not describe all the sugar interconversions involved in acceptor regeneration, but from Figure 2.10b you can see that five molecules of triose phosphate (C3) produce three molecules of ribulose phosphate (C5). Formation of RuBP from ribulose phosphate is another reaction of the C3 cycle that requires an input of energy (ATP).

- ❍ Using the information above and/or in Figure 2.10b, work out how many molecules of ATP and NADP.2H are required to fix *one* molecule of CO_2.

- ● Three molecules of ATP and two of NADP.2H: two molecules each of ATP and NADP.2H are required to reduce the *two* molecules of PGA produced by the initial carboxylation; one further molecule of ATP is used in the regeneration step.

- ❍ How many turns of the C3 cycle are necessary for the net synthesis of one molecule of hexose (6-carbon) sugar?

- ● Six: each turn of the cycle gives a net fixation of one molecule of CO_2 and you can see from Figure 2.10b that three turns give one molecule (net) of triose phosphate. Hence six turns gives one molecule of hexose.

Working out the steps in the C3 cycle was a biochemical *tour de force* and, quite properly, the US scientist Melvin Calvin, who led the research team (and after whom the cycle was named), was awarded the Nobel Prize for Chemistry in 1961. As an example of the classical approach to sorting out a biochemical pathway we describe the principles of Calvin's experimental method in Box 2.2 (overleaf), which could be read either now or at the end of Section 2.3.

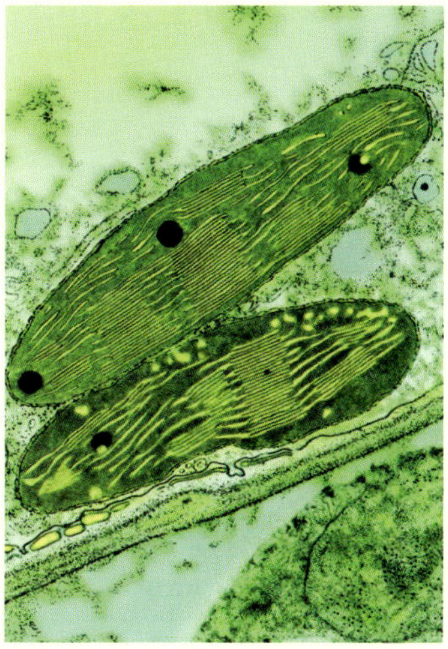

Figure 2.11 Coloured transmission electron micrograph of two chloroplasts in a leaf of a pea plant (*Pisum sativum*). Each chloroplast is seen cut lengthways and granules of stored starch are visible (small, pale areas).

STARCH AND SUCROSE SYNTHESIS

The main end-products of the Calvin cycle are the disaccharide sucrose (glucose-fructose), and starch (a polymer of glucose). Sucrose is synthesized in the cytosol, from where it is transported away in phloem (Chapter 1) and used or stored in other tissues. Starch is synthesized in chloroplasts when sucrose synthesis does not keep pace with the Calvin cycle and is stored there during the day (Figure 2.11), being broken down to glucose and used by the plant during darkness.

The starting point for both products is triose phosphate, which is first converted to glucose 1-phosphate. This intermediate is then 'activated' by reaction with ATP, for starch synthesis, or UTP (uridine triphosphate), for sucrose synthesis. The ADP-glucose and UDP-glucose thus formed are the immediate precursors for starch and sucrose synthesis, respectively, as illustrated in Figure 2.12. You can also see from Figure 2.12 that triose phosphate is exported from chloroplasts by a transport protein, the **phosphate translocator**, which is located in the inner chloroplast membrane and exchanges inorganic phosphate (P_i) in the cytosol for triose phosphate from the chloroplast. The phosphate translocator effectively regulates the ratio of P_i to triose phosphate which, in turn, is a major factor controlling and coordinating rates of starch and sucrose synthesis.

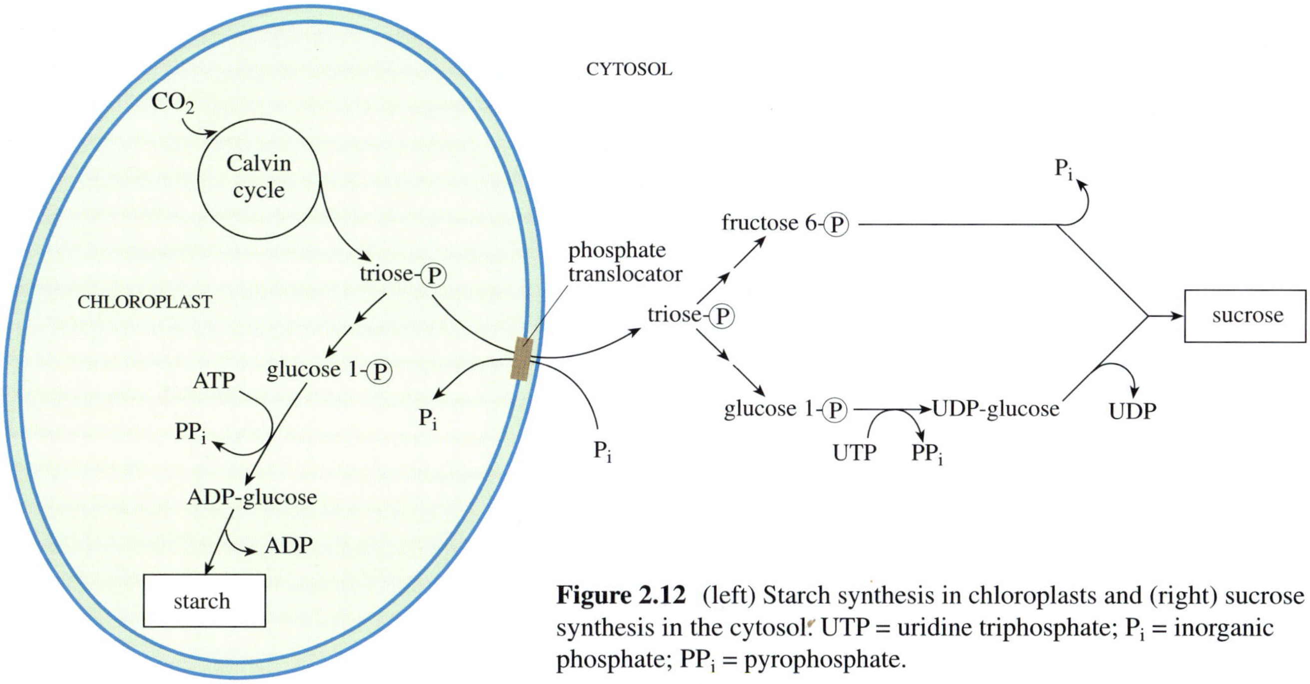

Figure 2.12 (left) Starch synthesis in chloroplasts and (right) sucrose synthesis in the cytosol. UTP = uridine triphosphate; P_i = inorganic phosphate; PP_i = pyrophosphate.

Box 2.2 Working out the C3 cycle

Research on the C3 cycle began in 1946, one year after the long-lived radioactive carbon isotope, ^{14}C, first became available from atomic reactors. Use of ^{14}C as a 'tracer' was vital for the success of this project, which involved three main types of experimental procedure.

(1) Cells that were photosynthesizing at a uniform rate were exposed for periods ranging from 5 seconds to a few minutes to $^{14}CO_2$. The cells were then rapidly killed in boiling methanol, the contents extracted and the ^{14}C-labelled compounds separated. The only biological material suitable for this kind of experiment was unicellular green algae such as *Chlorella*, which could be grown in uniform cultures, rapidly killed and, being in the group immediately ancestral to green plants (Chapter 1), was biochemically very similar to them. Use of algal cultures was a second factor vital to the success of the project.

(2) Having extracted ^{14}C-labelled compounds, the theory was that the compound(s) containing the greatest amount of ^{14}C after the shortest labelling period should be the first stable intermediate(s) of carbon fixation. To separate and identify the labelled compounds the (then) relatively new technique of two-way paper chromatography was used, which was the third element vital to the success of the project (but now superceded by much faster separation techniques). Figure 2.13 illustrates how autoradiography was used to determine the positions of labelled compounds after separation. The three-carbon compound 3-phosphoglycerate (PGA) was identified as the first-formed product at an early stage in the research, giving rise to the mistaken belief that the initial acceptor of CO_2 must be a *two*-carbon compound and a long, fruitless search for it!

❍ Do the autoradiograms in Figure 2.13b support the view that PGA is the first stable intermediate in carbon fixation?

● Yes, because PGA is the most heavily labelled compound (i.e. has the largest spot, which counting could show contains the most radioactivity) after the shortest labelling period.

(3) To confirm and clarify the steps in the C3 cycle, especially the regeneration stage, it was necessary to determine the position of ^{14}C atoms within labelled compounds after chemically degrading them. For example if you look back at Equation 2.3, you can see that the CO_2 carbon atom (pink box) becomes the carbon atom of the carboxylate group ($-COO^-$) of one of the two PGA molecules produced.

Having worked out the steps in the C3 cycle using techniques (1)–(3), final confirmation that the pathway existed was obtained by isolating the enzymes necessary to catalyse each proposed step. All the enzymes were identified.

Triose phosphate and 3-phosphoglycerate (PGA), derived directly or indirectly from the Calvin cycle, are also starting materials for the synthesis of both fatty acids and amino acids (Figure 2.10b). Fatty acid synthesis in green tissues occurs exclusively in chloroplasts, and in non-green tissues, in equivalent organelles called *plastids*, so chloroplasts/plastids and the C3 pathway are at the heart of biosynthesis in plants.

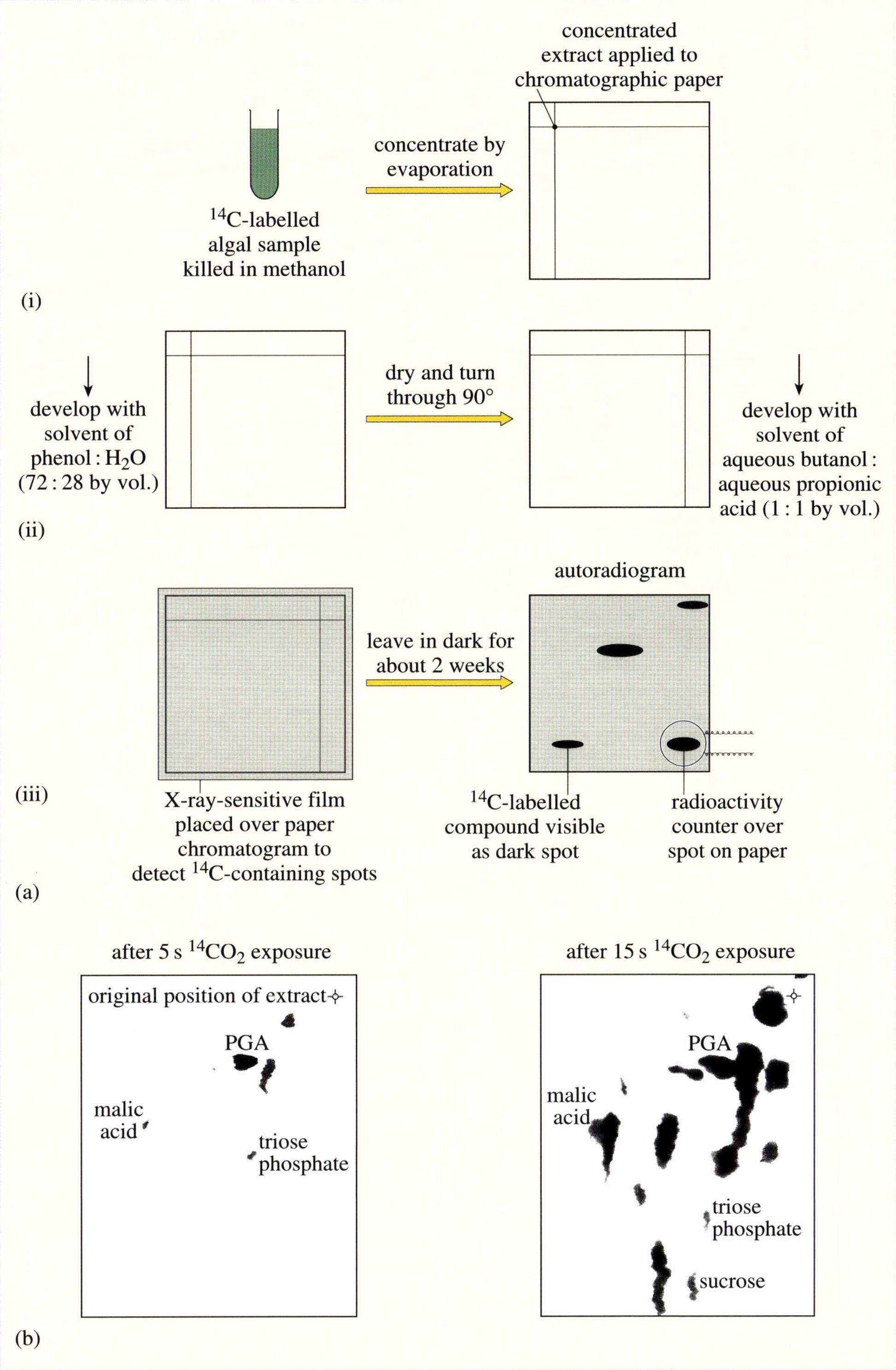

Figure 2.13 (a) Use of two-way paper chromatography to separate the products of carbon fixation after exposing *Chlorella* cultures to $^{14}CO_2$. (b) The autoradiograms for labelling periods of 5 and 15 seconds. PGA = 3-phosphoglycerate.

2.3.2 RUBISCO — THE PREMIER ENZYME

Rubisco has two claims to the title 'premier': it captures CO_2 in the first reaction of photosynthesis and it is the most abundant protein on Earth, comprising around half of all leaf protein. The full name of Rubisco is ribulose bisphosphate carboxylase/oxygenase, which actually conveys much information about the substrates and activity of the enzyme. You know already that RuBP is a substrate which Rubisco carboxylates (combines with CO_2). The '/oxygenase' indicates that Rubisco may, alternatively, oxygenate RuBP (combine with oxygen), the reaction being:

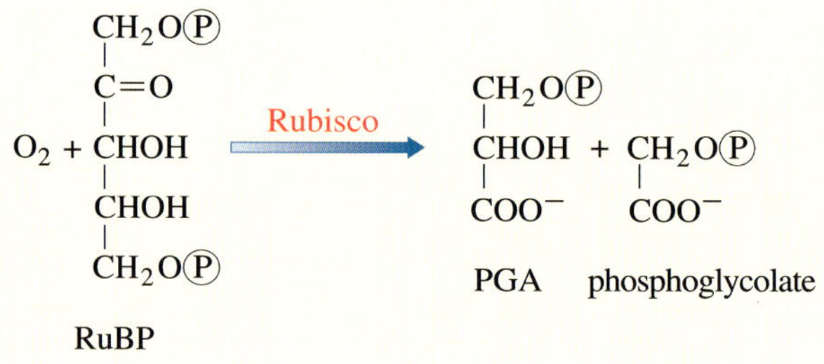

(2.4)

CO_2 and O_2 are thus competing substrates for Rubisco. The phosphoglycolate produced in the oxygenase reaction is the substrate of another cycle of reactions, the *C2 cycle*, which is discussed in Section 2.4.

STRUCTURE AND PROPERTIES OF RUBISCO

Rubisco is a very large enzyme with an M_r of about 560 000. In cyanobacteria and most eukaryotes, Rubisco comprises eight large subunits and eight small subunits which, in green plants, are encoded by chloroplast genes and nuclear genes, respectively. A chaperone protein is required to facilitate the assembly of all the subunits correctly in chloroplasts. The uniformity of the enzyme over such a wide taxonomic range indicates that it is very ancient and must have evolved in cyanobacterial ancestors when the atmosphere contained much more CO_2 than it does now, but no significant amounts of O_2.

The oxidase activity of Rubisco appears to have been incidental, you might even say an 'evolutionary accident'. At present-day levels of atmospheric O_2, the competing oxygenase reaction commonly reduces Rubisco carboxylation by about 30%. The only way in which most plants can sustain a reasonable rate of carbon fixation is by having very large quantities of Rubisco, hence its abundance. Some plants have evolved a mechanism that, at a cost, partially overcomes the problem of Rubisco inefficiency, by concentrating CO_2 within chloroplasts (Sections 2.5 and 2.6). There have also been evolutionary 'improvements' in Rubisco with respect to its specificity for CO_2 over O_2, i.e. the ratio of carboxylation to oxygenation rate. Some photosynthetic bacteria have a simpler form of the enzyme (made up of fewer subunits) with such low specificity that they cannot fix significant amounts of CO_2 in the presence of O_2 and, indeed, all of them are strict anaerobes. The specificity for CO_2 relative to O_2 increases from five in cyanobacteria to six in green algae to between eight and ten in flowering plants.

Because it plays such a key role in the C3 cycle, there has been much research on the control of Rubisco activity and much debate about whether the quantity or activity of this enzyme ever controls the overall rate of carbon fixation. We discuss these questions next.

2.3.3 Control of carbon fixation

Like respiration, a complex, multi-step process such as the C3 cycle involves control mechanisms that operate on different levels and have several components. Before examining these levels and components, it is useful to ask the questions: Why control? What is the point (from a plant's point of view) of being able to slow down or speed up the C3 cycle? What considerations affect the maximum potential rate of the cycle for a leaf? Think first about the overall function of photosynthesis: it is to trap light and convert it to chemical energy, which is then used to fix carbon, i.e. assimilate it into an organic form. Fixed carbon is either stored or used to synthesize new materials required for growth or survival. So the rate of the C3 cycle should, as far as possible, match that of the light reactions and use up ATP and reducing power as fast as they form, as happens in shady conditions when low light (i.e. low PPFD) limits the overall rate of photosynthesis.

However, from the discussion of sunflecks (Section 2.2.2) you know that light flux may suddenly increase, requiring a capacity to speed up the C3 cycle within seconds. To accelerate the C3 cycle, and also to 'start up' the cycle promptly at sunrise, it is essential that appropriate amounts of active enzymes and intermediates are present — especially ribulose bisphosphate, the primary CO_2 acceptor. A powerful brake is required in order to achieve this state of readiness, so that the cycle slows down or stops suddenly and does not free-wheel in darkness.

- If the C3 cycle did free-wheel to a stop as darkness fell, what would happen to the pool size of RuBP?

- It would decline dramatically as CO_2 would continued to be fixed (so using up RuBP) but the rest of the cycle would grind to a halt as supplies of NADP.2H and ATP were used up. At sunrise, therefore, precious time would be wasted in replenishing the pool of RuBP.

Finally, we need to think about matching a plant or a leaf to its environment in the most 'economical' way, i.e. with optimal use of energy and resources. It takes a lot of resources to synthesize the enzymes of the C3 cycle and their levels ought, therefore, to match the expected maximum rate of the cycle. That rate depends on the environment: in shade, light levels determine how fast the cycle needs to turn but in the open, when light is in excess, the supply of CO_2 from the atmosphere or the levels of C3 cycle enzymes are the determining factor and much higher rates of cycling can be sustained. Thus obligate shade plants have considerably lower levels of C3 cycle enzymes than do obligate sun plants. Plants that experience frequent, large changes in light intensity (due to sunflecks, for example) tend to have intermediate levels of C3 enzymes. Overall, the genetic make-up of a plant and its capacity to respond to environmental signals (i.e. its phenotypic plasticity) determine the levels of C3 cycle enzymes.

Table 2.3 summarizes the different levels of control of the C3 cycle. Levels 2 and 3 are discussed further below.

Table 2.3 Levels of control in the regulation of the C3 cycle.

Level	Components affected	Effect
1 genetic controls and environmental factors (light)	amounts of enzymes (especially Rubisco)	determines maximum rate of cycling
2 coarse biochemical control (via light and other environmental factors)	activation state of Rubisco and four other enzymes	stops/slows down and starts/accelerates cycle
3 fine biochemical control (via light)	reaction rates and activity of enzymes	exerts fine control of rate of cycling

COARSE BIOCHEMICAL CONTROL (I): RUBISCO ACTIVATION

Rubisco activity is influenced by more environmental factors than is any other C3 cycle enzyme: light, CO_2 and O_2 concentration and temperature all affect its activity. Considering light, it has been known for many years that Rubisco is inactivated in darkness and activated in the light. The first clue about the mechanism came in the 1980s when a mutant of thale cress (*Arabidopsis thaliana*, an annual plant much used in plant molecular biology) was discovered in which light activation did not occur unless CO_2 levels were extremely high. The mutant lacked just one enzyme, which is now known as **Rubisco activase**. In the light, Rubisco activase removes substances (including RuBP) that bind to Rubisco in the dark and 'lock' it into an inactive form (Figure 2.14). Here, therefore, is a key mechanism that links Rubisco activity to light.

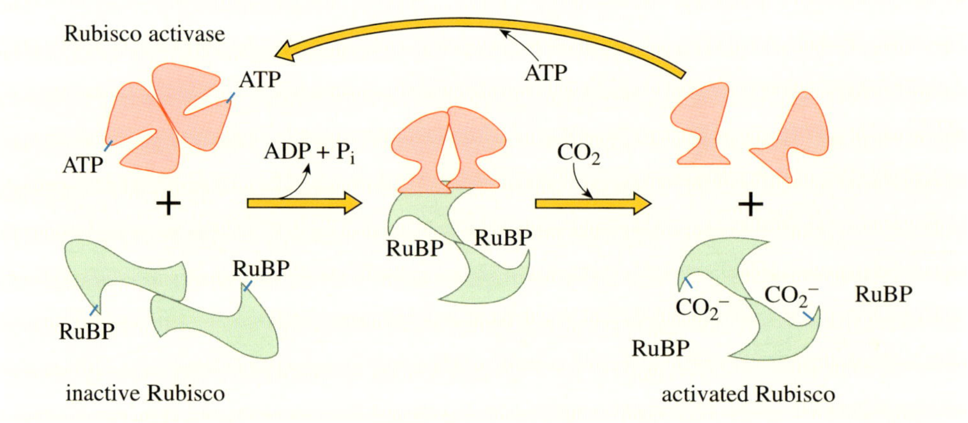

Figure 2.14 Activation of Rubisco in the light by Rubisco activase. The activase couples ATP hydrolysis with release of bound RuBP from inactive Rubisco, which is then activated by binding CO_2 at an allosteric site (i.e. distinct from the substrate-binding site).

CO_2 and O_2 concentration affect rates of carbon fixation by altering the ratio of carboxylase to oxygenase reaction rates of Rubisco. Rising temperature also tends to reduce carboxylation rate and increase the oxygenase reaction rate of Rubisco, because of reduced solubility of CO_2 relative to O_2 at higher temperatures and because the affinity of Rubisco for CO_2 relative to O_2 decreases. Since atmospheric concentrations of CO_2 (a greenhouse gas) are now rising and increased global temperatures are predicted, the effects on Rubisco activity are of considerable interest.

- What are the possible effects of raised [CO_2] in the atmosphere and increased global temperatures on Rubisco activity and net carbon fixation?

- Rising [CO_2] should increase carboxylase activity and net carbon fixation but rising temperatures could oppose these increases, at least partially.

The final outcome is, therefore, impossible to predict at present and the situation is further complicated by the possibility of altered rainfall patterns and, in some areas, decreased water availability for plant growth.

COARSE BIOCHEMICAL CONTROLS (II): LIGHT-ACTIVATION OF OTHER ENZYMES

Four enzymes in the C3 cycle are inactivated in darkness and activated in light by a common mechanism: three enzymes are involved in RuBP regeneration and one in the conversion of PGA to triose phosphate. The common mechanism is the **ferredoxin–thioredoxin system**, which was identified in the early 1990s and involves covalent modification of disulfide (—S—S—) groups. In the light, when the enzymes are active, their disulfide groups are reduced (to —SH SH—) but in darkness they are oxidized (back to —S—S—) and the enzymes are inactive. Ferredoxin is a soluble electron acceptor linked to photosystem I (Section 2.1) and is therefore reduced in the light and oxidized in darkness. Reduced ferredoxin in turn reduces thioredoxin, which in turn reduces the disulfide groups of the C3 cycle enzymes (Figure 2.15 overleaf).

The ferredoxin–thioredoxin system is the main component of the powerful 'brake' that stops the C3 cycle in darkness and allows it to start up again in the light. It has another function, however: inactivation in the light and activation in darkness of an enzyme that controls the breakdown of sugars in chloroplasts. Thus the ferredoxin–thioredoxin system can be seen as coordinating carbohydrate synthesis and breakdown, so that synthesis predominates in the light and breakdown in darkness.

FINE BIOCHEMICAL CONTROLS

The mechanisms described here generally act to slow down or speed up the C3 cycle rather than stop or start it. Firstly, several C3 enzymes (including Rubisco) have a high pH optimum (around pH 8) and some, including Rubisco, show enhanced activity with increased concentrations of magnesium ions (Mg^{2+}).

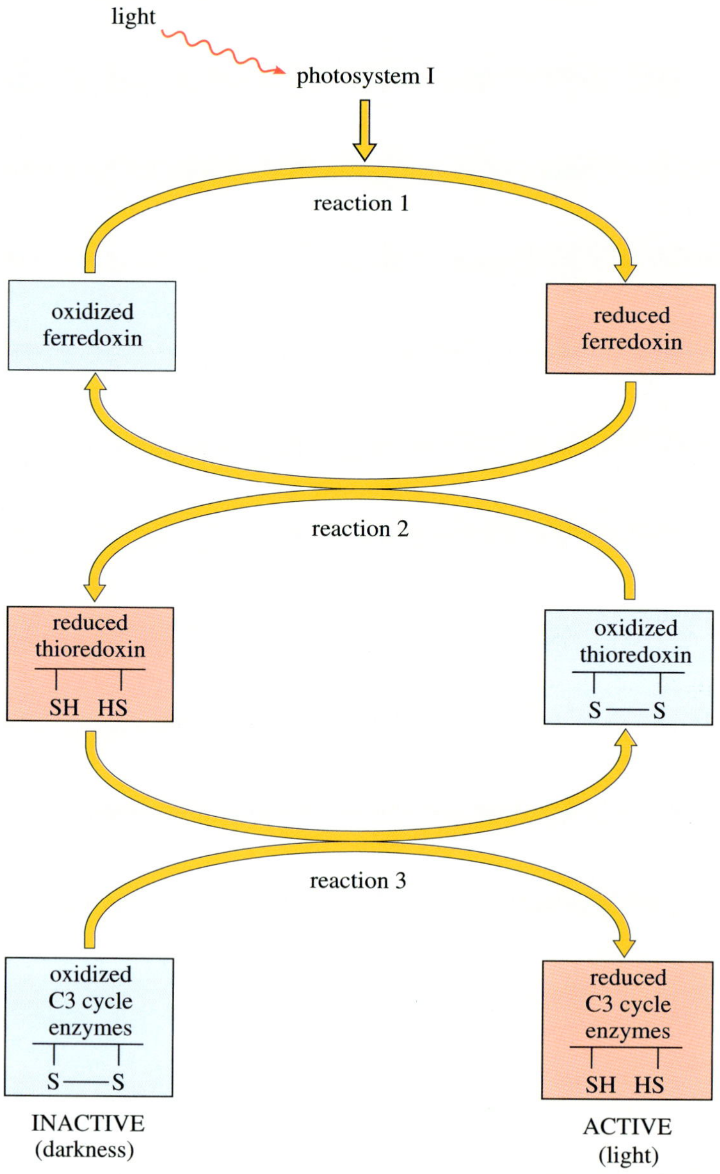

Figure 2.15 The reduction and hence activation of certain C3 cycle enzymes in the light by the ferredoxin–thioredoxin system.

❍ What happens during the light reactions of photosynthesis that affects the pH of the stroma?

● Protons are pumped from the stroma (hence raising stromal pH) into the thylakoid space or lumen, where pH falls.

The pumping of protons *out of* the stroma during the light reactions is accompanied by a flux of Mg^{2+} ions *into* the stroma, so changes in both pH and ion concentrations in the light tend to increase the activity of C3 enzymes.

A second type of fine control operates via levels of ATP and NADP.2H. The reduction stage (Figure 2.10) is very sensitive to these levels and slows down if they fall, which is most likely to occur if the rate of the light reactions decreases.

Overall, there is remarkably effective control of carbon fixation, ranging from genetically fixed attributes of plants in particular environments (e.g. deep shade) to mechanisms that operate within seconds or minutes as light conditions change. What remains to be considered are the consequences of the oxidase reaction of Rubisco, which are significant for both carbon fixation and the light reactions.

SUMMARY OF SECTION 2.3

1 The Calvin or C3 cycle is the only pathway in eukaryotes that achieves a net fixation of carbon. It has three stages (carboxylation, reduction and regeneration) and uses three molecules of ATP and two of NADP.2H to fix one molecule of CO_2.

2 Triose phosphate from the C3 cycle is used to synthesize sucrose in the cytoplasm (for export) and starch in chloroplasts (for temporary storage). The phosphate translocator plays a key role in balancing and controlling these two processes.

3 Rubisco is a huge and very abundant enzyme that catalyses the first reaction of the C3 cycle, carboxylation of RuBP with CO_2 to give the 3-carbon intermediate, 3-phosphoglycerate (PGA). It also acts as an oxygenase, combining RuBP with oxygen to give PGA and phosphoglycolate. CO_2 and O_2 compete as substrates for Rubisco.

4 For maximum efficiency and economy, the rate of the C3 cycle matches that of the light reactions and the cycle responds sensitively to changes in light flux.

5 Gross control of the C3 cycle is set by the amounts of enzymes (especially Rubisco). Coarse biochemical control, which starts or stops the cycle abruptly in light or darkness, respectively, operates by regulating the activity of Rubisco (via Rubisco activase) and other cycle enzymes (via the ferredoxin–thioredoxin system). Fine biochemical controls operate via pH and the levels of Mg^{2+}, ATP and NADP.2H, all of which influence the activity of certain C3 cycle enzymes.

2.4 THE C2 CYCLE

The C2 cycle is a direct result of the oxygenase reaction of Rubisco (Equation 2.4, Section 2.3.2) and metabolizes the phosphoglycolate produced by that reaction. The cycle has long been known as **photorespiration** because it operates only in the light and involves uptake of O_2 and release of CO_2, but any resemblance to true or 'dark' respiration ends there — no energy is released during the C2 cycle, but rather some ATP is *used*. For this reason, the term photorespiration is now discouraged and **C2 cycle** or, more fully, *oxidative photosynthetic carbon cycle* is preferred.

At current atmospheric levels of O_2 (21%) and CO_2 (0.036% or 360 parts per million, p.p.m.), the oxygenase reaction of Rubisco reduces net carbon fixation by between 25 and 50%, so the C2 cycle is by no means a minor pathway. We need to look more closely at what this pathway does (Section 2.4.1) and then consider further its biological function (Section 2.4.2).

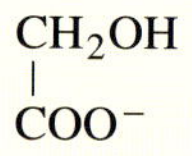

glycolate

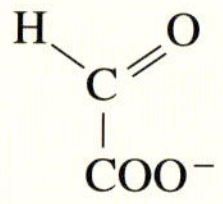

glyoxylate

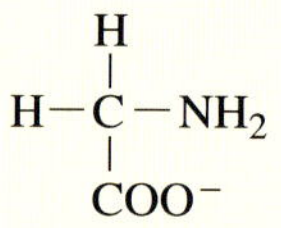

glycine

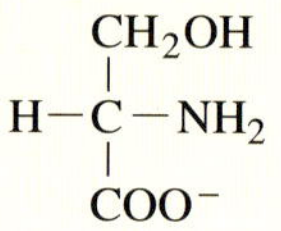

serine

2.4.1 Reactions of the C2 cycle

It has taken far longer to work out the details of the C2 cycle than it did for the C3 cycle — and no wonder, for the C2 cycle involves three organelles: chloroplast, peroxisome and mitochondrion. Figure 2.16 shows a simplified version and the structures of the key intermediates are given on the left. The main point to notice is that, for every two molecules of phosphoglycolate (2 × C2) produced from ribulose bisphosphate, one molecule of phosphoglycerate (C3) is returned to the C3 cycle, i.e. three-quarters of the carbon is salvaged.

Points worth noticing about the C2 cycle are that it involves oxidation, decarboxylation and amination/deamination steps.

- ❍ Starting from phosphoglycolate, where does the first oxidation step occur? Describe the reaction.

- ● It occurs in peroxisomes, where glycolate is oxidized by molecular oxygen to yield glyoxylate and hydrogen peroxide (H_2O_2).

The potentially damaging hydrogen peroxide is rapidly broken down by peroxisome enzymes to oxygen and water. The amination step, i.e. addition of an amino, $-NH_2$, group (from an amino acid) is next, in which glyoxylate is converted to the 2-carbon amino acid glycine.

- ❍ Describe what happens to the glycine.

- ● It is transported to a mitochondrion where, from two molecules of glycine, one molecule of serine is produced and one molecule each of ammonia (NH_3) and CO_2 are released.

These reactions, with decarboxylation and oxidation of half the glycine, mean that three of the original four carbons entering the cycle (from two molecules of phosphoglycolate) now reside in the amino acid serine. Serine moves back to the peroxisomes where it is deaminated and the 3-carbon intermediate produced is eventually converted to glycerate.

- ❍ Describe the last step in the C2 cycle.

- ● Glycerate moves to the chloroplast where it reacts with ATP and is converted to 3-phosphoglycerate (PGA), which enters the C3 cycle.

The salvage of three carbon atoms is now complete. Furthermore, the valuable nitrogen released as ammonia (full red arrow) is salvaged by reactions in the chloroplast, where NH_3 is reincorporated into amino acids, a process which uses both ATP and reducing power (as reduced ferredoxin). Overall, the C2 cycle plus amino acid regeneration use almost as much ATP and reducing power as does the C3 cycle.

The pathway was worked out partly using a similar approach to that used for the C3 cycle (Box 2.2), i.e. following the fate of O_2 labelled with the heavy ^{18}O isotope and by isolating enzymes. However, use of C2 cycle mutants in *Arabidopsis* was also important for the final characterization of the pathway.

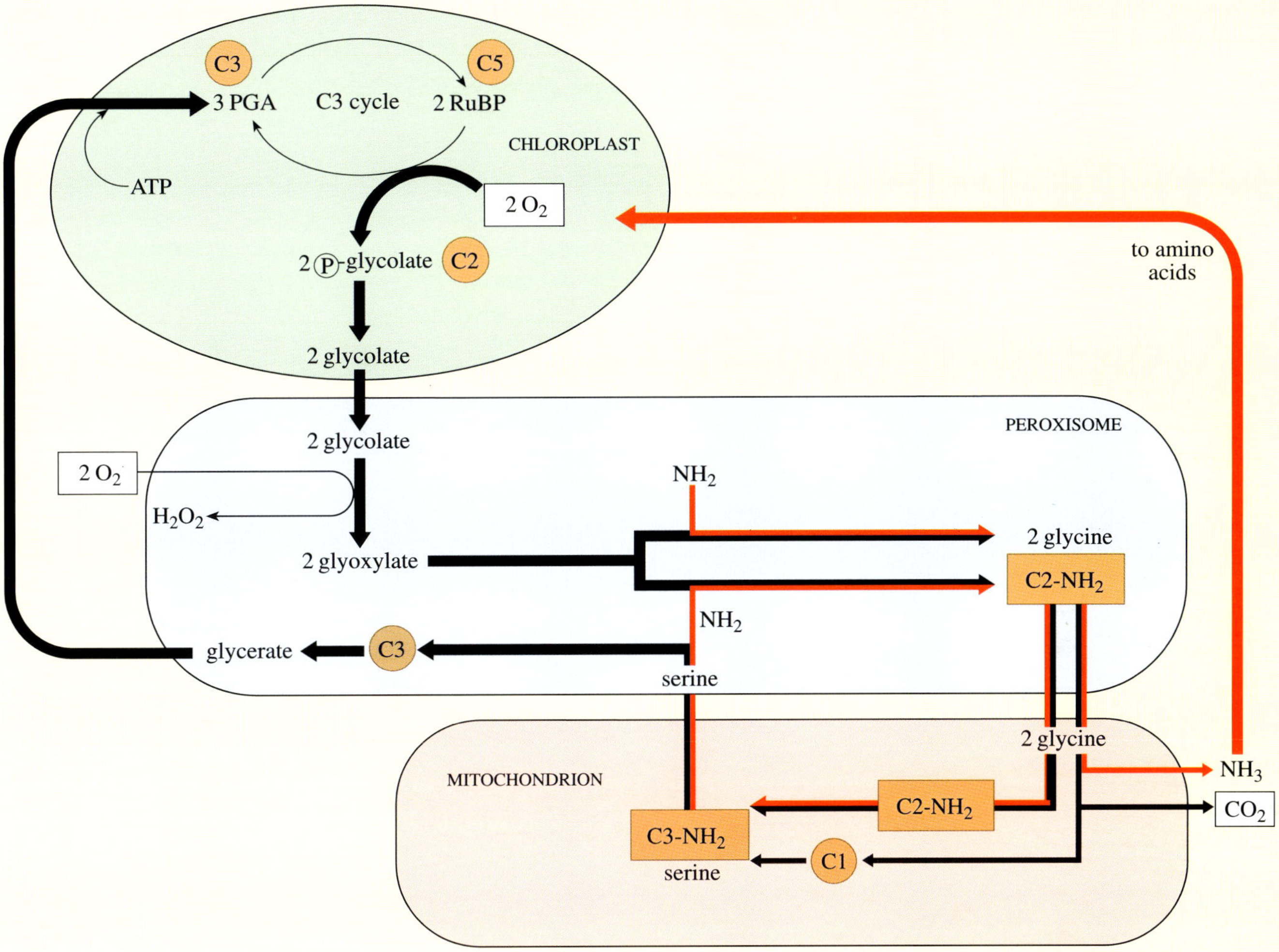

Figure 2.16 Outline of the C2 cycle. See text for explanation.

2.4.2 Biological significance of the C2 cycle

In the past, 'photorespiration' was widely regarded as a wasteful process or, at best, a necessary evil (in that it disposed of phosphoglycolate but salvaged only 75% of the carbon). By the late 1990s, a radically different view was emerging. The C2 cycle is now considered by some biologists to be an integral part of photosynthetic carbon metabolism and in a 1997 review of his life's work on the C2 cycle, N. E. Tolbert wrote:

> Let us develop the realization that the oxygenase activity of Rubisco and the subsequent C2 cycle are essential and equal parts of photosynthetic carbon metabolism as the CO_2 decreases or the O_2 increases. The combination of the C2 and C3 cycles provides a check and balance on net photosynthesis and atmospheric concentrations of CO_2 and O_2. Photosynthetic carbon metabolism has its … alternate

electron acceptor in O_2 fixation. Photosynthesis is self-limiting by balancing the atmospheric CO_2 to O_2 ratio within limits set by the specificity of Rubisco. At lower CO_2 or higher O_2 than the [compensation points], plants cannot grow.

Tolbert (1997)

Tolbert's argument, therefore, is that O_2 uptake and CO_2 release by the C2 cycle are at least as important as heterotroph respiration in determining the ratio of these two gases in the atmosphere. Figure 2.17 illustrates the interlocking nature of the C3 and C2 cycles, which currently operate in a ratio of about 3 : 1.

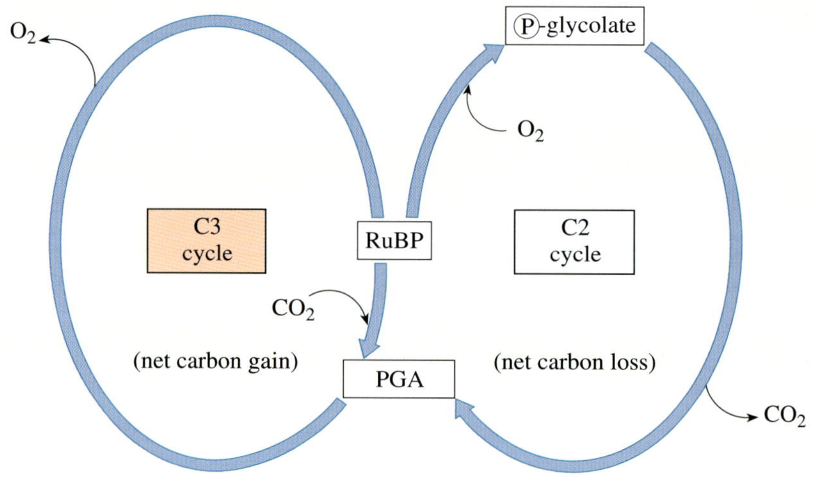

Figure 2.17 The linked nature of the C3 and C2 cycles. The flow of carbon in a leaf and the balance of O_2 and CO_2 in the atmosphere are both determined to a large extent by the balance between these mutually opposing cycles.

The *compensation points* mentioned in the Tolbert quotation are discussed further in Section 2.6 but, in brief, they are the lowest (for CO_2) or highest (for O_2) atmospheric concentrations below or above which net carbon fixation cannot be achieved. For example, atmospheric O_2 levels 300 Ma ago are thought to have been much higher than they are now (possibly 35%, cf. 21%), which means that to achieve net carbon fixation by Rubisco and the C3 cycle, CO_2 levels must have been around 0.07% (700 p.p.m.). As CO_2 decreased over geological time, so too must O_2 levels have done; otherwise C3 plants could not have survived. The relatively small number of terrestrial plant species (C4 and CAM plants) that solved the problem of CO_2/O_2 competition by concentrating CO_2 around Rubisco did not evolve until about 7 Ma ago.

Tolbert's view is one way of looking at the 'usefulness' or wider relevance of the C2 cycle. Another view is that the cycle plays an important role as a 'safety valve', protecting plants against photoinhibition, especially in conditions of high light intensity and temperature and low CO_2 levels.

❍ Bearing in mind that photoinhibition tends to increase when the utilization phase fails to keep pace with the light reactions (Figure 2.9), suggest an explanation for this proposed protective role of the C2 cycle.

- The conditions when the protective role would be most prominent are those when CO_2 supply is strongly limiting for Rubisco carboxylation and the C3 cycle. Hence utilization of ATP and reducing power by the C3 cycle falls or fails to keep pace with the light reactions. But the oxygenase reaction and the C2 cycle would be promoted in these conditions and, since this cycle also utilizes ATP and reducing power in chloroplasts, it could, at least for a short time, take over as the utilization phase.

This question of the usefulness, or otherwise, of the C2 cycle is of more than academic interest. Because of current concerns to increase world crop production, considerable research effort has been directed towards increasing the carboxylation efficiency of Rubisco and thereby reducing O_2 uptake and carbon loss via the C2 cycle. Rubisco mutants with a higher specificity for CO_2 have been identified in the unicellular green alga *Chlamydomonas reinhardtii* and it has been suggested that it might be possible to engineer such an 'improved' Rubisco that could be introduced into crop plants. Before embarking on such a project, however, it should be absolutely certain that a reduced C2 cycle really would be advantageous in both the short and the long term.

SUMMARY OF SECTION 2.4

1 The C2 cycle metabolizes phosphoglycolate, produced by the oxygenase reaction of Rubisco with RuBP, returning 75% of the carbon to the Calvin cycle as phosphoglycerate. In the process, O_2 is taken up, CO_2 is released and ATP and reducing power are utilized. Photorespiration is an alternative name for this cycle.

2 Reactions of the C2 cycle occur in chloroplasts, peroxisomes and mitochondria and involve oxidation, decarboxylation and amination/deamination. Oxygen is used in peroxisomes; CO_2 is released in mitochondria; and there is cycling of nitrogen between all three organelles, with NH_3 passing from mitochondria to chloroplasts.

3 The C2 cycle may play a role (a) in regulating the balance of O_2 and CO_2 in the atmosphere (Tolbert's view); and/or (b) by acting as a safety valve and temporary utilization phase, which protects against photoinhibition by utilizing ATP and reducing power when CO_2 availability is low.

2.5 CARBON DIOXIDE-CONCENTRATING SYSTEMS

Whatever the potential usefulness of the C2 cycle, it does, nevertheless, reduce net carbon fixation in C3 plants. Improved selectivity of Rubisco for CO_2 (Section 2.3.2) alleviated but by no means removed the problem. However, some plants, algae and cyanobacteria have evolved a different kind of solution: they increase the ratio of CO_2 to O_2 at the site of Rubisco by concentrating CO_2 at this site.

Angiosperms with CO_2-concentrating mechanisms first became abundant about 7 Ma ago. They are called **C4 plants** (Section 2.5.2), because CO_2 is fixed initially into a 4-carbon intermediate and then released (and concentrated) at the site of Rubisco; most are grasses or sedges. During this concentration process, the relative amounts of the stable carbon isotopes ^{12}C (the common form) and ^{13}C (a rarer form) that are fixed into plant tissues are altered: much less ^{13}C is incorporated in C4 plants compared with C3 plants. Measuring the $^{12}C : ^{13}C$ ratio in plant remains by the technique of mass spectrometry has allowed us to pinpoint the time when C4 plants first became widespread.

A second group of land plants uses the same principle for CO_2 concentration (initial fixation into a 4-carbon intermediate plus re-release), but has a slightly different mechanism. The mechanism (described in Section 2.5.3) is called *Crassulacean acid metabolism*, usually abbreviated to *CAM*, and named after the family Crassulaceae in which it was first discovered. CAM occurs in non-angiosperms and a far greater range of angiosperm families than does the C4 pathway, so it probably evolved earlier than the latter, but CAM plants have never been sufficiently abundant to allow detection in the fossil record by $^{12}C : ^{13}C$ analysis.

For aquatic photosynthesizers, i.e. cyanobacteria, many algae and some plants (e.g. pondweeds, *Potamogeton* spp., that have become secondarily aquatic), a different type of CO_2-concentrating mechanism has evolved and for different reasons (selective pressures). We describe these reasons and the nature of the CO_2-concentrating mechanism in Section 2.5.1.

2.5.1 AQUATIC ORGANISMS

The problem for aquatic photosynthesizers is twofold: first, CO_2 diffuses much more slowly in water than in air so, in still water, CO_2 supply rapidly becomes limiting. Second, at pH values in the range 7–8, most of the dissolved CO_2 is converted to hydrogen carbonate, HCO_3^- (see Figure 2.18); so free CO_2 is almost unavailable.

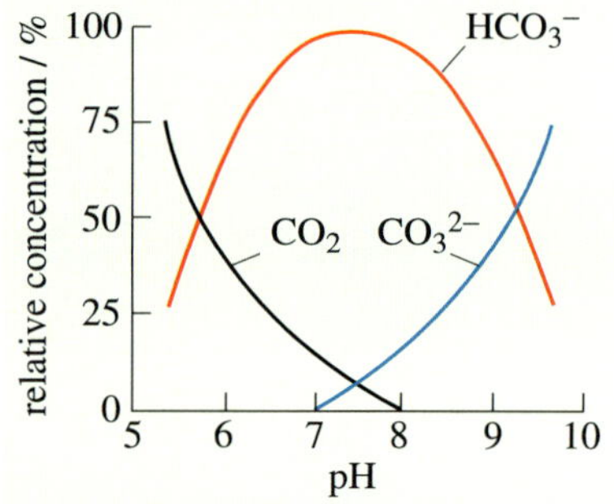

Figure 2.18 The relationship between pH and the $CO_2/HCO_3^-/CO_3^{2-}$ equilibria.

The pH of seawater is around 7.5 and that of most lowland freshwater bodies is usually between 7 and 8, so it follows from Figure 2.18 that HCO_3^- is the dominant form of inorganic carbon. The CO_2-concentrating mechanism in aquatic organisms involves the use of HCO_3^- and the release of CO_2 from it at the site of Rubisco. Key elements of the mechanism are active, membrane-bound pumps and use of the enzyme **carbonic anhydrase**, which catalyses the reversible reaction:

$$HCO_3^- + H^+ \rightleftharpoons H_2O + CO_2 \tag{2.5}$$

The simplest and best understood system for taking up HCO_3^- ions, concentrating them in the cell and then releasing them at the site of Rubisco is that found in cyanobacteria and illustrated in Figure 2.19a. In the plasma membrane there are inorganic carbon (C_i) pumps which transport both HCO_3^- and CO_2 into the cytoplasm against a concentration gradient (a secondary active transport process). The cytoplasmic concentration of inorganic carbon may be several thousand times greater than in surrounding water.

❍ Given that cytoplasmic pH in the light is about 8, in what form is inorganic carbon present?

- From Figure 2.18, most of it (around 90%) is present as HCO_3^-.

HCO_3^- moves by diffusion to structures called *carboxysomes* where Rubisco is located and it is here that carbonic anhydrase releases CO_2. Carboxysomes are surrounded by a protein shell (not a membrane) and in some way that is not understood, they restrict the outward diffusion of CO_2.

The situation is more complicated in eukaryotes (algae and higher plants), where the chloroplasts concentrate CO_2 as in cyanobacteria, but the cytoplasm has an additional CO_2-concentrating system (Figure 2.19b). There is an HCO_3^- active transporter in the plasma membrane and often a carbonic anhydrase which is located on the inside of the cell wall and appears to release CO_2 from HCO_3^-. Carbon dioxide then diffuses into the cell down a steep concentration gradient. There are other carbonic anhydrases in both cytoplasm and chloroplast, but much disagreement about what their function is.

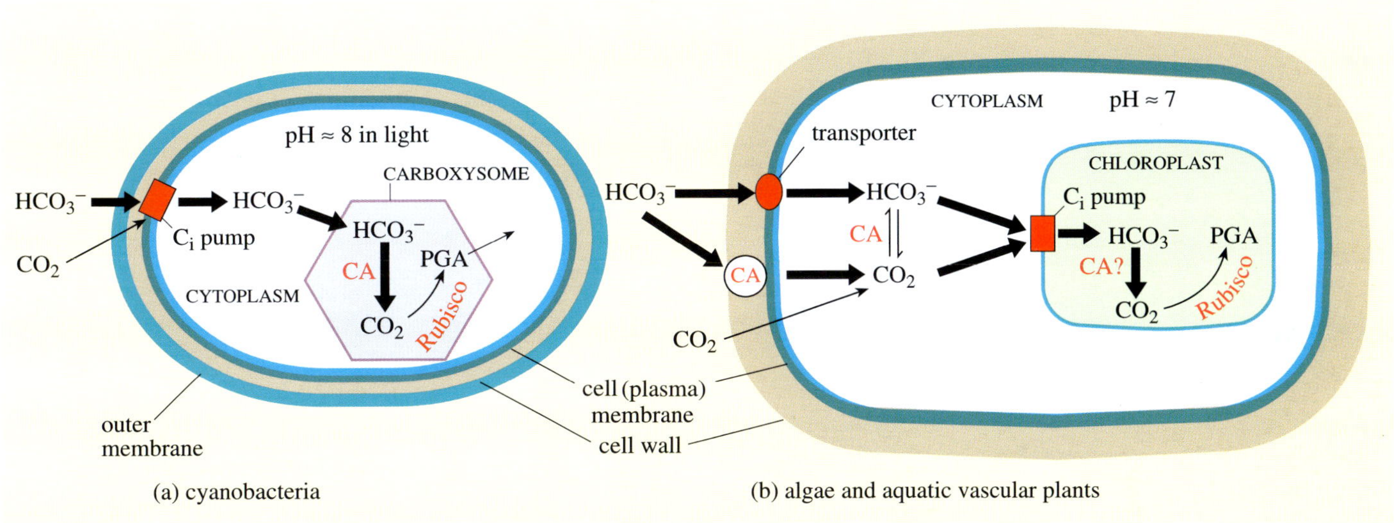

Figure 2.19 Models of how the CO_2-concentrating mechanism may work in (a) cyanobacteria and (b) algae and aquatic vascular plants. CA = carbonic anhydrase. (Note that the outer membrane and cell wall of cyanobacteria present no significant barrier to the entry of CO_2 and HCO_3^-.)

Possession of CO_2-concentrating mechanisms in aquatic organisms means that they effectively suppress the oxygenase reaction of Rubisco. The system is simple and highly effective, so it is puzzling that C3 plants have not retained from their algal ancestors a similar system to concentrate CO_2 within chloroplasts. Terrestrial C3 plants possess a chloroplast carbonic anhydrase, but lack the C_i pump. Instead, they have evolved the much more complex systems described in Sections 2.5.2 and 2.5.3.

2.5.2 C4 PLANTS

C4 species comprise only 1% of the known species of flowering plants, but they include some of the most abundant tropical grasses and some important crop plants (maize and sugar-cane, for example). The grass and sedge families (Poaceae and Cyperaceae, respectively) are especially rich in C4 species, but altogether 16 families of both dicotyledons and monocotyledons contain C4 members. These plants include herbs and shrubs, but no large trees, and the majority occur in open, sunny habitats in the lowland tropics and subtropics.

The two distinctive features of C4 plants are a special kind of leaf anatomy and an extra biochemical pathway (the C4 cycle), which fixes CO_2 and then re-releases it. We show here how this combination of features achieves effective concentration of CO_2 at the site of Rubisco and the C3 cycle.

LEAF ANATOMY

Comparing leaf sections of typical C3 and C4 species (Figure 2.20), the most obvious difference is the presence in the C4 leaf of a distinct layer of cells around the vein (or vascular bundle). These **bundle sheath** cells contain more and larger chloroplasts than the other (mesophyll) cells and they usually have a thicker cell wall which may even be suberized (Chapter 1) at the junction with mesophyll cells. However, there are numerous plasmodesmata (the cytoplasmic channels that link cells across walls) at this junction. This cell arrangement in C4 plants is commonly referred to as **Kranz anatomy** (after the German for wreath, which is what the bundle sheath looks like) and you can often detect it by holding a leaf to the light and looking for darker green bands around veins. It was first observed by the German physiologist Haberlandt in 1884.

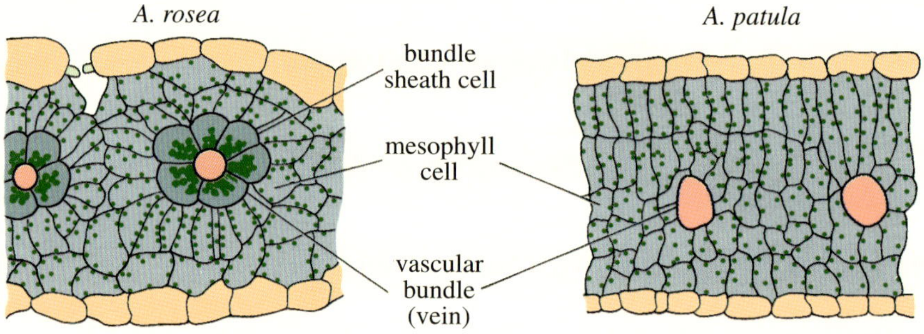

Figure 2.20 Schematic drawings sections of leaves of *Atriplex rosea* (a C4 plant) and *A. patula* (a C3 plant).

Mesophyll cells in a C4 leaf are rarely more than two cells away from a bundle sheath cell because C4 leaves are often thinner with veins closer together than C3 leaves. At the ultrastructural level, there are also differences in the chloroplasts of bundle sheath and mesophyll cells: in many species, the chloroplasts of the bundle sheath cells contain relatively few grana.

❍ How does this structural feature affect the balance between PSI and PSII (Section 2.2.1)?

● Bundle sheath cell chloroplasts are deficient in PSII, which is localized on grana.

PSII is the site of O_2 release in photosynthetic light reactions, so less O_2 is produced in bundle sheath cells. This biochemical difference is one of many that distinguish bundle sheath and mesophyll cells, which cooperate to bring about the C4 cycle.

THE C4 CYCLE

The structural and biochemical differences between bundle sheath and mesophyll cells all relate to the fact that initial CO_2 fixation occurs in the mesophyll and re-release of CO_2 with 'C3' or photosynthetic fixation by Rubisco occurs in the bundle sheath. The spatial separation of activities allows CO_2 fixed by many mesophyll cells to be concentrated at the site of Rubisco in relatively few bundle sheath cells. Rubisco and the C3 cycle operate only in bundle sheath cells, which are also the major site of starch synthesis.

The C4 cycle is thus an addition to the C3 cycle. Figure 2.21 shows the former in outline.

Figure 2.21 Outline of the C4 cycle. CA = carbonic anhydrase; PEP = phosphoenolpyruvate; and abbreviations for the C3 cycle as in Figure 2.10.

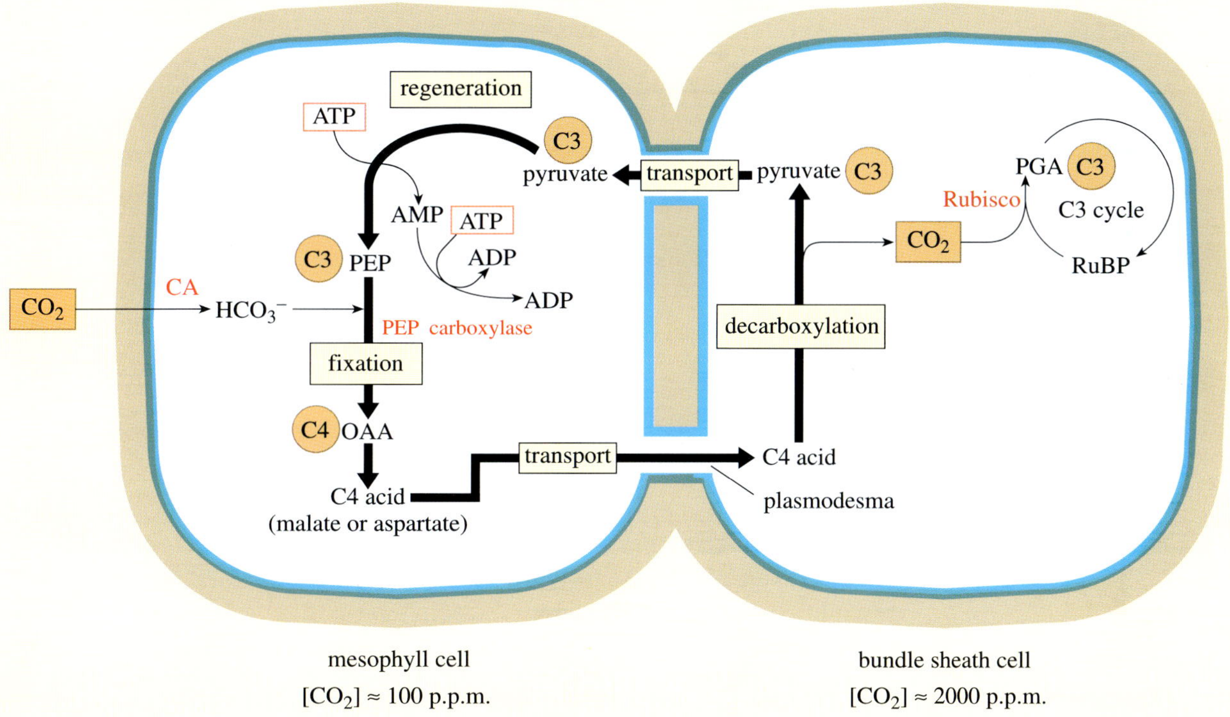

Starting at the left of Figure 2.21, the first important reaction after entry of CO_2 into the leaf via stomatal pores is conversion of CO_2 to HCO_3^- by the action of carbonic anhydrase (Equation 2.5). This step is vital because the cytosolic enzyme **PEP carboxylase**, which brings about the initial fixation, interacts with HCO_3^- (not CO_2) to carboxylate the 3-carbon intermediate phosphoenolpyruvate (PEP). You may recognize PEP as an intermediate in glycolysis. Carboxylation of PEP yields the 4-carbon intermediate, oxaloacetate (OAA), completing the *fixation stage* of the cycle.

What happens next varies between C4 species, some reducing OAA to malate and others converting it to aspartate. The 4-carbon acid then moves by diffusion via plasmodesmata into bundle sheath cells, completing the *first transport stage*.

The last three stages are:

- *decarboxylation* of the 4-carbon acid to release CO_2 in bundle sheath cells, where thickened walls may help to reduce outward diffusion of the gas;
- movement (the *second transport stage*) of the residual 3-carbon acid back to the mesophyll;
- *regeneration* of PEP ready to start the cycle again.

You should try to remember these bare bones of the C4 cycle and bear in mind also that the cycle requires an input of energy and the synthesis of several new enzymes.

❍ (a) What is the energetic cost (ATP and reducing power) of one turn of the C4 cycle? (b) What is the total energetic cost of fixing one molecule of CO_2 into carbohydrate in C4 plants?

● (a) Two molecules of ATP are required, one to produce PEP from pyruvate and one to regenerate ADP from AMP. No reducing power is required. (b) 5ATP + 2NADP.2H, i.e. the sum of costs for the C4 cycle (2ATP) and the C3 cycle (3ATP + 2NADP.2H).

The extra energetic cost of the C4 cycle represents a trade-off: well worth it if CO_2 is in short supply — when light levels are high, for example — and especially if high temperatures favour the C2 cycle, but a powerful disadvantage in other conditions.

Water conservation and the ecology of C4 plants

We mentioned earlier that C4 plants thrive in hot sunny habitats, but a common feature of such places is shortage of water. C4 plants are particularly efficient in their use of water and are especially common in seasonally dry areas such as the African savannah. The reason hinges on the fact that the surface pores (stomata) through which CO_2 enters leaves are also the route by which water is lost through evaporation. The apertures of stomata can be adjusted (described in Chapter 3) and water is conserved if they are only partially open. Despite restricting CO_2 entry, C4 plants achieve respectable rates of photosynthesis in this state.

By comparing the mass of water transpired per unit mass of dry weight increase (the **transpiration ratio**), it is possible to assess quantitatively the relative efficiency of C3 and C4 plants in conserving water during photosynthesis. The transpiration ratio is 450–950 : 1 for C3 species and 250–350 : 1 for C4 species. This difference is impressive, but for plants growing in *extremely* dry habitats a different photosynthetic system has evolved, for which the transpiration ratio is only 18–125 : 1. This system, which allows CO_2 concentration for photosynthesis to occur with the minimum loss of water, is discussed next.

2.5.3 Crassulacean acid metabolism (CAM)

If reducing water loss is of paramount importance, then the best time for stomatal pores to open is at night, when the air is cooler and more humid, but the snag is that photosynthesis needs light. A group of plants, mostly succulents with fleshy leaves or stems (e.g. cacti), have evolved an ingenious mechanism which solves this problem and is termed **Crassulacean acid metabolism** or **CAM** for short.

If you chew a leaf taken from a CAM plant at night, it tastes sharp and acidic but this taste disappears during the day. Herein lies the explanation of the CAM strategy. CAM plants open their stomata and fix CO_2 mainly at *night*, using PEP carboxylase (as in C4 plants) and producing malate. The malate is *stored* in cell vacuoles as malic acid (hence the sharp taste of leaves), which during the day is released into the cytoplasm, decarboxylated and the CO_2 produced fixed by Rubisco and the C3 cycle. Stomata remain closed during the day and the thick cuticles typical of CAM plants ensure that very little water or CO_2 is lost from leaves. Daytime CO_2 levels may reach 2.5% (25 000 p.p.m.) within CAM leaves, so here is a very effective CO_2-concentrating mechanism.

Follow through these steps of CAM by studying Figure 2.22, and also note its defining characteristics:

- diurnal (day–night) fluctuation in malic acid content;
- CO_2 fixation from the atmosphere occurring mainly at night;
- stomata open at night but closed for most of the day.

❍ From Figure 2.22, what is happening in late afternoon?

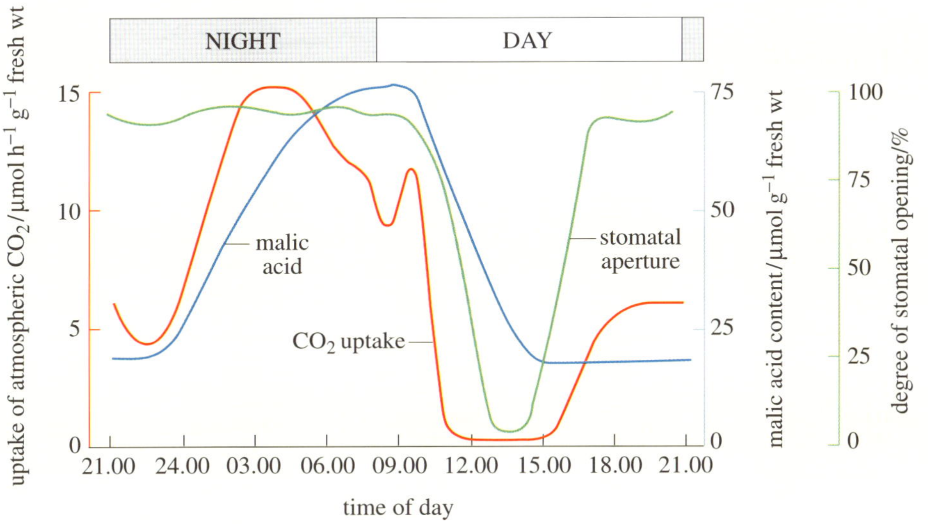

Figure 2.22 Changes in a typical CAM plant, during night and day, of the rate of uptake of atmospheric CO_2, malic acid content and the degree of stomatal opening.

● Atmospheric CO_2 uptake starts to increase just after 3 p.m. (15.00). At this time, the stored malic acid is largely used up, but by about 4 p.m. quite a large proportion of stomata are open. So CO_2 must be entering leaves and being fixed directly by Rubisco, as in C3 plants.

A phase of C3 metabolism is widespread in CAM plants and the C2 cycle operates at these times. Some species, e.g. pineapple, described as *facultative CAM species*, may switch from CAM to C3 metabolism or a mixture of both, depending on water supply and temperature. CAM is thus a more flexible system compared to that in C4 plants.

The key difference between CAM and C4 plants is that, in CAM, initial CO_2 fixation and the C3 cycle operate at *different times* but in the same cells, whereas in C4 plants they operate at the same time but in *different cells*. Details of CAM are shown in Figure 2.23, which you should compare with Figure 2.21 (C4).

❍ How do C4 and CAM plants differ with respect to regeneration of the primary acceptor, PEP?

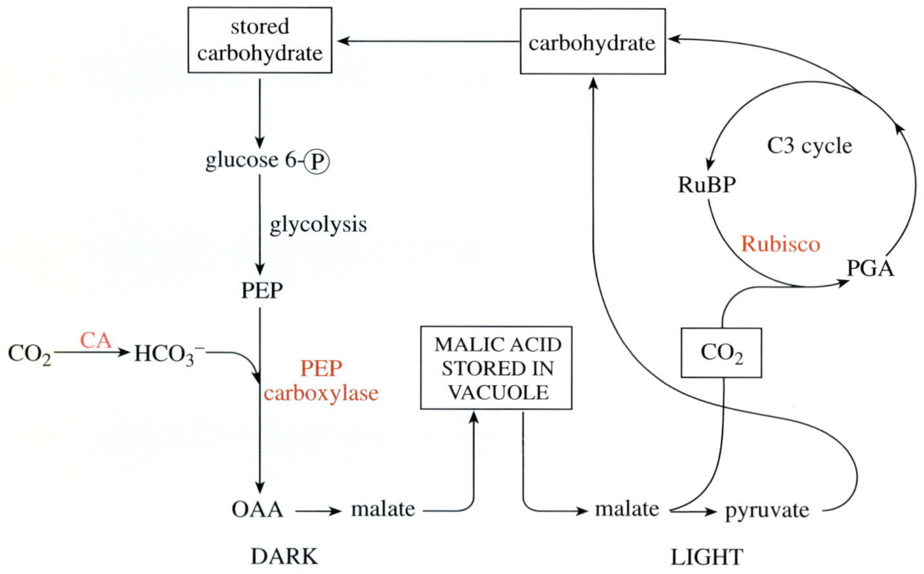

Figure 2.23 Outline of the reactions in Crassulacean acid metabolism (CAM) in dark and light.

● In CAM plants, PEP is regenerated in the dark by glycolysis, using stored carbohydrate. Carbohydrate is produced and stored in the light from the pyruvate produced by malate decarboxylation. In C4 plants, this pyruvate is used directly for regeneration of PEP.

Another diagnostic feature of CAM plants, therefore, is a diurnal fluctuation in the levels of storage carbohydrate, which is often starch but may be soluble hexose sugars. Storage carbohydrate levels rise during the day and fall at night, which is the opposite direction to malic acid levels (rise at night and fall in the day). Accumulation of malic acid in the vacuole requires energy and operates by secondary active transport linked to proton pumping: one malate ion enters the vacuole from the cytoplasm for every two protons pumped in and at the low vacuolar pH, malate is converted to malic acid. The additional energetic cost of malate transport in CAM means that it is energetically even more expensive than the C4 cycle: such efficient conservation of water has its price. Furthermore, there is a limit to the amount of malic acid that can be stored, which usually determines the overall photosynthetic capacity of CAM plants, traditionally regarded as 'slow growers'.

CAM plants do indeed grow slowly in very arid conditions and, in extreme drought, may adopt a pure survival strategy, without growth, in which stomata remain closed all the time. There is, however, diurnal fluctuation of malic acid linked to fixation and release of *respiratory* CO_2, a phenomenon called *CAM-idling*. At the other end of the scale, crops such as pineapple, a facultative CAM species, and species of *Agave* (Agavaceae) and *Opuntia* (cacti, Cactaceae) that are cultivated in Central and South America, exceed the most productive C3 crops and are not far behind C4 crops (Table 2.4). Given their highly efficient use of water, which can tide them over dry spells, it has been predicted that CAM plants could become increasingly important as crops for animal feed, human consumption and many other purposes.

Table 2.4 Annual productivities of the most productive CAM, C3 and C4 crops. Values are above-ground dry weight in tonnes per hectare per year and, for CAM species, are based on years with substantial rainfall or with irrigation. Average values relate to four species at several locations. Data from Nobel (1994).

Type and species	Location	Productivity / t ha^{-1} y^{-1}
CAM species		
Agave salmiana	Mexico	42
Opuntia ficus-indica	Chile, Mexico	47–50
average		**44**
C3 crops		
oil palm (*Elaeis guineensis*)	Malaysia	40
alfalfa (*Medicago sativa*)	Arizona and California, USA	30–34
average		**36**
C3 tree crops		
Cryptomeria japonica	Japan	44
Monterey pine (*Pinus radiata*)	New Zealand	34–38
average		**40**
C4 crops		
napiergrass (*Pennisetum purpureum*)	Central America	70
sugar-cane (*Saccharum officinarum*)	Guyana, Hawaii, Australia	50–67
average		**52**

The greater metabolic diversity of CAM plants compared with C4 plants is matched by their taxonomic diversity. About 20 000 species of angiosperms, roughly 8% of the total, show some version of CAM. These include not only typical desert succulents, such as cacti, agaves and euphorbias, but also many orchids and bromeliads that grow as epiphytes in the canopy of tropical forests. In the 1980s, tropical trees of the genus *Clusia*, which develop like strangler figs (climbing up other trees, eventually enveloping and killing them) were shown to have facultative CAM. We describe below one example which illustrates the diversity of CAM species.

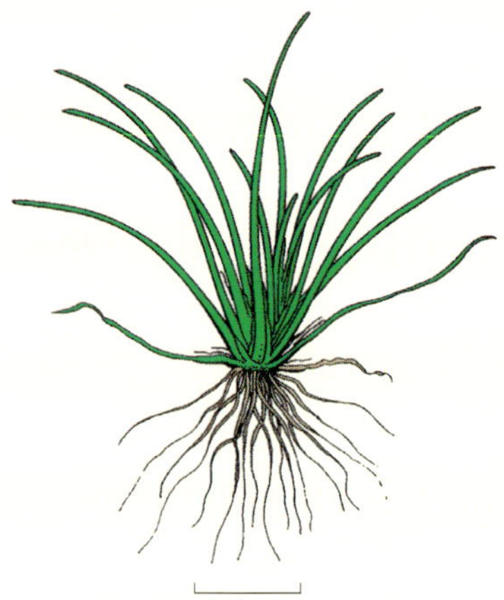

Figure 2.24 *Isoetes* sp. (a quillwort), a CAM plant that grows submerged in acid lakes.

Isoetes

Isoetes spp., commonly known as quillworts, are members of the Lycophyta (Chapter 1). Some species grow submerged in shallow, acid lakes (Figure 2.24) and show CAM. It appears that in these lakes, CO_2 availability becomes very low during the day but is high at night and possession of CAM is related to fluctuations of inorganic carbon sources.

❍ Why would HCO_3^- not be a viable alternative source of inorganic carbon in this habitat?

● Because, at low pH, most inorganic carbon is present as CO_2 (Figure 2.18).

Much (probably most) CO_2 is obtained via the roots of aquatic *Isoetes* by diffusion from lake sediments and it is now known that tropical alpine *terrestrial* quillworts also obtain CO_2 in this way and also show CAM. Figure 2.25 shows the best-known of these species, *Isoetes andicola*, which is native to the Peruvian Andes and characterized by having 96% of the biomass underground, with just the leaf tips having chlorophyll and completely lacking stomata! Possession of CAM allows such species to continue fixing CO_2 during the night and then boosting day-time levels when CO_2 supply from sediments continues. Possibly this strategy helps to reduce O_2 competition during the day because, in the absence of stomata, O_2 is removed only by respiration and outward diffusion from roots. The full significance of CAM for such plants is still not fully understood.

Clearly, the adaptive significance of CAM varies for different species and molecular phylogenetic evidence indicates that this mode of photosynthesis has evolved several times in different plant lineages. It has probably played a significant role in the diversification of plants.

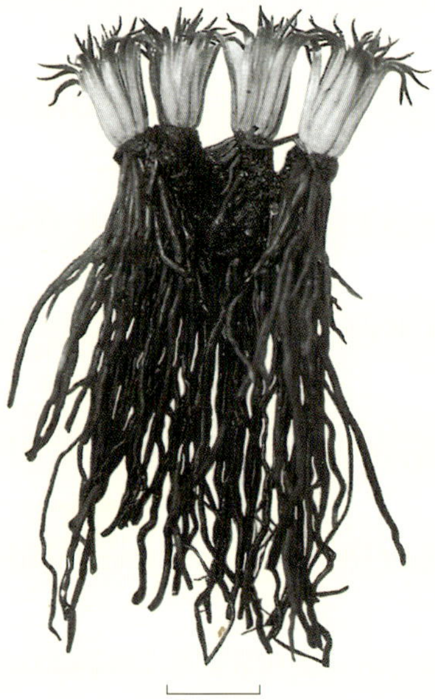

Figure 2.25 *Isoetes andicola*, a tropical alpine terrestrial species from the Peruvian Andes. Only the darker leaf tips contain chlorophyll. Note the enormous root system.

Summary of Section 2.5

CO_2-concentrating systems raise [CO_2] at the site of Rubisco and hence minimize the oxygenase reaction and the C2 cycle. There are three types:

- In aquatic photosynthesizers (cyanobacteria, some algae and some aquatic plants), inorganic carbon (C_i) pumps and carbonic anhydrase are used.
- In C4 plants, a combination of Kranz anatomy and the C4 cycle are involved. CO_2 is fixed initially into a 4-carbon acid in mesophyll cells and is released in bundle sheath cells at the site of Rubisco. An extra two ATP molecules are required to fix one molecule of CO_2 in these plants, which are mostly grasses and sedges from open tropical habitats. Their water use efficiency is better than that of C3 plants.
- In CAM plants there is temporal separation of initial CO_2 fixation and operation of the C3 cycle. CO_2 is fixed and stored in vacuoles as malic acid at night and released for use by Rubisco during the day. Taxonomic and structural diversity is much higher among CAM plants compared with C4 plants, and CAM is also a more flexible system, often operated facultatively. CAM plants have very low transpiration ratios (high water-use efficiency) because stomata can remain closed during the day. They include many desert succulents.

2.6 THE PHYSIOLOGY OF PHOTOSYNTHESIS

In this section we move to another level of study, plant physiology, where photosynthesis as a whole, i.e. light reactions + carbon fixation and the C2 cycle, is usually studied in leaves, whole plants or stands of plants. At this level (level 2 in Table 2.1), it is easier to see how plants adapt to different habitats or climatic conditions and how mechanisms such as the C4 cycle affect growth. Measurements are usually of net photosynthesis (*NP*) in terms of CO_2 uptake or O_2 release, i.e. gas exchange (Table 2.1).

- Over a period of several hours, O_2 release (in relative units) was 16 units in the light and uptake was 5 units in the dark. From these data and using Equation 2.2 (Section 2.1), what were (a) *NP* and (b) apparent gross photosynthesis, and (c) why was the value of *GP* apparent and not actual?

- (a) *NP* = 16, the net release of oxygen in the light. (b) Since *GP* = *NP* + *R* (from Equation 2.2) and O_2 uptake in the dark measures *R*, *GP* is apparently 16 + 5 = 21. (c) However, the data do not allow any estimate to be made of O_2 uptake by the C2 cycle in the light, so the actual value of *GP* would be higher.

We now consider how *NP* is influenced by four environmental factors: light, temperature and levels of CO_2 and O_2. The first three of these vary considerably in different habitats or conditions, whilst the last, atmospheric O_2 levels, is relatively constant today but varied over geological time.

2.6.1 COMPENSATION POINTS AND THE EFFECTS OF LIGHT, CO_2 AND O_2

When environmental conditions are such that *GP* = *R*, then net photosynthesis is zero and a plant is said to be at its **compensation point**. The point may be defined in terms of either light intensity or the CO_2 concentration at which it is reached and, as explained below, acts as a useful marker of how well plants are adapted to prevailing conditions.

EFFECTS OF LIGHT ON PHOTOSYNTHESIS

Light and the supply of CO_2 are both factors that may limit the rate of net photosynthesis. Figure 2.26 shows how net photosynthesis changes with increasing light flux (PPFD, Section 2.2.2) at a fixed CO_2 level, and you should notice four points:

1. When the light flux is low, *NP* increases linearly with PPFD, i.e. photosynthesis is light-limited.
2. The response curve flattens off above a certain PPFD, indicating that some other factor (usually CO_2 supply) and not light is now limiting. Photosynthesis is described as light-saturated or CO_2-limited.
3. At a certain, low PPFD, *NP* is zero, i.e. CO_2 uptake equals CO_2 release (*GP* = *R*) and this light flux defines the **light compensation point**.

4 When PPFD falls below the light compensation point there is a net *release* of CO_2 (*R* exceeds *GP*). The rate of CO_2 release in total darkness (where the curve intercepts the vertical axis) is the 'dark' respiration rate (and you should mark this point on Figure 2.26).

Figure 2.26 The change in net photosynthesis with increasing light flux (PPFD) and a fixed $[CO_2]$.

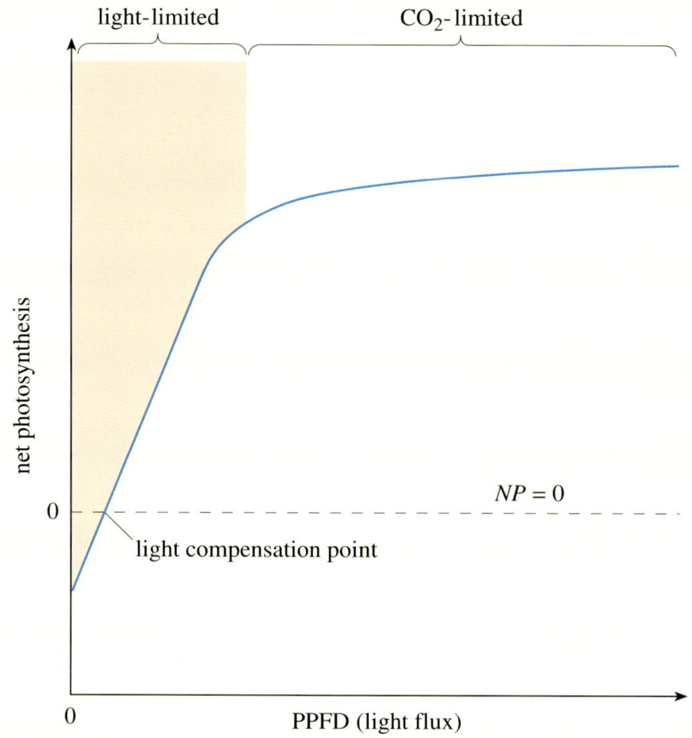

The light compensation point is lower in shade plants (or leaves) than in sun plants (Figure 2.27), so it provides a useful way of characterizing adaptation to light conditions. Two features of shade plants explain their ability to achieve net carbon fixation at lower light fluxes than do sun plants.

- ❍ Which one of these features was discussed at length in Section 2.2?
- ● At low light levels, the biochemical and structural characteristics of shade plants allow them to absorb and utilize light with much greater efficiency than do sun plants.

Of even greater importance in explaining their low light compensation point is the low respiration rate of shade plants: they have thin leaves with fewer cells per unit area than in sun leaves, which in energetic terms makes them very cheap to run. Overall and as you might expect, shade plants are photosynthetically superior to sun plants at low light fluxes. However, the trade-off is seen in the relative performance of sun and shade plants at *high* light fluxes (Figure 2.27). For reasons discussed in Section 2.2, shade plants become light-saturated at much lower irradiances than sun plants and are far more likely to suffer from

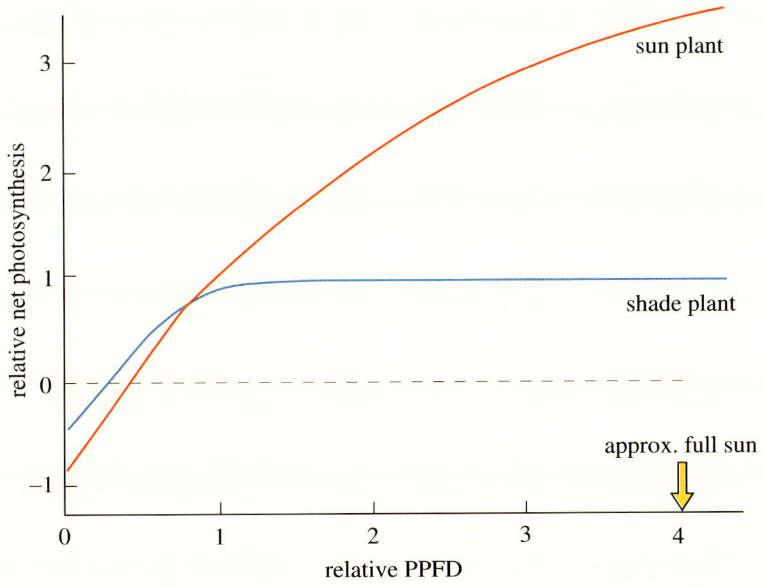

Figure 2.27 Typical photosynthetic responses of sun and shade plants to increasing PPFD.

photoinhibition. So sun plants are photosynthetically superior at high light intensities. The physiological consequences of acclimation, i.e. the ability of some plants to adapt to different light conditions during development (Section 2.2.2), is illustrated in Figure 2.28, which shows that orache (*Atriplex patula)* plants raised at low PPFD behave like shade plants, whilst those raised at high PPFD behave like sun plants. This example illustrates well the principle of phenotypic plasticity (p. 69).

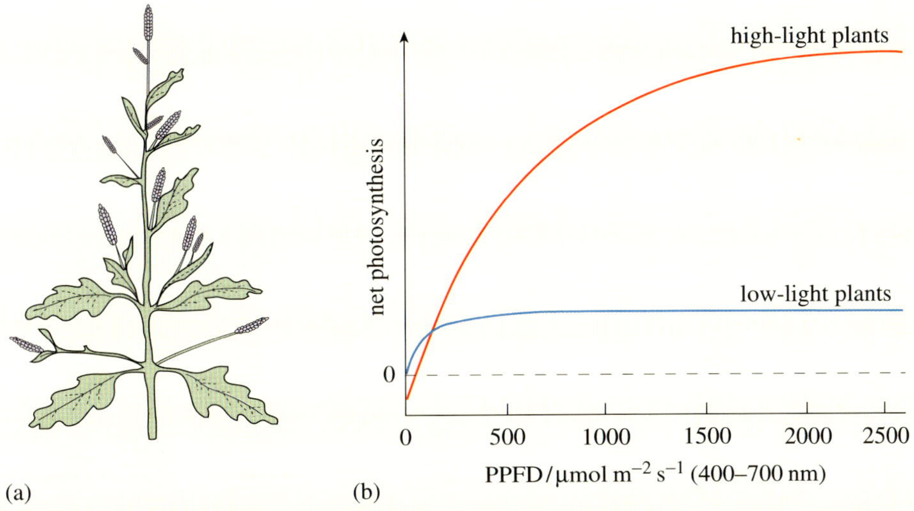

Figure 2.28 (a) An orache (*Atriplex patula)* plant. (b) Light acclimation in orache plants which were raised at low and high PPFD of 92 and 920 μmol m^{-2} s^{-1} (400–700 nm), respectively.

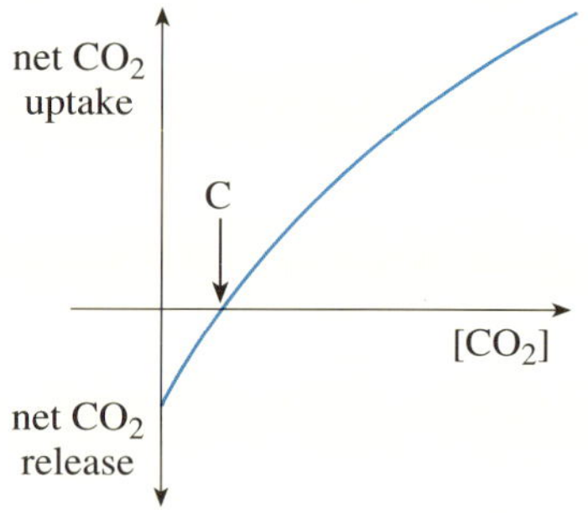

Figure 2.29 The CO_2 compensation point (C): the CO_2 concentration at which there is no net uptake or release of CO_2, i.e. $GP = R$.

EFFECTS OF CO_2 ON PHOTOSYNTHESIS

The idea of a compensation point, at which $GP = R$, can be extended to plant responses to changing CO_2 concentrations. If net photosynthesis is measured at a fixed (saturating) light flux, fixed $[O_2]$ and over a range of CO_2 concentrations, the concentration at which $NP = 0$ defines the **CO_2 compensation point** (Figure 2.29).

A low CO_2 compensation point means that a plant utilizes low concentrations of CO_2 very efficiently and also has a low respiration rate. Plants with a low light compensation point also have low respiration rates but there is one major difference: when $[CO_2]$ is low and PPFD is high, the C2 cycle operates, so low 'respiration' means strong suppression of the C2 pathway and not a low rate of 'dark' respiration.

- How can the C2 cycle can be suppressed?

- By concentrating CO_2 within the leaf at the site of Rubisco and hence suppressing the competing oxygenase reaction which provides the substrate for the C2 cycle (Section 2.4).

In Table 2.5 you can see that C4 plants and also the green alga *Chlorella*, both of which have a CO_2 concentrating mechanism (Section 2.5), do indeed have low CO_2 compensation points. By contrast, C3 plants — which lack such mechanisms — have high CO_2 compensation points.

Table 2.5 CO_2 compensation points for various plants and *Chlorella*.

Species	Type of plant	CO_2 compensation point / p.p.m.
sugar-cane (*Saccharum officinarum*)	C4	0 (approx.)
maize (*Zea mays*)	C4	1.3 ± 1.2
Chlorella (a unicellular alga)	(C3)	< 3
sunflower (*Helianthus annuus*)	C3	53
barley (*Hordeum vulgare*)	C3	55–65
temperate tree (*Acer platanoides*)	C3	55

At high light intensities, C3 plants are photosynthetically inferior to C4 plants (i.e. have lower rates of net photosynthesis) whenever conditions favour the Rubisco oxygenase reaction and the C2 cycle. What matters is the ratio of $[CO_2]$ to $[O_2]$ within leaves in the intercellular spaces: the lower the ratio, the greater the rate of the oxygenase reaction. The ratio can be lowered experimentally by reducing the external $[CO_2]$, and you can see in Figure 2.30 that for two species of *Atriplex*, the C4 species performs better than the C3 species at external CO_2 concentrations less than about 700 p.p.m.

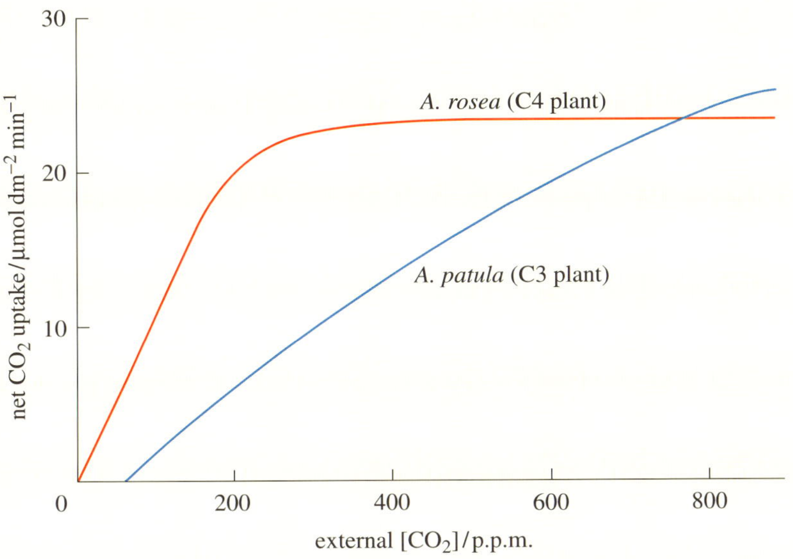

Figure 2.30 The effect on net photosynthesis of a C3 and a C4 species of *Atriplex* of changing the external CO_2 concentration. Experiments were carried out at light saturation and 27 °C.

❍ What is the trade-off for the C4 species?

● The C4 species is photosynthetically inferior (having a lower rate of CO_2-saturated photosynthesis) at CO_2 concentrations above about 700 p.p.m., indicating that there is some 'cost' with this strategy (discussed in Section 2.5).

Given that atmospheric $[CO_2]$ is already about 360 p.p.m. and is predicted to rise well above this value during the 21st century, there are considerable implications for the ecology of C4 plants. As their photosynthetic advantage over C3 plants disappears, C4 plants may, for example, lose out whenever the two types are in competition.

EFFECTS OF O_2 ON PHOTOSYNTHESIS

For all species that lack a CO_2-concentrating mechanism, O_2 levels profoundly affect net photosynthesis through their action on the Rubisco oxygenase reaction and the operation of the C2 cycle. Relative changes in net carbon fixation and in the CO_2 compensation point with changing $[O_2]$ are illustrated in Figure 2.31.

❍ From Figure 2.31a, by how much is net carbon fixation reduced at present atmospheric levels of O_2 compared with that at 1–2% O_2?

● By about one-third. *NP* at 21% O_2 (the present atmospheric level) is about 10 units and at 1–2% it is about 15 units.

This reduction at 21% O_2 is a severe disadvantage for C3 plants and the selective advantage of CO_2-concentrating mechanisms is clear. You can also see in Figure 2.31b the linear rise in CO_2 compensation point with $[O_2]$ for C3 plants, in stark contrast to the situation in C4 plants, where it hardly changes at all.

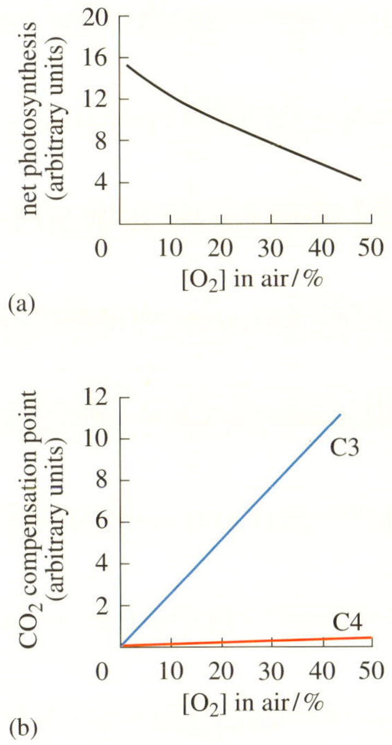

Figure 2.31 The effect of O_2 concentration on: (a) net photosynthesis (carbon fixation) and (b) the CO_2 compensation point in a C3 leaf and, for comparison, a C4 leaf measured at 25 °C and 360 p.p.m. CO_2. Values are relative and in arbitrary units.

These different physiological responses of C3 and C4 plants suggest that C4 plants are generally superior to C3 plants in hot, sunny and, often, dry conditions — which is indeed where many C4 plants grow naturally (Section 2.5). C3 plants still dominate in cooler climates and in shady habitats, where they are photosynthetically superior. Furthermore, all large trees are C3 plants, probably because photosynthesis of the tree *as a whole* is light-limited, with only the outer layer of leaves exposed to full sun and the many layers of inner leaves shaded to varying degrees.

In terms of their photosynthetic capacity, therefore, herbaceous or shrubby C3 plant are adapted to a cool and/or low-light climate, whereas C4 plants are adapted to a warm, high-light climate. There are many exceptions, however: *Spartina anglica* is a C4 grass common on British saltmarshes and *Larrea divaricata* is a C3 shrub that is dominant in some North American deserts. Physiological adaptation of plants to their normal environment is an important general principle and we describe in Section 2.6.2 a further illustration of this principle.

2.6.2 PHOTOSYNTHESIS AND TEMPERATURE

Temperature is one of the environmental conditions that varies over a very wide range on a global scale and it affects virtually all aspects of plant growth and survival. The main types of world vegetation (tropical rainforest, savannah, temperate deciduous forest, etc.) are largely determined by the interaction of temperature and rainfall, and distribution boundaries, such as the tree line on mountains or in the Arctic, also depend ultimately on temperature. At the biochemical level, the effects of temperature on membrane properties, enzyme activities and the rates of chemical reactions are of greatest significance — you have already seen how temperature influences the oxygenase activity of Rubisco (Section 2.3) and hence the C2 cycle and net photosynthesis (Section 2.4.1). The photosynthetic machinery is damaged by extremes of high or low temperature, mainly by effects on membrane-bound enzymes.

Key point to refer back to in C4 plants.

- How does low temperature interact with high light fluxes to cause photosynthetic damage?

- These conditions often lead to severe photoinhibition or even irreversible photo-oxidation (Section 2.2.3).

The precise value of 'extreme' temperatures in this context varies greatly for plants from different regions, with tropical species damaged by chilling temperatures of around 10 °C. So, clearly, plants must be adapted to all aspects of the thermal regime in their natural environment — not only to temperature extremes but also to the optimum temperature, at which the rate of net photosynthesis is maximal. We describe below some examples that illustrate such temperature adaptation.

Look first at Figure 2.32.

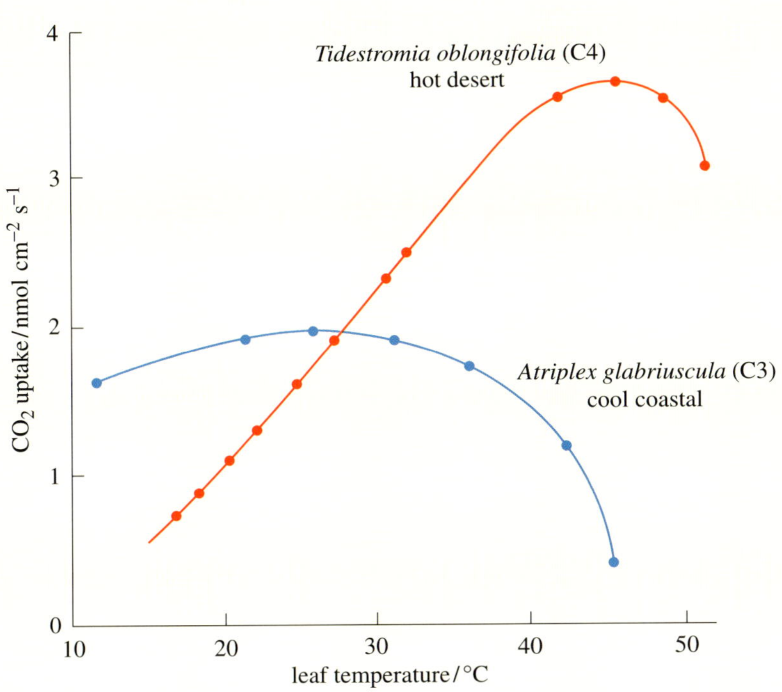

Figure 2.32 Temperature dependence of photosynthesis for the desert plant *Tidestromia oblongifolia*, a C4 species, growing in summer in Death Valley, California; and *Atriplex glabriuscula*, a C3 species, grown under a temperature regime simulating that of its native cool, coastal habitat.

(a) What are the optimum temperatures for net photosynthesis for *T. oblongifolia* and *A. glabriuscula*? (b) How does Figure 2.32 illustrate photosynthetic adaptation to temperature?

(a) The optimum temperature is about 46 °C for *Tidestromia* and about 23 °C for *A. glabriuscula*. (b) Death Valley is a notoriously hot environment and *T. oblongifolia* has a much better photosynthetic performance at high temperatures (a higher temperature optimum) compared with *A. glabriuscula* which, however, performs better at lower temperatures that match its normal environment. These plants are genetically adapted to different thermal regimes.

The optimum temperature for photosynthesis is not a fixed characteristic, however, and just as plants acclimate to different light environments, depending on the conditions under which they grow (Figure 2.30), so also do they show **temperature acclimation**. The ability to acclimate is genetically determined and varies widely between species, but is best developed in plants that experience large changes in temperature over their growing season. At Barrow, Alaska, for example, the mean temperature increases by 14 °C from early spring to the warmest time and the optimum temperature for photosynthesis of three mosses that grow there increases from 12–13 °C to 19–21 °C.

The two important general conclusions from this section and much of this chapter are as follows:

- Environmental factors may interact in complex ways to influence the rate of photosynthesis and different factors may be limiting in different environments or for different plants in the same environment.

- Plants show varying degrees of photosynthetic adaptation to their native environment; often, these adaptations act to minimize the impact of major stresses (e.g. high temperature) or of dominant rate-limiting factors.

Perhaps the most striking photosynthetic adaptations are the CO_2-concentrating systems, which influence photosynthetic responses to many other environmental variables, including temperature and light, and also have a powerful influence on the efficiency of water use (Section 2.5).

SUMMARY OF SECTION 2.6

1 At the physiological level, net photosynthesis (and hence growth) may be limited by the availability of light or CO_2 or by temperature. Plants may be genetically adapted to a limited range of environmental conditions or show phenotypic plasticity, having a capacity to acclimate to a wide range of conditions.

2 Light compensation points indicate plant adaptation to prevailing light intensity; CO_2 compensation points indicate the efficiency of CO_2-concentrating mechanisms in strong light.

3 Shade plants have lower light compensation points than sun plants because they use light more efficiently at low PPFD and have low respiration rates. The trade-off is that their *NP* is lower than that of sun plants at high PPFD.

4 The low CO_2 compensation point of plants with CO_2-concentrating mechanisms results from their suppression of the Rubisco oxygenase reaction and the C2 cycle. C4 and CAM plants have higher *NP* than do C3 plants when conditions favour the C2 cycle, but may perform less well than C3 plants in cool, low light conditions.

5 Current atmospheric concentrations of O_2 reduce *NP* significantly in C3 plants in conditions of high light and temperature, but have no such effect on C4 and CAM plants.

6 The optimum and limiting temperatures for photosynthesis vary depending on the usual habitat of a plant or the conditions under which it was grown.

2.7 PHOTOSYNTHESIS AND THE FUTURE

There is broad agreement among scientists that the global environment is changing: atmospheric CO_2 concentrations and average temperatures are increasing; the length of the growing season is increasing in many areas; and patterns of precipitation are likely to change. So what are the implications for plant photosynthesis, crop production and the survival of natural communities?

Consider first temperature.

❍ How, if at all, might increases in global mean temperatures affect photosynthesis and growth in C3 plants?

● From Section 2.6.2 you know that many plants have broad temperature optima which match conditions in their local environment. So the direct effect of raised temperature on photosynthesis is not likely to be great. On the negative side, it could increase rates of the C2 cycle; on the positive side, it could extend the growing season for temperate species. The net effect is thus likely to be negative for tropical species and positive for temperate species, *provided* that they have adequate supplies of water and nutrients for growth.

Because they suppress the C2 cycle and have better water use efficiency than C3 plants, growth of C4 plants is more likely to benefit from increased temperatures, again provided that they have adequate water and nutrients. Altered rainfall patterns, with drier summers or longer dry seasons, could well be the most important factor affecting crop production.

Now consider the effects of rising CO_2. An increase in net photosynthesis and growth might be expected for any plants that were not limited by light, temperature or shortage of water or nutrients.

- Are the effects on C3 and C4 plants likely to be of similar magnitude?

- No: the effect on C3 plants is likely to be greater because of reduction of carbon losses via the C2 cycle.

In natural communities, enhanced growth of C3 plants could alter the competitive balance and lead to reductions in C4 species.

Clearly, there is no easy answer to the question posed at the beginning of this section and much current research is investigating the effects on photosynthesis and growth of global climate change. However, an important point emphasized above is that plant growth depends not only on rates of photosynthesis but also on supplies of water and mineral nutrients. The next two chapters consider these subjects.

REFERENCES

Nobel, P. S. (1994) *Remarkable Agaves and Cacti*, Oxford University Press, New York, Oxford.

Powles, B. and Björkman, O. B. (1981) Leaf movement in the shade species *Oxalis oregana* II. Role in protection against injury by intense light, *Carnegie Institute of Washington Yearbook*, **80**, pp. 63–66.

Tolbert, N. E. (1997) The C_2 oxidative photosynthetic carbon cycle, *Annual Review of Plant Physiology and Plant Molecular Biology*, **48**, pp. 1–25.

FURTHER READING

Taiz, L. and Zeiger, E. (1998) *Plant Physiology* (2nd edn), Sinauer Associates, Inc. Sunderland, Massachusetts. [An excellent textbook intended for honours-level undergraduates.]

Hall, D. and Rao, K. K. (1994), *Photosynthesis* (5th edn), Cambridge University Press. [Available in paperback; gives useful descriptions of techniques and particularly strong on the biochemical aspects of photosynthesis.]

WATER AND TRANSPORT IN PLANTS

3

3.1 INTRODUCTION

The soft tissues of land plants consist, on average, of 90–95% water, all of which is absorbed from the soil by roots (or from air in the case of certain epiphytes) and then moves to the stems, leaves and other tissues. Most (95% or more) of the water absorbed is not retained in the plant, however, but evaporates through stomatal pores (Chapters 1 and 2) on the leaf surfaces, a process called **transpiration**: rapidly transpiring leaves can lose their own weight in water every *hour*. This apparent waste of water does not reflect bad plant design but is an inevitable consequence of being a photosynthetic organism on land.

- ❍ From your study of Chapter 2, why does loss of water inevitably accompany photosynthesis?

- ● Open stomata (recall that these pores can be open or closed) are necessary to allow *entry* of CO_2 but water vapour from intercellular spaces then passes out of leaves by this route.

Plants function in ways that minimize the conflict between CO_2 gain and water loss. For example, stomatal pores are usually open only in the light so that transpiration ceases at night. In conditions of severe water shortage, however, stomata may close during the day when conserving water takes precedence over photosynthesis. Plants also show many adaptations which act to minimize water loss when stomata are open (discussed in Section 3.6) and water supply (i.e. precipitation) is, along with temperature, a controlling factor that determines the broad type of vegetation — forest, grassland, desert, etc. — in different geographical regions. It is because humans so often grow crops outside their 'normal' vegetation zone and/or try to mitigate the effects of local droughts that irrigation is by far the largest consumer of water on a global scale.

Transpiration also performs two vital functions in land plants:

- It acts to cool leaves because some of the radiant energy falling on their surface is used to evaporate water (and is lost as latent heat of evaporation). In hot, high-light environments, such cooling can be important for survival.

- By inducing a flow of water through the plant (the **transpiration stream**), transpiration also promotes the transport to leaves of mineral nutrients absorbed by roots and carried in solution.

So transpiration is not an unmitigated evil but, nevertheless, it is tightly controlled in many plants by mechanisms that regulate stomatal aperture (Section 3.5).

In the first half of this chapter we address some fundamental questions about plant water relations, including: where and by what mechanisms water moves in plants (Section 3.2); what the *driving forces* of water movement are and what determines how fast and how much water moves through plants, even when it is to the tops of tall trees (Sections 3.3 and 3.4). At the end of the chapter, after discussing stomatal control and the problems of water shortage (Sections 3.5 and 3.6), we use information from Chapter 2 and this chapter for a transport case study about phloem, the tissue involved in the long-distance movement of sugars (Sections 3.7 and 3.8). The basic principles described in this chapter apply to all vascular plants and the evolution of different structures and control systems have allowed these plants to colonize virtually every terrestrial habitat and to range in size and form from tiny herbs to gigantic trees.

3.2 THE PATHWAY OF WATER MOVEMENT

You already know that water moves from soil to roots to stems to leaves but we need to consider now the precise pathway followed, the tissues involved and the type of movement (diffusion or mass flow). As a revision exercise from earlier chapters and from your own experience (if you grow plants or arrange flowers), try to answer questions (a)–(c) below *before* looking at Figure 3.1.

❍ (a) In what tissue does water move through stems from roots to leaves?

(b) Where is this tissue located within roots and hence in what direction must water move having entered a root from the soil?

(c) Where is this tissue located within leaves and how and in what form does water entering a leaf by this route reach stomata?

● (a) Vascular tissue and, more precisely, xylem vessels or tracheids (Chapter 1).

(b) In the centre of the root (Chapter 1, Figure 1.45) so that water entering a root must move radially across it from epidermis to stele.

(c) In the leaf veins, which are usually located between the upper (palisade) mesophyll and the lower mesophyll (spongy parenchyma) (Figure 1.30). To reach stomata, water must move in liquid form through cells and/or along cell walls and then evaporate into an air space from where it can diffuse as a gas (water vapour) to the stomata.

Check this pathway with Figure 3.1 but bear in mind that some water reaching leaves recirculates back to roots (and other organs) via sugar-transporting phloem (Chapters 1 and 2).

Now consider the type of water movement that may occur: *mass flow* (movement of water and solutes together in one direction because of differences in pressure); or *diffusion* (random movement of water molecules in all directions with a net flux from regions of higher to lower free energy, which represents the potential for movement). Mass flow is the type of movement that occurs when a solution is sucked up a straw or pumped along a pipe, so it can be quite fast: the flux of water is proportional to the pressure gradient and the fourth power of the 'pipe' radius. Diffusion, by contrast, is rapid over small distances (up to 1 mm) but exceedingly slow over long distances (i.e. 1 m or more) and it would take many years for water to diffuse from roots to the leaves of a tall tree. Clearly, therefore, water movement in xylem is by mass flow. However, when water enters the cytoplasm of a living cell through the cell wall, it usually does so by diffusion.

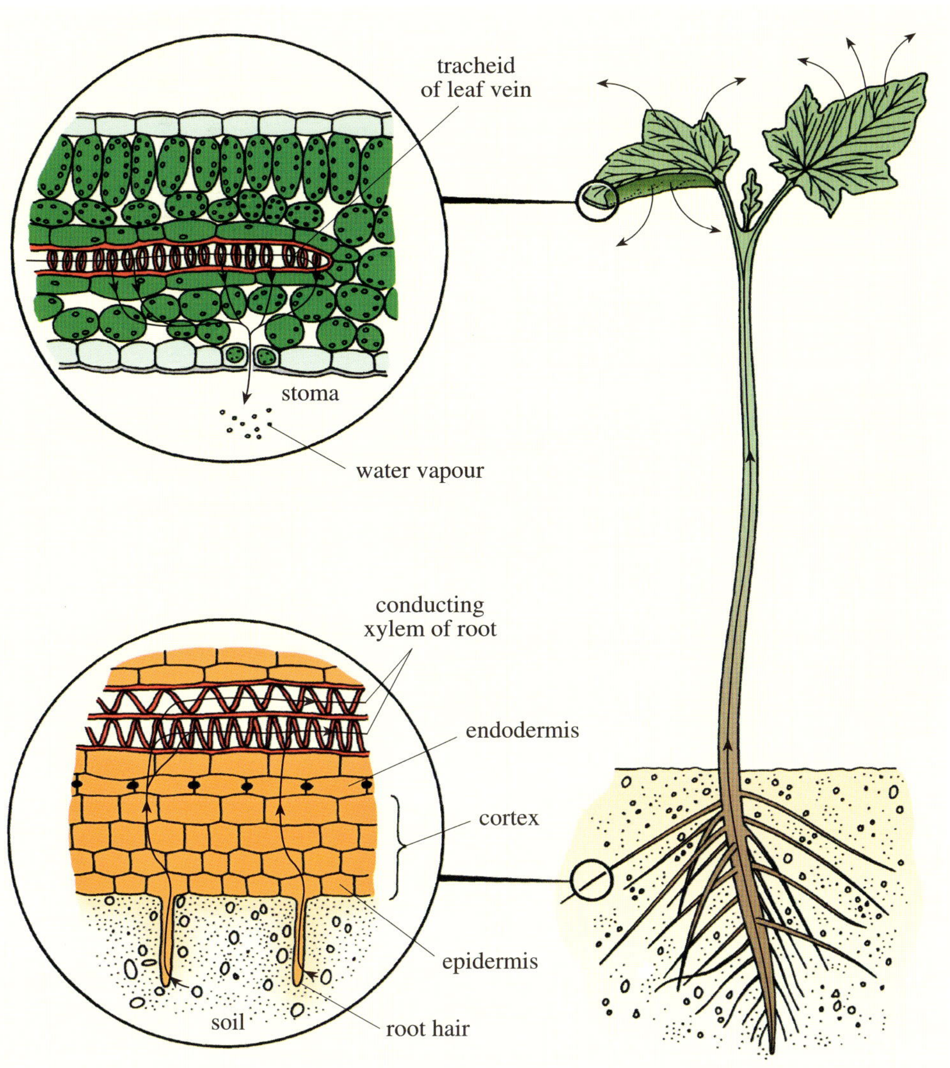

Figure 3.1 The pathway of water movement through a plant from roots to leaves. Black arrows show the pathway in the whole plant (right) and details of the pathway in roots and leaves are shown in the large circles (left).

❍ In most cells, what barrier can be crossed only by passive diffusion?

● The cell membrane (plasma membrane or plasmalemma) between the cell wall and the cytoplasm.

Unlike many solute molecules water is never *actively* transported across membranes via transport molecules, although its movement may be facilitated by special water-selective channels (aquaporins), which are discussed further in Section 3.2.1. During radial movement across a root from soil to xylem in the central stele, water must usually diffuse across at least one cell membrane although, for most of the journey, it can move along the cell walls by mass flow. This cell wall pathway is described as the **apoplast**. We discuss the movement of water across roots in more detail in Section 3.2.1.

When water moves across leaves (from xylem in veins to intercellular spaces and the outside atmosphere) its pathway also involves a mixture of diffusion into cells and movement in the apoplast. The latter route, mass flow through the apoplast, dominates when leaves have open stomata and are transpiring rapidly.

3.2.1 ROOT SYSTEMS AND WATER MOVEMENT ACROSS ROOTS

For nearly 150 years plant physiologists have been arguing about which parts of a root system take up most water and the precise path by which water moves from the soil to the root xylem. The questions are interesting in their own right but, equally, they are relevant to agriculture (and gardening) because they affect how plants are cultivated and bred so as to optimize water use. Two things are essential for effective water uptake by land plants: (i) there must be intimate contact between soil and roots (hence the importance of 'firming in' transplanted seedlings); and (ii) unless the soil is permanently very wet, roots must grow constantly.

- ❍ Why is root growth so important?

- ● Plant demand for water is often so high that uptake by roots dries out the soil locally; root growth therefore ensures that new volumes of soil are constantly exploited.

If a four-week-old wheat seedling is removed very carefully from soil, the root system appears something like that illustrated in Figure 3.2a.

The tightly adhering soil (or **rhizosheath**; *rhizo* = Greek for root) not only ensures close contact of root and soil but also has an important anchoring function. It is stabilized by mucilage derived either from the root cap (Figure 1.33c) or from certain bacteria. The rhizosheath forms over that part of a root where the epidermis

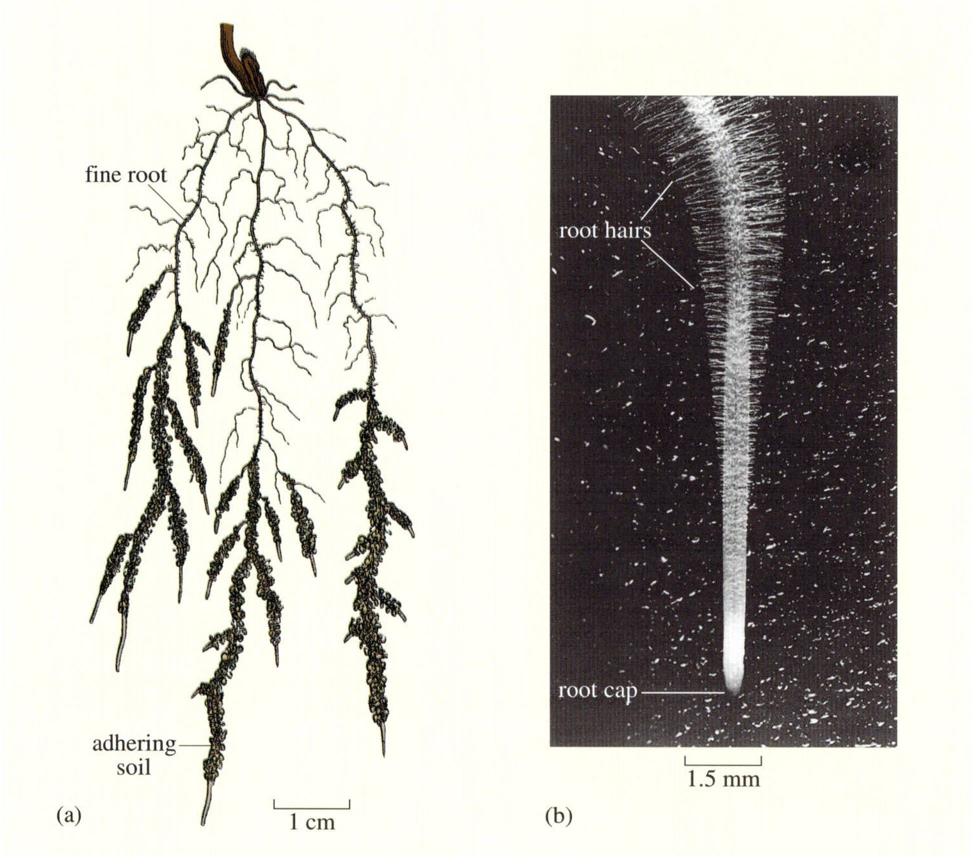

Figure 3.2 (a) The root system of a four-week-old wheat seedling. Note the tightly adhering soil some distance behind root tips. (b) The root tip of a primary (framework) root in a radish seedling.

is intact and root hairs (Figure 3.2b) are present and is a major site for the uptake of water and mineral nutrients (Chapter 4). It is present on both framework roots and fine roots (Figure 3.2). **Framework roots** are those which develop initially from the seed or subsequently from the underground part of the stem; they grow throughout life and hence are described as *indeterminate*. **Fine roots** (only a few of which are visible in Figure 3.2a because they are so easily torn off upon uprooting) develop from framework roots and are mostly 3–10 cm long with *determinate* growth, i.e. they lose their root cap and apical meristem and stop growing, although continuing to function as uptake organs. In fact, it has been shown that fine roots in total have about 30 times the length of framework roots and, consequently, are far more important for water and ion uptake (McCully, 1999). They may proliferate to an astonishing degree in patches of soil where there are locally high levels of nutrients such as nitrate (Figure 3.3), apparently in response to a nitrate-sensing system in the meristems that switches on certain genes. In addition, fine roots play an important role in times of drought. In many plant families, drought-resistant primordia of fine roots develop during drought and rapidly grow and become active once the soil is re-wetted, even if the meristem of the framework root has died.

Most studies of root function have been carried out with framework roots, however, because they are so much larger and easier to handle. The sequence of changes that occurs along a framework root as it grows, including development of fine roots, is illustrated in more detail in Figure 3.4.

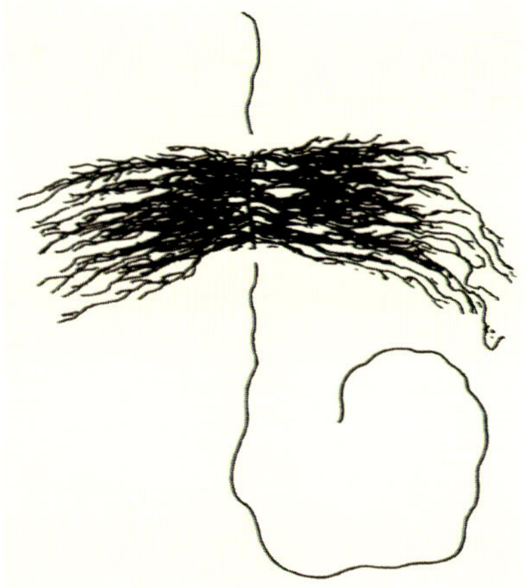

Figure 3.3 Localized proliferation of lateral and fine roots on a framework root of barley which was induced to grow through a zone of high nitrate concentration (1.0 mmol l^{-1} compared with 0.1 mmol l^{-1}).

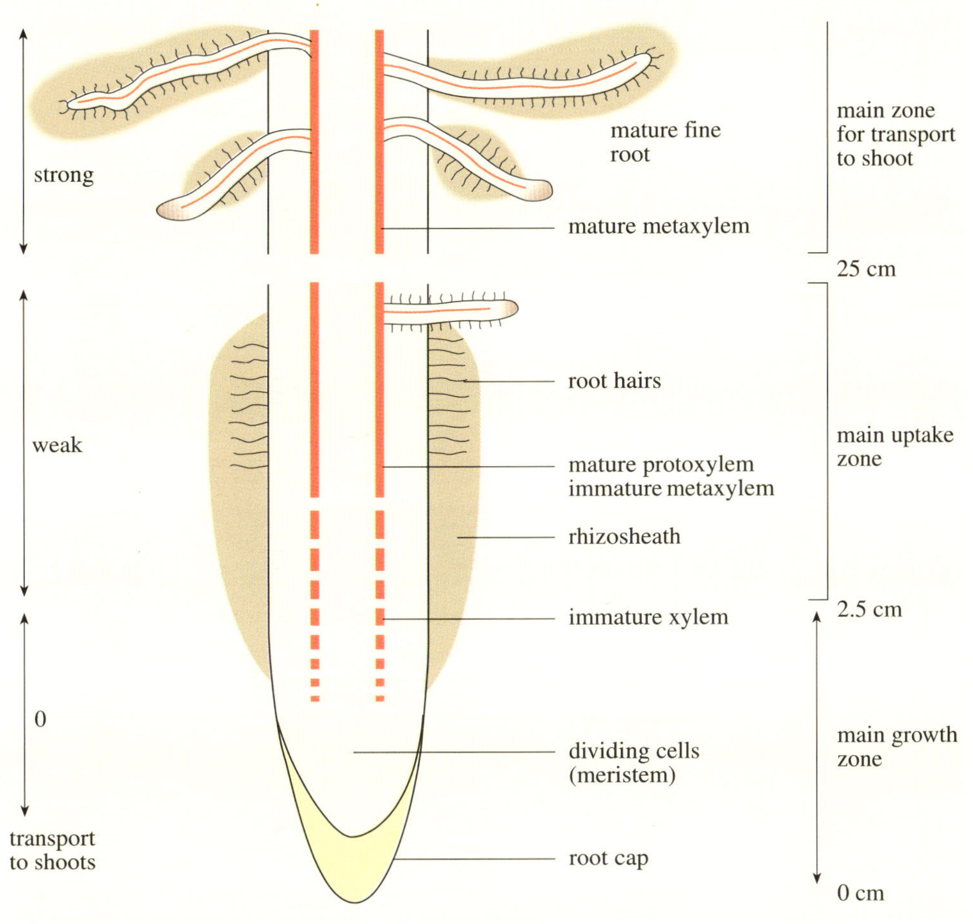

Figure 3.4 Diagram of a framework root of maize (*Zea mays*) in longitudinal section to show developmental changes and some effects on water uptake and transport to shoots.

❍ Maturation of xylem vessels means that they lose living cell contents and the end walls break down. Why, therefore, does maturation of large metaxylem vessels correspond to the main transport zone in Figure 3.4?

● Only when they are mature can xylem vessels conduct water by mass flow to the shoot. Because of their greater diameter, large metaxylem vessels conduct water much faster (recall that mass flow is proportional to the *fourth* power of the radius).

In a typical maize root, conducting capacity to the shoot increases 1800-fold when large metaxylem vessels mature. What we need to consider now is the pathway of radial water transport from soil to xylem, which is essentially the same for both framework and fine roots.

RADIAL WATER TRANSPORT

Figure 3.5 shows three possible pathways for water movement across the root cortex. The apoplastic (cell wall) pathway (Figure 3.5a) was mentioned earlier.

❍ Using Figure 3.5, describe the other two pathways.

● The **symplastic** pathway (Figure 3.5b) involves movement within cell cytoplasm and from cell to cell via the plasma membrane-lined pores (plasmodesmata, Chapter 1) that pass through cell walls. The transcellular path (Figure 3.5c) also involves movement within cells but water moves between cells mainly across the walls and membranes and not via plasmodesmata.

❍ So for each of the three pathways, how many membranes must be crossed by water as it moves across the epidermis and cortex as far as the endodermis?

● For the apoplast pathway, none; for the symplastic pathway, one (at the epidermis if that is where water enters the path); for the transcellular pathway, many. For this last path, two membranes are crossed for each cell traversed (one as water enters and one as it leaves and more if water enters the vacuole, as shown in Figure 3.5c).

It has been argued that all three of these pathways can be used for radial water transport up to the endodermis, although to differing extents in different conditions and different species (Steudle and Peterson, 1998). When transpiration is rapid, the apoplastic pathway may dominate, except in those species where membrane permeability to water is so high that it is almost as easy for water to move across membranes as along cell walls. If transpiration is slow or stops (e.g. at night), the symplastic plus transcellular paths tend to dominate and are the *only* pathways usually available for water to cross the endodermis.

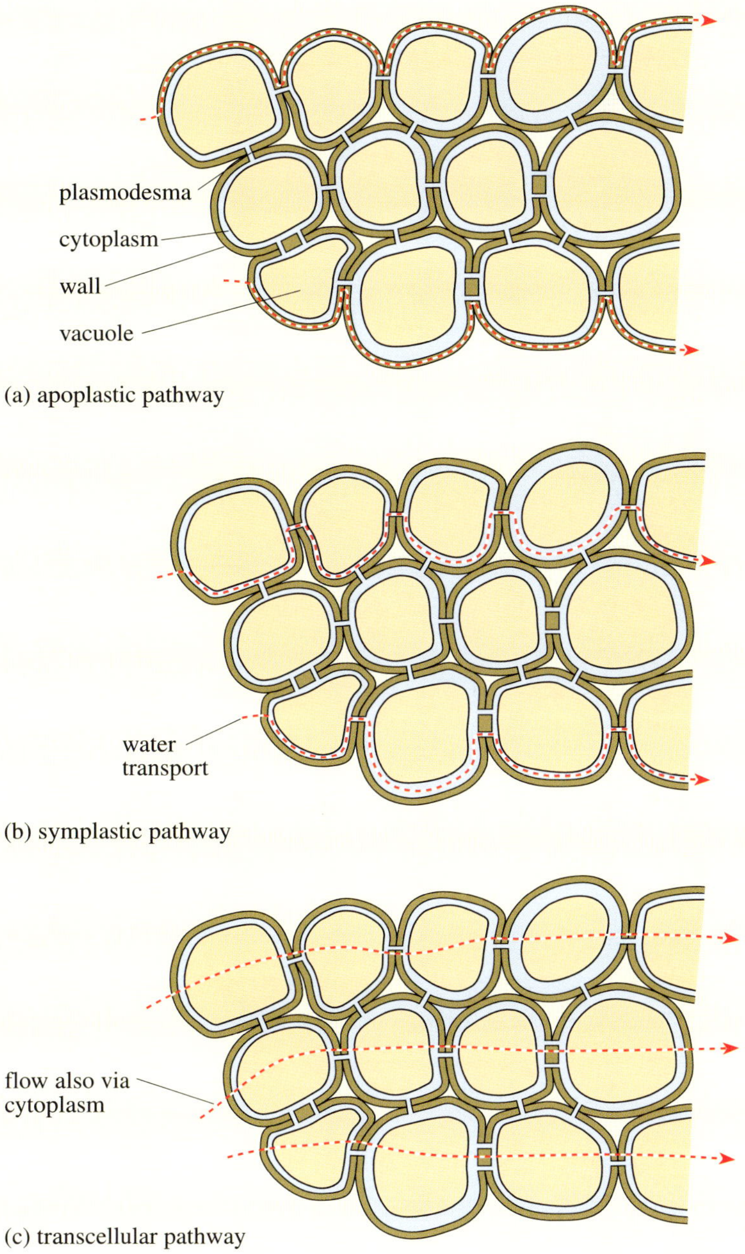

Figure 3.5 Three pathways available for water transport across the root cortex.

❍ From Figure 3.6a and Chapter 1, why is the apoplastic pathway not available for water to cross the endodermis?

● Because the radial walls contain a waterproof, suberized strip (the Casparian strip, to which the plasma membrane is firmly attached) which blocks the apoplastic pathway.

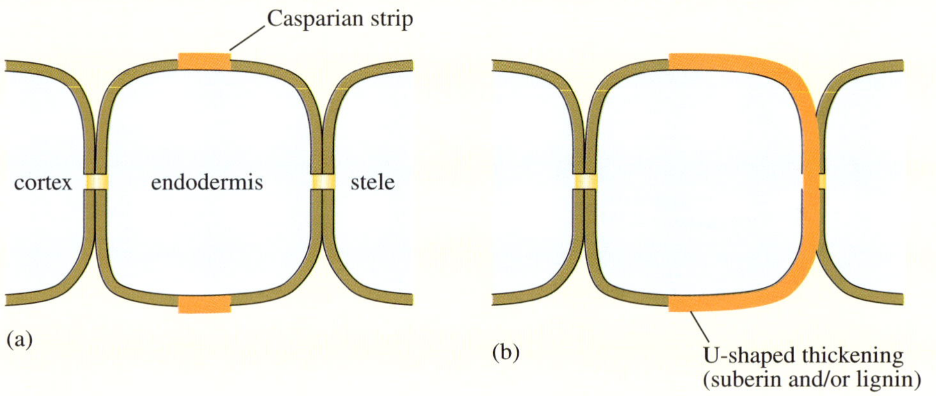

Figure 3.6 Transverse sections through an endodermal cell of maize in (a) the uptake zone and (b) the zone where large metaxylem vessels are mature.

In maize and some other grasses, crossing the endodermis becomes even more difficult in older parts of roots where the large metaxylem vessels are mature. Figure 3.6b illustrates why this is so: all the inner endodermal walls — radial, transverse and tangential — become thickened and waterproofed by the deposition of suberin and/or lignin. In addition, another layer of cells (the *exodermis*), lying just inside the epidermis, may also develop suberized layers on at least the radial walls, although it is still not clear how much of a barrier to apoplastic water movement this layer presents. Water can cross the heavily suberized endodermis only where lateral roots emerge or via special passage cells which lack thickened walls but still have a Casparian strip: there is some evidence that, at these sites, control over water movement is exerted by the availability of **water pores** or **aquaporins** in the plasma membrane. Aquaporins are protein channels which facilitate water movement across membranes; their availability seems to depend on metabolic activity, which may possibly be mediated via the reversible phosphorylation of the channel-forming protein. In effect, they can 'fine-tune' water uptake, increasing or decreasing water flow as they open or close or are added to or withdrawn from the plasma membrane. They may be especially important in times of drought or when soil salinity rises.

An obvious question to ask, however, is *why* do barriers to water movement, as in the endo- and exodermis, occur in roots? In fact the simple endodermis, with Casparian strips only, is a relatively weak barrier to water movement but very effective at blocking apoplastic solute movement. Solutes (e.g. inorganic ions) are transported, often actively and selectively, by what are essentially one-way channels into the stele, and Casparian strips ensure that they cannot then leak out. By contrast, water moves more easily in both directions across endodermal membranes and plasmodesmata and, especially if the soil is very dry, can move out of the stele and out of the root. This water outflow is most likely to occur at night (for reasons explained in the next section) and has the effect of moistening the rhizosheath, which helps to sustain microbial activity and the uptake of ions from the soil. Plants whose roots penetrate into deep, moist soil may take up deep-lying water at night and release it into the drier surface soil. This phenomenon, known as **hydraulic lift**, is particularly important in some desert habitats (Section 3.6) but occurs in temperate regions too. Trees may redistribute hundreds of litres of water each night by hydraulic lift and herbs and shrubs growing close to the trees have been shown to obtain up to 60% of their water from that released into surface soil by adjacent tree roots.

So much for the pathway of water movement across and along roots. However, to understand why water moves in a particular direction and at a given rate we need to consider the forces that cause movement and the nature of resistances to movement. These topics are considered in the next sections.

SUMMARY OF SECTION 3.2

1. Water taken up from the soil moves radially across roots to the xylem and then, by mass flow, up to the leaves.
2. Effective water uptake by roots requires constant root growth and close contact with soil particles, which is facilitated by formation of a rhizosheath. Most water uptake occurs via fine roots, which branch from the larger, framework roots.
3. Radial water transport across roots from epidermis to endodermis may involve any or all three of the apoplast, symplast and transcellular pathways, depending on plant species and environmental conditions.
4. Water movement across the endodermis and, if present, the exodermis necessarily occurs via cell membranes or plasmodesmata because of the waterproof thickening on radial cell walls. Aquaporin availability may control and fine-tune water flow across the cell membranes in roots.
5. Whereas solute movement into the stele is essentially one way, water can move both into and out of the stele across the endodermis.
6. Deep-rooted plants may distribute a substantial quantity of water into the surface soil by hydraulic lift.

3.3 WATER POTENTIAL AND THE DIRECTION OF WATER MOVEMENT

3.3.1 WATER POTENTIAL

You may already know some of the factors that cause water to move. Water flows down a river; it can be sucked up a straw or ejected from a syringe, and if a stem segment of a wilted plant is floated in distilled water, the segment slowly becomes firm as water enters its cells.

❍ For each of the examples above, state the nature of the force that causes water movement.

● Pressure resulting from gravity causes river flow; pressure, either negative (tension) or positive, causes movement in straw or syringe; and osmosis due to differences in solute concentration causes entry into wilted plant tissue.

For plants, we can ignore gravitational force because it is small in relation to the roles of hydrostatic pressure and solute concentration in water movement. The capacity of water to move is defined by its **water potential**, Ψ (Greek letter psi); water *moves down gradients of water potential*, from regions of higher to those of lower Ψ. Ψ is a measure of the free energy of water and usually expressed in units of pressure (pascals, Pa or megapascals, MPa). It is a *relative* measure: just as altitude is measured relative to sea-level, so water potential is relative to that of a standard — pure liquid water at ambient temperature and pressure — which is arbitrarily set at zero.

❍ From the earlier example of pure water moving into a wilted stem segment, is Ψ_{stem} above or below that of the outside water?

● It must be below, because water moves down gradients of water potential.

The driving force is the difference in water potential, $\Delta\Psi$ (where Δ, the capital Greek letter delta, means 'difference in'), between the stem segment and the distilled water outside. It follows that, since Ψ for pure water is zero, the stem cells must have a *negative* value of Ψ. This principle is important: with rare exceptions, *living cells have a negative water potential*. To explain this observation we need to dissect out the components of water potential.

3.3.2 The components of water potential

You already know that pressure, P (more precisely, hydrostatic pressure), and solute concentration influence water movement, so how do they affect water potential? A positive pressure increases the tendency of water molecules to move and, therefore, increases Ψ. An important point to note is that hydrostatic pressure in this context is defined as that *above or below atmospheric pressure*, which is taken as zero.

Conversely, solute molecules attract polar water molecules and increase hydrogen bonding between remaining water molecules, thus reducing their free energy and tendency to move. Solutes, therefore, decrease Ψ. The effect of solute concentration is described by the term **osmotic pressure**, which has the symbol π (Greek letter pi) (Swithenby and O'Shea, 2001). Recall that when two systems are separated by a semipermeable membrane (i.e. one that allows free passage of water but not of solutes), there is a net diffusion of water (i.e. **osmosis**) from the system with the lower to that with the higher solute concentration.

We now have the simplest equation which defines water potential and which you should remember:

$$\Psi = P - \pi \qquad (3.1)$$

❍ What is the water potential of a cup of salt solution of osmotic pressure 1 MPa?

● −1 MPa. P here is zero (atmospheric) so, from Equation 3.1, $\Psi = 0 - 1 = -1$.

In the next section, Equation 3.1 is applied to living plant cells, but first we need to refine and modify the equation so that it can be used for a wider range of situations, including non-living systems such as xylem or soil. Membranes are rarely completely semipermeable (i.e. allowing no passive diffusion of solute molecules) and diffusion of solute molecules from more to less concentrated solutions reduces π of the former. Membrane leakiness is allowed for by multiplying π by a term $\boldsymbol{\sigma}$ (Greek letter sigma), the **reflection coefficient**, which has a value of 1 for a truly semipermeable membrane and 0 for membranes equally permeable to water and solutes (or if no membrane is present). Equation 3.1 then becomes:

$$\Psi = P - \sigma\pi \qquad (3.2)$$

Another factor that can affect water potential is the presence of colloids or solid surfaces covered by a film of water. Water molecules tend to stick to surfaces, which lowers free energy and hence Ψ. Such adsorption or *matric* effects are negligible in living, fully hydrated cells but can be very significant in dry soil or seeds, for example. To allow for adsorption effects, a term, **matric pressure**, m, is included in Equation 3.2.

- Is m added to or subtracted from the right-hand side of Equation 3.2?

- Subtracted because, like π, matric pressure tends to decrease Ψ.

The final form of the equation then becomes:

$$\Psi = P - \sigma\pi - m \qquad (3.3)$$

Table 3.1 summarizes the factors that affect the components of water potential.

Table 3.1 Factors that affect water potential.

Factor	Symbol	Measured in terms of:	Effect when increased
hydrostatic pressure	P	pressure above (e.g. turgor) or below (tension) atmospheric	raises Ψ
solutes	π	osmotic pressure	lowers Ψ
interfaces or colloids	m	matric pressure	lowers Ψ

3.3.3 LIVING CELLS, OSMOSIS AND TURGOR

Figure 3.7 illustrates a critical difference between animal and plant cells when they absorb water by osmosis. Because plant cells have relatively rigid cell walls, swelling due to entry of water by osmosis is opposed as the internal hydrostatic pressure, P, which in this special case is called **turgor pressure**, rises. Turgor pressure can be defined as the pressure (above atmospheric pressure) that is exerted by the protoplast on the cell wall or, equally, the pressure exerted by the wall on the protoplast — the two are numerically identical.

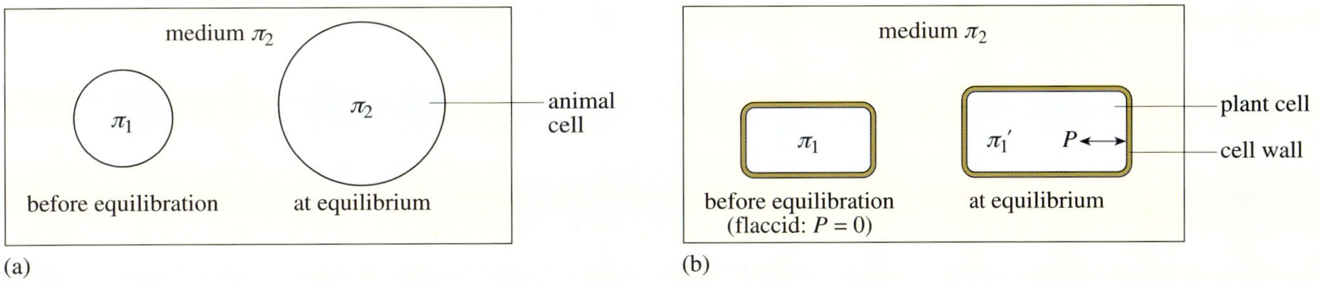

Figure 3.7 Comparison of (a) a wall-less (e.g. animal) cell and (b) a walled (e.g. plant) cell when placed in a solution, at atmospheric pressure, of osmotic pressure π_2 which is lower than that of the cells (π_1). The plant cell is initially flaccid, i.e. turgor pressure $P = 0$.

- ❍ Using appropriate terms, describe what happens to (a) the animal and (b) the plant cell in Figure 3.7 when placed in solution π_2. For each, define cell water potential at equilibrium.

- ● (a) The animal cell swells due to influx of water by osmosis until, at equilibrium (when water influx equals efflux), the internal osmotic pressure equals that of the outside solution and $\Psi = -\pi_2$ (as in the earlier calculation for the cup of salt solution). (b) The plant cell swells until the wall can stretch no more so that, at equilibrium, cell osmotic pressure, π_1', is still below π_2 and P has risen from 0 to a positive value. $\Psi = P - \pi_1'$, at equilibrium, assuming $\sigma = 1$ and m is negligible.

Thus the water potential of typical animal cells depends only on their osmotic pressure whereas, for plant cells, Ψ depends on both π and P. Turgor is important for support in non-woody plant tissues because turgid cells are stiff. It is also vital for plant growth because the expansion of cells depends on stretching young, pliable cell walls by internal (i.e. turgor) pressure.

Figure 3.8a summarizes the changes that occur in cell volume and in π and P as the external water potential changes. Starting at the left side, with the cell at equilibrium in pure water ($\Psi = 0$), cell volume and turgor are at a maximum and $P = \pi$. It follows that the higher the solute concentration in a cell (and hence π), the greater the turgor which can be generated, a relationship which becomes very important when we consider transport in phloem (Section 3.7).

- ❍ How could you have deduced that $P = \pi$ for a cell in pure water using Equation 3.1?

- ● $\Psi_{\text{cell}} = 0$ (as for the external solution), so $0 = P - \pi$ and hence $P = \pi$.

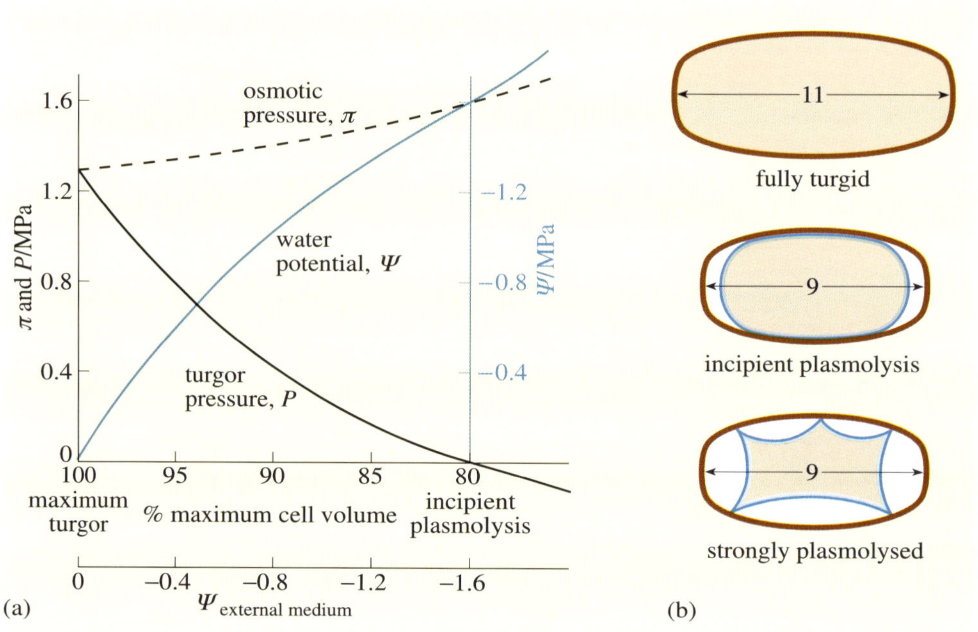

Figure 3.8 (a) The relationship between volume, water potential, osmotic pressure and turgor pressure of a cell with rather elastic cell walls. Changes are related to the external water potential with which the cell is in equilibrium (bottom axis). (b) Diagrams to illustrate the appearance and relative sizes of a cell at full turgor, incipient plasmolysis and when strongly plasmolysed (values are relative arbitrary units).

As the external water potential (and that of the cell which is in equilibrium) falls, turgor declines rapidly, the cell shrinks, there is an increase in π as solutes become more concentrated, and eventually (right hand side of Figure 3.8a) a state of **incipient plasmolysis** is reached. At this point, the walls can contract no further, so cell volume is at a minimum, and turgor is zero. The plasma membrane begins to pull away from the walls (Figure 3.8b, middle). A further fall in Ψ causes strong plasmolysis when cell contents contract towards the centre of the cell (Figure 3.8b, bottom) and it is clear from Figure 3.8a that P becomes negative. Cells may be irreversibly damaged if this state is reached.

❍ At incipient plasmolysis: (a) how would the *appearance* of a rooted, herbaceous plant (e.g. a tulip) change? (b) what is the relationship between Ψ and π? (c) what would be the effect on the rate of plant growth?

● (a) The plant would droop and appear wilted because of the lack of cell turgor. (b) They are numerically equal, which can be seen in Figure 3.8a or calculated from Equation 3.1 ($\Psi = 0 - \pi$, so $\Psi = -\pi$). (c) Growth would cease since a positive turgor pressure is required to cause cell expansion.

In fact, growth is very sensitive to small decreases in turgor and may cease well before incipient plasmolysis is reached.

Water therefore diffuses into or between living plant cells, down water potential gradients that depend on turgor and osmotic pressure. What determines the *rate* of movement, however, is the permeability of cell membranes to water, a property described as **hydraulic conductivity, L_p**. Water flux, the volume (in m^3) crossing unit area (in m^2) of membrane per unit time ($m^3\ m^{-2}\ s^{-1}$) simplifies, by cancelling out the metres, to flow rate ($m\ s^{-1}$) and:

flow rate ($m\ s^{-1}$) = hydraulic conductivity ($m\ s^{-1}\ MPa^{-1}$) × driving force (MPa).

$$\text{water flux or flow rate} = L_p \times \Delta\Psi \qquad (3.4)$$

So the flow of water across a root, for example, could be increased by increasing either hydraulic conductivity or the water potential gradient and there is evidence that a hormonal regulator, abscisic acid (Chapter 5), the concentration of which increases in times of water stress, actually does both.

❍ Describe at least one way in which L_p could be altered.

● Through the activation or synthesis of aquaporins (Section 3.2.1). More general changes in membrane properties could also affect L_p.

The hydraulic conductivity of root cell membranes certainly varies widely, not only within a root but also at different times of day and between species; the maximum value for the bean *Phaseolus coccineus*, for example, is almost 40 times greater than that for barley or wheat. In fact, so permeable to water are cell membranes in *P. coccineus* roots that it is just as easy for water to cross roots via the transcellular pathway as via cell walls (the apoplastic route, Section 3.2). Usually, pathways that lack cell membranes (e.g. cell walls, soil, xylem) have a much greater hydraulic conductivity than pathways that include membranes. In the next section we consider these 'non-living' pathways in more detail but, first, pause to consider how the water relations of living plant cells are measured.

3.3.4 MEASURING Ψ, P AND π FOR PLANT CELLS

The methods available for studying plant water status have improved dramatically since around 1980 and resulted in major advances in understanding how and where water moves. Particularly important have been:

- microsurgical techniques that allow sampling and measurements from single cells;
- very sensitive, electronic systems that allow measurement of small changes in, for example, turgor and solute concentrations; and
- most recently, non-invasive methods (such as the use of nuclear magnetic resonance (NMR) imaging) that allow cells or tissues to be studied without disturbance.

We describe here the principles of methods used for the direct measurement of water potential and of P and π in living cells, with details of some techniques in Boxes 3.1 and 3.2. Methods used for studying xylem are described in Section 3.4.

MEASURING Ψ DIRECTLY

If plant tissue is placed xin a solution and there is no net water movement into or out of the tissue (so that tissue volume, length or weight does not change), then tissue and external solution are in equilibrium and their water potentials are equal. If you know Ψ_{ext}, you also know the *average* water potential of the tissue. Box 3.1 describes a method (known as a psychrometric method) based on this principle but where, instead of placing tissue *in* a solution of known Ψ, it is placed in a sealed chamber and allowed to come to water vapour equilibrium with the solution.

BOX 3.1 A PSYCHROMETRIC METHOD TO MEASURE WATER POTENTIAL

As the water potential of a solution falls, fewer water molecules evaporate from it in unit time, thus causing a fall in vapour pressure (i.e. the pressure of water in the gas phase in equilibrium with the solution). Ψ_{tissue} is related directly to vapour pressure (or relative humidity) at equilibrium. For this method, tissue is sealed inside a chamber (or psychrometer; psychro derives from the Greek meaning 'to cool'; Figure 3.9a) with a droplet of solution of known Ψ, left until air in the chamber is saturated and then the *temperature* of the droplet monitored. If the droplet has the same water potential as the tissue, its temperature does not change. If the droplet has a higher (less negative) water potential, water evaporates from it causing cooling, diffuses into the air and is absorbed by the tissue. The reverse happens if $\Psi_{solution}$ is lower (more negative) than Ψ_{tissue}: the solution is warmed as water moves through the vapour phase from tissue to solution. In practice, measurements are made with a series of solutions and a graph obtained as shown in Figure 3.9b.

❍ What is the water potential of the tissue from Figure 3.9b?

● About −1.2 MPa: this value corresponds to that of the solution at which there was no temperature change.

Temperature of the droplet is measured by a very sensitive thermocouple and the whole instrument is maintained at constant temperature. If the tissue is crushed and a drop of its sap used instead of whole tissue, the osmotic pressure of the sap can be measured by this method. Knowing Ψ and π for the tissue, turgor pressure P can be calculated from Equation 3.1.

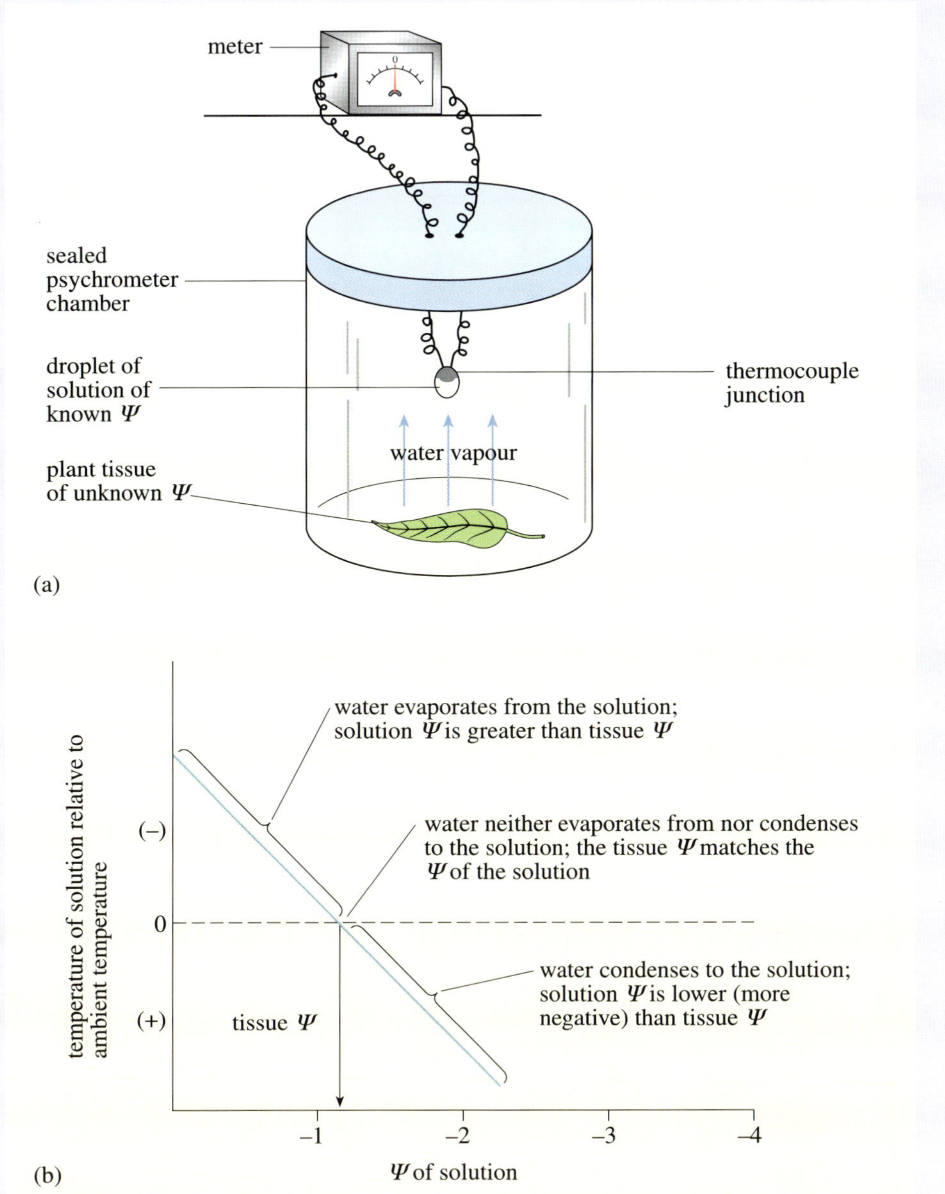

Figure 3.9 The psychrometric method for measuring water potential: (a) experimental set-up; (b) graph showing temperature of the droplet plotted against its water potential (in MPa). Data from Taiz and Zeiger (1998).

MEASURING π AND P

An alternative to the psychrometric method described in Box 3.1 for measuring the solute concentration in sap (i.e. average π) is *cryoscopic osmometry*. In essence, you measure the freezing point of sap and compare it with that of pure water (0 °C): solute molecules depress freezing point below 0 °C and the higher the concentration, the greater the depression.

However, both techniques described so far measure *average* values of Ψ or π when, for a full understanding of plant water relations, the values for individual cells are needed. Such single-cell measurements are now possible and are described in Box 3.2.

Box 3.2 The pressure probe and single-cell sampling

The pressure probe was developed during the 1960s for use with very large algal cells and Figure 3.10 illustrates how this early version worked. It cannot be used with smaller cells because too high a proportion of cell sap is lost in the capillary, but Figure 3.11 illustrates how this problem can be avoided in more modern instruments. The key change is that the capillary is now filled with silicone oil and inserted into an oil reservoir which is linked to a pressure sensor and a remote-controlled piston. As cell turgor pushes the oil meniscus up the capillary, counter pressure can be applied via the piston and measured by the sensor. The counter pressure required to return the meniscus to the cell wall gives a measure of cell turgor.

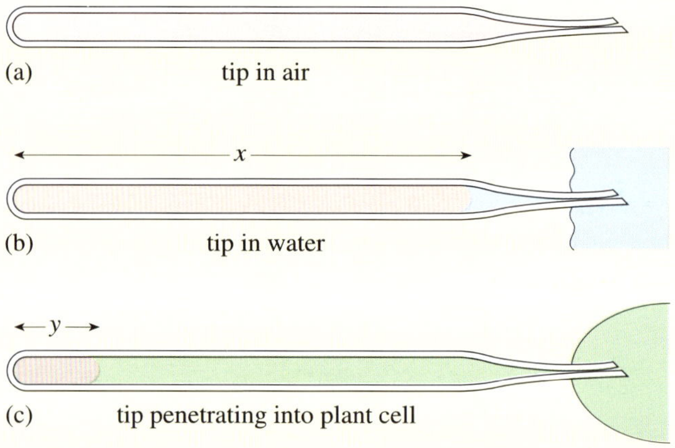

Figure 3.10 Principle of the early pressure probe used to measure turgor in giant algal cells. A small glass capillary pipette closed at one end is used (a). The tip of the pipette is first placed in water (b) and then inserted into the vacuole of the test cell (c). Turgor pressure, P, compresses air in the capillary pipette and the amount of compression $(x - y)$ is proportional to P.

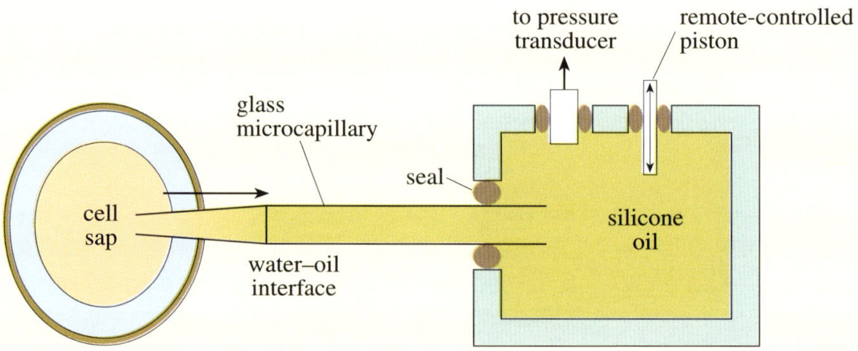

Figure 3.11 A diagram of a cell pressure probe suitable for use with small, higher-plant cells. Counter pressure is applied via the piston until the cell sap/oil meniscus is at the cell wall.

Pressure probes have been adapted so that samples of sap from single cells can be obtained for analysis (Single Cell Sampling and Analysis, SiCSA), e.g. of solute content. Osmotic pressure of single cells can thus be measured. Probes may also be attached to excised root tips in order to measure positive pressures in xylem (root pressure), discussed in Section 3.4.2.

Knowing turgor and osmotic pressure for single cells or the average values for pieces of tissue, Ψ can be calculated from Equation 3.1. Slowly, as techniques have improved, a clearer picture is emerging of water potential gradients within living plant tissues and the effects of environmental changes on such gradients.

SUMMARY OF SECTION 3.3

1 Water potential, Ψ, is a relative measure of the free energy of water and pure water has a value of 0. Water moves down gradients of water potential at a rate that depends on $\Delta\Psi$ and hydraulic conductivity, L_p.

2 Living cells usually have a negative water potential. Its value depends on hydrostatic pressure above atmospheric (turgor, P) and solute concentration (osmotic pressure, π), which depends in turn on the reflection coefficient σ of membranes. In systems with a high solid:liquid ratio (e.g. soil), matric pressure is also a contributor. Equation 3.3 summarizes the interactions.

3 Turgor is essential for the expansion growth of plant cells and for support in non-woody tissues.

4 Average values of Ψ or π for tissues can be measured by psychrometric methods (Box 3.1) and P can then be calculated from Equation 3.2. Values of P and π for single cells can be obtained using a pressure probe.

3.4 WATER FLOW IN SOIL AND XYLEM

Because there are no semipermeable membranes in soil or mature xylem, water movement here depends on gradients of pressure (xylem) or matric potential (soil); the term $\sigma\pi$ is lost from Equation 3.2 because $\sigma = 0$.

3.4.1 MOVEMENT THROUGH SOIL

Soil is basically a mixture of particles which are surrounded by a film of water and have gaps containing either air or water between them. When plant roots take up water they cause local drying of the soil which causes water to adhere more tightly to soil particles. The resultant lowering of matric potential acts like a negative pressure or suction and water potential is reduced: $\Psi = -m$ in soil. So water moves from wetter to drier parts of soil down gradients of matric potential, partly by diffusion but mainly by mass flow (Section 3.3.1).

How fast water moves through soil to roots depends on the steepness of the water potential gradient and on the **hydraulic conductivity of the soil** (equivalent to Equation 3.4). Soil hydraulic conductivity is a measure of the ease with which water moves through it and it depends both on the type of soil (e.g. sand or clay) and on water content.

○ From your own experience, which would you expect to have the higher hydraulic conductivity at equal water contents: a sandy soil or a clay-rich soil?

● A sandy soil. Think how much faster water drains through sand than through clay.

Clay particles are much smaller than those of sand, so there is a greater surface area to bind water and smaller channels between particles. So clay binds water tenaciously and also has a high water-holding capacity — which is why clay soils are described as 'heavy'. As soil dries out, water potential falls (as *m* rises) and hydraulic conductivity decreases many fold, so plant roots must develop an even lower water potential if they are to take up water. Maximum effectiveness is achieved by many fine roots ramifying through the soil, especially in surface soil, which tends to dry out most readily but is also richest in minerals. By increasing the surface area for water uptake, the fine roots act to reduce water flux, which equals flow/(area × time). Some plants that grow in drought-prone or fast-draining soils (e.g. sand dunes) have both a network of surface roots plus one or more deeply penetrating roots which can tap water in lower soil layers, and water may be redistributed to the dry surface layers using hydraulic lift (Section 3.2). The rhizosheath (Section 3.2.1) also plays an important role during drought because it maintains root–soil contact as roots shrink (sometimes by up to 50%) in drying soil. Rhizosheaths are prominent in desert cacti.

3.4.2 Movement through xylem: the ascent of sap

That water can move through xylem from roots to the top of a tall tree, perhaps a hundred metres high, is truly remarkable and, even today, arguments still rage about how it is done. The most widely accepted mechanism was first proposed in the 1890s and is called the **cohesion–tension theory**, which argues as follows:

1. Transpiration from leaves generates a gradient of water potential through leaf cells to veins and causes water to move out of xylem.
2. The result is a lowering of water potential in vein xylem, which means that hydrostatic pressure is lowered (since *P* is the only component of Ψ in xylem); a suction force, i.e. negative pressure or *tension*, is created which is the driving force for the transpiration stream.
3. Tension in leaf xylem is transmitted all the way down to the roots *provided* that continuous columns of water are maintained in the xylem, an important proviso as you will see in the next section. Continuous water columns under tension are possible because (a) the strong, lignified cell walls of xylem conducting cells do not collapse under tension; (b) water molecules adhere strongly by hydrogen bonding to the walls of xylem conduits, so the water column does not pull away from the walls; and (c), most important of all, hydrogen bonding ensures the *cohesion* of water molecules to each other, holding the water column together and preventing water from vaporizing at the low pressures experienced.

Such a mechanism requires a gradient of water potential in xylem (i.e. a pressure gradient) of up to 3 MPa in order to move water against the forces of gravity and frictional resistance from the roots to the top of a tree 100 m tall (Taiz and Zeiger, 1998). The modern controversy has been over whether such large pressure gradients actually exist. Using a long-established technique, the pressure chamber, the measurements indicate that they do; but data obtained using a pressure probe, as described for living cells in Box 3.2, suggest that they do not.

The **pressure chamber** (or **pressure bomb**) method is illustrated in Figure 3.12. A twig or shoot is cut, whereupon water in the xylem contracts away from the cut surface because of the low xylem pressure. The twig is clamped inside a pressure chamber with the cut end protruding into air and the chamber is pressurized, raising water potential, until water is forced along xylem towards the cut surface. The chamber pressure at which water just reaches this surface should exactly equal the original xylem tension.

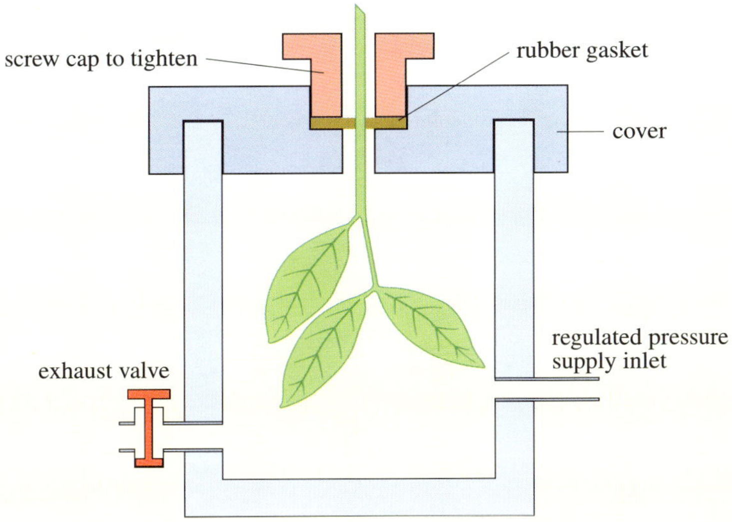

Figure 3.12 A pressure chamber or pressure bomb. Compressed gas is used to pressurize the sealed chamber.

Pressures of around −2 MPa have been measured in xylem using the pressure chamber, values that are sufficiently low to explain water movement up moderately tall plants. With the xylem pressure probe, however, measured xylem pressures are not found below −0.6 MPa, which is not low enough to explain such movement. So either the xylem pressure probe is unable to measure lower xylem pressures or some mechanism in addition to, or instead of, that proposed by the cohesion–tension theory must operate. Current opinion generally favours the first of these two explanations (e.g. Tyree, 1997), although it is not clear *why* the xylem pressure probe does not measure low pressures. The most likely explanation seems to be that the probe causes cavitation in xylem, a subject we discuss next.

XYLEM CAVITATION AND EMBOLISM

Despite cohesive forces, water columns under tension in xylem are somewhat unstable, commonly described as metastable. The lower the pressure, the greater the instability. If xylem pressure becomes too low or if shoots are wounded by grazers or jarred suddenly, metastable water may vaporize locally and a cavity containing water vapour and some air can form in a xylem conduit. This process is called **cavitation** and it leads to more air coming out of solution, forming a bubble or **embolism**, which expands to block the conduit and blocks water flow. An embolized tracheid or xylem vessel is dysfunctional.

Figure 3.13 illustrates what happens during cavitation and embolism. Notice that cavitation produces a clicking sound as the walls vibrate following pressure increase. In the 1970s, special microphones were developed that allowed these ultrasonic clicks to be heard, enabling the frequency of cavitation to be measured in living plants. The frequency was far higher than previously thought: in corn (*Zea mays*), for example, embolism reduced water flow by 50% during a single day and in sugar maple saplings (*Acer saccharum*) flow reduction in the trunk was 31% by early autumn and 60% by the following spring, with many small twigs completely blocked (Tyree and Sperry, 1989). Damage on this scale is potentially disastrous and three questions can be asked. What determines plant vulnerability to embolism? What conditions cause cavitation? How do plants recover from embolism?

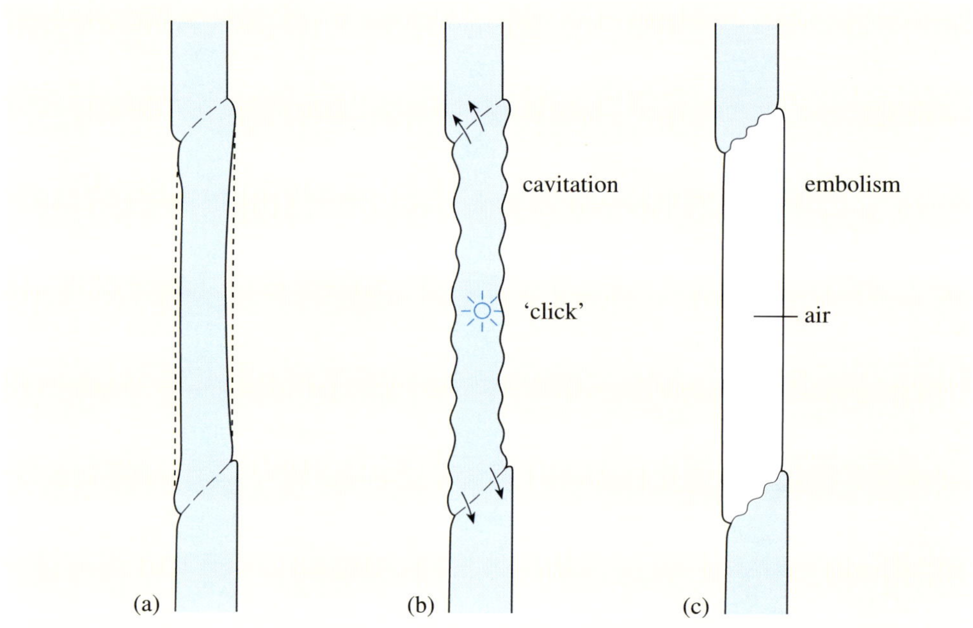

Figure 3.13 Representation of cavitation and embolism in a xylem vessel. (a) Under extreme tension (low pressure), the walls are strained inwards from the dotted line. (b) A cavitation 'bubble' filled mainly with water vapour forms and the strained walls vibrate, producing sound waves. Water exits to adjoining vessels. (c) Air comes out of solution and a gas bubble forms.

1 *Vulnerability*

First, *xylem structure* is important. Wide conduits are more likely to cavitate than narrow ones, so plants with relatively few, wide, long vessels are not only more susceptible but also lose a higher proportion of their conducting system if a vessel embolizes. Recall (Chapter 1) that conifers have tracheids but no vessels.

❍ What are the advantages and disadvantages to conifers of having no xylem vessels? What is the trade-off?

● First, bearing in mind that tracheids are both narrower and shorter than vessels (Chapter 1), conifers are likely to be less susceptible to cavitation than non-conifers. However, because of their larger diameter and greater length, vessels offer less resistance to water flow and so allow greater volume flow. Conifers may be unable to supply water fast enough to rapidly transpiring leaves and the needle-like leaves of conifers do indeed act to restrict transpiration rates.

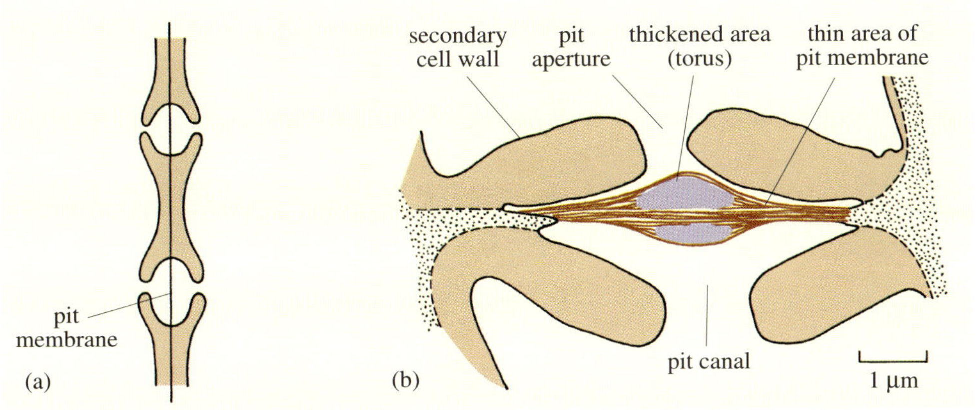

Figure 3.14 Structure of bordered pits in xylem. (a) Simple type; (b) more complex type with a thickened central torus, found in conifers. The pit membrane is the remains of the middle lamella plus primary wall and, when pressed sideways against the pit aperture, it prevents air bubbles passing from one xylem element to another.

Second, the *permeability and strength of the pit membrane* (see Figure 3.14) greatly affect vulnerability to embolism. Pits in xylem walls allow water to move sideways and bypass a blocked conduit (Figure 3.15) and the more permeable the pit membranes, the easier is sideways flow. However, pit membranes are also the crucial barriers that prevent air bubbles spreading from an embolized conduit to another (Figure 3.14) and there is now strong evidence that, at very low xylem pressures, this barrier becomes less effective. Tiny air bubbles squeeze through pores in pit membranes of embolized conduits, triggering cavitation in adjacent conduits and the bigger the pores (i.e. the more porous the membrane), the more likely is such 'air seeding'. Pore size correlates roughly with vessel or tracheid diameter so that here is another example of a trade-off between ease and speed of water flow and risk of cavitation and embolism. The high rates of cavitation measured by acoustic detection are caused largely by air seeding from occasional, accidentally embolized xylem elements.

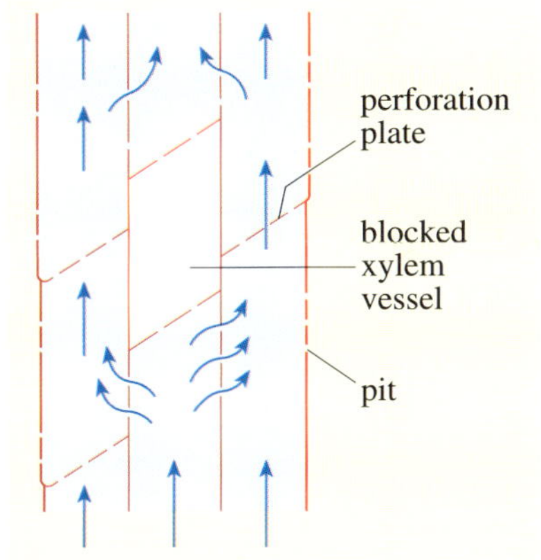

Figure 3.15 Diagram to illustrate how sideways flow of water through pits in xylem elements can circumvent a blocked conduit.

2 *Causes of cavitation and embolism*

Two conditions are mainly responsible for high rates of cavitation. (a) *Water stress*, associated with high rates of transpiration and low xylem pressures, promotes air seeding as described above. Drought greatly increases the risk of cavitation and plants that grow in dry habitats have evolved several mechanisms that reduce the risk (Section 3.6.1). (b) *Freezing* of xylem sap in winter leads to extensive formation of air bubbles when thawing occurs and widespread embolism in woody plants. A third, less common factor, is *pathogen-induced embolism* (c). For example, embolism is the first damage caused by the Dutch elm disease fungus that has devastated British elm trees, and the rapid wilting seen in *Clematis* wilt disease is probably caused by fungus-induced embolism. The mechanism is thought to be through release into xylem sap of surfactants — substances such as oxalic acid which lower surface tension and thereby facilitate air-seeding at pit membranes.

3 *Recovery from embolism*

For herbaceous plants, some means of removing embolisms during the growing season is essential for survival. The usual mechanism is through **root pressure**, a *positive* hydrostatic pressure in xylem. The air in an embolism goes back into solution if xylem pressure rises to or just below atmospheric pressure, which occurs most commonly through root pressure at night. Stomatal pores close at night (Chapter 2) and transpiration stops, but provided the plant is reasonably well watered, active ion uptake and water influx continue. The build up of ions in root xylem parenchyma, from where they diffuse into xylem vessels, lowers water potential below that of the external medium and water flows across the root into xylem at a rate which matches that at which salts enter xylem. Thus xylem P gradually rises until it becomes positive and a column of liquid rises upwards. Table 3.2 shows data that illustrate the nature of the water potential gradients which drive water into xylem when there is slow transpiration (Stage 1) or almost none (Stage 2). In effect, the living cells of the root act like a single unit separated from xylem and soil by semipermeable membranes.

Table 3.2 Data for a slowly transpiring plant showing stages in the development of root pressure. Units are MPa and note that the osmotic pressure of xylem sap is taken into account when considering water movement *into* xylem.

	Root		Wet soil adjacent to root
	Xylem	Cortex	
Stage 1			
m	negligible	negligible	0.03
π	0.10	0.50	negligible
P	–0.30	+0.40	-
Ψ			
	gradient of Ψ along which water flows		
Stage 2			
m	negligible	negligible	0.03
π	0.30	0.50	negligible
P	+0.05	+0.40	-
Ψ			
	gradient of Ψ along which water flows		

❍ Using Equation 3.3 (assuming $\sigma = 1$) calculate water potential values in Table 3.2 and add arrow heads to the lines indicating the direction of the water potential gradient.

● For Stage 1, $\Psi = -0.4$, -0.1 and -0.03 from left to right; for Stage 2 the comparable values are -0.25, -0.1 and -0.03. In both cases, the arrow head is at the left end of the line indicating a gradient of Ψ from soil to xylem.

Root pressures are usually small (0.05–0.50 MPa) but they are sufficient to push water slowly through xylem and induce re-filling of embolized conduits. An interesting consequence of root pressure is the phenomenon known as **guttation**. You may have noticed drops of liquid looking rather like dew hanging from the tips of leaves at night or in humid conditions when transpiration is low. In fact, these are guttation fluid forced out of the vein endings by root pressure and through stomata or, in some cases, through specialized hairs called *hydathodes* onto the leaf surface.

In trees, root pressures are usually insufficient to refill embolized vessels during the growing season, and to prevent xylem pressures becoming too low during the day, stomata may be closed. Alternatively, or in addition, non-conducting tissue in the trunk can act like a huge water reservoir, supplying water to the xylem conduits during the day and filling up at night; trunk diameter may, indeed, fall in the day and rise at night. However, some woody plants such as birch, *Betula*, and grape vine, *Vitis*, develop considerable root pressure in early spring before buds burst and growth starts. This 'rising of the sap' is so pronounced in vines that sap may drip for several days out of cut branches and frothing is seen as air is expelled and embolized vessels re-fill with water. The other and more important way in which woody plants may recover from winter embolism caused by freezing is through the growth of new xylem cells in spring.

Susceptibility to cavitation, tolerance of embolism and ability to recover from it are major factors influencing the type and distribution of land plants and, particularly, their tolerance of drought and freezing. The other factor which influences strongly where plants can grow is their control of water loss from leaves, which is discussed next.

SUMMARY OF SECTION 3.4

1. In the absence of membranes, water movement through soil and xylem depends on gradients of matric and hydrostatic pressure, respectively.
2. Rates of water movement in soil depend on water content and soil type, which determine soil hydraulic conductivity. The smaller the soil particles, the lower the hydraulic conductivity.
3. The widely accepted mechanism for water movement in xylem to the tops of tall trees is the cohesion–tension theory.
4. The pressure chamber (or bomb) is the most reliable method for measuring negative pressures in xylem.
5. Low pressures in xylem cause instability of the water column, which can result in cavitation and embolism, blocking conduits.
6. Vulnerability to cavitation and embolism is influenced mainly by xylem structure (width of conduits) and the permeability and strength of pit membranes (affecting air seeding).
7. Cavitation and embolism may be caused by water stress (causing low xylem P), freezing of xylem sap and by pathogens.
8. Recovery from embolism in herbaceous plants is through root pressures developed at night as a result of active ion uptake by roots. This mechanism operates in some woody plants in spring but is usually inadequate during the growing season.

3.5 Transpiration and stomatal control

When plants transpire, most of the water taken up by roots evaporates from leaves as water vapour (Section 3.1) and it is the difference in the potential of water vapour (not water) that drives transpiration. The main factor influencing this gradient is the water vapour content or **relative humidity** (**r.h.**) of the outside air. Relative humidity measures water content relative to that of saturated air ($c_{wv}/c_{wv(sat)}$, usually expressed as a percentage) and is the chief determinant of water vapour potential, the other factor being temperature: the higher the leaf temperature, the lower (more negative) is Ψ. There is usually a large difference between the saturated air within a leaf (r.h. close to 100%) and the atmospheric humidity, which in temperate regions is usually around 50–70%.

The flux of water vapour during transpiration (J_{wv}) depends on the driving force, $\Delta\Psi$ (or, at constant temperature, Δr.h.) and the ease with which water vapour diffuses from leaf to atmosphere, which can be expressed either as conductance, g, or its reciprocal, resistance, r, as follows:

$$J_{wv} = \Delta\Psi \times g = \Delta\Psi / r \qquad (3.5)$$

Since there is a large and relatively constant driving force for transpiration, the factor that usually controls water loss is g (or r), so we need to examine these factors more closely.

3.5.1 Resistance to water loss

The shoots of land plants are covered by a waxy and essentially waterproof cuticle (Chapter 1) which offers very high resistance (low conductance) to water loss. So the main pathway by which water vapour diffuses out of leaves is via open stomatal pores (Figure 3.16).

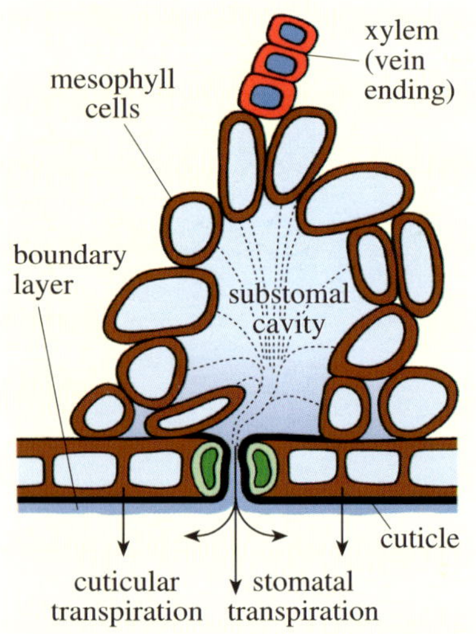

Figure 3.16 Section through part of a leaf showing the outward diffusion pathways for water vapour (black arrows). The arrows show stomatal and cuticular transpiration. Note that most of the water evaporates from the walls of cells close to the xylem vein ending.

The operative word here is 'open': stomata provide a low resistance path when pores are open but resistance rises to the same value as the cuticle when pores close. **Stomatal resistance**, r_s, thus varies depending on the pore diameter, and Section 3.5.3 discusses how pore diameter is controlled.

In addition to r_s, a second resistance to water loss arises because of the presence of still, almost water-saturated air that covers the leaf surface, the **boundary layer** (Figure 3.16). **Boundary layer resistance**, r_b, depends on the thickness of the boundary layer, l, which is proportional to leaf width, w, and wind velocity, v.

$$r_b \propto l \propto w/v \qquad (3.6)$$

❍ From Equation 3.5 decide: (a) whether boundary-layer resistance is a constant or variable resistance; (b) whether the flat leaf of a sycamore or the needle leaf of a pine has the higher r_b?

● (a) It is a variable resistance because it depends on wind speed, which varies. (b) The sycamore leaf because it has the greater width.

Various structures and processes allow plants to increase boundary layer thickness, for example the presence of hairs, the positioning of stomata inside pits and the ability to roll up leaves so that the surface bearing the stomata is enclosed (Figure 3.17).

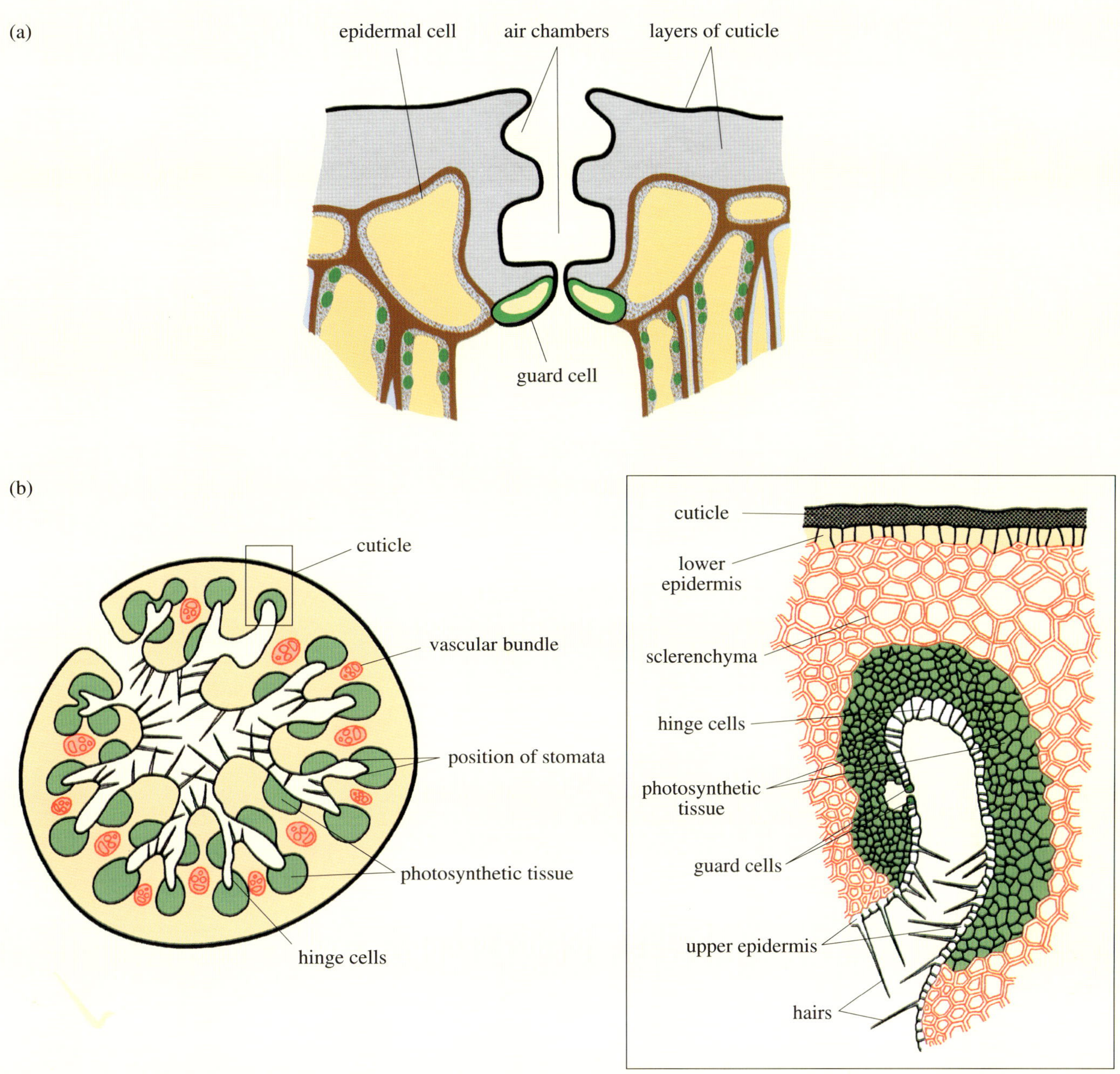

Figure 3.17 Mechanisms by which the boundary layer thickness may be increased. (a) Stomata are deeply sunk below the leaf surface in the desert plant *Dasylirion* sp. (b) Rolled-up leaf of marram grass (*Ammophila arenaria*), which grows on sand dunes. Turgor loss by the hinge cells causes the leaf to roll up, enclosing the surface bearing the stomata. The enlarged diagram shows a stoma within a fold.

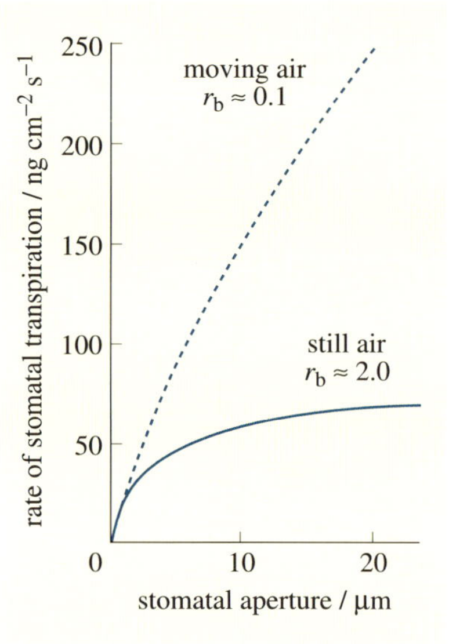

Figure 3.18 The relationship between the rate of stomatal transpiration and the diameter of the stomatal pores in still and moving air. The units of r_b are s cm^{-1}.

Because r_s and r_b act sequentially (i.e. in series), the total resistance to water vapour diffusion can be obtained by summing them. Generally, stomatal resistance is considerably greater than that of the boundary layer and so can be regarded as the controlling factor. However, look at the experimental results in Figure 3.18.

❍ Describe how transpiration rate varies with stomatal aperture in (a) moving and (b) still air. In each case indicate whether r_s or r_b exerts the stronger control.

● (a) In moving air, the rate of transpiration increases almost linearly with stomatal aperture, so r_s clearly exerts the stronger control. (b) In still air, it is only when stomata have a very small aperture and are almost closed that they influence transpiration rate significantly; boundary layer resistance otherwise exerts the main control.

In fact 'in nature' air is hardly ever really still and r_b rarely rises above 1.7 s cm^{-1}. So, in general, *stomatal aperture is the dominant factor controlling the rate of water loss from leaves*. Next we describe the mechanisms by which stomatal aperture is controlled.

3.5.2 The mechanism of stomatal movement

The structure of stomata (singular, stoma; Greek for 'mouth') is closely linked to their function as closeable pores, so we shall consider structure first.

The structure of stomata

Each stoma consists of a pore surrounded by two kidney-shaped or (in grasses) dumb-bell-shaped **guard cells** (Figure 3.19 and you saw these in plant sections studied in Chapter 1). Adjacent epidermal cells are intimately involved in guard cell functioning and are referred to as *subsidiary cells*; the whole — guard cells plus subsidiary cells — is called the *stomatal complex*.

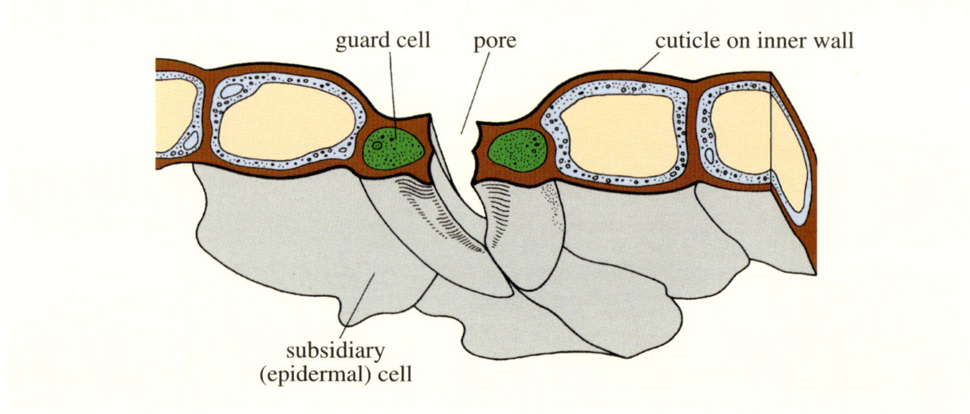

Figure 3.19 Section through a stoma on the undersurface of a leaf. Notice that the cuticle extends round the guard cells and some way along the inner surface of other epidermal cells.

The diameter of a pore depends on the shape of the guard cells which, in turn, depends on the properties of their cell walls and on their turgor (Section 3.3.3) relative to that of neighbouring cells. Key properties of guard cells are:

1. They can rapidly and reversibly alter their turgor, which causes the volume of the cells to change, sometimes doubling as water uptake occurs and turgor increases above that of adjacent cells.
2. Guard cell shape at high and low turgor depends on wall properties. Bundles of inelastic cellulose molecules (microfibrils) are arranged such that the inner wall of the guard cell (next to the pore) is less elastic in a longitudinal direction than the outer wall. In addition, the inner wall is often thickened. The net effect is that kidney-shaped guard cells behave like radial tyres: the cross-section can change its shape but not its circumference (Figure 3.20a). So when turgor increases, the outer wall elongates more than the inner wall and the guard cells become bow-shaped (pores open); when turgor decreases, the cells are more or less straight (pores closed). For dumb-bell-shaped guard cells in grasses, the bulbous ends expand but not the thick-walled stretch between them so that a slit-like pore opens up in this central region (Figure 3.20b).

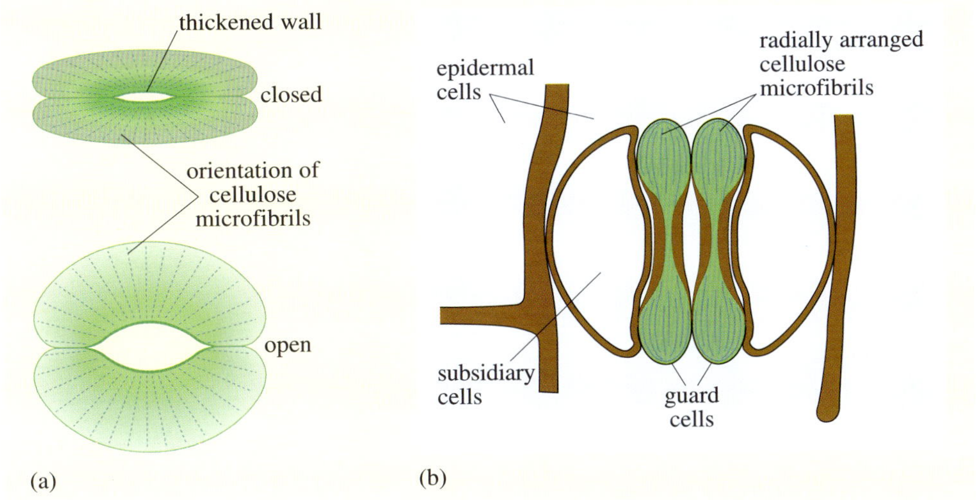

Figure 3.20 (a) Closed and open stoma with kidney-shaped guard cells and (b) closed stoma with dumb-bell-shaped guard cells. Note the radial arrangement of cellulose microfibrils (dashed lines) and the thickened walls adjacent to pores.

Guard cells may differ from other epidermal cells in two further ways: (i) often they are not linked by plasmodesmata to adjacent cells, i.e. they are symplastically isolated; and (ii) they contain chloroplasts, standing out under the microscope as the only green cells in epidermal strips. Both of these characteristics are thought to be important in regulating stomatal aperture, as discussed below. So guard cells are highly specialized epidermal cells and the problem of how stomata open and close boils down to a question of how guard cells change their relative turgor.

CHANGES IN GUARD CELL TURGOR

Having considered what the structure of guard cells tells us about how stomata work, we now move on to another, physiological level of explanation. When stomata open, the key event is a massive increase in the solute content of guard cells — by a factor of four in broad bean leaves, for example.

- ❍ Why should increasing solute content affect guard cell turgor and hence stomatal opening? (Think back to Section 3.3, Equation 3.1 and Figure 3.8.)

- ● From Equation 3.1 ($\Psi = P - \pi$), an increase in solute content raises osmotic pressure and hence lowers water potential. As Ψ becomes more negative, water moves into guard cells down a gradient of water potential and turgor pressure, P, rises until equilibrium is reached (Figure 3.8).

The increase in osmotic pressure may involve different solutes depending on species, environmental conditions and even time of day. Typically, stomata have a daily rhythm of opening (around dawn) and closing (at dusk). For the dawn opening, there is a rapid increase in the concentration of specific ions in guard cells.

- ❍ From Figure 3.21, what is a major cation involved in stomatal opening?

- ● Potassium: K^+ levels increase over ten-fold.

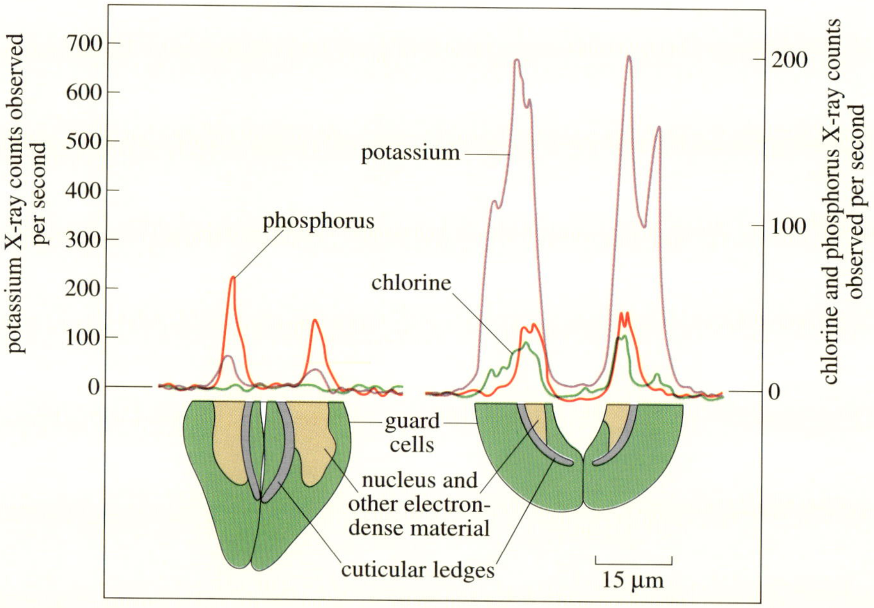

Figure 3.21 Profiles of the relative amounts of potassium (purple lines), chlorine (green line) and phosphorus (red line) in guard cells of a closed and open stoma. Data were obtained by electron-probe microanalysis of freeze-dried cells. This technique involves scanning the material with a fine beam of electrons; atoms of different elements emit X-rays of characteristic wavelengths which can be measured to assess their concentration. Note the different scales for potassium compared with chlorine and phosphorus.

At dawn (and in many experimental situations) potassium ions move into guard cells from the cell walls and surrounding cells when stomata open and they move out if stomata close. The key event leading to K^+ uptake is *activation of a membrane-bound H^+-ATPase*, which actively pumps protons out of guard cells — in other words, stomatal opening is a classic chemiosmotic mechanism (see Furth, 2001). The electrochemical gradient produced by proton export allows passive inward movement of potassium ions down a gradient of electrical charge, i.e. secondary active transport that depends directly on active proton pumping. K^+ uptake occurs through selective potassium channels in the plasma membrane, which are 'opened' in response to voltage across the membrane and to signals such as calcium level and pH in the cytoplasm. A second type of K^+ channel transports K^+ into the vacuole, where ions are stored.

- ❍ Given the above mechanism, why are guard cells symplastically isolated?
- ● Movement of ions into guard cells cannot be countered by outward diffusion via plasmodesmata.

So far, this type of stomatal opening can be represented by Figure 3.22a. Protons, derived mainly from water, move out of guard cells leaving behind hydroxyl ions (OH^-) so that, as external pH falls, intracellular pH rises and the membrane potential rises (inside of the cell becomes more negative) leading to K^+ influx. In the long term, however, OH^- cannot act as a balancing anion for K^+ because intracellular pH is strictly controlled, so there must be other balancing anions. One such anion is chloride, which you can see from Figure 3.21 also rises during stomatal opening; Cl^- ions enter guard cells along with protons (H^+-Cl^- co-transport; see Swithenby and O'Shea, 2001) and powered by the pH gradient. In addition, you can see from Figure 3.22b that malate synthesized within the guard cells (as described for C4 plants in Chapter 2) may act as a second balancing anion; there is variation both within and between species as to which of these two anions predominates. Events during stomatal closure when K^+, Cl^- and malate are the main osmotic solutes are illustrated in Figure 3.22c. Note that ions enter and leave the vacuole and cytoplasm by different sets of channels.

Figure 3.22 A summary of ion movements and metabolism in guard cells during K^+-dominated stomatal opening (a, b) and closure (c). Broken arrows indicate secondary active transport inwards and passive diffusion outwards; yellow arrows indicate primary proton pumping dependent upon ATP. Malate levels are indicated by the height of the red rectangle with malate synthesized by CO_2 fixation via PEP carboxylase, as described for C4 plants in Chapter 2.

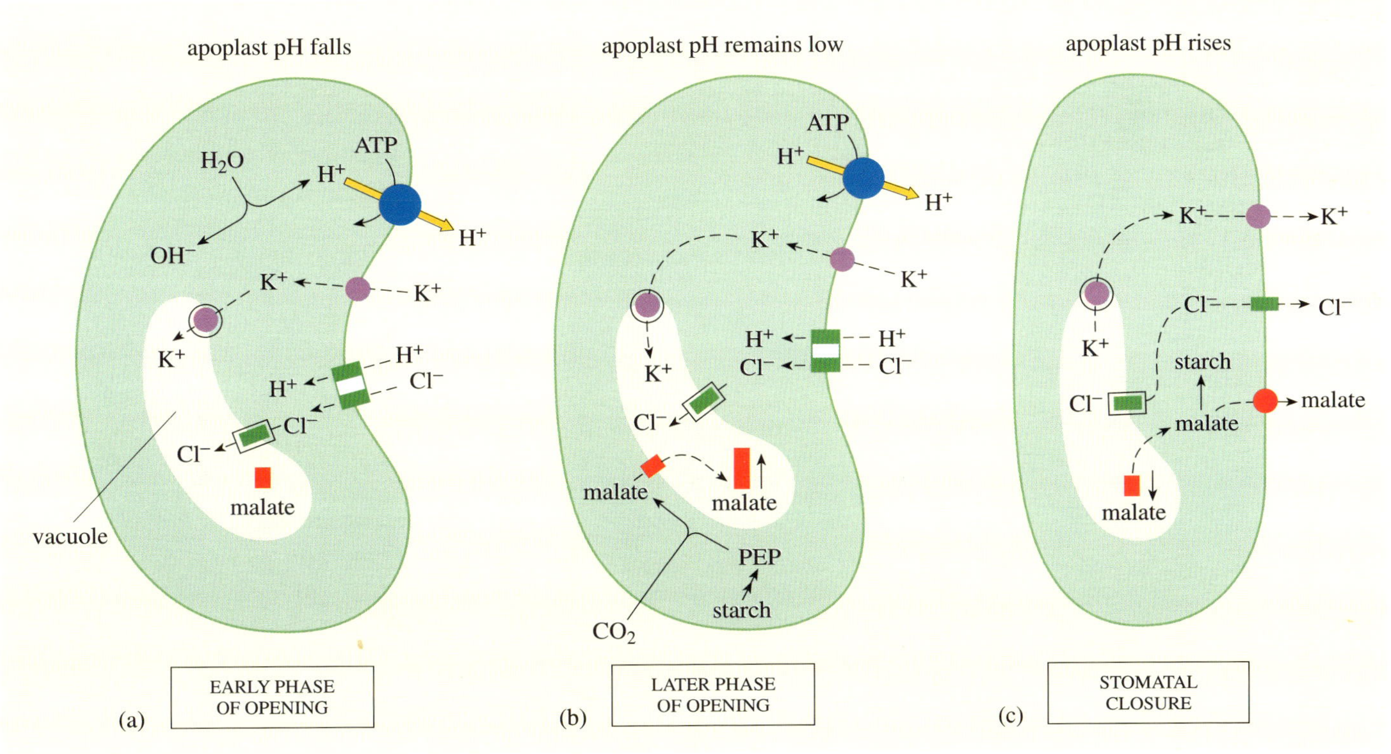

Nearly all the molecular research on stomatal movements — for example, characterizing the nature, properties and control of ion channels — has focussed on the mechanism just described and used isolated guard cells or sheets of epidermal tissue. But look at the data in Figure 3.23 (from Talbott and Zeiger, 1996), which were obtained using whole plants and detaching leaves just before analysis.

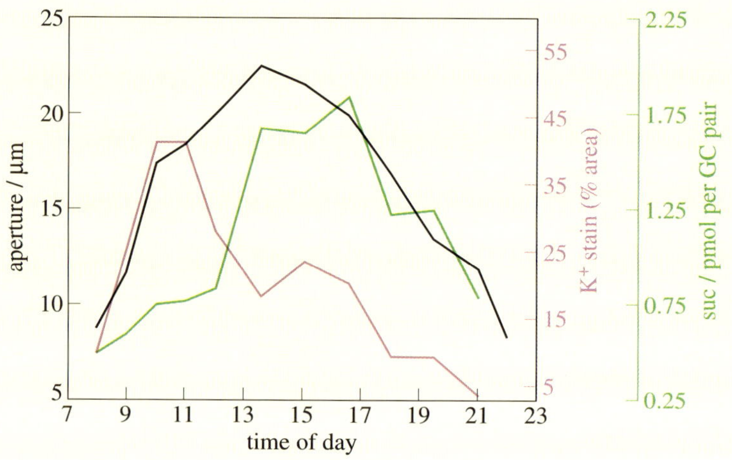

Figure 3.23 Stomatal aperture (black line), and K^+ (purple line) and sucrose (green line) content of guard cells in broad bean, *Vicia faba*, over a daily cycle of stomatal movements. Plants were grown in a controlled environment chamber and leaves sampled at intervals. Sucrose content is expressed as picomoles per guard cell pair and K^+ content as the % of guard cell area covered by a K^+-specific stain. Data from Talbott and Zeiger (1996).

❍ What conclusions do you draw about the solutes involved in guard cell turgor and stomatal aperture in broad bean?

● During the morning, the increase in stomatal aperture correlates closely with increasing potassium levels in guard cells. However, around mid-day, K^+ levels begin to fall, although stomata remain open, and sucrose levels in guard cells increase. Sucrose is the dominant solute during the afternoon.

A *sucrose-dependent phase* of guard cell osmotic regulation has been confirmed in a wide range of species, raising a whole string of questions, only some of which as yet have answers. The sucrose seems to derive from stored starch or directly from the C3 cycle in guard cell chloroplasts, although there is some evidence that it may enter guard cells from surrounding tissues. What controls sucrose levels and the switch from the potassium to the sucrose phase is unknown, but the latter always follows the former: thus if stomatal opening is delayed by experimental manipulation until the afternoon, a K^+-dependent phase still precedes the sucrose phase. Why plants have two forms of osmotic regulation for guard cells is still unclear, so we shall move on and consider other questions. First, at the evolutionary level, the role of stomata — why do plants have them? Second, at the physiological level, what is the range of environmental signals that controls stomatal aperture?

3.5.3 STOMATAL EVOLUTION AND THE CONTROL OF STOMATAL APERTURE

The stomatal story so far has suggested that land plants evolved stomata because of selective pressures to restrict water loss while providing a means for the entry of atmospheric CO_2 into leaves. So one could argue that plants that are never short of water or that obtain CO_2 from somewhere other than the atmosphere should not 'need' stomata. Consistent with this hypothesis, there are no stomata in certain species of *Isoetes* (Lycophyta), which obtain CO_2 from the soil (Chapter 2), nor in some parasitic, non-photosynthetic flowering plants such as bird's nest orchid, *Neottia nidus-avis*. Stomata are also absent in submerged aquatic plants, and are permanently open in floating-leaved species such as water-lilies (e.g. *Nymphaea alba*, *Nuphar lutea*) and duckweeds (*Lemna* spp.) (Woodward, 1998).

Evidence for the importance of CO_2 availability as a selective force in stomatal evolution comes from studying fossil plants, where stomata are clearly visible in the well-preserved cuticle (Figure 3.24b). When land plants first appeared, 450–400 Ma ago, estimated CO_2 levels were approximately 10 times higher than at present and these early plants had very low frequencies of stomata (left side of Figure 3.24a, blue data points). As CO_2 levels fell (300 Ma ago), rose again (250 Ma) and then fell progressively up to the present, stomatal frequencies broadly tracked these changes, so there is an *inverse* relationship between stomatal frequency and the concentration of atmospheric CO_2 (Figure 3.24a).

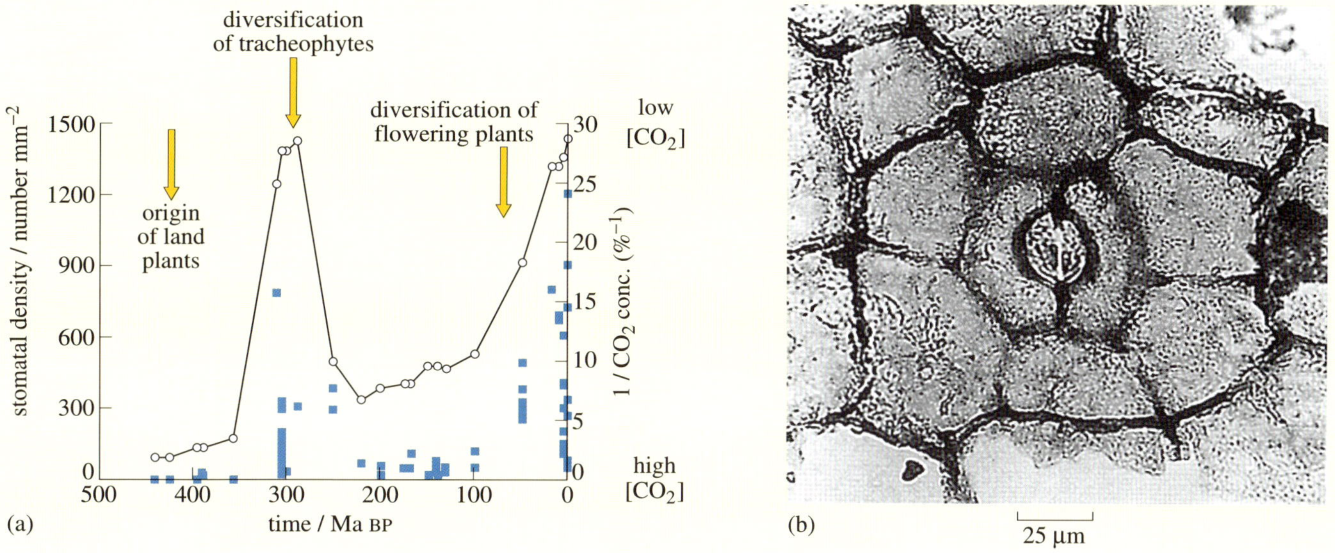

Figure 3.24 (a) Fossil records of stomatal density (blue squares) and estimated inverse CO_2 levels (black line) at the times of the fossil records, plotted on an inverse scale of concentration. Data from Beerling and Woodward (1997). (b) Fossilized cuticle of the Devonian lycophyte *Drepanophycus spinaeformis* (about 370 Ma) showing a stoma with guard cells.

Interestingly, it was during the periods of low CO_2 levels and high stomatal densities that plants showed greatest diversification, especially of large, tree-like forms (horsetails, ferns, seed ferns and conifers around 300 Ma ago, and flowering plants during the recent period). A possible explanation (Woodward, 1998) is that large plants require high stomatal densities (a) to produce a strong transpiration stream and hence to power water and nutrient transport up tall plants (when stomata are open); and (b) (when stomata are closed) to provide flexible protection, especially against cavitation in xylem, from the damaging effects of water shortage. So even if the evolution and density of stomata was determined by the need for CO_2, they must also have become essential for transpiration and protection.

Against this background, we can now examine the complex signalling systems that control stomatal aperture.

Given the dual role of stomata described above, it is not surprising that two groups of opposing signals regulate stomatal aperture. One group affects aperture in relation to the photosynthetic demand for CO_2 while the second group reduces aperture or causes closure when water supply is low and there is a danger of cavitation and desiccation. In the first group are light and CO_2 and in the second group are atmospheric humidity, soil water potential and sometimes temperature. A third sort of signal, shortage of mineral nutrients (nitrate, phosphate or sulfate), causes reduced stomatal aperture but does not fit clearly into either category.

LIGHT AND CARBON DIOXIDE: LINKS TO PHOTOSYNTHESIS

Carbon dioxide

Low CO_2 within leaves often increases stomatal aperture and high CO_2 decreases it which, if intercellular CO_2 serves as a marker for photosynthetic activity, ties in neatly photosynthetic demand for CO_2 with stomatal aperture. Species vary considerably in their sensitivity to CO_2 but, on average, a doubling of atmospheric CO_2 concentration decreases stomatal conductance (a proxy for aperture) by around 40%. That CO_2 concentration is sensed within guard cells is shown by the ability of isolated pairs of guard cells to respond to the gas, and recent evidence (Zeiger and Zhu, 1998) suggests that the sensing could involve levels of a chloroplast pigment, zeaxanthin, which is also involved in photoprotection (Chapter 2) and in stomatal responses to light.

Light

When plants are well-watered and grown in a relatively humid atmosphere, stomatal aperture matches the flux of light (photosynthetically active radiation, PAR, 400–700 nm, equivalent to PPFD, see Chapter 2) very closely (Figure 3.25) and stomata open during the day and close at night.

Two different systems are involved in perceiving light. First, PAR promotes stomatal opening, being absorbed by chlorophyll pigments in guard cell chloroplasts and probably acting through provision of ATP energy and organic solutes (e.g. malate). This system is thought to be of more importance when light levels are relatively high in the middle of the day and seems to be essential for very wide stomatal opening.

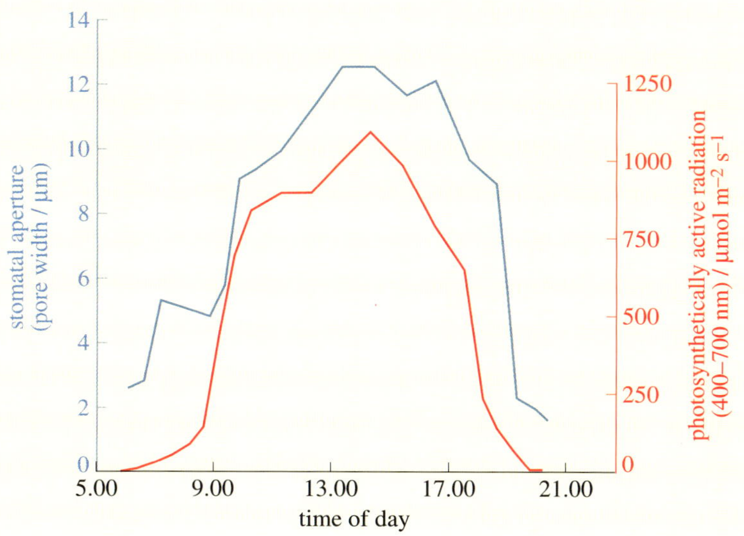

Figure 3.25 Changes in stomatal aperture on the lower surface of broad bean leaves, *Vicia faba*, and in the amount of photosynthetically active radiation (PAR) incident on the leaf. Data from Srivastava and Zeiger (1995).

Second, there is a blue light-dependent system which is thought to depend on absorption by the xanthophyll pigment, zeaxanthin, in chloroplasts. A model proposed by Zeiger and Zhu (1998) of how this system might work is illustrated in Figure 3.26 and described in the legend. You do not need to remember details of this model except to note that blue light activates stomatal opening by stimulating proton pumping and starch hydrolysis to produce malate. The blue-light photosystem is very sensitive to the intensity of blue light but saturates at a lower flux density than the PAR system and does not promote such wide stomatal opening as the latter. It is thought to trigger rapid opening of stomata at dawn (when light is composed largely of blue wavelengths) and during brief exposures to sunflecks (Chapter 2). In the tropical lady's slipper orchids, *Paphiopedilum* spp., which grow in very shady habitats, the guard cells have colourless plastids instead of chloroplasts and their response to light is apparently mediated largely through the blue-light photosystem.

❍ How is this feature of *Paphiopedilum* adaptive for a plant that grows in deep shade?

● In deep shade, photosynthesis is limited by the availability of light and not that of CO_2 (Chapter 2), so wide stomatal opening via the PAR system may be unnecessary for obtaining sufficient CO_2.

The role of zeaxanthin in stomatal control is quite separate from its role in the photoprotective xanthophyll cycle (Chapter 2) but it mediates a range of other blue-light responses, including the bending of shoots towards light (phototropism), which are discussed in Chapter 5.

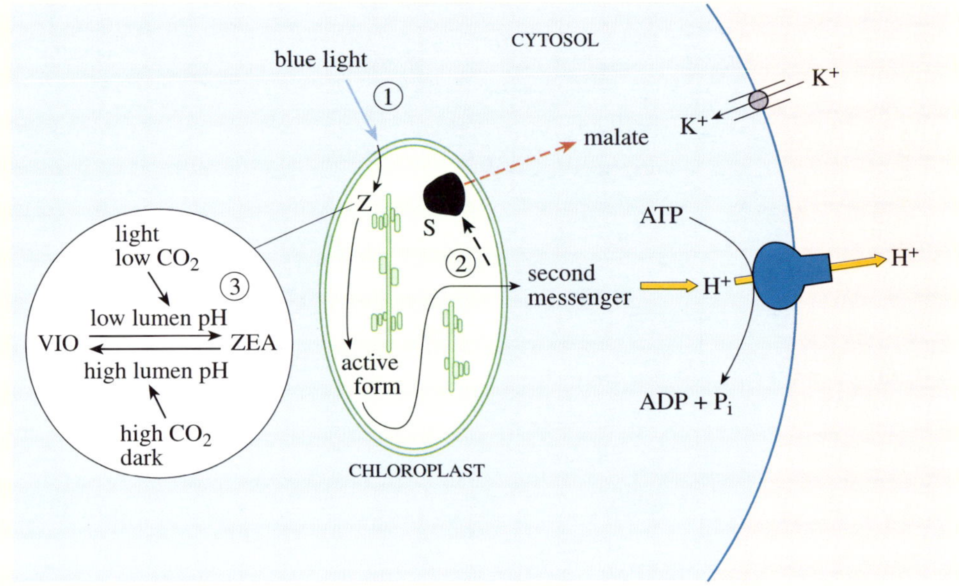

Figure 3.26 Zeiger and Zhu's model of how blue light causes stomatal opening. (1) The membrane-bound chloroplast pigment zeaxanthin Z absorbs blue light and is converted to a form which initiates a cascade of reactions. (2) The cascade activates the plasma membrane proton pump via a second messenger and hydrolysis of starch S to provide malate or, possibly, sucrose. Either or both of these events can increase solute levels in guard cells. (3) Levels of zeaxanthin in chloroplasts depend on pH in the thylakoid lumen: low pH (caused by photosynthesis in light and by low CO_2) promotes the formation of zeaxanthin (ZEA) formation from violaxanthin (VIO); high pH (caused by darkness and/or high CO_2) promotes the reverse reaction.

ABSCISIC ACID AND LINKS TO WATER RELATIONS

If leaves become water stressed because water supply does not keep up with transpiration, then three undesirable consequences may follow: leaf turgor falls so that cell expansion cannot continue; xylem pressure falls, increasing the risk of cavitation; and photosynthesis may be inhibited through reductions in ATP supply and CO_2 fixation (independent of CO_2 supply). For many plants, reducing stomatal aperture at the first signs of water stress is critical for survival and overrides the need for CO_2. Figure 3.27 illustrates patterns of stomatal closure that reflect the need for water conservation.

The immediate signal for stomatal closure linked to water stress is a rise within guard cells of the growth regulator **abscisic acid**, **ABA**, which is often described as a stress hormone. We consider first the mechanism by which ABA acts to reduce guard cell turgor, a subject of intensive research in the 1990s. ABA first binds to a receptor on the guard cell plasma membrane that initiates two changes: a rise in concentration of cytoplasmic calcium ions (released from the vacuole) and a rise in cytoplasmic pH of around 0.3 units. Both these changes cause a rapid efflux of K^+ and balancing anions out of the vacuole and then across the plasma membrane by activating appropriate efflux channels and inhibiting influx channels on the plasma membrane (Figure 3.28). The loss of ions causes a fall in guard cell turgor and partial or complete closure of stomata.

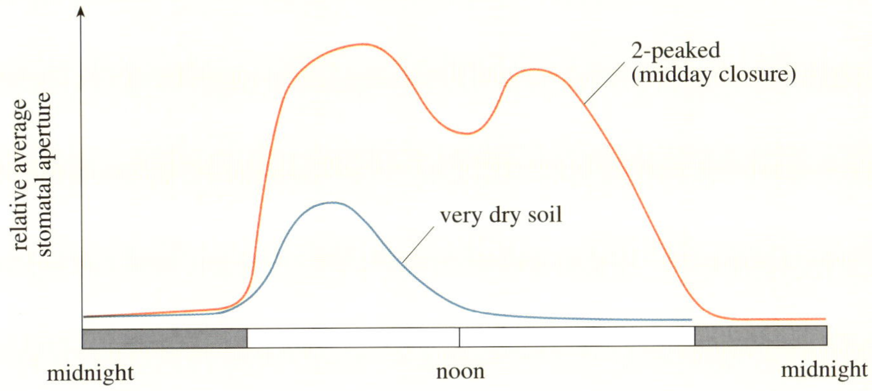

Figure 3.27 Patterns of stomatal opening and closure when there is moderate water stress (midday closure, upper curve, a pattern often seen in trees) and severe water stress due to very dry soil (morning-only opening, lower curve, a pattern often seen in herbs and shrubs at the end of a dry season).

- ❍ With this model of ABA action, what problem can you foresee if stomatal closure by ABA occurs in the afternoon (as it often does)?
- ● In the afternoon, the main solute in guard cells is sucrose and not K^+ plus anions. ABA would, therefore, have to cause different sorts of changes — conversion of sucrose to starch, for example, or loss of sucrose across plasma membranes.

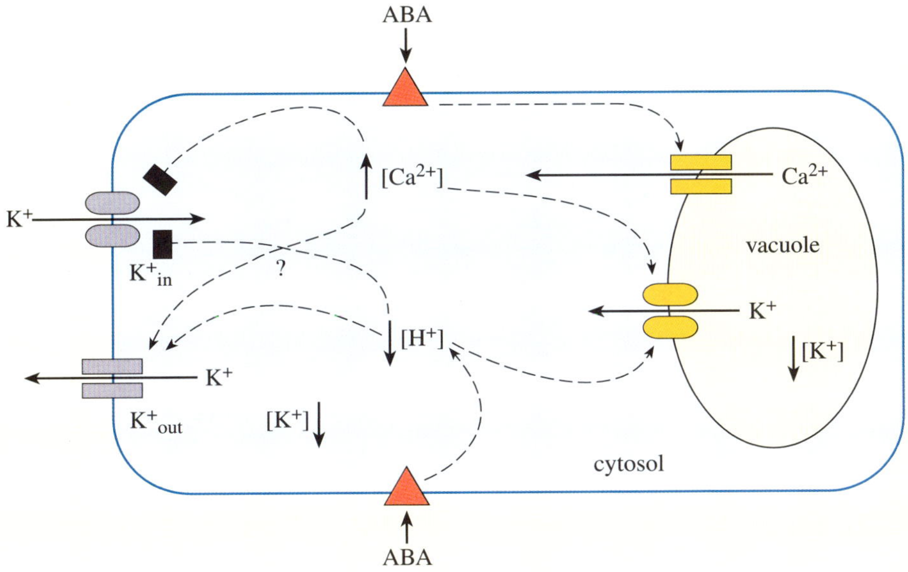

Figure 3.28 A model of how ABA causes stomatal closure by promoting loss of ions from guard cells, hence reducing turgor. Within the cell, upward or downward pointing arrows indicate a rise or fall in concentrations respectively; dashed lines terminated by a bar or arrow indicate inhibition or activation of a pump or channel respectively.

Apart from this question of how ABA causes loss of sucrose from guard cells, there is a reasonably clear picture of how it acts, which seems to be common to a wide range of plants. Far less clear, and with much variation between plants, are the mechanisms by which ABA levels around guard cells are regulated and a state of water shortage is signalled in the first place. Facts on which there is broad agreement are:

1 ABA is synthesized continuously in *roots* and moves up to leaves in xylem.

2 Within leaves, ABA is taken up mostly by mesophyll cells, where it is broken down and inactivated.

3 The entry of ABA into root xylem and leaf mesophyll and its release into the cell wall (apoplast) compartment (from where it can reach guard cells) is influenced by pH both within and outside cells.

In general, regulation of stomatal aperture seems to depend primarily on water availability in the soil (Ψ_{soil}), which in turn affects root water potentials, pH and the synthesis and release to root xylem of ABA. For some plants, the water status of the leaf (Ψ_{leaf}) seems to play little or no part in determining whether or not stomata close in response to mild water stress; all that matters is the ABA supply from the roots. Such plants are described as *anisohydric* (from the Greek, *an* = not, *iso* = the same, *hydric* = water), meaning that the leaf water potential is not constant but depends on the availability of water to the roots, as illustrated in Figure 3.29 for sunflower, *Helianthus annuus*.

Figure 3.29 Effects of soil water supply in sunflowers on (a) stomatal conductance (mol m^{-2} s^{-1}), (b) leaf water potential and (c) ABA concentration in xylem sap (μmol m^{-3}). Plants were grown in the field and either well watered (red line) or subjected to mild (blue line) or severe (purple line) soil water deficit. Error bars indicate interval of confidence at the 95% probability level. Data from Tardieu *et al*. (1996).

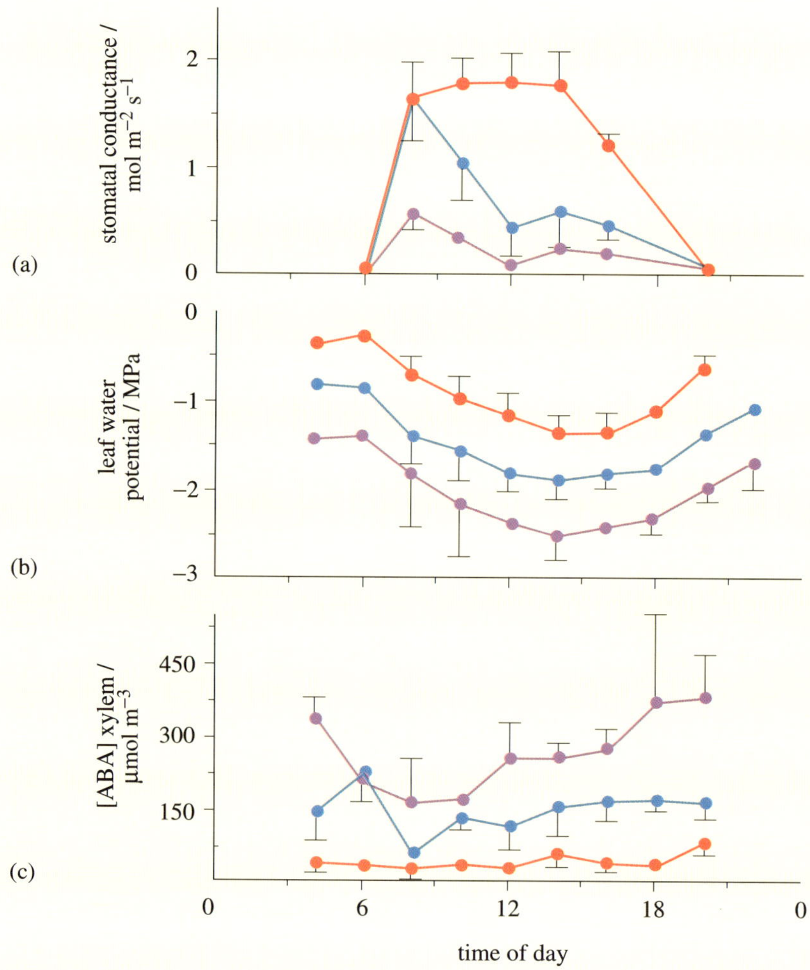

❍ From Figure 3.29a describe how stomatal aperture is influenced by soil moisture.

● Stomatal aperture relates to stomatal conductance so high conductance equates to wide aperture. When well watered, these sunflowers showed the typical pattern (Figure 3.23) of opening in the morning, remaining widely open all day and closing in late afternoon. With mild soil water deficit, stomata open widely only in the morning, partially close at noon and remain so until full closure. With severe soil water deficit, stomata open slightly in the morning and remain almost closed for the rest of the day.

These three patterns of stomatal opening match three different leaf water potentials (Figure 3.29b) and varying concentrations of ABA in xylem sap (Figure 3.29c). Other experiments confirmed that $[ABA]_{xylem}$ regulated stomatal conductance, and independently varying Ψ_{leaf} and atmospheric humidity had little effect on conductance in anisohydric plants (Tardieu and Simonneau, 1998). Similar behaviour occurs in almond and peach trees (*Prunus* spp.), soya bean, barley and wheat.

In other plants, however, leaf water potential during the day remains constant, irrespective of soil water supply. Such plants include lupin (*Lupinus* sp.), maize, poplar trees (*Populus* sp.), pea and sugarcane and are described as *isohydric* (Figure 3.30).

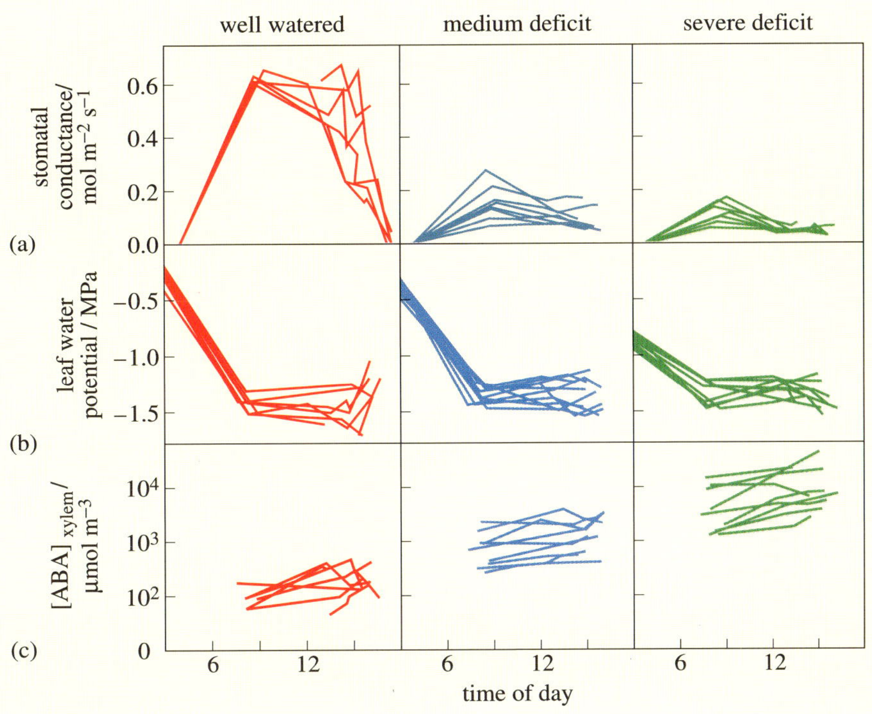

Figure 3.30 Effects of soil water supply in poplar saplings (*Populus euramericana*) on (a) stomatal conductance, (b) leaf water potential and (c) ABA concentration in xylem sap. Plants were grown in a greenhouse and either well watered (red lines) or subjected to mild (blue lines) or severe (green lines) soil water deficit. Each line relates to a single plant. Data from Tardieu and Trejo (1998).

Isohydric plants progressively close stomata in the afternoon, as leaves become warmer, air humidity falls and transpiration rate tends to increase. However, such plants have also been shown to reduce root hydraulic conductivity in the afternoon as part of a diurnal cycle of root L_p, a change which would reduce water movement to leaves and hence transpiration. The end result is that leaf water potential remains constant during the day (Figure 3.30b). ABA delivery to guard cells may increase because less ABA is taken up by mesophyll cells and, overall, the plants seem to regulate stomatal conductance by an interaction between water supply ($[ABA_{xylem}]$) and rate of water loss. If these subtle controls on stomatal aperture fail and leaves reach the point of incipient wilting, then an emergency mechanism operates: ABA is synthesized within leaf cells and released in large amounts, causing instant stomatal closure.

Shortages of major nutrients (N, P and S) cause reductions in stomatal aperture in isohydric plants and, like the afternoon closure, have been shown to correlate with changes in root hydraulic conductivity (Clarkson *et al.*, 2000). The change in L_p seems to be caused by reduced aquaporin availability in cells of the stele (Section 3.2.1) but how, or if, this change influences ABA supply to leaves is not yet known.

We have discussed stomata in some detail because they provide a classic case study of control in plants, operating at a range of levels and involving interactions between internal and external (environmental) signals. Stomatal density varies on evolutionary timescales in response to the need for CO_2; stomatal aperture varies on a 24 h cycle in response to light and $[CO_2]$ as conditions for photosynthesis change; aperture also varies as plant water status varies, overriding the photosynthetic controls so that xylem cavitation and leaf desiccation are avoided. There is broad uniformity in these mechanisms but diversity among highly specialized plants such as the tropical lady's slipper orchid or CAM plants.

❍ Recall the pattern of stomatal opening in CAM plants (Chapter 2). What key signal for stomatal opening must be overridden in these species?

❍ The light signals. Stomata in CAM plants are closed during the day and open at night. Aperture is still sensitive to $[CO_2]$ and to water status, however.

In the next section we look at the whole range of structures and mechanisms (including stomatal control) that allow land plants to survive periods of water shortage and grow in very inhospitable habitats.

Summary of Section 3.5

1 The rate of transpiration is determined mainly by stomatal aperture (i.e. stomatal resistance or conductance) except in very still air when boundary layer resistance becomes the controlling factor.

2 Because of their cell wall structure, guard cell shape varies with turgor such that stomata open when turgor is high and close when it is low.

3 The turgor of guard cells (and hence stomatal aperture) depends on solute content. Dawn opening involves secondary active influx of potassium ions

due to activation of a plasma membrane H^+-ATPase, with chloride and/or malate ions as balancing anions. Later in the day, these ions may be replaced by sucrose as the solute controlling turgor.

4 Over geological time there is an inverse relationship between atmospheric [CO_2] and stomatal density. Stomata are also essential, especially in tall plants, for the transpiration stream that carries water and nutrients up the shoot and as a rapid-response system that (by closure) protects against xylem cavitation.

5 The environmental and internal signals that control stomatal aperture relate to the demand for CO_2 and the need to reduce water loss; nutrient stress also acts to reduce stomatal conductance.

6 If plants have adequate water, low [CO_2] within leaves and light promote stomatal opening. The light response is mediated by a PAR-based system and/or a blue-light photosystem based on zeaxanthin.

7 ABA is the main signal causing stomatal closure in response to water shortage. It is synthesized in roots and its effect on guard cells may (isohydric plants) or may not (anisohydric plants) be influenced by leaf water status. In emergencies, ABA is synthesized in leaves and causes instant stomatal closure.

3.6 SURVIVING WATER SHORTAGE

Plant survival and the yields of many crops depend strongly on the availability of water. So an understanding of how plants cope with periods of water shortage has both scientific and practical relevance. Two sorts of drought can be distinguished: when there is an actual shortage of water in the soil (**true drought**); or when water is present but unavailable to plants because, for example, it is too salty or is frozen (**physiological drought**). We consider true drought first.

3.6.1 TRUE DROUGHT

The ability of plants to survive in very dry habitats has been studied mainly in natural deserts. However, many habitats in temperate regions resemble mini-deserts.

❍ What kinds of habitats resemble mini-desert in the UK?

● Habitats where there is little or no soil (e.g. on rocks, walls or very shallow soils); habitats such as sand dunes which drain rapidly and freely.

We shall discuss mainly desert plants but bear in mind that temperate region plants may have similar adaptations to drought although often in less extreme forms.

Plants show adaptations to drought at various levels that range from the life cycle, through whole-plant structure to the cellular level. Table 3.3 shows a broad classification of plants that avoid water shortage in various ways and those that tolerate it.

Table 3.3 The strategies by which desert plants survive water shortage.

Strategy	Example
Avoidance	
1 Dormancy (shed leaves or survive as seeds or underground organs, e.g. tubers)	drought-deciduous shrubs or trees and short-lived desert ephemerals
2 Water tapping (deep roots extend to water table)	*Acacia* spp.; mesquite (*Prosopis* spp.)
3 Water storage (succulence of leaves or stems)	cacti, agaves, desert species of *Euphorbia*
4 Desiccation (tissues dry out completely and recover when re-wetted)	many mosses, some ferns and lycophytes, resurrection plants, seeds
Tolerance	
Xerophytes (continue to photosynthesize during drought without major structural changes)	perennial evergreen desert shrubs and grasses

AVOIDING WATER SHORTAGE

For plants with strategies 1 and 4 (Table 3.3), there are often few or no visible features that improve water uptake or restrict water loss. The main feature of *desert ephemerals*, for example, is that seeds germinate only after prolonged rainfall and plants then grow very fast (many are C4 plants, Chapter 2) and complete their life cycle in a few weeks before the soil dries out. Their adaptation to water shortage thus relates to their life cycle.

Drought-deciduous shrubs (strategy 1) are much more variable (Figure 3.31). At one extreme are those which regularly produce large leaves in the cooler or wetter season (usually winter) and shed leaves, becoming dormant, before the drought

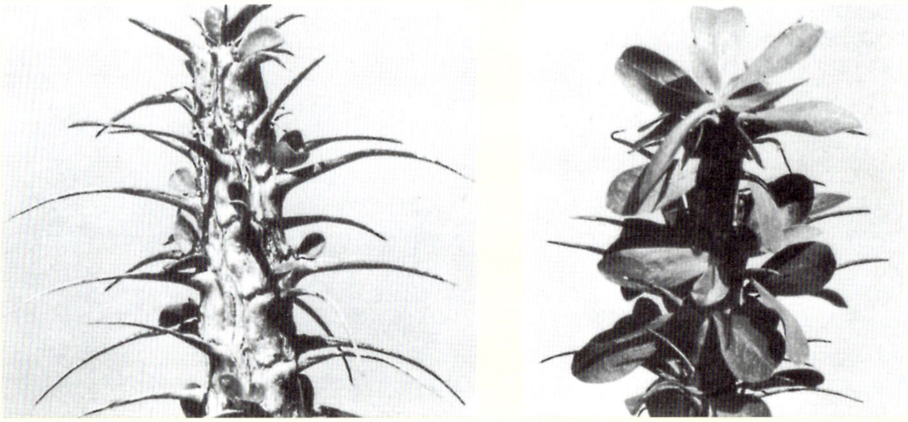

(a) (b)

Figure 3.31 Ocotillo (*Fouquieria splendens*). (a) A young branch which is sprouting new leaves after losing its previous crop. (b) A branch in full leaf after adequate watering. Note the spines, which are the midribs and petioles of old primary leaves.

season (usually summer). At the other extreme are species such as *Encelia farinosa* (Asteraceae, the brittlebush of North America) which has large (50 cm^2), smooth leaves in the winter season that are replaced by small (as small as 0.3 cm^2), hairy leaves in summer, a phenomenon called leaf polymorphism. The hairs on summer leaves reflect light, so reducing heat load and transpiration, and although these leaves have a much lower photosynthetic capacity compared with winter leaves, they still allow moderate carbon fixation in the dry season. In between these extremes are species such as the ocotillo (*Fouquieria splendens*), which has opportunistic leaf production and produces several crops of leaves a year after rain, shedding them as drought returns (Figure 3.31). These stem photosynthesizers, after shedding wet-season leaves, maintain low rates of photosynthesis because the green stems, which generally lose less water via stomata, are more tolerant of high temperatures than are leaves. Overall, these drought-deciduous species avoid water shortage by virtue of their growth patterns and morphology, rather than by physiological or biochemical adaptations.

In contrast, the *desiccation-tolerant* strategy (item 4 in Table 3.3) involves extreme biochemical specialization. Whereas most plants die if their water potential falls too low, tissues of these **resurrection plants** can dry out to a crisp but recover within hours of re-wetting. Many mosses and a few ferns (Figure 3.32), lycophytes and angiosperms show this strategy. They have no special mechanisms for preventing water loss or increasing uptake but have biochemical mechanisms — that are still not fully understood — which allow cell desiccation and recovery.

Plants showing the *water-tapping* strategy (2) in its purest form also have few adaptations of shoots against water loss but they have remarkable root systems that may penetrate as much as 50 m to perennial groundwater in deserts. Figure 3.33 shows a UK example.

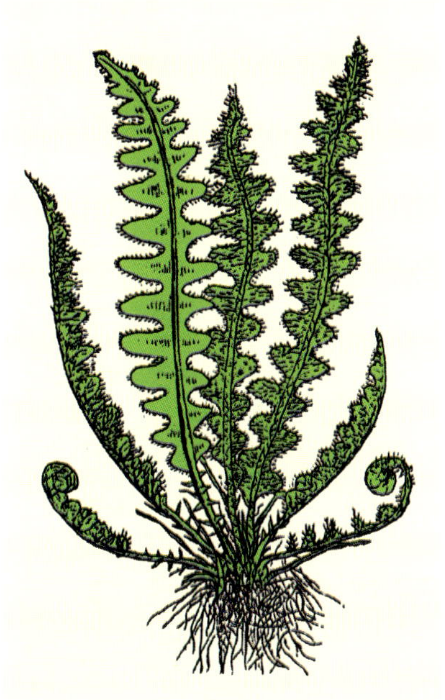

Figure 3.32 The rustyback fern *Ceterarch officinarum*, a resurrection plant.

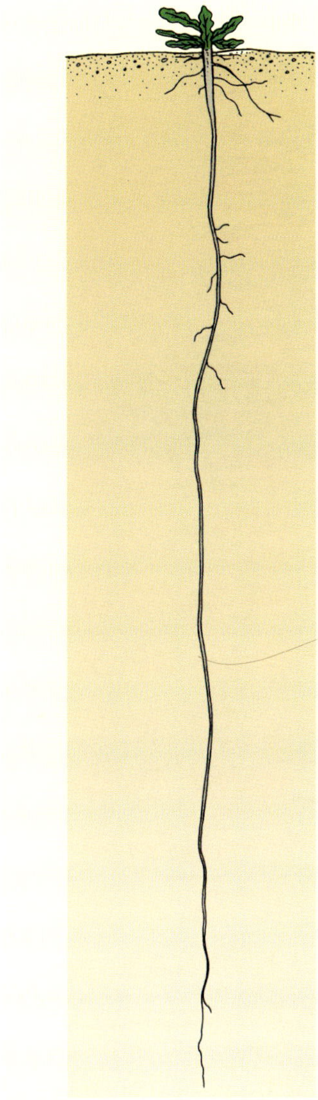

Figure 3.33 The deeply penetrating root system of a one-year-old seedling of cat's ear (*Hypochoeris radicata*) growing on a sand dune.

Seedlings of plants with a water-tapping strategy can establish only during wet periods when their roots grow at a phenomenal rate. However, there is a problem for these plants in that mineral nutrients are often concentrated in the upper soil layers which may become bone dry. Hydraulic lift (Section 3.2) is thought to facilitate nutrient uptake in this situation. At night when transpiration stops, water uptake from deeply penetrating roots allows the water potential of surface roots to rise above that of the surrounding dry soil so that water may flow out of these roots. Such moistening of the surface soil allows nutrient uptake to occur when the water is reabsorbed. When seedling roots are growing downwards through dry soil but have not reached the water table, it is thought that *reverse hydraulic lift* operates: water from moist upper parts of the soil moves down roots and so allows the root tips to extend. Some water tappers (e.g. certain *Acacia* spp.) do not actually reach the permanent water table but only the deeper soil layers, and such plants are vulnerable to water shortage in prolonged drought. They may show xerophytic features or drop leaves when water stressed.

Succulence (*water storage* — strategy 3) is a highly specialized adaptation to water shortage in terms of structure, physiology and biochemistry. In effect, succulents avoid water shortage by storing it, when available, in specialized parenchyma cells in their stems (e.g. cacti (Cactaceae), Figure 3.34) or leaves (e.g. agaves (Agavaceae), sedums (Crassulaceae)). However, they also have many features that ensure water is lost very slowly.

❍ From information in Chapter 2 and this chapter, identify one adaptation of succulents that involves both biochemical and physiological features.

● CAM (crassulacean acid metabolism), which involves fixing CO_2 and opening stomata at night (when conditions are cooler and less water is transpired).

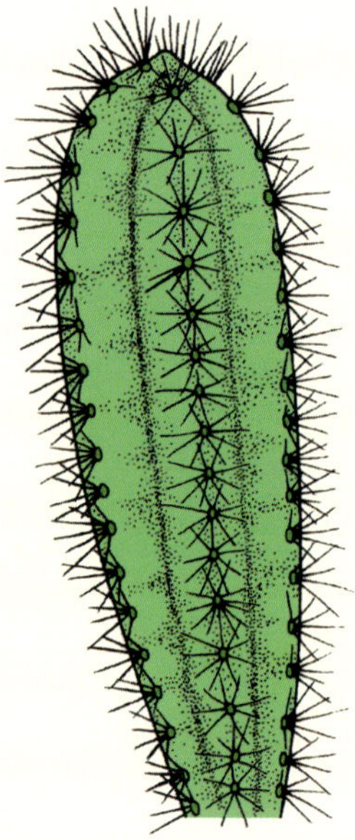

Figure 3.34 A desert cactus (*Cereus* sp.) which has leaves reduced to spines and stores water in the green, swollen stems.

In fact, many succulents show *facultative* CAM in that they can switch from daytime CO_2 fixation via the C3 pathway when water is plentiful to CAM during drought. In extreme drought, CAM plants may also resort to *CAM idling*, a strategy in which stomata remain permanently closed but respiratory CO_2 is recycled internally (by CAM) and dry weight remains constant. Absence of daytime transpiration means that succulents have no transpirational cooling and hence may heat up dramatically on sunny days: tolerance of high shoot temperatures (around 50 °C in some cacti) is a feature of many succulents.

Other characteristics of succulents relate to their root systems and water uptake. Succulents have shallow, extensive roots which absorb water very efficiently from the surface soil. As this soil dries out, fine roots die and only waterproof anchoring roots remain, but new ‘rain roots’ are produced remarkably quickly when the soil is rewetted. In the most extreme habitats, for example, the rainless Atacama desert in South America, soil is never wet but there are periodic fogs which deposit water drops on shoots. *Tillandsia* spp. survive in such places by absorbing water through specialized hairs or scales on the leaf surface and have virtually no root system. *Tillandsia usneoides*, the famous Spanish moss, lives in this way as an epiphyte, festooning trees and overhead wires throughout a large region from the southern USA to Argentina (Figure 3.35).

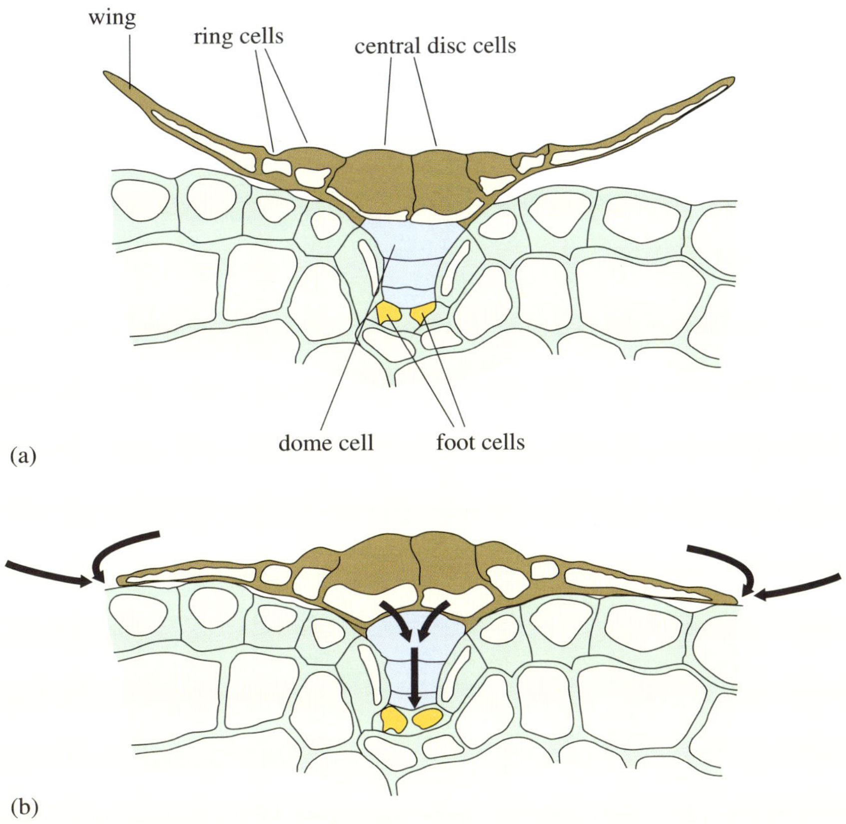

Figure 3.35 Water-absorbing scales on the surface of Spanish moss, *Tillandsia usneoides*. (a) A cross-section of a dry scale, and (b) in the process of water absorption. When water lands on the disc cells they swell, forcing the wings down and creating a suction which draws water under the wings and into the central dome and foot cells (arrows).

Succulents are most abundant in semi-deserts where there are moist periods twice a year that allow recharging of water storage tissue. Such habitats also support non-CAM tree species such as the baobab *Adansonia digitata*, which stores water in its greatly swollen trunks. Succulents also occur as epiphytes in tropical forests, growing high up on trees and without access to the soil (e.g. many orchids and bromeliads). An interesting recent observation was that a CAM bromeliad, *Aechmea magdalenae*, grew on the shady forest floor of seasonally dry Central American rainforest (Skillman *et al*., 1999). Experiments showed that not only does *Aechmea* survive and grow better during the dry season than C3 pathway species but it also has a more rapid photosynthetic response to sunflecks (Chapter 2). Once again, photosynthesis and water relations are seen to be closely linked.

TOLERATING WATER SHORTAGE: XEROPHYTES

Xerophytes (zero`-fites, from the Greek *xeros*, dry) are plants that remain metabolically active during drought by a combination of restricting water loss, efficient water uptake and high tolerance of low tissue water potentials. Typical examples are evergreen desert shrubs (Figure 3.36) and grasses, and we list below some of their key characteristics.

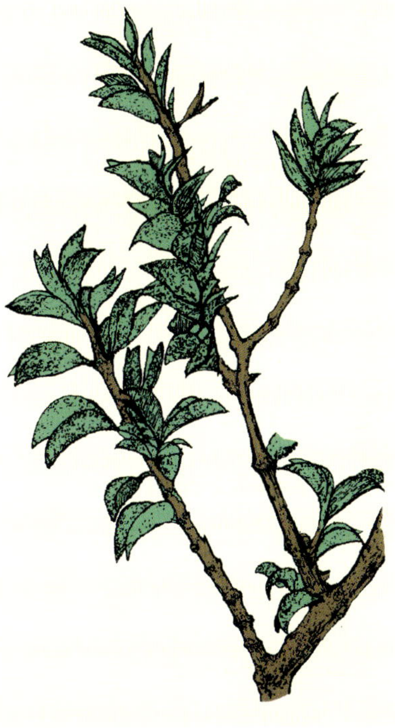

Figure 3.36 A xerophytic desert shrub, the creosote bush, *Larrea tridentata*, from Northern and Central America.

1 Xerophytes often have relatively small leaves (minimizing the surface for water loss), which have a vertical orientation (reducing light absorption and heating in strong sun).

2 Stomata do not close until leaf water potential is much lower than in non-xerophytes and stomata may be protected in ways that minimize water loss (Figure 3.17).

3 Tissue water potentials can fall to very low values without damage to living cells or cavitation in xylem.

4 Low water potentials without loss of turgor are achieved either by accumulating solutes (raising osmotic pressure, see Figure 3.8) or by having elastic cell walls which allow cells to shrink.

In Figure 3.37 you can see how much higher are osmotic pressures of evergreen desert shrubs at both plasmolysis and full turgor compared with other desert species. The low water potentials thus achieved allow xerophytes to absorb water from almost dry soils that have very low matric pressures. The process of lowering water potential by accumulating solutes is described as **osmoregulation** and is achieved by a combination of accumulating ions in the vacuole and organic solutes in the cytoplasm (described further in Chapter 4). Roots are extensive but not especially deeply penetrating in xerophytes, although the deepest roots sometimes supply water to surface roots and soil by means of hydraulic lift, as described for water tappers above.

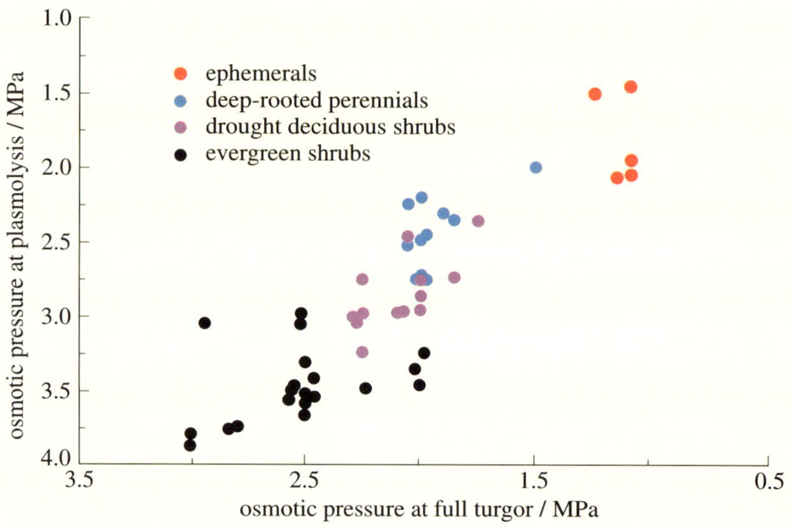

Figure 3.37 The relationship between osmotic pressure at plasmolysis (which equals water potential) and osmotic pressure at full turgor (when $\Psi = 0$) for four different groups of desert plants in North American deserts. Data from Monson and Smith (1982).

In fact shortage of water (or nutrients) causes many 'ordinary' (non-xerophyte) plants, including crop species, to develop more extensive root systems: the dry-weight ratio of roots to shoots may increase several fold, greatly increasing the capacity for water and nutrient uptake.

3.6.2 Physiological drought

Saline soils, which often occur in deserts but also in salt marshes, make water uptake more difficult because the water potential at the root surface is low. Plants adapt to this situation by osmoregulation (Section 3.6.1), attaining an even lower water potential than the soil by accumulating solutes. Freezing conditions present a similar problem because water in the soil and/or in xylem becomes unavailable. In this situation of *frost drought* stomata close and water is withdrawn from leaf cells into intercellular spaces, thus preventing the lethal formation of ice crystals inside cells. This partial desiccation causes drooping of evergreen leaves which you may have noticed during severe frosts.

Cell membranes seem to be protected against the damaging effects of high solute concentrations by the presence of protective solutes, which include certain oligosaccharides and the amino acid proline. In cabbage, for example, allowing leaves to absorb proline can make them frost resistant. Not all plants can develop freezing resistance in this way and those that do undergo changes in cell biochemistry in autumn, a process called **cold hardening** or **cold acclimation**. A major aim in agriculture has been to increase the cold hardiness of autumn-sown cereals, which yield up to 40% more than spring-sown varieties but cannot be grown in large areas of the USA because of limited freezing resistance. Increasing cold hardiness in winter wheat by chemical treatment or breeding to create new varieties would have a significant impact on world food production.

We have now completed the survey of plant water relations. In the next two sections we move on to consider an aspect of plant transport which requires a knowledge of water relations: solute transport in phloem.

Summary of Section 3.6

1. Plants may survive true drought by avoidance or tolerance.
2. Avoidance mechanisms include dormancy, water tapping, water storage and desiccation. Apart from succulent CAM species, plants may show few or no mechanisms that improve water acquisition or reduce water loss whilst remaining metabolically active.
3. Tolerance mechanisms are seen in xerophytes. Plants remain metabolically active despite low tissue water potentials and often have mechanisms that minimize water loss. Root systems are extensive and may utilize hydraulic lift.
4. During physiological drought due to salinity, plants sustain water uptake by osmoregulation that lowers cell water potential. Surviving frost drought and damage due to freezing conditions involves cold hardening: cells become partially desiccated and specific solutes accumulate that protect membranes.

3.7 PHLOEM STRUCTURE AND FUNCTION

To function properly, plants must constantly move substances around from one organ to another. You have seen (Section 3.1) that ions and water taken up by roots move to the shoots in xylem. Similarly, the products of photosynthesis (**assimilates**) and metabolites of nitrogen and sulfur, usually amino acids and thiols such as glutathione, must be transported from the organs where they are synthesized or stored (sources) to the places where they are used (sinks). Such **source to sink** transport occurs in phloem. So xylem and phloem provide the plumbing system of plants that allows long-distance transport (**translocation**) between organs of water, solutes and signalling compounds such as growth regulators.

Our concern here is with phloem translocation. Not until 1928 was it established with certainty that phloem is the only tissue involved in assimilate transport and not until the late 1970s was a consensus reached about the mechanism of transport. Research since then has focused on the mechanisms by which sugars are loaded into and unloaded from phloem and the control and coordination of the system so that supply of materials from sources meets the demands of sinks. We begin, however, by looking more closely at phloem structure because it provides the essential foundation for an understanding of function.

3.7.1 PHLOEM STRUCTURE

You know from Chapter 1 that phloem is located in vascular tissue and contains three types of living cells: phloem parenchyma, sieve tube elements and companion cells (Figure 3.38). Phloem parenchyma serves mainly as 'packing' but the other two cell types are intimately involved in translocation.

SIEVE TUBE ELEMENTS

Translocation actually takes place through these highly specialized cells. In angiosperms, they link up to form long conduits called **sieve tubes**, the end walls (**sieve plates**) having large pores which you saw when studying Chapter 1. During development, sieve tube elements lose their nuclei and ribosomes, the tonoplasts break down and so do internal membranes of mitochondria and plastids. Ultimately, the main components of sieve tube elements are a thick cellulose wall, a plasma membrane and a watery sap usually containing large amounts of a special protein. This **P-protein** (P = phloem) exists as fibrils and plays a role in protecting plants from phloem damage.

Protection is needed because sieve tubes have a very high turgor and if nibbled into or cut may bleed sap profusely. Deposition of P-protein and an insoluble polysaccharide called callose (glucose polymer) is used to plug wounds. Such deposition causes great problems when trying to study phloem microscopically (especially by EM) because it is difficult to avoid during tissue preparation. Arguments raged for years about whether or not sieve plate pores were partially blocked by P-protein or callose, because unobstructed pores are essential for one of the proposed (now widely accepted) mechanisms of phloem transport. There is now convincing evidence that pores are *not* blocked in functional sieve tubes.

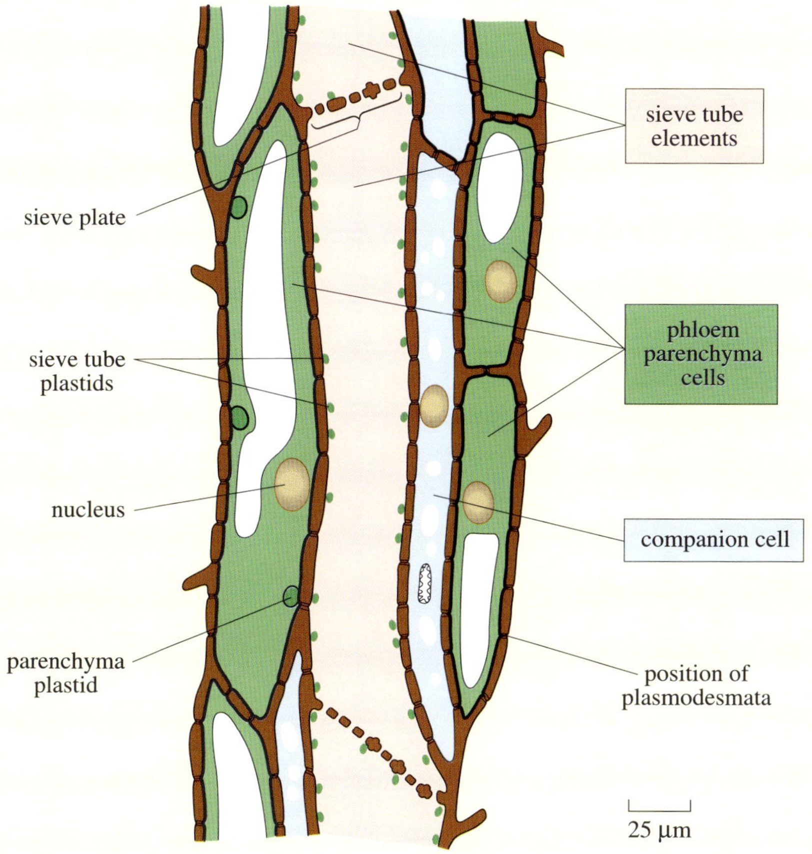

Figure 3.38 A longitudinal section of phloem tissue from the stem of *Nicotiana tabacum* (tobacco plant).

COMPANION CELLS

Sieve tube elements are always associated with one or more companion cells to which they are linked by numerous plasmodesmata (Figure 3.38). Companion cells have a full complement of cell organelles and 'service' the sieve tube elements by passing to them ATP, proteins and other essential molecules.

❍ Why do sieve tube elements need such help?

● Because they lack nuclei, ribosomes and functional mitochondria. Any replacement P-protein, enzymes or substrates required for cell maintenance have to be supplied from other cells.

Three types of companion cells are now recognized; ordinary companion cells, transfer cells and intermediary cells. *Ordinary companion cells* have smooth walls and few or no plasmodesmatal (i.e. symplastic) connections to surrounding cells other than the sieve tube element. *Transfer cells* (Chapter 1) have the same disposition of plasmodesmata but the walls adjacent to other cells have numerous ingrowths which greatly increase their surface area. **Intermediary cells** have smooth walls but numerous plasmodesmata connecting them to surrounding cells (the companion cell shown in Figure 3.39 is of this type). The significance of these arrangements relates to the loading of sugars into phloem (Section 3.8.2) because whereas the first two cell types can collect solutes from the cell walls (apoplast) and pass to the sieve tube, only the latter can obtain them via the symplast. Transfer cells are highly specialized for scavenging solutes from the apoplast, and are found in many situations where such transfer occurs, for example adjacent to xylem conducting cells from which they transfer solutes to other cells, including phloem (Figure 3.39). Active (energy-requiring) transport of solutes occurs across the plasma membrane of the convoluted wall while transfer via the plasmodesmata is by passive diffusion.

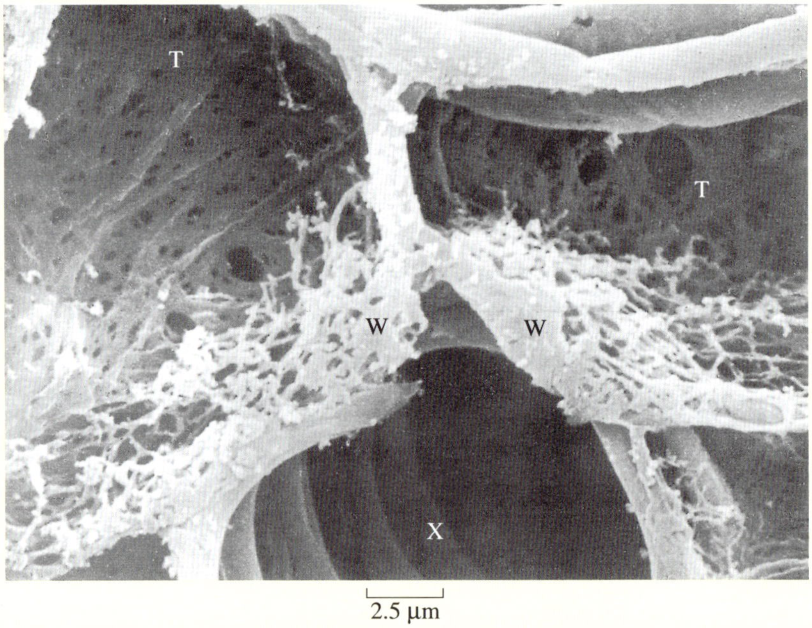

Figure 3.39 A scanning electron micrograph of part of a vascular bundle in the stem of *Tradescantia*. Cytoplasm has been digested away so that only cell walls remain. Two transfer cells (T) abut onto a xylem element (X) and the wall ingrowths (W) lie adjacent to this element.

3.7.2 EXPERIMENTAL STUDIES AND PHLOEM FUNCTION

Now that you know something about phloem structure we consider questions relating to function. For example, what is the composition of phloem sap and how fast and in what directions does it move? Also described in this section are some of the techniques used to study translocation. The earliest experiment was conducted in 1679, before the existence of phloem was known, and introduced the useful technique of ring barking or **girdling** (removing bark and soft tissues which include phloem) external to the wood of a tree. The Italian, Malpighi, girdled a woody shoot and his results and conclusions are described in Figure 3.40.

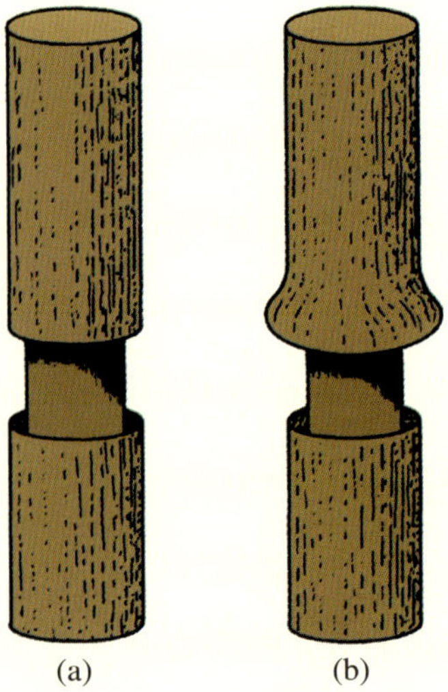

Figure 3.40 Malpighi's experiment. (a) Girdling a woody shoot which leaves xylem intact but removes phloem. (b) A few weeks after girdling, the tissue on the upper side has swollen provided that green leaves were present in the light. Malpighi concluded that nutrients were being 'elaborated' by leaves and transported down the stem, which, since the transpiration stream in xylem rose up the stem, indicated that another tissue was involved in the transport of nutrients out of leaves.

Experiments in the 1930s identified phloem as the tissue involved in translocation out of leaves and, in 1945, the availability of the heavy carbon isotope ^{13}C was used to demonstrate the direction and flexibility of phloem transport, both up and down stems (Figure 3.41).

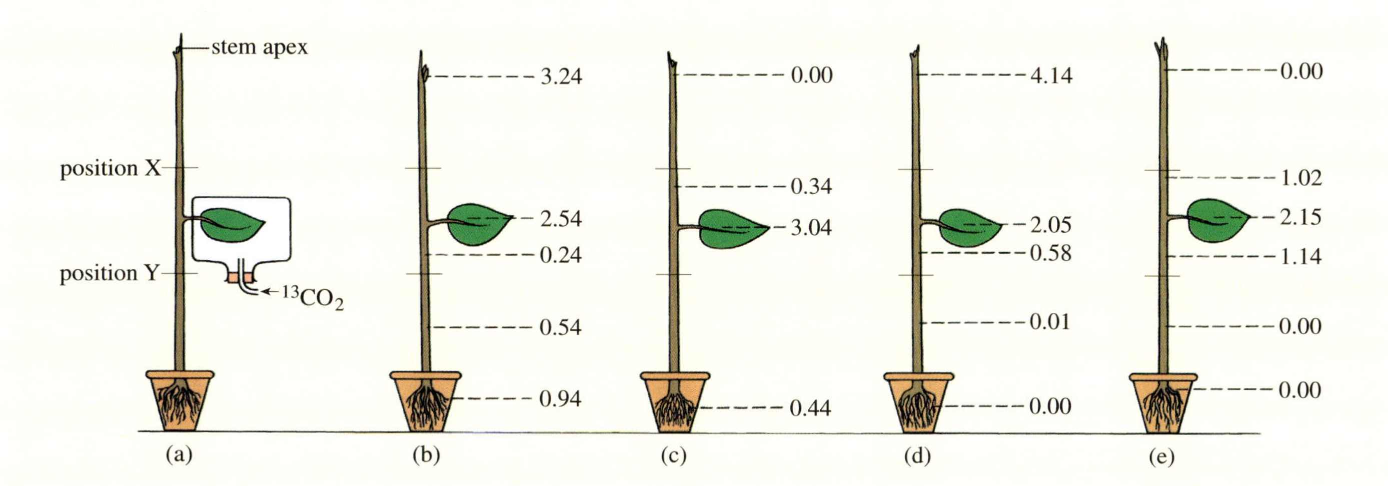

Figure 3.41 The experiment of Rabideau and Burr (1945) using French bean (*Phaseolus vulgaris*). (a) The system for supplying $^{13}CO_2$ to a leaf (other leaves were removed) and the positions (X and Y) where the stem was girdled in some plants. (b)–(e) The relative distribution of ^{13}C after fixation of $^{13}CO_2$ by the leaf and translocation, with and without girdling at X and/or Y.

- ❍ Look at the data in Figure 3.41b–e showing the distribution of ^{13}C and decide whether the girdles were applied at X alone, Y alone, both positions or neither. After checking your answer, label the marked positions on Figure 3.41.

- ● For the plant shown in Figure 3.41b, no girdles were applied: the marker moves both up and down the stem but mainly upwards. For Figure 3.41c, d and e, the positions of girdles were at X alone, Y alone and at both and X and Y respectively.

When radioactive ^{14}C became available in the 1950s it was possible to use autoradiography to show that sieve tubes were the conduits used in translocation (Figure 3.42) and then information about the composition of phloem sap and rates of transport began to accumulate. In a few species (e.g. castor bean, *Ricinus* sp., and lupins, *Lupinus* spp.) sap for analysis can be obtained simply by cutting into phloem and collecting the exudate which flows out due to the high pressure within sieve tubes. But in most species, cut phloem is rapidly sealed by P-protein or callose and the possibility of contamination by surrounding tissues is always present. A more elegant and precise way of tapping phloem involves the use of sap-sucking insects such as aphids and leaf hoppers, the **stylet technique** (Figure 3.43).

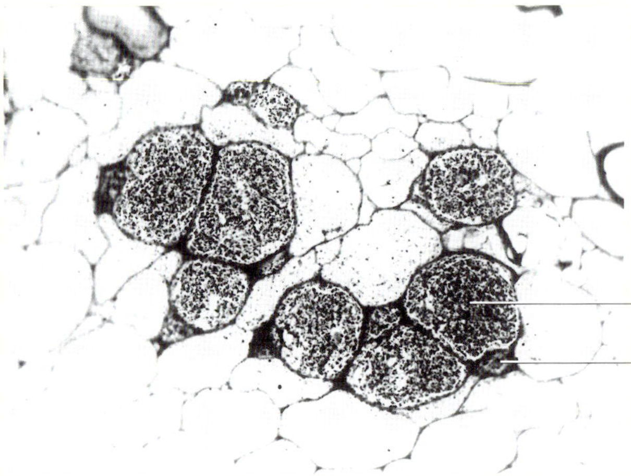

Figure 3.42 Autoradiographic evidence that assimilates from leaves are transported in sieve tubes. ^{14}C-labelled assimilates are localized in sieve tubes and companion cells of *Ipomoea hederacea* (morning glory). A transverse section of stem is shown, 10 cm below a single leaf that was supplied with $^{14}CO_2$ for six hours.

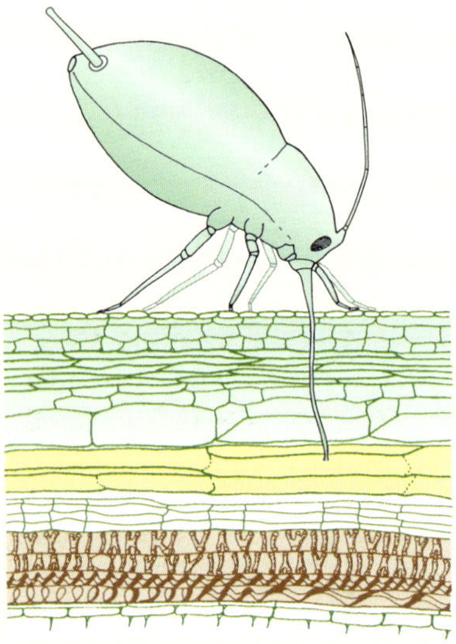

Figure 3.43 Diagram of an aphid in feeding position with its stylets inserted into a sieve tube element. Phloem tissue is coloured yellow.

Sap suckers such as aphids feed by inserting their tubular mouthparts (stylets) into a *single* sieve tube so that the high-pressure sap surges up them. If a feeding aphid is anaesthetized (to prevent withdrawal of stylets) and the body severed from the stylets, phloem sap continues to exude from the cut stylets, often for several days, and can be collected for analysis. Aphid saliva is thought to contain inhibitors that prevent deposition of P-protein or callose. The amounts of sap collected in this way, though small, are adequate for chemical analysis and the technique can also be used, in combination with radioactive tracers, to measure rates of translocation and the effects on the translocation process of treatments such as cooling. In this treatment radioactively-labelled sugars are injected into phloem at a known distance from exuding stylets and the time taken for the label to reach the stylets is recorded.

Composition of phloem sap

Compared with xylem sap, phloem sap is a much more concentrated solution of considerably higher pH. Xylem sap is typically dilute and slightly acid (about 0.01% (w/v) solids and pH 6.0) whereas phloem sap contains 15–30% (w/v) dissolved solids and has a pH around 7.2–8.5. Usually, more than 90% by weight of phloem solutes are non-reducing sugars, of which the disaccharide sucrose (glucose + fructose) is by far the most common. In some species, however, considerable amounts of 'unusual' sugars, such as raffinose, are present, with one or more galactose molecules added to the sucrose, and sugar alcohols such as mannitol may also be present. You will see later that this observation is significant in relation to phloem loading (Section 3.8.2). Figure 3.44 shows the composition of phloem sap and, in addition to the components shown, trace amounts of plant growth regulators, proteins and even viruses may be present.

❍ The sucrose concentration in phloem sap is considerably greater than that in surrounding tissues. What does this gradient suggest about the mechanism by which sucrose enters sieve tubes?

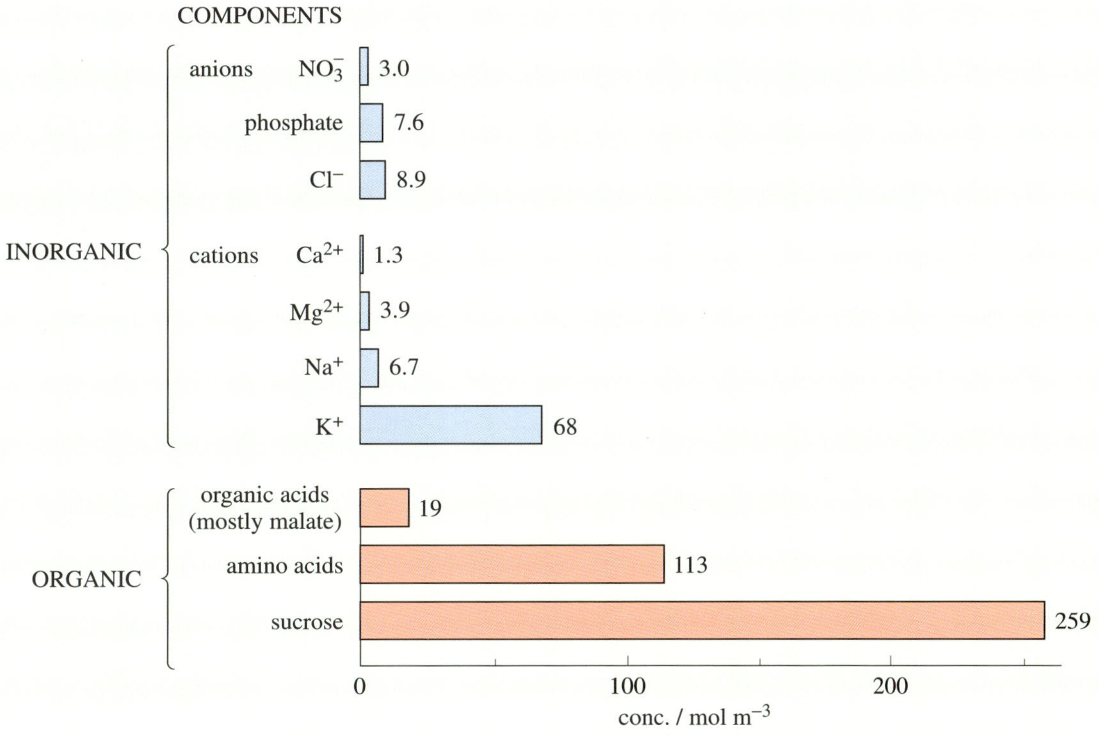

Figure 3.44 The average composition of phloem sap from *Ricinus* (castor bean plant) obtained by cutting and repeatedly shaving the stem.

- Because sucrose entry is against (or 'up') a concentration gradient, it probably requires an energy input, i.e. sucrose is loaded actively into sieve tubes by some kind of active transport.

- How does the high solute content of sieve tubes help to explain their high turgor?

- High solute content means high osmotic pressure and, therefore, low water potential (Equation 3.1). Water enters phloem from surrounding tissues because of the low water potential and hence the turgor rises. Recall from Figure 3.9a that the higher the value of π, the higher is P at full turgor.

Notice in Figure 3.44 that nitrogen is transported in phloem mainly as amino acids rather than as nitrate, and potassium is by far the most abundant ion. Magnesium, phosphate, sodium and chloride ions are all commonly present in phloem sap, but calcium is only ever present in very small amounts because it tends to form insoluble phosphates at the pH of the sap.

This differential mobility of ions in phloem has implications for their distribution around the plant. Bear in mind that ions absorbed from the soil are carried in xylem to all transpiring organs, irrespective of the organs' 'need' for ions. Most ions are re-exported from older, non-growing leaves (source organs) to sink regions such as the shoot apex, flowers or fruits, but calcium and iron cannot be redistributed in this way.

❍ If crops suffer from calcium deficiency, which parts of the plant are most likely to show deficiency symptoms?

● The later-formed sink organs, i.e. shoot tips, young leaves, flowers and fruits. Shoot tips and fruits are often the worst affected. These organs transpire relatively little and receive minimal xylem input but cannot receive calcium in phloem, redistributed from older leaves.

RATES OF PHLOEM TRANSPORT

Transport velocities of sugars in phloem are commonly in the range 3–150 cm h^{-1}, averaging about 100 cm h^{-1}. For short periods, and often in experimental situations, velocities of 500–1500 cm h^{-1} have been recorded, with velocities in the *Arenga* palm reaching an astounding 7.2 m h^{-1}. Of more significance to the plant than transport velocity, however, is solute flux, that is, the amount of solute reaching an organ via phloem in unit time, which largely determines how fast an organ can grow. Solute flux depends on the total area of phloem sieve tubes and the **specific mass transfer rate** or **SMT** (solute mass passing through unit cross section of phloem in unit time) which can be expressed as:

SMT (g cm^{-2} h^{-1}) = sap concentration (g cm^{-3}) × average velocity (cm h^{-1})

Measured values for SMT are mostly around 0.5–6.3 g cm^{-2} h^{-1} but for the cut inflorescence stalk of the *Arenga* palm reached 99 g cm^{-2} h^{-1} and, over a period of 130 days, 252 kilograms of sucrose were collected in bleeding sap! Phloem transport can, therefore, deliver a lot of sugar and at high velocities, which exceed by around 10^5 the rate at which sugar could diffuse along sieve tubes; so whatever the mechanism of phloem transport, it is *not* simple diffusion. We consider next what the mechanism is thought to be.

SUMMARY OF SECTION 3.7

1 Phloem is the tissue involved in long-distance transport of solutes, especially assimilates, from sources to sinks.

2 In angiosperms, translocation occurs within sieve tubes, which interact closely with companion cells that may be specialized as transfer or intermediary cells. Sieve tubes have a high turgor and readily become blocked by deposition of P-protein or callose.

3 Stem girdling, use of isotopically labelled solutes, autoradiography and the stylet technique are examples of techniques used in studies of phloem transport.

4 Phloem sap is slightly alkaline and has a very high solute content. The major solute is sucrose but unusual sugars such as raffinose are present in some species. Certain ions and nitrogen, in the form of amino acids, commonly occur.

5 Average transport velocity in phloem is about 100 cm h^{-1} and solute flux is measured as specific mass transfer rate (g cm^{-2} h^{-1}).

3.8 THE MECHANISM AND CONTROL OF PHLOEM TRANSPORT

Since about 1980, the majority of research workers have accepted one model as best describing the mechanism of phloem transport: the **pressure flow hypothesis**. We describe it below and consider why, for most of the twentieth century, arguments raged about its validity.

3.8.1 THE PRESSURE FLOW HYPOTHESIS

This hypothesis was first proposed by the German physiologist Münch in 1930 and, although elaborated upon somewhat since then, it remains an essentially simple concept. The main propositions are:

1 The driving force for phloem transport is a *gradient of hydrostatic pressure within sieve tubes*: sieve tubes at the source end of a pathway have a higher turgor than those at the sink end. Movement of water down a gradient of water potential is still the rule but the only component of Ψ that matters *along* a sieve tube is pressure, just as it does in xylem.

2 The pressure gradient is set up through the active movement of solutes into sieve tubes of source organs. Water then enters by osmosis, generating high turgor, whilst, at the sink end of the pathway, solutes leave (actively or passively) along with water, and turgor is relatively low. These concepts are illustrated in Figure 3.45. Note that energy is expended only to load (and possibly unload) sieve tubes and none is required along the pathway to sustain transport.

3 Movement along sieve tubes is by mass flow, driven by the pressure gradient.

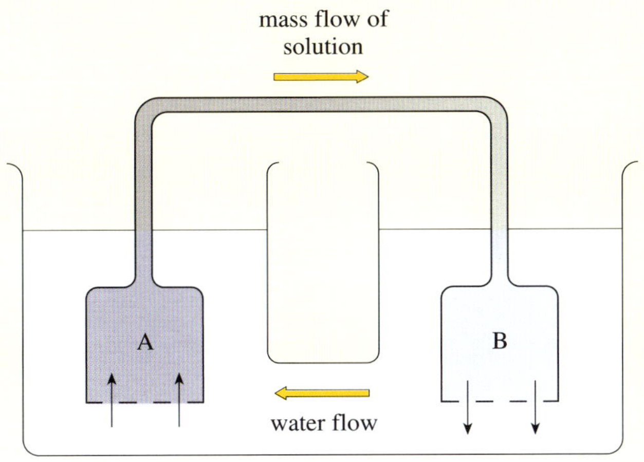

Figure 3.45 A model to illustrate the pressure flow hypothesis. A represents a source, in which there is a higher concentration of solutes than in the sink (B). Water enters A by osmosis across the semipermeable membrane (dashed), generating a hydrostatic pressure (turgor) which causes mass flow along the connecting tube to B. Because the osmotic pressure (solute concentrations) is higher at A than at B, water is forced out of B across the semipermeable membrane by reverse osmosis. In nature, active unloading of sieve tubes at sinks can lead to higher solute concentrations outside so that water flows out by normal osmosis.

PREDICTIONS OF THE PRESSURE FLOW HYPOTHESIS

Most of the controversy surrounding the pressure flow hypothesis stemmed from evidence which contradicted its two main predictions. These predictions are:

1 *There should be a pressure gradient along sieve tubes sufficient to support the observed rates of transport.* Measurements of sieve tube turgor have been made at different points along the source–sink pathway using either fine needles or exuding aphid stylets (Section 3.7.2) to which pressure-measuring devices were attached. Results show that a pressure gradient is present (0.043–0.050 MPa m^{-1} in an oak, for example) and is sufficient to account for observed rates of transport *provided the pathway has a low resistance*. Pathway resistance depends overwhelmingly on the numbers and dimensions of sieve plate pores and whether pores are blocked by P-protein or callose. Early EM studies of phloem often showed a majority of pores blocked (Figure 3.46) and it was, therefore, argued that pressure flow alone could not explain phloem transport. However, as explained in Section 3.7.1, it is notoriously difficult to prepare phloem for the EM without causing P-protein or callose deposition and later work using confocal microscopy of living, functional phloem showed that pores were *not* blocked. For angiosperms, this prediction of the pressure flow hypothesis is fully supported but the situation differs for gymnosperms, which have more primitive sieve cells in which pores are indeed blocked by membranes. So a question mark still hangs over whether or how the pressure flow hypothesis operates in gymnosperms.

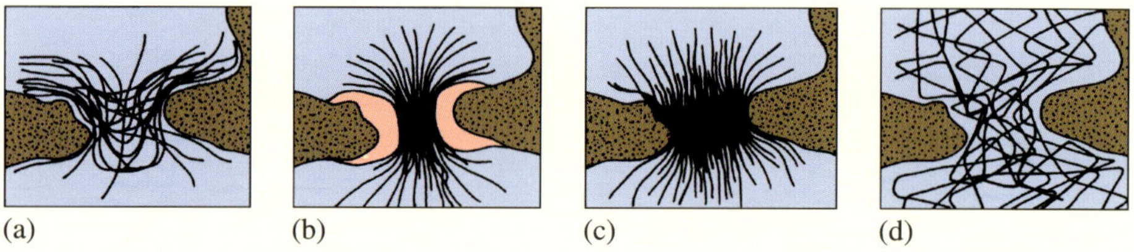

Figure 3.46 Arrangements of P-protein filaments (black) and callose (pink) in sieve pores that have been observed in the EM. Such blocked pores are incompatible with the operation of a pressure flow mechanism alone.

2 A second prediction is that *water and solutes should move together in the same direction and at the same rate down a sieve tube*. This necessary corollary of mass flow means, for example, that if two markers such as radioactively-labelled sugar and K^+ are introduced simultaneously into a sieve tube, they should move at the same rate along it. Experiments purporting to show that they did not were mostly explained as due to the markers entering different sieve tubes with different sinks. True *bidirectional flow* in which solutes in a single sieve tube move in opposite directions has never been demonstrated.

Other experiments have shown that localized cooling along a source–sink pathway, which reduces energy supply from respiration, does not greatly affect the rate of phloem transport. Only a reduction in the energy supply for phloem loading would be predicted to inhibit transport according to the pressure flow hypothesis. So, at least for angiosperms, the pressure flow hypothesis is consistent with experimental findings and all the known facts about phloem transport. For a proper understanding of phloem transport, however, we need to consider further the key processes of phloem loading and unloading.

3.8.2 PHLOEM LOADING

Phloem sap in sieve tubes has a very different composition (Section 3.7.2) to the cytosol of surrounding cells; some solutes (especially sucrose) are present at much higher concentrations. It follows that phloem loading must be (a) *selective* and (b) *active*, i.e. requiring expenditure of metabolic energy. The sensitivity of phloem loading to low temperature and to metabolic inhibitors provides supporting evidence for (b). But how is selective, active loading achieved? Figure 3.47a illustrates one mechanism, described as **apoplastic loading**, for which there is good evidence in many families of predominantly herbaceous plants (including Fabaceae, Asteraceae and Brassicaceae). Solutes such as sucrose move from source cells towards phloem via plasmodesmata along a symplast route (Section 3.2) and then, probably on reaching the companion cell or possibly the sieve tube element, efflux into the cell wall (apoplast) and are actively loaded into phloem.

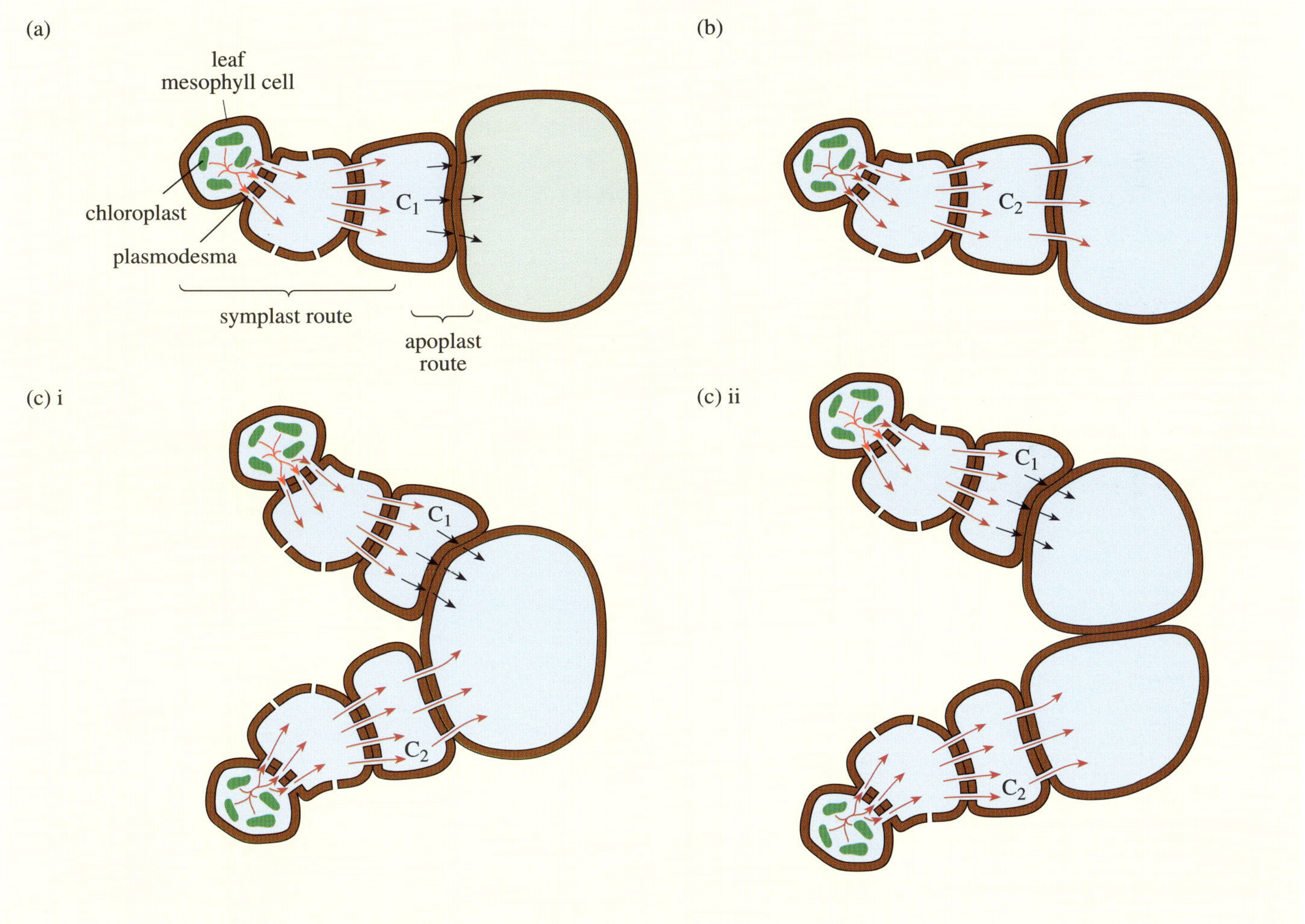

Figure 3.47 Mechanisms of phloem loading. (a) Apoplastic loading: solutes move in the symplast via plasmodesmata (red arrows) from leaf mesophyll (or other source) cells to the companion cells (C), and then enter the sieve tube by the apoplast with active transport (black arrows). (b) Symplastic loading: solutes move from source cells to sieve tubes entirely via the symplast. (c) Combined apoplastic and symplastic loading, (i) into the same sieve tube element, (ii) into different sieve tube elements.

In some families of predominantly woody plants, however, the mechanism shown in Figure 3.47b, **symplastic loading**, seems to operate.

❍ From Figure 3.47, identify two key differences between apoplastic and symplastic phloem loading.

● (i) Plasmodesmatal connections are present between all cells along the pathway from source cells to sieve tubes in symplastic loaders but in apoplastic loaders they are not. (ii) The companion cells of symplastic loaders are of the intermediary type (Section 3.7.1) and linked by plasmodesmata to both sieve tubes and surrounding cells; in apoplastic loaders, however, companion cells are of the ordinary or transfer cell type and lack plasmodesmatal connections either to surrounding cells or, as in Figure 3.47, to sieve tubes.

In some plants, both types of phloem loading occur, sometimes into the same sieve tube and sometimes into different sieve tubes (Figure 3.47c).

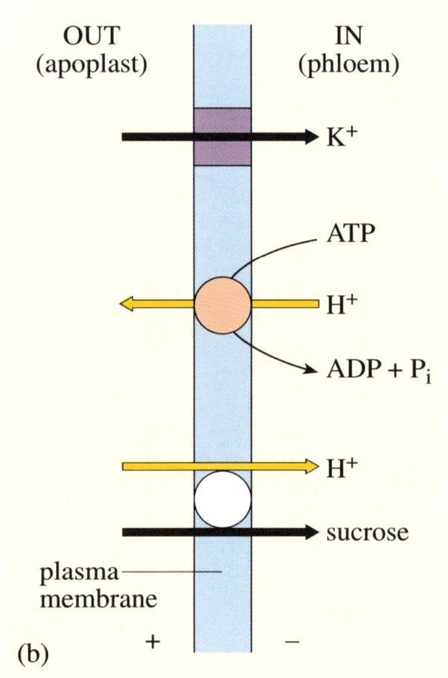

Figure 3.48 Sucrose–proton co-transport in apoplastic phloem loading. The primary active efflux of H^+ ions occurs via the ATPase (pink circle) and secondary active transport of sucrose is achieved with coupling to H^+ via a sucrose transporter (white circle). Secondary active influx of K^+ and other solutes may also occur.

So what are the advantages and disadvantages of these different mechanisms of phloem loading? In apoplastic loading, solutes move from the apoplast via specific transporters using secondary active transport. An electrochemical gradient is produced by primary active pumping of protons out of the receiving cell and sucrose, for example, enters that cell from the apoplast by **sucrose–proton co-transport** (Figure 3.48). It is clear why energy is needed for this process and how selectivity can be achieved by the availability of transporters; glucose, for example, does not enter phloem because there are no transporters available to load it. Conversely, the gene controlling synthesis of the sucrose–H^+ transporter is very strongly expressed in phloem tissue.

However, it is far less clear how symplastic loading works.

❍ What problem can you see for symplastic loading in concentrating sucrose within sieve tubes?

● If sucrose moves via plasmodesmata down its concentration gradient, it would have to enter sieve tubes against its concentration gradient to accumulate in them.

The mechanism of symplastic loading is still a source of controversy but an interesting possibility, the **polymer trap mechanism**, was suggested by Turgeon (1991) and is illustrated in Figure 3.49.

Study Figure 3.49 and note the sites of formation and route of sugar molecules through the schematic plant structure illustrated, then read on.

Sucrose synthesized in leaf mesophyll cells moves via plasmodesmata to the intermediary (companion) cell where it combines with galactose to form a 3-unit sugar, raffinose. Further reactions may yield even larger sugars (oligosaccharides). These sugar polymers are too large to diffuse back through

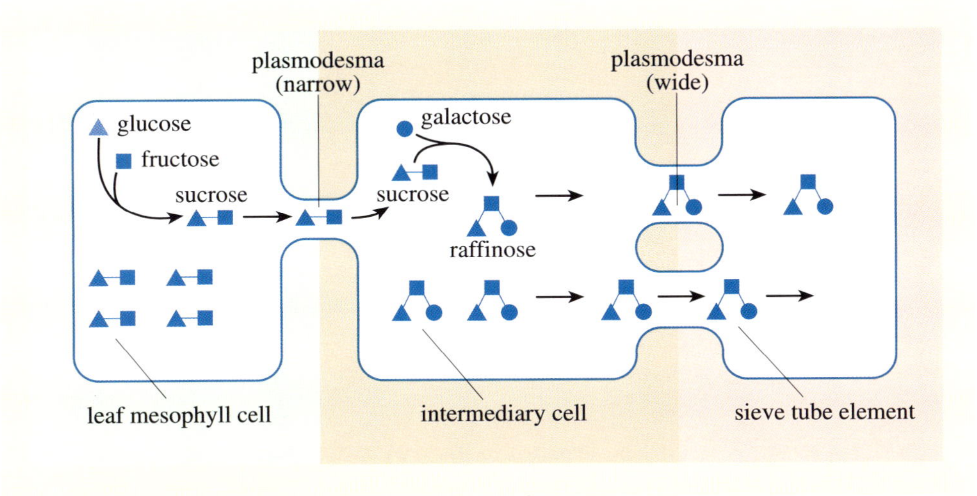

Figure 3.49 The polymer trap mechanism of symplastic phloem loading.

the plasmodesmata used for entry (hence they are 'trapped') but can pass through larger plasmodesmata into sieve tubes as their concentration rises in the intermediary cells. Recall (Section 3.7.2) that phloem sap sometimes contains 'unusual' sugars (e.g. raffinose) and it is in species with intermediary cells and symplastic phloem loading that they occur. Not all data are consistent with the polymer trap mechanism so it remains a hypothesis that needs further testing, but it does provide explanations for the specificity of symplastic phloem loading and the energy requirement (for oligosaccharide synthesis).

❍ What three predictions arise from the polymer trap mechanism relating to:
(a) relative sucrose concentration in intermediary and mesophyll cells;
(b) location of enzymes for the synthesis of raffinose and other oligosaccharides;
(c) permeability of plasmodesmata linking intermediary cells to outer cells?

● (a) Sucrose concentration should be lower in intermediary cells than in mesophyll cells; (b) the enzymes should be located mainly in intermediary cells; (c) these plasmodesmata should exclude molecules larger than sucrose.

Apoplastic phloem loading is thought to be more 'advanced' than symplastic loading because it occurs in later-evolved plant families. Furthermore, apoplastic loading prevails in temperate and arid regions whereas symplastic loading prevails in tropical rainforests, suggesting that it has disadvantages in dry and/or cool conditions. There is evidence, for example, that at temperatures below 10 °C, plasmodesmata tend to become blocked by callose deposition in chilling-sensitive rainforest plants. Possibly also, the synthesis of oligosaccharides is especially sensitive to cool temperatures and there is indeed evidence that symplastic loaders are less efficient in temperate climates, having lower mass transfer rates than apoplastic loaders. It appears, therefore, that apoplastic loading evolved after symplastic loading and has facilitated the colonization by plants of drier, cooler habitats.

3.8.3 Phloem unloading

The growth of a sink organ — roots, flowers, seeds, developing leaves etc. — depends, to a great extent, on the amount of assimilates that it receives, a measure of its *sink strength*. A major aim of plant breeders has been to increase sink strength of harvestable organs such as fruits or storage organs in crops and, if you compare crops with their wild relatives, harvestable organs are always much bigger in the crop plants. So ultimately, sink strength is under genetic control and is an aspect of plant development; proximately, however, it is influenced strongly by the metabolic activity of the sink and its capacity to unload phloem, which is our concern here.

Mechanisms and control of phloem unloading

Phloem unloading involves efflux of solutes from sieve tubes followed, usually, by transport via parenchyma cells, leading to their eventual metabolism or storage in sink cells. For terminal sinks, two types of phloem unloading have been identified:

(i) *Entirely symplastic* from sieve elements to cells that use or store assimilates (Figure 3.50a). Movement occurs via plasmodesmata by diffusion or mass flow and down a potential gradient, with sieve tubes having a high turgor and receiving cells lower turgor. Control of the unloading flux depends, therefore, on the hydraulic conductivity of plasmodesmata and on the capacity of receiving cells to maintain low turgor by using or storing assimilates (e.g. as starch). A majority of sink organs seem to use this mechanism.

(ii) *Symplastic with an apoplastic step* after sieve element unloading. The point along the pathway where symplastic transport stops and assimilates move into the apoplast varies and, sometimes, transfer cells retrieve solutes from the walls (Figure 3.50b). This mechanism is known to operate in two situations. First, in seeds and symbionts (including mycorrhizal fungi and parasites), that is, where

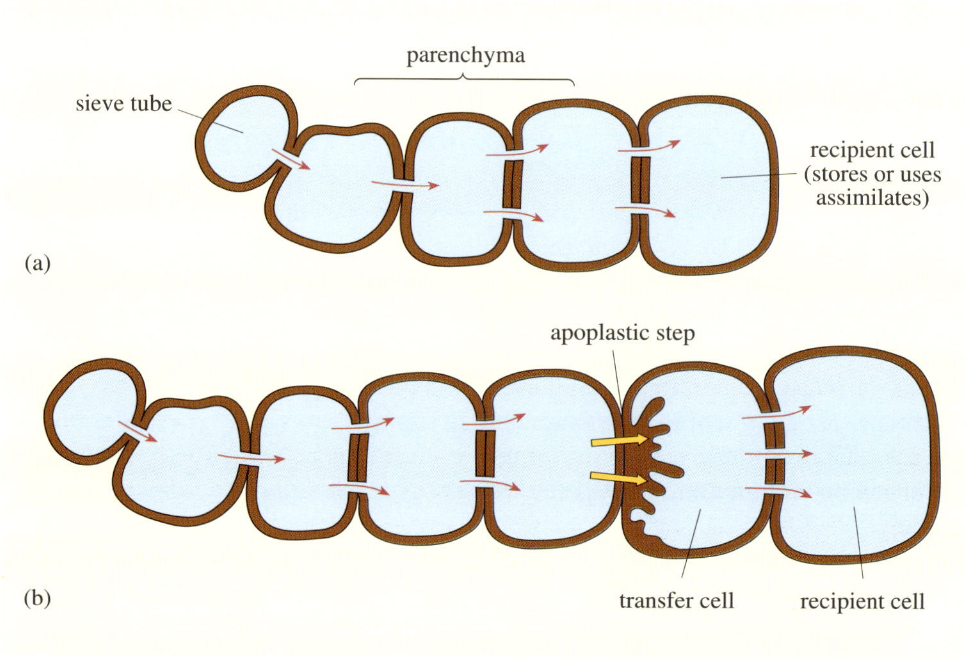

Figure 3.50 Phloem unloading: (a) entirely symplastic; (b) symplastic with an apoplastic step.

the sink has a different genome and is effectively non-self so that, inevitably, there is no symplastic link to the host or parent. Second, in storage organs that store sucrose (rather than starch), for example the stems of sugar cane and roots of sugar beet. The same constraints operate here as for phloem loading because sucrose must be accumulated against its concentration gradient.

A variety of mechanisms operate to sustain assimilate efflux into the apoplast and uptake into sink cells. Efflux may be entirely passive, by simple or facilitated diffusion, or may be partially active (via an H^+–sucrose co-transport system); developing seeds commonly have cell-wall invertase which converts sucrose to glucose and fructose.

❍ How might wall-bound invertase facilitate sucrose efflux into the apoplast during phloem unloading?

● By removing sucrose from the walls, a steep concentration gradient is maintained from cytosol to wall and, hence, a high rate of diffusion.

Uptake from the apoplast of both sucrose, and glucose plus fructose, generally seems to be (secondarily) active and proton coupled. The activity of the transporters involved in uptake is thought to be regulated by cell turgor so that turgor acts as an indicator of sink demand for assimilates: when sinks no longer 'require' assimilates, turgor rises and phloem unloading slows down or stops.

Together, the metabolic activity of sinks — how fast they use or store assimilates — and the efficiency of phloem unloading determine the rate at which solutes leave sieve tubes and hence their turgor. The lower the turgor of terminal sieve elements, the steeper the pressure gradient from source to sink and the greater the mass transfer rate. However, a steep gradient can be maintained only if the rate of phloem *loading* keeps pace and a fall in sieve tube turgor in source organs has, indeed, been found to stimulate phloem loading. The whole system, therefore, is highly integrated.

Integration extends beyond phloem, however. Consider, for example, the following observations:

1 When potato tubers begin to form, the rate of photosynthesis in the leaves increases.

2 If young tubers are removed from a potato plant, photosynthesis in the leaves declines.

Similarly, the presence of mycorrhizal fungi in plant roots has been shown to increase the rate of photosynthesis. Clearly, there is feedback from sinks to sources that influences overall metabolic activity of the sources, although the control mechanisms are still not understood. During its life, a plant must coordinate assimilate supply to a wide range of sinks, whose 'demands' vary as they grow; the process is called **assimilate partitioning**. The initiation of a sink (when it starts to grow) and its termination (when it stops growing or storing) is determined largely by growth regulators (Chapter 5) so we start to move from the study of plant transport into studying development and growth. Before that point, however, there remains one key area of study that relates to how plants obtain and distribute essential requirements: mineral nutrition, the subject of Chapter 4.

SUMMARY OF SECTION 3.8

1 The pressure flow hypothesis is now accepted as the mechanism of phloem transport. Movement occurs by mass flow driven by a gradient of hydrostatic pressure that arises through active loading of solutes into sieve tubes in source organs and their (active or passive) removal in sink organs.

2 Key predictions of the pressure flow hypothesis — an adequate pressure gradient along sieve tubes, unblocked sieve plates, absence of bidirectional flow within single sieve tubes, and insensitivity of transport to metabolic inhibition along the pathway — have been supported by experimental studies.

3 Phloem loading requires an energy input and may be apoplastic (using sucrose–proton co-transport) or symplastic (via plasmodesmata and possibly using the polymer trap mechanism). Apoplastic loading is thought to be a later-evolved mechanism that works better in drier, cooler habitats.

4 Phloem unloading may be entirely symplastic or involve an apoplastic step that requires proton-coupled secondary active transport.

5 Assimilate partitioning involves coordination not only of phloem loading and unloading but also of the metabolic activity of sinks and sources.

REFERENCES

Allen, G. J., Amtmann, A. and Sanders, D. (1998) Calcium-dependent and calcium-independent K^+ mobilization channels in *Vicia faba* guard cell vacuoles, in *Stomatal biology*, A. Hetherington and W. Davies (eds), *Journal of Experimental Botany*, **49**, Special Issue, pp. 305–318.

Beerling, D. J. and Woodward, F. I. (1997) Changes in land plant function over the Phanerozoic: reconstructions based on fossil records, *Botanical Journal of the Linnean Society*, **123**, 137–53.

Clarkson, D. T., Carvajal, M., Henzler, T., Waterhouse, R. N., Smyth, A. J., Cooke, D. T. and Steudle, E. (2000) Root hydraulic conductance: diurnal aquaporin expression and the effects of nutrient stress, *Journal of Experimental Botany*, **51**, pp. 61–70.

Fischer, R. A. (1971) Role of potassium in stomatal opening in the leaf of *Vicia faba*, *Plant Physiology*, **47**, pp. 555–8.

Furth, A. (2001) Making ATP, in *The Core of Life*, *Vol. I*, J. Saffrey (ed.), The Open University, Milton Keynes, pp. 209–240.

McCully, M. E. (1999) Roots in soil: unearthing the complexities of roots and their rhizospheres, *Annual Review of Plant Phys*iology, **50**, pp. 695–718.

Monson, R. K. and Smith, S. D. (1982) Seasonal water potential components of Sonoran Desert plants, *Ecology*, **63**, pp. 113–123.

Rabideau and Burr, (1945) *American Journal of Botany*, **32**, Botanical Society of America.

Skillman, J. B., Garcia, M. and Winter, K. (1999) Whole plant consequences of Crassulacean acid metabolism for a tropical forest understory plant, *Ecology*, **80**, pp. 1584–93.

Steudle, E. and Peterson, C.A. (1998) How does water get through roots? *Journal of Experimental Botany*, **49**, pp. 775–788.

Srivastava, A. and Zeiger, E. (1995) Guard cell zeaxanthin tracks photosynthetically active radiation and stomatal apertures in *Vicia faba* leaves, *Plant Cell Environment*, **18**, pp. 813–817.

Swithenby, M. S. and O'Shea, P. (2001) Membranes and transport, in *The Core of Life, Vol. I*, J. Saffrey (ed.), The Open University, Milton Keynes, pp. 107–164.

Taiz, L. and Zeiger, E. (1998) (2nd edn) *Plant Physiology*, Sinauer Associates Inc., Sunderland, Mass., p. 89.

Talbott, L. D. and Zeiger, E. (1996) Central roles for potassium and sucrose in guard-cell osmoregulation, *Plant Physiology*, **111**, pp. 1051–7.

Tardieu, F., Lafarge, T. and Simmoneau, Th. (1996) Stomatal control by fed or endogenous xylem ABA in sunflower: interpretation of observed correlations between leaf water potential and stomatal conductance in anisohydric species, *Plant, Cell and Environment*, **19**, pp. 75–84.

Tardieu, F. and Simonneau, T. (1998) Variability among species of stomatal control under fluctuating soil water status and evaporative demand: modelling isohydric and anisohydric behaviours, in *Stomatal biology*, A. Hetherington and W. Davies (eds), *Journal of Experimental Botany*, **49**, Special Issue, pp. 419–432.

Tardieu, F. and Trejo, unpublished data, in Tardieu, F. and Simmoneau, T. (1998) Variability among species of stomatal control under fluctuating soil water status and evaporative demand: modelling isohydric and anisohydric behaviours, *Journal of Experimental Botany*, **49**, Special Issue, *Stomatal biology*, A. Hetherington and W. Davies (eds), pp. 419–432.

Tezara, W., Mitchell, V. J., Driscoll, S. D. and Lawlor, D. W. (1999) Water stress inhibits plant photosynthesis by decreasing coupling factor and ATP, *Nature*, **401**, pp. 914–917.

Turgeon, R. (1991) Symplastic phloem loading and the sink–source transition in leaves: a model, in *Recent Advances in Phloem Transport and Assimilate Compartmentation*, J. L. Bonnemain, S. Delrot, W. J. Lucas and J. Dainty (eds), Nantes, France, Ouest Editions, pp. 18–22.

Tyree, M. T. (1997) The Cohesion–Tension theory of sap ascent: current controversies, *Journal of Experimental Botany*, **48**, pp. 1753–65.

Tyree, M. T. and Sperry, J. S. (1989) Vulnerability of xylem to cavitation and embolism, *Annual Review of Plant Physiology*, **40**, pp. 19–38.

Woodward, F. (1998) Do plants really need stomata? in *Stomatal biology*, A. Hetherington and W. Davies (eds), *Journal of Experimental Botany*, **49**, Special Issue, pp. 471–480.

Zeiger, E. and Zhu, J. (1998) Role of zeaxanthin in blue light photoreception and the modulation of light–CO_2 interactions in guard cells, in *Stomatal biology*, A. Hetherington and W. Davies (eds), *Journal of Experimental Botany*, **49**, Special Issue, pp. 433–442.

FURTHER READING

Taiz, L. and Zeiger, E. (1998) (2nd edn) *Plant Physiology*, Sinauer Associates Inc., Sunderland, Mass. [An excellent textbook that covers most of the material in this chapter, often at a more advanced level.]

Smith, S. D., Monson, R. K. and Anderson, J. E. (1997) *Physiological Ecology of North American Desert Plants*, Springer. [A textbook that examines the features of desert plants and relates morphology to physiology.]

Plant mineral nutrition

4

4.1 Introduction

It has already been established that all living things require a source of energy and a range of chemical elements with which to construct and maintain themselves. Plants use photosynthesis to obtain their energy from light and to obtain carbon, hydrogen and oxygen from carbon dioxide and water. Packaged in the form of sugars, these **organic nutrients** are supplemented by **mineral nutrients** which are additional chemical elements that are obtained in the form of inorganic ions or molecules, mainly from the soil. It has been known for more than 2000 years that adding nutrients to the soil in the form of ash or lime improves plant growth, but it was not until the 20th century that research provided an explanation for these effects. We now know that the simple presence of an element in a plant does not imply that it is essential. As impressive as plants can be in acquiring the inorganic nutrients they need from the soil, they are not perfectly selective so that, in addition to essential nutrients, they may take up minerals that are redundant or even toxic.

The term **essential mineral element** (or nutrient) was coined by Arnon and Stout in the late 1930s. They proposed that three criteria must be met if an element is to be considered essential.

1 A given plant must be unable to complete its life cycle in the absence of the element.
2 The function of the element cannot be performed by another.
3 The element must be directly involved in plant metabolism, for example, as a component of an essential constituent such as an enzyme, or it must be required for a distinct metabolic step such as an enzyme reaction. Elements that can compensate for the toxic effects of other elements, or which simply replace mineral nutrients in some of the less specific functions, such as maintenance of osmotic pressure, are not essential but can be described as **beneficial elements**.

For seed plants, 13 mineral elements are apparently universally essential, while a further three are known to be essential to a limited number of species. Some elements are needed in relatively large quantities. These **macronutrients** are either constituents of organic compounds such as protein and nucleic acids, or act as osmotica (i.e. contribute to the osmotic pressure of cells or organelles). The **micronutrients** are required in much smaller quantities and include enzyme cofactors and components of electron transport proteins, etc. With continuous improvements in analytical techniques, it is quite possible that more elements may be added to the list of micronutrients. Table 4.1 lists the mineral nutrients, some of their important functions, the form in which they are commonly absorbed by plants and the average relative concentration in dry tissues.

Table 4.1 Table of essential mineral nutrients for seed plants, showing the form in which they are absorbed, the average relative concentration in dry tissues and some examples of their important functions. Forms absorbed less commonly are shown in brackets. Note that Na, Si and Ni are not essential for all plants.

Element (symbol)	Form absorbed by plants	Mean relative concentration in dry tissue	Important functions (not necessarily exhaustive)
Macronutrients			
nitrogen (N)	NO_3^- nitrate (NH_4^+ ammonium)	1000	component of proteins and nucleotides
potassium (K)	K^+	250	osmoregulation maintenance of electrochemical equilibria regulation of enzyme activity: e.g. in protein synthesis, ATPases; effects on protein conformation
calcium (Ca)	Ca^{2+}	125	stabilizes cell walls and membranes; second messenger with important roles in cellular control and coordination
magnesium (Mg)	Mg^{2+}	80	constituent of enzymes, e.g. ATPases, and chlorophyll; role in regulation of pH and charge balance within cells
phosphorus (P)	$H_2PO_4^-$ (HPO_4^{2-}) (PO_4^{3-}) phosphates	60	constituent of nucleic acids, phospholipids, ATP and ADP; role in protein synthesis, membranes and energy transfer as well as regulatory role through phosphorylation reactions
sulfur (S)	SO_4^{2-} sulfate	30	component of proteins and glutathione (an important antioxidant)
Micronutrients			
chlorine (Cl)	Cl^- chloride	3	osmoregulation, electrochemical equilibria and enzyme regulation, e.g. in photosystem II
iron (Fe)	Fe^{2+} (Fe^{3+})	2	component of redox systems: electron carriers, enzymes, e.g. cytochromes, catalases; also needed for protein synthesis
boron (B)	H_3BO_3 boric acid or BO_3^{3-} borate	2	precise function uncertain, but seems to play role in cell elongation, nucleic acid synthesis and membrane function
manganese (Mn)	Mn^{2+}	1	role in photosystem II; component of the antioxidant superoxide dismutase

zinc (Zn)	Zn^{2+}	0.3	component of enzymes, e.g. carbonic anhydrase
copper (Cu)	Cu^{+} (Cu^{2+})	0.1	component of plastocyanin, role in electron transfer
molybdenum (Mo)	MoO_4^{2-} molybdate	1×10^{-3}	component of nitrate reductase and so has a key role in nitrogen metabolism
sodium (Na)	Na^{+}	variable	essential in a few, but not all, plants and requirements never as high as in animals
silicon (Si)	SiO_3^{2-} silicate	variable	essential in some, e.g. grasses, as cell wall component, but not all plants
nickel (Ni)	Ni^{2+}	variable	essential in some, but not all, plants

❍ Which of the elements listed in Table 4.1 as essential to all plants are absorbed as cations (positively charged) and which as anions (negatively charged)? Are there any atypical elements?

● K, Ca, Mg, Fe, Mn, Zn and Cu are absorbed as cations. P, S, Cl, B and Mo are absorbed as anions; N can be taken-up as either cationic NH_4^{+} or anionic NO_3^{-}.

Plants need to have just the right amounts of these elements in just the right places within their cells, tissues and organs if they are to flourish. Too much or too little of these nutrients and the plant may suffer toxic effects or deficiency. Certain forms of mineral toxicity are of global importance, and are discussed later in the chapter (see Sections 4.6.1–4.6.3). Table 4.2 (overleaf) lists some symptoms that plants may exhibit if they lack adequate supplies of particular elements.

❍ Look at Table 4.2 and list the nutrient deficiencies a plant may be suffering from if it displays some signs of chlorosis (yellowing of the leaves).

● It may be suffering from a deficiency of any of the following mineral nutrients: N, Mg, K, Mn, S or Fe.

It follows that plants need mechanisms for locating, taking up, distributing and regulating the levels of mineral elements within their tissues. Just how plants achieve such selectivity is the subject of Sections 4.2–4.5.

Environments differ too. Consequently, evolution has generated species and locally adapted populations (**ecotypes**) in which these basic systems are adjusted to suit local conditions. Examples of these adaptations are mentioned throughout the chapter, but Section 4.6 deals with three examples of adaptation to potentially toxic concentrations of minerals in the soil, which are of both global significance and largely anthropogenic (i.e. caused by humans), namely toxicity resulting from metal extraction, excess salinity from irrigation, and aluminium toxicity from acid precipitation. Section 4.7 then goes on to discuss how this naturally occurring variation may be exploited to improve both agricultural efficiency and sustainability as well as facilitating the restoration of degraded areas.

Table 4.2 Symptoms observed in flowering plants suffering from deficiencies of specific mineral nutrients.

Element deficient	Symptoms
	Effects generalized over whole plant, but older and lower leaves most affected; symptoms include drying of lower leaves
N	Plant light green; lower leaves yellow, drying to light brown colour; stalks short and slender if element is deficient in later stages of growth
P	Plant dark green, often developing red and purple colours; stalks short and slender if element is deficient in later stages of growth
	Effects mostly localized, with older and lower leaves most affected; symptoms include mottling, but minimal drying of lower leaves
Mg	Mottled or chlorotic (yellowing) leaves, typically may redden; sometimes with dead spots; tips and margins turned or cupped upward; stalks slender
K	Mottled or chlorotic leaves with small spots of dead tissue, usually at tips and between veins especially at the margins of leaves; stalks slender
Zn	Dead spots generalized, rapidly enlarging, generally between veins; leaves thick; stalks with shortened internodes
	Newer or bud leaves affected; symptoms localized; terminal bud dies following distortions at tips or bases of young leaves
Ca	Young leaves of terminal bud at first hooked, then dying back at tips and margins; stalk at terminal bud dies last
B	Young leaves of terminal bud become light green at bases; in later growth, leaves become twisted; stalk finally dies back at terminal bud
	Newer or bud leaves affected; symptoms localized; terminal bud survives
Cu	Young leaves permanently wilted without spotting or chlorosis; twig or stalk just below tip and seedhead often wilt in later stages
Mn	Young leaves not wilted; chlorosis with spots of dead tissue scattered over the leaf; smallest veins remain green producing a checkered or net-like effect
S	Young leaves not wilted; chlorosis causes young leaves to be entirely light green; dead spots sparse or absent
Fe	Young leaves not wilted, but they are chlorotic, although principal veins remain green; stalks short and slender, dead spots sparse or absent

SUMMARY OF SECTION 4.1

1 Mineral nutrients are obtained from solutions surrounding the plants' absorptive surfaces (usually the roots).

2 Thirteen elements are known to be essential to all plants. Of these, six are called macronutrients and are required in relatively large quantities, and seven are called micronutrients and are required in relatively small quantities by all plants.

3 Plants suffer deficiency symptoms if the supply of one or more of the nutrients is inadequate.

4 Excessive quantities of the micronutrients can be toxic to certain plants.

4.2 MINERAL NUTRIENT UPTAKE

Ions can be absorbed over the whole surface of submerged plants (such as pondweeds) and of non-vascular plants (bryophytes). However, for most vascular plants ion uptake is largely confined to the roots, where ions are absorbed along with water from the dilute solution that surrounds soil particles. It is true that small amounts of ions can be absorbed from rainwater by leaves (**foliar feeding**, i.e. the spraying leaves with a solution of fertilizer, depends on this absorption route) but, in general, the action starts in the roots. The question asked here is: how do ions move from the soil solution to the growing parts of the shoot, where there is a high demand for mineral nutrients?

To reach the growing tip of a shoot, a mineral element must first cross the root, radially, from the epidermis to the stele (Figure 4.1), and then move upwards to the shoot in the conducting cells of the xylem.

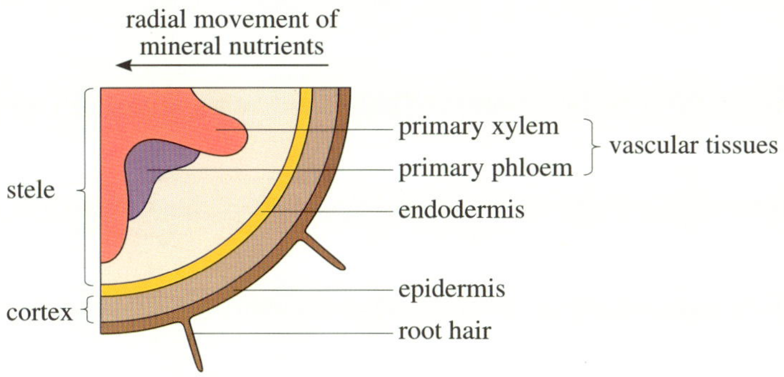

Figure 4.1 Part of a transverse section (TS) of a herbaceous root showing the radial movement of mineral nutrients from the external solution towards the vascular tissue.

4.2.1 APOPLASTIC TRANSPORT

Ions first enter the root by diffusing into the apoplast of the root cortex (Chapter 3). Structurally, cell walls can be likened to wicker baskets, in that they provide strength and rigidity even though the weave is full of holes. The spaces between the fibres in the cell wall have a maximum diameter of around 5 nm, which is big enough to let low molecular mass solutes such as K^+ and Ca^{2+} ions, sucrose, amino acids and organic acids, pass between them. The solutes do not all move at the same speed: the pectic materials in the walls carry an array of fixed negative charges (due to the dissociation of carboxylic acid), therefore cations can move more readily into the apoplast than anions such as NO_3^- and particularly SO_4^{2-}, which are repelled and so diffuse much more slowly than cations. However, cations such as K^+ and Ca^{2+} cannot pass entirely freely through the spaces within the cell walls because the carboxylate groups act as cation exchangers, i.e. they bind cations reversibly. Within the cell walls, the apparent free space is divided into the **water free space (WFS)**, which is freely accessible to ions and uncharged molecules, and the **Donnan free space (DFS),** where cation exchange and anion repulsion take place. Ion distribution within the DFS is similar to that which occurs in soils at the surfaces of negatively charged clay particles (Section 4.2.4). Divalent cations such as Ca^{2+} are preferentially bound to these cation exchange sites and so diffuse more slowly than monovalent cations. However, high molecular mass solutes (such as metal compounds, organic toxins, viruses and other pathogens) are too big to pass through the gaps between the fibres and so are excluded from the cell walls.

The main barrier to solute movement in the apoplast of roots is the endodermis, the innermost layer of cells of the cortex.

- ❍ From your knowledge of endodermal structure from Chapters 1 and 3, why does the endodermis pose a problem for apoplastic transport?

- ● The endodermal cell wall develops a suberized band, the Casparian strip, running right round the cell.This strip constitutes an effective barrier to the passive movement of solutes into the stele through the apoplast.

The plasma membrane of the endodermal cell becomes very firmly attached to the Casparian strip by special proteins, which bridge the wall and the membrane (Figure 4.2) (Clarkson, 1993). This attachment is a crucial feature of endodermal design. It ensures that material passing from cortex to stele must cross a membrane. Only by this means can uptake become selective. However, calcium is a special case, in that the path followed is primarily apoplastic (see Section 4.2.2 below).

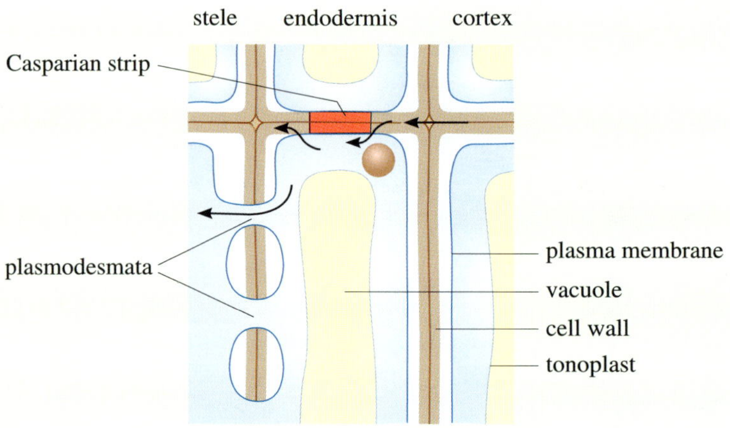

Figure 4.2 A partly plasmolysed cell illustrates the attachment of the plasma membrane and the Casparian strip. The cell is connected to its neighbours by plasmodesmata. Black arrows show how solutes moving along cell walls are diverted into the cytoplasm by the Casparian strip.

4.2.2 CROSSING CELL MEMBRANES

In most situations, there is a considerable difference between the mineral nutrient content of the external solutions and the mineral nutrient requirements of the plant cells. Therefore, *nutrient uptake by plant cells must be selective*. This principle of **ion selectivity** is illustrated in Figure 4.3 for giant cells of the protoctist alga *Hydrodictyon*. The size of these cells makes them easy to study using ion-selective microelectrodes. By inserting the electrodes into different cell compartments the concentration of specific ions can be quantified.

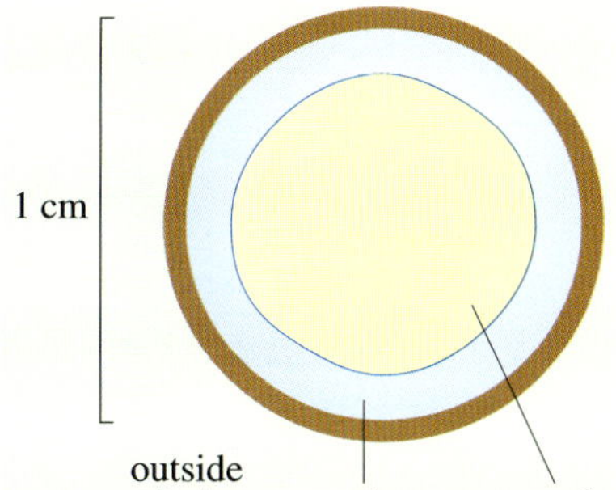

	outside solution	cytoplasm	vacuole
[K^+]	0.1	93	40
[Na^+]	1.0	51	17
[Cl^-]	1.3	58	38

Figure 4.3 A giant algal cell (*Hydrodictyon*) showing values for ion concentrations, measured as mmol l^{-1}, in different cell compartments and in the external solution.

❍ Are the ions listed in Figure 4.3 present in the cytoplasm of *Hydrodictyon* in the same proportions as they are in the external solution?

● No, in the external solution the order of abundance is $Cl^- > Na^+ > K^+$, in the cytoplasm the order is $K^+ > Cl^- > Na^+$.

It should be noted that *Hydrodictyon* can grow in brackish waters and probably 'needs' Na^+ as an osmoticum. Most land plants are selective in excluding Na^+ much more effectively than this alga does (see Section 4.6.2). This example also illustrates another characteristic of ion uptake, namely that of **accumulation**. The concentration of mineral elements can be much higher in the plant cell sap than in the external solution. The concentrations of the ions K^+, Na^+ and Cl^- are many times higher (from 50 to 1000 times) in the cytoplasm of *Hydrodictyon* than in the external solution. The data in Figure 4.3 also illustrate a third important phenomenon.

❍ Are the ions listed in Figure 4.3 at the same concentration in the vacuole as they are in the cytoplasm?

● No, all three — K^+, Na^+ and Cl^- — are more concentrated in the cytoplasm (between 1.5 and 3 times more) than in the vacuole.

This ability to maintain different concentrations of elements in different cell compartments (compartmentation) is important, and will be returned to in later sections.

It is generally agreed that such selectivity and accumulation require both *specific binding sites* and an *energy supply* to provide a driving force (although it should be remembered that not all ions require active transport into the cell: passive, facilitated diffusion of ions into cells via transport proteins (**uniports**) is quite common). The principal site for selective, active uptake of cations, anions and other solutes is in the plasma membrane of individual cells. The various mechanisms of membrane transport are dealt with in some detail in Swithenby and O'Shea (2001). However, plants differ from animals in some important ways that are explained below.

MECHANISMS OF MEMBRANE TRANSPORT: GENERATING THE DRIVING FORCE

Primary active transport generates an overall electrochemical potential gradient which then drives the uptake of other ions via ion-specific transport proteins (carriers and channels) to which the primary pumps are coupled (secondary active transport). Animal cells utilize the sodium pump and, to a lesser extent, proton pumps in the form of H^+-ATPases for primary active transport (Swithenby and O'Shea, 2001).

In marked contrast to animals, *vascular plants* apparently possess *no primary active Na^+ transport*. Instead, like fungi and bacteria, it is mainly the activity of the *proton pump* that powers the movement of solutes across membranes (pump 1, Figure 4.4). Plants also differ from animals in their possession of a large, fluid-filled vacuole, the membrane of which (tonoplast) also possesses mechanisms for primary and secondary active transport. At the tonoplast, primary active transport occurs via one of *two distinct proton pumps*: an H^+-ATPase (pump 2, Figure 4.4, which is very different from the one in the plasma membrane) and an inorganic phosphatase, **H^+-PP_iase** (pump 3, Figure 4.4: PP_i stands for inorganic pyrophosphate, in which phosphate ions are linked together in pairs; PP_i is produced when ATP is converted into AMP). The energy for H^+ pumping comes from the conversion of the pyrophosphate dimer to two phosphate momomers. The proton pumps in plasma membranes and tonoplasts pump H^+ into the apoplast and vacuole, respectively.

- ❍ What effect does this pumping have on the charge balance and pH of the cytoplasm relative to the vacuolar and external solutions?

- ● The movement of H^+ out of the cytoplasm into the vacuole or out of the cell makes the cytoplasm relatively more negatively charged and more alkaline than the neighbouring compartments. (As a rule, the pH of the cytoplasm is 7.3–7.6, the vacuole 4.5–5.9 and the apoplast about 5.5.)

These gradients of charge and pH produce the electrochemical potential gradient that drives the movement of other solutes across membranes in secondary active transport.

Figure 4.4 also illustrates another form of primary active transport (pump 4); one that is driven by electron transport (as occurs in photosynthetic and respiratory electron transport) rather than phosphate ions. As Figure 4.4 suggests, there is some evidence that proton pumping out of plant cells, including roots, may be linked to an electron transport chain in the plasma membrane that is commonly referred to as a **transmembrane redox pump**. This system may also be involved in the uptake of iron. In most soils, dissolved iron is present as Fe^{3+}, but it is taken up by roots as Fe^{2+}. What happens is that a reducing agent, released at the root surface, converts Fe^{3+} into Fe^{2+}. Thus, Fe^{3+} could serve as the terminal electron acceptor for the chain, becoming reduced to Fe^{2+} when it does so. A model indicating how both proton secretion from roots, and Fe^{3+} reduction may be linked to a transmembrane redox pump is shown in Figure 4.5.

The only other ions that may undergo primary active transport in vascular plants are Ca^{2+} and Cl^-, but these ions are pumped *out* of the cytoplasm, not *in* (see below for the special case of calcium).

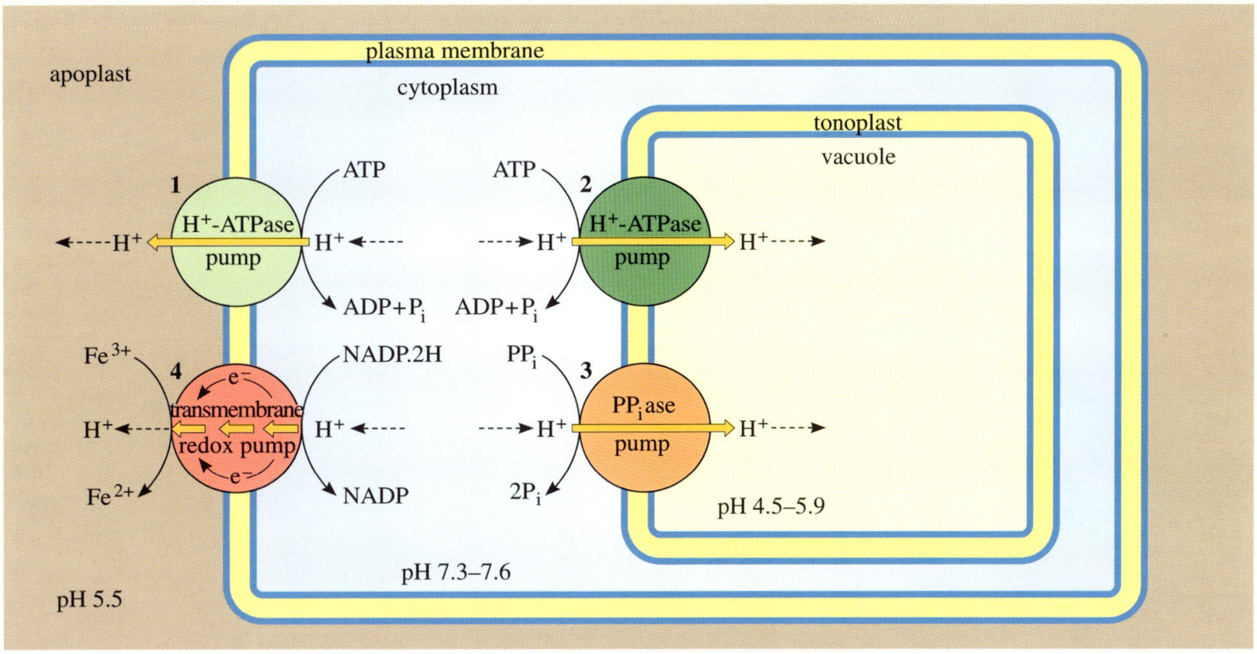

Figure 4.4 A model for the location and functioning of proton pumps and transmembrane redox pumps involved in primary active transport in plant cells. See the text for details of the different types of pump.

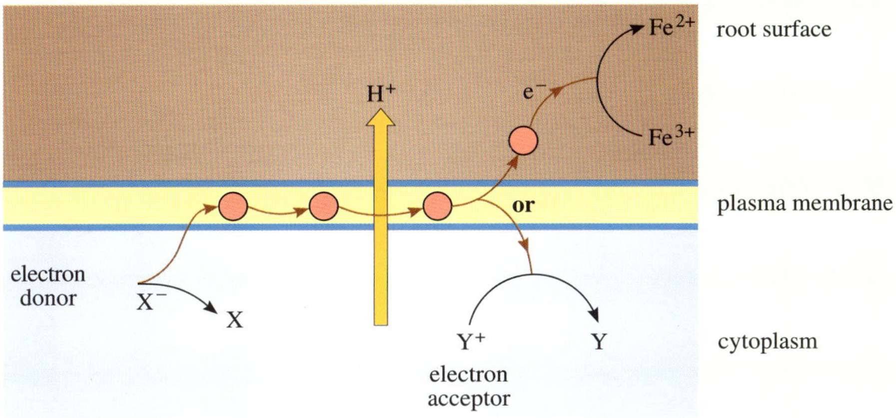

Figure 4.5 A model for the transmembrane redox pump in the plasma membrane of plant root cells, linked to proton secretion and iron reduction. Reduction of Fe^{3+}, is shown as a possible alternative to reduction of an intracellular substrate, Y^+.

SECONDARY ACTIVE TRANSPORT: SELECTIVE PASSAGE THROUGH MEMBRANES

Secondary active transport occurs via membrane proteins that have properties which place them somewhere along a continuum between ion carriers and ion channels.

In ion carriers, the transported substance binds initially to a specific site on the protein. This causes a conformational change in the protein, which exposes the substance to the solution on the other side of the membrane. Transport is complete when the substance dissociates from the protein's binding site. This form of transport can be active or passive.

In ion channels, the proteins function as selective pores in the membrane. The size of a pore and the density of surface charges on its interior lining determine its transport specificity. The transporters have 'gates' that open and close the pore in response to external signals. Transport through the membrane by this means is always passive and up to a million times faster than transport by ion carriers.

Membrane proteins with channel-like properties are a relatively new discovery in plant cell membranes, even though they have been known in animal cells since the 1930s. In addition to a role in ion uptake, they play an important part in Ca^{2+} signalling and the operation of guard cells. They also appear to have a role in ion loading into the xylem (see Section 4.2.4), phosphate uptake in mycorrhizal associations (see Section 4.5.3) and organic acid efflux (see Section 4.6.3).

Although a particular transport protein is usually specific for the kinds of substances it transports, under some circumstances it can transport related substances. For example, in plants, a K^+ transporter on the plasma membrane may transport Rb^+ (rubidium) and Na^+ in addition to K^+, but K^+ is usually preferred. However, this imperfect selectivity does not normally cause problems unless the competing ions are unusually abundant in the environment, such as occurs in saline conditions (see Section 4.6.2)

These transport proteins can act as uniports, symports or antiports.

❍ Which of the three transport proteins in Figure 4.6 is operating as a symport, which an antiport and which a uniport?

● A is a symport: the passive flow of H^+ ions is coupled to the active movement of substrate A in the *same* direction, but against its own electrochemical potential gradient. B is a uniport: the solute moves *passively* down its own electrochemical potential gradient. C is an antiport, in which the passive movement of H^+ ions is coupled to the pumping of another solute in the *opposite* direction but against its own electrochemical potential gradient.

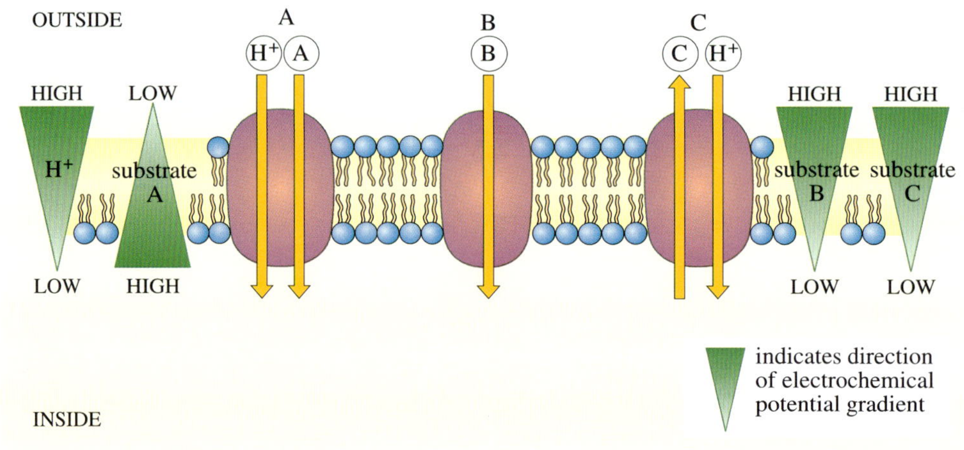

Figure 4.6 Model for movement of solutes through plant membranes. (A) The energy dissipated by a proton moving back into the cell is coupled to the uptake of one molecule of a substrate (e.g. a sugar) into the cell. (B) A membrane protein allows a substance to cross the membrane in the direction from high to low concentration, i.e. down its concentration gradient, and without any input of energy. (C) The energy dissipated by a proton moving back into the cell is coupled to the active transport of a substrate (e.g. Na^+), out of the cell. In (A) and (C), the substrate under consideration is moving against its gradient of electrochemical potential.

SOLUTE UPTAKE

Most cations diffuse into the root cell via specific ion channels operating as uniports. However, this system does not work for K^+ at low external concentrations, because it would operate against a strong concentration gradient. Thus, an *active* 'high-affinity K^+ uptake system' is required and probably takes the form of an active symporter. Other solutes such as Cl^-, NO_3^- and $H_2PO_4^-$ (Table 4.1), amino acids and sugars appear to enter the cell (down a charge gradient) via specific proton symporters. Figure 4.7 shows results from a glucose-uptake experiment that provide evidence for this last conclusion.

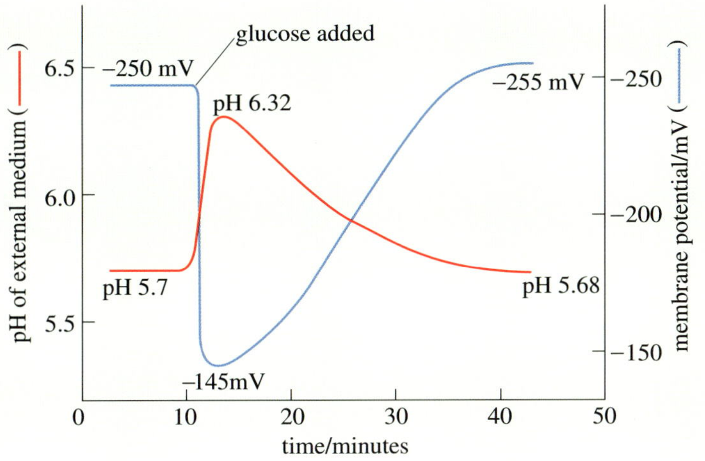

Figure 4.7 Evidence for a glucose–proton symport is shown by simultaneous measurements of the pH of the medium that bathes the surface of the aquatic plant duck-weed (*Lemna gibba*) and the membrane potential of one cell. The early portions of the curves show steady values of pH and membrane potential, conditions that change when 50 mmol l^{-1} glucose is added to the solution. Data from Novacky *et al.* (1980).

- ❍ What happened to the membrane potential and external pH when glucose was supplied to and taken up by the plant cells (that were bathed in a simple solution of mineral salts)?

- ● There was a simultaneous reduction in membrane potential and an increase in external pH.

The observed increase in pH indicates that protons are disappearing from the medium at the same time that the membrane potential of the cell is decreasing. The decrease in membrane potential is due to the positive charges (H^+) that move into the cell along with glucose. These observations are predicted by a glucose–proton symport if glucose is cotransported with a proton into the cell. The membrane depolarization was short-lived, however, because the reduced membrane voltage allowed the H^+ pump to work faster and thereby restored the membrane voltage and pH gradient in the presence of continuing glucose uptake.

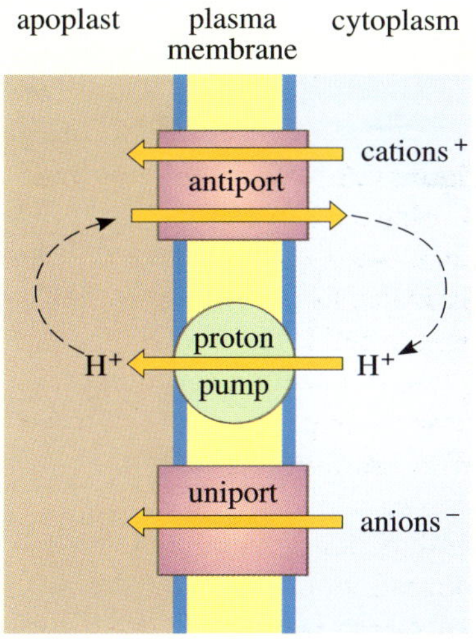

Figure 4.8 A model for the export of mineral nutrients via transport proteins in the plasma membrane of plant roots. Note that the solutes are transported against their own concentration gradient only in the case of the antiport.

ION EXPORT

Cations are exported from cells via antiports. This mechanism enables salt-resistant plants to get rid of unwanted sodium ions in saline conditions. Anions diffuse from the cell into the surroundings, down their own potential gradient, i.e. by anion uniport (see Figure 4.8).

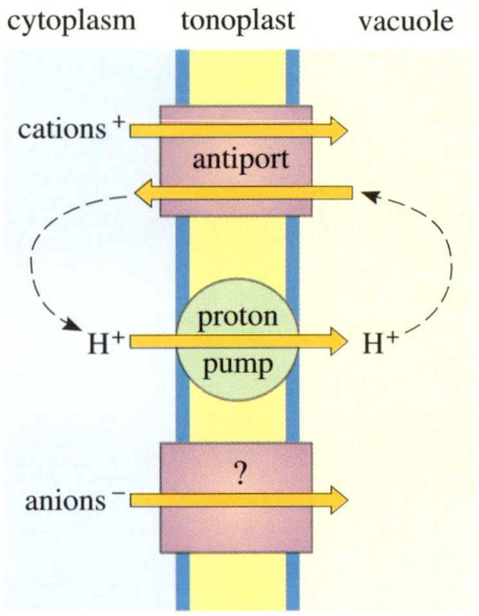

Figure 4.9 A model for the movement of ions into the vacuole via transport proteins in the tonoplast of plant cells. Note that the cations are actively transported against their own concentration gradient but the anions may be moving passively down a charge gradient.

THE ROLE OF THE TONOPLAST

Controlled movement of cations into the vacuole via antiports is important for both turgor regulation through high vacuolar K^+ concentrations, and also the maintenance of low cytosolic concentrations of Na^+ and Ca^{2+}. It is not yet certain how anions enter the vacuole, but they may follow their own electrochemical gradient as the vacuole is positively charged relative to the cytoplasm (see Figure 4.9).

CALCIUM: A SPECIAL CASE

Calcium is an extremely abundant element in soils, indeed, it is unusual in that it is one of the few ions present in the environment at higher concentrations than in the plant tissues. Powerful homeostatic mechanisms operate to keep cytosolic concentrations of Ca^{2+} low, because it can be toxic; even small fluctuations in cytosolic Ca^{2+} concentration drastically alter the activities of many enzymes. Ca^{2+}-ATPases pump calcium out of the cytoplasm into the cell wall (a primary active transport system) and a H^+/Ca^{2+} antiport causes movement of Ca^{2+} into the vacuole (a secondary active transport system) (Figure 4.10). Thus very little Ca^{2+} moves across the cortex in the cytoplasm; instead it moves passively by diffusion along its own concentration gradient via the apoplast (i.e. within the cell wall).

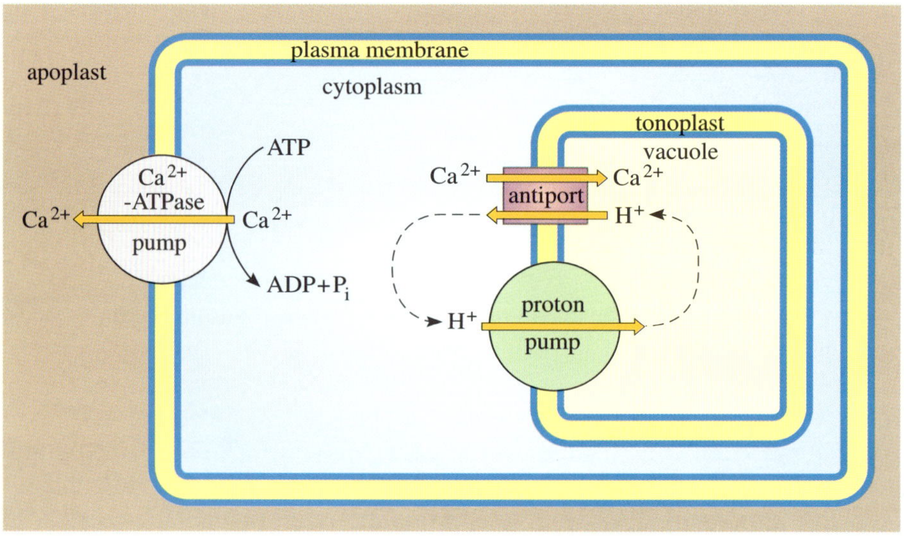

Figure 4.10 A model showing the export of Ca^{2+} from the cytoplasm via both a primary calcium pump into the apoplast and a secondary antiport into the vacuole.

Quite how the Ca^{2+} ions negotiate the endodermis and its Casparian strip is not entirely certain: perhaps Ca^{2+} enters the endodermal cytoplasm on the cortical side and is pumped out into the cell wall on the other side, a kind of symplast loop, or maybe Ca^{2+} moves across in the apoplast in the few regions where there is no 'waterproofing' of the endodermal wall, i.e. close to the root tip or where secondary roots grow out. Either way Ca^{2+} uptake and transport to the xylem are relatively insensitive to inhibitors of respiration compared with ions transported in the symplast, which suggests that calcium uptake is primarily passive. However, despite its toxicity, Ca^{2+} plays a very important role within the cell. It is hugely important in primary cell wall structure, where it is required in macronutrient quantities, a paradox that the plant struggles to solve, not always successfully. Hence, Ca-deficiency disorders are amongst the most common maladies in horticultural crops. Calcium also has a key role in signal transduction within cells. Perhaps the very mechanisms that permit the tight control over its intracellular distribution predispose it to a role as a second messenger.

4.2.3 Transport within the cytoplasm

Once nutrients have crossed the plasma membrane and entered the cytoplasm of the cortical cells in the root, the ions then move across the cortex by diffusion through the symplast, and may equilibrate with reservoirs of ions accumulated in cell vacuoles.

❍ From Section 3.2.1, what structures enable substances to be transported from cell to cell across the cortex without moving out of the cytoplasm or crossing a plasma membrane?

● Movement occurs from cell to cell via the *plasmodesmata* — the narrow channels containing cytoplasm and lined by the plasma membrane — that cross cell walls (see Figure 4.2).

Some mineral nutrients may remain in the plant in an unchanged state (e.g. K^+, Na^+, Cl^-) while others are incorporated directly into organic molecules after transport to their final destination (e.g. phosphate, iron, Ca^{2+}). However, the utilization of nitrogen and sulfur depends on chemical reduction and assimilation into organic molecules, i.e. they must be metabolized, just as carbon is metabolized when fixed in photosynthesis. The reduction reactions for nitrate and sulfate are energetically very expensive. Only plants and certain microbes perform these reactions and so are able to survive with entirely inorganic sources of nitrogen and sulfur. Other organisms must obtain pre-metabolized N and S in organic compounds, either from their food or from symbiotic microbes in their guts.

4.2.4 Release of ions into the xylem

Once ions have crossed the plasma membrane and entered cells near the root surface, some remain and are used there, or are shunted into the vacuole, but the majority move on; they cross the cortex in the symplast and eventually enter the lignified conducting elements of the xylem. This release into fully differentiated non-living xylem vessels represents a retransfer from the symplast into the apoplast. There is still uncertainty about how the ions are loaded into the xylem vessels, but current evidence suggests that after active uptake of ions from the apoplast near the root surface or nearer to the endodermis, ions move passively across the root and then, similar to guard cells at closing, ions are released into the xylem sap through ion transport proteins (Figure 4.11, overleaf).

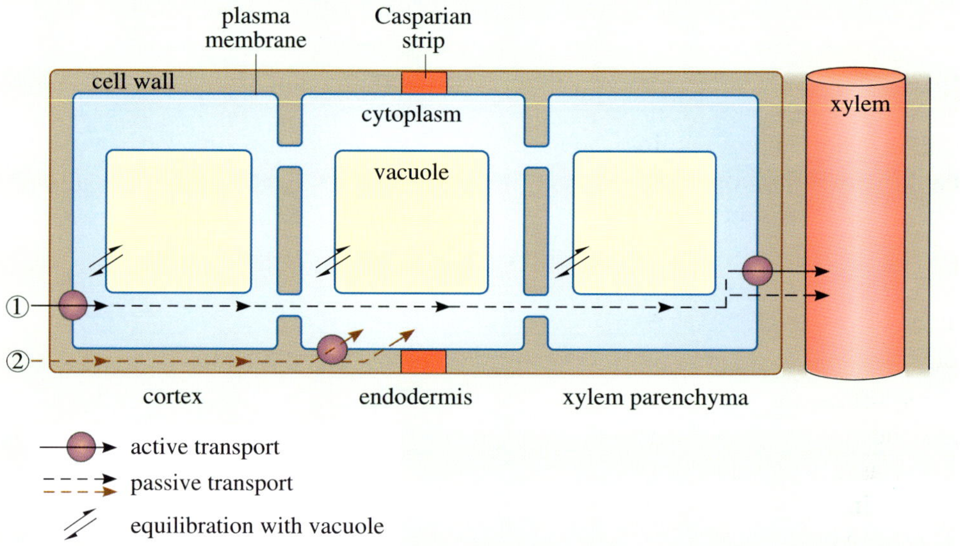

Figure 4.11 A model for symplastic (1) and apoplastic (2) pathways of radial transport of ions across the root and into the xylem vessels.

Details of the mechanism are currently under intensive investigation. Ions do not 'leak' into the xylem vessels. Instead, the transfer is under tight metabolic control through regulation of the plasma membrane H^+-ATPase and/or ion efflux channels. The ion movements through the membrane are regulated by both the membrane potential and the cytosolic calcium concentration. There is general agreement that xylem loading is regulated separately from the ion uptake in cortical cells, which has important implications for the control and regulation of transport (see Section 4.4.1).

It does not follow that the biochemical apparatus for mineral uptake necessarily determines the rate at which a whole plant absorbs mineral elements from the soil. Net uptake of nutrients depends on numerous other factors, including environmental availability, internal demand and the capacity of the plant to forage for nutrients. These factors are the subjects of the next three sections.

SUMMARY OF SECTION 4.2

1. The Casparian strip of the endodermis blocks diffusion of ions through the apoplast in both directions, i.e. into and out of the root.
2. Therefore, with the possible exception of calcium, the uptake of ions into roots requires ions to cross the plasma membrane of at least one root cell.
3. It is at this step that selectivity of the absorption process operates.
4. Selective membrane transport needs a supply of energy, e.g. proton-pumping ATPases (primary active pumps), and ion-specific carriers (for secondary active transport).
5. The number and distribution of these carriers largely determine which ions get in where.
6. Transport to the shoot requires the same sort of factors operating in the xylem parenchyma adjacent to conducting cells.
7. Within the symplast, nutrients move from cell to cell via plasmodesmata.

4.3 AVAILABILITY OF IONS

Common sense suggests that the internal concentration of elements in plants must be influenced by their availability in the soil. However, the absolute concentration of a mineral element within the soil is a poor indicator of how available it is to plants. The availability of individual nutrients is affected by several factors related to the chemical and physical environment, and the pH of the soil is one of the most important.

4.3.1 PH OF THE SOIL

Soil pH is determined by the concentration of hydrogen ions in the soil solution, which is affected by the relative abundance of basic cations, i.e. ions of the alkaline earth and alkali metals such as Ca^{2+}, Mg^{2+}, Na^+ and K^+. Soils rich in these basic cations have higher pH values than those with lower levels. Water, percolating down through the soil, tends to take the basic cations with it, leaving H^+ ions in their place.

❍ Would you expect areas of high rainfall to have higher or lower soil pH values than areas of low rainfall, if all other things were equal?

● High rainfall areas would be expected to have lower soil pH values because, as soils are progressively leached by the rainwater, basic cations are replaced by H^+ and are lost.

Areas with low rainfall would have high pH

Particles of organic matter and especially clay possess many negative surface charges, to which cations are attracted. Clay particles greatly influence the physical and chemical properties of soil. Clay minerals have a crystalline structure composed of several plate-like layers (Figure 4.12), and, in some, these plates may move apart in the presence of water to expose their internal surfaces.

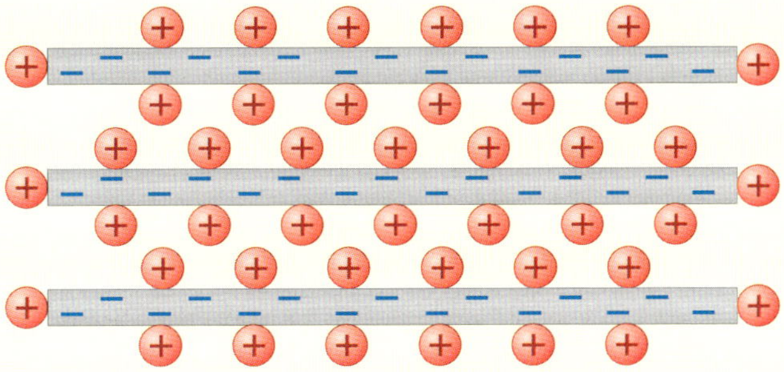

Figure 4.12 Diagrammatic representation of the plate structure of clay minerals. The silicate layers of the clay minerals are negatively charged and surrounded by the layer of exchangeable cations which include H^+, K^+, Na^+, Ca^{2+} and Mg^{2+}.

The presence of these negatively charged particles affects the distribution of ions in the soil solution. Cations such as H^+, K^+, Na^+, Ca^{2+} and Mg^{2+} are attracted to the particle surfaces and form a layer of positive charges around them; together this arrangement is known as the **electric double layer**. Low-valency cations are less strongly held by the particles than high valency ones, but all of them can be exchanged with other charged soil components, including the soil solution. Anions in the soil solution, e.g. Cl^-, NO_3^-, etc. are repelled by the clay particles. However, sand is largely uncharged, and so sandy soils are more readily leached than clay soils. This has implications for soil fertility.

❍ In the light of this observation, would you expect sandy soils to be generally more or less fertile than clay soils?

● Sandy soils would tend to be less fertile, because they are more readily stripped of their basic cations. However, clay soils are susceptible to loss of anions such as NO_3^- by leaching.

Gardeners know that sandy soils are generally less fertile, more rapidly exhausted by successive crops and more acidic than clay soils, and are well aware that the addition of compost and manure to soils not only adds nutrients, but improves their nutrient retention properties. The pH of the soil can affect ion availability in a number of ways, for example, if present in particular combinations, some ions can precipitate out of solution as insoluble salts, which makes them unavailable to plants, e.g. phosphates of iron or aluminium. Alternatively, some elements can be present in the soil in several ionic forms, but often only one of these is readily taken up by roots, e.g. iron and phosphorus. Furthermore, the form most readily absorbed may change as the pH changes. For example, N exists as both NO_3^- and NH_4^+ in the soil but at low pH values NH_4^+ is more readily available to plants, while NO_3^- is more easily absorbed at higher pH values.

Figure 4.13 shows how the availability of nutrients changes with the pH of the soil.

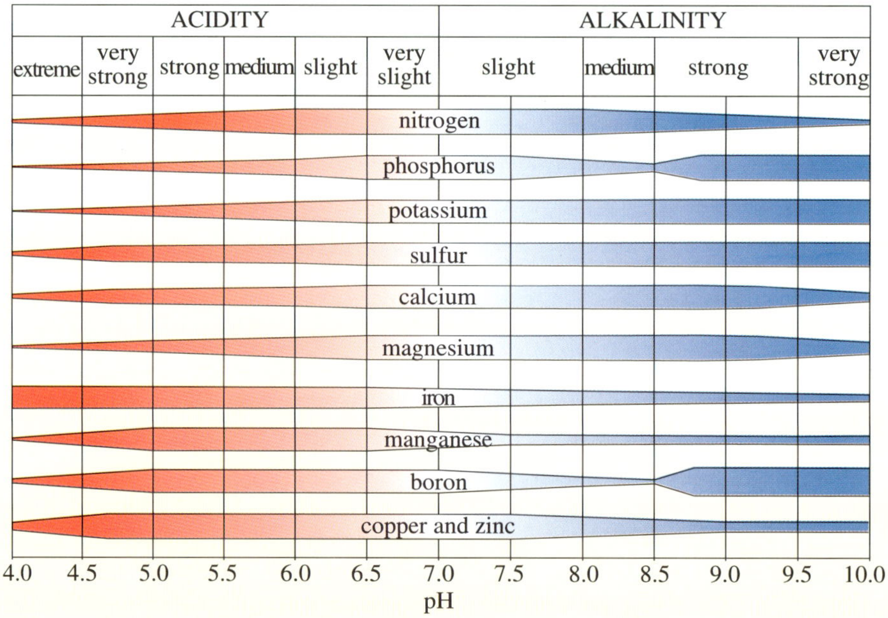

Figure 4.13 The relationship between the pH of the soil and the availability of mineral nutrients: the wider the bar, the greater the availability.

- ❍ Which macronutrient and which micronutrients are most likely to be in short supply on moderately alkaline soils?

- ● The macronutrient phosphorus and the micronutrients iron, manganese, boron, copper and zinc.

The ecological distribution of many plants is strongly influenced by soil pH. Most plants are adapted to grow well at around pH 6.5, at which most essential elements are readily available. If the pH rises above 7.5, as it does in soils overlying chalk and limestone, then elements such as P, Fe, Mn, B and Zn become relatively unavailable and so there is a potential for deficiency. At pH values below 6.0, these same micronutrients may reach toxic concentrations, and Ca, Mg and P can become unavailable. Acid conditions are typically found in the peaty or heavily leached soils overlying quartz-rich rocks such as granite, e.g. on Dartmoor. At acid pH, aluminium toxicity can become a serious problem too. This element is not an essential nutrient, but is one of the most abundant in the Earth's crust. Aluminium toxicity seriously limits the agricultural potential of acid soils, a problem that is being exacerbated by the increase in acid precipitation (the so-called acid rain). This problem is discussed in detail in Section 4.6.3.

Plants adapted for growth on calcareous soils are known as **calcicoles** (lime-lovers), e.g. cowslip (*Primula veris*) and rock-rose (*Helianthemum nummularium*). They are often capable of surviving on acid soils, but do not grow well, possibly because they are particularly susceptible to the deficiency of major nutrients and/or toxicity by micronutrients. Conversely, plants adapted for growth on acid soils are known as **calcifuges** (lime-haters) and include species typical of upland moors and sandy heaths such as bilberry *(Vaccinium myrtillus)*, heathers (e.g. *Calluna vulgaris* and *Erica cinerea*) and *Rhododendron* spp.

These plants are adapted to withstand aluminium toxicity but, if they are grown on alkaline soils, they commonly show severe yellowing, called **lime chlorosis**, which is caused by a deficiency of iron. This condition may be linked to the fact that aluminium is thought to enter plants either via magnesium channels or, in grasses, via the iron-transport system. If Fe is in short supply, grasses release non-protein-forming amino acids, called **phytosiderophores**, that form stable complexes with Fe^{3+}. These complexes are then taken up into the root cells via specific transporters in the plasma membrane. Thus, if calcicoles protect themselves from Al^{3+} by lowering the number of potential uptake sites, they may be particularly susceptible to Mg or Fe deficiency (both of which would lead to chlorosis), when Fe and Mg become less available at higher pH. This theory may also work in reverse to explain why calcicoles are very susceptible to metal toxicity when grown in acid conditions. However, a second theory cites NH_4^+ toxicity as a prime reason for the poor performance of calcicoles on acid soils, and the influence of this factor should not be ignored.

4.4 Regulation of internal concentrations of mineral nutrients

While the nutrient content of plants may be greatly affected by their availability in soil, plants can regulate their own internal mineral content to some extent. At the cellular and tissue levels, key locations for regulation are the cell membranes, where ion movements are under active control. This **intracellular regulation** involves the transport proteins in the cell membranes (see Section 4.4.1). However, the regulatory system can affect events at the root system level too; plants can adopt strategies that optimize exposure of the roots to the mineral elements, depending upon local conditions. These strategies can include:

- mechanisms that change the availability of ions in the soil;
- changes to root architecture;
- symbiotic associations with microbes and other plants.

These strategies for optimizing the acquisition of mineral elements, that involve extracellular events and the root system as a whole, are customarily grouped together under the term **nutrient foraging** (see Section 4.5), to distinguish them from intracellular regulation.

4.4.1 Intracellular regulation

Plants possess feedback mechanisms that regulate the net rate of uptake of many mineral nutrients, and these are summarized in Figure 4.14.

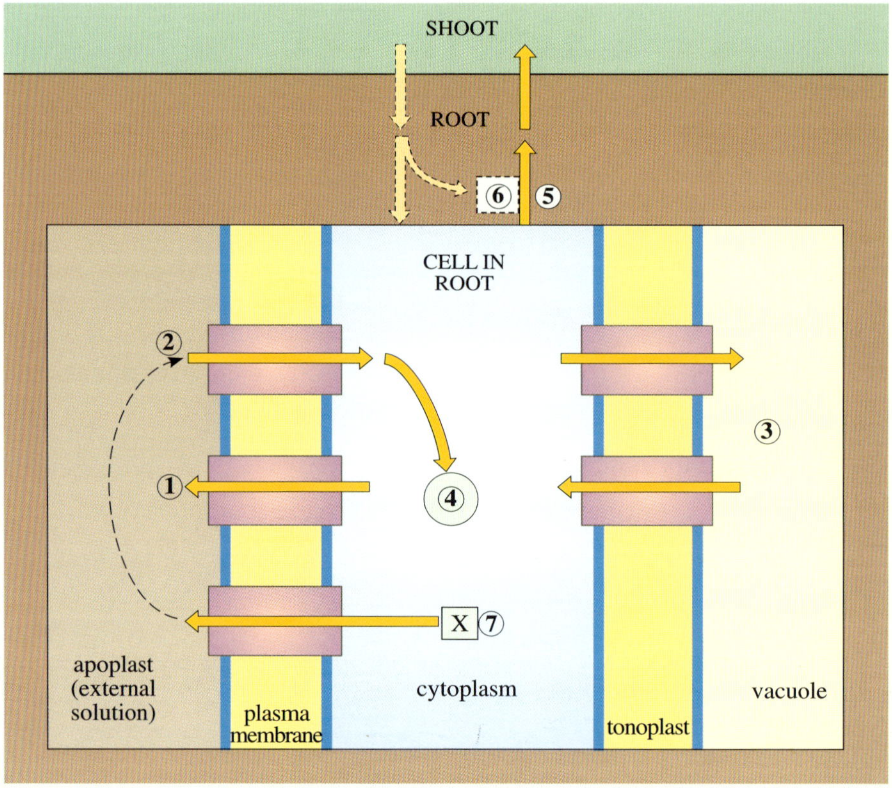

Figure 4.14 A model of internal feedback regulation mechanisms on ion uptake by roots at cellular, tissue and whole root level: (1) efflux, (2) influx, (3) vacuolar concentration, (4) transformation and incorporation into the cytoplasm, (5) xylem transport to the shoot, (6) feedback regulation from the shoot, (7) nutrient deficiency/toxicity — enhanced exudation of organic solutes, X (e.g. organic acids).

The net rate of uptake of an element is determined by the balance between *influx* and *efflux* (i.e. the rate of movement into or out of the cell, tissue or root concerned). When plants are deprived of nutrients, the net rate of uptake can be increased by either decreasing the efflux (1), or increasing the influx (2) (which is probably the more important of the two). Experiments have shown that, when plants are deprived of P, K or S for a few days, there is often an increase in the number of carrier proteins (probably resulting from increased expression of the genes that encode them), rather than an increase in their affinity for the ions, although changes in the affinity of the carriers for the ions is not unknown. The response induced by nutrient deprivation requires additional protein synthesis. Figure 4.15 shows what happens to both sulfate and phosphate influx when barley is deprived of external sulfate. (Remember, plants take up sulfur in the form of sulfate.) The pattern for sulfate uptake is very much as expected; its influx increases rapidly within 3–5 days of deprivation (Figure 4.15a), but decreases drastically within a few hours and is lost within one day when the ion is resupplied (Figure 4.15b).

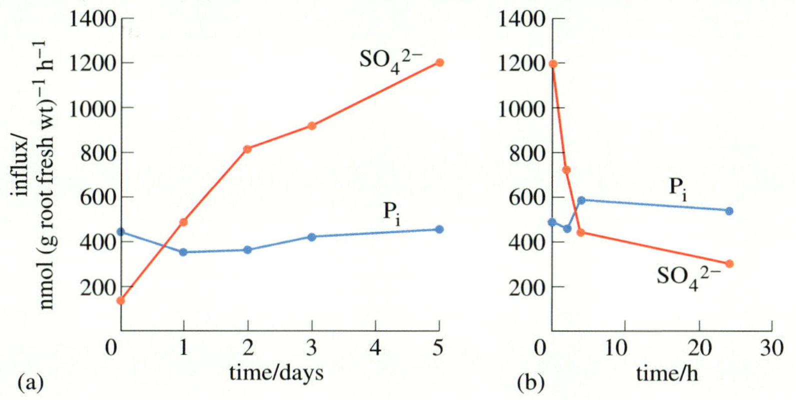

Figure 4.15 Time course of the influx of sulfate (SO_4^{2-}) and phosphate (P_i) into roots of barley plants. (a) Deprived of external sulfate supply for up to 5 days. (b) Resupplied with sulfate for up to 1 day. Data from Clarkson and Saker (1989).

However, the pattern for phosphate uptake is different.

❍ Look again at Figure 4.15. What effect does depriving the plant of sulfate have on phosphate uptake?

● The availability of sulfate has very little effect on phosphate influx, which remains almost constant throughout the experiment.

❍ What does this observation imply about the carrier proteins for sulfate and phosphate, and the nature of the induced response to sulfur deficiency?

● It implies that phosphate is taken up via a different carrier protein from sulfate, and that the *response induced by deficiency is specific to the element involved.*

The mechanism for activating the response, i.e. inducing protein synthesis, may be related to changes in the concentration of elements in the vacuole (3), the cytoplasm (4) or the shoot (5) (Figure 4.14). Sulfate influx, for example, is influenced by changes in the concentration of SO_4^{2-} in the vacuole and sulfur compounds such as the amino acid cysteine in the cytoplasm, while nitrate influx is regulated by NO_3^- in the vacuole and by NH_4^+ or nitrogen compounds such as glutamine in the cytoplasm. Uptake of several elements, including K, P, Fe, N and S, is influenced by conditions in the shoot. After a period of nutrient deprivation, it appears that when the nutrient is resupplied, its accumulation in the vacuole or cytoplasm of the root cells (which ultimately regulates influx at the plasma membrane) is delayed until the shoot's requirements have been met. This adaptability is just as well, or the root would be effectively starving the shoot of nutrients. The concentration of mineral nutrients in the phloem sap may feed back information about the nutrient status of the shoot to the root (6).

Finally, deficiency (or excessive concentrations) of certain key elements in the root tissues may induce additional root responses (7). They may take a variety of forms, but essentially involve: the release of substances (**root exudates**) into the apoplastic spaces and rhizosphere, which make elements more or less available for uptake; changes in root morphology, in particular the branching pattern and overall size of the root system relative to the shoot; and also changes in receptiveness to formation of mutualistic symbioses with soil microbes, i.e. nutrient foraging. These factors are the subject of the next two sections.

Summary of Sections 4.3 and 4.4

1. The concentration of elements in plant tissues is determined by the availability of the elements in the environment and the internal nutrient demand of the plant.
2. Soil pH is one of the major environmental factors affecting nutrient availability. Soils rich in basic cations such as Ca^{2+} and K^+ tend to have higher pH values than those deficient in these ions.
3. Sandy soils are more readily leached by rainwater than clay-rich soils and so tend to be more acidic.
4. P, Fe, Mn, B, Cu and Zn can be unavailable to plants on moderately alkaline soils, and available at toxic concentrations on acid soils. Al^{3+} can be toxic on acid soils, a problem that is exacerbated by acid precipitation.
5. Plants adapted to grow on base-rich calcareous soils are called calcicoles, and those adapted to grow on acid soils are called calcifuges. Calcifuges may suffer lime chlorosis on alkaline soils as a result of iron deficiency.
6. Plants influence their internal nutrient concentrations through intracellular regulation and nutrient foraging.
7. Net nutrient uptake is the difference between influx and efflux. Specific nutrient deprivation can induce the synthesis of particular, additional transport proteins.
8. The activity of transport proteins in the cell membranes and production of specific root exudates are determined by feedback about the nutrient status of the plant from the cytoplasm, vacuole and shoot.

4.5 NUTRIENT FORAGING

The term **nutrient foraging** encompasses those responses by the root system, in terms of root exudates, root architecture and mutualistic symbioses, that enable a plant to optimize its mineral nutrient uptake in any given set of environmental circumstances.

4.5.1 THE ROLE OF ROOT EXUDATES

You encountered root exudates in a discussion of the rhizosheath in Section 3.2.1. Root exudates comprise both high and low molecular weight solutes that are released or secreted into the soil by the root cap (Chapter 1) and adjacent subapical cells of the epidermis. The high molecular weight components are mainly **exoenzymes** (i.e. enzymes that act outside the cell membrane) and **mucilage** (which is a gelatinous material composed of polysaccharides). The low molecular mass components include organic acids, e.g. citric and malic acids, sugars, phenolics and amino acids. In the natural state, the root exudates become mixed with microbes and mineral particles, and this *mélange* is termed **mucigel** (Figure 4.16).

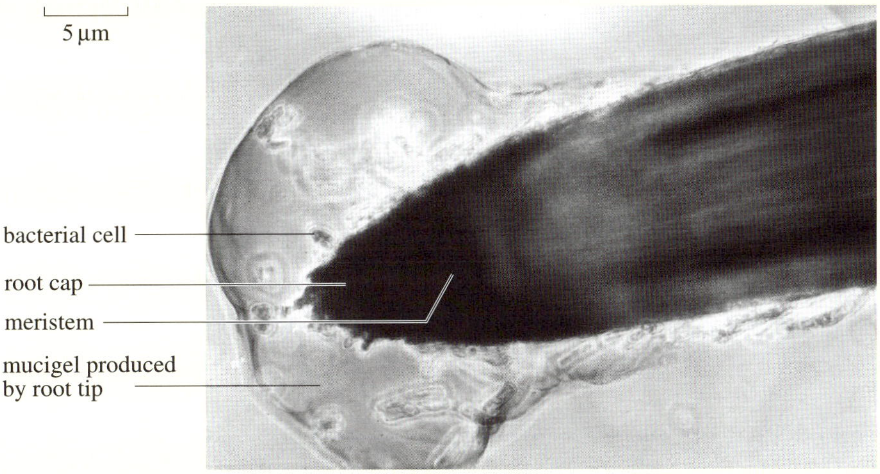

Figure 4.16 Light microscope image of a maize root tip showing the layer of mucigel containing bacteria and cells sloughed off the root cap.

In addition to protecting root tips from desiccation and lubricating their passage through the soil, root exudates also play an important role in nutrient foraging. They enhance nutrient uptake from impoverished soils by making elements more available, and as you will see later, protect roots from potentially toxic concentrations of certain elements. Mucilage release, which occurs from surface cells near root tips, influences nutrient availability indirectly by affecting soil structure. By bridging the gaps between roots and soil particles, the intimate root–soil contact necessary for nutrient uptake is maintained.

CASE STUDY — RAPE AND PHOSPHORUS SCAVENGING

You deduced from Figure 4.13 that phosphorus and a range of micronutrients including Fe, Mn, B and Zn are commonly in short supply in moderately alkaline soils. The active secretion of protons lowers the pH at the root surface which can make these elements more available. Rape (*Brassica napus*) is one of the species that is particularly effective in obtaining phosphate from P-deficient soil. When all available P (i.e. that which is not locked away in an insoluble form) has been absorbed, the rate of organic acid secretion (such as malic and citric acids) is increased. Table 4.3 shows what happens to organic acid exudation when rape is grown for seven days without or with phosphorus.

Table 4.3 Organic acids in exudates from different root zones of rape (*Brassica napus* L.) plants grown for seven days without or with phosphorus. Data from Hoffland *et al.* (1989).

		Organic acids in exudates/ nmol (cm root)$^{-1}$ (2 h)$^{-1}$	
Phosphorus supply	Root zone	Malic	Citric
–P	apical	0.87	0.27
	basal	0.20	0.13
+P	apical	0.15	0.06
	basal	0.03	0.03

- Looking at the data in Table 4.3, which region of the root is most important for the exudation of citric and malic acids?

- Both malic and citric acids are produced in far greater quantities by the apical zone of the root than the basal zone.

These acids solubilize phosphates that are almost insoluble at higher pH values, increasing by up to 10-fold the uptake of P. The acids work not only by lowering the rhizosphere pH due to the increase in H^+ ions, but also by releasing phosphate from charged surfaces in the soil by **ligand** (anion) **exchange** (ions tend to associate preferentially with the ligand to which they bind most strongly). Citrate, for example, releases phosphate from clay surfaces by this means. However, binding of aluminium and iron, as well their release, mobilizes the phosphate from iron and/or aluminium phosphates. Citric and malic acids form relatively stable compounds with Fe^{3+} and aluminium, thereby increasing the solubility and rate of phosphorus uptake (Figure 4.17). Binding of aluminium is also involved in overcoming aluminium toxicity (Section 4.6.3). In the same way, acid secretion helps to solubilize otherwise unavailable iron and manganese from their insoluble phosphates.

However, plants, including rape, also have a more specific means for obtaining phosphate from soil. Between 30% and 70% of total soil phosphate is present as a component of organic matter (P_{org}). Much of this is mobilized by soil microbes, but hydrolysis of P_{org} is also mediated by **acid phosphatase enzymes** produced by plant roots. Figure 4.18 shows the acid phosphatase activity in the rhizosphere of rape grown in a silt loam soil.

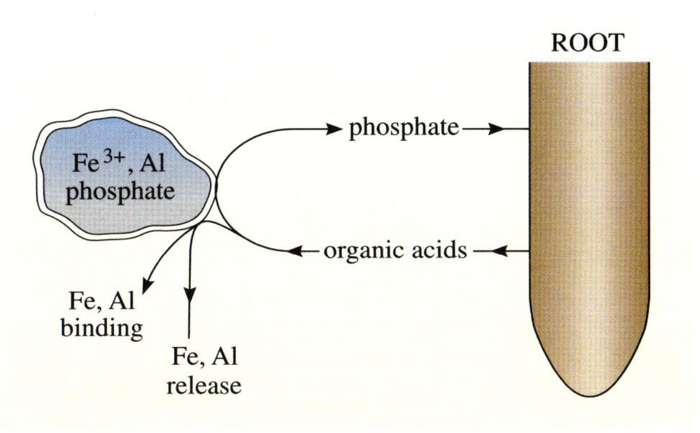

Figure 4.17 Solubilization of sparingly soluble iron and aluminium phosphate by root exudates.

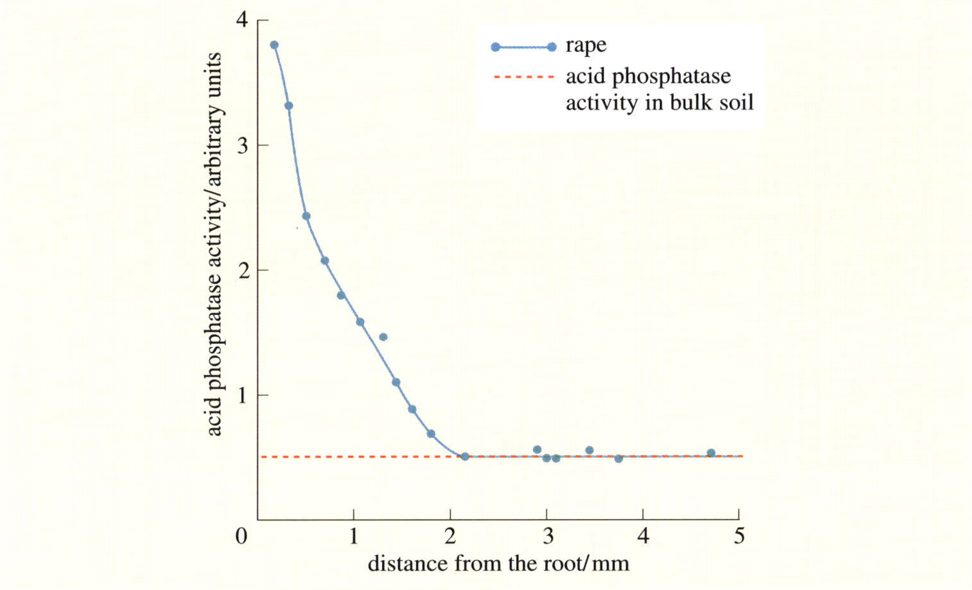

Figure 4.18 Acid phosphatase activity in the rhizosphere of rape grown in a silt loam soil. Data from Tarafdar and Jungk (1987).

- ❍ Approximately how far from the root is plant-derived acid phosphatase activity detectable in rape?

- ● About 2 mm, at which distance the acid phosphatase activity returns to the background level in the bulk soil.

Thus, by secreting organic acids and acid phosphatase enzymes, rape is able to scavenge effectively for P when it is in short supply.

4.5.2 NUTRIENT FORAGING: THE IMPORTANCE OF ROOT ARCHITECTURE

From the previous sections you might reasonably conclude that the most important factors in determining whether plants absorb sufficient quantities of nutrients would be the cellular responses to nutrient demand such as the number and properties of proton pumps and ion carriers in the roots, or the composition of the root exudates, but Figure 4.19 (overleaf) indicates that this assumption is not necessarily true.

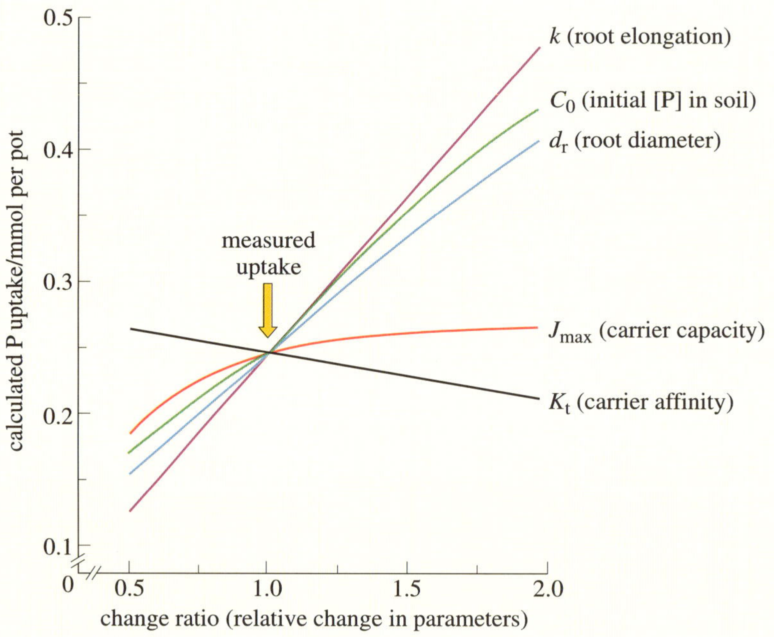

Figure 4.19 Effect of changing different variables on the predicted uptake of phosphorus by pot-grown soya beans on a nutrient-rich soil. K_t and J_{max} are the affinity and transport capacity, respectively, of the phosphate transport protein; C_o is the initial concentration of phosphate in the soil; k is the rate of root elongation; and d_r is the root diameter. Predicted (i.e. calculated) P uptake correlates with real measurements of value 1.0 on the change ratio scale.

The graph illustrates the results of a modelling exercise into phosphorus uptake by soya bean plants (*Glycine max*). It shows how phosphorus uptake by the plants, growing in nutrient-rich soil, would be expected to change when individual root and soil variables are changed. The scale on the vertical P-uptake axis is fairly straightforward, but that of the horizontal axis is a little more complex. It is expressed in terms of a change ratio. Basically, doubling the amount of a particular variable increases the change ratio from 1 to 2, and halving it reduces the change ratio from 1 to 0.5. Thus the lines with the steepest gradient represent the factors that have the greatest effect on P uptake.

- What variable influences the rate of P uptake most strongly?

- The rate of root elongation, k: P uptake approximately doubles (from 0.25 to 0.5) when this factor is doubled (calculated change ratio increases from 1 to 2).

Root diameter (d_r) and the initial concentration of P in the soil solution (C_o) also have large effects on uptake rate, but changes in ion carriers — their affinity for phosphate (K_t) and transport capacity (J_{max}) — have hardly any effect at all. These effects mean that properties of the root system, e.g. growth rate and root diameter, as well as ion concentration in the soil solution, may be more important for the uptake of phosphorus than properties of the ion-specific carriers. It must be emphasized that this situation applies only to *normal* soils; there is good evidence that changes to ion transport systems do play an important role in ion uptake where potential deficiency (Section 4.4.1), or toxicity of soils, are the case (Section 4.6.2). Here we shall concentrate on the other factors that influence the ability of plants to forage for nutrients.

However, before considering these factors in some detail, it must be emphasized that root architecture is influenced by several factors other than nutrient availability. For example, roots provide anchorage, so the structure of the root system is affected by the size of the plant and the nature of the rooting medium. Life history also influences root structure; the roots of woody shrubs differ from those of annual weeds, and both differ from the roots of herbaceous perennials. Consequently, root responses to nutrient availability are also constrained by these other factors.

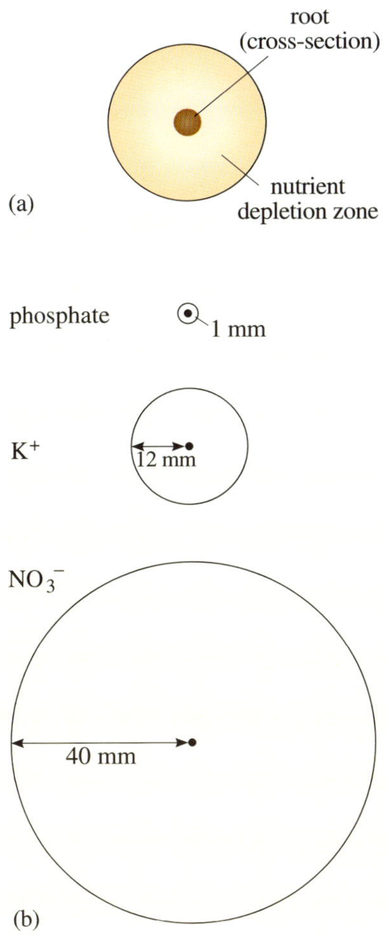

Figure 4.20 (a) Nutrient depletion zone of a root. (b) Sizes of nutrient depletion zones for three ions.

ROOT ELONGATION AND NUTRIENT DEPLETION ZONES

Roots continue to grow throughout the growing season by cell division in the meristem and elongation of the cells produced: as Figure 4.19 shows, the rate of root elongation has a powerful influence on ion uptake. To understand why, consider what happens when a root extends into 'new' soil. At first, ion uptake occurs at a rate that depends mainly on the concentration of ions in the soil solution. This process lowers ion concentrations adjacent to the root surface, setting up a concentration gradient down which ions diffuse towards the root. However, uptake proceeds much faster than diffusion so that a region that is depleted of ions — the **nutrient depletion zone** — gradually extends out around the root, as illustrated in Figure 4.20a.

This zone can be regarded as 'exhausted' soil and, once established, the rate of ion uptake falls considerably, even if the root continues to take up water at a constant rate, because ions and water diffuse independently of each other. The width of the depletion zone shows little increase after about 5 days, but its radius differs greatly for different ions (Figure 4.20b). This variation reflects the different mobilities, or rates of diffusion, of ions through the soil, which depends on the strength of binding interactions between ions and electrically charged components of soil (clay and organic matter). The more mobile an ion is, the wider its depletion zone.

- From Figure 4.20b what can be deduced about the relative mobility of nitrate and phosphate ions?

- The depletion zone of nitrate is wider than that of phosphate which implies that nitrate is more mobile than phosphate. In fact, nitrate is 1000 times more mobile than phosphate, because phosphate binds much more strongly to soil components than nitrate does.

Consequently, it is essential that roots grow continuously into new areas of unexploited soil if ion uptake is to be maximized. This growth is particularly important for relatively immobile ions such as phosphate and zinc, because the volume of soil depleted by a single root is so small. It is also important that one root does not grow into the depletion zone created by another, which is one reason why the geometry of the root system matters.

THE GEOMETRY OF ROOT SYSTEMS AND INDIVIDUAL ROOTS

If root density is high, depletion zones overlap and roots compete for nutrients. This can happen at quite low densities for mobile ions such as nitrate and sulfate, which have wide depletion zones. Therefore, if these nutrients are limiting growth, wide, even spacing between root branches is desirable in terms of plant economy, i.e. extracting maximum nutrients from a given volume of soil for the minimum dry weight of roots. Another desirable feature from this point of view is a root system with many fine branches, as in the fibrous roots of grasses, rather than one with a few thick branches, as you often find in tree seedlings, for example, because the fine branching maximizes surface area for a given biomass of root. Figure 4.21 shows two identical areas containing different root systems.

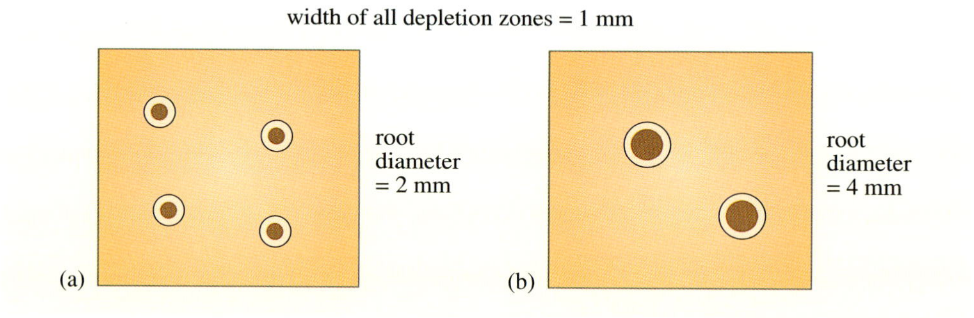

Figure 4.21 Identical areas containing (in cross-section): (a) four roots of diameter 2 mm and (b) two roots of diameter 4 mm. All roots have a depletion zone that is 1 mm wide.

❍ From the data in Figure 4.21 work out for (a) and (b): (i) the total areas of root cross-section (for a cylindrical root, area is proportional to the volume of root tissue produced which gives an indication of the plant's 'expenditure' on roots); (ii) the total areas of depletion zones (again, for a cylindrical root, the area is proportional to the volume of soil exploited and so gives a measure of nutrient uptake); (iii) relative nutrient uptake per unit root area (this gives a measure of 'root economy', i.e. how efficiently a given amount of root tissue exploits the soil).

Note: the area of a circle is πr^2 (where r is the radius and π (pi) a value of about 3.14).

● (i) Total root area in (a) is $4 \times \pi \times 1^2 = 12.6\ \text{mm}^2$ and in (b) is $2 \times \pi \times 2^2 = 25.1\ \text{mm}^2$.

(ii) Total areas of depletion zones are obtained from:

(area of roots + depletion zones) – (area of roots).

For (a) this is:

$(4 \times \pi \times 2^2) - 12.6 = 50.2 - 12.6 = 37.6\ \text{mm}^2$.

For (b) it is:

$(2 \times \pi \times 3^2) - 25.1 = 56.5 - 25.1 = 31.4\ \text{mm}^2$.

(iii) For (a), relative uptake per unit root area is: $37.6/12.6 = 3.0$ and for (b), it is: $31.4/25.1 = 1.25$.

So it is more than twice as efficient to have four roots of diameter 2 mm than to have two roots of diameter 4 mm!

In reality, root systems are inevitably a compromise. If relatively immobile nutrients such as phosphate are growth-limiting, then closely packed root branches may be necessary to satisfy plant demand — even though many of these branches are of little use for nitrate uptake because depletion zones for nitrate overlap.

The degree of root branching may also vary if the distribution of soil nutrients is uneven, as shown in Figure 4.22. This capacity for local variation in geometry greatly increases the foraging capacity of root systems.

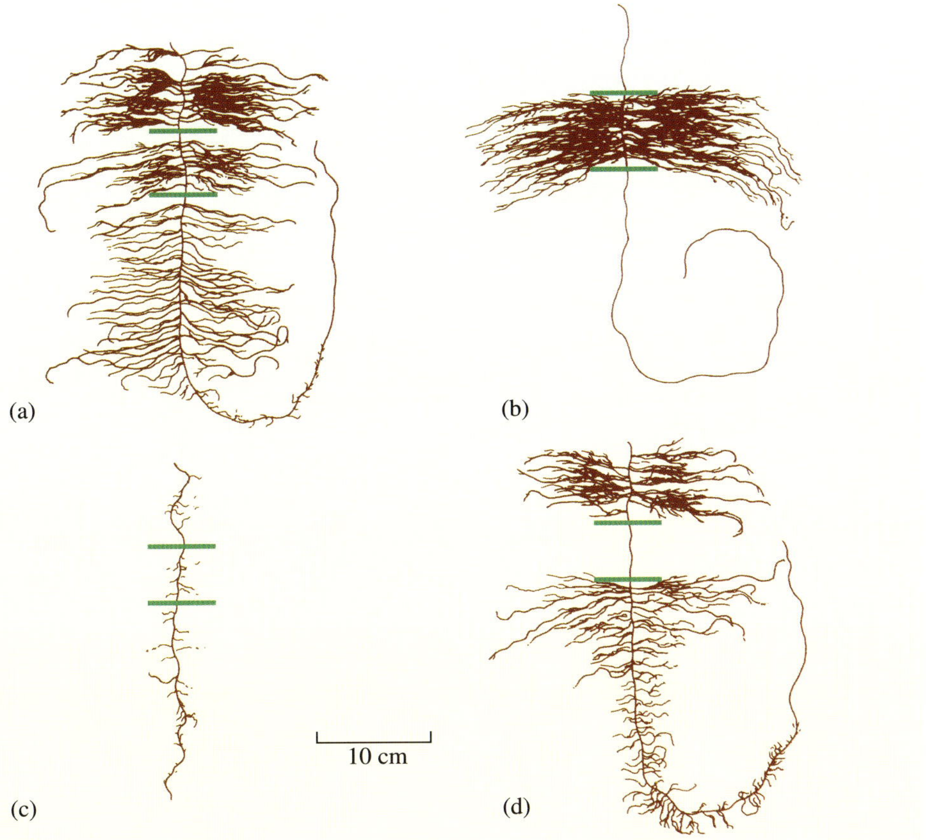

Figure 4.22 Changes in the amount of lateral branching along one major root of barley, induced to grow through three successive zones, each containing either 'high' (1.0 mmol l^{-1}) or 'low' (0.01 mmol l^{-1}) nitrate. The central zone is marked by two horizontal green bars. The locations of 'high' and 'low' nitrate were: (a) high, high, high; (b) low, high, low; (c) low, low, low; (d) high, low, high. The experiment was carried out over 26 days.

A mechanism by which individual roots increase their foraging power is through the development of root hairs (Figure 4.23). These fine extensions from single epidermal cells are usually from 0.5 to 8.0 mm long and increase the absorption area of root but, since they grow initially within the depletion zone, their effectiveness increases sharply when they extend beyond this zone.

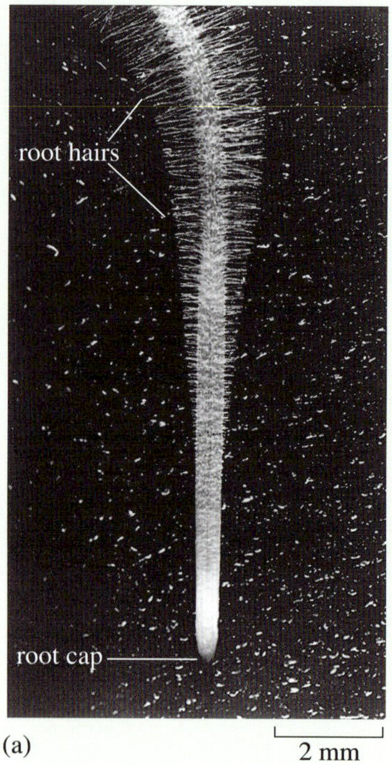

(a)

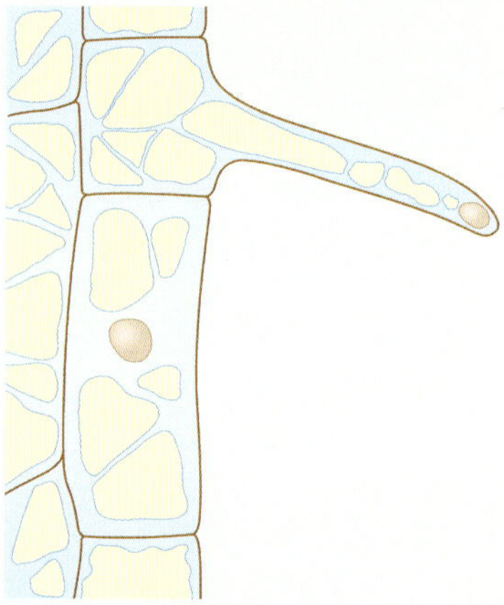

(b)

Figure 4.23 (a) Root tip of a radish seedling showing the development of root hairs. (b) Diagram of epidermal cells in longitudinal section to show a root hair growing as an extension of a single cell.

- ❍ For which ion(s) are root hairs most likely to extend beyond the initial depletion zone?

- ● Ions such as phosphate, which have a very narrow depletion zone (Figure 4.21a), or possibly, for long root hairs, ions such as K^+, or NH_4^+ which also bind quite strongly to soil particles.

It follows that root hairs are most effective in the absorption of relatively immobile nutrients, such as phosphate, whose concentration near the epidermal surface is low. Indeed, root hair length has been shown to be inversely related to [P_i] in the medium bathing the roots in several species, including rape and *Arabidopsis*. However, phosphate uptake is influenced far more by another very common mechanism: formation of symbiotic associations such as mycorrhizas (see below).

4.5.3 Nutrient foraging: microbial symbioses

Given the apparent importance of many fine roots to efficient nutrient absorption, it is perhaps surprising that when plants, especially trees and shrubs, are dug up from field and garden, they often don't seem to have very extensive systems of fine roots. One of the main reasons is that the majority of plants form mutualistic symbiotic associations with soil microbes and leave much of the nutrient acquisition to them. (Two exceptions that don't form associations are the cabbage family, Brassicaceae, and the nettle family, Urticaceae.) This enhanced mineral nutrition is a particular feature of **mycorrhizal** symbioses (from the Greek *mykos*, fungus and *rhizon*, root), in which certain specialized fungi grow in very intimate contact with the fine roots of the 'host' plant.

Mycorrhizal symbiosis

It is astonishing, but not widely known, that soil fungi colonize the roots of about 90% of land plants to form mutualistic mycorrhizas and play a central role in the capture of nutrients from the soil. More than 6000 fungal species are capable of establishing mycorrhizas with about 240 000 plant species, yet despite this diversity, very few anatomical types of mutualistic plant–fungus interaction are produced. There are many different variations on the theme, but basically, mycorrhizas fall into two groups: the **endomycorrhizas** (Figure 4.24a), in which the fungal hyphae form a loose weft of hyphae over the surface of the root, but they also penetrate the cell walls and produce structures of various forms that lie within an infolded but *intact* plasma membrane; and the **ectomycorrhizas** (Figure 4.24b), in which the fungal hyphae do not penetrate any cell walls. The hyphae form a dense mantle over the surface of the root tips (Figure 4.25a) and hyphae ramify between the cells of the cortex to form the **'Hartig net'** (Figure 4.25b). The endomycorrhizas are further split into the **ericoid** mycorrhizas, i.e. those of the heather family and its allies, and the **arbuscular mycorrhizas (AM)** (typical of most other herbaceous plants) in which the hyphae that penetrate the cell walls and invaginate the plant plasma membrane are highly branched, forming structures called arbuscules.

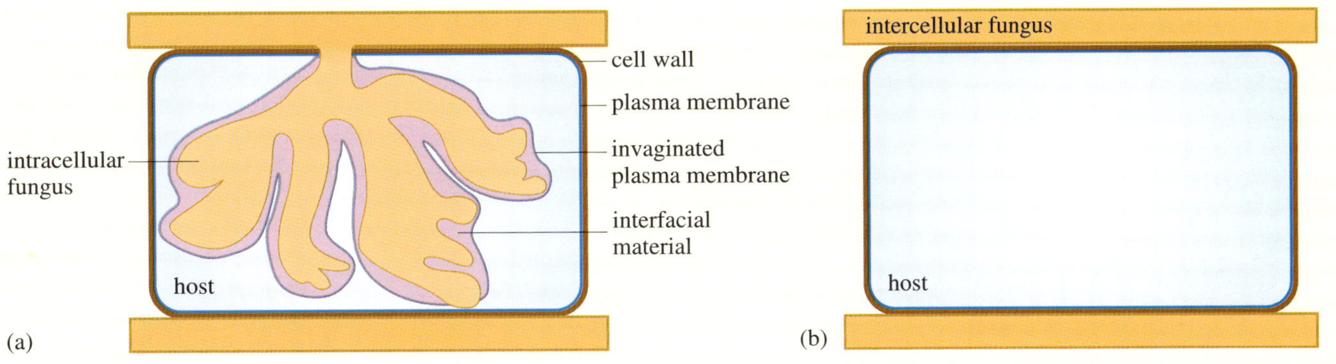

Figure 4.24 Diagrams to show the two different types of contact or interface between plant and fungus in mycorrhizal associations, depending on whether the fungus is (a) intracellular (endomycorrhizal) or (b) intercellular (ectomycorrhizal). In (a) the intracellular fungus is separated from the host cytoplasm by the invaginated host plasma membrane and by interfacial material. In (b) the walls of both partners are physically in contact, but remain intact.

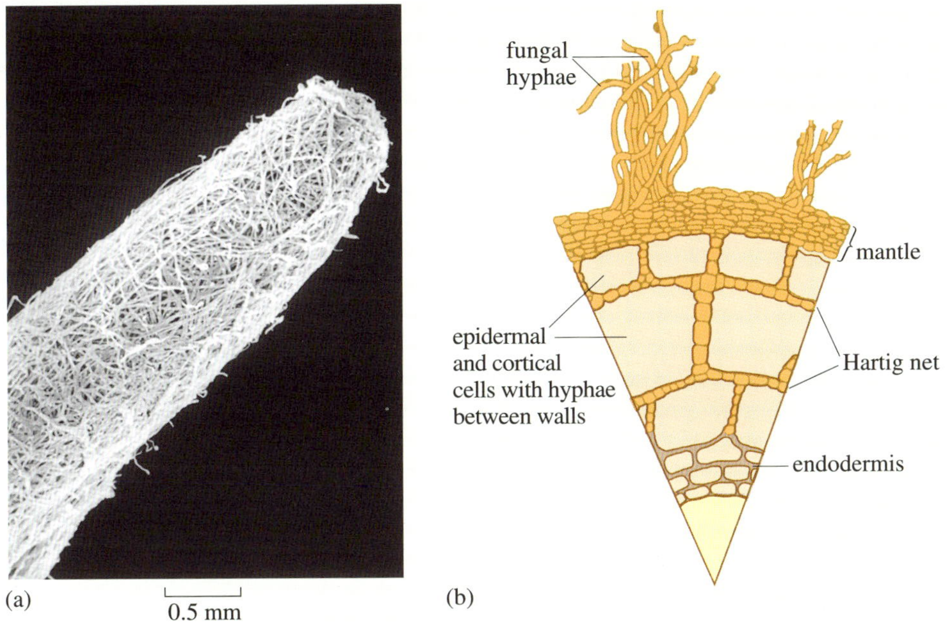

Figure 4.25 (a) Scanning electron micrograph (SEM) of an ectomycorrhizal root tip between the fungus *Paxillus involutus* and birch (*Betula* sp.). Note how the fungal hyphae cover the root tip to form the sheath or mantle. (b) Diagram of a TS of an ectomycorrhizal root of pine (*Pinus maritima*). Fungal hyphae form an outer mantle from which they extend into the soil. They also penetrate between the cells of the cortex and epidermis to form the Hartig net.

In all these cases (we are omitting mycorrhizas of the orchid family, which are a special case), the fungus benefits from the association because the host plant supplies it with carbohydrates, mostly in the form of hexose sugars, and the host plant benefits because the fungus provides it with an enhanced mineral nutrient supply, as shown in Table 4.4.

Table 4.4 The growth and nutrient content of pine seedlings (*Pinus elliotti*) with and without ectomycorrhizal fungi.

	Growth/ g dry wt plant^{-1}	Macronutrients/mg plant^{-1}		
		N	P	K
No mycorrhiza	0.26	2.4	0.22	2.27
+ Ectomycorrhiza	2.81	38.9	3.9	35.6

❍ From the data in Table 4.4 what is the net effect of the mycorrhizal association on host growth?

● Mycorrhizal plants have much higher growth than non-mycorrhizal plants — mycorrhizas increase growth by over 10-fold.

There are several reasons why the fungal partner enhances nutrient supply to the host. The network of fungal hyphae that extends away from the roots into the surrounding soil (the mycelium), is much more effective than the plant roots at scavenging nutrients in soils of low pH and nutrient concentration. This difference arises partly because the hyphae are much narrower than even the root hairs of the plants, and so, for a given mass of tissue, the fungi can exploit a much greater mass of soil. It has also been shown that some of the fungi can acquire mineral nutrients from sources that are unavailable to the higher plants. They can solubilize otherwise insoluble phosphates and some can acquire nutrients from *organic* remains that they digest using exoenzymes such as proteases. The precise nutritional relationship between the host and fungus varies depending on the type of mycorrhiza involved. These variations are summarized in Table 4.5.

Table 4.5 Differences in nutritional relationship between mycorrhizal types.

Type of mycorrhiza	Nutritional characteristics
Ectomycorrhizas	Can decompose organic carbon — less dependent on host plant for C than other mycorrhizas. Can decompose proteins to obtain N. Important source of N and P to the host plant.
Ericoid mycorrhizas (endomycorrhizas)	Can decompose organic carbon and proteins well, especially in acid conditions. Important source of N to the host plant. Supply of P to the host is less important than in AMs and ectomycorrhizas.
Arbuscular mycorrhizas (AMs) (endomycorrhizas)	Poor decomposers of organic carbon and proteins — highly dependent on host plant for both C and N. Supply host with P which they scavenge effectively.

In addition, fungi can take up nutrients against steep concentration gradients and translocate them towards the host. The nutrients can be passed on to the plant or stored within their fungal hyphae, which may serve as a reservoir for times of scarcity, enabling the plants to overcome seasonal variations in availability.

Plant roots, of course, release sugars as a normal component of root exudates. The intimate relationship between the fungal hyphae and the cortical cells of the plant roots, gives the mycorrhizal fungi an excellent opportunity to out-compete other microbes for this valuable resource. By converting the hexose sugars into trehalose and sugar alcohols such as mannitol (Figure 4.26), the fungi are able to maintain a concentration gradient down which more sugars follow passively from the plant. But, how the host plants induce the fungi to release large amounts of phosphate is less clear. Cellular membranes do not normally 'leak' phosphate. It is thought that much of the phosphate efflux may occur via ion channels in the plasma membrane of the fungal hyphae, which the plants somehow manage to keep in the 'open' state. Phosphate would then diffuse down a steep concentration gradient out of the fungus. However, how the plants might activate the fungal ion channels is not yet known.

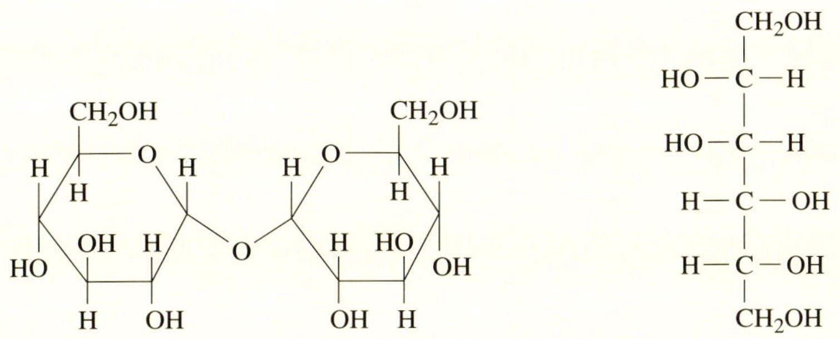

Figure 4.26 Structure of (a) the disaccharide sugar trehalose and (b) the sugar alcohol mannitol.

In some ectomycorrhizas, 25–30% or more of host net production passes to the fungus, making the association costly to higher plants. This apparent drain on plant productivity may not be as bad as it seems, because evidence is emerging that the 'cost' may be offset by an increase in photosynthesis in leaves, perhaps due to greater activation of Rubisco (Section 2.3). However, the formation of mycorrhizas is most cost-effective if soil nutrients are in short supply. Furthermore, not all fungal partners are equally beneficial to the host plants. In recent years, with the emphasis in agriculture and forestry shifting towards 'low' input systems, which means less use of fertilizer, ensuring that crops have the most effective mycorrhizal partners is receiving more attention. Research is going on to determine if the yield of plantation trees can be improved by inoculating saplings with particular ectomycorrhizal strains of fungus in the plant nurseries. Figure 4.27 (overleaf) shows the effect of inoculation with different fungal partners (in the nursery) on the height of Douglas fir trees, for two years after transplantation to a non-fertilized, nutrient-poor, acid upland soil, that had previously been used as a larch plantation (Le Tacon *et al.*, 1992).

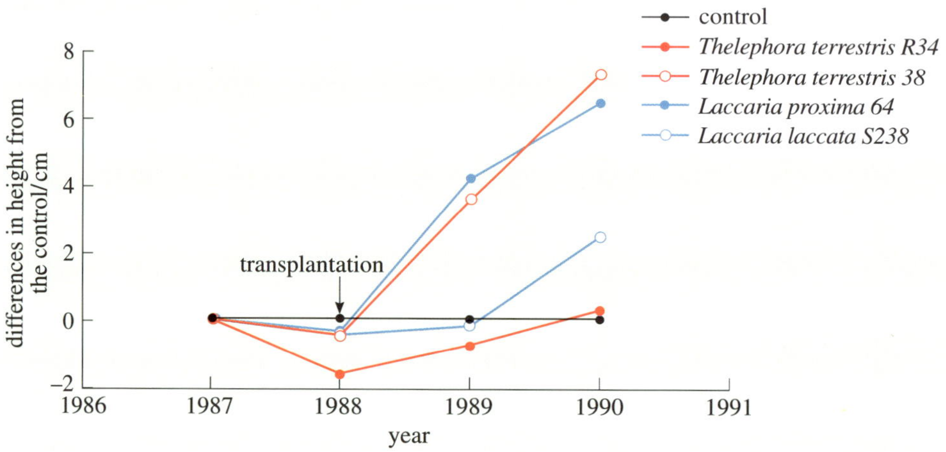

Figure 4.27 Growth of containerized Douglas fir (*Pseudotsuga menziesii*) seedlings, mycorrhizal with four different fungal strains, two years after planting out in an infertile soil of low pH. (Tree height is expressed as differences from the control without mycorrhizas.) Fungal strains include: *Thelephora terrestris R34*, *Thelephora terrestris 38*, *Laccaria proxima 64* and *Laccaria laccata S238*. Data from Le Tacon *et al*. (1992).

- Do all of the inoculated strains increase growth of the fir trees in comparison with the uninoculated control plants?

- No, two strains, *Thelephora terrestris 38* and *Laccaria proxima 64* enhance tree height considerably: one strain, *Laccaria laccata S238,* enhances it a little and another strain, *Thelephora terrestris R34*, is actually detrimental to the tree, at least over the first couple of years after transplanting.

This sort of research is of particular benefit in the tropics; in tropical America, for example, over 40% of soils are infertile and acidic, and inoculating soil with particular *endo*mycorrhizas has greatly improved the growth of many crops, including tea and coffee.

NITROGEN FIXATION

The biggest reservoir of nitrogen on earth is nitrogen gas in the atmosphere (which is 80% N_2) but, unfortunately, plants cannot use it!

- What forms of nitrogen can plants use?

- Nitrate and/or ammonium ions (Section 4.1).

Certain prokaryotes, however, can 'fix' gaseous nitrogen (Ridge, 2001), by reducing it to ammonia and some of these nitrogen fixers form symbiotic associations with plants. The prokaryote supplies N as NH_3 to the plant and in return obtains photosynthetic products. On the roots of peas, beans and other members of the Fabaceae, there are pinkish nodules (Figure 4.28a) inside which live N-fixing bacteria known as rhizobia (Figure 4.28b).

The pink colour results from the presence of leghaemoglobin, an oxygen-binding protein that matches O_2 supply to O_2 use (for respiration) and so maintains very low levels of O_2 in the nodule; its presence is essential, because N-fixation is an anaerobic process and would be poisoned by O_2. The process of N-fixation by the bacteria is made possible by the fact that the bacteroid membrane is impermeable to O_2. The bacteria depend for their energy supply entirely on carbon compounds from the host, so — as in mycorrhizas — there is a substantial 'cost' to the host. The payoff is that most of the ammonia produced by N-fixation passes into the host root, where it is assimilated into amino acids and amides.

Some woody plants, including alder (*Alnus* spp.), sea buckthorn (*Hippophaë rhamnoides*) and sweet gale (*Myrica gale*), have root nodules containing N-fixing actinomycetes (also prokaryotes, MacQueen *et al.*, 2001). And in *Sphagnum* moss, cycads (gymnosperms) and some liverworts (bryophytes), N-fixing cyanobacteria live symbiotically in pouches within the green tissues. In nearly all these examples, the host plant often grows on nutrient-poor soils where there is a particular shortage of nitrogen — acid, waterlogged conditions or free-draining sands, for example. However, on agricultural soils, legume crops such as clover (*Trifolium* spp.) have long been used as 'living fertilizers' because when they die and decay the nitrogen content of the soil is increased: improvements may be possible by inoculating soil with particularly 'good' strains of *Rhizobium*. Another aim for the future is to produce N-fixing *cereal* crops by genetic engineering, either by introducing bacterial genes (and there has been some recent progress with this technique) or by introducing legume genes necessary for establishing a root nodule symbiosis (which appears to be difficult, perhaps impossible). The aim is to achieve high yields of grain with low inputs of nitrogenous fertilizer.

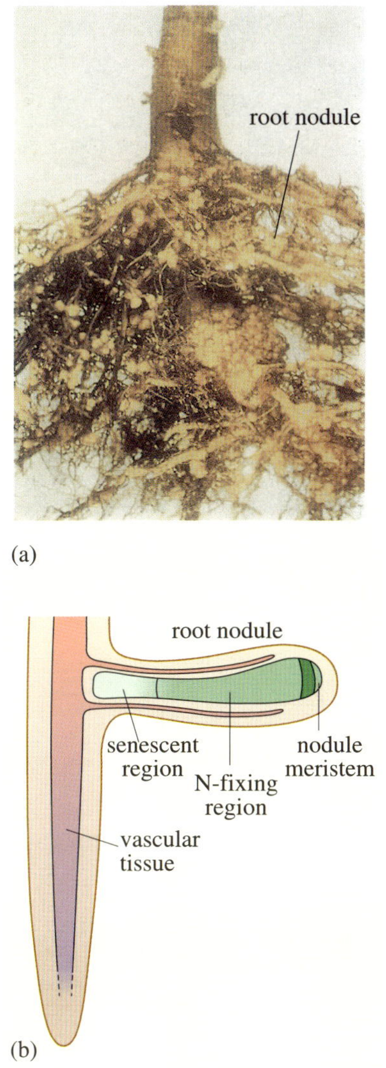

Figure 4.28 (a) Legume roots showing root nodules. (b) Diagram of a root plus nodule in longitudinal section.

SUMMARY OF SECTION 4.5

1. Plants enhance their capacity to scavenge for nutrients through nutrient foraging, which involves root exudates, root architecture and various mutualistic associations with microbes.
2. Plant root exudates comprise a polysaccharide mucilage, various exoenzymes and a range of low molecular weight components. These exudates become colonized by soil microbes to form mucigel. Root exudates enhance nutrient uptake through improved contact with soil particles, and a variety of chemical reactions with soil components.
3. Rape is a very effective P scavenger: organic acid exudation makes P more available by lowering soil pH and releasing ions through ligand exchange; acid-phosphatase enzymes digest P_{org}.
4. Root architecture can have a very important influence on mineral nutrient uptake on 'normal' soils: the size and growth rate of the root system, the thickness of roots, the position of root branching, and the presence of root hairs can all affect how efficiently the roots find and absorb mineral nutrients.
5. Mycorrhizas are mutualistic symbioses between fungi and the roots of seed plants. The fungus obtain carbohydrates from the plant and the plant obtains mineral nutrients from the fungus. In endomycorrhizas the fungal mycelium penetrates cell walls of the root cortex to form feeding structures, while in ectomycorrhizas the fungal mycelium is strictly extracellular.
6. Mycorrhizal fungi have access to soil nutrients that are unavailable to the host plant. Their fine hyphae explore the soil more efficiently than plant roots can. Protease enzymes are part of the fungal nutrient-scavenging armoury. Not all mycorrhizal fungi are equally effective at enhancing the growth of the host plant.

7 Rhizobial bacteria form nitrogen-fixing nodules with the roots of leguminous plants. The bacteria invade plant root cells to form nodules in which atmospheric nitrogen is converted into ammonia under anaerobic conditions. The associated plant obtains some of this fixed nitrogen in return for supplying the microbial symbionts with carbohydrates. Other nitrogen-fixing mutualistic symbioses include: N-fixing actinomycetes with some woody plants, and N-fixing cyanobacteria with some lower plants.

4.6 Toxic soils

Humankind has spent much of its recent history exploiting soils for its own advantage and by so doing often degrades them. Intensive or inappropriate agricultural methods can destroy the soil structure leading to erosion and the depletion of the soil microbial flora and fauna. Other human activities can result in the soil becoming toxic to much plant life: mining and smelting of metal ores generates extensive spoil heaps; irrigated land often suffers from **salinization**, caused by the build-up of salts in the surface layers; and industrial activity often has detrimental effects on soils over a wide area, e.g. through the so-called acid rain. Pressures of population, and the promise of subsidies, encourage farmers to take marginal land into cultivation. Consequently, cultivars are needed that can produce good yields in unfavourable conditions. Fortunately, for every anthropogenic soil 'problem' created, there is usually a naturally occurring parallel situation where nature has already produced plants capable of thriving in similar conditions. This section considers some of these 'problem' soils and examines how evolution has adapted the basic systems for nutrient acquisition and distribution already described to cope with specific **edaphic** (soil-related) conditions.

4.6.1 Metal mining and mycorrhizas

Soils containing potentially toxic concentrations of metals such as lead, zinc and copper are found on ore outcrops, or at sites where the ores have been mined, smelted or otherwise processed. Despite the fact that some of these metals are essential nutrients, when present in excess amounts, they are toxic to plant growth. Many plant species are known to have evolved metal tolerance in response to exposure to raised concentrations. The inherent mechanism of aluminium-resistance is explored in some detail in Section 4.6.3. However, perhaps contrary to expectation, it has been found that mycorrhizal fungi can ameliorate metal toxicity to higher plants.

❍ Why might mycorrhizal amelioration of metal toxicity be contrary to expectation?

● Because mycorrhizal fungi are good scavengers for nutrients that are in short supply, it might be expected that they would exacerbate metal toxicity, not ameliorate it.

For example, ectomycorrhizal birch (*Betula* spp.) have higher growth rates and lower concentrations of zinc in their shoots than non-mycorrhizal birch when grown in raised zinc concentrations. However, whole organ studies revealed increased, rather than decreased, zinc concentrations in the root systems of mycorrhizal birch, which has led to the hypothesis that the fungus protects the associated birch plant by accumulating zinc within the fungal component of the mycorrhizal root system. To investigate this hypothesis three experiments involving X-ray microanalysis were performed (Denny and Wilkins, 1987). X-ray microanalysis is summarized in Box 4.1, which you should read now.

Box 4.1 X-ray microanalysis

In a transmission electron microscope (TEM), a beam of electrons is focused onto the specimen. Different parts of the specimen absorb or transmit the electrons to differing extents. By carefully focusing the emergent beam of electrons an image can be generated on a screen. When the beam of electrons hits the specimen, some of the incident electrons cause a proportion of the orbital electrons in the specimen to be ejected. The gap created is immediately filled by an electron from a higher energy shell. In so doing, the transferring electron releases its excess energy as an X-ray photon. The emitted X-ray has a fixed wavelength and characteristic energy because each electron exists in a precisely defined energy level. Consequently, each element produces a unique X-ray energy spectrum by which it may be identified, i.e. the 'characteristic radiation'. Some elements may produce more than one peak in the spectrum corresponding to the transfer of different electrons. A second type of X-ray radiation is produced when incident electrons interact with the nucleus of the atom. Electrons scattered in the field surrounding the charged nucleus lose energy in the form of X-rays with energies produced randomly over the entire range. This continuous radiation is called 'continuum' or 'white' radiation. It is a function of all the atoms present in the analysed volume of the specimen, and can be used to measure specimen thickness. Figure 4.29 illustrates diagrammatically how the two kinds of X-ray are generated.

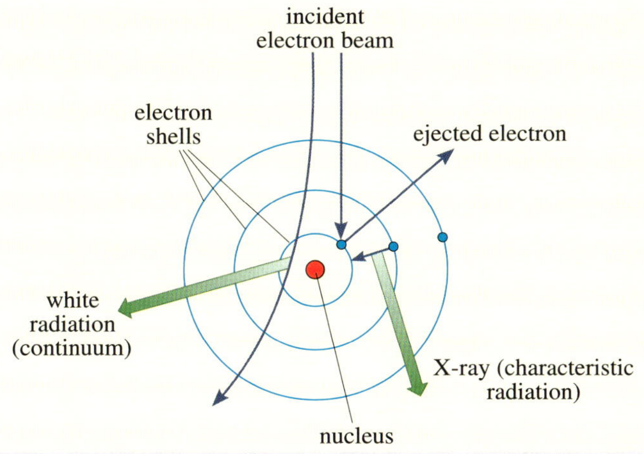

Figure 4.29 Production of characteristic and white X-rays when electrons in the beam of an electron microscope interact with atoms in the specimen.

These two types of X-ray can be used to analyse very small areas of the specimen both qualitatively and quantitatively. However, it is only really applicable for the analysis of elements with an atomic number of at least 10 and preferably quite a bit higher, which means it is good for investigating the distribution of transition metals (30 elements from the *d* block of the periodic table, e.g. Cu, Ni, Zn, Fe), but useless for common biological elements like C, O and N. Two approaches are most useful for the analysis of biological material.

1 Spot X-ray microanalysis

In this technique, the specimen is fixed, embedded in resin and then sectioned at around 90 nm in thickness. The sections are mounted on support grids and examined using a TEM modified with the installation of an X-ray detector just to one side of the specimen (see Figure 4.30).

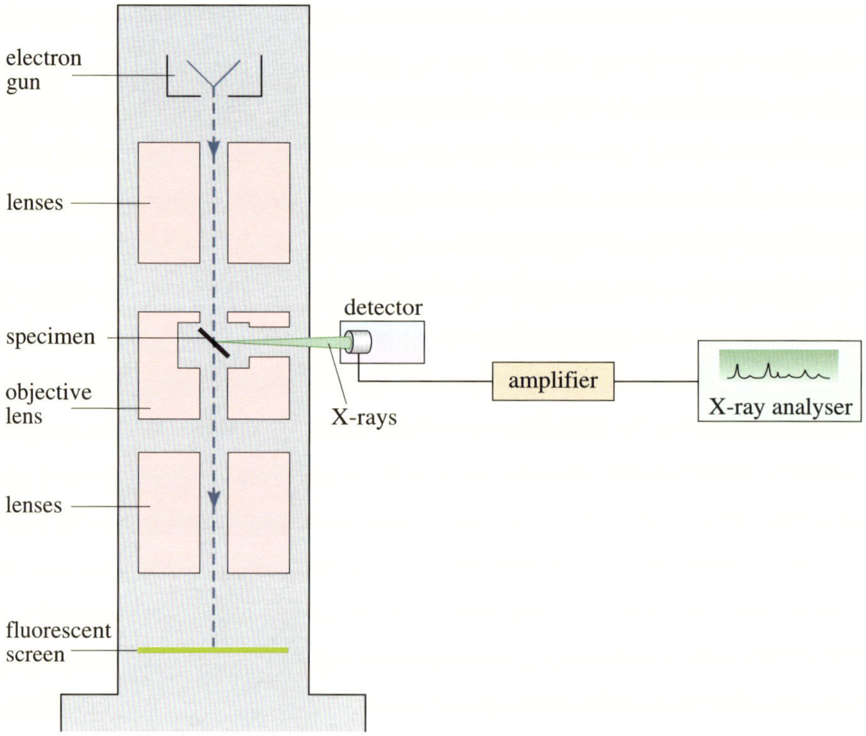

Figure 4.30 Schematic representation of a TEM with equipment for X-ray microanalysis attached.

The electron beam can be focused onto the tissue or cellular component of interest and the X-rays produced are collected by the detector and processed by a multichannel analyser to generate a spectrum such as that shown in Figure 4.31.

In theory the relative concentration of an element can then be found by finding the ratio between the area under the largest characteristic peak for that element (E on the diagram) and the amount of white radiation under a fixed area of the spectrum containing no characteristic peaks (marked W on the diagram). The absolute concentration of the element can then be found by comparing this value with one taken from a standard of known concentration.

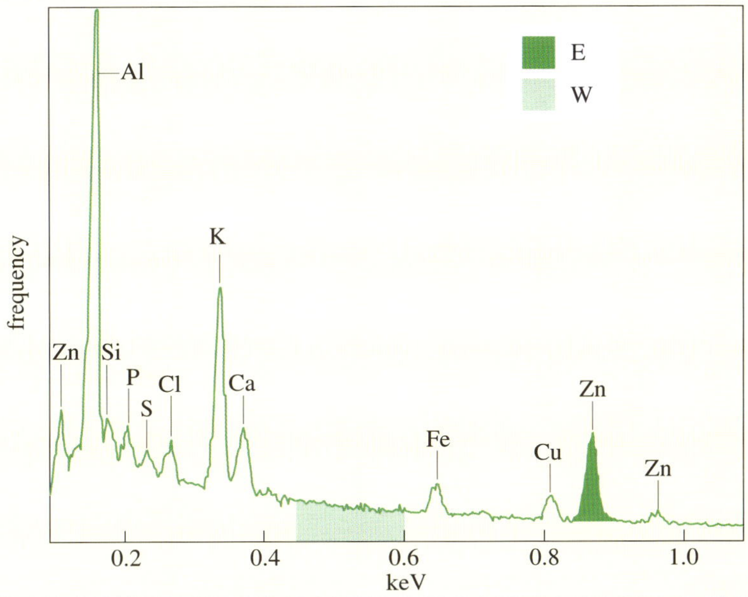

Figure 4.31 Sample spectrum from X-ray microanalysis of a section of root tissue from a birch (*Betula* sp.) plant grown at elevated zinc concentrations. Notice the peaks of 'characteristic' radiation, including one for zinc (E) overlying the 'white' or 'continuum' radiation (W). The *x*-axis is calibrated in kiloelectronvolts (keV), which indicate the energy level of the X-rays received by the detector. The *y*-axis indicates the relative frequency of the X-rays of different energies received by the detector.

2 STEM X-ray mapping

In this technique, slightly thicker sections are cut, around 1 μm. To produce the scanning transmission electron image (STEM), the electrons transmitted through the section are collected by a detector passing back and forth across the field and processed to produce a televison image. A complementary X-ray map, of the same area, is generated when the X-rays of just one element are collected from the area being analysed and processed to produce an image showing the spatial distribution of the element (see Figure 4.33 for an example of such data).

In practice, both these techniques are dogged by potential artefacts. Specimen preparation is particularly crucial, because conventional preparation methods for electron microscopy (EM) induce massive changes to the composition of the specimen. For instance, most EM stains contain heavy metals which obviously have to be avoided. Techniques have been developed to minimize loss of light elements and the introduction of exotic elements. In addition, X-ray spectra also include signals coming from the grid supporting the specimen and other parts of the machine and, if the specimen is too thick the signal can be distorted, so methods have had to be developed to eliminate these extraneous influences from the raw data and subsequent analysis. However, X-ray microanalysis has proved very useful in a number of cases, as described in the text.

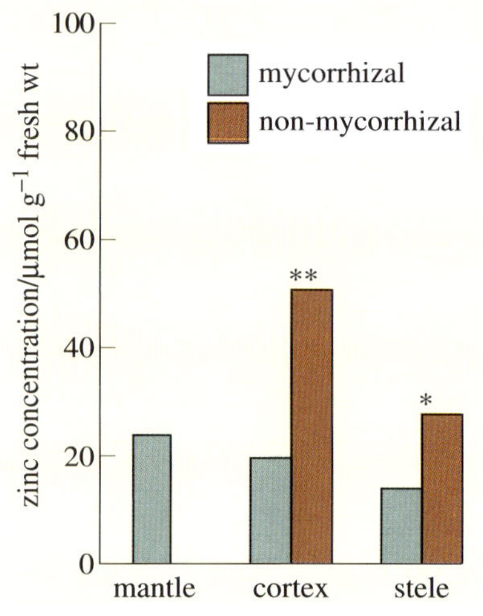

Figure 4.32 Mean zinc concentrations in three separate root tissues of *Betula* sp. grown at elevated zinc concentration with and without the presence of the mycorrhizal fungus, *Paxillus involutus*, measured by X-ray microanalysis. ** indicates a difference significant at 1% level ($P < 0.01$), * indicates a difference significant at 5% level ($P < 0.05$). Data from Denny and Wilkins (1987).

In Experiment 1, the tissue concentrations of zinc were measured, using spot analysis on thin sections of root from birch clones grown, in aseptic conditions, at elevated zinc concentrations, with and without an isolate of the ectomycorrhizal fungus *Paxillus involutus*. The results of the experiment are shown in Figure 4.32.

- ❍ How do the concentrations of zinc in the cortex and stele of mycorrhizal and non-mycorrhizal plants compare?
- ● The concentration of zinc in the root tissues of mycorrhizal plants was significantly lower than that in the non-mycorrhizal plants.

In Experiment 2, sections of mycorrhizal root that had been exposed to raised zinc concentrations, were mapped for zinc using a STEM system. Figure 4.33a shows a STEM image of a section containing a cortical cell and adjacent mantle hyphae while Figure 4.33b shows an X-ray map of the same section. In Figure 4.33b zinc concentration is proportional to the density of white dots.

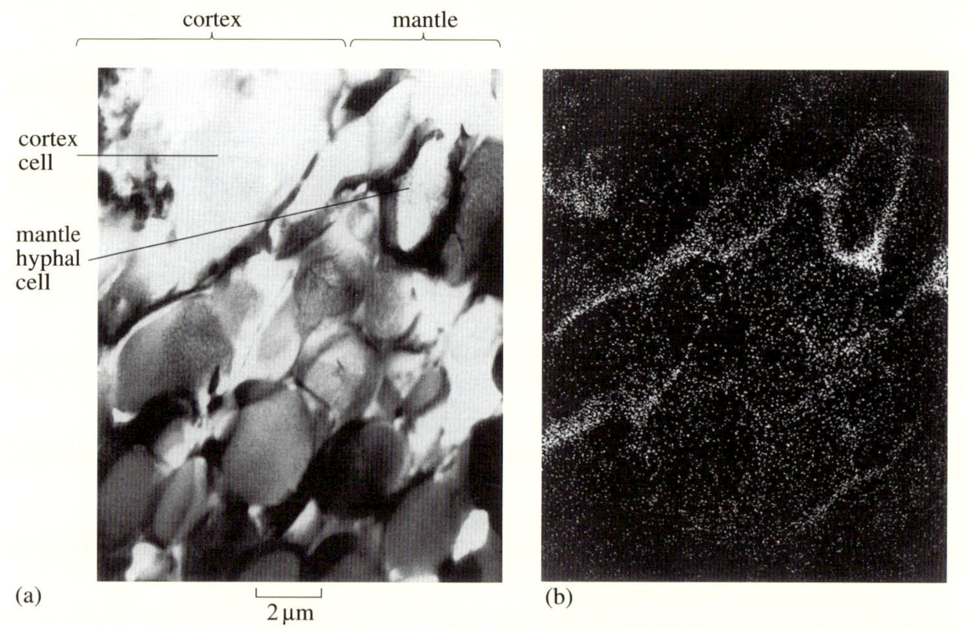

Figure 4.33 (a) STEM image of TS of zinc-treated, freeze-substituted *Betula* mycorrhiza, showing a plant cortex cell and a number of mantle hyphal cells. (b) X-ray map for zinc of the area in (a). Note: freeze-substitution is a preparation technique designed to preserve the *in vivo* concentrations and distribution of ions, as far as possible.

- ❍ Where is the zinc accumulating?
- ● Zinc is accumulating in the hyphal cell walls and interhyphal spaces. It is not accumulating in the hyphal cytoplasm or within the root cells of the birch.

- ❍ Are these observations from the first two experiments consistent with the hypothesis?

- Yes, it would be expected that the zinc concentration would be lower in the root tissues of the mycorrhizal plant, and that zinc would be accumulating around the fungus.

However, these observations do not explain why the overall root concentrations of zinc were higher in the roots of mycorrhizal than non-mycorrhizal plants in whole organ studies.

- ❍ Why do the results of Experiments 1 and 2 not explain where the excess zinc was?

- These whole-organ studies showed that root systems of mycorrhizal plants contain more zinc than non-mycorrhizal root systems. But in Experiment 1 the concentration of zinc in the hyphal mantle of the mycorrhizal roots was roughly similar to the concentration of zinc in the root as a whole.

In order to explain this apparent paradox, Experiment 3 compared the zinc concentration using spot analysis of thin sections of hyphae of the mantle (man) and those of the mycelium extending out into the growth medium (em). The results are summarized in Figure 4.34.

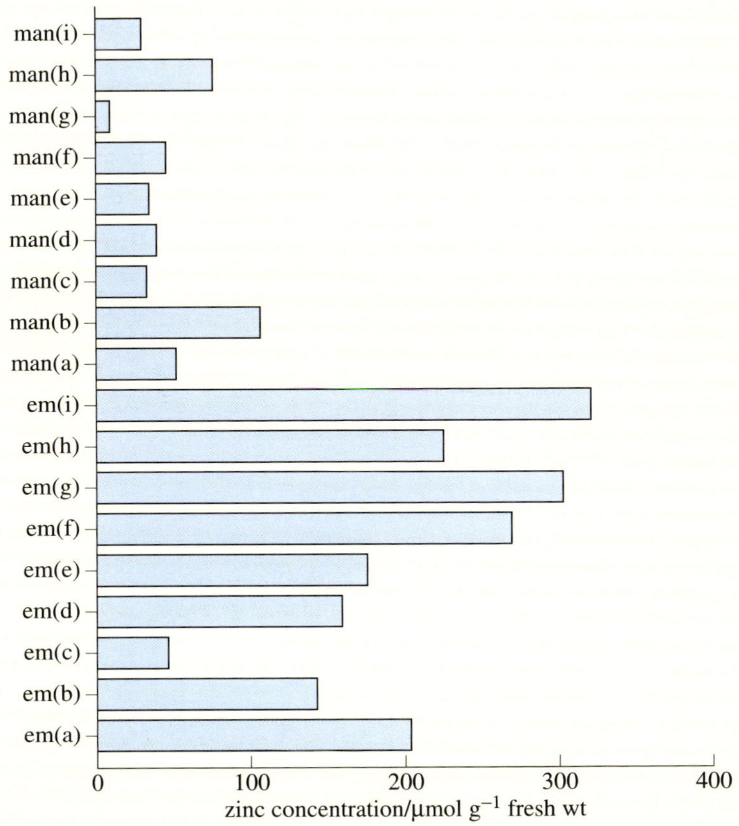

Figure 4.34 Mean zinc concentration in tufts of external mycelium [em(a)–(i)] and mantle hyphae [man(a)–(i)] of ectomycorrhizal *Betula* sp. grown at elevated zinc concentrations. Each bar represents the mean of five hyphae. The overall differences between em and man hyphae are significant at the 0.01% level. Data from Denny and Wilkins (1987).

❍ How do the zinc concentrations in the hyphal mantle and external mycelium compare?

● The concentrations of zinc in the external mycelium were generally significantly higher than those in the hyphal mantle.

❍ Do these findings support the hypothesis that the fungus was protecting the associated birch plant by accumulating zinc within the fungal tissues?

● Taken as a whole, yes, they do support the hypothesis.

However, it does not appear that the fungus controls the distribution of zinc by accumulating it within the cytoplasm of mantle hyphae. Given that we know the metal is not translocated along the hyphae, these results have been interpreted as suggesting that zinc in the soil solution is passively adsorbed onto the surface of the hyphae. This process removes zinc from the soil solution, so that the surfaces of the plant roots with mycorrhizas are exposed to a lower zinc concentration than those of non-mycorrhizal roots.

4.6.2 Saline soils: salty solutions

Saltmarshes are interesting examples of specialized communities that occur naturally on soils of little agricultural value. But, worldwide, artificial salinization of irrigated agricultural soils through poor water management practices is a serious problem. Yields of crops such as rice are severely limited in areas, such as parts of the Indian subcontinent, that already struggle to produce enough food to feed their populations. Whether the saline conditions have arisen naturally or through human activity, the problems they engender are the same.

Most vascular plants find high concentrations of Na^+ (and to a lesser extent Cl^-) harmful: elevated salt concentrations in the soil solution make it difficult for plants to take up water by osmosis, which can create conditions of water deficit (refer back to Section 3.6.2 on physiological drought); excessive uptake of Cl^- and Na^+ can lead to ion toxicity, e.g. by inhibiting enzyme reactions; while nutrient imbalances can result from Na^+ and Cl^- depressing the uptake of other ions or impairing the internal distribution of mineral nutrients, especially K^+ and Ca^{2+}.

Growth on such damp, saline soils requires special adaptations. If you were to visit a British saltmarsh with an experienced botanist, you would find a characteristic community of plants. Indeed, many of the species present in naturally occurring sites such as saltmarshes are so finely tuned to saline conditions that they can grow nowhere else. These **halophytes**, as they are called, often have a distinctive morphology. However, your botanist companion, in addition to encouraging you to examine the plants closely with a hand lens, may well urge you to taste them too. Plants such as the glassworts (*Salicornia* spp.) are very juicy and a little salty to the taste. **Succulents** like these have thick, fleshy leaves and stems (Figure 4.35), which lower exposure to salt when submerged by reducing the surface area to volume ratio of the plants. But succulence also enables large amounts of salt to be stored in the vacuoles in a well-diluted form, so that the salt concentrations in the cytoplasm are not damagingly high.

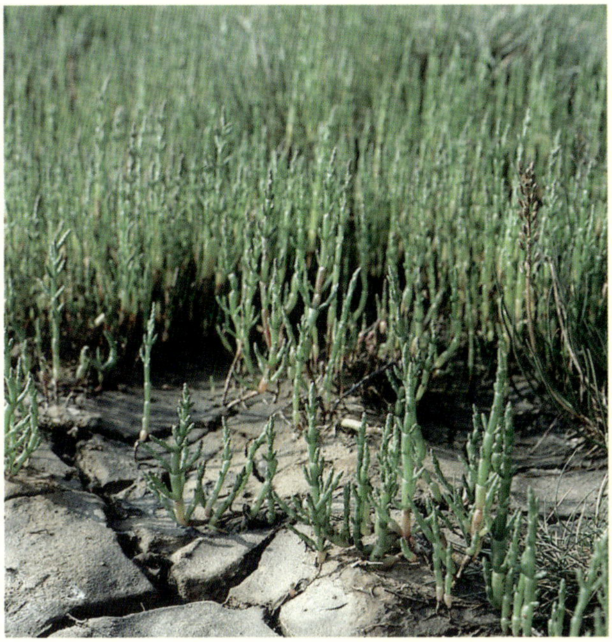

Figure 4.35 *Salicornia* sp. on a saltmarsh, showing succulent stems and leaves.

On the other hand, sea-lavender (*Limonium* spp., Figure 4.36a) has quite tough leaves that can taste very salty if licked because the salt concentration of the active photosynthetic tissue is reduced by salt extrusion. These leaves may be encrusted with salt because excess salts are secreted onto the leaf surface through special **salt glands**, from where it can be washed off by rain or dew (Figure 4.36b shows a salt gland of sea-lavender).

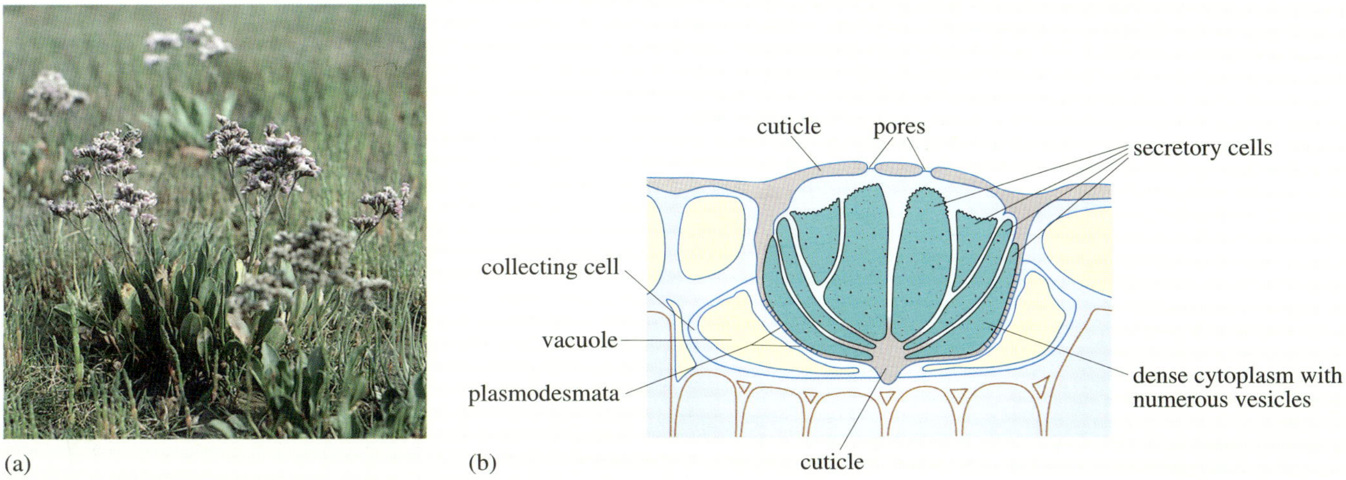

Figure 4.36 (a) Sea-lavender (*Limonium latifolium*), growing on a British saltmarsh. (b) A salt gland of sea-lavender. Na^+ and Cl^- ions accumulate in the vacuoles of the collecting cells, then move passively via plasmodesmata into the complex of secretory cells, which is largely surrounded by an impermeable cuticle except for a few surface pores. The secretory cells have the dense cytoplasm and corrugated outer wall characteristic of transfer cells and, in some way (probably by active transport at the plasma membrane), secrete salt onto the leaf surface.

In further contrast, shrubby seablite (*Sueda fruticosa*, Figure 4.37) and sea arrow-grass (*Triglochin maritima*) only taste salty if older leaves are chewed well. These species do not possess such elaborate salt extrusion mechanisms. They only taste salty if chewed well because they dump (*sequester*) the excess ions within the cell vacuoles of leaves destined for shedding.

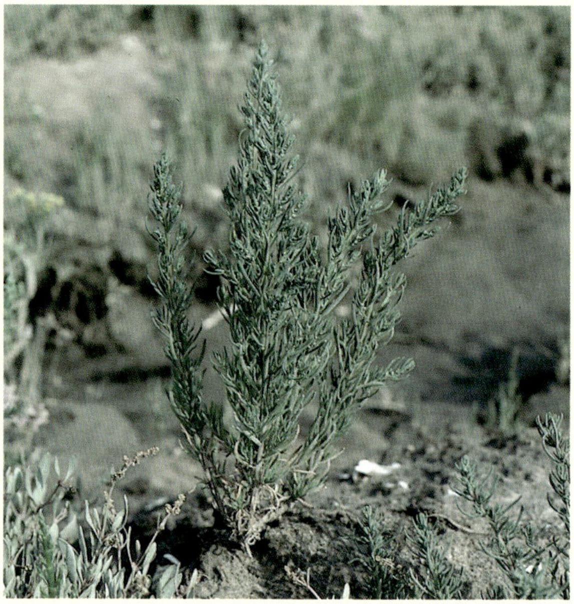

Figure 4.37 Shrubby seablite (*Sueda fruticosa*) growing on a British saltmarsh.

However, you may also find some populations of species on the saltmarsh that are more typical of 'normal' soils, such as rye grass (*Lolium perenne*). **Glycophytes** is the name given to conventional species with salt-adapted populations, and these salt-adapted individuals do not taste unusually salty: salt does not seem to reach the shoot. In fact, the root tissues do not contain elevated concentrations of salt either. Clearly, different saltmarsh plants find different ways of dealing with the problem of excess salt in the environment.

- ❍ On the basis of the 'taste-test' given above, can you speculate as to a major difference between halophytes and glycophytes in terms of their salt-resistance strategies?

- ● Salt-resistant glycophytes tend to exclude salt from their tissues by controlling uptake into the plant at the roots, while halophytes often take up a lot of salt, but then minimize the toxic effects, e.g. by restricting the salt to locations, such as the leaf surfaces, where it can do little harm.

Salt-resistant plants are described as **excluders** and **includers**, depending on which of these two strategies they practise. It follows from this that while salt glands and succulence, etc. may be the most dramatic manifestations of salt resistance, they are not necessarily essential for it. So what is?

FUNDAMENTALS OF SALT RESISTANCE

Plants do not have Na^+-pumps in their membranes and Na is not an essential element, therefore exclusion of Na^+ ions, as exhibited by most glycophytes, would seem to be the simplest solution to the problem. But if Na is not needed, how do Na^+ ions get into a plant and cause a problem in the first place? The data from work on the woody shrub *Phillyrea latifolia* give a clue to how this can work (Gucci *et al.*, 1997). Figure 4.38 shows what happens to the Na^+ and K^+ content of this shrub when the plant is exposed to rising salt concentrations.

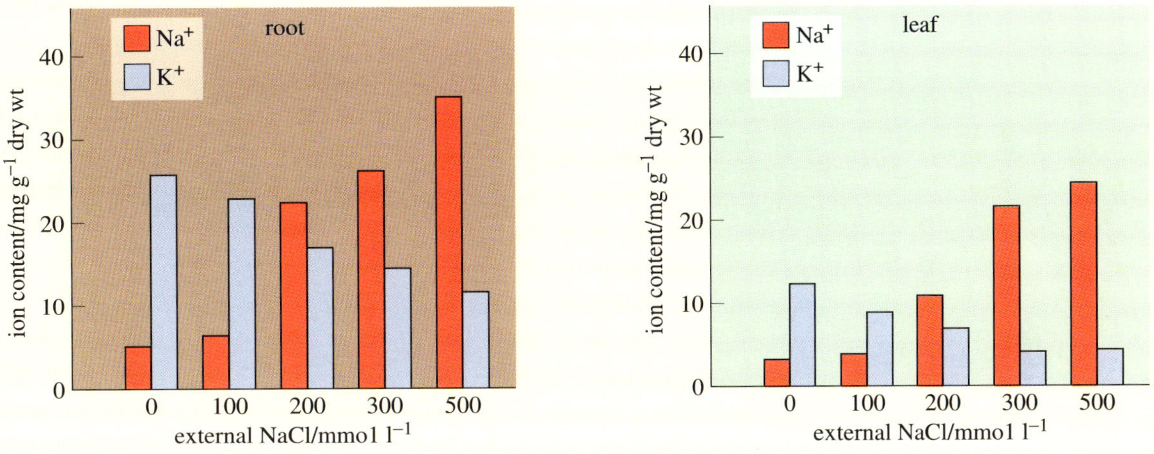

Figure 4.38 Na and K content of root and leaf tissue of *Phillyrea latifolia* plants, grown under glasshouse conditions. Tissue was sampled at the end of a period of salt treatment. Histograms are means of six (root) or nine (leaf) replicates. (*Note*: there was no treatment at 400 mmol l^{-1}). Data from Gucci *et al.* (1997).

- ❍ As the external salt concentration rises, what happens to the Na^+ and K^+ content of the tissues?

- ● The concentration of Na^+ rises and that of K^+ falls in the roots and leaves.

It appears that the Na^+ ions out-compete the K^+ ions for specific binding sites on the K^+ transport proteins, thereby gaining entry to the plant cells via the K^+ uptake system and, in so doing, cause K^+ deficiency. Consequently, reducing Na^+ uptake probably means having to reduce the number of K^+ binding sites.

- ❍ What implications would fewer K^+ uptake sites have for the vigour of the plant?

- ● The plant would have an intrinsically low growth rate, because of K^+ deficiency.

In fact, this resistance strategy is adopted by most graminaceous (i.e. members of the grass family) glycophytes, probably because it is genetically easy to achieve. A mutation at a single locus determining the density of K^+ uptake sites can markedly increase an individual's salt resistance. It also explains why salt-resistant individuals are commonly found, at low frequencies, in populations growing on non-saline soils.

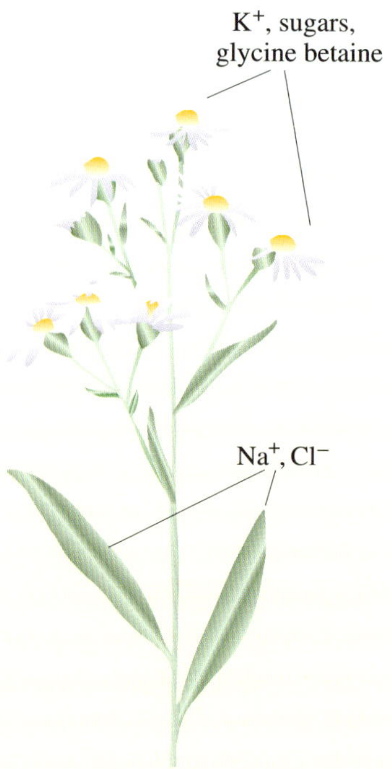

Figure 4.39 Drawing illustrating the distribution of solutes used to balance the osmotic pressure of various components of sea aster exposed to saline conditions.

- ❍ Why should such salt-resistant mutants be present at *low* frequencies on normal soils?

- ● Because their lack of vigour and slow growth rates would make them poor competitors against wild-type plants.

The lack of vigour caused by excluding K^+ (as well as Na^+) is likely to be compounded by the fact that the plants must expend valuable resources on synthesizing alternative solutes that can raise the osmotic pressure of the cell contents sufficiently to permit uptake of water by osmosis. In glycophytes, these **compatible solutes** are commonly proline, D-sorbitol and mannitol, partly because they are largely non-toxic, water soluble and lack a net charge, and partly because they are already present as a normal component of cell contents.

Inclusion, as practised by halophytes, is energetically cheaper than exclusion because it uses Na^+ ions to raise the internal osmotic pressure so that water can be taken up. However, many more mechanisms are required to protect sensitive sites from Na^+-toxicity and overcome the problems of K^+-deficiency. Consequently, genetic control of Na^+-inclusion is multigenic and the species involved are necessarily salt specialists. For example: many halophytes utilize a particularly effective compatible solute, **glycine betaine**, to protect their most sensitive, subcellular components. Sea aster (*Aster tripolium*) uses Na^+ and Cl^- for osmotic adjustment in the leaves, but protects its flowers with K^+, glycine betaine and sugars (Figure 4.39).

Many halophytes have overcome the problem of potassium deficiency by being very efficient in their use of K^+. By substituting Na^+ for K^+ in some cellular roles, many halophytes can overcome both the problem of excessive Na^+ and that of K^+ deficiency. They use the abundant Na^+ for osmotic adjustment in the vacuoles and so conserve the K^+ for its essential metabolic roles. **Natrophilic** species, e.g. members of the goosefoot family (Amaranthaceae), reduce their need for K^+ further, by substituting Na^+ for K^+ in cellular processes such as protein synthesis. The essence of salt-inclusion then, is effective internal compartmentalization and mobilization of ions, the capacity for which resides in enhanced membrane transport.

The upshot is that succulence and salt glands may help plants to flourish in saline habitats, but these features are not fundamental to salt resistance. More important are enhanced membrane transport functions that enable the plants (whether halophytes or glycophytes) to protect their salt-sensitive sites from excessive exposure to Na^+ and Cl^- ions and use the scarce nutrients efficiently. Furthermore, it is probably through genetic manipulation of the ion-transport sites in terms of their distribution and, perhaps more importantly, their specificity in cell membranes that the development of salt-resistant crops will be achieved.

4.6.3 Aluminium toxicity: precipitating an acid problem

Aluminium is the third most abundant element in the Earth's crust. Its chemistry is very complex: at neutral to mildly acid pH values it exists as insoluble aluminosilicates and oxides, but at pH values less than 5.5 it is released into the soil solution as Al^{3+}, which is the main **phytotoxic** form. Consequently, aluminium toxicity is a major factor limiting crop productivity on acid soils, including the heavily leached soils of the tropics, which comprise 40% of the world's arable lands. But aluminium toxicity is becoming a more widespread problem, because soil acidification results from some common agricultural practices as well as from acid precipitation caused by burning fossil fuels (Figure 4.40). Gaseous oxides of carbon, nitrogen and sulfur are released during combustion and combine with moisture in the air to form acids, such as carbonic, nitric and sulfuric, which then fall to the ground in rain and snow, etc.

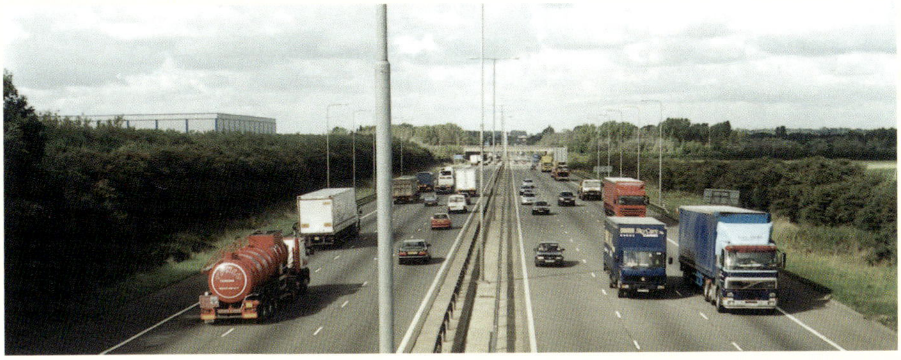

Figure 4.40 Burning of fossil fuels such as diesel and petrol releases gaseous oxides of carbon, nitrogen and sulfur; these combine with moisture in the air to form acids, such as carbonic, nitric and sulfuric, which then fall to the ground in precipitation.

Aluminium toxicity causes inhibition of root growth at the meristem which leads to problems of water and nutrient acquisition. Although the mechanisms of toxicity are poorly understood, we know that Al^{3+} can form complexes with many common and important cellular components, e.g. ATP, RNA, proteins, carboxylic acids and phospholipids. We also know that significant amounts of Al^{3+} can enter the symplast rapidly enough for aluminium toxicity to involve a direct symplastic interaction between aluminium and cellular components. The diameter of the Al^{3+} ion is most similar to Mg^{2+}. Consequently, Al^{3+} uptake probably occurs most often via the Mg^{2+} channels and it may also interfere with Mg^{2+}-regulated processes such as phosphate transfer reactions, cytoskeletal interactions and signal transduction events.

Fortunately, many plants exhibit genetic-based variability in aluminium sensitivity and plant breeders have exploited this variability to develop aluminium-resistant cultivars of crops. It is known that control of aluminium resistance can be multigenic, in which there are one or two major genes and a number of minor genes controlling a number of resistance mechanisms. Al-resistant cultivars exhibit higher root growth rates and higher rates of protein synthesis than Al-sensitive lines. Aluminium resistance would seem to result primarily from exclusion of aluminium from the root apex because resistant lines accumulate less aluminium in the root tips.

MECHANISMS OF ALUMINIUM RESISTANCE

Current evidence suggests that, unlike salt resistance, differences in ion-uptake transport proteins in the plasma membrane do not represent the principal resistance mechanism. In contrast, Al^{3+}-exclusion seems to be achieved through changes to root exudates: agents such as organic acids present in the root exudates appear to bind to the Al^{3+} ions making them both less toxic and less readily taken up. The emerging data tell an interesting story.

EVIDENCE FOR RESISTANCE THROUGH BINDING OF ALUMINIUM

Aluminium-resistant French beans (*Phaseolus* sp.) have been found to exude citrate from their roots; maize (*Zea mays*) releases citrate and inorganic phosphate, which forms insoluble aluminium phosphates. However, most of the work has been done on wheat (*Triticum aestivum*); this species secretes mostly malate ions, but also phosphate in some circumstances.

Figure 4.41 shows the rates of malate exudation from roots of two wheat cultivars — Al-resistant Atlas and Al-sensitive Scout — when seedlings are challenged with raised aluminium concentrations in the external solution (Huang *et al.*, 1996).

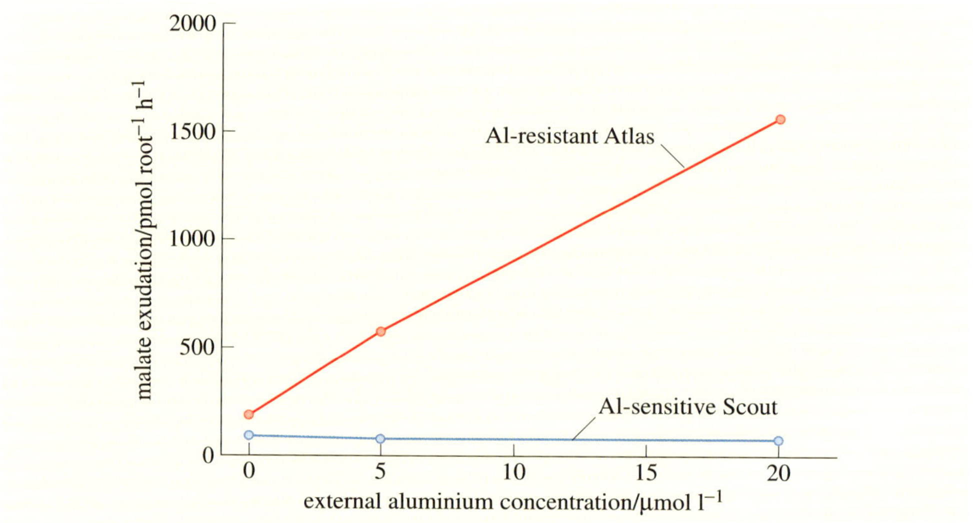

Figure 4.41 Influence of different concentrations of Al on the rate of malate exudation from roots of intact wheat seedlings. Data from Huang *et al.* (1996).

❍ How does malate exudation in Atlas differ from that in Scout?

● Malate production in Atlas is proportional to the aluminium concentration in the external solution while that in Scout remains low and constant.

Thus, the Al-resistant cultivar responds to elevated aluminium concentrations with enhanced malate exudation, but the non-resistant cultivar does not. It has also been shown that malate efflux is triggered specifically by Al^{3+}, but not La^{3+}, Sc^{3+}, Mn^{2+} or Zn^{2+}, and is localized at the root apex (*note*: La denotes lanthanum and Sc denotes scandium).

❍ How do these two observations support the hypothesis that malate secretion is a mechanism of aluminium resistance?

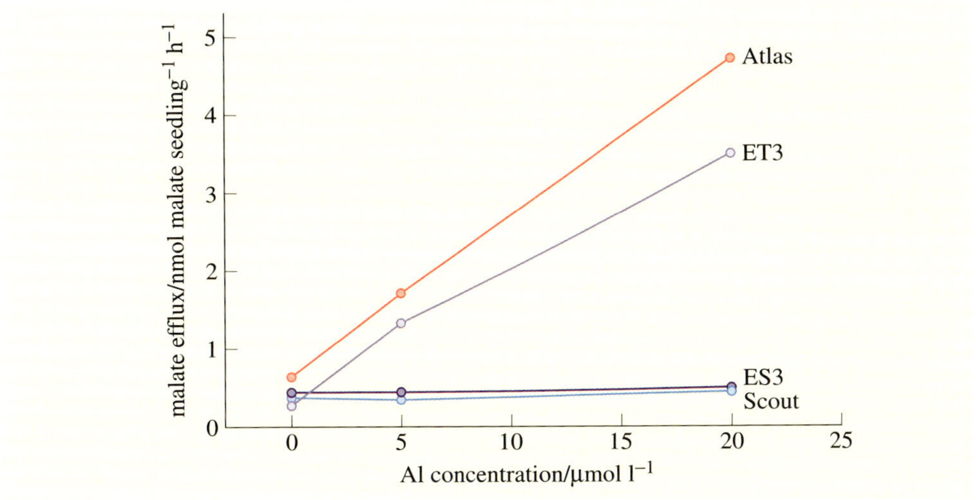

Figure 4.42 Effect of Al concentration on malate exudation in the two Al-resistant (Atlas and ET3) and two Al-sensitive (Scout and ES3) wheat genotypes. Seedlings were exposed to Al for 7 h. Pooled data are of two separate experiments with five to seven replicates. Data from Pellet *et al.* (1996).

- The first implies that malate secretion is a *specific* response to Al, and the second that it is restricted to the plant parts most sensitive to Al toxicity.

However, the really crucial evidence needed to prove that malate secretion is the primary mechanism of aluminium resistance, is a demonstration that high rates of Al-triggered malate efflux are associated with alleles for Al resistance in genetic studies. Al resistance was investigated in two wheat cultivars: Al-resistant Atlas and Al-sensitive Scout, in which resistance is multigenic, and also in two near-isogenic lines, Al-resistant ET3 and Al-sensitive ES3 (i.e. they differ only in the presence or absence of a single Al-resistance gene at the *ALT*-1 locus) (Pellet *et al.*, 1996).

Malate efflux was found to be proportional to the concentration of aluminium in the bathing solution in both resistant lines. Malate efflux by the sensitive genotypes was consistently low at all aluminium concentrations (Figure 4.42).

- ❍ Did the two Al-resistant genotypes produce similar malate efflux responses?

- Malate efflux was slightly, but significantly higher in Atlas, the multigenic strain.

Atlas also exhibited enhanced phosphate release (see Figure 4.43).

- ❍ How did phosphate efflux compare in the two near isogenic lines?

- Phosphate efflux by ET3 and ES3 were not significantly different from each other and only slightly greater than for the Al-sensitive Scout genotype.

As enhanced phosphate efflux is not a feature of Al-resistance in ET3, this characteristic cannot be controlled by the *ALT*-1 locus. Therefore, enhanced phosphate efflux in the resistant Atlas must be controlled by A1-resistance alleles at one or more additional loci. Figure 4.44 shows that the enhanced phosphate efflux was also localized to the root apex.

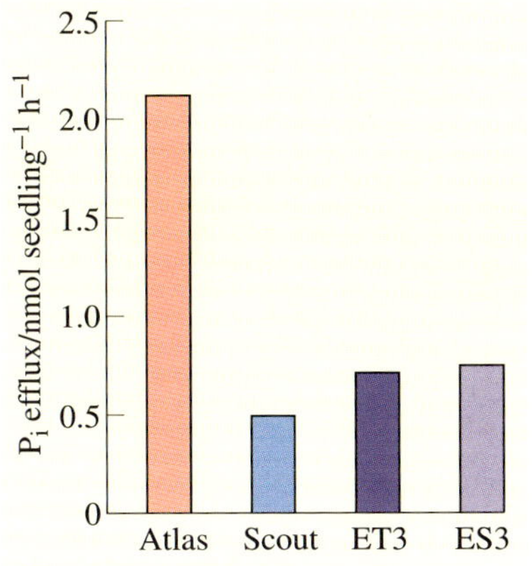

Figure 4.43 Constitutive phosphate exudation in the two Al-resistant (Atlas and ET3) and two Al-sensitive (Scout and ES3) wheat genotypes. Rates are averages over three Al concentrations (0, 5 and 20 µmol l^{-1} Al). Seedlings were exposed to Al for 7 h. Pooled data are of two separate experiments with five to seven replicates. Data from Pellet *et al.* (1996).

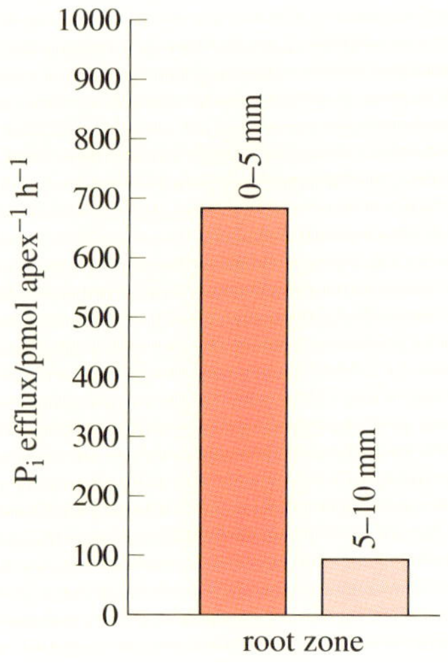

Figure 4.44 Phosphate exudation in two different segments of excised root of Al-resistant Atlas (wheat cultivar), measured from root tips. (*Note*: 1 pmol = 1×10^{-12} mol.) Data from Pellet *et al*. (1996).

Furthermore, both malate and phosphate have been shown to ameliorate aluminium toxicity: addition of these ions to toxic solutions of aluminium protects aluminium-sensitive roots from toxicity.

❍ What do the results from these experiments suggest about the genetic basis for Al resistance in the wheat cultivar Atlas?

● These results provide physiological evidence that Al resistance in Atlas is controlled by at least two genes. The primary mechanism is the exudation of malate ions (a mechanism controlled by the *ALT*-1 locus in Scout and ET3), but it appears that both malate and phosphate exudation processes act in concert to enhance Al exclusion and Al resistance in Atlas.

Overall, there seems to be convincing evidence that exclusion of aluminium is a major mechanism of aluminium tolerance, and that it involves secreting binding ligands in the form of organic acids such as malate and citrate, with phosphate efflux representing a back-up resistance mechanism in some varieties where resistance is multigenic. Small differences in aluminium binding properties of the plasma membrane and cell wall do exist in some cases, but they are probably controlled by minor resistance genes as their effects are likely to be comparatively small.

Organic acids are produced by all plants. Malic acid, for example, plays a role in internal translocation of cations, pH homeostasis and scavenging for soil minerals, especially iron. It is also a metabolite in the TCA cycle and in C4 metabolism (Section 2.5.2). Therefore aluminium resistance requires only a modification to the malate regulatory system. However, enhanced synthesis of organic acids inevitably imposes a cost on Al-resistant plants, and if P is in short supply, secreting phosphate is also an expensive option. Consequently, it is not surprising that Al-resistant plants are less vigorous competitors, and exist at low frequencies, in populations found on 'normal' soils.

Summary of Section 4.6

1. Many metallic, essential elements can become toxic at high concentrations, such as at ore outcrops or in spoils from metal mining and extraction.
2. Mycorrhizas have been found to ameliorate zinc toxicity.
3. X-ray microanalysis has been used in experiments to shed light on the mechanism of ectomycorrhizal amelioration of zinc toxicity.
4. It appears that the zinc ions are adsorbed to the surface of the fungal mycelium, thereby lowering the concentration of the metal in the soil solution which results in the associated plants being exposed to less of the metal.
5. Saltmarshes are dominated by halophytic plants that specialize in living in saline habitats. They exhibit a number of ingenious mechanisms, e.g. salt glands and succulence, for disposing of excess Na^+ and Cl^- ions in their environment.
6. Glycophytes are conventional plants with some salt-resistant populations, that may occur on saltmarshes.

7 Most glycophytes adopt a salt-exclusion strategy of resistance to excess salinity which avoids salt toxicity but requires the synthesis of large amounts of compatible solutes to overcome the water deficit problem. This strategy is genetically simple to achieve, but tends to lead to nutrient deficiency and low growth rates.

8 Most halophytes adopt a salt-inclusion strategy which is energetically cheaper than salt-exclusion, but requires enhanced membrane transport functions in many locations, to enable the Na^+ and Cl^- ions to be restricted to sites where they are harmless, and K^+ etc., to be used very efficiently.

9 Natrophils can substitute Na^+ for K^+ in some cellular processes. Halophytes protect their most sensitive sites with glycine betaine, a compatible solute restricted to water-stress specialists. Such complete and sophisticated adaptation involves many genes.

10 Enhanced membrane transport functions are fundamental to all salt-tolerance mechanisms. The key to developing salt-resistant crops probably lies in the genetic manipulation of the specificity and/or distribution of membrane-bound ion-transport sites.

11 Aluminium toxicity is a widespread and serious problem in soils of low pH, a problem that is being exacerbated by acid precipitation.

12 Aluminium toxicity is associated with the Al^{3+} cation: it causes root stunting, and can combine with and interfere with the activity of many important cellular components.

13 Experimental research has revealed that the principal mechanism of aluminium resistance is the enhanced release of organic acids at the root surface in response to elevated concentrations of Al^{3+} in the soil. These acids then bind to, and thereby neutralize, the Al^{3+} cations.

4.7 CROP DEVELOPMENT

Over the millennia, certain types of plants have been selected for use as crops while others have not. Why should some species make better crops than others?

Figure 4.45 shows the growth responses of three native plant species to increasing phosphate availability.

- ❍ Which species shows greatest increase in growth rate in response to increased P supply and which the smallest?

- ● Nettle *(Urtica dioica)* shows greatest increase in growth rate and wavy hair grass *(Deschampsia flexuosa)* the least.

Plants such as nettle (*Urtica dioica)* are typical **nutrient-responsive** plants. They are capable of very high growth rates, but require high levels of mineral nutrients to be available in order to achieve those rates. (Nettles are typically found in drainage ditches at the edges of fertilized fields, where they can benefit from the nutritious run-off from the fields.) Wavy hair grass (*Deschampsia flexuosa*) is a typical **nutrient-insensitive** plant that can maintain higher growth rates in conditions where nutrients are in short supply, but are incapable of increasing

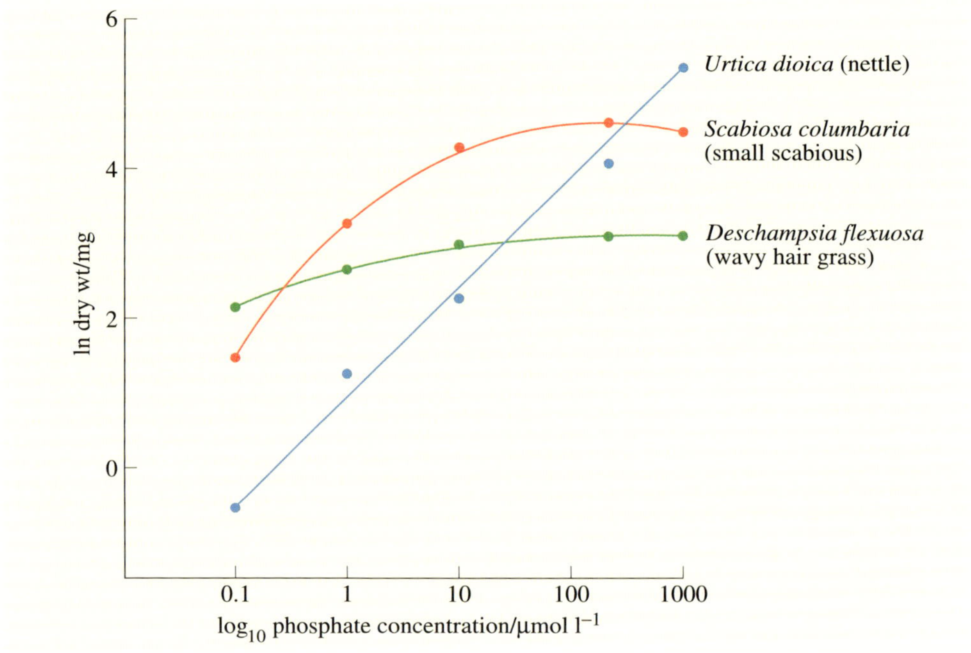

Figure 4.45 Growth response of three ecologically contrasted wild species to phosphate concentration in the growing medium, after 6 weeks. Data from Rorison (1968).

their growth rates much, even when there are abundant nutrient supplies. (Wavy hair grass grows in acid heaths, moors and open woods.) *Scabiosa columbaria* (the small scabious) is interesting in that it shows roughly intermediate growth rates, but also shows a decline in growth rates at high phosphate availability. This particular species stores up to 80% of its phosphate in inorganic form, so the fall in growth rate probably reflects luxury uptake when it is abundant, with the plant storing up phosphate for use in times of shortage. The small scabious is found in dry calcareous grassland and rocky places, i.e. habitats in which phosphate deficiency is quite common.

Species adapted to nutrient-poor soils such as those that are calcareous, acid and saline, tend to be nutrient-insensitive and have low intrinsic growth rates. Remember, plants adapted to toxic soils often have reduced capacity for nutrient uptake; reduced potassium uptake may be the cost that salt-resistant species pay when they limit sodium uptake; similarly calcifuges may have reduced Fe/Mg uptake as a result of limiting aluminium uptake. These species cannot respond to large increases in the supply of major nutrients, but can scavenge effectively for minor nutrients in short supply. Species adapted to nutrient-rich soils have the ability to make use of superabundant major nutrients, but are not as good at scavenging for potentially deficient minor nutrients. Consequently, the high species diversity in chalk grasslands is maintained by the effective exclusion of nutrient-responsive grasses such as cocksfoot (*Dactylis glomerata)* and perennial rye-grass *(Lolium perenne)* which would otherwise smother and out-compete the slow-growing calcicolous species that are adapted to survive with very low nutrient availability. This interaction also explains why old hay meadows are such sensitive habitats. They are nutrient-poor but floristically rich; as soon as the meadows are treated with fertilizers to boost the yield of hay, the nutrient-responsive species shoot up and exclude the nutrient-insensitive meadow flowers.

Crop species tend to be of the nutrient-responsive type, selected because of their fast growth rates and thus their potential for high yields. But therein lies a problem: with ever increasing human populations there are pressures for higher and higher yields. However increasing salinization and acid precipitation coupled with a desire to avoid the excessive use of artificial fertilizers and pesticides, etc. create conditions that nutrient-responsive plants are less well suited for than are nutrient-insensitive plants. What is the solution?

Traditional crop breeding required selective breeding from individuals or populations that demonstrated particularly favourable characteristics. But there are several problems associated with this method: it is very lengthy and rather haphazard, only a proportion of the progeny from a cross are likely to display all of the desirable characteristics and these progeny may show unforeseen disadvantages. Furthermore, not all crosses are feasible because, generally, hybridization is only possible between closely related lines. An alternative method for genetic enhancement of cultivars may be to try using biotechnology to transfer specific genes from one line to another. This approach should be quicker and produce more reliable results (see Chapter 5). Indeed, modern cytogenetics allows quantitative trait loci to be identified and shunted around. These loci are regions of chromosomes which contain genes that control such factors as performance under conditions of N-deficiency, drought and salinity stress. Such loci have been identified in wheat, maize and rice and put on the chromosome maps. For multigenic traits, modern techniques that allow whole chromosomes or chromosome arms to be relocated are a major hope and are subject to a worldwide research effort. Therefore, these methods have the potential to increase resistance to toxicity such as that caused by salinity or aluminium, or to improve uptake efficiency for scarce nutrients such as iron and phosphate (see Section 4.5.1). They may even imbue plants with the capacity to form symbiotic associations that they would not have naturally.

A completely different strategy may be to ensure that crops are inoculated with the most suitable microbial symbionts. Careful selection of mycorrhizal partners can boost yields considerably (see Section 4.5.3). Finally, it may be advantageous to look for new species with crop potential from among the groups of plants specifically adapted to particular problem conditions.

SUMMARY OF SECTION 4.7

1 Plants can be classified as nutrient-responsive or nutrient-insensitive, depending on whether they exhibit a rapid growth response to added nutrients.

2 Most crop plants fall into the nutrient-responsive category, because they are able to generate high yields, but only in heavily fertilized conditions.

3 In the light of modern concerns about agricultural sustainability, the current trend is to look for ways of feeding the population that avoid the extensive use of pesticides and artificial fertilizers.

4 Modern cytogenetics and biotechnology may have the capacity to produce crops that can produce high yields on less fertile soils, while avoiding pests and diseases through genetic resistance mechanisms.

5 Mutualistic symbionts, such as mycorrhizal fungi and N-fixing bacteria, may also offer some solutions to this problem.

REFERENCES

Clarkson, D. T. (1993) Roots and the delivery of solutes to the xylem, *Philosophical Transactions of the Royal Society of London Series B*, **341**, pp. 5–17.

Clarkson, D. T. and Saker, L. R. (1989) Sulphate influx in wheat and barley roots becomes more sensitive to specific-binding reagents when plants are sulphate-deficient, *Planta*, **178**, pp. 249–257.

Denny, H. J. and Wilkins, D. A. (1987) Zinc tolerance in *Betula* spp. IV The mechanisms of ectomycorrhizal amelioration of zinc toxicity, *New Phytologist*, **106**, pp. 545–553.

Gucci, R., Aronne, G., Lombardini, L. and Tattini, M. (1997) Salinity tolerance in *Phillyrea* species, *New Phytologist*, **135**, pp. 227–234.

Hoffland, E., Findenegg, G.R. and Nelemans, J. A. (1989) Solubilization of rock phosphate by rape. II. Local root exudation of organic acids as a response to P-starvation, *Plant Soil*, **113**, pp. 161–165.

Huang, J. W., Pellet, D. M., Papernik, L. A. and Kochian, L. V. (1996) Aluminium interactions with voltage-dependent calcium transport in plasma membrane vesicles isolated from roots of aluminium-sensitive and -resistant wheat cultivars, *Plant Physiology*, **110**, pp. 561–569.

Le Tacon, F., Alvarez, I. F., Bouchard, D., Henrion, B., Jackson, R. M., Luff, S., Parlade, J. I., Pera, J., Stenstrom, E., Villeneuve, N. and Walker, C. (1992) Variations in field response of forest trees to nursery ectomycorrhizal inoculation in Europe, in *Mycorrhizas in Ecosystems*, D. J. Read, D. H. Lewis, A. H. Fitter and I. J. Alexander (eds), CAB International, London.

MacQueen, H., Burnett, J. and Cann, A. (2001) The study of microbes, in *Microbes*, H. MacQueen (ed.), The Open University, Milton Keynes, pp. 1–63.

Novacky A., Ullrich-Ebercus, C.I. and Luttge, U. (1980) pH and membrane potential changes during glucose uptake in *Lemna gibba* G1 and their response to light, *Planta*, **149**, pp. 321–326.

Pellet, D. M., Papernik, L. A. and Kochian, L. V. (1996) Multiple aluminium-resistance mechanisms in wheat, *Plant Physiology*, **112**, pp. 591–597.

Ridge, I. (2001) Microbial metabolism, in *Microbes*, H. MacQueen (ed.), The Open University, Milton Keynes, pp. 65–97.

Rorison, I. H. (1968) The response to phosphorus of some ecologically distinct plant species. I. Growth rates and phosphorus absorption. *New Phytologist*, **67**, pp. 913–923.

Swithenby, M. and O'Shea, P. (2001) Membranes and transport, in *The Core of Life Vol. I*, J. Saffrey (ed.), The Open University, Milton Keynes, pp. 107–164.

Tarafdar, J. C. and Jungk, A. (1987) Phosphatase activity in the rhizosphere and its relation to the depletion of soil organic phosphorus, *Biology and Fertility of Soils*, **3**, pp. 199–204.

FURTHER READING

Marschner, H. (1995) *Mineral Nutrition in Higher Plants* (2nd edn), Academic Press, London. [Translated from the original German, this is an incredibly broad and deep treatment of the subject that includes lots of original research data, but it is rather a heavy read.]

Read, D. J., Lewis, D. H., Fitter, A. H. and Alexander, I. J. (1992) *Mycorrhizas in Ecosystems*, CAB International, London. [Collection of papers, by most of the current researchers in the field, on ecological aspects of mycorrhizal biology.]

Smith, F. A. and Read, D. J. (1997) *Mycorrhizal Symbiosis* (2nd edn), Academic Press, San Diego. [Standard textbook on mycorrhizal structure and function.]

Taiz, L. and Zeiger, E. (1998) *Plant Physiology* (2nd edn), Sinauer Associates Inc., Sunderland, Massachusetts. [A good general book which covers topics in this chapter.]

PLANT GROWTH AND DEVELOPMENT

5

5.1 INTRODUCTION

During the course of its life cycle, a flowering plant passes through a series of pre-programmed developmental stages that begins with seed germination and ends with senescence. Both the nature and the timing of these events are under genetic control. Being sessile organisms, plants have to tolerate the environmental conditions to which they are exposed and, as a consequence, they have evolved the ability to adapt their programme of differentiation and growth. The extent of such *plastic development* or *phenotypic plasticity* varies widely between plant species but, in general, is much more pronounced than in most animals.

In this chapter we outline some of the developmental events that a plant undergoes and discuss the ways in which the environment can influence them. The advances taking place in developmental genetics and the increasing expertise in sequencing plant genomes are leading to a rapid increase in our understanding of the mechanisms by which the environment can influence plant growth. In particular, the study of mutants and transgenic plants is enabling plant biologists to pose critical questions about the regulation of developmental plasticity and its control.

In addition to the written material in this chapter, there is a CD-ROM 'Plant Gene Manipulation' that provides you with the opportunity to design and carry out some experiments in a 'virtual' laboratory. The first exercise takes you through techniques for manipulating flower colour and the second enables you to undertake the genetic engineering of a tomato fruit to improve some of its characteristics. These exercises are designed to complement the text and can be attempted at any time during study of this chapter, although by leaving it to the end you will have studied all the theoretical background first.

5.2 EMBRYOGENESIS, SEED FORMATION AND GERMINATION

The life cycle of a flowering plant commences when one of the sperm nuclei emerging from the pollen tube fuses with the egg cell in the ovary to form a diploid zygote, while the other fuses with the two central nuclei to form a triploid endosperm (Figure 1.24). At the beginning of embryo development (**embryogenesis**), the first two divisions of the zygote occur in a periclinal orientation (parallel to the main axis) producing a filament of two then four cells (Figure 5.1). The initial division takes place asymmetrically and results in the formation of a small apical cell and a larger basal cell. This unequal division places the daughter nuclei into different environments and is a commonly observed event that establishes polarity in plants. The apical cell forms the **proembryo** while the basal cell develops into the **suspensor** and remains attached to the maternal tissue.

Once the proembryo reaches the four-cell stage, divisions occur in both periclinal and anticlinal (at right angles to the main axis) planes and result in the formation of a sphere of cells. This globular structure has no discernible organs but the cells at this stage are already arranged into discrete layers, and once the heart stage (Figure 5.1) is reached in dicotyledonous plants, rudimentary cotyledons or seed leaves can be identified. Further development leads to the formation of a torpedo and then a walking-stick shape by which time the major features of the seedling can be identified (Figure 5.1).

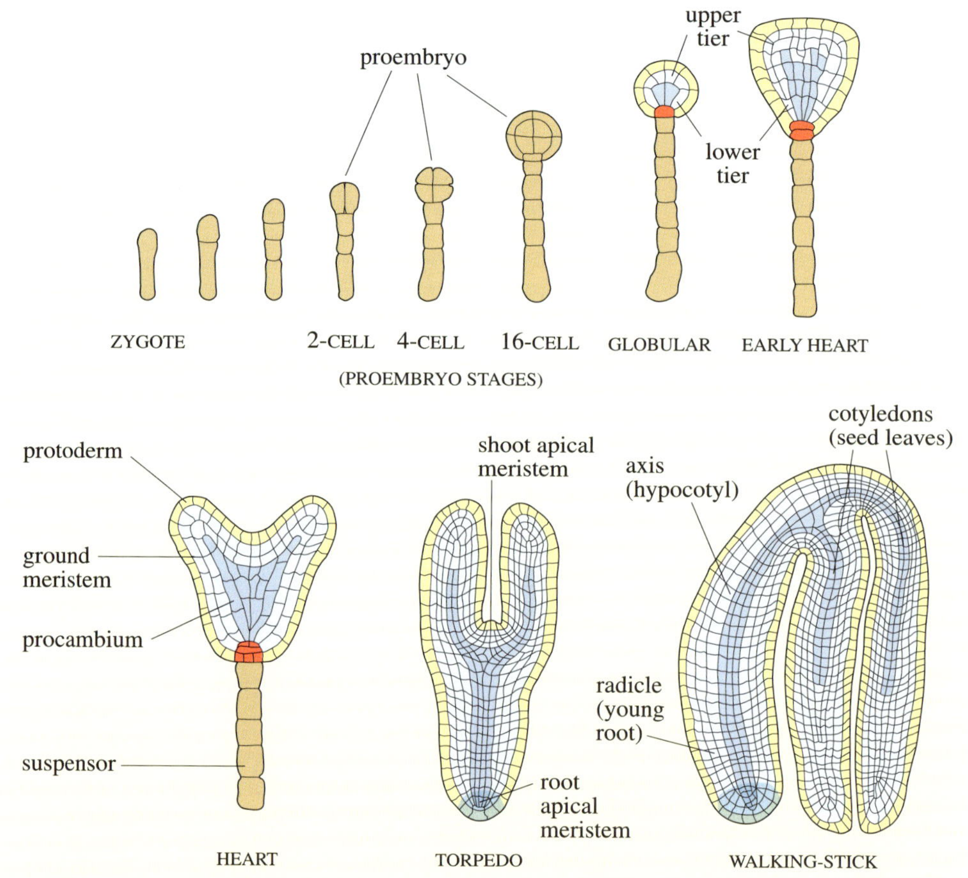

Figure 5.1 Embryogenesis in a typical dicot (*Arabidopsis*). Early stages are named according to the number of cells in the proembryo, later stages by the shape of the embryo. At the globular stage, transverse divisions along an apical–basal axis divide the proembryo into an upper tier and a lower tier of cells. Signs of tissue differentiation into three fundamental cell layers are also evident at this stage: the protoderm (which gives rise to the epidermis), the ground meristem (giving the cortex) and the procambium (giving the pith and stele). The root and shoot apical meristems become evident at the early heart and heart stages respectively but are labelled here at the torpedo stage.

- ❍ From Figure 5.1 and information in Chapter 1, describe the main components of the embryo at the walking-stick stage.

- ● It comprises three cell layers: an outer protoderm underlain by ground meristem with a central strand of procambium. There is an axis (the hypocotyl) with a radicle (young root) and root apical meristem at one end and a shoot apical meristem and two nutrient-storing seed leaves (cotyledons) at the other end.

In this section we consider the control of embryogenesis (5.2.1), general features of seed germination (5.2.2) and finally a case study of barley grains (5.2.3) which illustrates the role of plant growth regulators and changes in gene expression in germination.

5.2.1 REGULATION OF EMBRYOGENESIS

The process of embryogenesis begins with a single cell and ends with a multicellular structure with discrete organs and tissues arranged in a highly precise way. Although few of the molecular and biochemical events associated with embryogenesis have been established, the study of mutants in *Arabidopsis* (see Box 5.1) and maize (*Zea mays*) is providing clues. Two types of mutants have been characterized. The first group results in such major disruptions to the development of the embryo that they prove lethal. Some of these mutated genes encode key regulators in embryogenesis while others may generate defects in general metabolic functions. The second group is termed **pattern mutants** as they lead to rearrangements in the structure of the embryo. It has been estimated that perhaps as many as 4000 genes are required for embryogenesis to take place in *Arabidopsis* but only 1% of them are involved in the design of the basic body plan.

BOX 5.1 *ARABIDOPSIS* AS A MODEL PLANT SYSTEM

Arabidopsis thaliana, or thale cress (family Brassicaceae), is a small weed with a generation time of only 6 weeks (Figure 5.2). It can be readily cultivated in the laboratory and one individual produces many thousands of seeds. The genome of this plant is small, with a haploid size of 100 megabase pairs of DNA and by 2001 had been sequenced in its entirety. The challenge for plant scientists is to identify the function of the approximately 30 000 genes that have been sequenced. One way to achieve this goal is to generate mutants where individual genes have been 'knocked out' or switched off by mutagens that may delete or rearrange either a single base or a substantial amount of DNA, and to determine the impact of such mutations on the phenotype of the plant. Genes that play crucial roles in events such as growth are easy to identify but those that have more subtle effects are much more difficult. Mutants have been identified (Figure 5.2) that exhibit defects in the development of embryos, roots, leaves and flowers, as well as stomata, cuticular waxes and root hairs. Further details can be found at http://nasc.nott.ac.uk/ (2001).

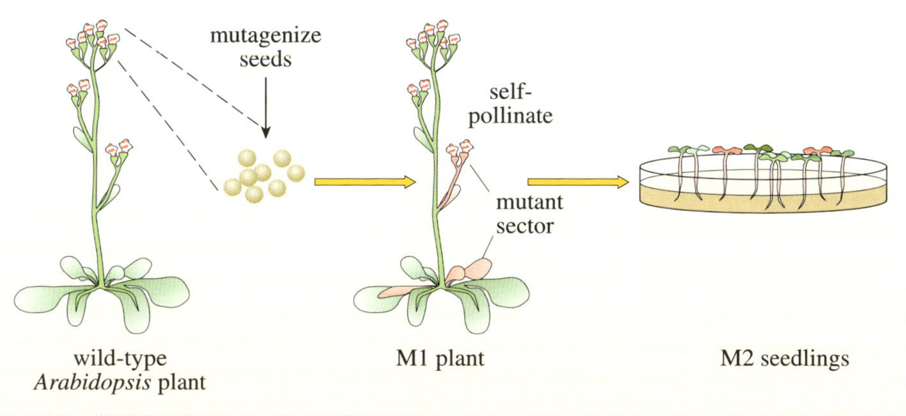

Figure 5.2 Generating and identifying mutants in *Arabidopsis*. Seeds are treated with a mutagen (e.g. a chemical such as ethyl methane sulfonate) and germinated to give M1 plants. Because the shoot apical meristem of the embryo is multicellular when mutagenized, only certain cells carry mutations (in a heterozygous state) and these cells give rise to recognizable mutant sectors in the M1 plants. Flowers in mutant sectors are self-fertilized and give rise to M2 seedlings, of which one-quarter carry recessive mutations in a homozygous state. Such homozygous mutants can be propagated as true breeding lines.

PATTERN MUTANTS

Pattern mutations are thought to occur in the master regulator genes, which determine the organization of the embryo (equivalent to the body plan in animals). A current model (or hypothesis) about embryo organization is illustrated in Figure 5.3. It proposes that the structure of a dicotyledonous embryo is established along two axes. (i) An apical–basal axis that can be divided into five domains: the shoot apical meristem (SAM), cotyledons, hypocotyl (primary shoot), radicle (embryonic root) and root apical meristem (RAM). These domains are established by the early transverse divisions of the embryo. (ii) A radial axis comprising three fundamental layers, L1, L2 and L3, which specify epidermal cells, cortical cells and the vascular tissue (shown as the protoderm, ground meristem and procambium respectively, in Figure 5.1).

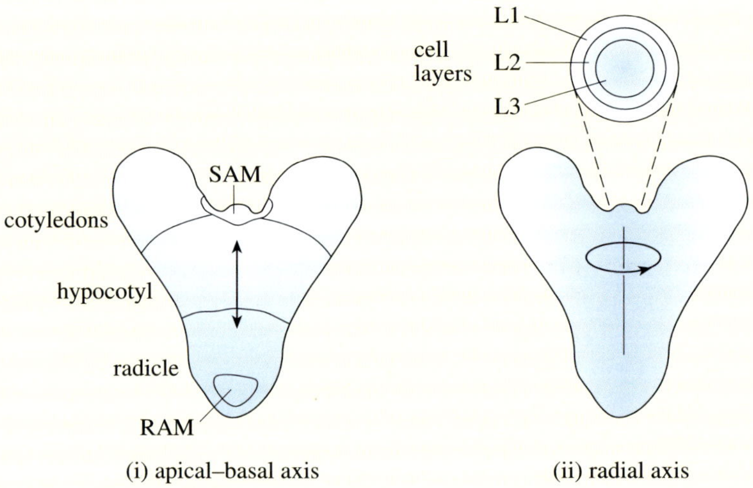

Figure 5.3 Body plan and segmentation pattern proposed for *Arabidopsis* embryos along (i) an apical–basal axis and (ii) a longitudinal axis. SAM and RAM are shoot and root apical meristems, respectively.

Several mutants have been identified that appear to lack some of the domains along the apical–basal axis (Figure 5.4). In *gurke** mutants, for example, the apical region is eliminated and the mature embryo has no cotyledons or shoot apex. This defect was traced back to misdivision in the early heart stage (Figure 5.1).

- ❍ Which domains are missing in the *monopteros* and *fackel* mutants (Figure 5.4)?

- ● In *monopteros* the root apical meristem, radicle and part of the hypocotyl are missing, i.e. the basal part of the embryo, and there is also only one instead of two cotyledons. In *fackel* the hypocotyl is missing.

It is thought, therefore, that the wild-type genes *GURKE*, *MONOPTEROS* and *FACKEL* are involved in some way in determining the apical–basal axis pattern of the embryo. Identifying such genes and finding out what they do helps in assembling the complex jigsaw of biochemical events that regulate embryogenesis.

*Note that the convention in plant genetics is to use lower case italics for recessive mutants with an initial capital letter if the mutant is dominant. The names of wild-type genes are given capital italic letters.

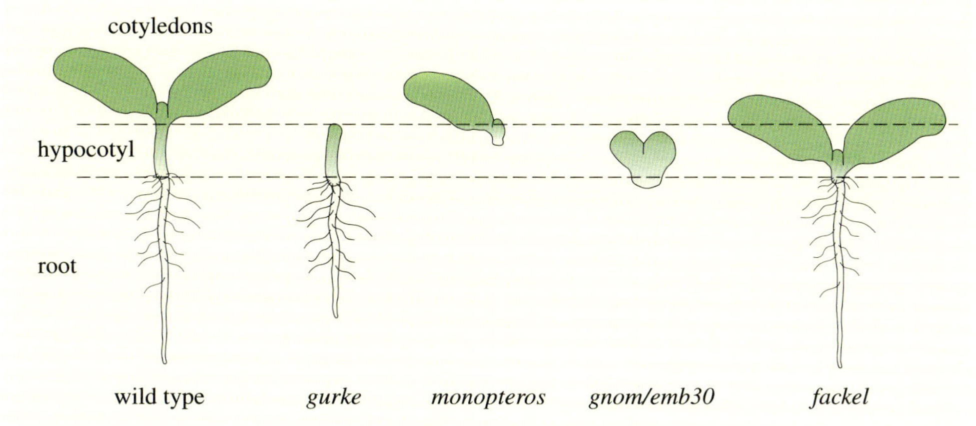

Figure 5.4 Seedling phenotypes of some *Arabidopsis* embryonic pattern mutants. With the exception of *gnom/emb30*, mutants are interpreted to have deletions of various segments along the apical–basal axis of the embryo. The mutant *gnom/emb30* is thought to have defects in establishing an apical–basal axis.

5.2.2 Seed formation and germination

The embryo may be the critical part but it is only one component of the developing seed. The triple fusion event at fertilization initiates the formation of the endosperm tissue, which progresses through a series of stages (Chapter 1) whilst embryogenesis is taking place (Figure 5.1). The endosperm provides a store of materials that nourish the embryo and which may either be absorbed into the cotyledons during embryo development or provide a source of storage reserves that are retained in the mature seed. Mature seeds may, therefore, have nutrient stores either in their cotyledons or in endosperm. During germination the endospermic reserves surrounding the embryo are gradually mobilized and used to drive seedling emergence and establishment.

During the development of the seed, the embryo enters a period of dormancy during which time the average water content of its tissues falls below 15%. This phase is critical as it reduces the likelihood of germination on the mother plant. There is convincing evidence that an endogenous regulator abscisic acid (ABA) plays a role in maintaining dormancy; mutants that lack the capacity either to synthesize ABA or respond to it germinate directly on the plant (Figure 5.5).

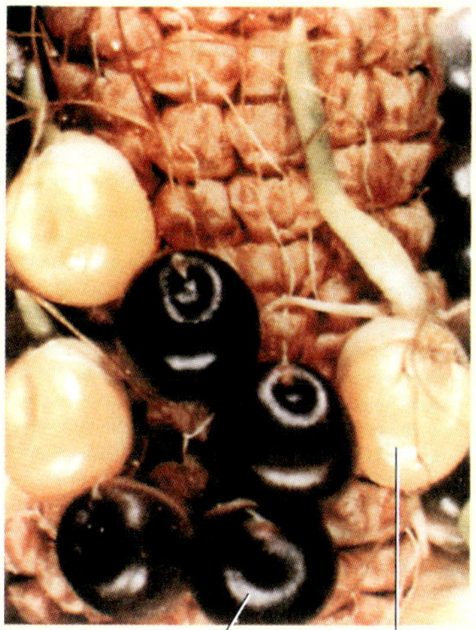

Figure 5.5 Part of a maize cob showing the effects of the *viviparous-1* mutation. Mutant seeds germinate prematurely on the cob (i.e. they are viviparous).

❍ What other role of ABA did you learn about in Chapter 3?

● ABA is a regulator of stomatal aperture and increases in ABA level cause stomata to close when water is in short supply.

The duration of the dormant phase varies from species to species. In cereals such as wheat and barley it is so brief that, in damp conditions, preharvest germination can take place, making the grain unsuitable for flour milling or brewing. In contrast, seeds of many weed species can remain dormant for months or even years in the soil.

❍ What advantages might there be for seeds of the arable weed, wild oat (*Avena fatua*) to remain dormant for up to seven years when seeds of the cultivated oat (*Avena sativa*) can germinate immediately after shedding in suitable conditions?

- Dormancy ensures that germination of seeds is spread out over a protracted period of time and increases the likelihood of seedling establishment and survival to maturity. Although cultivated crops originated from weed relatives, the dormancy phase has been reduced by farmers selecting for seed that exhibits a more synchronous emergence after planting. Many weed species exhibit deep dormancy while their cultivated relatives do not.

Three principal environmental factors, *water availability, light* and *temperature*, determine whether and when a seed germinates.

WATER AVAILABILITY

Seeds have a low moisture content when they are shed and the first process that needs to occur prior to germination is the **imbibition** (taking in) of water. This process is regulated by the permeability of the seed coat (testa) and driven by the low water potential of the seed due to its high matric pressure (Chapter 3). The process of imbibition takes place even if the seed is dead (non-viable). Seeds of xerophytes, plants that grow in arid environments, germinate rapidly in response to rainfall and so exploit the short-lived conditions that are favourable for seedling growth and establishment. Seeds with thick waxy coats take up water slowly which may impede germination to such an extent that they remain dormant until the testa has undergone some degradation in the soil. For example, it is recommended to gardeners that a portion of the seed coat of sweet pea (*Lathyrus odoratus*) seeds is removed manually (called 'chitting') to enhance and synchronize germination.

- In what other ways might the testa inhibit germination?

- It might limit the necessary gaseous exchange between the embryo and its environment; it might prevent the leaching of a germination inhibitor from the embryo or endosperm; or it might act as a physical barrier to restrict radicle emergence.

In fact, all of these effects occur in certain seeds.

LIGHT

One explanation of why light is such an important regulator of germination is that it provides critical information to the seed about its environment. **Photoblastic species**, those that require a light stimulus to germinate, commonly have seeds with few storage reserves that remain dormant in the soil until they are exposed to a brief flash of light. Two wavelengths of light regulate the timing of germination in such seeds; red light (approximately 660 nm) promotes, and far-red (approximately 720 nm) inhibits. While there are naturally more red than far-red wavelengths in sunlight, this situation is reversed under a leaf canopy, where chlorophyll absorbs the former wavelengths but not the latter. As a consequence, photoblastic seeds remain dormant when shed under conditions of extensive canopy shading. This phenomenon is particularly important for tropical rainforest trees where seeds are shed under extreme shade and may lie dormant on the forest floor until a break in the canopy forms above them.

TEMPERATURE

In temperate regions many seeds are shed towards the end of the growing season. The requirement of a minimum duration of chilling before germination takes place (known as **after-ripening**) followed by a period of warmth ensures that germination does not take place until the spring.

5.2.3 THE GERMINATION OF BARLEY GRAINS

The importance of the process of malting to the brewing industry has resulted in a considerable amount of research being devoted to understanding how barley germination is regulated. Although barley grains do not require after-ripening, germination is accelerated by a short period of dry storage immediately after harvest. Once this time has passed, germination occurs rapidly, at ambient (15–20 °C) temperature, in the presence of an adequate supply of water.

The food reserves in the barley grain are stored in the endosperm tissue (Figure 5.6) and consist primarily of starch and protein. The mature endosperm is made up of dead storage cells, but is surrounded by a layer of metabolically active cells called the **aleurone**. The aleurone cells play a critical role in barley germination and particularly in controlling the mobilization of storage reserves within the endosperm.

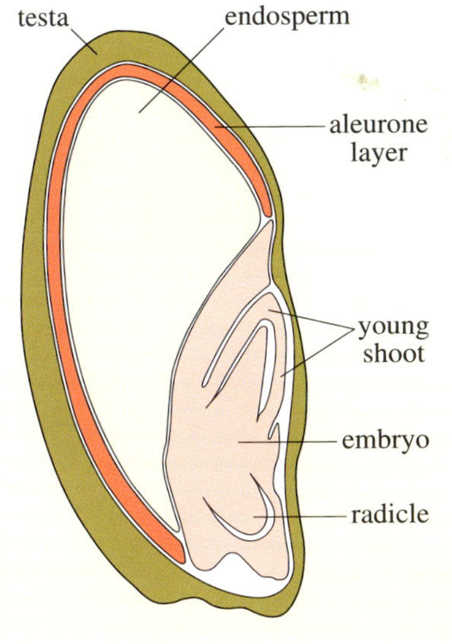

Figure 5.6 Longitudinal section through a barley grain.

❍ Why would the reserves of the seed need to be broken down in a regulated manner?

● The growth of the embryo is fuelled by nutrients supplied by the endosperm which need to be supplied at a rate that can be used effectively by the emerging seedling. Excess supply of sugars and amino acids might leach out of the seed, where they would be lost to the plant but would provide an excellent substrate for growth of bacteria or fungi.

The first visible sign of germination is the emergence of the radicle through the testa. However, this event is preceded by a series of biochemical reactions that include the hydrolysis of some of the starch stored in the endosperm to yield glucose. This monosaccharide is critical for both ATP synthesis, via respiration, and as a source of carbon skeletons for growth. A key enzyme that releases glucose from the starch is **α-amylase**. A simple test for the production of α-amylase is to cut barley grains in half transversely and place the two pieces, cut surface down, on a layer of agar containing starch. After 24 hours the half-grains can be removed and iodine solution poured on to the agar. Those areas where the α-amylase has diffused into the agar and degraded the starch do not stain blue. A typical result obtained after carrying out this experiment is shown in Figure 5.7 (overleaf).

❍ Which of the following hypotheses could account for the result seen in Figure 5.7?

(i) Absorption of water activates α-amylase which is present in the endosperm cells.

(ii) Absorption of water stimulates the embryo to produce α-amylase.

(iii) Absorption of water stimulates the embryo to secrete a substance that induces the production of α-amylase in other parts of the seed.

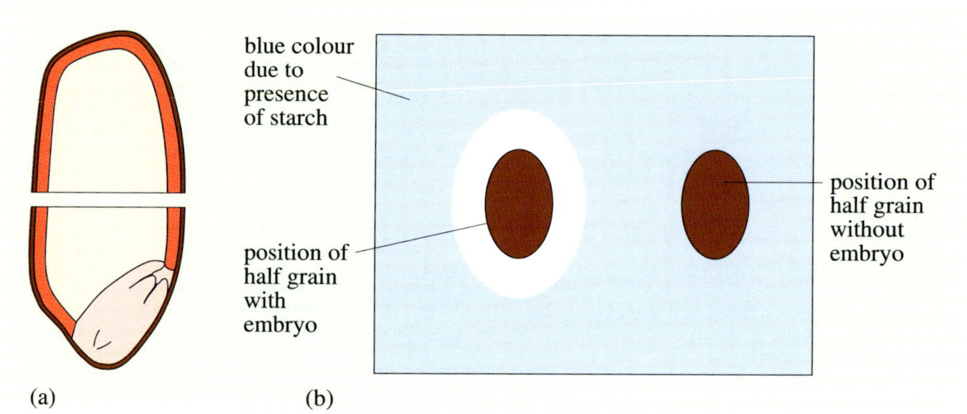

Figure 5.7 Experiment to test for α-amylase production. (a) Barley grains were halved transversely and the two halves placed, cut surface down, on agar containing starch. (b) 48 h later the grain halves were removed and the agar stained with iodine to test for the presence of starch.

- Only explanation (i) can be discounted as half-grains without embryos fail to secrete α-amylase into the agar. Both hypotheses (ii) and (iii) are equally plausible although the latter has more complexity.

- Suggest an experiment that would allow you to differentiate between hypotheses (ii) and (iii) using the starch gel technique.

- Embryos could be dissected out from the endosperm and placed directly on to the starch agar to determine whether they can produce α-amylase directly.

In practice it is difficult to remove all traces of the endosperm from the embryo but a variant of this experiment showed that hypothesis (iii) is correct. When the embryo plus a small amount of endosperm was incubated alone, no starch was hydrolysed but when incubated in close proximity to an embryo-less half grain (endosperm + aleurone), starch was hydrolysed by the half grain. Thus the embryo stimulates the production and secretion of α-amylase by cells of the aleurone layer. The enzyme (plus other hydrolytic enzymes) then diffuses into the endosperm tissue converting starch into glucose which is then absorbed by the embryo to fuel growth. The substance that the embryo produces is called **gibberellic acid (GA)** and is one of a small group of molecules that are thought to regulate plant growth and development. These compounds are known as plant growth regulators (PGRs) — see Section 5.3. Plants contain a large variety of GA structures (gibberellins) but only a few of these such as GA_1 and GA_3 are physiologically active. The remainder are components of the highly complex biosynthetic pathways.

GA biosynthesis in barley embryos begins approximately 24 hours after imbibition and the sequence of events thereafter is shown in Figure 5.8. In addition to stimulating α-amylase production, GA also induces the aleurone cells to secrete other enzymes necessary to break down starch and peptidases that act on the storage proteins within endosperm cells. The aleurone layer can be removed from the barley grains that have previously imbibed water, which are then treated with cell-wall-degrading enzymes to release aleurone **protoplasts** (i.e. wall-less cells). These protoplasts respond to GA just like the intact tissue and secrete α-amylase (Figure 5.9).

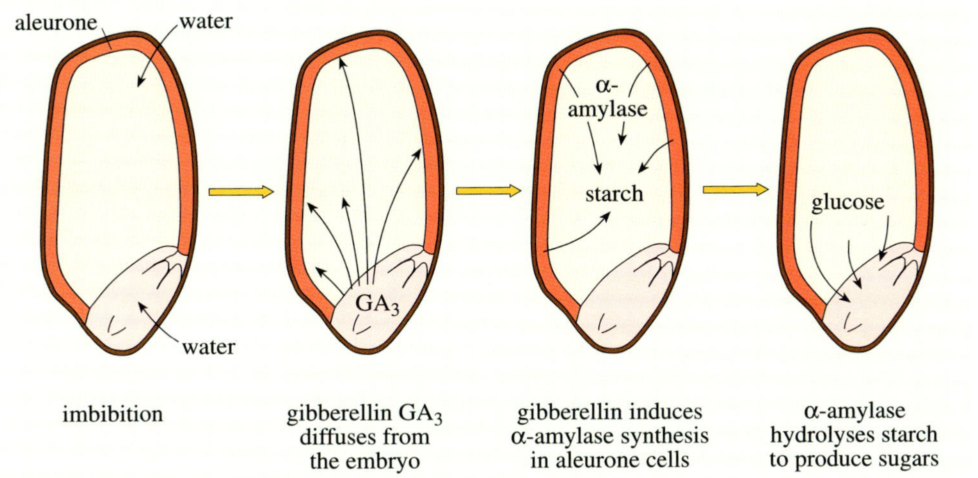

Figure 5.8 Stages in the mobilization of starch reserves in a barley grain.

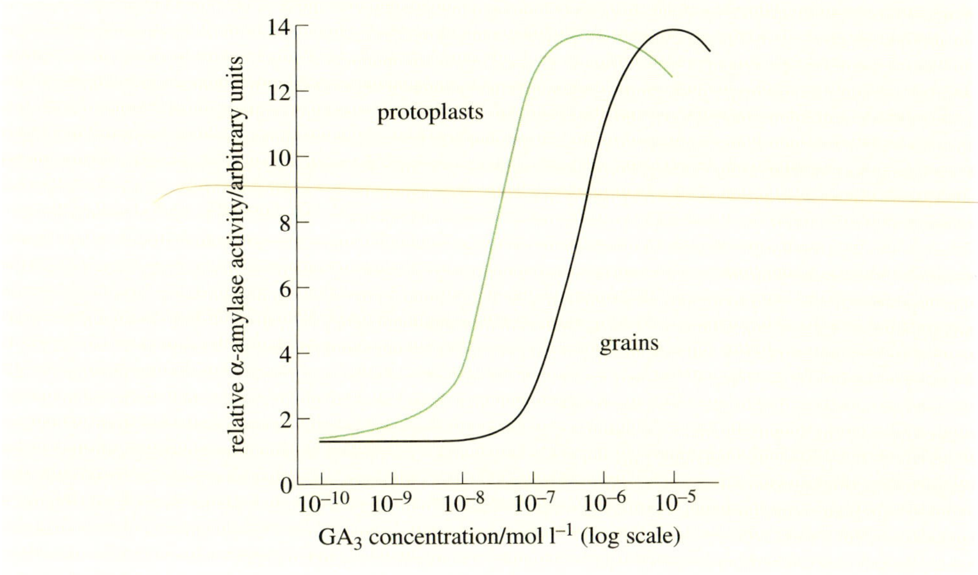

Figure 5.9 Dose–response curve of barley grains and of aleurone protoplasts to gibberellin GA$_3$ with respect to α-amylase activity.

- ❍ Explain the observation in Figure 5.9 that aleurone protoplasts secrete α-amylase in response to lower concentrations of GA$_3$, supplied externally, than do intact seeds.

- ● Much of the GA$_3$ that is applied to intact grains fails to enter the seed and reach the aleurone cells. As a consequence a much higher concentration of the PGR must be applied to obtain the response.

This type of observation is typical of what happens when scientists work with whole plants and is one explanation why high concentrations of PGRs often appear to be necessary to induce changes in only a few cells.

BARLEY GERMINATION AND GENE EXPRESSION

It is now clear that barley germination is the consequence of a coordinated series of changes in gene expression. One of the earliest genes that is **upregulated** (switched on) encodes an enzyme (GA 20-oxidase) that regulates a critical step in the biosynthesis of active GA. This observation, and the fact that barley seeds germinate, albeit at a slower rate, in the presence of GA biosynthesis inhibitors suggest that this PGR may not be the sole trigger for germination but acts to coordinate the process. The increase in α-amylase activity induced in aleurone cells by GA is known to be the result of an increase in gene transcription. Aleurone protoplasts can be induced to take up DNA which is then expressed transiently in a promoter-dependent manner (a promoter is the sequence upstream of a gene that is required for transcription, see Silva-Fletcher, 2001). As the protoplasts respond to GA by synthesizing α-amylase, the regulatory features of the promoter can be examined to determine which parts of it may play a role in regulating GA-specific expression. By careful genetic analysis using a β-glucuronidase (GUS) **reporter gene** (Swithenby, 2001) it has been possible to identify three critical domains in the promoter and these have been described as the GA-responsive gene-complex.

SUMMARY OF SECTION 5.2

1. The life cycle of a flowering plant begins when sperm nuclei fuse with the egg cell and the binucleate central cell. Polarity is established after asymmetric division of the zygote into apical and basal cells. The apical cells form the proembryo.
2. Embryogenesis is not well understood but the study of mutants is throwing light upon the process. Using *Arabidopsis* as a model system and studying its mutants and those of other plants is helping to elucidate the processes involved.
3. The embryo is only one part of the developing seed. The endosperm provides a store of nutrients for the developing embryo. Seeds may remain dormant for long periods (probably under the influence of ABA) or germinate quickly, sometimes even on the mother plant.
4. Environmental factors affecting germination are water, light and temperature. Water uptake is regulated by the permeability of the testa and when the water content is under 15% the seeds remain dormant. Light is detected in the red/far-red range. Some seeds require chilling before germination.
5. Seed germination is a coordinated series of events regulated by changes in gene expression. An early upregulated gene encodes an enzyme which has a critical role in the pathway of GA biosynthesis. GA may not initiate germination but it may regulate it.

5.3 PLANT GROWTH REGULATORS AND PLANT DEVELOPMENT

As the example of germination shows, the development of a plant requires a pre-determined programme of events to take place, which is frequently coordinated in response to either an environmental or genetic signal. The compounds **auxin**, gibberellins, **cytokinins**, **ethylene** and abscisic acid (ABA) have been identified as playing critical roles in plant development and are variously described as plant hormones, **plant growth regulators (PGRs)** or plant growth substances. However, none of these terms can be considered as an ideal description of their function. The word hormone was originally applied in animal systems to define a molecule that had a specific site of synthesis, a particular target tissue, and a transport system that was capable of delivering the compound from one site to another. In plants, there is good reason to believe that synthesis and response may often take place *within the same cell* and only the auxin, **indoleacetic acid (IAA)** has a polar transport system (i.e. occurring in one direction across living cells) capable of regulating delivery. Other regulators move chiefly either in the xylem (e.g. ABA, cytokinins) or phloem (e.g. gibberellins) and their delivery is dependent upon rates of transpiration or on sink strength. Ethylene (C_2H_4) is a gas and moves largely by diffusion, making it difficult to view its movement from one site to another as either targeted or controlled. For this discussion we describe all these compounds as plant growth regulators or PGRs.

5.3.1 Use of mutants to study the role of PGRs in plant development

Later sections discuss the roles of specific PGRs during plant development and Table 5.1 gives a summary of their main effects. Until recently, much of the evidence that these compounds play critical roles has come from monitoring the impact of inhibitors of PGR biosynthesis or action on developmental events. Thus the application of silver ions (which block ethylene action) delays fruit ripening of climacteric fruit, flower senescence and abscission (Section 5.6). Similarly the use of paclobutrazol (which inhibits gibberellin biosynthesis) delays cereal germination and reduces internode elongation. However, the use of inhibitors is fraught with difficulties in that many of these compounds are not specific and their effects could be attributable to other biochemical actions that they bring about. A more elegant strategy is to isolate mutants that have an impaired ability to produce a specific PGR or respond to it. Many of these mutants have been isolated in *Arabidopsis* using screens that have been established to identify a particular phenotypic characteristic. For instance ABA plays a critical role in regulating stomatal aperture and mutants that have a reduced ability to synthesize this PGR should exhibit a 'wilty' phenotype in environments where water supply is limited. ABA biosynthetic mutants have, indeed, been isolated in this way.

❍ If a mutant shows signs of deficiency of a PGR, is it necessarily unable to synthesize the compound?

● No, an alternative cause for the observed phenotype is that the mutant is unable to respond to the PGR.

It is possible to distinguish between a biosynthetic mutant and an insensitive mutant by determining the response after application of the PGR.

❍ How may mutants help us understand how a specific PGR is synthesized?

● By identifying a defective gene for an enzyme involved in PGR synthesis it should be possible to determine information about the step in the biosynthetic pathway of the PGR that is blocked.

Alternatively if the mutation affects how a PGR acts, identifying a relevant gene may reveal how the PGR is perceived (its receptor) or how its effect is transduced. A spectrum of mutants has now been isolated with specific developmental abnormalities that have been linked to either the biosynthesis or action of a specific PGR.

A critical stage in mutant isolation is the development of an appropriate screen. If the search were for a compound that is critical for cell growth, the screen would identify genetic dwarfs. Mutants that produce reduced levels of gibberellins fall into this category and although auxins are also known to regulate cell elongation, no IAA mutants have been found that are genetic dwarfs. A possible explanation is that plants that produce reduced amounts of auxin are not able to survive; alternatively the role of IAA in regulating cell expansion may need to be reconsidered. Mutants that are not able to import or export IAA from their cells have been isolated and these exhibit an **agravitropic** phenotype, i.e. they do not respond in the usual way to gravity, which supports a role for IAA in plant responses to gravity (see Section 5.4.1).

Table 5.1 Examples of the effects of plant growth regulators on plant growth and development.

Plant growth regulator	Effect	Developmental event
auxins, e.g. indoleacetic acid, IAA	promote	elongation of coleoptile and shoot cells
	promote	apical dominance (suppression of lateral buds by the apex)
	promote	adventitious root formation on stems
	promote	ethylene synthesis
	inhibit	abscission
gibberellins, e.g. gibberellic acid, GA	promote	internode elongation (especially in dwarf and rosette plants)
	promote	seed germination
cytokinins	promote	cell division
	promote	cell expansion in leaves and cotyledons
	inhibit	apical dominance (promotes lateral bud growth)
	inhibit	leaf senescence
abscisic acid (ABA)	promotes	stomatal closure
	inhibits	germination
	promotes	leaf senescence
ethylene	promotes	ripening of climacteric fruit
	promotes	abscission
	promotes	senescence of leaves and flowers
	promotes	lateral cell expansion in stems of land plants and cell elongation in submerged aquatics
brassinosteroids	promote	elongation of shoots
	promote	pollen tube growth
	inhibit	root growth

The isolation of a new class of PGR — brassinosteroids

During the 1990s a number of dwarf mutants were identified in *Arabidopsis* that did not seem to be deficient in gibberellins or auxin or insensitive to these PGRs. Some of these mutants also showed abnormal responses to light or its absence and, for example, showed a light-grown morphology when grown in darkness. Thus after 7 days in darkness they had the short hypocotyl, expanded cotyledons and true leaves typical of light-grown plants instead of the etiolated morphology typical of dark-grown seedlings. One of these **photomorphogenetic** mutants (Section 5.3.2), *de-etiolated2* (*det2*), has been identified and found to result from a mutation in the gene that encodes a protein similar to a key enzyme involved in steroid synthesis in mammals. A group of compounds termed the **brassinosteroids** had previously been isolated from *Brassica* species and shown to have growth-promoting activities when applied to plants. It now turns out that the mutant *det2* is deficient in brassinosteroids and mutant isolation and analysis has proved that these compounds play an important role as PGRs *in vivo*. Brassinosteroids promote cell elongation but are not able to rescue GA-deficient dwarf mutants, which suggests that the two PGRs regulate the expansion of cells using different mechanisms.

5.3.2 Mechanism of action of PGRs

The effects of PGRs are specific and to some extent they can be considered as targeted to certain types of cells. Many of the changes caused by PGRs involve the expression of new genes and some mechanism must exist for cells to perceive a certain PGR and then respond to it. Receptors for such molecules could be associated with membranes such as the plasma membrane or be freely soluble within the cytoplasm. Attempts to isolate receptors using radioactively labelled PGRs have not been successful, perhaps because the number of receptors may be low and binding is a reversible reaction. In the late 1990s, however, major strides have been made in our understanding of the mechanism of action of PGRs using the mutant approach. We describe here one example that involves ethylene.

Isolation and characterization of PGR receptors — the ethylene story

Ethylene is an important regulator of processes such as fruit ripening, senescence and abscission (Table 5.1). In addition, it plays a role in the mediation of a plant's response to stress (e.g. infection or mechanical damage). The fact that ethylene is a gas makes it particularly useful as a coordinator of a developmental response because it diffuses rapidly from one part of a plant to another. When applied to young seedlings grown in the dark, ethylene induces a specific syndrome of effects known as the *triple response*. Two aspects of this response are shown in Figure 5.10 in *Arabidopsis* seedlings.

- From Figure 5.10 identify two effects of ethylene on stem growth in *Arabidopsis* seedlings.

- Elongation of the stem is strongly inhibited, but lateral growth is promoted (note in Figure 5.10a that the stem is wider and it may form a distinct apical swelling).

These two effects of ethylene are part of the triple response. The third can be seen only at lower ethylene concentrations (below 10 p.p.m.) when more elongation growth occurs but the stem grows horizontally instead of vertically (a phenomenon called diageotropism). Another effect of ethylene that you can see in Figure 5.10a is the increased curvature of the apical hook. Such growth changes may help seedlings to push through compacted soil, a condition which stimulates ethylene synthesis, and (by diageotropism) grow round solid objects.

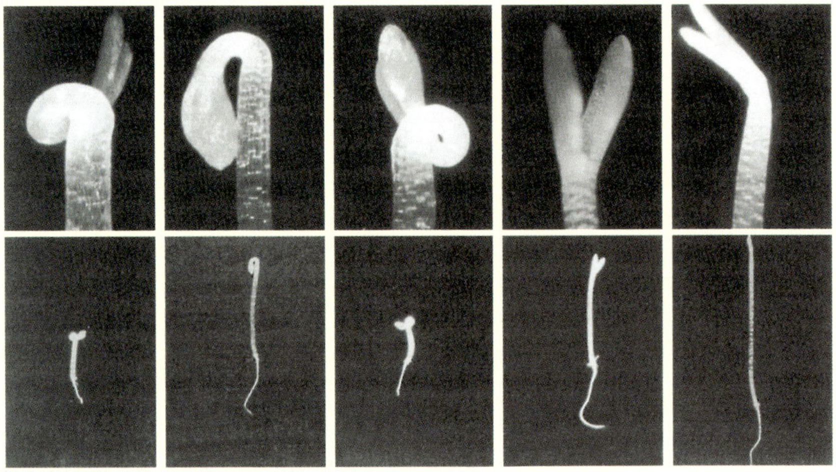

Figure 5.10 Effects of ethylene on the growth of *Arabidopsis* seedlings and the behaviour of triple response mutants. The lower panels show whole seedlings; upper panels are higher magnifications showing details of the apical region of the seedlings. Three-day-old seedlings were grown in the dark in the presence or absence of ethylene (10 p.p.m.). (a) and (b) wild type + and – ethylene; (c) mutant *eto1*–1 (*ethylene overproducer1*–1, which shows a triple response in the absence of ethylene because it synthesizes abnormally large amounts); (d) mutant *hls1*–1 (*hookless1*–1, which has altered sensitivity to ethylene at the apex and does not form a hook in the absence of ethylene); (e) mutant *ein2*–1 (*ethylene insensitive2*–1, which does not show a triple response in the presence of ethylene).

The triple response has been used as a screen for *Arabidopsis* mutants that are insensitive to ethylene; seedlings that continue to elongate in the presence of the gas (Figure 5.10e) can be readily identified and characterized. The first mutant identified in this way was termed *ethylene resistant1* (*Etr1*) and, suprisingly, the mutation was found to be dominant.

❍ Why is it unusual that a mutation rendering a plant unresponsive to a PGR is dominant?

● Mutations normally impair the function of a gene and, in a heterozygous plant, the absence of a functional gene on one chromosome is normally masked by the gene on the other chromosome that is transcribed and translated to give a functional protein.

The *ETR1* gene is now thought to encode a protein which acts as an ethylene receptor — the first PGR receptor to be identified — and, intriguingly, it acts in a very similar way to the two-component regulatory systems that are used in bacteria to sense and respond to chemicals in the environment. The bacterial system comprises a *sensor* protein, which perceives the chemical and transmits a signal to a *response regulator* protein, which initiates a response. Communication between these two components is via protein phosphorylation: the sensor phosphorylates one of its own histidine residues (acting as a histidine kinase) and then transfers the phosphate to an aspartate on the response regulator. Equivalents of both these proteins occur in the C-terminal region of the ETR1 protein and, in addition, the N terminus has three hydrophobic, membrane-spanning domains, which are the site of ethylene binding. The top part of Figure 5.11 illustrates the set-up and also shows that the ETR1 protein functions as a dimer. A further four ethylene receptor proteins have been isolated, raising the possibility that different receptors may regulate different developmental events in different tissues.

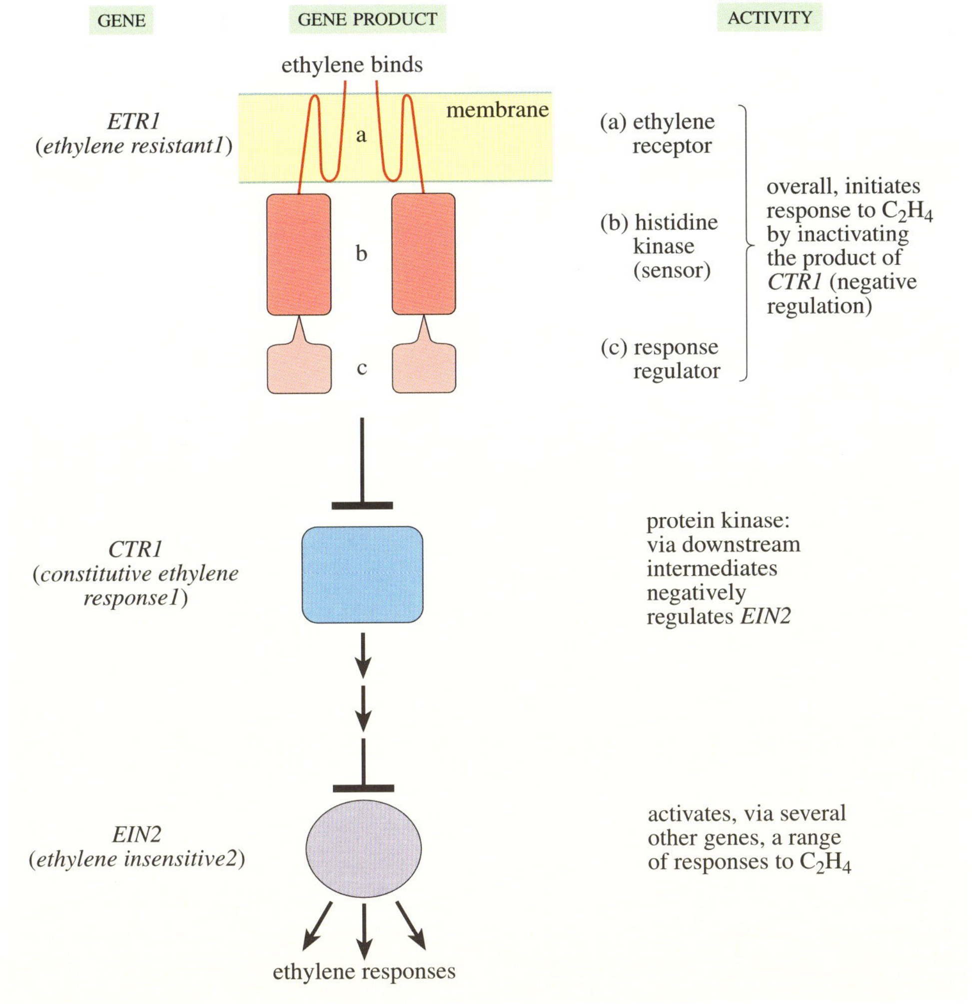

Figure 5.11 A model for the action of ethylene (C_2H_4) involving a two-component receptor encoded by *ETR1*.

Having identified the *ETR1* gene, can we explain why, if rendered non-functional by mutation, it is dominant? The answer has come from the identification of a mutant that shows a triple response in the absence of ethylene, the *ctr1* (*constitutive triple response1*) mutant. The protein product of the normal *CTR1* gene is a protein kinase which acts to block ethylene responses, i.e. it is a *negative regulator,* and mutation of this gene causes permanent (or constitutive) activation of ethylene responses. From Figure 5.11 you can see that *CTR1* acts after (downstream of) *ETR1* which, when its product binds ethylene, acts to block the action of *CTR1:* so there is negative regulation of a negative regulator!

Now think what may happen with *etr1* mutants: the product of the mutated *ETR1* gene (even if 'diluted' by product from the unmutated allele) no longer acts to block *CTR1*, either because it fails to bind ethylene or, if it does, fails to respond.

❍ What would be the next step?

● Because the negative regulator *CTR1* is now permanently active, all responses to ethylene would be blocked.

A spectrum of genes in the ethylene action pathway has now been identified using the mutant approach (Figure 5.11) and this strategy is proving an effective way of dissecting PGR signalling mechanisms in plants. Further rapid advances are expected now that the *Arabidopsis* genome has been sequenced and can be compared with those of other organisms that have been fully sequenced (currently those of yeast, *Drosophila* and the nematode, *Caenorhabditis*) (*Arabidopsis* Genome Initiative, 2000). For example, the ethylene receptors which resemble bacterial two-component histidine kinases so closely are thought to have been derived from cyanobacteria by lateral transfer from chloroplast to nucleus; no equivalents occur in fungal or animal genomes. But the downstream *CTR1* component of the pathway resembles a kind of gene (MAP kinases, see Clements and Saffrey, 2001) that is widespread in animals as a component of cellular signalling pathways. So plants have evolved a unique signalling pathway by combining a receptor derived from bacteria with an ancient (i.e. conserved) eukaryotic relay component.

At least 20 other MAP kinase genes were found in *Arabidopsis* and it seems likely that the signalling pathways of abscisic acid and cytokinins have a MAP kinase component. Other sorts of kinases function as actual receptors, receptor serine/threonine kinases, for example. Such receptors are widespread in animals and at least 340 genes code for receptor Ser/Thr kinases in *Arabidopsis* but only rarely is the ligand for the receptor known in plants. So comparative analysis of genomes has produced a situation where we know the genes for many receptors or putative receptors but not the signal molecules they bind and, conversely, there are some well-known signal molecules (such as auxins) for which no receptors are known. Matching receptors to signal molecules, sorting out the signalling pathway and linking that pathway to final physiological responses (cell expansion, leaf fall or flowering, for example) are challenges for the future.

5.3.3 PGRs and intercellular signalling

We have already seen that the environment plays a critical role in providing signals to a plant that can influence its developmental programme. Thus factors such as quality and quantity of light may regulate the timing of germination or flowering, and the direction from which gravity and light fall upon a plant can alter patterns of growth. However, many of the environmental signals perceived by plants are related to stresses such as water, nutrient or oxygen availability and pathogen attack. There is convincing evidence that PGRs can act as signals in response to stress and often these compounds move from one tissue to another. For instance, water deficit around the roots has been shown to bring about an increase in ABA concentration within the xylem sap and this PGR moves as a consequence of transpiration to the leaves where it brings about stomatal closure and limits further water loss (Chapter 3). In response to surplus water around their roots (i.e. waterlogging), plants such as tomato undergo elevated growth on the upper surfaces of leaf stalks (petioles) and, as a consequence, the aerial parts droop. This phenomenon is known as **epinasty** and is the result of elevated ethylene production by the leaves. The intercellular signal is thought to be a soluble precursor of ethylene called aminocyclopropane carboxylic acid (ACC) which moves in the transpiration stream from waterlogged roots to the shoots where it is converted to the gas.

- The conversion of ACC into ethylene requires oxygen. How does this information explain why ACC can signal to leaves that roots are waterlogged?

- The amount of oxygen present around waterlogged roots is greatly reduced. The unoxidized ACC is transported from the roots to the aerial parts of the plant where the ambient oxygen concentrations enable it to be converted into ethylene.

Amphibious plants and the 'flood response'

Waterlogging is a major stress for land plants but for those that grow in aquatic environments it can be tolerated. Indeed petiole growth of certain amphibious, floating-leaved plants such as *Nymphoides peltata* (the fringed waterlily) is stimulated by submergence (Figure 5.12). The growth of the stem or leaf petiole continues to occur more rapidly under water until the leaf lamina breaks the water surface and it is accumulation of ethylene in submerged tissues that causes the growth stimulation. Accumulation occurs because ethylene diffuses about 10 000 times more slowly through water than in air.

- From what you know about the triple response to ethylene (Section 3.3.2), why is this growth stimulation in submerged tissues surprising?

- Ethylene acts as a powerful *inhibitor* of elongation growth in the triple response, the exact opposite of its effect on submerged tissues.

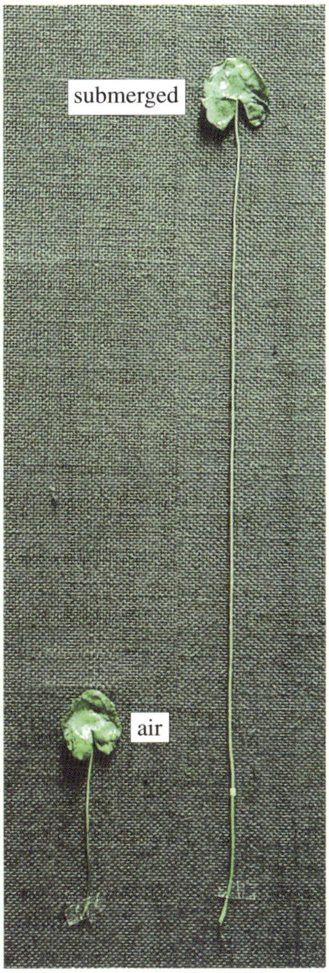

Figure 5.12 Leaves of *Nymphoides peltata* showing greatly increased elongation of the petiole when grown submerged (right) compared with growth in air (left).

A similar effect, called the **flood response**, can be seen in several grassland species. For example, the creeping buttercup (*Ranunculus repens*) commonly grows in fields that experience flooding. On waterlogging, the petioles of newly produced leaves elongate so that the leaf blade extends beyond the surface of the floodwater enabling the plant to survive by extending into an aerobic environment. Species of docks (the genus *Rumex*) form a gradient from strictly terrestrial to amphibious. For instance *Rumex acetosella* (sheep's sorrel) grows on dry sandy soils while *R. palustris* (marsh dock) is often found by the banks of rivers. Submergence of the flood-tolerant *R. palustris* leads to elevated shoot elongation while the flood-intolerant *R. acetosella* shows no such response. In both species, submergence leads to an accumulation of ethylene in the petiole tissues but only in *R. palustris* is shoot elongation stimulated by this gaseous PGR. This observation indicates that the response to a PGR can be markedly influenced by the phenomenon of sensitivity. The sensitivity could be simply related to the number of receptors available to bind the PGR. A homologue of the ethylene receptor *ETR* has been isolated in *R. palustris* and has been found to be upregulated (switched on) by low concentrations (3%) of oxygen. Whether the absence of a flooding response in *R. acetosella* is due to low levels of expression of this gene is not yet known.

SUMMARY OF SECTION 5.3

1 During plant development, events take place in a specified order in response to genetic or environmental signals. PGRs (auxin, cytokinins, gibberellins, brassinosteroids, ethylene and abscisic acid) play a critical role. In plants, synthesis and response to PGRs may take place in the same cell. Only IAA (auxin) has been shown to have a transport system; ethylene, being a gas, diffuses in an unregulated way and other PGRs undergo long-distance transport in xylem and/or phloem.

2 Mutants are used to investigate the role(s) of PGRs, their synthesis and mode of action. Brassinosteroids, which promote cell elongation, were shown to be PGRs using a dwarf mutant that was found not to be deficient in or insensitive to GA but deficient in brassinosteroid.

3 The effects of PGRs are very specific and often involve the expression of new genes. All PGRs are thought to have specific receptors but this area is not well understood in plants.

4 A recent study of mutants has shown that several types of ethylene receptor exist, closely resembling bacterial two-component sensors, which act as histidine kinases. These receptors are thought to have originated by lateral gene transfer from the cyanobacterial genome of chloroplasts. Hundreds of other putative receptors have been identified in the fully sequenced genome of *Arabidopsis* that resemble receptors found in animals and yeast, but the role of these receptors and the ligands they bind are mostly unknown.

5 There is evidence that PGRs can mediate responses to environmental stress and pathogen attack. Elongation of stems or petioles occurs in flooding-tolerant plants during submergence, caused by accumulation of ethylene and upregulation of an ethylene receptor at low [O_2].

5.4 SEEDLING DEVELOPMENT

The seedling is perhaps the most critical stage in the life cycle of a plant. Not only may it have to grow swiftly to penetrate layers of soil but also it must respond to an array of stimuli once it emerges, if growth and reproductive potential are to be optimal. To this end, the seedling is equipped with a multitude of sensors that provide information about the environment in which it is growing. A **tropism** is defined as the directional movement of a plant in response to a unilateral stimulus. Two of the most crucial signals are *gravity* and *light*, hence **gravitropism** and **phototropism**. Immediately after germination it is the former stimulus that orientates the direction of growth while the latter dictates the rate at which growth occurs and the direction of shoot growth above the soil.

5.4.1 RESPONSES TO GRAVITY

A primary root is described as **positively gravitropic** in that it grows in the direction of the gravitational pull (i.e. downwards) while a shoot is **negatively gravitropic** as it extends in the opposite direction (i.e. upwards) (Figure 5.13a).

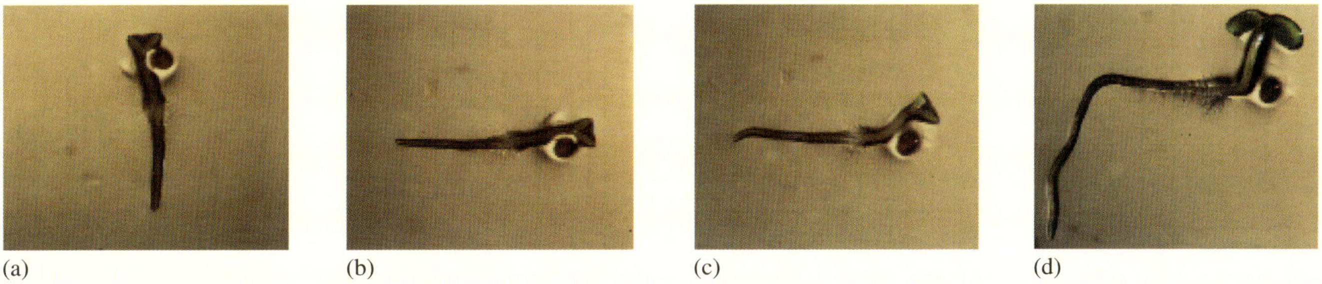

Figure 5.13 Gravitropism of the root and seedling shoot (hypocotyl) in *Arabidopsis*. (a) Three days after germination on a vertical agar medium, the root and hypocotyl grow vertically downward and upward, respectively. (b) After rotation of the culture dish by 90°, root and hypocotyl develop gravitropic curvatures. (c) Curvatures developed after 3 h. (d) 24 h after gravistimulation, the curvatures are completed: root and hypocotyl again grow vertically downward and upward, respectively.

Other parts of the plant may grow at an angle to gravity, including branches of trees or lateral roots. The simplest way to determine the natural position of a plant organ is to reorientate it and examine how it responds (Figure 5.13b–d). The final angle reached by the plant may be a compromise between its response to gravity and to other signals such as light. The response to gravity can be broken down into three distinct events: first, the plant organ must perceive the direction in which the stimulus is acting (**graviperception**); secondly, a signal must be generated and finally, there must be differential growth in response to the signal.

GRAVIPERCEPTION

There is a considerable body of evidence to support the hypothesis that graviperception in plants is mediated by the sedimentation of starch grains or starch-filled plastids **(amyloplasts)** that are denser than the surrounding cytoplasm. The basis of this assertion is that they are the only organelles that change their position rapidly enough to account for the fast response times (less than 5 min) that have been determined for gravitropism.

Sedimenting starch grains are present only in certain cells within the plant. In roots, they can be located within the root cap (Chapter 1) in a file of cells termed the *columella* (Figure 5.14). The cap not only provides information about the direction in which the root is growing but also protects the apical meristem from abrasion and produces mucilage that aids the passage of the root tip through the soil.

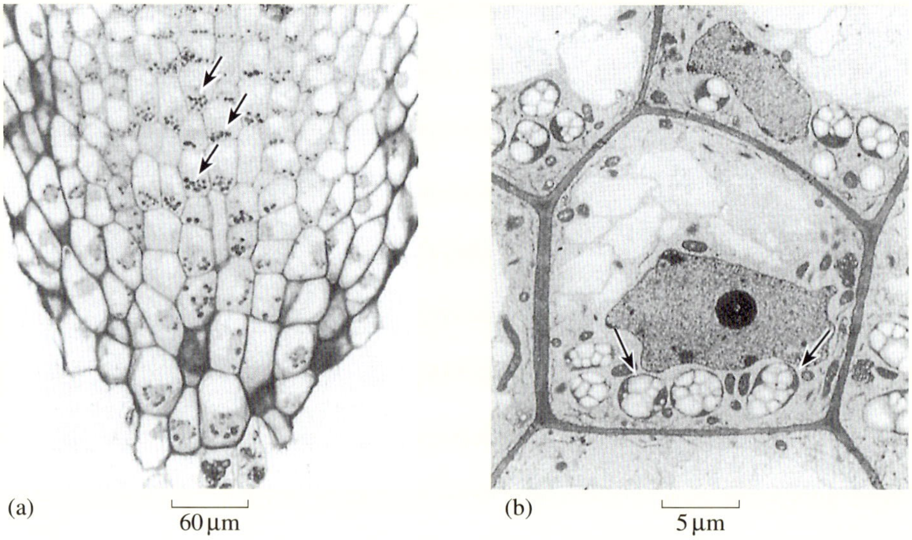

Figure 5.14 The root cap and root gravitropism. (a) LS of a root cap of French bean, *Phaseolus vulgaris*. Cells in the centre of the cap (columella) contain numerous starch-laden amyloplasts located in the lower part of the cells (indicated by arrows). (b) Magnified view of a single cell from the columella in (a); arrows indicate amyloplasts that have sedimented to the bottom of cells.

In shoots of dicotyledonous plants the sedimenting amyloplasts can be found in a ring of cells that encircles the vascular tissue and is known as the *starch sheath* or shoot endodermis. If this layer is absent then the shoot is unresponsive to gravity. In the inflorescences (flowering shoots) of cereals, bending is restricted to the stem nodes (joints) and starch grains are found here in cells adjacent to the vascular tissue.

It is not clear how the movement of a starch grain is able to provide information about a plant's orientation. It seems likely that, rather than the motion itself, it is the direction in which the amyloplasts sediment that is important for a specific signal to be generated (see Figure 5.15). Evidence is accumulating that sedimentable amyloplasts are enmeshed in a dense network of microfilaments connected to cell components such as microtubules and endoplasmic reticulum. The pulling action generated by the movement of the starch grains could then lead to the activation of membrane channels enabling ions such as Ca^{2+} to move from one cellular compartment to another and generate a local signal.

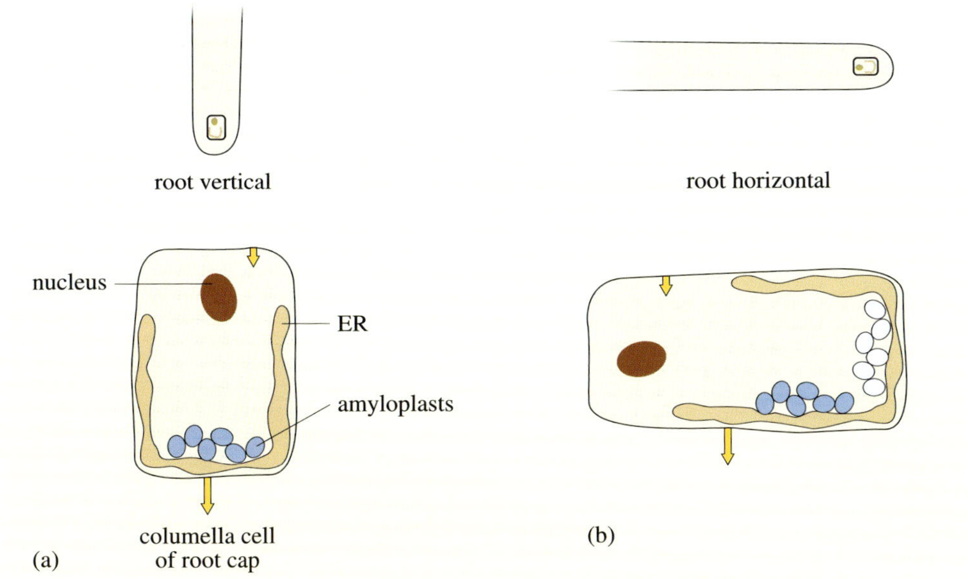

Figure 5.15 Gravity sensing in the root cap. (a) When the root is vertical, amyloplasts (dark blue) in the columella cells of the root cap sediment to the physical bottom of the cells. Upon gravistimulation (b), amyloplasts sediment from their position prior to stimulus (light blue ellipses) to the new physical bottom of the cell. The columella cells are thought to perceive gravity by sensing the tension and pressure that exist between the plasma membrane and the cell wall on opposing flanks of the cell. Gravity is represented by yellow arrows.

THE NATURE OF THE SIGNAL(S)

Although we can identify the cells that perceive gravity, these are not the cells that respond to the stimulus by undergoing differential elongation. For instance, the cells of the columella region in the root must transmit the gravitational signal to the rapidly elongating tissue that lies behind the apical meristem. Similarly it is likely that the endodermal (starch sheath) cells of the shoot pass a signal to the cortical or epidermal cells that results in differential expansion.

The nature of the signal(s) has not yet been identified. However, in view of the fact that the stimulus must regulate growth, the spotlight has fallen on the PGR auxin, indoleacetic acid (IAA). This hypothesis was originally proposed over 75 years ago and has been the subject of research and debate ever since (see Section 5.5). However, recent work using mutants of *Arabidopsis* that fail to respond to gravity has provided further support that IAA plays a key role in gravitropic bending, at least in roots. It is believed that IAA is synthesized in young leaves and is then transported in the phloem to the root apex. On arriving at the tip IAA is then redistributed to the cells of the cortex where it regulates cell division and elongation as well as lateral root development. IAA transport down the root from the tip takes place from cell to cell via a precisely controlled mechanism that involves influx and efflux carriers (**polar transport**). An influx carrier at the plasma membrane allows the undissociated form of IAA (IAA—H) to be taken up and an efflux carrier that is specifically located at the bottom of the cell allows the ionized form of the auxin (IAA^-) to be excreted. Mutations in the genes for either of these carriers render plants unresponsive to gravity. These observations strongly support a role for IAA in gravitropism. Whether it is the key link in the chain or only one component of it is not yet clear.

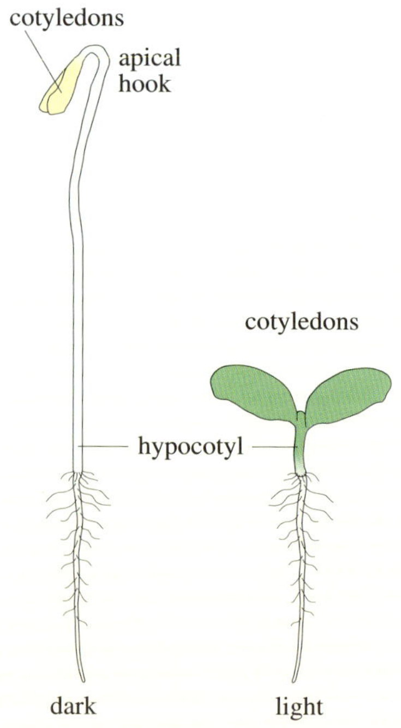

Figure 5.16 Comparison of *Arabidopsis* seedlings grown in the dark and light. Etiolated seedlings have long hypocotyls (seedling stem), apical hooks (at early stages) and unexpanded, unopened seed leaves (cotyledons). Light-grown seedlings have short hypocotyls, lack an apical hook and have green cotyledons that are opened and expanded.

5.4.2 Responses to light

In addition to gravity, light is an important signal for regulating seedling development. Seedlings growing in the dark exhibit a specific pattern of development and are described as **etiolated**. Etiolated dicotyledonous seedlings show rapid elongation growth, limited leaf expansion, lack chlorophyll and are commonly hooked at the apex (Figure 5.16). These features ensure that the seedling emerges into the light as quickly as possible without damaging the photosynthetic apparatus or the apical meristem. A single flash of light may initiate the switch from etiolated to de-etiolated growth, so there must be very sensitive systems that perceive light.

❍ From Figure 5.16, what effect does light have on cell expansion in the hypocotyl (stem) compared with the cotyledon (leaf)?

● Light inhibits elongation of cells within the stem but promotes the expansion of cells within the leaf.

This difference between leaf and stem is an example of how the same environmental signal can promote contrasting responses during plant development. It is likely that the perception mechanism is similar but the way that the signal is transduced may be different between the cells of stems and leaves.

Light perception

Responses to light are always mediated by pigments, which act as light receptors and absorb particular wavelengths. **Photomorphogenesis**, the changes in growth in response to light, can be promoted by far-red, red, blue and UV wavelengths and two sorts of pigments are involved in light perception. The pigment **phytochrome** initiates responses to red and far-red light while **cryptochrome** initiates responses to the blue part of the spectrum (including the response of guard cells to blue light, Chapter 3).

Several phytochromes occur, each composed of a polypeptide part (**apoprotein**), which varies for different phytochromes, and a **chromophore** (the light absorbing pigment). Each phytochrome can exist in two, interconvertible forms: a biologically inactive, red-light absorbing form (P_r) or a biologically active, far-red-light absorbing form (P_{fr}). Conversion between these two forms is driven by light (Figure 5.17a).

❍ In Figure 5.17b which curve shows the absorption spectrum of P_r and which that of P_{fr}? Check your answer and then label the curves in Figure 5.17b.

● The red line is the absorption spectrum of P_r: it is the phytochrome formed after absorption of saturating far-red light. The blue line is the absorption spectrum of P_{fr}, formed after absorption of saturating red light, and with an absorption maxima of 730 nm.

Phytochrome interconversion can be viewed as a switch. If the switch is on and P_{fr} predominates, then events such as leaf expansion and chlorophyll biosynthesis are stimulated. If the equilibrium is in the direction of P_r, then the switch is off and stem growth is promoted by other regulators. Phytochrome is synthesized in the P_r form and so dark-grown seedlings only synthesize P_r when emerging into the light.

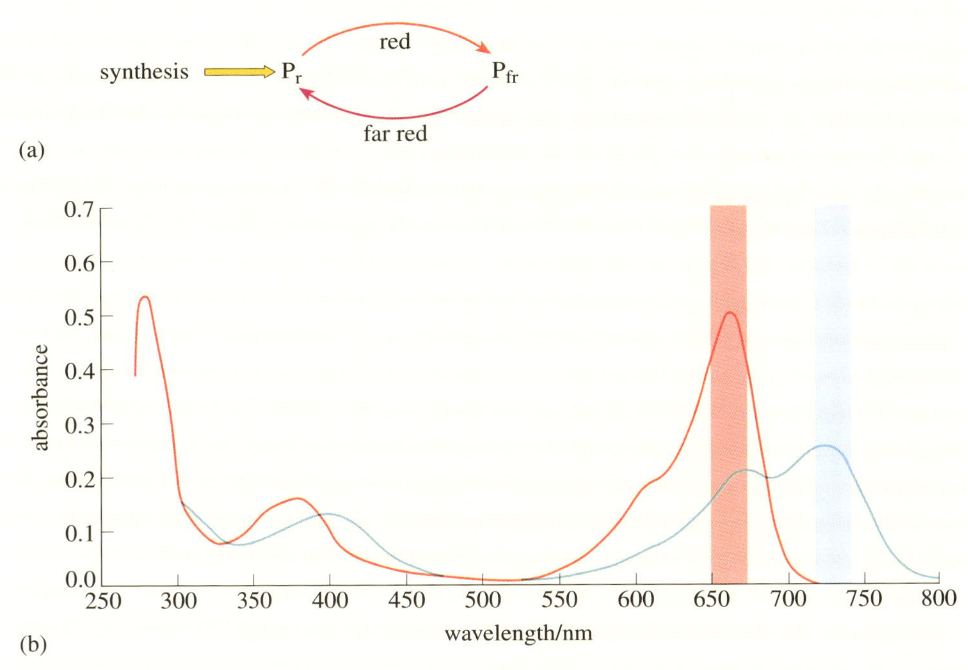

Figure 5.17 (a) Phytochrome interconversion: when P_r absorbs red light it is converted into P_{fr}. When P_{fr} absorbs far-red light, it is converted into P_r. (b) The absorption spectra of purified rye phytochrome after exposure to saturating red or far-red wavelengths. The coloured bars show the absorption maxima of the phytochromes.

The absorption spectra of P_r and P_{fr} overlap (Figure 5.17b) and therefore the ratio of P_{fr} : P_r is dependent upon the wavelength of light to which the plant is exposed. Normally a plant would be growing in an environment where white light predominates, which would cause the equilibrium to be in the direction of the formation of P_{fr}. However, plants growing under vegetational shade are exposed to far-red-enriched light as a consequence of the chlorophyll in the leaves above them reflecting the green and absorbing the red and blue wavelengths. This shade environment drives the equilibrium towards P_r and as a consequence plants may behave as if they were in the dark and exhibit rapid stem elongation until they emerge from the canopy shade. Not all plants respond to shade in this way and some such as bluebell (*Hyacinthoides non-scriptus*) and dog's mercury (*Mercurialis perennis*) are specifically adapted to growing under conditions where the levels of light are low. Such plants are described as *shade tolerant* and exhibit no increase in stem elongation in response to far-red light (see Figure 5.18).

❍ In Figure 5.18 explain why dog's mercury is shown as the most shade-tolerant species and groundsel as the most shade-intolerant (a shade avoider).

● As the proportion of far-red light increases (decrease in the P_{fr} : P_{total} ratio), dog's mercury shows the least increase in stem extension rate whereas groundsel shows the greatest increase.

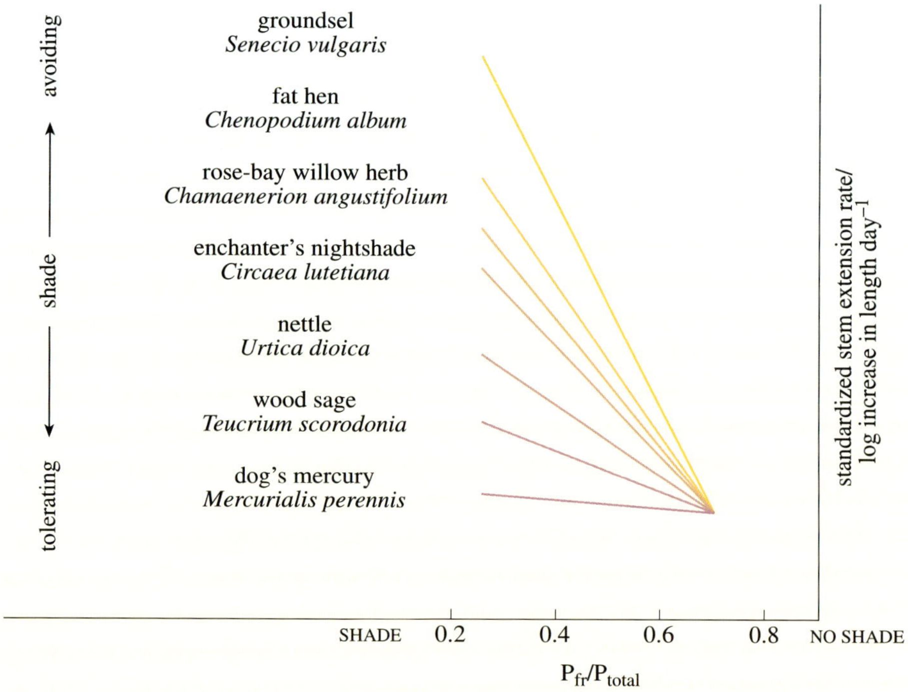

Figure 5.18 The relationship between stem extension rate and estimated phytochrome photo-equilibrium (ratio of $P_{fr} : P_{total}$) for a range of herbaceous plants. Data from Briggs *et al.* (1982).

In addition to its effects on seedling growth, light can also have a dramatic effect on germination (Section 5.2.3). The germination of photoblastic seeds is inhibited by far-red light and as a consequence such seeds remain dormant under a canopy. However, once the vegetation has died back or been otherwise removed, germination takes place as the seeds become exposed to white light. This phenomenon seems to be important for weed species where seed reserves are commonly low and also forest species whose seedlings emerge rapidly when a clearing develops due to the death of a mature tree. Phytochrome is also involved in the regulation of flowering (Section 5.6.2), leaf movements (as described for *Oxalis* when exposed suddenly to strong light, Section 2.2.3) and aspects of growth and development in mosses and ferns. So it is an important and ancient regulatory system in plants.

In addition to canopy shade, time of the day may also influence the spectral quality of the light. For instance, there is an increase in the relative proportion of blue wavelengths at dawn due to light scattering which is thought to provide a signal, perceived by cryptochrome, that promotes stomatal opening just before the sun comes up (Chapter 3, Section 5.3). Major changes in spectral composition are also found with increasing depth of water, which is important for the growth and development of aquatic plants and algae. In unpolluted waters, both the quality and quantity of light that penetrates are reasonably constant over the first 10–20 m whereas, in polluted waters, these parameters can change rapidly; the shorter green and blue wavelengths are absorbed much more rapidly (at shallower depth) in polluted water.

PHOTOTROPISM

It is not only the wavelength of light that provides critical signals for the regulation of plant growth and development but also the *direction* from which it comes. The bending of plants 'towards' light (*phototropism*) can be viewed by anyone who places a plant on a window sill. In practice, bending results from light inhibiting stem growth so that the shaded side grows faster, bringing about the characteristic growth towards light. The wavelengths of light most effective at inducing this response are in the blue part of the spectrum and the ability of a plant to move out of directional shade is critical for the optimization of photosynthetic capacity. The response occurs quickly (within about 10 min) and, apart from the nature of the signal, phototropism has close parallels to gravitropism (Section 5.4.1). This observation was not lost on the original workers in this field, who proposed that phototropic bending was the consequence of an accumulation of endogenous (naturally present) growth promoters on the shaded side of the shoot. In the next section we follow the history of research on phototropism, which provides a classic case study of how PGR action was investigated before the use of mutants and molecular techniques became widespread.

SUMMARY OF SECTION 5.4

1 The seedling is the most critical stage in the plant life cycle and responds to gravity and light as well as the presence of water and warmth.

2 Primary roots are positively gravitropic in that they grow towards the gravitational pull, whereas shoots are negatively gravitropic, growing upwards. Lateral roots and shoot grow at varying angles to gravity.

3 Plants perceive gravity by the sedimentation of amyloplasts, which generate a signal instructing cells in the growing zone to expand in a particular direction. Amyloplasts are found only in certain cells e.g. the columella of root caps and starch sheath of stems. The nature of the signal is unknown but may be IAA moving in a polar way from the root or stem tip.

4 Light regulates seedling development in several ways. The photoreceptors include phytochromes and cryptochrome.

5 Phytochrome is synthesized in the light and switches from an inactive, red light absorbing form, P_r, to an active, far-red absorbing form, P_{fr}. P_{fr} causes etiolated seedlings to change into a de-etiolated state as they emerge from the soil; stem growth is inhibited and leaf expansion and chlorophyll synthesis are promoted.

6 In shade under plants, where the proportion of far-red light is increased and the ratio of P_r to P_{fr} is high, seedlings adapted to well-lit habitats show etiolated growth patterns. Seedlings adapted to shady habitats do not show this response.

5 Phototropism (bending towards light) is mediated by blue light absorbed by cryptochrome. The response allows movement out of shade, which maximizes photosynthesis. Phototropism has close parallels to gravitropism.

5.5 Phototropism and auxin: a cautionary tale

The evidence about PGR action in phototropism was collected over a long time span to provide a model that explained how plant organs such as stems or coleoptiles (the protective sheath in which the developing stem grows in monocotyledons) bend towards a source of light. Similar models have been proposed for stem and root bending in response to gravity (gravitropism, Section 5.4.1) and touch (thigmotropism).

As you progress through this section you will be asked to assess the validity of experimental data and you will develop the 'standard' model or explanation. We then go on to explore just how the 'standard' explanation fares in the light of other evidence and further analysis of the data. The purpose of this short case study is not to provide a factual summary of how phototropism works, but to give you the opportunity to explore the issues and assumptions that underlie the experimental evidence.

The story starts with a set of observations by Charles Darwin and his son Francis Darwin (1880), and their findings (Experiment 1) are summarized in Figure 5.19:

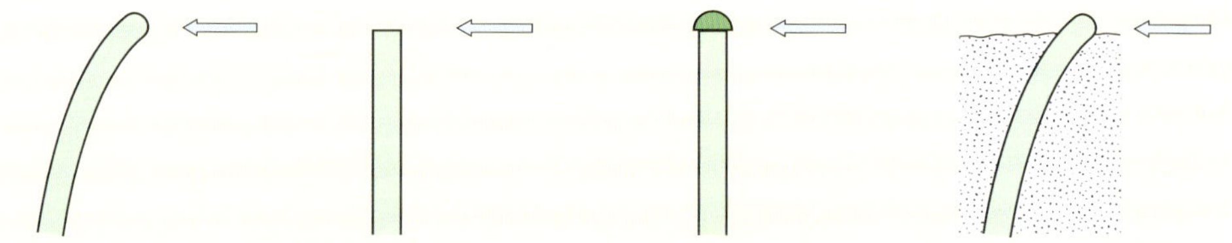

Figure 5.19 The Darwins' observations which suggested that the tip of the coleoptile acts as the 'site of perception' for unidirectional light (arrow) and the growing region below the tip acts as the 'effector'.

- ❍ Compare observation 1 with observation 2; then compare observation 1 with observation 3. What do these comparisons suggest about the nature of phototropism?
- ● The seedling responds to unilateral light by growing towards it only if the tip of the seedling is intact and exposed to the stimulus.

- ❍ Compare observation 3 with observation 4. What does this suggest?
- ● The stimulus need only be received at the tip of the seedling; the response occurs lower down.

The implication that the receptor (= tip) and site of response (= growth region below the tip) are two separate zones is a key feature of the explanation of how the response occurred. Although the Darwins did not propose any specific model to account for their observations, other investigators who followed up this work inferred that there must be some 'influence' passing from the tip to the growth region (as reasoned earlier for the gravitropic response, Section 5.4.1).

Over the 30 years following these initial observations, series of experiments were carried out by several investigators, working independently, in an attempt to elucidate the nature of this 'influence'.

The results of these investigations are summarized below. Note from the date in brackets on each heading how painfully slow progress appeared to be!

Experiment 2 (1913)

The tip of the coleoptile was removed, and a small amount of gelatine was placed on the cut surface. The tip was then replaced and the coleoptile subjected to unilateral light (Figure 5.20).

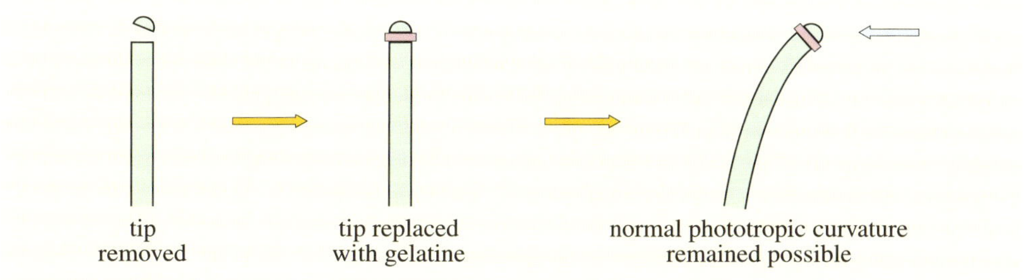

Figure 5.20 An early experiment (Experiment 2) investigating phototropic bending in seedlings.

- ❍ What can be inferred by comparing the result in Figure 5.20 with that of 'observation 2' from the Darwins' experiment (Figure 5.19)?

- ● The phototropic response can be re-established by replacing the excised tip on a gelatine-covered cut surface of the growing region of the coleoptile. The 'influence' inferred from the Darwins' experiment can diffuse from the tip through the gelatine to the growth region. Thus the 'influence' must be chemical in nature rather than a structural link between 'receptor' and 'effector' zones.

Experiment 3 (also 1913)

A small sheet of mica (a glass-like material) was inserted part-way into the coleoptile between the tip and growing region. The coleoptile was then placed in unilateral light, coming either from the side where the mica had been inserted or from the opposite side (Figure 5.21).

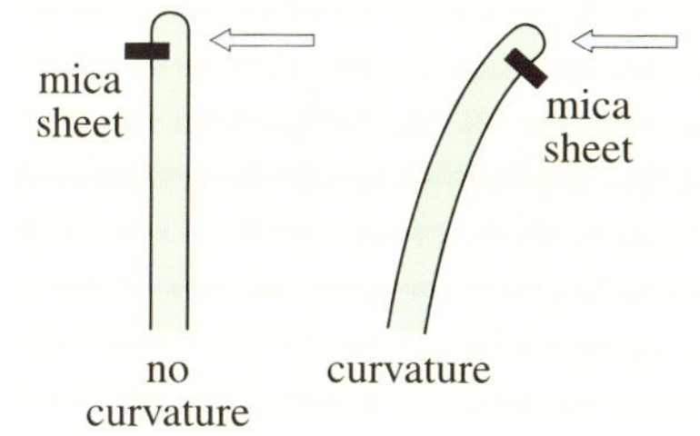

Figure 5.21 Results of Experiment 3.

- ❍ Describe the results. What, if anything, can be inferred from the results about the nature of the chemical diffusing from tip to growing zone?

- ● Where the chemical can diffuse down the shaded side of the coleoptile, normal phototropic bending occurs. Where the chemical is prevented from diffusing down the shaded side, straight growth continues in the growth region. One interpretation of these observations is that the chemical is a growth promoter.

Experiment 4 (1919)

The tip of the coleoptile was cut off and then replaced asymmetrically on the cut surface of the growing zone. The coleoptile was then placed in *all-round* illumination (Figure 5.22).

Figure 5.22 Results of Experiment 4.

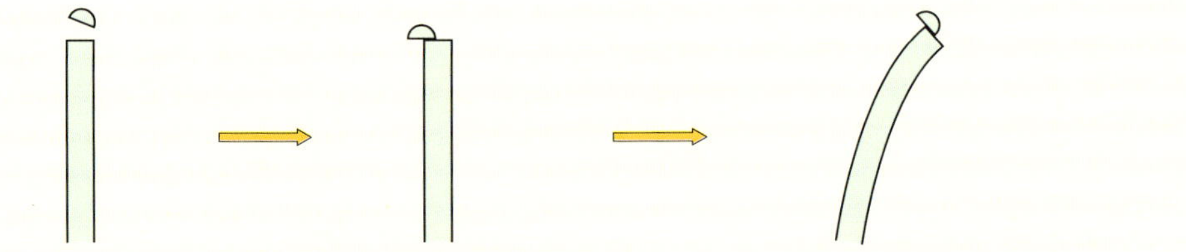

- ❍ Can you suggest an explanation for the results of Experiment 4?

- ● This experiment also supports the idea that the chemical produced in the tip is a growth promoter. Where it diffuses down one side only, even in all-round light, that side seems to grow at a faster rate, producing curvature similar to that observed when unilateral light is shone onto an intact coleoptile.

The search then began for the nature of the growth promoter, but it was not until 1926 that Fritz Went obtained from cut coleoptile tips a substance which seemed to fit the bill. The substance was collected from cut tips of *Avena* (oat) coleoptiles placed onto agar blocks (Figure 5.23). When these blocks were placed asymmetrically on decapitated coleoptiles the bending response was similar to that described in Experiment 2. Moreover, the angle of curvature was shown to be dependent on the amount of 'hormone' collected in the agar block. Indeed the angle of the curvature induced in the coleoptile became the means of measuring the amount of 'hormone' obtained from other tissues (one of the first examples of biological assay, or bioassay).

The curvature induced by the 'hormone' seemed to match results obtained by adding IAA to agar blocks which were then placed asymmetrically on decapitated coleoptiles; the more IAA added to the block the greater the angle of curvature produced, as shown in Figure 5.23c. It was not until much later (early 1970s) that other techniques showed that IAA was present naturally in coleoptiles.

- ❍ From the above experiments and information, suggest a mechanism by which IAA could control the phototropic response.

- ● Curvature of the coleoptile or stem could be caused by the asymmetrical distribution of auxin produced in the tip and transported down to the growth zone to a greater extent on the shaded side than on the lit side. Where IAA is present in larger quantities, the cells expand more, causing uneven growth rates and resulting in curvature towards the light source.

The idea was proposed by Went (working on phototropism) and independently by a Russian, Cholodny (working on gravitropism) and become known as the **Cholodny–Went theory**. A main preoccupation with workers exploring this theory was to establish whether the asymmetrical distribution of the auxin occurred by (A) lateral transport from the lit side to the shaded side or (B) breakdown of the auxin on the 'inside' bend region. (Figure 5.24).

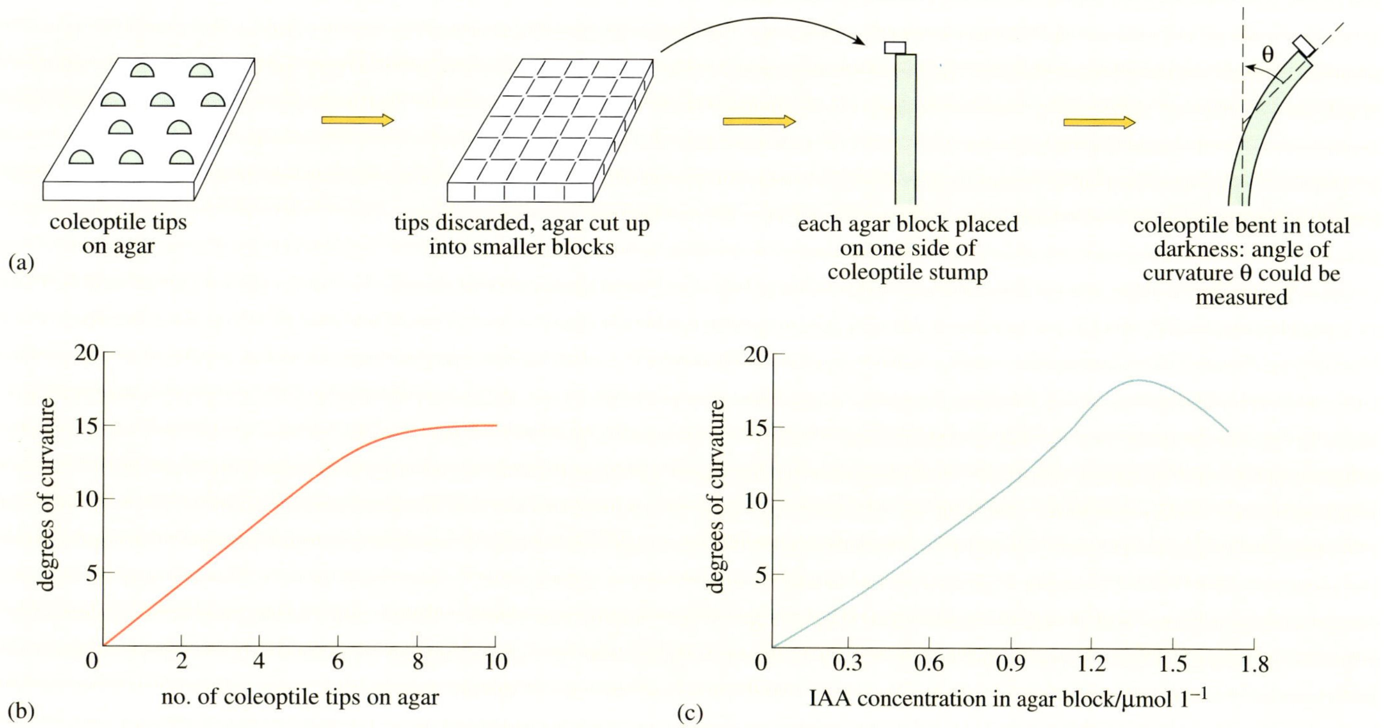

Figure 5.23 Experiments which suggested that tropic curvature of oat coleoptiles is due to unequal distribution of IAA. (a) Outline of the experimental procedure. (b) Results obtained using different numbers of coleoptile tips on the agar blocks. (c) Results obtained using different concentrations of IAA on the agar blocks.

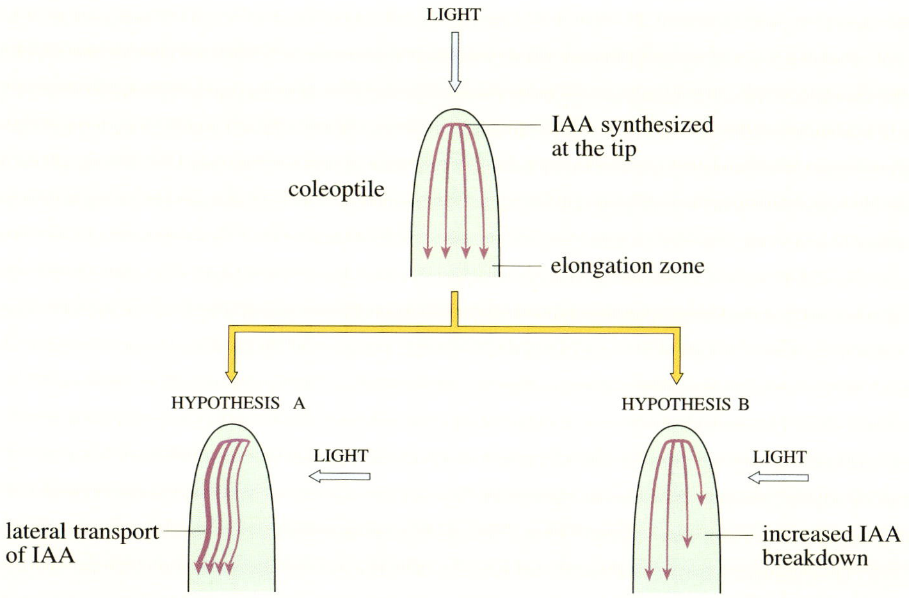

Figure 5.24 Two hypotheses (A and B) explaining how unequal levels of IAA occur on the light and dark sides of phototropically stimulated maize coleoptile.

❍ Bearing in mind that IAA diffuses out of coleoptile tips and can be collected in agar blocks, suggest an experiment that might distinguish between hypotheses A and B above.

- Place coleoptile tips on agar blocks and keep in darkness or with illumination from one side. Allow IAA to diffuse into the blocks and, after a suitable period of time, assay blocks for IAA. Hypothesis A predicts that the same amount of IAA would be present in blocks in darkness and with unilateral illumination whereas hypothesis B predicts that *less* would be present in unilateral illumination due to IAA destruction on the illuminated side.

The results of such experiments, using a bioassay to measure IAA, were inconsistent with hypothesis B and broadly supported hypothesis A. Indeed, by splitting the receiver blocks using a sheet of mica during the collection period, it was shown that about twice as much IAA appeared to diffuse from the shaded side as from the lit side of laterally illuminated tips (Figure 5.25). The accumulation of this sort of evidence, spanning over 50 years work, supported the Cholodny–Went theory that a PGR (here identified as IAA) controlled the tropic response.

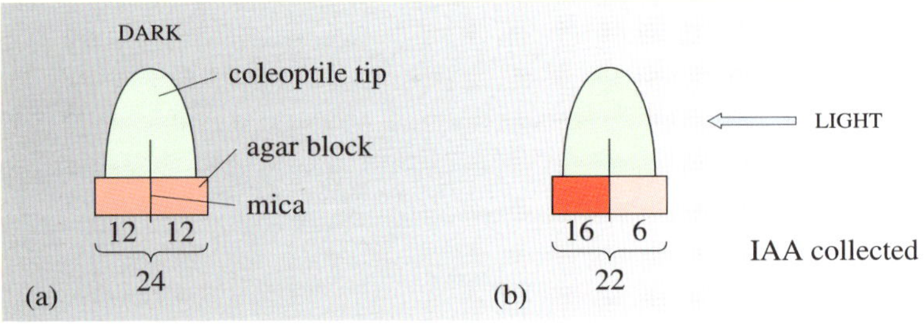

Figure 5.25 The results of collecting IAA over a 3 h period from maize coleoptile tips held in darkness or illuminated from one side. IAA diffused into agar blocks which were split by a mica sheet and the two halves of the blocks were bioassayed separately. Each number is a relative IAA concentration which is the mean of at least 40 bioassay measurements.

- Summarize the main features of the Cholodny–Went model.

- (a) A chemical, in this case IAA, is produced at the tip (receptor of light zone). (b) The IAA diffuses downwards to the growth zone ('target cells'). (c) Uneven distribution of the IAA causes uneven cell enlargement in the two sides (shaded and lit) of the growing zone, resulting in curved growth.

You may feel quite convinced by the evidence presented so far — indeed, you will find this explanation given as the only model for tropic responses in many older textbooks. However, consider the following observations about phototropism.

Figure 5.26 shows the results of measuring *growth rate* on two opposite sides of a coleoptile both before and after stimulation by unilateral light.

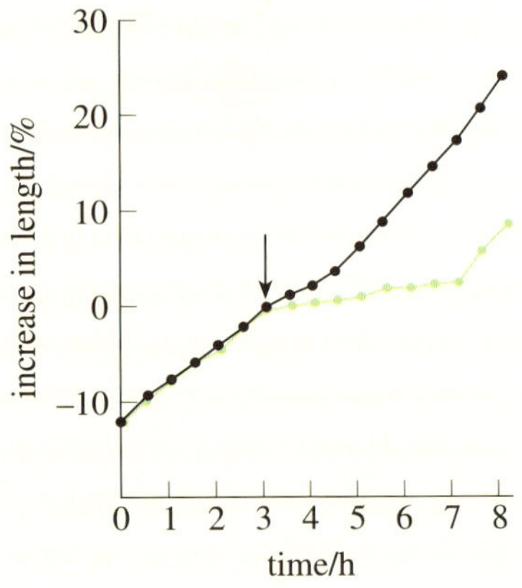

Figure 5.26 Growth of both sides of *Avena* coleoptiles before and after unilateral phototropic stimulation (indicated by the arrow). Growth on the illuminated side is shown in green and that on the shaded side in black. (Increase in length is expressed as a percentage of the length measured at the start of unilateral illumination.)

- What happens to the growth rate of the shaded side after stimulation has occurred? Is this outcome predicted by the Cholodny–Went model?

- The growth rate (shown by the slope of the line) on the shaded side remains virtually identical to the rate before stimulation; the Cholodny–Went theory would predict an increase in growth rate due to the presence of increased levels of IAA.

- What happens to the growth rate on the illuminated side?

- There is an almost immediate 'stop' to growth on the illuminated side, followed by a restoration of original growth rate some time later.

Similar graphs have been obtained from experiments on a wide range of coleoptiles and stems; phototropic and gravitropic responses all have the common feature of a 'stop' to growth on what becomes the 'inside bend'. This may sometimes be accompanied by an increase in growth rate on the 'outside bend' (by up to 10% of pre-stimulated growth rate), but the 'stop' (reduction in growth rate by up to 90% of the pre-stimulated rate) on the inside bend is the universal feature.

❍ How does the timing of the response shown in Figure 5.25 fit with a hormone-based theory?

● The graph suggests that the response to unilateral light is almost immediate; the production and redistribution of IAA in this time span would be impossible.

❍ Look at Figure 5.27 showing the measurement of growth rate along zones of a coleoptile subjected to unilateral light. Do these data support a hormonal redistribution theory?

● No. A hormonal redistribution model would predict a 'wave' of differential growth passing down from the top zone to lower zones as the redistribution takes effect; the fact that each zone responds simultaneously to the unilateral light conflicts with this sort of model. Simultaneous reactions of all zones along the length of the coleoptile or stem strongly suggest a direct effect of the stimulus on the growing cells.

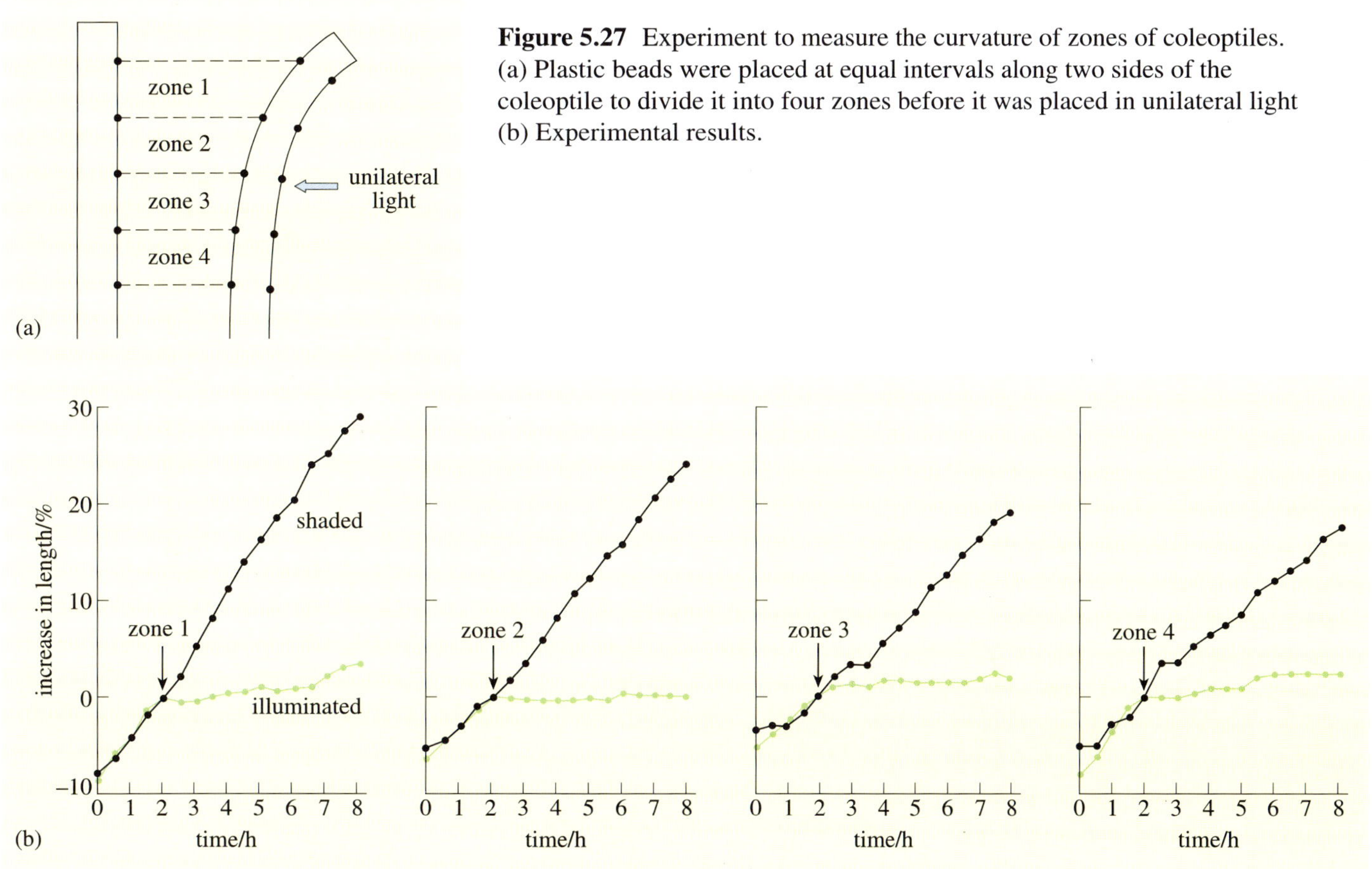

Figure 5.27 Experiment to measure the curvature of zones of coleoptiles. (a) Plastic beads were placed at equal intervals along two sides of the coleoptile to divide it into four zones before it was placed in unilateral light (b) Experimental results.

The experiment shown in Figure 5.25 was later repeated, measuring IAA activity on the illuminated and shaded sides using the bioassay technique but then comparing these results with a direct chemical assay (thin-layer chromatography, a technique unavailable when the experiment was first carried out). The results of the bioassay confirmed the original finding: the *activity* of IAA on the illuminated side was about 38% of that on the shaded side. However, the *actual amount* of IAA present in both sides was the same.

Such findings cause severe problems for the original Cholodny–Went theory because uneven growth is occurring even though there is no lateral gradient of IAA in the growing zone.

- ❍ How could the activity of IAA in the receiver blocks differ on the illuminated and shaded sides even though the actual amount does not change?

- ● Inhibitors that reduce the activity of IAA might be unevenly distributed between the illuminated and shaded sides.

There is some evidence that inhibitors are present and unevenly distributed but their chemical nature is still unknown. Alternatively, PGRs, including IAA and inhibitors, have nothing to do with tropic curvatures! In this situation the options are: either abandon the Cholodny–Went theory altogether, or attempt to modify it to fit the new evidence. Before we explore each option further, let's consider how our original interpretation of the early experiments led us (and indeed everyone else at the time!) to such misleading conclusions.

The first reason is that some of the 'experiments' are really observations and lack proper *controls*. For instance, in Experiment 4 (Figure 5.22), an alternative explanation is that the 'offset' tips allowed greater evaporation of water from the cut surface of the growth zone — hence differential shrinkage of the coleoptile cells could have produced the curvature!

- ❍ Suggest an appropriate control for Experiment 4.

- ● Some cut coleoptiles could have offset non-porous blocks placed on them and curvature of these coleoptiles should be compared to the experimental set with offset tips. If curvature is due to evaporation then both sets will bend to the same degree.

The other reason why we have been misled by the early experiments is due to the underlying assumptions of the model devised to explain the initial observations.

- ❍ With the benefit of hindsight, suggest three, possibly misleading, assumptions in the interpretations of the experiments.

- ● *Assumption 1*: that the site of perception is separated from the site of response. The early observation may have supported this assumption, but appropriate experiments (with controls) need to be performed to establish that the two sides are separate rather than assuming that this would be a feature of the model. Alternative hypotheses suggest a direct effect of light on the responding cells, and do not need an explanation based on a 'hormone' moving between tip and growing zone at all. The early observations could have alternative explanations: cut the growing tip off and you might expect that the whole developing system would be disrupted!

Assumption 2: that there is only one explanation of differential growth — more IAA accelerates cell elongation in a very localized way. However, differential growth could be caused by any of the following: inhibition of growth on one side; a combination of inhibition and acceleration on either side; inhibition on both sides to different extents; acceleration on both sides to different extents — or any combination of these mechanisms! So early investigators assumed their model was the only explanation when others were possible.

Assumption 3: that there was a 'cause and effect' mediated by a hormone-like chemical — that redistribution of IAA *caused* elongation. In fact, the timing of the response is crucial here — some more recent investigators argue that any detectable shift in the amount of IAA across responding tissue occurs after the response has started! This 'cause-and-effect' assumption is based on what was known about animal hormones and communication systems, where a rise in a hormone level has specific effects on target organs.

Herein lies the fundamental problem with the model: the explanation is based on 'animal-like' properties of hormones. But there are alternatives to the idea that cells respond to changing levels of hormone-like chemicals.

The fact that PGR levels often do not change dramatically in the way that some animal hormones do has led some workers to suggest that the mechanisms of PGR action are fundamentally different from those of animal hormones. The tissues may not be responding in the 'animal-like' manner of target tissues to changes in hormone level but rather changing their *sensitivity* to fairly static PGR levels. The fact that in many experiments artificially high levels of PGR need to be added suggests that the plant system is geared not to respond to the small changes in internal PGR concentration.

The sensitivity of a cell to a PGR can be altered in several ways, some of which were discussed in Section 5.3. First, the amount of PGR transported to the receptor sites on the cell membrane or within the cell could be altered. Secondly, the number of receptor sites could be increased or decreased, so altering the receptivity of the cell to unchanging PGR levels in much the same way as receptor regulation occurs in animal cells. A third possibility is that the events occurring after the PGR has bound to a receptor could be altered. Cells could thus have a different capacity to respond at different times during their development. These possibilities are summarized in Figure 5.28.

The concept of *response capacity* helps to explain the wide range of responses shown by different cells to the same PGR. Different cells may have different receptors capable of binding a particular PGR; in each case the formation of a PGR-receptor complex would stimulate a different sequence of events within the cell, so producing a different response (Figure 5.28c).

We can now return to the two options considered regarding the conflicting evidence for Cholodny–Went theory — either abandon it completely or modify it. There are proponents for each strategy!

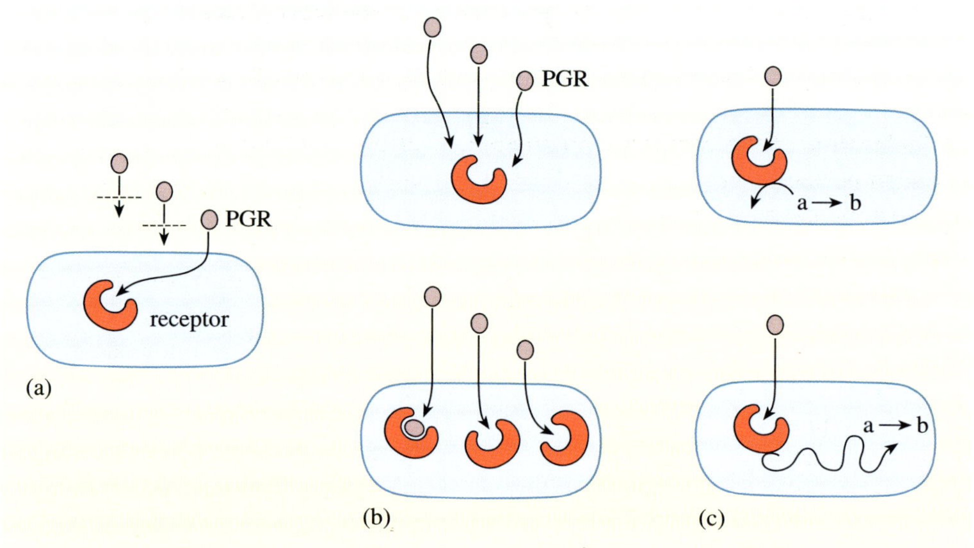

Figure 5.28 Three ways in which the sensitivity of the cell to a PGR could be altered.
(a) Different amounts of PGR transported to receptor sites.
(b) Different numbers of receptors.
(c) Different post-binding effects.

❍ How could the theory be modified and still provide an explanation for phototropic bending?

● Instead of uneven distribution of IAA causing uneven growth rates, we could suggest that IAA levels stay the same but the cells on either side become differentially *sensitive* to the IAA already present.

The alternative is to abandon the theory altogether and propose a direct effect of light on cells, i.e. elongation is inhibited as a direct consequence of unilateral light on cells. There is still no consensus but the use of mutants — with deficient receptors, or inability to produce IAA or other PGRs, for example — is the most promising way forward. For gravitropism, such studies clearly indicate a role for IAA (Section 5.4.1) but the nature of that role is still unclear.

Summary of Section 5.5

1 Early experiments with coleoptiles suggested that phototropic bending occurs because a growth regulator (IAA), produced at the tip, becomes unevenly distributed between expanding cells under unilateral illumination, causing uneven cell elongation and hence curvature. This view is summarized in the Cholodny–Went theory.

2 Later experiments were inconsistent with Cholodny–Went and showed that growth is inhibited on the illuminated side, rather than being stimulated on the shaded side, and that levels of IAA do not vary across coleoptiles, although activity in bioassays may do.

3 Misleading interpretation of early experiments arose because of inadequate controls and incorrect underlying assumptions. The status of the Cholodny–Went theory is still unresolved but use of mutants is the most promising way forward.

5.6 FLOWERING AND FLOWER DEVELOPMENT

One of the major changes that a plant undergoes is the change from a vegetative to a flowering state. In some species this event is restricted to a particular time of the year while in others flowering may take place over an extended period of time. The coordination of reproductive development not only fosters outbreeding but also ensures that flowering and the availability of insect pollinators can be synchronized. Two environmental stimuli that have been shown to have a profound impact on the timing of flowering are *temperature* and *day length*. Temperature can affect the ability of a plant to enter the reproductive phase and for some species a period of low temperature (a few weeks at or below 5 °C) is critical for flower development to take place. Such plants are described as requiring **vernalization** and crops such as winter barley and winter wheat fall into this category. Intriguingly, the cold treatment does not induce the development of floral organs directly but in some way has a permanent impact on the programme of development such that the plant flowers many months later.

5.6.1 PHOTOPERIODISM

For many plants, the critical signal for regulating the timing of flowering is day length. Plants that require a specific day length for flowering to be triggered are called **photoperiodic**. Such a species may be classified as either a **short-day plant (SDP)** or a **long-day plant (LDP)** depending on whether it requires less than a maximum or more than a minimum number of hours of daylight (i.e. the critical day length) for flowering to occur (Figure 5.29).

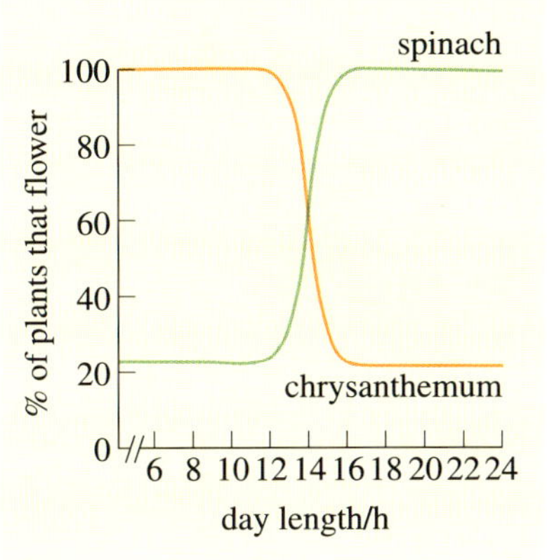

Figure 5.29 The relationship between day length and flowering in chrysanthemum and spinach.

❍ In Figure 5.29 which species is the SDP and which is the LDP?

● Chrysanthemum is the SDP because it flowers when day length is less than about 14 h; spinach is the LDP and flowers when day length is greater than about 14 h.

If a species has an absolute requirement for either a short day or a long day it is described as being an *obligate* photoperiodic plant. However, if flowering is only accelerated by inductive conditions, it is termed a *facultative* photoperiodic species.

❍ What properties does day length have that make it such a valuable stimulus for coordinating reproduction in both plants and animals?

● It is an unambiguous signal, indicating the time of year, that is unaffected by day to day variations in other climatic conditions. In addition, by comparing the length of one day with the next it is possible to determine whether the days are lengthening (i.e. spring) or shortening (i.e. autumn).

WHICH IS MORE IMPORTANT: THE LENGTH OF THE LIGHT PERIOD OR THE LENGTH OF THE DARK PERIOD?

Although the terms used to describe photoperiodic plants place the emphasis on the duration of the light phase (i.e. SDP and LDP) it was thought that the length of the dark period was critical for flowering. In an experiment to determine which component of the photoperiod was crucial for flowering, a controlled environment experiment was carried out using populations of soya beans (*Glycine max*) exposed to fixed periods of light followed by a varying period of dark. Soya bean is a short-day plant and the durations of the light phases chosen were 4 h or 16 h, with 20 h and 8 h of darkness, respectively.

- ❍ Which day length would be predicted to stimulate flowering in soya beans: (a) 4 h or (b) 16 h?

- ● Soya beans should flower under (a) since, being an SDP, a day length of 16 h might be expected to be above the critical duration to trigger flowering. In practice 4 h promotes flowering but the short period of illumination limits the extent of photosynthesis and, therefore, the response is limited.

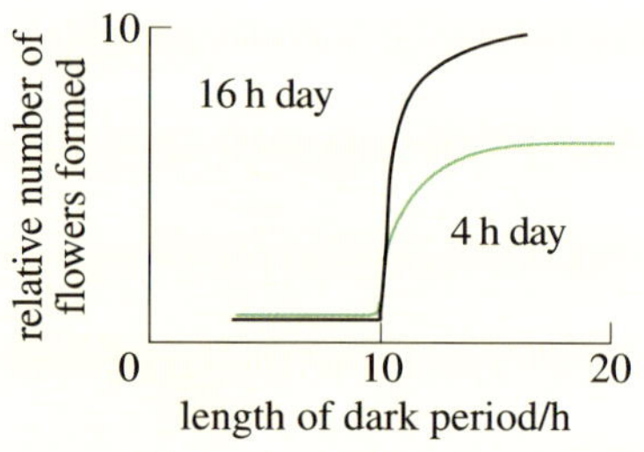

Figure 5.30 The formation of flowers by soya bean plants given a constant 16 h or 4 h period of light in association with different lengths of dark period.

By keeping the duration of the light phase constant but varying the length of darkness in the cycle it is possible to determine whether the night period has a significant effect on flowering (Figure 5.30). It was discovered that if plants were given cycles containing 10 h of darkness or less, flowering did not take place. However, above 10 h, flowering was induced and reached an optimum in response to cycles containing 16 h of light followed by 16 h darkness. Although this observation tells us that the duration of the dark period is a crucial component of the photoperiod, lengthening of the dark period beyond 20 h causes flowering to decline. It turns out that the length of both the light and dark periods are important and consequently the nomenclature SDP and LDP has been retained.

DOES THE DARK PERIOD HAVE TO BE CONTINUOUS?

We know from the experiments described above that in order for an SDP such as soya bean to flower it must experience a cycle containing *more* than 10 h of darkness. A question that has been posed is whether this dark period has to be continuous. By interrupting the night with brief flashes of light (night breaks) it has been found that the impact of such a treatment is dependent upon the timing of the stimulus. Exposure to light is most disruptive in the middle of the night with flowering being completely prevented at this time by a stimulus lasting only a few minutes (Figure 5.31, red curve). Intriguingly if an LDP is grown under SD, then flowering can be induced by exposure to a night break.

- ❍ What evidence in Figure 5.31 supports this last statement?

- ● The blue curve (for an LDP grown under short days) shows that interrupting the dark period can induce flowering with optimal induction about mid-way through the dark period.

Further experiments have shown that the most effective wavelength for interrupting the dark period to inhibit flowering in SDPs is red light (660 nm) with the effect of this wavelength being reversed by far-red light (720 nm).

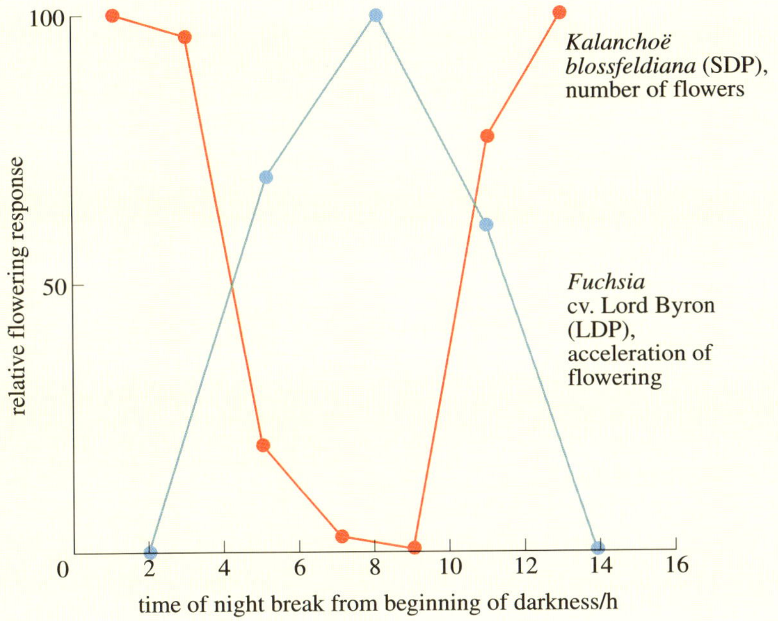

Figure 5.31 Effects of brief light interruption at different times during the dark period, on flowering (measured as number of flowers or acceleration of flowering) in a short-day plant (SDP) and in a long-day plant (LDP), both grown under short-day conditions. Data from Hart (1988).

- What does this red/far-red reversibility tell us about the likely identity of the pigment that perceives day length?

- A diagnostic feature of the pigment phytochrome is red/far-red reversibility (Section 5.4.2). So phytochrome is likely to be involved in regulating the response of SDP and LDP to day length.

5.6.2 How is phytochrome involved in time measurement?

The results of the night-break experiment and the demonstration that phytochrome is involved allow us to formulate a hypothesis about how plants may be able to measure day length accurately. Daylight contains more red than far-red light and, as a consequence, drives the phytochrome equilibrium towards the formation of P_{fr} (see Figure 5.17). During the night, phytochrome undergoes a phenomenon termed **dark reversion** that results in a decline in the level of P_{fr} in a plant and a rise in P_r (Figure 5.32). As the inductive effect of the night can be disrupted by a brief flash of red light it can be concluded that P_{fr} must be inhibitory to flower development in SDP.

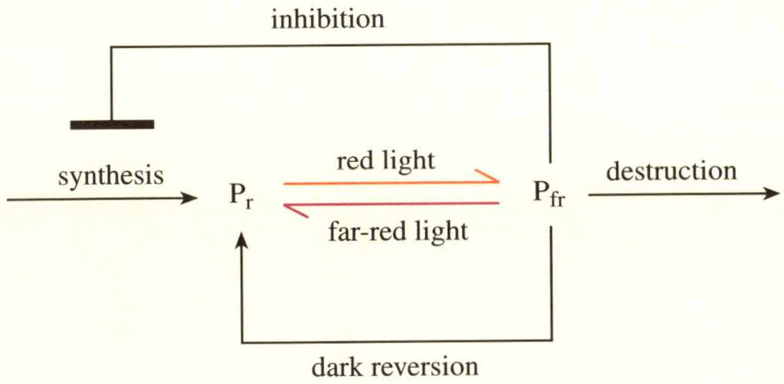

Figure 5.32 Phytochrome conversions, synthesis and destruction. P_r requires red light for its synthesis, which is inhibited by P_{fr}. P_{fr} levels decline at night due to dark reversion to P_r and to destruction.

From these observations it is possible to construct a hypothesis stating that it is the level of P_{fr} that dictates whether flowering takes place. According to this **'hour-glass' model** (where the hour-glass acts like an old-fashioned egg timer), at the end of the light period, levels of P_{fr} are high and inhibitory to flowering. During the night they decline (rather like the level of sand in an hour-glass) and if they fall below a threshold amount (i.e. the sand runs out), flowering is no longer inhibited. The time it takes to fall to below the threshold is the **critical night length**, i.e. in soya beans it would be more than 10 hours. Figure 5.33 illustrates this model for a plant with a critical day length of 12 h.

- In Figure 5.33, which regime would allow flowering according to the 'hour-glass' model?

- None: either the critical day length is not reached (a), or the essential dark period is too short (b) or is interrupted (c), with the result that P_{fr} does not fall below the critical level.

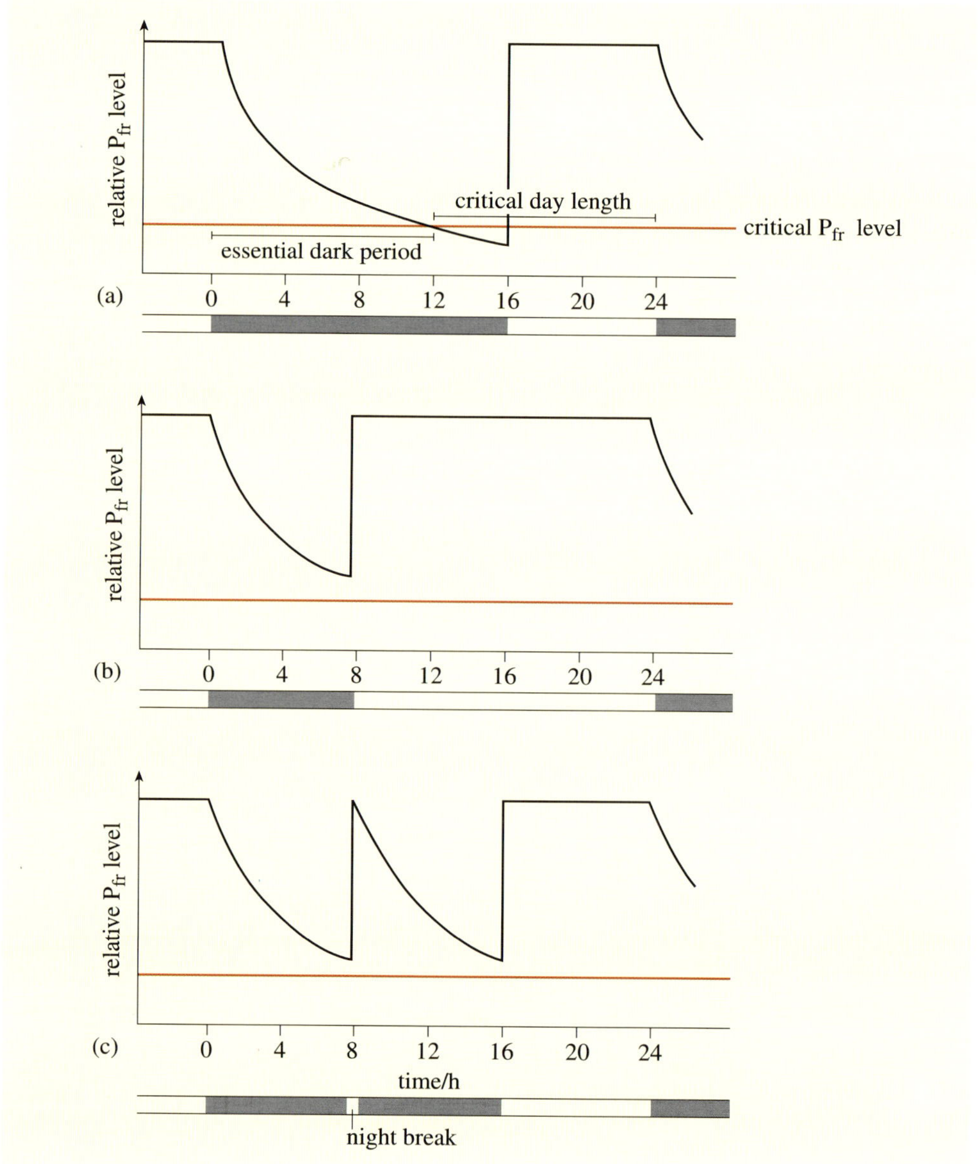

Figure 5.33 Changes in P_{fr} predicted for an SDP with a critical day length of 12 h (i.e. with 12 h dark in a 24 h cycle). (a) Given 16 h dark and 8 h light. (b) Given 8 h dark and 16 h light. (c) As (a) but with 5 min light in the middle of the dark period. In this experiment the essential dark period is equivalent to the critical night length.

❍ How could you test this 'hour-glass' hypothesis?

● One stratagem would be exposure to far-red light. This treatment would be predicted to reduce the level of P_{fr} below the threshold and trigger flowering in the absence of a long night. Unfortunately such an effect is not observed and therefore we need to refine the 'hour-glass' hypothesis.

Clearly the level of P_{fr} is only one component of the flowering machinery and another would seem to be an *endogenous clock*. Thus we can envisage P_{fr} as part of the chiming mechanism that must be coupled to the clock in order for us to be able to tell the time, the endogenous rhythm being the mechanism that keeps the clock ticking — the **clock hypothesis**.

5.6.3 Flowering and endogenous rhythms

Changes linked to an internal clock are called **endogenous rhythms** and play an important role in the life cycle of a plant. Rhythms such as the drooping of leaves at night (sleep movements) have a cycle length of approximately 24 hours and are described as circadian (*circa dies* — approximately one day). These **circadian rhythms** are maintained in the absence of external cues although stimuli such as light act to entrain the rhythm to around 24 hours. If an experiment to examine the critical length of the dark period in soya beans is continued over 3 days it becomes clear that flowering is associated with a circadian rhythm (Figure 5.34). During parts of the cycle, dark is inhibitory to (24 and 50 h, i.e. cycle length of 32 and 58 h) whilst at other times it strongly promotes (16 and 40 h, i.e. cycle length of 24 and 48 h) flowering. This observation suggests that both the level of P_{fr} and the time in the cycle when it is naturally low may be critical for flowering to be initiated, lending support to the clock hypothesis.

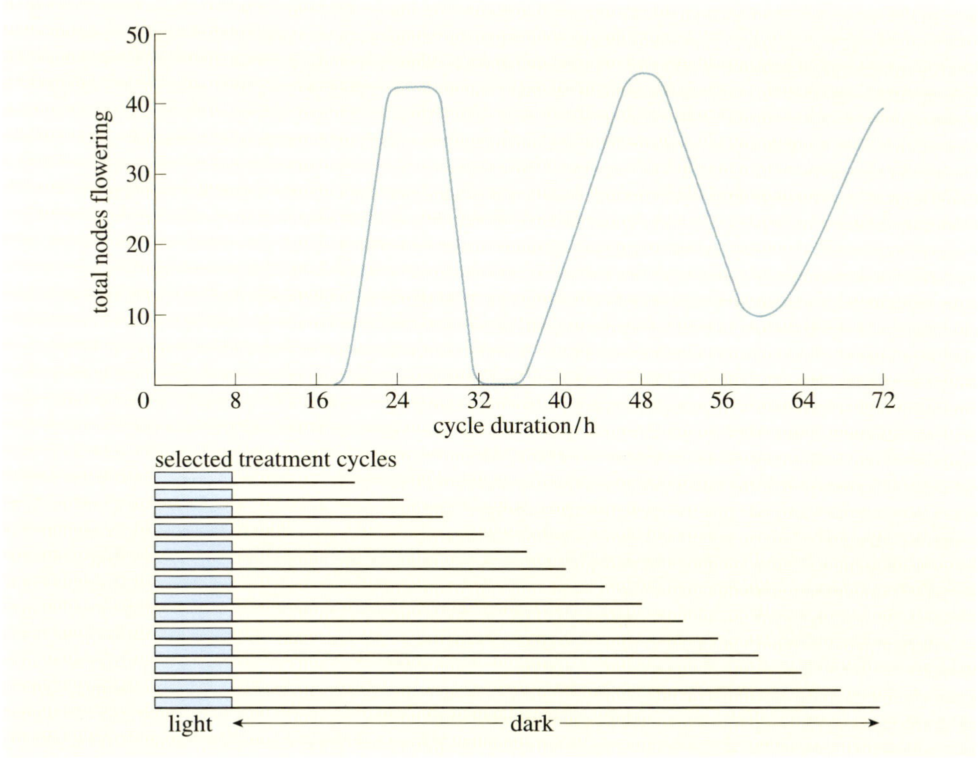

Figure 5.34 Flowering in soya bean (an SDP) and circadian rhythms. Plants were exposed to treatment cycles consisting of 8 h light and dark periods of different lengths; the number of nodes that flowered is plotted against the total length of a cycle. Data from Hart (1988).

5.6.4 WHERE IS THE FLOWERING STIMULUS PERCEIVED?

You have already seen that day length is critical for flowering in photoperiodic plants and that the pigment that mediates this behaviour is phytochrome. An important question that remains to be answered is the site of perception of the day length signal. The classic experiment that was undertaken to answer this question was carried out on garden chrysanthemum. This species is an SDP and its horticultural importance as a flower crop makes it a useful target for experimental manipulation. If the leaves of a single-stemmed chrysanthemum are removed from the upper third of the plant and the remaining leaves enclosed inside a light-proof chamber, it is possible to expose the upper and lower halves to contrasting photoperiods (Figure 5.35).

❍ (i) What happens when the whole chrysanthemum is exposed to either long days or short days? (ii) Which part of the plant perceives the photoperiodic signal?

● (i) Being an SDP, under long days the plant remains vegetative (a), whilst under short days flowering is initiated (b). (ii) The site of perception must be the leaves, as flowering takes place if they are exposed to SD but not if they are maintained under LD (Figure 5.35c and d).

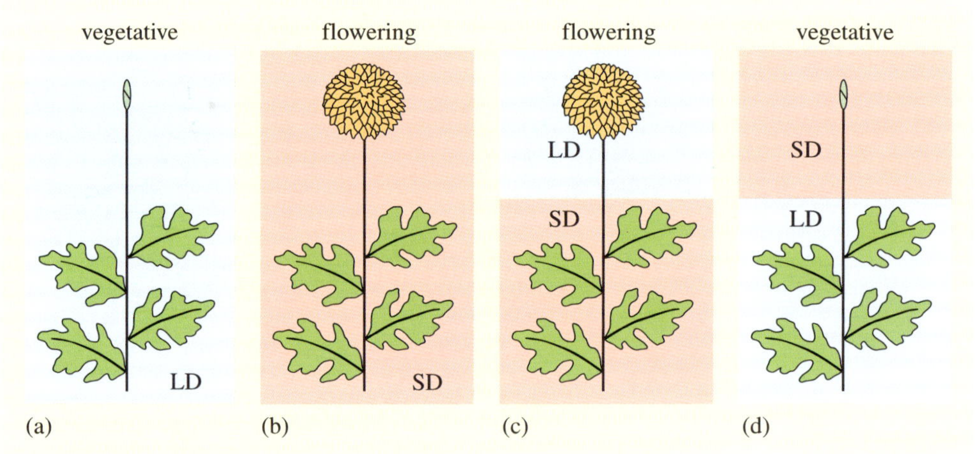

Figure 5.35 The effect of giving a flower-inducing treatment (short days) to the leaves and to the shoot apices of chrysanthemum.

Treatment of only a single leaf is sufficient for flowering to be induced in species such as rye (*Secale cereale*) (LDP) and cocklebur (*Xanthium strumarium)* (SDP). Furthermore, in *Xanthium,* exposure of whole plants to only a single SD treatment is sufficient for flowering to be induced although in most species the extent of flower development is dependent upon the number of inductive cycles received.

5.6.5 EVIDENCE FOR A TRANSMISSIBLE FLOWERING STIMULUS

Although the leaves of a plant perceive the photoperiodic stimulus, the development of the flower usually occurs at the shoot apex. This observation suggests that a floral signal must be transmitted from the leaves to the shoot apex where it triggers the conversion from a vegetative into a reproductive state. Further evidence to support this assertion has come from experiments where a single induced leaf when grafted on to a plant maintained under non-inductive conditions has been shown to promote flowering. The flower-inducing substance has been given the name **florigen**. Many of the grafting experiments have been carried out on *Xanthium* as it seems to be particularly sensitive to photoperiodic stimuli; however, similar observations have been made on LDPs. In general a successful graft union can only be established between members of the same species, but it has proved possible to graft the shoot of the LDP *Sedum spectabile* onto the SDP *Kalanchoë blossfeldiana*. When the composite plant was maintained under short days, the pattern of flowering is as shown in Figure 5.36.

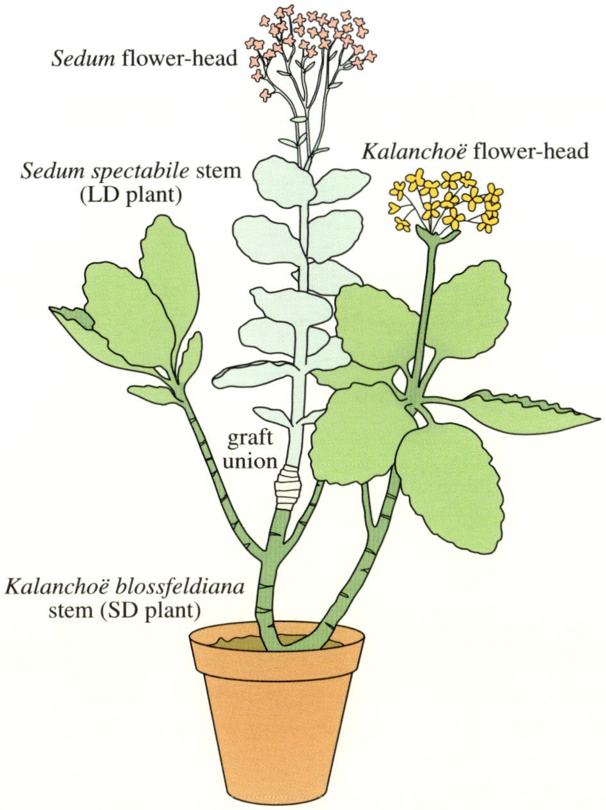

Figure 5.36 The result of grafting together portions of long-day and short-day plants (*Sedum* and *Kalanchoë*, respectively) and keeping the composite plant under short-day conditions.

- ❍ How could you explain the result that both species developed flowers?
- ● *Kalanchoë* is an SDP so, when maintained under short days, florigen is produced and flowering takes place. This stimulus passes across the graft union and induces the development of flowers in *Sedum*.

Another conclusion from this experiment is that the flowering stimulus, i.e. florigen, acts in the same way in both SDP and LDP. It seems as if florigen is transported from the leaves to the apex via the phloem since, in successful grafting experiments, contact between a donor leaf and a recipient plant must be maintained long enough for vascular connections to become established. Moreover, if the stem above an induced leaf is steam girdled to kill the phloem tissue (Chapter 3) then flowering does not take place even under inductive photoperiods.

Knowing the identity of the tissues in which florigen moves, it would seem feasible to isolate it from the content of phloem sap in plants prior to and after exposure to inductive photoperiods. Many scientists seek to isolate and characterize florigen. However, as yet no one has successfully isolated a compound that has proved to have the characteristics predicted for a flowering 'hormone' and attempts to promote flowering using any of the known plant growth regulators have also been unsuccessful. One possible explanation is that florigen might be a mixture of more than one compound or a balance between a flower promoter and an inhibitor. Other PGRs can, indeed, promote flowering in certain species. For example, ethylene may induce flowering in pineapple (*Ananas comosus*) and GA can cause flowering and 'bolting' in some rosette-type LDP.

EVIDENCE FOR THE EXISTENCE OF FLOWERING INHIBITORS

Although an induced leaf when grafted on to an uninduced plant can promote flowering the effect is most noticeable if all the other leaves above the graft union are removed. The most likely explanation for this observation is that the other leaves interfere with the floral stimulus and either affect its transport to the apex or inhibit its action. The relative importance of promoters and inhibitors in the induction of flowering remains to be resolved.

5.6.6 THE IDENTIFICATION OF GENES THAT REGULATE FLOWERING

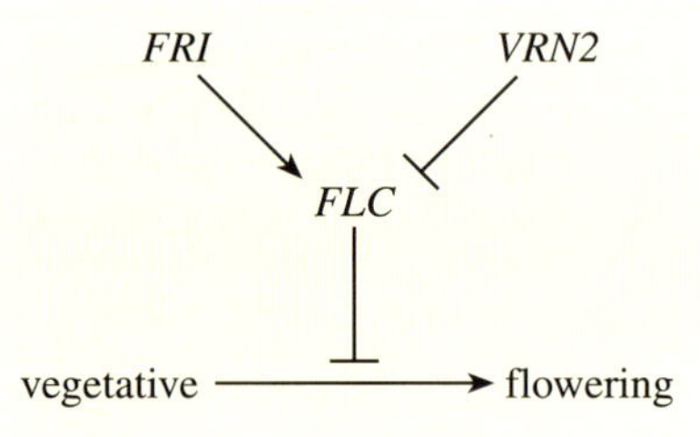

Figure 5.37 Model of the interactions between three genes that influence flowering in *Arabidopsis*.

The search for critical regulators of flowering using the strategies described above has had limited success. Recently researchers have focussed on the model plant *Arabidopsis* in an attempt to identify mutants with altered flowering characteristics. A dominant gene termed *FRIGIDA* (*FRI*) has been found to be responsible for causing late flowering in some ecotypes and has been shown to be critical in controlling the vernalization response of this species. A second gene *FLOWERING LOCUS C* (*FLC*) also delays flowering while a third gene *VERNALIZATION2* (*VRN2*) has been isolated that mediates the inductive response to low temperatures. By analysing the mutants it has been shown that *FRI* promotes and *VRN2* inhibits the synthesis of the *FLC* gene product (Figure 5.37), which appears to be an inhibitor of flowering.

The regulation of processes such as flowering appears to be the consequence of a balance of influences and as an increasing number of genes involved in the process are identified, stimuli such as florigen and perhaps antiflorigen may be characterized.

5.6.7 FLORAL PATTERNING

Induction of flowering is just the first stage in the sexual reproductive process. The second phase is the conversion of the apex from a vegetative to a flowering state. Floral organs arise in four concentric rings or whorls (Figure 5.38a) and the development of each whorl is a consequence of the expression of a specific temporal and spatial pattern of **homeotic genes**. Homeotic genes encode proteins that determine organ identity and the process is analogous to the formation of the body plan in the early embryos of animals.

By studying mutants of *Arabidopsis* and *Antirrhinum* (snapdragon) that exhibit abnormal flower development, such as petals differentiating where carpels should be, it was possible to devise a mechanism to account for floral patterning. This hypothesis, now called the **ABC model**, proposes that three classes of homeotic genes exist and the combination of their expression determines the identity of the different floral organs. Class A genes operate in whorls 1 and 2, Class B in whorls 2 and 3, and Class C genes in whorls 3 and 4. For instance, expression of Class A in whorl 1 leads to the formation of sepals; in whorl 2 both Class A and B are expressed and petals are formed; in whorl 3 stamens develop as a consequence of the combined action of Class B and C genes; and finally in whorl 4 the action of Class C leads to the development of carpels (Figure 5.38b). In addition, the action of A genes *suppresses* that of C genes in whorls 1 and 2 while C activity suppresses A in whorls 3 and 4.

The ABC hypothesis enables the phenotypes of various homeotic mutants to be predicted.

- ❍ What would the flower of a Class B mutant look like?
- ● Sepals would replace petals in whorl 2 and carpels replace stamens in whorl 3.

This is precisely what is seen in the *apetala3* mutant of *Arabidopsis* (Figure 5.39c).

- ❍ What would the flower of a Class A mutant look like?
- ● Because A suppresses C activity in whorls 1 and 2, carpels would replace sepals in whorl 1 (only C activity effective here) and stamens would replace petals in whorl 2 (i.e. B + C activity) (see Figure 5.39b).

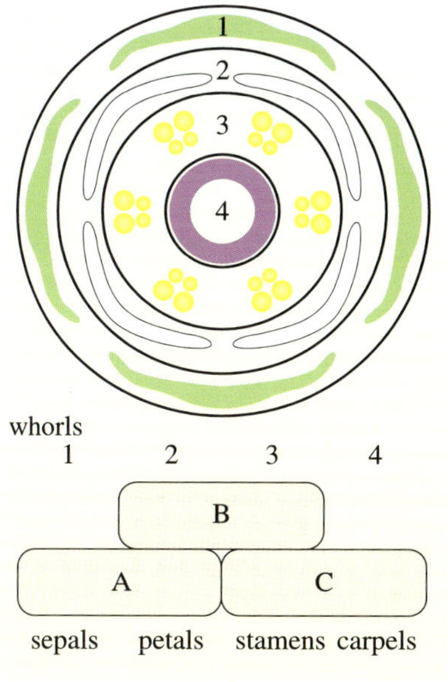

Figure 5.38 (a) The four whorls of organs in an *Arabidopsis* flower: whorl 1, sepals; whorl 2, petals; whorl 3, stamens; whorl 4, carpels (fused to form a gynoecium). (b) Simple representation of the ABC model demonstrating that floral organs are specified by the overlapping action of class A, B or C homeotic genes in whorls 1 to 4.

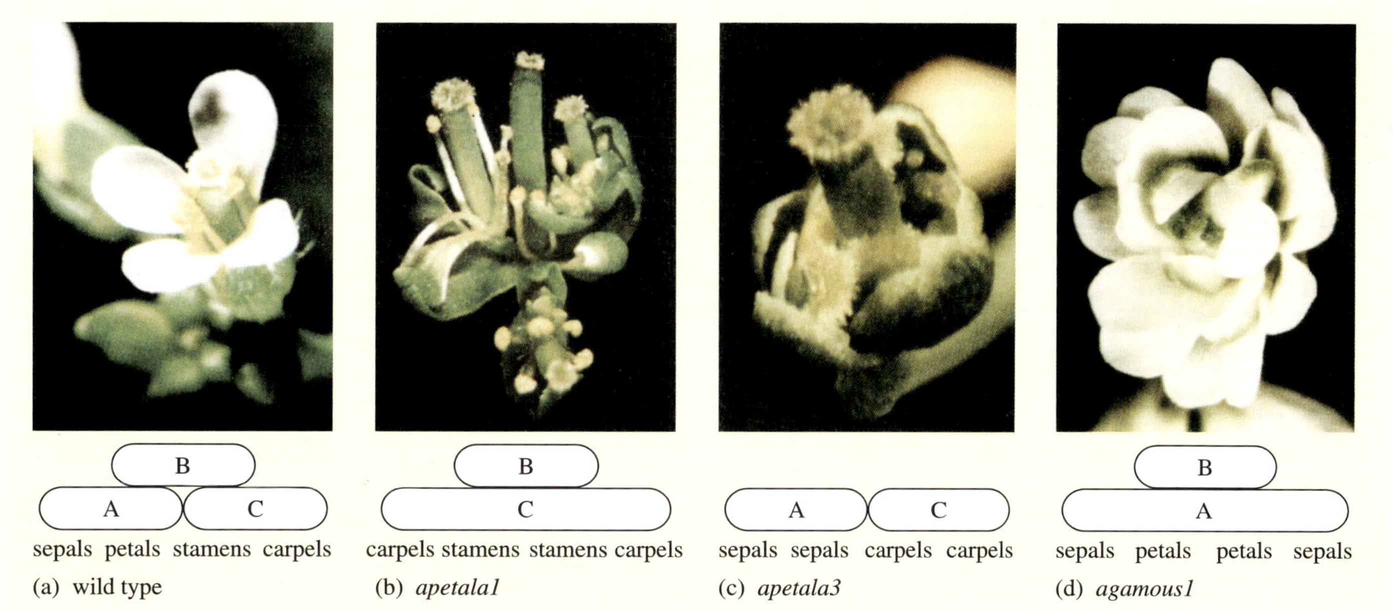

Figure 5.39 Flower phenotypes of floral homeotic mutants in *Arabidopsis*. (a) Wild type; (b) class A mutant *apetala1*; (c) class B mutant *apetala3;* (d) class C mutant *agamous1*. Below each photograph is the interpretation of phenotype according to the ABC model.

A spectrum of floral homeotic genes have now been isolated and cloned. All have been found to encode transcription factors (i.e. proteins that switch other genes on or off) containing a characteristic 55–60 amino acid sequence termed a MADS box, which includes a DNA-binding domain.

However, recent research (2000–2001) indicates that the ABC model is too simple and that other genes are required for flower formation. Thus, although mutant plants with loss of function for A, B and C class genes transform all floral organs into leaves (i.e. ABC genes are *necessary* for flower formation), transgenic plants in which A, B and C genes are switched on in all parts of the plant, do not show the reverse transformation of leaves into floral organs (i.e. ABC genes alone are not *sufficient* to specify flowers). Honma and Goto (2001) confirmed that the missing factor was a fourth class of genes (termed E genes — D genes are concerned only with ovule specification) whose protein products interact with those of A, B and C genes. The ABCE model is shown in Figure 5.40a.

- ❍ Write out the specifications for the four types of floral organs according to the ABCE model.

- ● Sepals, A; petals, A + B + E; stamens, B + C + E; carpels, C + E.

- ❍ What would you expect to observe in mutant plants with loss of function for E genes?

- ● All flower organs should look like sepals (because only sepals do *not* require the expression of E genes).

By studying how the protein products of A, B, C and E genes interact, Honma and Goto found that they associate in fours and a model of how they might bind to different pairs of genes is shown in Figure 5.40b. The details of the model are described in the figure legend. Because four classes of genes are involved whose products associate in tetramers, the name **quartet model** has been given to this model of floral organ specification. Up to 100 MADS-box genes may exist in the *Arabidopsis* genome and many are thought to play key roles in the differentiation of plant organs in addition to the development of flowers.

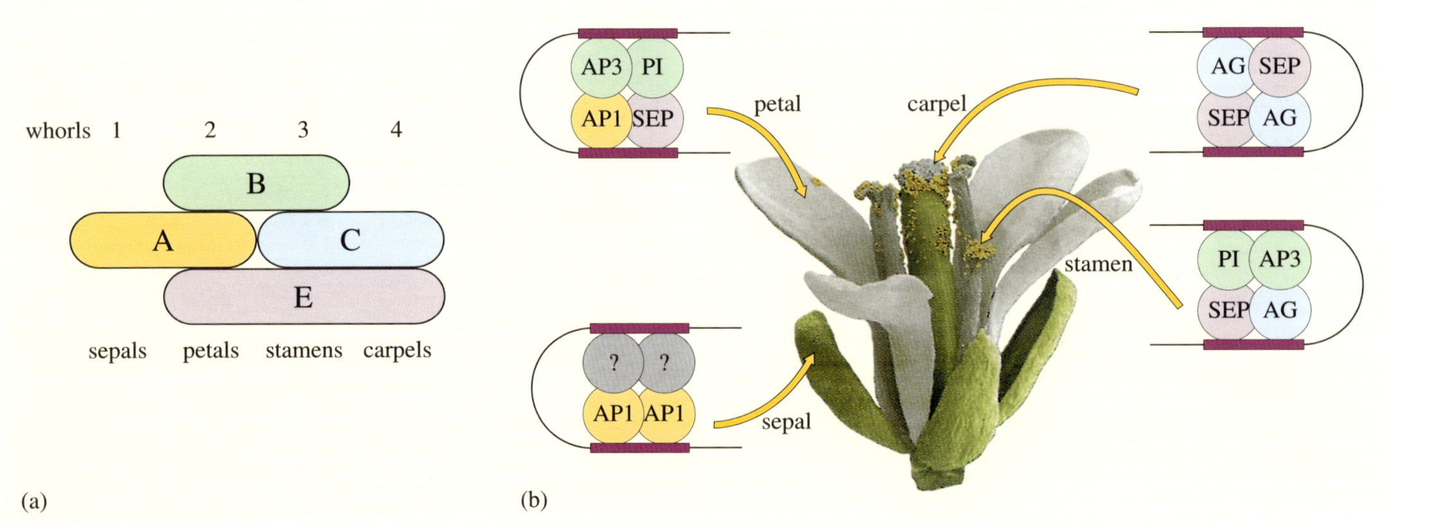

Figure 5.40 (a) The ABCE or quartet model showing how interactions between the products of four sets of MADS-box genes might control flower pattern. (b) A more detailed and still tentative version of the quartet model. Proteins encoded by the ABCE genes interact in fours. The protein quartets act as transcription factors and bind to the promoter regions (shown in purple) of different genes depending on the composition of the quartet. Binding occurs to two sites on the same DNA strand, brought into close proximity by DNA bending. The exact structures and composition of the quartets are still uncertain and, in particular, the nature of components marked with question marks and specifying sepals is unknown.

Conclusion

Recent studies on flower development have revealed that the process can be split into two consecutive phases. The first is the switch from vegetative to reproductive development that may be under the control of such stimuli as temperature and photoperiod. The second is the initiation of individual flowers and the development of a specific floral pattern. Using modern strategies of molecular genetics, key genes have been identified for both these phases and the challenge for the future is to identify how the expression of these genes is regulated and the way in which the encoded proteins interact.

Summary of Section 5.6

1. The time of year when a plant changes from a vegetative to a flowering state is determined most commonly by temperature and/or day length.
2. Photoperiodic plants respond to changes in day and night length: both stimuli are important and the pigment that detects these changes is phytochrome.
3. Phytochrome exists in two forms: P_r and P_{fr}. In red or day light the equilibrium shifts to P_{fr} and at night this process is reversed at a controlled rate. It is the level of P_{fr} that is critical: flowering is inhibited when P_{fr} levels are high.
4. The hour-glass model postulates that P_{fr} levels must fall below a critical value at night in order that flowering be induced, but this model alone cannot explain certain observations. An endogenous (circadian) 24 h rhythm is also involved; the level of P_{fr} and the time in the cycle when it is naturally low are critical for flowering initiation.
5. Day length perception occurs in the leaves and a floral-inducing substance termed florigen travels to the apex in the phloem. Florigen has yet to be isolated and identified. It may not be a single substance since evidence from mutants suggests that there are floral inhibitors as well. Consequently, flowering is a balance between these influences, superimposed on the natural plant rhythms.
6. Floral patterning is the result of sets of homeotic genes working together. The original ABC model with three sets of genes has now been superseded by the ABCE or quartet model. Predictions can be made as to the results of changing the expression of these genes on development in the four concentric whorls that comprise a flower. A similar control system operates to control the development of the body plan in animals.

5.7 Fruit ripening, abscission and senescence

In this final section we consider developmental changes that occur towards the end of a plant's life or the life of certain organs. All these changes are programmed and under genetic control; often they are of considerable importance in agriculture and horticulture.

5.7.1 FRUIT RIPENING

The ripening of a fruit is a critical phase in the development of many flowering plants. When the fruit is growing its main role is to nurture and protect the developing seeds. However, once the seeds have matured the function of the fruit changes dramatically, the main objective being to maximize the dispersal of the seeds (Chapter 1). To this end, cell-wall cohesion in fleshy fruits must be reduced so that the seeds can be released. Moreover, for animal-dispersed fruits, potential seed distributors must be enticed to eat the fruit and take ingested seeds to sites some distance from the mother plant: the germination of some seeds is facilitated by passage through the gut of an animal. The fruit is often made more attractive to a potential consumer by changing colour and producing an appetising smell and taste; such changes have been enhanced in crop fruits eaten by humans. However, some fleshy fruits remain green when ripe (e.g. some apples and pears, melons and (on the outside) tropical mangoes).

❍ Suggest possible reasons why some fleshy, animal-dispersed fruits remain green.

● The animal disperser may lack colour vision or the colour may be equally or more attractive to undesirable animals that destroy the seeds without dispersing them, such as wasps in the UK.

The point is that colour change is a genetically controlled character that arises through natural or artificial selection. There are also, of course, many non-fleshy fruits whose seeds are dispersed by wind, e.g. dandelion (*Taraxacum officinale*) and sycamore (*Acer pseudoplatanus*) or gravity, often combined with some kind of violent discharge (projectile dispersal), eg. sweet pea (*Lathyrus odorata*) and lupin (*Lupinus albus*).

5.7.2 CHANGES DURING FRUIT RIPENING

Fruits can be classified into two groups depending on the sorts of changes they undergo during ripening. **Climacteric fruit** produce a large rise in respiration as ripening proceeds and such fruit include tomatoes, bananas and avocados. **Non-climacteric fruit** exhibit no such increase and many members of the citrus family, strawberries and grapes belong to this group. In addition to a rise in respiration, climacteric fruit also exhibit an elevation in *ethylene* production at the onset of ripening. Ethylene is an important PGR and application of the gas to unripe climacteric fruit (but not to non-climacteric fruits) stimulates their ripening. This effect explains the adage that the easiest way to ripen a fruit is to place it in a container with one that is already ripe.

❍ Would placing a ripe orange in a bag of green tomatoes speed up the ripening of the tomatoes?

● No, oranges belong to the citrus family whose non-climacteric fruits do not exhibit a rise in ethylene production. The tomatoes ripen faster under the influence of a rise in the level of ethylene. Put a ripe banana in the bag instead; bananas give off a lot of ethylene.

Because ripening is an event that finally leads to the degradation (breakdown in structure) of the fruit it was initially proposed that it was the consequence of a series of uncontrolled events culminating in hydrolysis of the cells. It is now clear from studies of the biochemical and physiological changes that accompany the process that it is the result of a highly coordinated sequence of events. Further evidence to support this hypothesis comes from the isolation of mutants that exhibit a reduced rate of ripening. For instance, tomato fruits of the mutant *Never ripe* (*Nr*) neither soften nor accumulate the red–yellow pigment **lycopene** (a carotenoid) while another mutant *ripening inhibitor* (*rin)* can stay a greeny-yellow colour for over a year without exhibiting signs of ripening. Both these mutants have a single gene that is non-functional and which is responsible for the reduced capacity to ripen. The identity of the *RIN* gene product is unknown but the *NR* gene encodes an ethylene receptor and plants of the mutant genotype are unable to respond to the gas. This observation confirms that ethylene plays a central role in the ripening process in climacteric fruit.

Ripening can be broken down into a series of events. The first is the **downregulation** (switching off) of genes that are critical for fruit maturation, encoding proteins that are crucial for chlorophyll production and stabilization. The other changes relate to genes that are upregulated (switched on) and the proteins they encode are involved in cell wall breakdown and pigment biosynthesis and also in the conversion of osmotically inactive carbohydrates (e.g. starch) to sugars, the production of organic acids, and the production of volatile molecules and, in the case of climacteric fruit, enzymes involved in the biosynthesis of ethylene.

5.7.3 RIPENING IN TOMATO: A CASE STUDY

A considerable amount of research has been carried out on fruit ripening in tomatoes.

- What practical advantages are there in using tomato as an experimental fruit?

- Tomatoes can be grown in a greenhouse (where they can be isolated). They can be grown and ripened in a single season and the fruit is of commercial interest.

In addition, the technology for generating transgenic tomato plants is well established and genetic manipulation enables specific questions to be addressed. In tomato, cell division within the fruit ceases approximately 2 weeks after pollination and is followed by a period of 3–4 weeks of cell expansion, after which time the fruit reaches its maximum size. As a consequence, the process of ripening can be studied in a tissue where cell division is no longer taking place. During ripening a series of physiological and biochemical changes take place (Table 5.2).

Central to these changes is an elevation in ethylene production that is the result of an increase in expression of genes that play a regulatory role in the biosynthesis of the gas. If the action of the gas is blocked by silver ions (which interact with the ethylene receptors) or by mutation, as in *Nr* above, then ripening is inhibited. Suppression of ethylene production also reduces the rate at which ripening takes place and has been achieved in transgenic tomato plants by the use of antisense technology (Silva-Fletcher, 2001). Use of this technology is also shown in the *Plant Gene Manipulation* CD-ROM.

Table 5.2 Major physiological and biochemical changes that occur during tomato fruit ripening.

Increase in ethylene biosynthesis
Changes in gene expression
Increased respiration (the 'climacteric')
Loss of thylakoids and photosynthetic enzymes
Degradation of chlorophyll
Synthesis of pigments, especially lycopene
Changes in organic acid metabolism
Increases in activities of polysaccharide-hydrolysing enzymes, particularly polygalacturonase
Depolymerization of cell wall polyuronides
Softening
Increased susceptibility to pathogen attack

Fruits of such ethylene-deficient plants ripen slowly; however, the process can be accelerated by exposure to the gas.

❍ How would the ability to control fruit ripening benefit both growers and consumers?

● This technology would reduce spoiling or loss due to infection in transit and ensure that fruit is in good condition when it reaches the shops. Over 50% of a fruit harvest can be lost in transit, especially in hot countries.

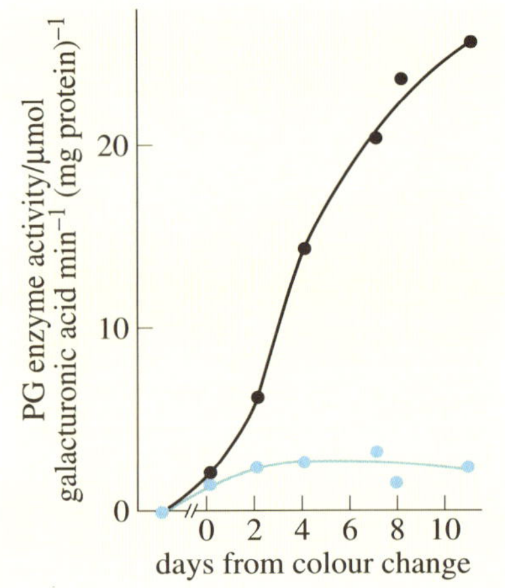

Figure 5.41 Polygalacturonase (PG) activity in control tomato fruit (black line) and in fruit of tomato plants carrying an antisense version of the gene encoding PG (blue line). The production of pigments during ripening was similar in the two sets of fruit. The break in the *x*-axis represents an indeterminate period (several days) during which the fruit remained green. Data from Smith *et al.* (1988).

Softening in tomato is the consequence of the degradation of the **middle lamella** (the outer part of the original, primary wall) between adjacent fruit cells. Since the middle lamella acts to hold cells together, its removal is analogous to removing the mortar between bricks in a wall. The middle lamella is largely composed of **pectin** (a polymer of galacturonic acid) and the enzyme that degrades this polysaccharide is **polygalacturonase (PG)**. Green tomato fruits contain negligible amounts of PG but there is a marked increase in the activity of this enzyme as the fruits turn from yellow to red. It is now clear that this rise in activity is the result of an increase in accumulation of PG mRNA and that the transcription of the PG gene is promoted by ethylene. An antisense RNA strategy has been applied to prevent the translation of PG mRNA and has resulted in the production of transgenic plants that produce barely detectable amounts of PG (Figure 5.41). Ripe fruits from these plants exhibit some softening, and this observation suggests that PG may be only one component in a cocktail of hydrolytic enzymes that is responsible for cell-wall degradation. Processed transgenic tomato fruit, where PG activity is diminished, contain more insoluble solids per ripe fruit as a consequence of the reduced breakdown of the pectin. The puree from such genetically modified (GM) plants was the first GM food product to be sold in the UK when it was launched in 1997.

5.7.4 ABSCISSION

Abscission is the process by which plant parts are shed. During the lifetime of a plant a range of organs and tissues are shed including leaves, flowers, floral parts and fruit. The process is similar to fruit ripening in that degradation of the middle lamella occurs but abscission takes place at discrete sites termed **abscission zones** (Figure 5.42). Moreover, there is good reason to believe that, as in the ripening of climacteric fruit, ethylene plays a critical role in the timing of organ shedding. The two principal enzymes that have been linked with abscission are **cellulase** and polygalacturonase (PG). Cellulase is thought to degrade β-1,4 linked glucans (glucose chains) within the cell wall while PG probably attacks the pectin-rich middle lamella. The increase in enzyme activity is the result of elevated rates of transcription of the genes encoding these hydrolytic enzymes and expression is restricted specifically to the cells that comprise the abscission zone. In addition to wall-degrading enzymes, there is a marked accumulation of peptides that are classified as protective or pathogenesis-related.

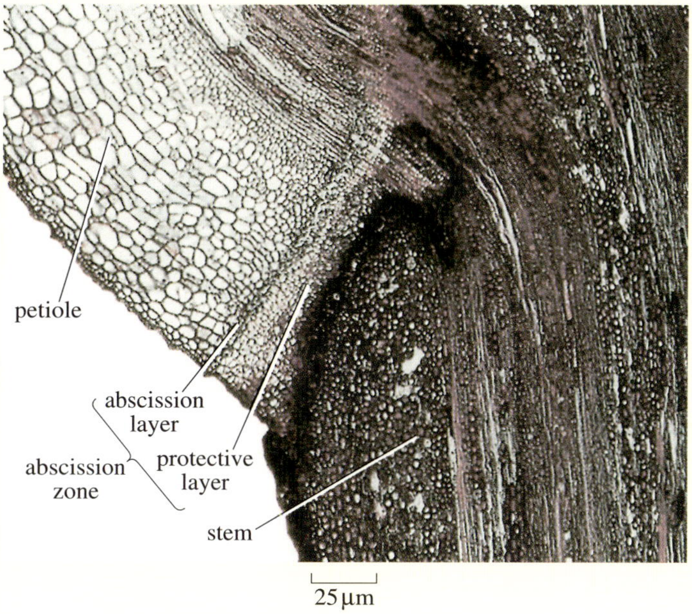

Figure 5.42 Section through an abscission zone at the base of a leaf stalk (petiole).

- ❍ Why would there be more pathogenesis-related proteins at abscission sites?

- ● Accumulation of these proteins would help protect the plant from invasion by pathogenic (disease-causing) fungi or bacteria once abscission had occurred exposing a 'cut' surface.

5.7.5 SENESCENCE

Senescence means aging that ultimately leads to death and there are many different senescence processes that take place in plants (Figure 5.43). Senescence can occur in individual cells, for example during the development of lignified xylem elements (Chapter 1); it can affect a whole organ such as a leaf or flower; or the whole plant may die, as takes place at the end of a one-season life cycle in annual plants. Although these processes may be regulated in different ways, it is clear that senescence is a consequence of a highly coordinated dismantling of the cellular components. Associated with the process is the degradation of cell contents (proteins, lipids, nucleic acids etc.) resulting in the release of nitrogen, phosphorus and carbon as well as other minerals released from the senescing cells. Much of this material is redistributed to the rest of the plant either for new growth or for storage.

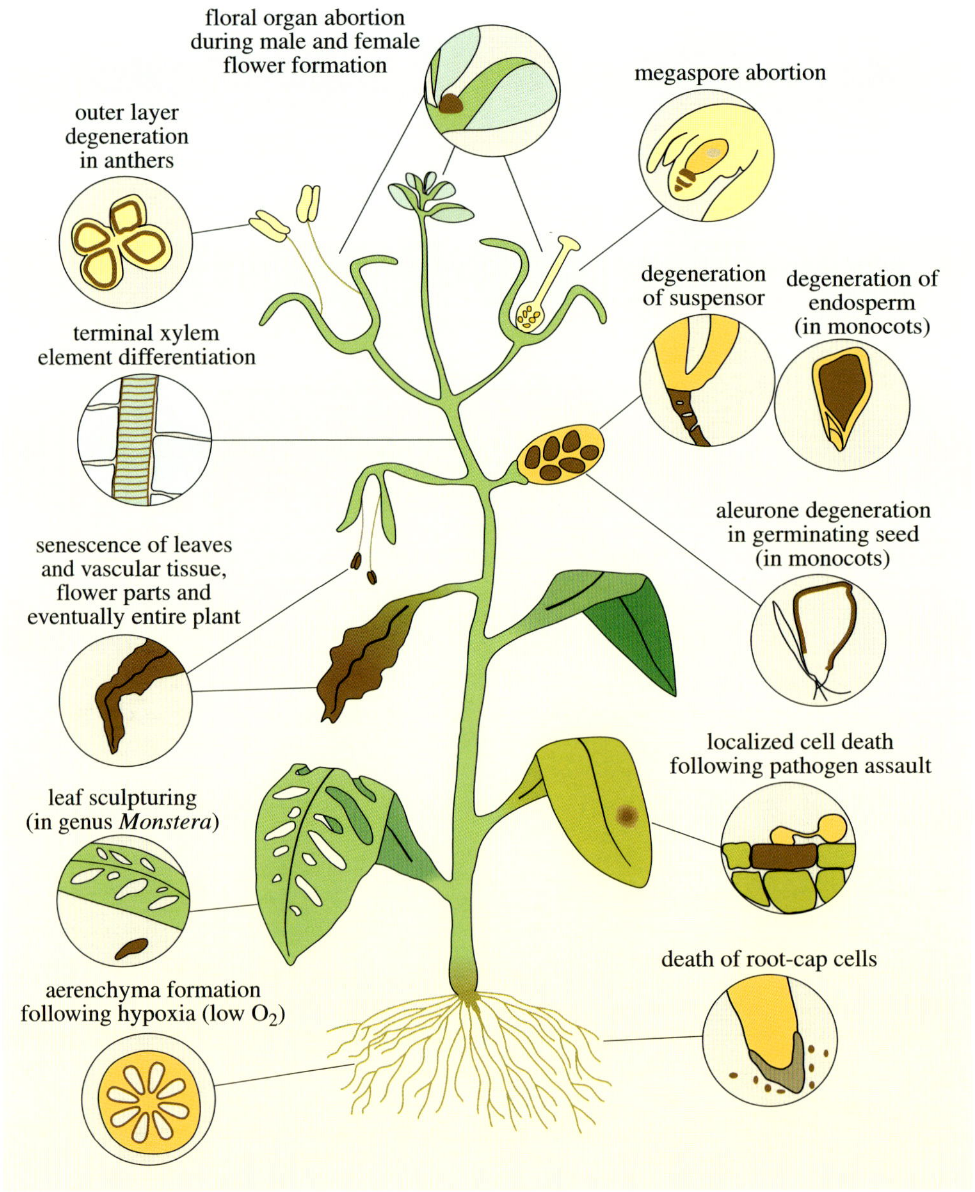

Figure 5.43 Senescence events in flowering plants. The scheme indicates the cells, organs and tissues in a plant that undergo cell death during normal development. Brown areas are those where programmed cell death (apoptosis) is thought to occur. *Note:* aerenchyma is a tissue in which large air spaces develop due to the breakdown of cells.

WHAT FACTORS INDUCE SENESCENCE?

Senescence can be induced by a range of different stimuli. Some are pre-programmed whilst others are the consequence of environmental signals. For instance, premature leaf senescence can be induced by nutrient stress due to a lack of nitrogen or phosphorus. Exposure to oxidative chemicals such as ozone or radiation such as UV-B promotes localized cell death that appears as necrotic spots on leaves and stems. Infection by pathogens may also induce senescence-like symptoms (Chapter 6). It is not clear whether this last effect is a consequence of pathogen growth at the site of infection mobilizing assimilates from the plant cells or a defensive response by the plant withdrawing nutrients from the site of infection and local apoptosis. Some pathogens produce cytokinins, a class of PGR that inhibits leaf senescence (Section 5.3), and causes a green 'island' at the site of infection. The similarities and differences between stress-promoted senescence and developmental senescence have yet to be completely resolved, but may eventually tell us whether the processes are induced in the same way and involve similar molecular and biochemical events.

Plants that are harvested while they are still growing, such as asparagus and broccoli and leafy crops such as lettuce and cabbage, undergo deteriorative changes such as loss of chlorophyll, protein degradation and membrane breakdown once removed from a water and nutrient source.

❍ How do you think an understanding of the regulatory processes of senescence would help growers in the agricultural industry and consumers?

● By identifying the critical biochemical and molecular events of senescence it may be possible to control the rate at which senescent changes occur so that the quality and shelf-life of these vegetables can be improved.

WHAT CHANGES OCCUR DURING SENESCENCE?

The most visible sign of leaf senescence is yellowing, which is the result of chlorophyll breakdown that reveals the carotenoid pigments. This phenomenon is probably quite a late stage in senescence and prior to it there is a decline in photosynthesis and the breakdown of proteins such as Rubisco (Chapter 2) which are mobilized from the cell. As the chloroplasts are dismantled, the thylakoid membranes become degraded and finally autolysis of the cell takes place. A spectrum of senescence-enhanced genes has been isolated which includes those coding for proteases and enzymes that may convert amino acids into forms for mobilization and transport in phloem. A number of protein kinases and transcription factors have also been isolated which may be involved in coordinating or even initiating the process.

Some types of senescence in plants exhibit features of **programmed cell death** or apoptosis, such as the maturation of xylem vessels, formation of holes in the leaf of *Monstera deliciosa* (Swiss cheese plant), and the death of cells surrounding a site of pathogenic infection that limits the spread of the disease (Figure 5.53). Apoptosis in animal cells (Saffrey, 2001) involves characteristic changes such as DNA fragmentation and membrane changes. Similar changes occur during the development of xylem elements and in the islands of cells which die at sites of pathogen invasion (the hypersensitive response, discussed in Chapter 6). The senescence of leaves and flowers appears to be slightly different in that the integrity of the nuclear DNA is maintained so that sequential steps in the process of dismantling the cellular machinery can be activated.

ROLE OF PLANT GROWTH REGULATORS IN THE REGULATION OF LEAF SENESCENCE

We have already seen that ethylene plays an important role during ripening of some fruits and in organ shedding. Leaf senescence in ethylene-insensitive mutant plants is delayed but once initiated, progresses at the same rate as in wild-type plants. This observation suggests that ethylene modulates the timing of leaf senescence but does not trigger the process. Treatment with cytokinins delays the phenomenon in many plants and it has been shown that this PGR is primarily synthesized in the roots and that the level in xylem sap declines at the time senescence is initiated. Further evidence to support a role for cytokinins in regulating the timing of leaf senescence has come from transgenic plants where overproduction of the PGR results in plants whose leaves exhibit a markedly delayed loss of chlorophyll.

FLOWER SENESCENCE

The senescence of flowers, especially those pollinated by insects, plays an important role in plant reproductive biology. Once pollinated, an open flower acts as a competitor for the attention of insects. Some flowers undergo petal abscission rapidly after pollination whilst others either wilt (morning glory — *Ipomea tricolor*) or modify their patterns of pigmentation (foxglove — *Digitalis purpurea*). Petals of carnation flowers lose turgor accompanied by a large rise in ethylene production. The ethylene originates from both the petals and the gynoecium and, if it is suppressed by downregulating one of the enzymes controlling biosynthesis of the gas, using antisense RNA technology, then the vase-life of the flower is increased dramatically.

SUMMARY OF SECTION 5.7

1. Fruit ripening, abscission and senescence all involve a series of coordinated events, primarily under genetic control and then modified by environmental signals.
2. Fleshy fruits are either climacteric, where a rise in ethylene production triggers a large increase in respiration, or non-climacteric, where such changes do not occur.
3. The tomato has been used as a model in studies of fruit ripening. Mutants such as *rin* and *Nr*, show that certain genes (e.g. those for chlorophyll synthesis) are down regulated during ripening and other genes (e.g. that for an ethylene receptor) are upregulated.
4. Transgenic manipulation of tomato using antisense technology has been used to produce fruits that do not soften and spoil during storage. The gene for polygalacturonase (PG), which causes fruit softening by degrading the middle lamella, is silenced in these plants.
5. Abscission involves cell wall breakdown in discrete zones due to the action of wall-degrading enzymes such as cellulase and PG. Ethylene may act as a trigger for abscission.

6 Senescence may occur in individual cells (xylem vessels), organs (leaf and flower parts) and at the whole plant level (annuals). It may be a developmental process controlled by environmental signals and PGRs such as ethylene and cytokinins, or may be induced by stress, such as nutrient shortage, pollutants or pathogens.

7 Genes that lead to breakdown of cell constituents (e.g. proteases) are upregulated during senescence. Senescence of individual cells, such as xylem vessels, resembles programmed cell death or apoptosis in animals except that DNA does not appear to fragment.

Conclusion

The aim of this chapter has been to describe specific phases of plant development and discuss how they are regulated. In particular the focus has been on the interaction between plants and the environment in which they carry out their life cycles. The application of genome analysis and molecular genetics together with the study of model organisms such as *Arabidopsis* and tomato has had a major impact on our understanding of the regulation of plant growth and development. We have entered a new green revolution whose consequences may have dramatic effects on the agricultural and horticultural industries.

References

Arabidopsis Genome Initiative (2000) Analysis of the genome sequence of the flowering plant *Arabidopsis thaliana*, *Nature*, **408**, pp. 796–815.

Briggs, W. R., Green, P. B. and Jones, R. L. (1982) Light quality, photoperception and plant strategy, *Annual Review of Plant Physiology*, **33**, pp. 481–518.

Hart, J. W. (1988) *Light and Growth*, Allen and Unwin, p. 178.

Honma, T. and Goto, K. (2001) Complexes of MADS-box proteins are sufficient to convert leaves into floral organs, *Nature*, **409**, pp. 525–529.

Clements M. and Saffrey, J. (2001) Communication between cells, in *The Core of Life, Vol. II*, J. Saffrey (ed.), The Open University, Milton Keynes, pp. 241–304.

Saffrey, J. (2001) Life and death of cells, in *The Core of Life, Vol. II*, J. Saffrey (ed.), The Open University, Milton Keynes, pp. 439–486.

Silva-Fletcher, A. (2001) Control of gene expression, in *The Core of Life, Vol. II*, J. Saffrey (ed.), The Open University, Milton Keynes, pp. 389–438.

Smith C. J. S., Watson, C. F., Ray, J., Bird, C. R., Morris, P. C., Schuch, W. and Grierson, D. (1988) Antisense RNA inhibition of polygalacturonase gene expression in transgenic tomatoes, *Nature*, **334**, p.724.

Swithenby, M. (2001) Exploiting microbes: biotechnology, in *Microbes*, H. MacQueen (ed.), The Open University, Milton Keynes, pp. 237–296.

FURTHER READING

Howell, S. H. (1998) *Molecular Genetics of Plant Development*, Cambridge University Press, Cambridge. [A textbook for advanced undergraduates or graduates. Useful if you want to learn more about plant molecular genetics and available in paperback.]

http://nasc.nott.ac.uk/ (2001). [This website, of the Nottingham *Arabidopsis* Stock Centre, has information on the *Arabidopsis* Genome Programme.]

Taiz, L. and Zeiger, E. (1998) (2nd edn) *Plant Physiology*, Sinauer Associates Inc. [A good general textbook that covers much of the material in this chapter.]

INTERACTIONS BETWEEN SEED PLANTS AND MICROBES

6

6.1 INTRODUCTION

Interactions between plants and microbes can take many forms, but they are often defined by the effect of the relationship on each of the organisms involved. They can range from mutually beneficial, (+,+), where both species gain some advantage, to mutually detrimental, (–,–), in which both species lose out in some way. Figure 6.1 illustrates the range of possible interactions in terms of the resulting balance of advantage between the organisms.

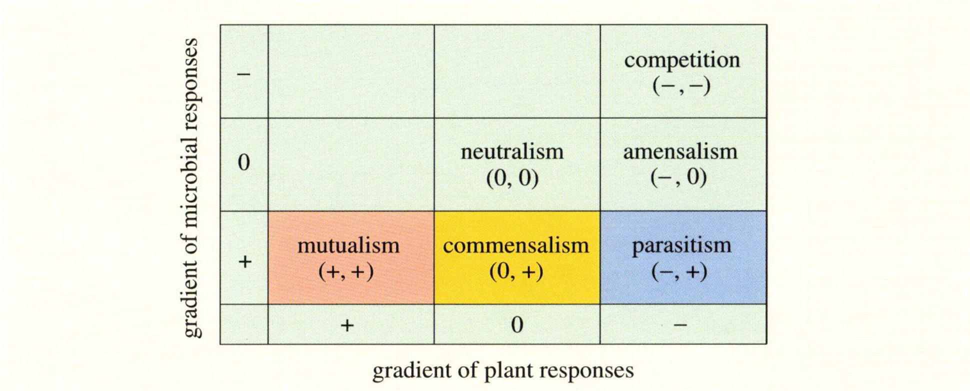

Figure 6.1 Range of possible types of interactions between plants and microbes, indicating the balance of advantage (modified from Johnson *et al.*, 1997).

In addition to **mutualism**, in which both species benefit, ecologically meaningful interactions include: **commensalism** (0,+), in which one species benefits and the other is not affected, **amensalism** (–,0), in which one species is adversely affected and the other is unaffected, **competition** (–,–), which is mutually detrimental because both species are disadvantaged by the relationship, and finally **parasitic**-type relationships (–,+), in which one species represents a food source and so is inhibited when the other species gains nourishment by consuming it (*predation* and *herbivory* also fall into this category, but are not really appropriate terms to use in plant–microbe interactions).

This chapter is concerned with interactions between seed plants — that is, gymnosperms and angiosperms (see Figure 1.3) — and microbes, such as fungi, bacteria and viruses. It will focus on the interactions represented by the highlighted region in the third row of Figure 6.1. In all these cases the microbe gains, but the effects on the plant can range from very beneficial to highly detrimental, in that the plant is inhibited in some way or even dies. You have already met the mycorrhizal and root nodule associations that benefit both partners in Chapter 4, and keen gardeners are only too well aware of the damage that can be done to plants when diseases like rust, mildew and potato blight flourish. Clearly, many of these interactions are of enormous economic significance to us and are worth studying for that reason alone, but current research is giving intriguing insights into these intimate and subtle relationships.

Many, but not all, of these interactions can be classified as **symbioses** — that is, associations between species that *live* together. Some symbioses date back to the emergence of the land plants; this time is long enough ago for the evolution of sophisticated systems of molecular communication that enable plants to distinguish friend from foe and regulate the interaction appropriately.

In the sections that follow you will learn about the different types of interactions that occur according to four fundamental criteria; be introduced to a range of illustrative case studies; learn more about how plants defend themselves against microbial diseases and how they recognize microbes. Then, Sections 6.7 and 6.8 introduce a couple of new, and somewhat controversial, areas of research, namely, how the nature of the relationship can change and how the existence of interplant connections via microbes can influence community dynamics as a whole.

6.2 Four dimensions of an interaction

There are thousands of specific interactions between plants and microbes, but each one can be described in terms of four dimensions to the relationship.

- *The balance of advantage* has already been mentioned above. Here we are concerned with mutualistic associations — for example, mycorrhizas and root nodules, in which both partners gain benefits from the interactions — and **pathogenic associations** (disease causing), in which only the microbe benefits, often by obtaining carbohydrates from the plant; in contrast, the host plant gains no benefits and may even suffer some damage. Disease-causing microbes are called **pathogens**. (A pathogen obtains nourishment from host tissues; if it can extract nutrients from living tissues, then it is also a **parasite**.)
- *Intimacy* can range from a loose, unstructured external association, to a very intimate, highly differentiated 'dual organ' (consisting of both microbial and plant tissue) following penetration of the plant's cell walls by the microbe.
- *Specificity*; a microbe may form a particular association with many plant species (broad **host range**), or with only one species, or even one race of a species (narrow host range).
- *Dependence*; some microbes and higher plants cannot function adequately in the absence of their partner, so are termed **obligate symbionts**. Alternatively, the organisms may be able to function quite well without the partner under certain conditions, in which case they are termed **facultative symbionts**.

The type of nutritional relationship that the microbe has with the plant can have very important effects on all of these dimensions. **Biotrophic** relationships (where the microbe lives with a live host) are symbiotic (MacQueen, Burnett and Cann, 2001), but may be mutualistic or parasitic. By contrast, **necrotrophic** relationships involve killing the host's cells, and then digesting them saprotrophically. Such relationships are always pathogenic and can be highly destructive.

❍ Classify each of the following types of interactions:

parasitic, mutualistic, pathogenic

in terms of the +/– system to denote balance of advantage (putting the plant experience first). Indicate whether they are biotrophic or necrotrophic.

● Parasitic interactions are –/+ symbioses involving biotrophic nutrition; mutualistic symbioses are +/+ relationships involving biotrophic nutrition, and pathogenic interactions are –/+ relationships involving either necrotrophic and/or biotrophic nutrition.

SUMMARY OF SECTIONS 6.1 AND 6.2

1 Some interactions between plants and microbes are beneficial to the plants, whereas others are detrimental to them. The balance of advantage between the participants in the interaction can be described by a +/– system of classification.

2 Plant–microbe interactions can be classified in terms of four dimensions: balance of advantage, intimacy, specificity and dependence.

3 Biotrophic interactions can be beneficial or detrimental to the plant, and are described as symbioses. Necrotrophic interactions are not symbioses, and are always pathogenic to the plant.

4 Plant–microbe interactions are of great economic significance to humans.

6.3 CASE STUDIES

The range of plant–microbe interactions is so diverse that it is only possible to scratch the surface when selecting case studies. The examples given here have been chosen to represent a range of contrasting characteristics in terms of the four dimensions listed above, and to extend the range of examples you have already met.

6.3.1 THE RHIZOSPHERE

You are already familiar with the **rhizosphere** from Chapters 3 and 4 (see also Walker, 2001).

❍ What is the rhizosphere?

● It is the part of the soil that is modified by the presence of roots.

❍ Why would the density of microbial life be orders of magnitude higher in the rhizosphere than the surrounding soil?

● Mucigel makes the root a rich source of nutrients for the soil fungi, bacteria and nematodes that inhabit this zone. It also causes soil particles to adhere to the root surface, forming the rhizosheath (Section 3.2.1).

The rhizosphere represents a loose, unstructured association between plants and microbes. Many of the microbes found there are non-specific in that they inhabit the rhizosphere of many plant types, and feed saprotrophically on the root exudates, exerting few direct effects on the associated plant. In the absence of the host, they survive in the soil as spores and other resting structures (i.e. ones with very low metabolic activity). Some or all may be stimulated to germinate and/or grow by the presence of the root exudates (see Section 6.6).

However, pathogenic microbes also exist in the soil as resting structures, and are similarly stimulated to grow towards the root surface by substances in the root exudates. They can be specific to a particular family of plants. The fungus *Sclerotinia cepivora*, for example, causes white rot in onion roots; it is attracted by compounds that are characteristic of the root exudates of members of the onion family. Ethanol is produced as a result of anaerobic metabolism in plants when waterlogging of the soil causes a poor oxygen supply to the roots. It can attract many pathogens such as the swimming spores of the parasitic protoctist *Phytophthora infestans* (a member of the Oomycota which causes potato blight; see Section 6.3.4), and stimulate the production of infection structures such as the rhizomorphs (MacQueen, Burnett and Cann, 2001) of honey fungus (*Armillaria mellea*).

The saprotrophic microbes may offer the associated plants some measure of protection from pathogens. Plant root exudates can include **siderophores**, which are low molecular mass, iron-binding agents (see Section 4.5.1) produced under iron-limiting conditions. They can limit the growth of microbes in the vicinity of roots by reducing the availability of iron, but soil-borne root-infecting fungi are often inferior to soil saprotrophic fungi in their ability to compete for resources.

❍ How can this superior competitive ability of soil saprotrophic fungi benefit the neighbouring plant?

● Growth of the pathogenic fungi is limited by a shortage of iron, a situation that is enhanced by the harmless saprotrophs out-competing the pathogens for the *limiting nutrient*. (If growth of organisms continues in a medium until a particular nutrient is exhausted, that nutrient is said to be *limiting*.) Therefore, the plants are exposed to fewer pathogens when saprotrophs are present.

Furthermore, saprotrophic soil fungi may also produce antibiotics that inhibit the growth of root-infecting fungi.

6.3.2 Rhizobia and root nodules

Rhizobia is a collective term embracing several genera of the Rhizobiaceae (Bacteria) which form nodules on legumes (Fabaceae); these genera are *Rhizobium, Bradyrhizobium* and *Azorhizobium*. Rhizobia are normal members of the rhizosphere microflora, but a small proportion of the population (by virtue of their possession of the p*Sym* plasmid) are capable of infecting the cells of the associated plant roots and forming root nodules.

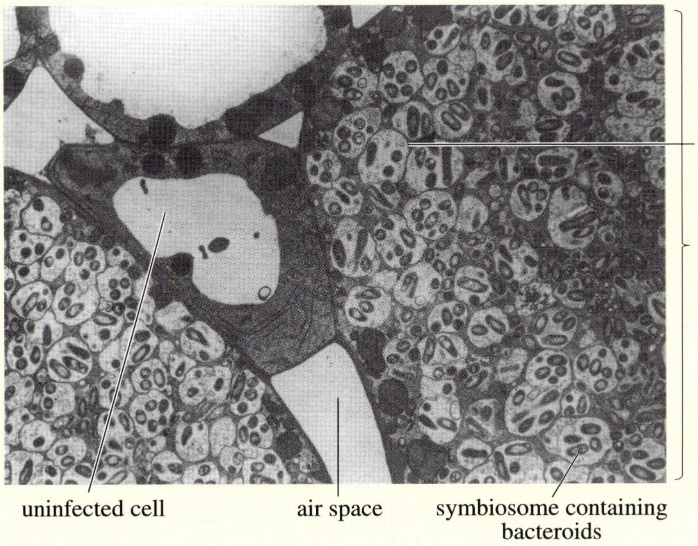

Figure 6.2 Electron micrograph showing cells in the infected zone of a soya bean root nodule. The infected cells containing large numbers of symbiosomes are clearly seen on either side of an uninfected cell and an air space. The peribacteroid membrane of a symbiosome is indicated in the right-hand infected cell.

- ❍ What function do root nodules have in plant mineral nutrition (Chapter 4)?
- ● The nodules are centres of nitrogen fixation by the rhizobia living within them.

Inside the infected root cells, the bacteria are enveloped in a membrane derived from the *plant* plasma membrane called the **peribacteroid membrane (PBM)**. Here they divide and differentiate to form nitrogen-fixing **bacteroids**. The organelle-like structure composed of PBM and bacteroids is called the *symbiosome*, and is the basic nitrogen-fixing unit of the nodule (Figure 6.2).

- ❍ In what other context is the term 'symbiosome' used?
- ● Many aphids contain bacterial symbiosomes, which synthesize essential nutrients that their diet does not supply (Pond, 2001).

A particular rhizobial species interacts with a limited range of plant species. The sequence of events leading to the formation of nodules is summarized in Figure 6.3.

Initial contact between rhizobia and the root hair cell is followed by root hair deformation (Figure 6.3a–d) and formation of an **infection thread** (Figure 6.3f): the plant cell wall next to the bacterium invaginates (turns in on itself) and grows to form a tube that extends through the root hair and cortex to provide access for

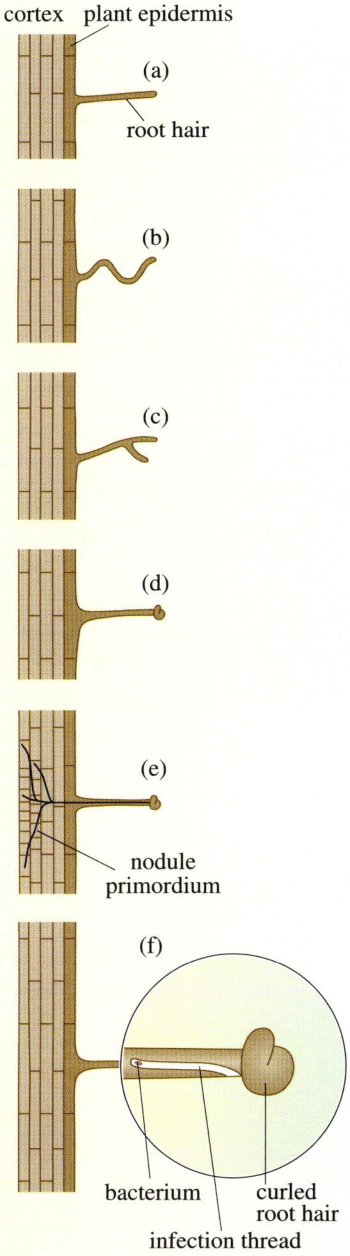

Figure 6.3 Initial stages in the rhizobia–legume symbiosis. Rhizobial signalling to host root hairs (a) leads to root hair deformation (b), branching (c) and curling (d). Mitosis in the root cortex ensues, which leads to the formation of the nodule primordium (e). Bacteria invade the plant cells through the infection thread (f), a plant-derived tube which delivers the bacteria into individual cells within the nodule primordium. At this point the bacteria differentiate into bacteroids.

the infecting rhizobium. Simultaneously, cortical cells divide mitotically, giving rise to the **nodule primordium** (site of cellular division and differentiation where an organ forms; Figure 6.3e). Infection threads grow towards the primordium. The infection threads then degrade, and the bacteria are taken into the cells of the developing nodule via endocytosis of the plasma membrane. Once inside the root cell, the bacteria divide and differentiate to form the bacteroids, while the PBM proliferates and differentiates until the infected cell is filled with symbiosomes. Note that the bacteria do not penetrate the PBM. Thus, even though the microbe penetrates the cell wall, it remains technically extracellular.

Infected cells in a mature legume nodule may house many thousands of symbiosomes. The PBM represents the physical interface between the symbionts. It originates from extensive synthesis and infolding of the plasma membrane. The new membrane bears resemblances to both plasma membrane and vacuolar membrane. All exchanges and communication must take place across the PBM; if it degrades, the symbiosome senesces.

- ❍ What do these last three sentences suggest about the properties of the PBM in terms of the control of its synthesis and its importance to the interaction?

- ● The PBM is synthesized by the plant, but its structure is a specific product of its interaction with the bacteria, and the symbiosis cannot function without it.

6.3.3 Arbuscular mycorrhizas

Ecto- or sheathing mycorrhizas were discussed in Chapter 4, but **arbuscular mycorrhizas (AM)**, are the most common type of mycorrhiza, occurring in around 80% of plant species (mostly herbaceous), which makes AM the most suitable types for potential exploitation in low-input agriculture programmes. AM fungi are members of the Ascomycota and form endomycorrhizas (see Section 4.5.3). Fossil evidence places their origin 350–450 Ma ago. Indeed, they may well have played a part in enabling early plants to colonize the land. As well as being one of the most ancient plant–microbe associations, they are also among the most intimate and subtle interactions.

Infecting hyphae can arise from three sources known collectively as **propagules**: spores, infected root fragments and hyphae growing from other infected plants. Large spores, with thick resistant walls and up to several thousand nuclei represent long-term survival structures, which can survive passage through the gut of various invertebrates, birds and mammals. Thus, they can be dispersed in animal droppings as well as by wind and water. AM fungi show little host specificity; individual plants can form associations with several AM fungi and vice versa. AM fungi are obligate biotrophs, displaying negligible growth in the absence of the host plant. (They are very poor digesters of complex carbohydrates like cellulose, unlike many ectomycorrhizas.) Consequently, soil disturbance by ploughing, tree felling, etc., disrupts the hyphal networks, and can result in much reduced infectivity of the soil and lower rates of nutrient uptake by plants. Table 6.1 shows the effects of disturbance of soil on the subsequent AM formation in experimental clover plants in three contrasting habitats.

Table 6.1 The effect of disturbing previously undisturbed soils on the subsequent formation of arbuscular mycorrhizas by clover plants (% root length colonized +/- standard error).

Soil	Mycorrhiza formation	
	Undisturbed	Disturbed
forest	28 ± 2.9	15 ± 4.4
heath land	11 ± 2.4	6 ± 1.5
pasture	52 ± 2.8	50 ± 4.3

- What is the effect of disturbance on the extent of arbuscular mycorrhiza formation in clover in the three habitats listed in Table 6.1?

- Disturbance reduces the proportion of infected plants by about a half in forest and heath land, but has no significant effect on AM formation on pasture land.

The explanation for this difference appears to be that infected root fragments and especially spores tend to be more robust than growing hyphae, which are destroyed by disturbance; root fragments and spores on pasture land are the predominant propagules, whereas hyphae are far more common in forests and heath land.

Infection begins when hyphae make contact with the plant root. The series of infection events is summarized in Figure 6.4. Hyphae do not grow directionally towards the root until they are very close to it, but, once contact occurs, the hyphae branch and spread over the root surface. After 2–3 days, round, almost swollen, disc-shaped **appressoria** are formed, which attach the hyphae to the root surface.

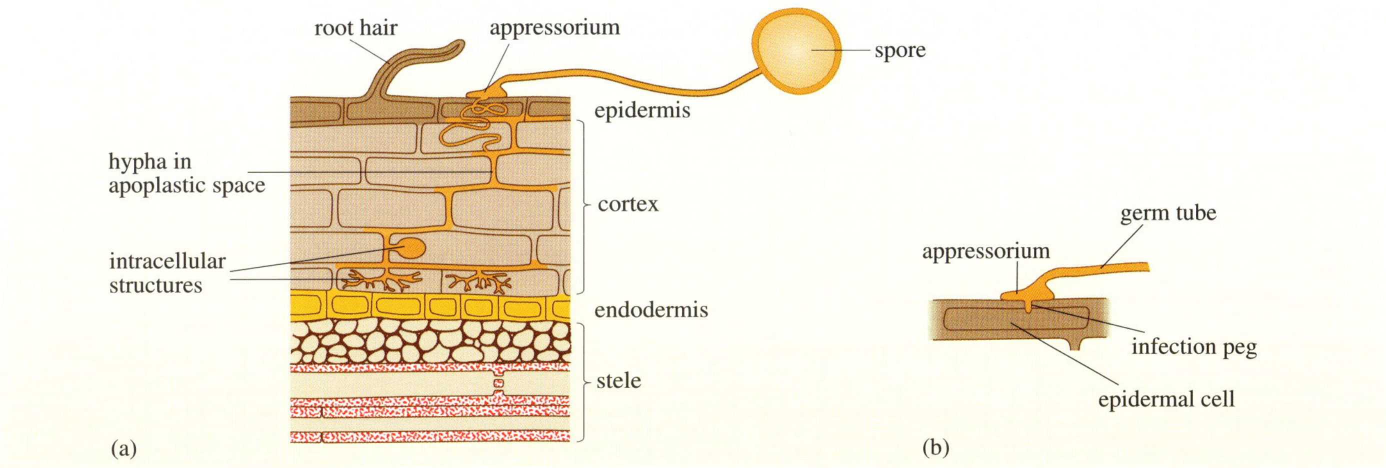

Figure 6.4 (a) Structures associated with infection of roots by arbuscular mycorrhizal fungi: infecting hyphae, from a large spore in the soil, penetrate the root epidermis using appressoria and infection pegs, then proceed to form branched arbuscules and intracellular vesicles in cells of the inner root cortex. (b) Detail showing an infection peg penetrating the cell wall of the plant root epidermal cell.

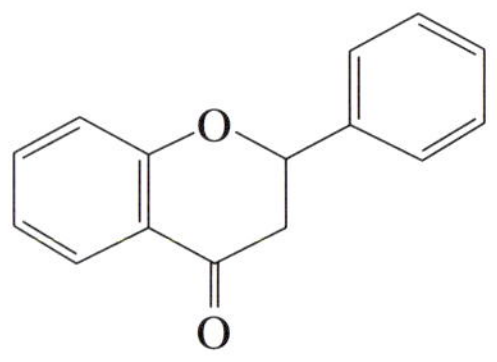

flavone (compound on which flavonoids are based)

Flavonoids from the plant stimulate the hyphae to breach the cell walls of adjacent epidermal cells by means of narrow **infection pegs**, using both mechanical pressure and some wall-dissolving enzymes (i.e. ones that can break down complex carbohydrates).

Other hyphae colonize the apoplastic spaces (Section 4.2.1), and enter other cells in a similar manner. **Arbuscules** are the branched structures that develop from the penetrating hyphae (Figure 6.5a). Like the nodulating rhizobia, the fungus does not penetrate the plant plasma membrane; the hyphae are enveloped in a **periarbuscular membrane (PAM)** that is derived from modified extensions of it (Figure 6.5b). The contents of both plant cell and the fungal hyphae show considerable rearrangement and many changes, all of which suggest that the interfaces around the arbuscules are sites of enormous cellular activity. The PAM continues to produce plant cell wall components, but they are not assembled into the typical rigid structure; they form a more fluid interfacial matrix between the PAM and the fungal cell wall.

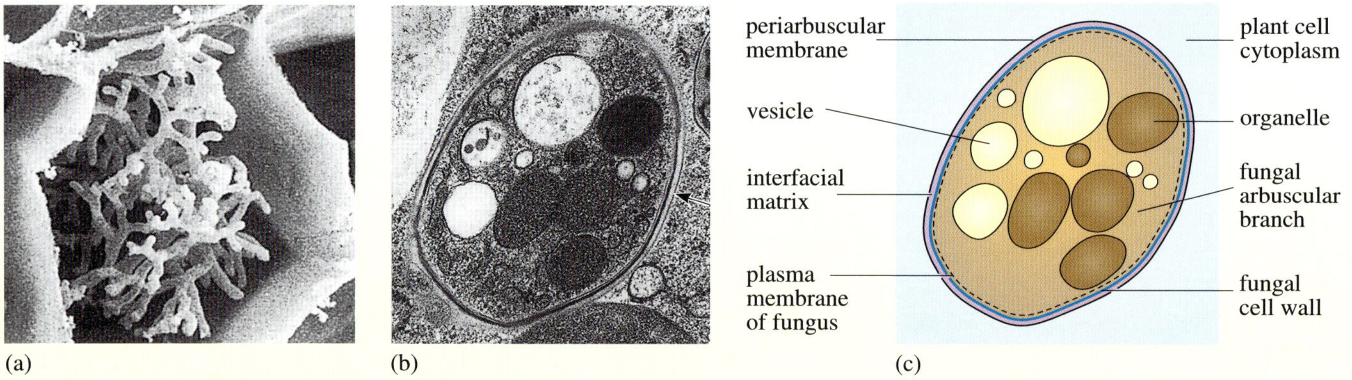

Figure 6.5 (a) Scanning electron micrograph of an arbuscule of *Glomus mosseae* within cells of *Liriodendron tulipifera*. Note how the hyphal branches fill the cell. (b) Transmission electron micrograph of an arbuscule branch surrounded by the invaginated host membrane, forming a periarbuscular membrane (PAM, arrowed); (c) line drawing of the situation shown in (b). Courtesy of P. F. Bonfante.

This interface zone is a new compartment, which is the structural expression of the symbiotic status. Its formation marks the successful colonization of plant cells by the AM fungi; it is through this zone that the two-way exchange of nutrients takes place, as indicated by strong H^+–ATPase activity in *both* PAM and fungal cell membrane.

- ❍ Why does H^+–ATPase activity in both membranes imply exchange of nutrients?

- ● H^+–ATPase enzymes are the primary proton pumps driving active transport across plant membranes (Chapter 4).

The association is dynamic: arbuscules only remain functional for 2.5–4 days, after which they senesce and collapse, though the plant cell remains functional. Meanwhile, other hyphae continue to initiate new arbuscules until as much as 90% of the root is colonized.

Functional arbuscules supply carbon for mycelial growth, so once they have formed, external hyphae can grow out into the surrounding soil to scavenge for mineral nutrients. In some cases thick-walled **vesicles** are formed, either in the soil or in dead plant tissues. These multinuclear bodies are rich in lipids, which is a characteristic of fungal resting structures. Interestingly, the density of vesicle formation is variable, but can be very high, especially on less fertile soils.

❍ Given that vesicle formation must represent a considerable investment in terms of energy and resources by the fungus, suggest an explanation for their greater abundance in conditions of low soil fertility.

● There is probably some sort of trade-off with the host plant: the more benefit the plant gains from the association in terms of mineral nutrient supply, the greater the supply of sugars to the fungus by the plant.

6.3.4 LATE BLIGHT OF POTATO

The roots are not the sole route of infection by microbes. Many organisms gain ingress to the plant via the shoots. Late blight of potatoes, caused by *Phytophthora infestans* (a member of the Oomycota), is found wherever potatoes (*Solanum tuberosum*) are grown . It is not the most serious disease in terms of lost production, but it is certainly the most notorious. It precipitated the potato famine in Ireland between 1845 and 1847 that resulted in the death or emigration of one-fifth of the population. (The political fallout from this event probably led to the birth of plant pathology as a scientific discipline.)

The fungus-like protoctist *Phytophthora* over-winters in tubers infected during the previous season. It needs only a few of these tubers to give rise to infected shoots, which then act as centres of infection from which the disease spreads.

Sporangia are borne on **sporangiophores** (special vertical hyphae that raise the sporulating structures above the growth medium) and are formed on the diseased leaves (see Figure 6.6a). They are blown onto healthy leaves, where they germinate, either by the formation of **germ tubes** (single emergent hyphae) or **zoospores** (spores that move with the aid of flagella; Figure 6.6b). After swimming for a time, the zoospores lose their flagella and then form germ tubes, which usually penetrate the epidermal walls of the potato leaf, or occasionally enter the stomata.

❍ What conditions are essential if zoospores are to be effective?

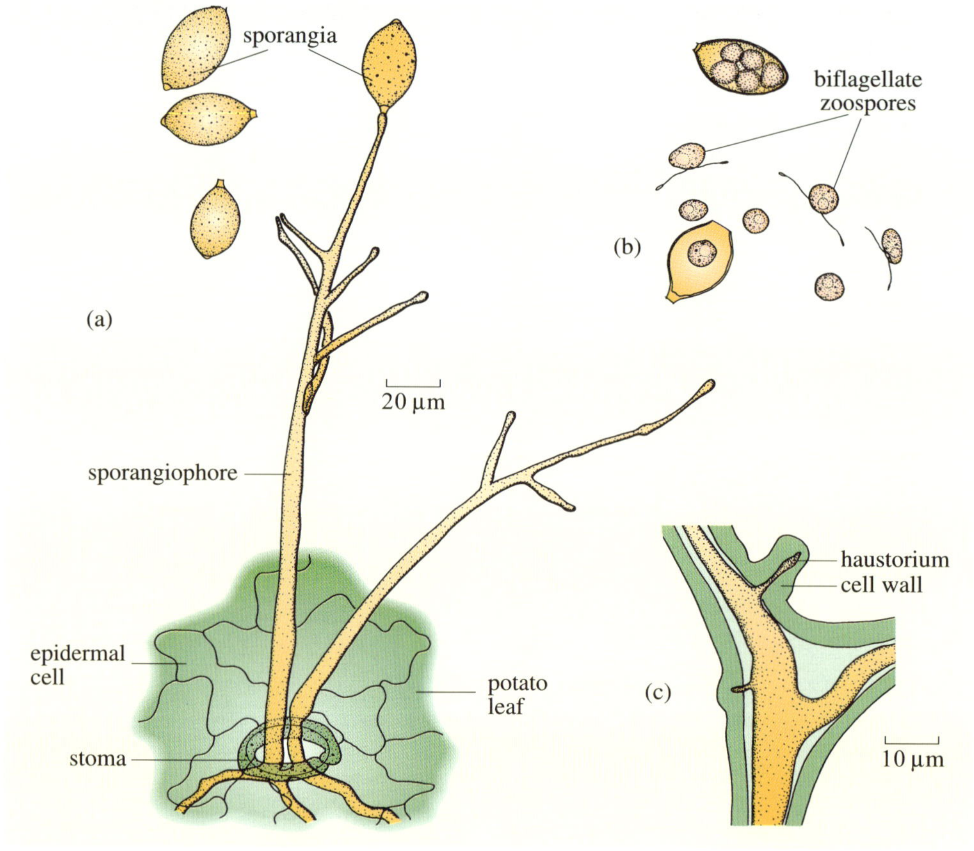

Figure 6.6 *Phytophthora infestans*. (a) Sporangiophores penetrating a stoma of a potato leaf. (b) Sporangial contents dividing and releasing zoospores. (c) Intercellular mycelium from a potato tuber showing the finger-like haustorium penetrating the cell walls; protoctist tissue is shown in brown.

- Enough moisture to allow the zoospores to swim to their site of attachment on the host.

An appressorium (see Figure 6.4) is formed at the tip of the germ tube, attaching the zoospore cyst firmly to the leaf. Penetration of the cell wall is via an infection peg using both mechanical pressure and enzymatic action. The mycelium develops within the leaf tissues. Initially the protoctist gains nourishment from the plant biotrophically via **haustoria** (singular **haustorium**), which are finger-like protuberances that penetrate the wall of the plant cells (Figure 6.6c). The haustorium has a characteristic interfacial zone between it and the plant plasma membrane. However, once the plant plasma membrane around the haustorium has been breached, the cell dies and the relationship becomes necrotrophic.

❍ In what ways do these haustoria resemble arbuscules of AM fungi, and in what way do they differ from them?

● The haustoria resemble AM arbuscules in that they form once the plant cell wall has been breached, and they are a means by which the microbe obtains nourishment biotrophically through a characteristic interfacial zone (provided the plant plasma membrane remains intact): but haustoria differ from arbuscules in that the microbe continues to gain nourishment from the plant, necrotrophically, once the plant plasma membrane has broken down.

The resulting lesions (wounds) have a dark green water-soaked appearance due to tissue disintegration, which is possibly aided by toxin secretion. As the lesion spreads, a zone of further sporangiophore production occurs, especially on the underside of the leaf. Sporulation is greatest in humid conditions.

❍ Why is it most advantageous to *Phytophthora* sp. for it to sporulate in humid conditions?

● Because moisture facilitates the spread of the disease via zoospores.

Potato yields suffer because of the damage to foliage, which reduces photosynthesis. Once 75% of the leaf tissue has been destroyed, tuber development ceases. The tubers can be infected directly by sporangia falling onto them. These infected tubers may rot quickly in storage, causing further loss of crop. Other *Phytophthora* spp. can produce sexual spores, which are large and capable of existing in the soil for long periods, indicating that these protoctists are largely dependent on the plant for their growth and reproduction. Nevertheless, in contrast to the AM fungi, they are not an entirely obligate group of symbionts in that they can be cultured fairly readily in the absence of the host, which may be related to the fact that such pathogenic interactions are of more recent origin than AM associations, and so are less likely to be so mutually dependent. However, although the relationship is not as intimate or finely regulated as the AM association, the degree of specificity is much greater. There is variation among potato cultivars in terms of their resistance to *P. infestans*, which itself infects only close relatives of the potato, although there are many other similar species that attack other plant taxa.

Farmers use a three-pronged attack to control potato blight. Spraying with pesticide at appropriate times can be effective, but is not very 'green'. Sound horticultural practice — namely protecting the tubers from infection by earthing up and removal of foliage before lifting the crop — is also useful, but is only suitable as a small-scale treatment. However, it is *breeding for resistance* that has most to offer the commercial grower. Host resistance is generated in cultivars by crossing *S. tuberosum* with a wild relative, *S. demissum*, which is highly resistant to the disease, but commercially useless.

❍ What implications does such selective breeding have for the maintenance of biodiversity?

● Biodiversity is worth maintaining because apparently commercially 'useless' species can act as a source of valuable genetic characteristics.

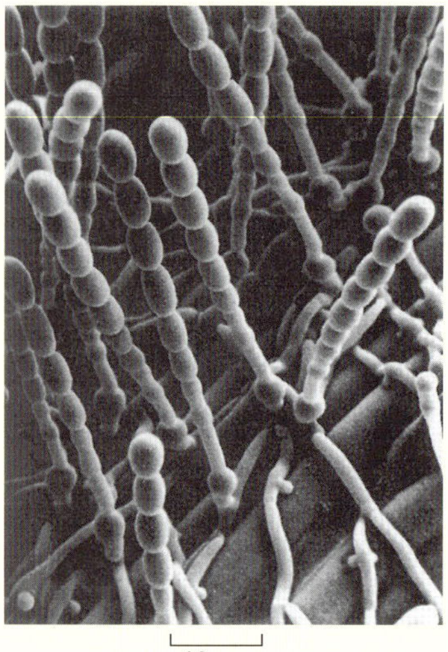

Figure 6.7 Scanning electron micrograph of infection by a powdery mildew fungus *Blumeria pisi* on pea (*Pisum sativum*). Fungal growth is confined to the epidermis. There is abundant development of conidia on the surface of the leaf, which are easily brushed off, giving a powdery appearance to infected leaves.

6.3.5 Powdery mildews (Erysiphales)

There are two groups of mildews, and both appear as grey infections of buds and leaves. The Peronosporales (Oomycota), or downy mildews, resemble grey, damp cotton wool, whereas the Erysiphales (Ascomycota) are taxonomically distinct and known as powdery mildews because of the powdery appearance of conidial spores (MacQueen, Burnett and Cann, 2001) on infected plants (Figure 6.7).

The Erysiphales are obligate parasites of flowering plants. Members of the *Blumeria* (or *Erisyphe*) genus cause mildew on many plant families with varying specificity: *B. polygoni* is very common on clover, but can infect many other legumes, giving it a very wide host range. On the other hand, *B. graminis* includes a number of host-specific forms (*formae speciales* or f.sp.); for example, *B. graminis* f.sp. *tritici* infects wheat (*Triticum* spp.) but not barley, whereas *B. graminis* f.sp. *hordei* infects barley (*Hordeum* spp.) but not wheat. Conidia germinate on wheat leaves within one to two days of landing, to form short germ tubes (Figure 6.8a).

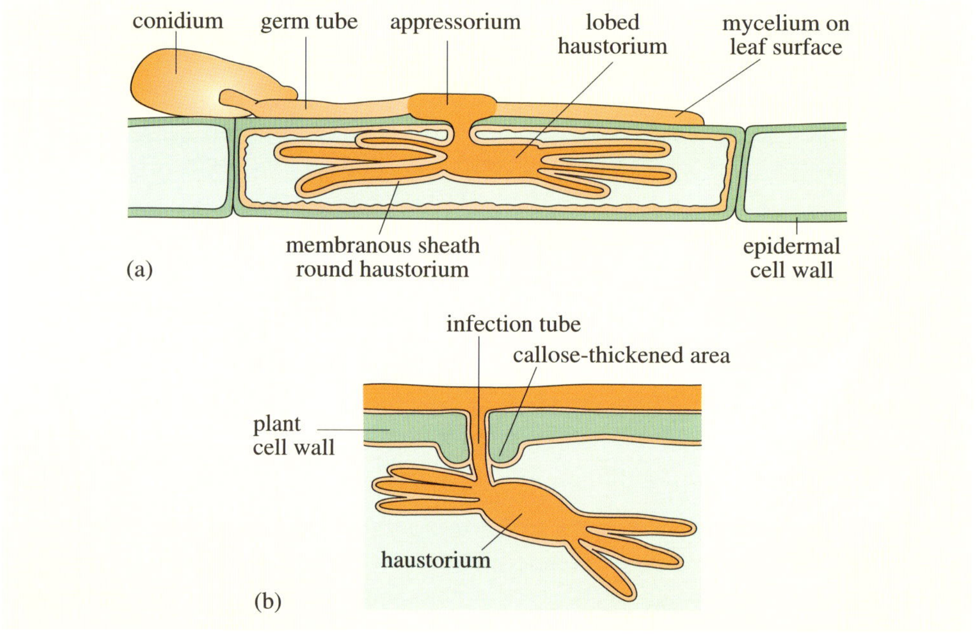

Figure 6.8 (a) Infection structures of *Blumeria graminis* on and in a host cell. (b) Section of an epidermal cell wall, showing a penetration point for a haustorium. Note the thickening of the cell wall due to callose deposition beneath the penetration point.

The germ tubes attach themselves to the epidermis by an appressorium. Beneath the point of attachment a fine infection tube breaches the host cell wall by means of mechanical and enzymatic digestion. The host cell wall may be thickened with **callose** beneath and around the infection tube (Figure 6.8b). Callose is a cell-wall carbohydrate produced in response to a variety of 'wounding' events, including damage to phloem sieve tubes (Section 3.7.1).

If the host is suitable, the infection tube enlarges within the epidermal cell to form an elongated, uninucleate haustorium. Haustoria of *B. graminis* have finger-like projections at each end (Figure 6.8b), but most are simple, rounded structures. The whole haustorium is enclosed in a 'sheath' comprising modified plant plasma membrane and vacuolar membrane with some matrix material sandwiched between. In a susceptible host, the infected cells remain alive and the fungus relies on the haustoria to extract carbohydrate biotrophically from the plant. Once haustoria are established, the mycelium spreads over the leaf surface, initiating new haustorial infections as it goes. When the fungus is established on the plant, it can start producing conidia. The spores are detached and dispersed by wind. The conidia of *Blumeria* spp. are unusual in their ability to germinate at low humidities, even at zero relative humidity. They have a very high water content (70% as opposed to 10% for most other airborne fungal spores), which may allow them to germinate at low humidity; this explains why powdery mildews are abundant in hot dry seasons.

Blumeria graminis can also reproduce via ascospores. Dark brown, globose bodies made up of several layers of cells, called **cleistothecia** (singular **cleistothecium**), each containing several asci are formed among a dense mass of mycelium on the lower leaves and leaf-sheaths of the cereal hosts (Figure 6.9). The ascospores are forcibly ejected from the asci when the cleistothecia crack open by swelling of the contents. The asci burst open at the top and the spores are squeezed out. The ascospores of *B. graminis* may germinate immediately, but they can also survive in the soil for up to 13 years.

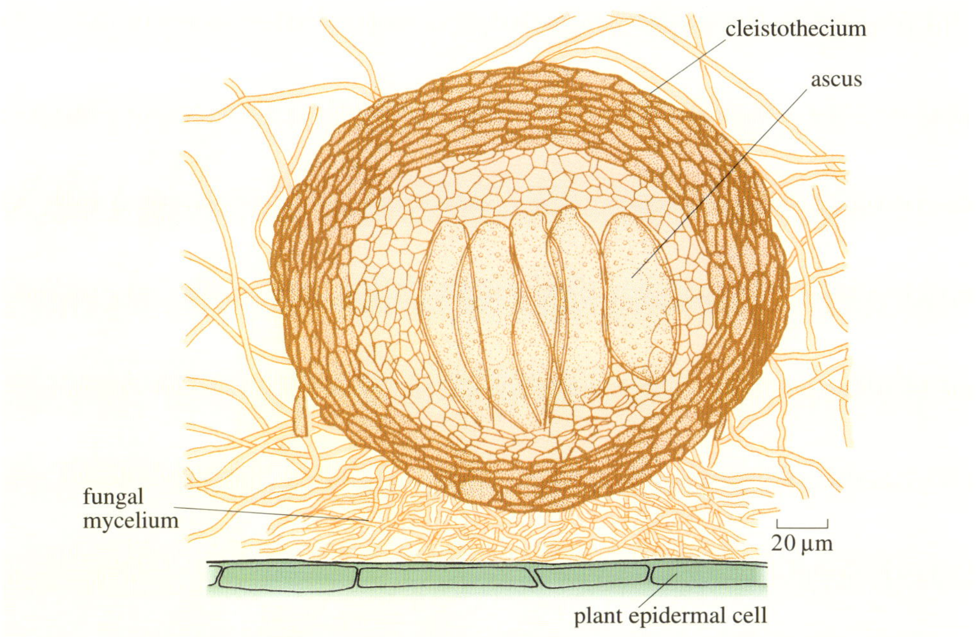

Figure 6.9 *Blumeria graminis*: section of cleistothecium containing several asci.

Mildew can affect crop yields because respiration is increased and photosynthesis is decreased in the infected plants. This reduces the amount of carbohydrate the leaves can export to the roots and ears. The disease can be controlled by dusting or spraying with fungicide, selective breeding or genetic modification of resistant host varieties.

6.4 PLANT–MICROBE INTERACTIONS: SOME GENERALIZATIONS

The examples described above allow us to make some generalizations about the interactions between plants and microbes. For example, most plants are exposed to two very different environments: the soil and the air. Therefore the surfaces they present are also different, adapted to the contrasting properties of these different environments.

Shoot surfaces present a waterproof outer layer, either cuticle or bark, perforated here and there by, respectively, stomata or **lenticels** (pores on woody shoots). Microbes arriving on a shoot surface must do so in a dormant state, suitable for airborne dispersal, such as a spore. In the soil, the plant is in continual contact with the microbes and animals that are active in the moist and stable conditions normally obtaining. The fine roots are not waterproofed, but are surrounded by mucilage. Soil microbes are not obliged to initiate growth from spores in a nutrient-poor, exposed environment, as airborne pathogens do. Unlike bacteria, which are relatively immobile in the soil, fungi and their protoctist look-alikes can approach the root directly, either as hyphae growing, or zoospores swimming, through the moist interstices of the soil. Mechanisms for effective dispersal and infection are particularly critical for an obligate symbiont that is host-specific; a random scatter-gun approach is too inefficient, and shoot-infecting microbes, in particular, need to be well adapted for infection of their host plants.

6.4.1 FINDING A HOST

There is a high degree of uncertainty about the final resting place of an airborne spore, although release of spores can be timed to coincide with conditions that increase the likelihood of encountering a suitable host in a suitable state. However, once a propagule has been dispersed, microbes increase their chances of finding a suitable host by responding to environmental stimuli. The response may be **thigmotropic** (i.e. stimulated by surface texture), as in the case of the barley rust fungus, *Puccinia hordei*, the germ tubes of which grow at right-angles to the longitudinal axes of the epidermal cells of the host leaf, initiating branches at junctions between cells (Figure 6.10).

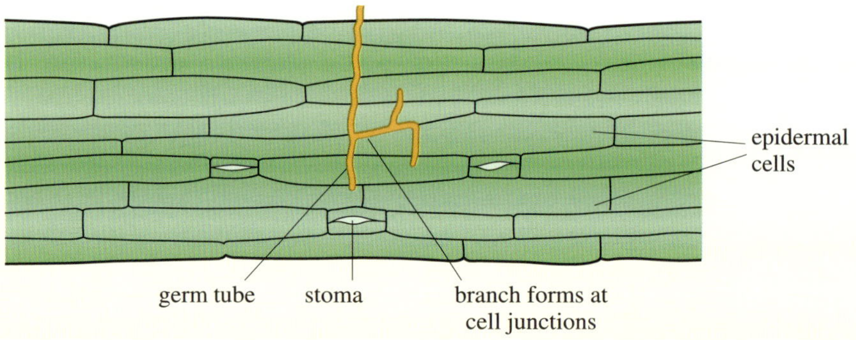

Figure 6.10 Plan view of a leaf surface, showing thigmotropic response of the rust fungus, *Puccinia hordei*, to a leaf surface. The germ tubes grow at right-angles to the longitudinal axes of the host's leaf, initiating branches at junctions between epidermal cells.

This growth pattern maximizes the chance of encountering stomata, through which the fungus enters the leaf. More frequently, the microbes respond to some compounds released by the plant; that is, there is a **chemotropic** response.

- ❍ Mutualistic AM fungi and rhizobia respond to flavonoids from their hosts; recall from Section 6.3.1 the type of compounds that honey fungus *(Armillaria mellea), Phytophthora* spp. and *Sclerotinia cepivora* respond to.

- ● Honey fungus and *Phytophthora* spp. respond to ethanol, which indicates an ailing and waterlogged host, and *Sclerotinia cepivora* responds to compounds specific to their hosts (members of the onion family).

6.4.2 Methods of infection

Whether mutualistic or pathogenic, many plant-infecting microbes exhibit common strategies for gaining entry to their hosts. Root-infecting fungi generally enter the apoplast of tissues, just behind the root tip. Those that limit themselves to intercellular penetration such as many bacteria and ectomycorrhizal fungi show no specialist features, but appressoria and infection pegs are employed by those that breach the plant cell walls. However, there are clear differences in approach between pathogens and mutualists. Necrotrophs make substantial use of enzymatic digestion of cell walls to facilitate ingress. The products of this digestion serve to nourish the fungus. Biotrophic fungal parasites, on the other hand, tend to rely more on mechanical pressure to force the infection peg through the cell wall. (Pressures up to 8 MPa have been recorded, the highest known in any eukaryotic cell.) These fungi make only limited use of wall-degrading enzymes. It appears that enzymatic digestion tends to invoke a more vigorous plant defence response than mechanical entry. Fragments of cell wall (composed of oligosaccharides) can act as warning signals to the plant that an intruder is attempting to force an entry (Section 6.6). Suffice it to say, the more 'softly softly' the approach by the microbes, the less likely it is that host defence responses will be triggered.

- ❍ In the light of these observations, would you expect AM fungi to make more extensive use of enzymatic digestion or mechanical pressure, when they penetrate the host cell walls?

- ● Strong defensive reactions by the host plant could be minimized by avoiding secretion of fungal proteins. AM fungi penetrate plant cells chiefly by mechanical pressure.

6.4.3 Nutritional relationships

There are clear similarities between the structure and function of arbuscules of AM fungi, the haustoria of pathogenic fungi like mildews, and even protoctists like *Phytophthora infestans* and the symbiosome of rhizobial nodules. Each of these structures provides a large surface area over which the exchange/uptake of materials can occur. Whether mutualistic or parasitic, biotrophic relationships can persist for long periods. In biotrophic associations, whether the microbe breaches the cell walls of the plant cells or not, the plasma membranes of the two organisms remain intact and functional. The microbe remains effectively outside the cell in the apoplastic space.

A key difference between parasitic and mutualistic associations lies in the activity of H^+–ATPases that drive solute transport across membranes. In parasitic associations, H^+–ATPases are absent from the plant plasma membrane involved in the interfacial zone of the haustorium, but not from the corresponding microbial membrane. These enzymes are present in normal amounts in plant cell membranes associated with mutualistic associations (AM and nodules).

- ❍ Suggest an explanation for this contrast.
- ● In mutualisms, there is reciprocal movement of nutrients, whereas in parasitisms there is unidirectional movement from the plant to the microbe.

Unlike biotrophic pathogens, many necrotrophs use toxins to assist in their attack on the host plant. The enzymes and toxins that the microbes produce help them to overcome the plant's defences. Both biotrophs and necrotrophs survive in the absence of their hosts either in the form of resting structures such as spores, or independently as saprotrophs.

Necrotrophic interactions can be likened to smash-and-grab robberies in which the plant 'victim' is unable, despite its best efforts, to prevent the aggressive assailant from taking what it needs (e.g. sugars). There is no subtlety about the events, and victims suffer considerable damage, if not death. In contrast, biotrophic parasites are more like sneak thieves or even confidence tricksters; they extract what they need without eliciting defensive responses from the host; instead they inveigle their way into forming an intimate relationship with the victim whose resources are depleted. Mutualistic symbionts are rather like paying guests that are welcomed more-or-less grudgingly, but only because the host needs assistance to meet its needs. In return for payment in the form of mineral nutrients, the fungus receives 'board-and-lodging' in the form of sugars from the host plant. Furthermore, the more benefit the host derives from the lodger, the more generous the 'meals' provided.

SUMMARY OF SECTIONS 6.3 AND 6.4

1 The rhizosphere represents a loose, unstructured association between plants and microbes, including harmless, non-specific, saprotrophs, which absorb the plant mucilage as a source of nourishment and some, more-or-less specific, potential pathogens. The saprotrophs may offer the associated plants some measure of protection from the pathogens.

2 Rhizobia possessing the p*Sym* plasmid can infect the Fabaceae, and produce root nodules, in which they fix nitrogen. The association is fairly specific, extremely intimate and mutualistic: the plant obtains nitrogen from the bacteria, which receive carbohydrates in return.

3 Arbuscular mycorrhizas are extremely ancient and intimate, mutualistic symbioses between the roots of most herbaceous land plants and certain ascomycotous fungi. The fungi exhibit a broad host range, but are obligate symbionts.

4 *Phytophthora infestans* causes the disease 'late blight' in potatoes. The oomycete protoctist infects the leaves of susceptible hosts, from which the pathogen obtains biotrophic and later necrotrophic nutrition. Spores isolated from the host can be cultured *in vitro*. The relationship is less obligatory but much more specific than AM symbioses.

5 Powdery mildews are obligate, fungal parasites of many flowering plants. The airborne spores infect the shoots of susceptible plants, where they form intimate associations involving the formation of haustoria. Fungal nutrition is biotrophic. Host range can be very narrow — that is, species, variety or strain specific.

6 Microbial mechanisms for dispersal and infection must be appropriate for the dispersal medium (soil or air) and the route of entry into the host (root, leaf or stem).

7 Microbes can promote infection of suitable hosts by responding to environmental stimuli such as surface texture or chemicals.

8 Specialist features such as appressoria and infection pegs or threads are employed by those microbes that penetrate plant cell walls by mechanical means. Extracellular, wall-degrading enzymes are an alternative or additional aid to breaching the cell wall, but are more typical of pathogenic microbes.

9 There are many similarities in the interfacial structures between plants and microbes in biotrophic symbioses, but one important difference is that mutualistic associations have H^+–ATPases on both the plant and microbial interfacial membranes, whereas these enzymes are restricted to that of the microbial symbiont in pathogenic associations.

6.5 Pathogens, virulence and resistance

Ever since the origins of agriculture in ancient Sumer, humans have been battling against the ravages of microbial diseases that destroy or taint crops. One of our main weapons has been to exploit the innate mechanisms of resistance to disease that plants display. However, beforc proceeding to discuss them in more detail, it is important to review the nomenclature, much of which you have already met, but which can be confusing. A *pathogen* is a species that is capable of causing disease; however, an organism that is pathogenic to one plant may not be to another. You know already that a pathogen's host range may be broad or narrow. Individual strains of a pathogenic species may be unable to establish infection in a potential plant host and cause no damage; that is, they are **avirulent**.

Correspondingly, certain host varieties are **resistant** to particular pathogen strains because an avirulent pathogen invokes a massive resistance response from the plant, which prevents the infection becoming established. In contrast, a virulent pathogen is able to establish an infection and cause disease, and a **sensitive** host is susceptible to the disease.

There is also considerable variation in the *degree* of susceptibility of a host and the strength of the resistance response. **Vertical resistance** confers total protection on a host variety against particular avirulent pathogen strains. **Horizontal resistance**, on the other hand, gives some measure of protection against a wide range of pathogens. In this case there is a much more generalized response involving only a proportion of the defence mechanisms and it is more likely to deter rather than destroy the pathogen. Indeed, quite a few of the defences induced in horizontal resistance can also be invoked by abiotic stresses such as wounding and toxic metals in the soil.

6.6 DEFENCE MECHANISMS IN SEED PLANTS

In many ways, plant defence mechanisms echo the way that animals respond to disease. Plants possess an impressive array of defence mechanisms to counter the undesirable invasion attempts by pathogenic microbes. Moreover, they are largely successful; most plants spend the majority of their lifetimes disease-free. Whether a plant suffers from a disease or not depends on the balance between the pathogen's ability to cause disease and the host's ability to defend itself against it. Some defences may be *constitutive*; that is, they are always there. They include the presence of a thickened cuticle or accumulated secondary metabolites with antimicrobial activity ('chemical barrier'; Davey and Gillman, 2001), which afford generalized protection throughout the lifetime of the plant. Other defences are *inducible*; that is, they are only apparent once the attempt to infect is underway. It is with these **inducible defences** that this section is concerned. The inducible plant defence system is very complex (look ahead briefly at Figure 6.19), so in an effort to make this subject easier to assimilate, parts of it are described in turn before the whole system is assembled.

6.6.1 CHANGES TO THE CELL WALL

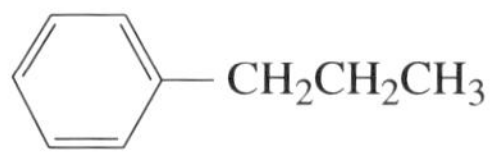

1-phenylpropane (structure on which phenylpropanoid compounds are based)

Substances may be added to the plant cell wall as a localized and rapid response to fungal invasion. These can include phenolic compounds like lignin, which are products of the **phenylpropanoid pathway** (Davey and Gillman, 2001), as well as carbohydrates such as **pectins** and callose, and several different kinds of protein including **peroxidase enzymes**. A common characteristic of most of these substances is that they have a greater capacity for cross-linking than the regular cell-wall constituents. This is illustrated by lignin in Figure 6.11. Cross-linking helps to strengthen the wall and make it less susceptible to microbial attack. Hydrogen peroxide (H_2O_2) is generated early on during a pathogen attack (Section 6.6.6), and acts as a substrate for this oxidative cross-linking of wall polymers. Highly localized deposition of callose thickens the inner side of the cell wall at the point where fungal hyphae or infection pegs attempt to enter the cell (Figure 6.8b). Peroxidase enzymes in the cell walls play a role in lignin synthesis, as well as other cross-linking reactions.

Tannins and lignin can also bind to proteins and in so doing can inhibit enzyme activity. In this way, the plant can deactivate the fungal enzymes designed to attack their tissues. (Thus, 'tanning' preserves leather by inhibiting the processes of microbial decomposition.)

Rapid reinforcement of the cell wall (e.g. with callose, as indicated in Figure 6.8b, at the point of contact with a pathogen, helps to slow the entry of the pathogen and give time for activation of other defences that require gene activation and *de novo* synthesis of defensive agents.

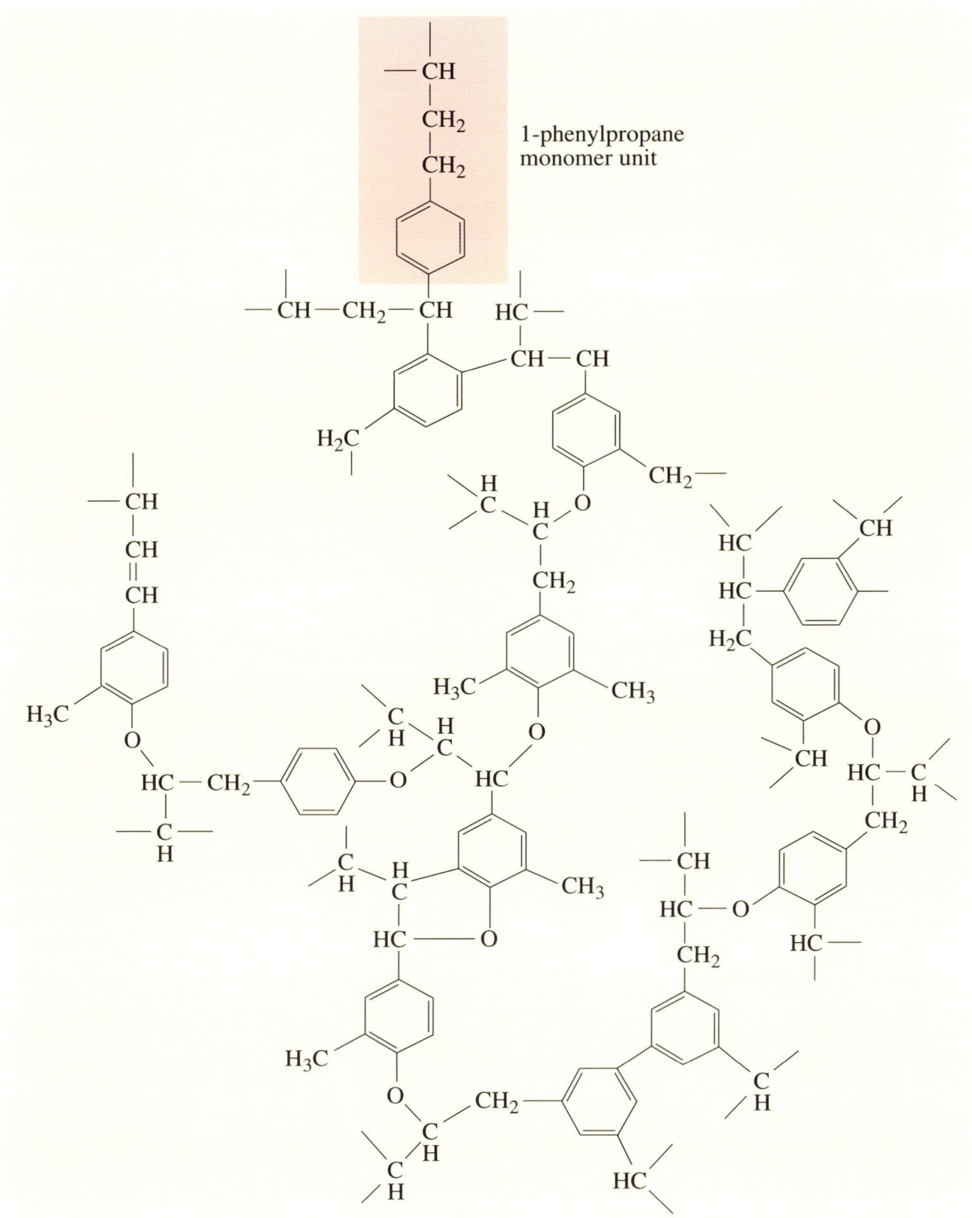

Figure 6.11 Part of the molecular structure of lignin, a complex three-dimensional polymer formed from phenylpropanoid subunits. The phenylpropanoid subunits are joined randomly in a three-dimensional, asymmetric network by various linkages.

6.6.2 PHYTOALEXINS

The phenylpropanoid pathway is also responsible for the production of many **phytoalexins**. Phytoalexins are low molecular mass compounds that are both synthesized by and accumulated in plant cells after exposure to microbes. (Some alkaloids (Davey and Gillman, 2001), are phytoalexins too.) They are all classed as secondary chemicals, but are an important part of the plant's defensive arsenal. Over 300 of them have been characterized; they have been found to belong to a wide range of different, though frequently related, compound classes including flavonoids and sesquiterpenes. However, individual plant families produce phytoalexins that belong to only two or three structural classes; for example, the legumes produce isoflavonoid derivatives, whereas the potato family produces sesquiterpenes.

❍ Recall from Section 6.4 another role for flavonoids besides plant defence.

● Root nodule-forming rhizobia are attracted to their legume hosts by the flavonoids in the plants' root exudates.

Phenylalanine ammonia lyase (PAL) and **chalcone synthase (CHS)** are both key enzymes involved in the synthesis of phytoalexins. PAL is the first enzyme of the phenylpropanoid pathway (Figure 6.12).

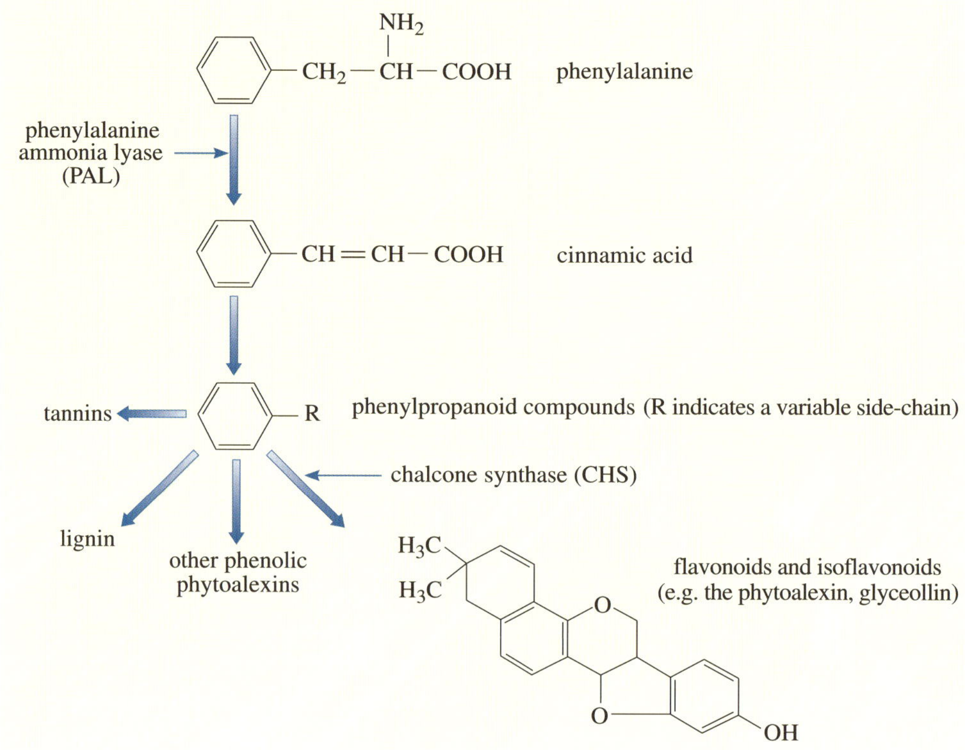

Figure 6.12 The phenylpropanoid pathway: cinnamic acid, produced from phenylalanine by the action of the enzyme phenylalanine ammonia lyase (PAL), is the precursor of many phenolic compounds such as lignin, tannins and some phytoalexins. The enzyme chalcone synthase (CHS) is the first one on the pathway for flavonoid and isoflavonoid derivatives such as glyceollin.

PAL converts phenylalanine to cinnamic acid, which is a precursor of a large number of phenolic compounds including lignin, tannins and phytoalexins. CHS is the first enzyme of the branch specific for flavonoids and isoflavonoid-derived phytoalexins such as glyceollin and medicarpin.

Phytoalexins are antibiotics of low potency and with fairly low specificity. They can be effective against bacteria, fungi, animal cells, viruses and even other plant cells. Most phytoalexins are lipophilic molecules; that is, they can dissolve in lipids, which means they can cross plasma membranes to an internal site where they exert their toxic effects. Phytoalexins are thought to give rise to radicals, which can damage DNA and disrupt membranes, and which can have various consequences for mineral uptake and signal transduction. They act only at the site of infection, where they inhibit the growth of pathogens, their accumulation being faster and greater when the plant is resistant to the pathogen than when it is sensitive.

Pathogens differ in their sensitivity to phytoalexins. Many fungi have the ability to metabolize phytoalexins to less toxic derivatives. It seems that the more virulent strains of particular pathogens can detoxify phytoalexins more effectively than less virulent strains. Figure 6.13 shows the results of research into the possible link between virulence in peas and the ability to detoxify the phytoalexin pisatin by the fungal root and stem pathogen *Nectria haematococca* (VanEtten and Tegtmeier, 1982).

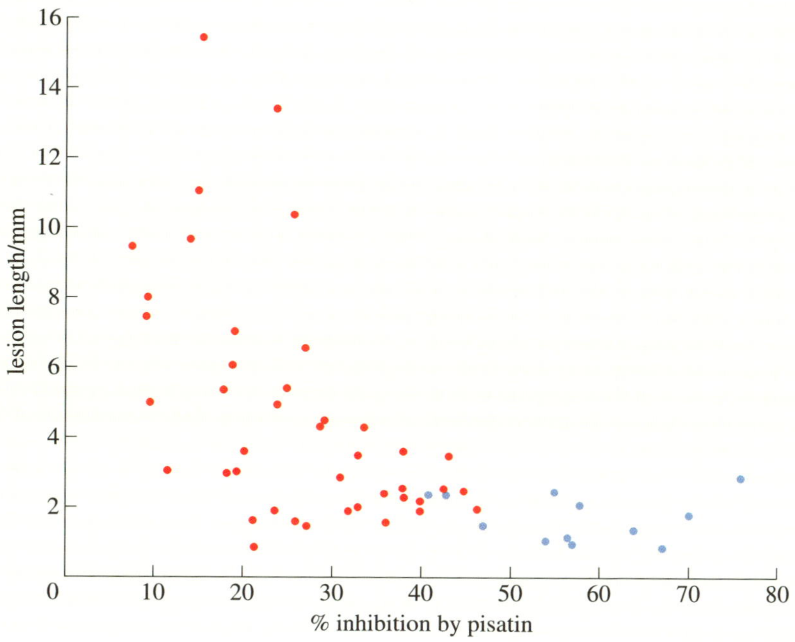

Figure 6.13 The relationship between sensitivity to pisatin (% inhibition by pisatin), virulence on pea in field isolates of *Nectria haematococca* (lesion length) and the ability to demethylate pisatin: each point represents one isolate; red dots indicate isolates able to demethylate pisatin, whereas blue dots indicate isolates unable to detoxify pisatin. Lesion length gives an indication of the damage caused by the isolates and hence their virulence. % inhibition indicates an isolate's sensitivity to the phytoalexin. (Data from VanEtten and Tegtmeier, 1982.)

All *N. haematococca* **isolates** that were unable to demethylate pisatin were highly sensitive to it and were low in virulence in peas. All the highly virulent isolates had the ability to demethylate, and thereby detoxify pisatin. No highly virulent isolate was sensitive to pisatin. However, a few isolates highly tolerant of pisatin were also of low virulence.

- ❍ What does this observation imply about the ability of microbes to detoxify phytoalexins and virulence?
- ● The ability to tolerate phytoalexins does not necessarily make a microbe pathogenic.

Some pathogens can synthesize 'suppressors' that can block the accumulation of phytoalexins at source. Such suppressors inhibit the accumulation of mRNA for both PAL and CHS, and so reduce the synthesis of pisatin in pea.

6.6.3 Hypersensitive response (HR)

The **hypersensitive response (HR)** involves the rapid death and collapse of cells challenged by a pathogen. This localized cell death at the site of attack serves to isolate the pathogen and can prevent its establishment and spread. It usually appears as small necrotic spots on a challenged leaf (Figure 6.14).

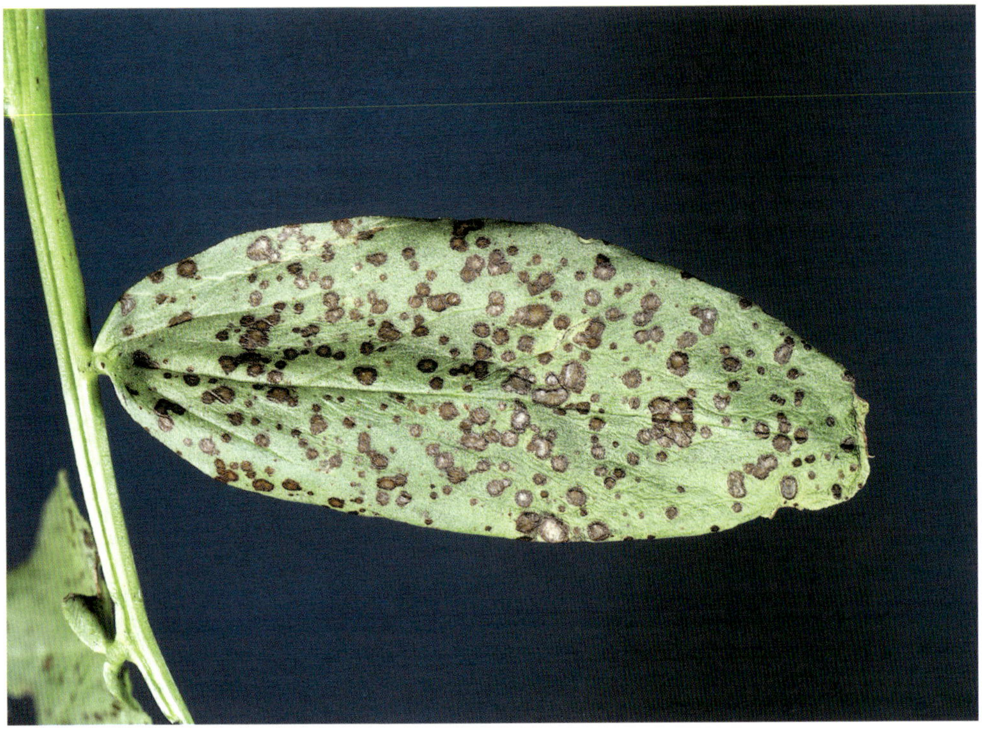

Figure 6.14 A plant with necrotic lesions (spots) caused by a hypersensitive response to attempted infection by a pathogen.

Such programmed cell death is an active, orderly process (Chapter 5). It is dependent on protein synthesis that is the outcome of recognition events at the point of contact between plant and pathogen. It can be likened to a tactical withdrawal by defending soldiers in a battle, in which crops are burnt and bridges destroyed behind the retreating forces in order to impede the advance of the enemy.

Cell death occurs in response to diverse pathogens apparently by at least two pathways. One route resembles the *apoptosis* (Saffrey, 2001) seen in animal systems, in which there is a sequential shutdown of cellular processes and condensation of organelles until the cell contents are reduced to a shrunken corpse. The other route resembles **necrotic cell death** superficially, in that it appears chaotic (there is cell swelling and rapid disintegration of cell contents); this is probably another example of programmed cell death.

- ❍ How effective might a hypersensitive response be against viruses, bacteria, obligate, biotrophic parasites, and necrotrophic pathogens?

- ● Viruses may be contained by HR if it affects the plasmodesmata through which the virus travels from one cell to another. HR might cause a decrease in growth and the long-term survival of bacteria if cell death involves dehydration. HR is likely to be effective against obligate parasites that depend on living cells to grow and develop. Necrotrophic pathogens may actually benefit from the release of nutrients from dead cells.

6.6.4 Pathogenesis-related proteins (PR-proteins)

The synthesis of many proteins is induced by the presence of potential pathogens. These **pathogenesis-related proteins (PR-proteins)** have been grouped into 11 families, PR-1 to PR-11, but the functions of many remain a mystery. PR-2, PR-3 and PR-11 are hydrolytic enzymes with β-1,3-glucanase or chitinase activities. These enzymes are stored within the vacuole of the cell and in the extracellular spaces until needed. This compartmentalization is important because both fungal and plant cell walls contain polymers composed of glucans. The problem is not so acute in the case of chitinases because, unlike fungal cell walls, plant cell walls do not contain chitin and so are unaffected by these enzymes.

❍ What danger would there be to the plant if its glucanases were distributed randomly?

● The plant might end up digesting its own cell walls.

PR-1 and PR-4 have antifungal activity, in so far as they may be toxic to fungi. Some of the other PR-proteins may be involved in the induction of systemic acquired resistance, described below.

6.6.5 Systemic acquired resistance

Table 6.2 shows the results of an experiment in which individuals from each of two groups of tobacco plants (*Nicotiana tabacum*), one of which had been previously exposed to infection by an avirulent strain of tobacco mosaic virus (TMV), were challenged by one of a number of tobacco pathogens. Resistance to infection is assessed in terms of lesion size, in which smaller lesions are taken as evidence of a hypersensitive response, and therefore indicate a resistant response by the challenged plant; large lesions are taken as evidence of a successful infection by the pathogen.

Table 6.2 The effect of earlier infection by an avirulent strain of TMV on resistance to subsequent infections by tobacco plants (*Nicotiana tabacum*). Small lesions are taken as evidence of a resistant response to the pathogen by the plant, whereas large lesions indicate a sensitive response.

Potential pathogen used to challenge the tobacco plants	Group A: control, previously uninfected plants	Group B: plants previously infected with TMV
virulent strain of TMV on *same leaf* as for first challenge on Group B	many large lesions	fewer smaller lesions
virulent TMV on a different leaf from that used for the first challenge on Group B	many large lesions	fewer smaller lesions
TEV (tobacco etch virus)	many large lesions	fewer smaller lesions
Pseudomonas tabaci, bacterial pathogen of tobacco	many large lesions	fewer smaller lesions
Perenospora tabacina (blue mould of tobacco)	many large lesions	fewer smaller lesions

❍ Using the data in Table 6.2, answer the following questions:

(a) What effect does previous infection by TMV have on resistance to attempted infection by: (i) virulent strains of the same pathogen, (ii) virulent strains of another viral pathogen, (iii) virulent strains of a bacterial pathogen, and (iv) virulent strains of a fungal pathogen?

(b) Is resistance restricted to only those parts of the plant that were subjected to the earlier infection?

● (a) Previous infection leads to: (i) smaller lesions and therefore increased resistance to virulent strains of the same pathogen. (ii) This induced resistance extends to other viral pathogens and (iii) also a broad range of bacterial pathogens and (iv) fungal disease agents.

(b) Resistance extends to the whole plant, not just the part previously exposed to infection (cf. rows 1 and 2).

Exposure of a plant to a pathogen seems to lead to a generalized increase in resistance to further pathogenic attack. This **systemic acquired resistance (SAR)** is analogous to the development of acquired immunity in animal systems (Davey and Gillman, 2001).

6.6.6 Coordination of defence responses

That plants possess a battery of cellular responses to attempted invasion by ever-present plant pathogens has been recognized for many years. However, more recently, attention has focused on a range of other changes induced by microbial infection. Some are components of the cellular protection system, but many are involved in signal transduction pathways, and so are responsible for the coordination of the major defence mechanisms. Cellular communication was discussed in Chapter 5 (see also Clements and Saffrey, 2001). Much of the early work was done on animal systems, but as research into plant systems progresses, it is becoming increasingly clear that there are some close parallels between the systems operating in plants and animals. Ion fluxes, an oxidative burst, nitric oxide and phosphorylation events are all implicated in the coordination of the plant defence system. Gradually the various elements of the system are being assembled into an overall, but still tentative, model for resistance regulation.

❍ What is the term used to describe a response to a stimulus that has not only a series of stages in which the chemicals involved in the first stage are activated by the stimulus (such as a pathogen), and these chemicals then activate the second stage and so on, but also the number of molecules recruited at each stage increases, thereby amplifying the response?

● The term is ‘cascade reactions’ (Davey and Gillman, 2001), and this is what occurs in the plant defence system.

Ion fluxes

One of the very first plant responses to the presence of an invader is a rapid flux of ions. There is an influx of extracellular Ca^{2+} into the cytoplasm (from either cell wall or soil) via activated calcium channels, and simultaneous, reciprocal movements of H^+ and K^+. Both Ca^{2+} and H^+ are at hugely greater concentrations outside the cell than in the cytoplasm. As soon as a disruptive pathogen penetrates the plasma membrane, and depolarizes it, rapid ion movements ensue. Ca^{2+} is thought to be involved in stimulating wall thickening, phytoalexin synthesis and hypersensitive cell death. Both cross-linking and callose deposition can be triggered by a Ca^{2+} signal involving calcium ion channels in the membrane at the point of contact. (The channels can be stretch-activated, so callose can be produced, as a protective layer, at points of friction too.)

Oxidative burst

The **oxidative** (or respiratory) **burst** (Davey and Gillman, 2001) is a characteristic early feature of the host response to microbial infection attempts. Figure 6.15 summarizes its role in plant disease resistance. Attempted infection by the pathogen leads to the activation of a membrane-bound NADP.2H oxidase (closely resembling that operating in activated mammalian neutrophils). This leads to the rapid generation of superoxide, ($O_2{\cdot}^-$), which is soon converted to other reactive oxygen species (Chapter 2) and hydrogen peroxide (H_2O_2), which tends to accumulate within challenged cells. Reactive oxygen species act as antimicrobial agents; many are very strong oxidants, which initiate chain reactions with many organic molecules, leading to massive cell damage. You already know that H_2O_2 acts as a substrate in oxidative cross-linking of cell walls (Section 6.6.1). In addition it stimulates the phenylpropanoid pathway and ion fluxes, activates genes encoding enzymes that *protect* the host cells from these effects (including **catalase**, which *removes* H_2O_2, and **glutathione S-transferase (GST)**, which removes dangerous radicals), as well as acting as a trigger for HR.

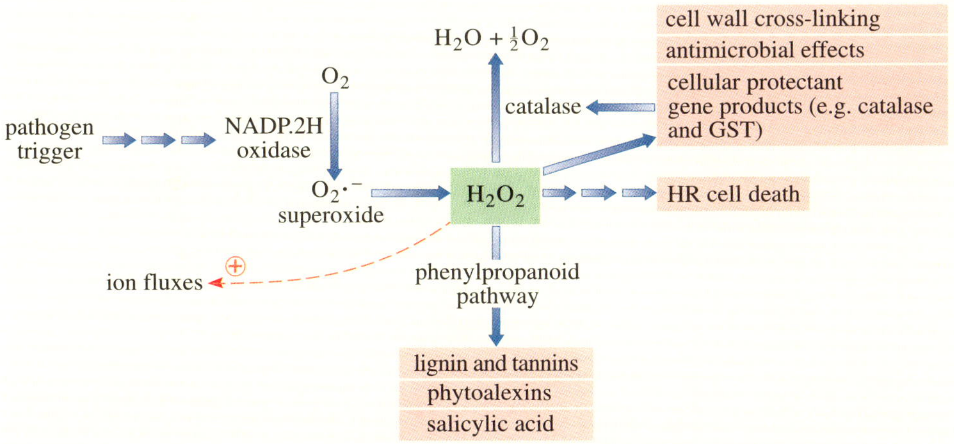

Figure 6.15 Schematic representation of the role of the oxidative burst in induced plant defences. The superoxide ion is rapidly converted to hydrogen peroxide (H_2O_2), which acts as a signal promoting a number of defence responses — for example, cell-wall cross-linking, phytoalexin synthesis and (if the signal is strong) a hypersensitive response (HR). H_2O_2 stimulates ion fluxes and also speeds its own removal by promoting the production of catalase. The broken red arrow indicates positive feedback.

Figure 6.16 illustrates the generalized kinetics for accumulation of H_2O_2 and induction of cell death in plant cells following bacterial inoculation. Both virulent and avirulent pathogens induce a rapid but weak, transient accumulation of H_2O_2 (phase I), which can induce generalized stress reactions such as phytoalexin stimulation, lignification and wall thickening. Only avirulent strains invoke a second, massive and prolonged oxidative burst between 3 to 6 hours after inoculation (phase II), which is sufficient to induce an HR.

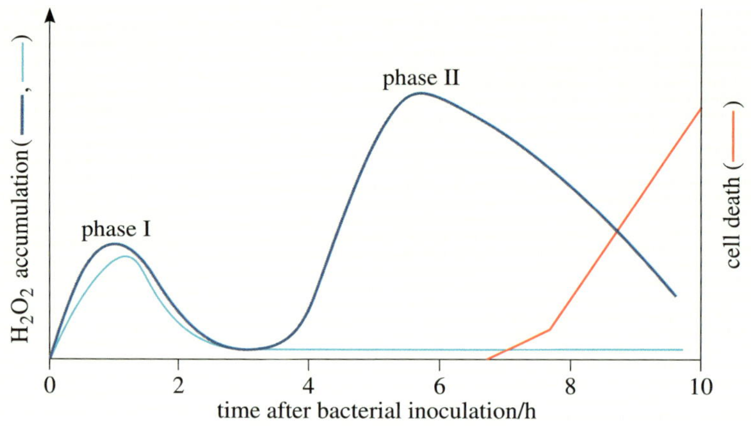

Figure 6.16 Kinetics of the accumulation of H_2O_2 and induction of cell death in plant cells following bacterial inoculation. The light blue line indicates H_2O_2 accumulation following inoculation with virulent pathogen or non-pathogen: no cell death results from this. The dark blue line indicates H_2O_2 accumulation following inoculation with avirulent or non-host pathogen. Cell death (as part of a hypersensitive response) follows the phase II peak in H_2O_2 production, and is indicated by the red line.

The phosphorylation poise

The oxidative burst is regulated by a balance between phosphorylation and dephosphorylation events, termed a **phosphorylation poise**. Protein phosphatase activity decreases reactive oxygen species production, and protein kinase enzymes work in the other direction (Clements and Saffrey, 2001) to increase it. Such a regulatory poise may be important for rapid induction and tight control of the magnitude and duration of the oxidative burst.

Accumulation of salicylic acid

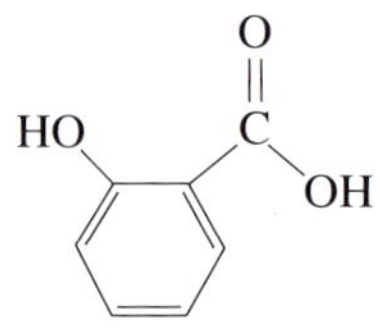

salicylic acid

Salicylic acid (Davey and Gillman, 2001), which is found in willow bark (Latin *salix*, willow), is a derivative of benzoic acid, and is another product of the phenylpropanoid pathway. (Acetylsalicylic acid will be known to you as 'aspirin'.) It accumulates locally and to a lesser extent systemically following inoculation with avirulent pathogens. It has no direct antimicrobial activity, but operates primarily as a signalling molecule with a number of roles. (It appears to be one cellular messenger that is unique to plants.) Its roles in defence coordination are summarized in Figure 6.17.

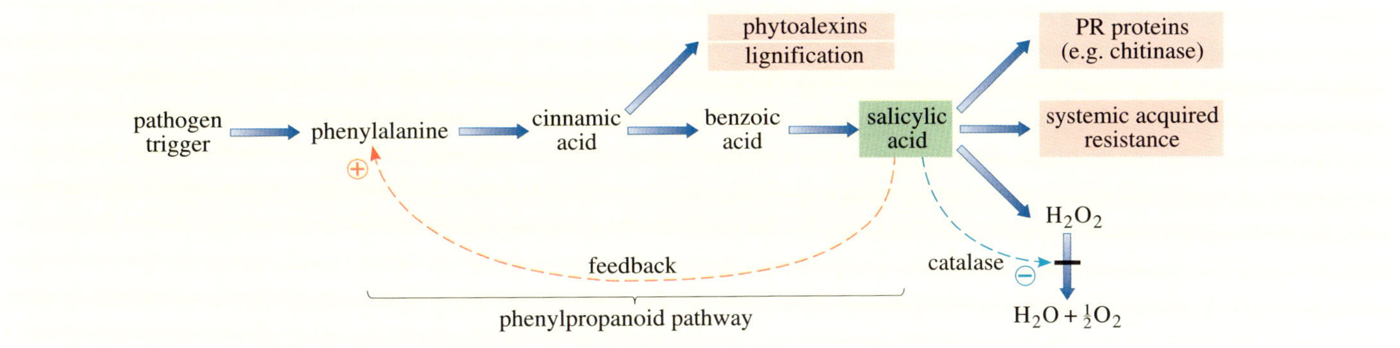

Figure 6.17 The role of salicylic acid in induced plant defence responses. Salicylic acid is a product of the phenylpropanoid pathway, and is involved in the activation of genes for PR-proteins and the development of systemic acquired resistance. It stimulates the phenylpropanoid pathway directly but inhibits catalase. The broken blue arrow indicates negative feedback.

Salicylic acid is implicated in the activation of genes for PR-proteins and the development of systemic acquired resistance. A build up of salicylic acid stimulates the phenylpropanoid pathway directly. It also binds to and inhibits catalase.

- Recall the reaction that catalase is a catalyst for, and using Figure 6.16, suggest what effect the inhibition of this enzyme may have on the plant defence response.

- Catalase speeds up the breakdown of hydrogen peroxide into water and oxygen. Inhibition of this reaction facilitates the accumulation of H_2O_2, which promotes cell-wall cross-linking, antimicrobial effects, activation of cellular protectant genes, the synthesis of lignin, tannins and phytoalexin, and even HR.

NITRIC OXIDE (NO)

Nitric oxide (NO) has only recently been added to the list of signalling agents involved in coordinating the resistance responses of plants, but it may be the most important. In animal systems it is known to regulate many aspects of cellular control including ion channels, phosphatases and transcription factors (Clements and Saffrey, 2001).

Recent evidence suggests that NO collaborates with reactive oxygen species to trigger transcriptional activation of plant defence genes and the hypersensitive response. Figure 6.18 summarizes the postulated role of NO in defence coordination. NO acts synergistically with reactive oxygen species to increase cell death in soybean cells. It can also activate PAL (phenylalanine ammonia lyase), which amplifies the activity of the phenylpropanoid pathway, leading to lignification (wall thickening), phytoalexin synthesis and the production of salicylic acid, which in turn then amplifies defence responses such as systemic acquired resistance, and production of PR-proteins such as chitinase and glucanases. Plants produce NO from the amino acid arginine using an NO synthase enzyme very similar to that found in animals. Furthermore, the effects of NO are mediated by guanylyl cyclase and cyclic GMP, which also mediate several NO responses in animals.

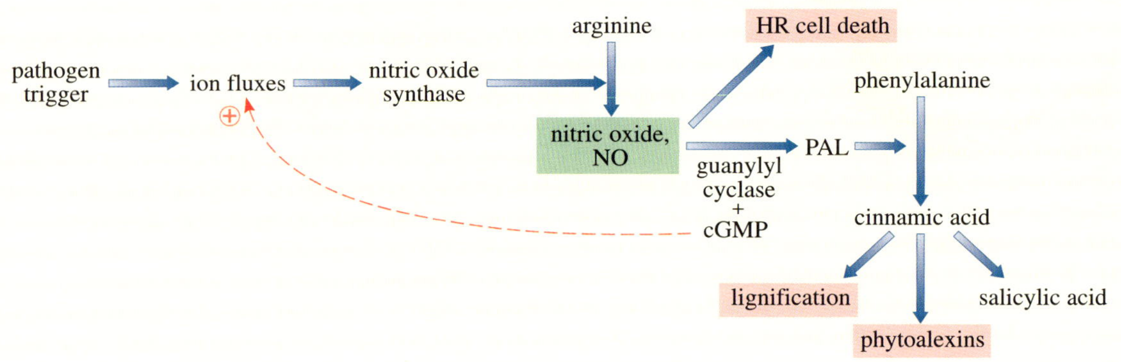

Figure 6.18 Ion fluxes stimulate the production of NO from the amino acid arginine. NO is involved in: inducing cell death (hypersensitive response) and activating PAL (phenylalanine ammonia lyase) which amplifies the activity of the phenylpropanoid pathway, leading to wall thickening, phytoalexin synthesis and the production of salicylic acid. Production of NO is enhanced by guanylyl cyclase and cGMP.

❍ What is the functional relationship between NO, guanylyl cyclase and cGMP?

● Inside the cell, the primary messenger NO binds to the enzyme guanylyl cyclase, which catalyses the production of the second messenger cGMP, which in turn promotes defence responses (Clements and Saffrey, 2001).

6.6.7 The plant defence system assembled

All of the defence mechanisms and signalling pathways described above can be assembled into an overall model for the plant defence system, which is summarized in Figure 6.19. It is a complicated system, so you may like to take a little time to check back and see where the various elements fit in.

The current view is that interaction between reactive oxygen species and NO establishes a means for fine-tuning the magnitude of the signals that flow through the defence-response pathway leading ultimately to an HR. Quite how it all works is not yet known. However, the balanced synthesis of NO and superoxide ion, $O_2{\cdot}^-$ allows the formation of **peroxonitrite radicals**, $NO_3{\cdot}^-$, which are extremely potent and capable of wreaking substantial cellular damage, possibly leading to cell death.

❍ From Figure 6.19, identify the elements of the coordination system (shown in green) that can influence:

(a) the hypersensitive response (HR);

(b) the development of systemic acquired resistance (SAR);

(c) the activation of cellular protectant genes, e.g. that producing catalase.

● (a) The HR is coordinated by ion fluxes, NO synthesis, the oxidative burst, the phosphorylation poise, and peroxonitrite radicals.

(b) The SAR is coordinated by all of the above (except peroxonitrite radicals) plus salicylic acid.

(c) The phosphorylation poise and the oxidative burst coordinate the activation of cellular protectant genes.

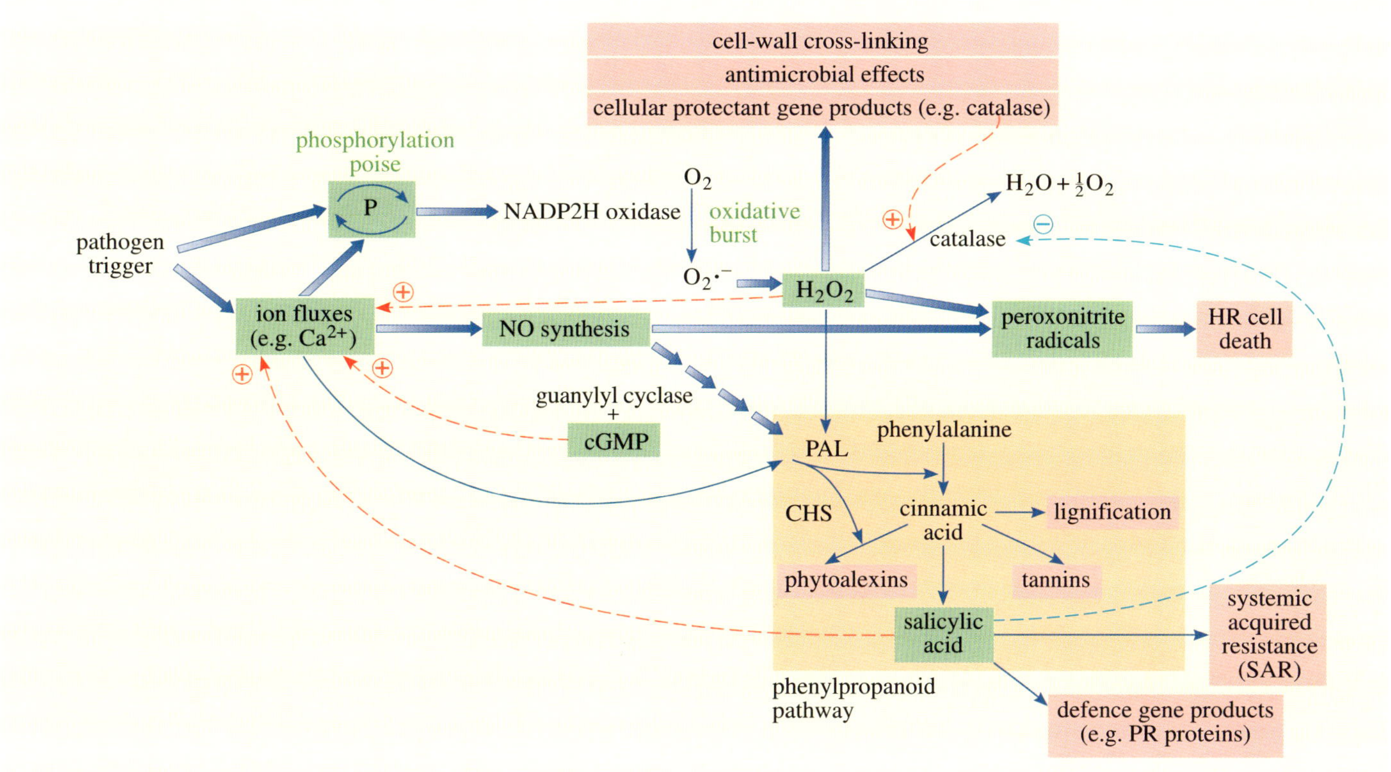

Figure 6.19 The induced plant defence system assembled. NO and the oxidative burst (and to a lesser extent ion fluxes, phosphorylation events and salicylic acid) combine to control generalized, phase I responses like cell-wall cross-linking, antimicrobial effects, the activation of cellular protectant and PR-protein genes, phytoalexin synthesis, and systemic acquired resistance (SAR). A strong signal can induce a phase II, hypersensitive response (HR). (PAL is phenylalanine ammonia lyase; CHS is chalcone synthase.)

As to the rest of the plant defence system, only reactive oxygen species are capable of inducing maximal expression of more generalized stress responses such as cell-wall cross-linking and glutathione S-transferase activity, but they are not the primary signals for rapid induction of defence genes encoding enzymes of the phenylpropanoid pathway. NO seems to have a central role in stimulating this pathway, and therefore influencing the synthesis of phytoalexins, lignin, tannins and salicylic acid, which, in turn, promotes the synthesis of PR-proteins, and development of systemic acquired resistance. No doubt, this is not the whole story: research is continuing to elucidate the missing elements in the model.

SUMMARY OF SECTIONS 6.5 AND 6.6

1 Only virulent strains of a pathogen can successfully establish a pathogenic infection on a sensitive host plant. Resistant hosts can respond to avirulent microbial pathogens with a strong, vertical resistance response, whereas a more generalized, horizontal resistance response can deter a wide range of potential pathogens.

2 Constitutive plant defences are always present, but induced defences are only activated in response to a challenge by a pathogen or more generalized wounding events, e.g. grazing by herbivores.

3 Induced defences include:

(a) reinforcement of the cell wall, e.g. by cross-linking with lignin, tannin, and the addition of callose;

(b) phytoalexins (low molecular mass, secondary chemicals), which act as mild antibiotics with low specificity, e.g. flavonoid derivatives like glyceollin and medicarpin;

(c) hypersensitive response — that is, the rapid collapse and death of cells challenged by a pathogen;

(d) pathogenesis-related proteins, some of which, like chitinases, have antimicrobial activity, and others which are involved in inducing other resistance responses;

(e) systemic acquired resistance — that is, a generalized increase in resistance, analogous to the development of immunity in animal systems, which makes the entire plant more resistant to a diverse range of pathogens following a single infection event.

4 The defence responses are coordinated by a complex signalling system involving ion fluxes, an oxidative burst, a phosphorylation poise, the accumulation of salicylic acid and nitric oxide.

6.7 Recognition and response

You now know a little more about the plant defence system, but, of course, plants do not always activate these defensive mechanisms when invaded by microbes; virulent pathogens can avoid, as well as disable, host defensive measures, and mutualists seem to avoid them almost entirely. Just as pathogens and symbionts can detect the presence of a potential host, so clearly the host plant can recognize the presence of the microbe and respond accordingly. So just how do plants distinguish between microbial friend and foe?

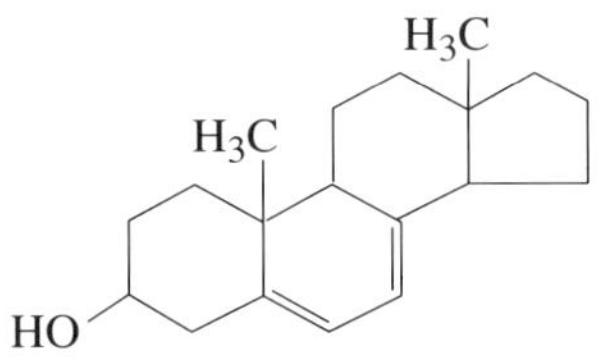

ergosterol

Certainly, plants have an exquisitely sensitive chemoperception system for substances derived from microbes. They can perceive many common cellular components such as certain oligosaccharides and lipophilic substances like ergosterol (the main sterol in most higher fungi) at threshold concentrations of 10^{-12}–10^{-10} mol l^{-1}. In fact, plant chemoperception systems resemble olfactory (smell) perception in animals, in that plants can recognize ‘non-self’ molecules characteristic of fungi and bacteria with a high degree of specificity, but some of them show rapid desensitization, leading to a refractory state — that is, one where further stimulation fails to elicit a response.

6.7.1 Recognizing pathogens

Factors that stimulate defence responses are called **elicitors**. We know that plants can be induced to synthesize and release antimicrobial compounds when exposed to common microbial components including cell-wall constituents such as polysaccharides, lipids and proteins, as well as enzymes that pathogens use to degrade the plant cell wall. They are termed **exogenous elicitors**, because they originate outside the host plant. In contrast, fragments of *host* cell wall also induce defence reactions (presumably because they are symptomatic of cell-wall damage caused by invading pathogens); such host-derived elicitors are termed **endogenous**. A high proportion of both kinds of elicitor are common to many plant–pathogen interactions and so are unlikely to be capable of inducing a vertical resistance response. (Remember, vertical resistance is highly specific as to pathogen race and host variety, and involves the full defence response including the HR.) The elicitors that induce an HR must be much rarer, more distinctive molecules, and the recognition mechanisms in the host plants are much more discerning.

As to the mechanism of recognition, some sort of signal/receptor arrangement would seem most likely. In the 1950s, H. H. Flor described his **gene-for-gene model**, which explains the genetic basis for vertical plant resistance to pathogens. He found that dominant **avirulence, *AVR*** genes in *Melampsora lini,* a fungal rust pathogen of flax, determine avirulence on flax containing dominant, complementary ***R* (resistance) genes**. It was postulated that the protein products of the *AVR* gene, later termed 'race-specific elicitors', are recognized by the products of *R* genes, which are receptors, and that a true match between the products of the *AVR* and the *R* gene provokes a resistant reaction. Figure 6.20 illustrates how this model is thought to work.

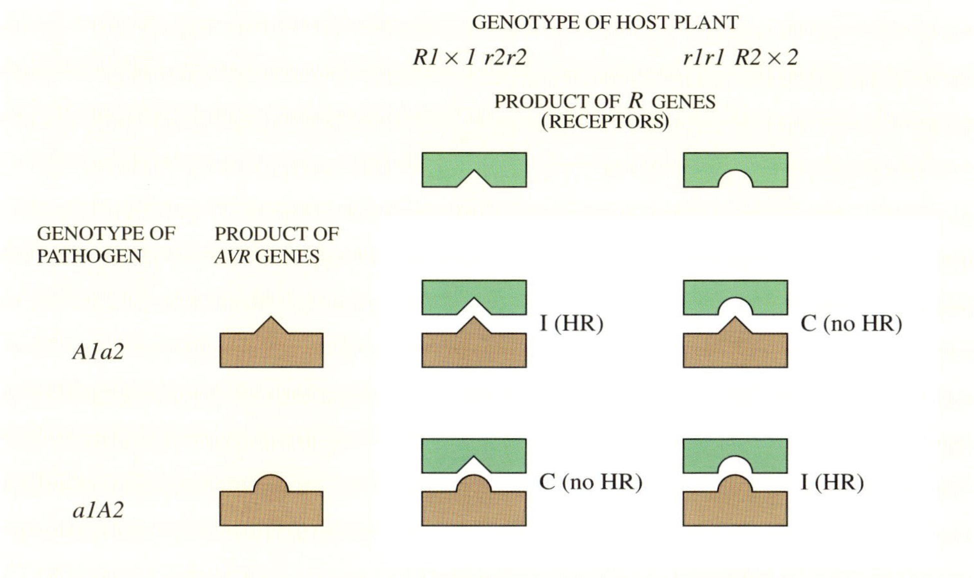

Figure 6.20 Diagram illustrating the gene-for-gene hypothesis for *AVR* ('avirulence') and *R* ('resistance') genes. The designation ×1 indicates that this allele can be either *R*1 or *r*1; ×2 indicates that this allele can be either *R*2 or *r*2. Abbreviations: I, incompatible interaction associated with the hypersensitive response (plant is resistant): C, compatible interaction not associated with the hypersensitive response (plant is susceptible); HR, hypersensitive response. Courtesy of De Wit, 1997)

Thus, **dominant** alleles of *AVR* genes (*A1* or *A2* in Figure 6.20) encode an antigenic molecule that, after recognition by a complementary receptor in a particular plant genotype, initiates the HR and other plant defence responses, including the accumulation of phytoalexins and PR-proteins, etc. It is important to realize that avirulence is not the result of the pathogenic race lacking something; it comes about because the avirulent pathogen produces something acting as a signal that is recognized by a resistant host.

- ❍ Look at Figure 6.20. What happens if either or both of the products of the *AVR* and *R* genes are missing or are not complementary?

- ● No HR is initiated because a signal molecule does not bind to a receptor. Therefore, the microbial infection may well become established.

The system shows significant parallels with the innate immune system found in animals (Davey and Gillman, 2001), but there are also some contrasts; for example, the animal system involves lots of cell movement, whereas in the plant system the cells are static.

AVR products may be recognized intracellularly or extracellularly depending on the life cycle of the pathogen. Structurally, they encode proteins that are involved in production of pathogenicity factors such as cell-wall degrading enzymes or ion channel blockers. A common feature of these elicitors is the presence of a cysteine-rich domain, which is thought to be the site involved in binding to receptors on the *R* gene product. *R* gene products, acting against very different pathogens, show a lot of structural homology. They all bear a leucine-rich repeating domain (LRR) towards one end, which is thought to represent the binding site of the receptor. The central portion may well be embedded in the plasma membrane (Figure 6.21), whereas the other end is involved in signal transduction, such as a protein kinase.

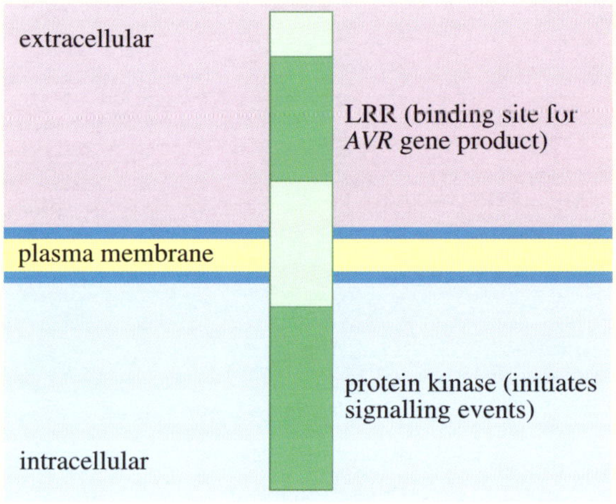

Figure 6.21 Schematic representation of a plant disease-resistance gene product (LRR = leucine-rich repeat).

❍ What sort of reactions do protein kinase enzymes catalyse?

● They catalyse the phosphorylation of proteins. (They are implicated in the phosphorylation poise regulation of the oxidative burst, see Section 6.6.6.)

The control of horizontal resistance is less well understood. Wall thickening, phytoalexin production and lignification can be induced by a range of factors like common cell-wall components, abrasion and toxic ions that cannot be described as race-specific. It is thought that they work either by generating ion fluxes directly, or perhaps through less specific binding to receptors, or binding to different receptors, in the plant plasma membrane, generating lower levels of signalling molecules.

6.7.2 Recognizing mutualists

Chemoperception of microbial substances also plays a role in mutualistic symbioses. The process of establishing arbuscular mycorrhizas and nitrogen-fixing nodules has already been described in some detail, but we now need to consider how these microbes manage to avoid the host defensive response.

Rhizobia and the host response

The establishment of nitrogen-fixing nodules in legumes starts with signal exchange. In the first step, flavonoids (produced by the phenylpropanoid pathway) are excreted by the plant and induce the transcription of *bacterial* nodulation genes (***NOD* genes**) by activating the promoter. The induction of these *NOD* genes lead to the synthesis of substances called **Nod factors**. These can induce various responses in the plant root, such as root hair deformation, depolarization of the root hair membrane potential (ion fluxes), induction of **nodulin** gene expression, and formation of nodule primordia; nodulins are plant proteins involved in nodule morphogenesis. Figure 6.22 illustrates a model to explain this 'molecular conversation' and how Nod factors may be detected (Heidstra and Bisseling, 1996).

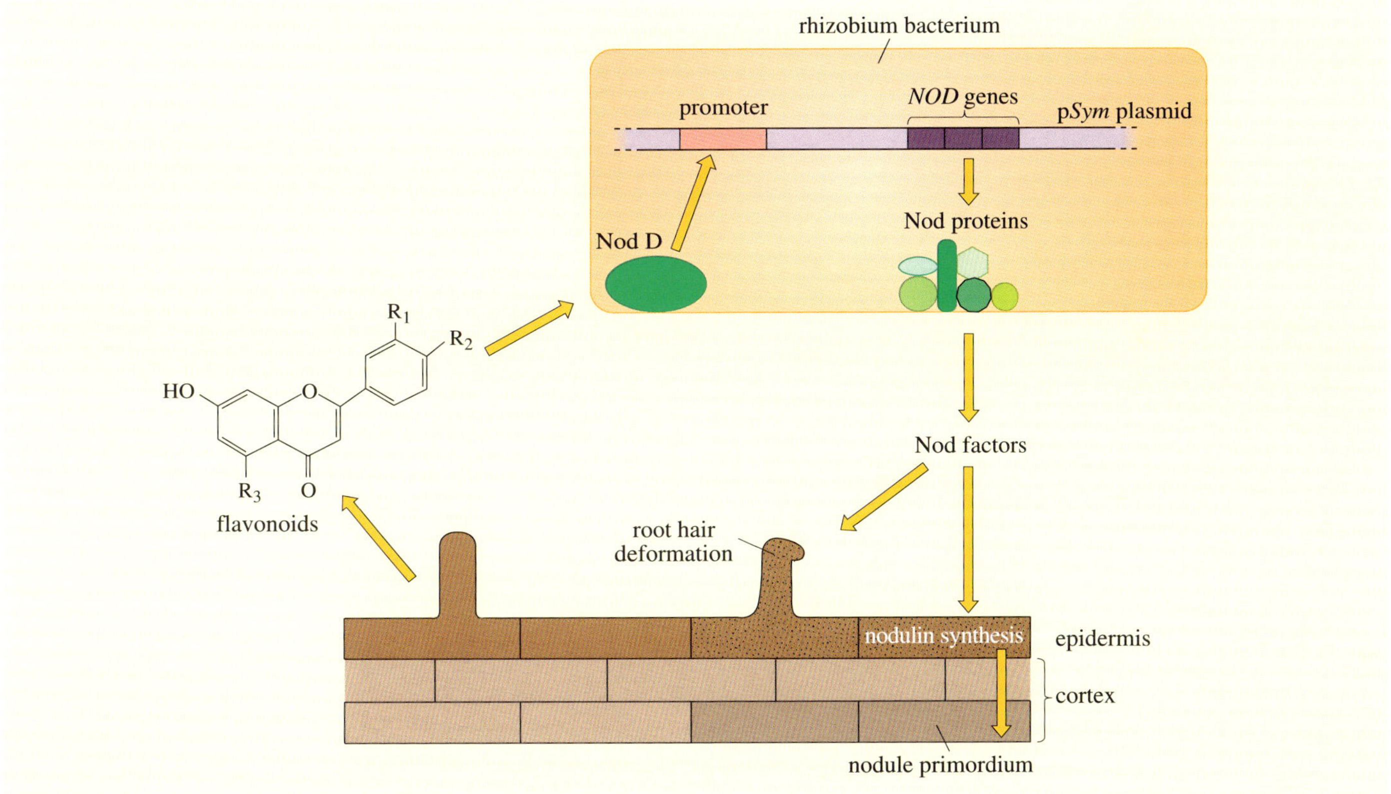

Figure 6.22 Early events in the legume–*Rhizobium* interaction. Flavonoids excreted by the plant induce the transcription of bacterial nodulation genes (*NOD* genes). Constitutively expressed *NOD D* gene product is a receptor for specific flavonoids. This complex then activates the other *NOD* genes. The Nod proteins are involved in the synthesis of Nod factors, which in turn induce responses like root hair deformation, nodulin gene expression and formation of nodule primordia.

NOD genes are present on the p*Sym* plasmid in those *Rhizobium* spp. capable of forming nodules. Each rhizobial strain possesses a range of *NOD* genes, some of which help to determine the host range of the bacterium. Most *NOD* genes need to be induced by the presence of flavonoids from the host plant. However, *NOD D* is expressed constitutively, and encodes a receptor for specific flavonoids. Different plants secrete different flavonoid inducers, thus providing a mechanism for host recognition by the rhizobial bacteria. The product of *NOD D* bound to its ligand then acts as an activator of the other *NOD* genes. The Nod-factor signal molecules generated bear a strong resemblance to chitin.

- ❍ Which types of organisms contain substantial quantities of chitin?
- ● Chitin is a major cell wall component of all fungi (but not the protoctist Oomycota). It is also found in the skeletons of arthropods.

Chitin is a polymer of β-1,4-linked *N*-acetylglucosamine (Figure 6.23), which can elicit a hypersensitive response (HR) on a large number of hosts (Section 6.6.3). But Nod factor recognition shows extreme host-specificity, and sets in motion the development of the nodules. Nod factor molecules have substitutions on the terminal β-1,4-linked *N*-acetylglucosamine units of the chitin molecule (Figure 6.23); these vary from one bacterial strain to another. So, chitin (unmodified β-1,4-linked *N*-acetylglucosamine) is a signal that plants interpret as evidence of a pathogen, but it is the additional modifications on Nod factors that perhaps coax the plant into accepting rhizobia as symbionts.

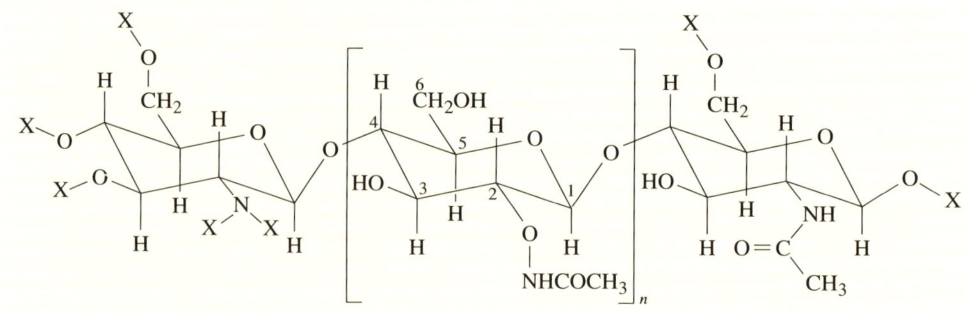

Figure 6.23 The general structure of Nod factors. The various substitutions on the *N*-acetylglucosamine units are indicated by the letter X; the nature of X depends on the particular bacterium.

The obvious implication is that a receptor must be involved in the perception of Nod factors, and evidence suggests that the Nod factor molecules are indeed recognized at the plant cell surface. Nod factors induce several changes in the host, including the synthesis of nodulins. Some nodulins resemble growth regulators such as cytokinins (Chapter 5), which would be consistent with a role as a diffusible signalling molecule involved in nodule primordium activation. The processes leading to nodule establishment may have evolved from those leading to pathogen recognition, but if so the process is not yet perfect. Only a small percentage of infections are successful. HR curtails the development of most attempts and activation of PAL and CHS enzymes is common. It appears that successful bacteria actively suppress the defences of the plant, rendering them more susceptible to infection.

ARBUSCULAR MYCORRHIZA FORMATION

Research into the role of genetic factors involved in recognition events in the formation of mycorrhizas has lagged somewhat behind that for plant–pathogen or the rhizobia–legume interactions, but enough data exist for some useful comparisons to be made. Pea mutants have been identified that are unable to form either nodules or AM associations.

❍ What does this observation imply about the role of the host genome in AM formation?

● AM formation must be partly under the control of the host genome.

Moreover, more than one gene is implicated, because symbiont development can be stopped at different stages. These so-called 'symbiosis' genes seem to have a general spectrum of action, since their mutation affects at least two types of plant–microbe interaction — nodules and mycorrhizas. However, there is some specificity, because they do not affect interactions with a range of pathogenic organisms. Other pea mutants can form mycorrhizas, but are unable to form nodules.

❍ What is the genetic implication of this finding?

● Additional symbiosis genes are implicated in the formation of mutualisms that are specific to either nodules or mycorrhizas.

AM fungi produce elicitors that induce transient and weak activation of defence mechanisms — that is, no HR — but there can be low activation of the phenylpropanoid pathway, callose production, PR-proteins production, etc. This response may include brief stimulation of flavonoid production, and several flavonoid/isoflavonoid intermediates of the phenylpropanoid pathway are known to stimulate hyphal growth or root colonization by AM fungi.

❍ In what other mutualistic associations do flavonoids act as signals between symbionts?

● In the rhizobial nodule associations (Section 6.3.2).

We know that mycorrhizal fungi apply mechanical pressure rather than cell-wall degrading enzymes when penetrating the host cell wall, but this difference cannot be the whole story. The weak defence response in AM formation is not due to symbiotic fungi lacking essential signal molecules, because they can elicit resistance responses in mutated host plants. Plant defence responses must be controlled or suppressed during establishment of the mycorrhizas. Exactly how this suppression is brought about is not clear yet, but results to date suggest that different mechanisms from those involved in plant–pathogen interactions must be operating. Indeed, it is possible to produce genetically modified plants with increased pathogen resistance without reducing their ability to form symbiotic associations with AM fungi.

In one of the more popular scenarios, the fungus is initially attracted by flavonoids in plant root exudates. As the hyphae approach the root tip, they encounter plant growth regulators (e.g. *zeatin*, a cytokinin), which induce changes in hyphal growth — such as altered branching patterns — necessary for the onset of mycorrhiza formation. The fungus produces oligosaccharides that coincide with a short-lived burst of plant defence responses — for example, the accumulation of chitinases, and the induction of systemic acquired resistance. The fungus also produces signalling molecules such as **hypaphorine**, which blocks root hair elongation and counteracts the effects of the plant growth regulator IAA, which stimulates hair production.

- ❍ Why is the lack of root hairs not detrimental to the plant?

- ● Root hairs are not needed by mycorrhizal plants because the fungus takes over their role in acquiring water and mineral nutrients.

However, the exact mechanisms involved at each stage remain to be fully elucidated, and are the subject of active research. Certainly, plant growth regulators seem to play a role. One possibility is that products of symbiosis-related plant genes, under the influence of a fungal activator, might limit directly the expression of defence genes. Alternatively, fungus-derived suppressor molecules, such as oligosaccharide derivatives, may be induced by activated symbiosis-related genes in the fungus, and may be responsible for the diminished host defence response.

6.7.3 Knowing the enemy: concluding remarks

Not all microbes elicit defence responses from the host plant. The reactions that occur, and the path that the interaction takes, is determined by a complex molecular conversation. Some aspects of the molecular conversation involved in establishing both mutualistic and parasitic associations are similar: the microbial components are attracted by exudates from the higher plant; the plant recognizes products from the microbe which either induce defence responses or initiate the establishment of the mutualistic structure. In the case of pathogenic interactions, it is in the interest of both parties to minimize recognition by the other, whereas in the case of mutualisms, it is in the interest of both parties to promote recognition by the other. Recognition of avirulent pathogens and rhizobial strains is very precise and specific, unlike recognition in mycorrhizal fungi and virulent pathogens.

Some, but not all, steps in the infection processes for mutualistic associations are controlled by common genetic determinants, whereas recognition of pathogens involves quite distinct groups of genes. Arbuscular mycorrhizas are thought to be the most ancient associations involving land plants, with coevolution leading to a progressively tighter interdependence between the two symbionts. It is possible that the evolution of mycorrhizas may have facilitated evolution of nodules since a number of genes are common to the early events in establishing both mutualisms. In contrast, pathogenic associations are thought to have evolved more recently and in reciprocal steps, rather like an arms race, in which the evolution of each new means of overcoming the host plant's defences by the pathogen is then matched by the evolution of a new defence mechanism by the plant (see Davey and Gillman, 2001).

Summary of Section 6.7

1 Plants have an exquisitely sensitive chemoperception system, which they use to distinguish between mutualists and pathogens by engaging in a more-or-less subtle molecular conversation with adjacent microbes.

2 The gene-for-gene model of vertical plant resistance involves a recognition event in which the product of an avirulence gene, in an avirulent pathogen, binds to a receptor, encoded by a complementary resistance gene, in a resistant host. This event initiates defence responses in the plant that prevent the infection becoming established.

3 Functional root nodules result from a very specific interaction between rhizobia and the roots of legumes involving flavonoids from the plant, which induce the production of Nod factors in the bacteria. Some Nod factors are modified chitin, and are recognized by receptors on the plant's roots as evidence of a mutualistic symbiont, which enables nodule formation to occur.

4 Arbuscular mycorrhiza formation is less specific, but involves some of the same plant genes that operate in nodule formation, and a response to flavonoids from the plant by the fungus.

5 How mutualists manage to minimize the host defence responses is not fully understood: the use of mechanical pressure rather than cell-wall degrading enzymes is only part of the story. Other plant and/or microbial genes must be involved in suppressing the host defence response.

6 Mutualisms appear to have resulted from coevolution by the symbionts, whereas pathogenic associations probably evolved in reciprocal steps, like an 'arms race'.

6.8 Mycorrhizas in the community

This chapter has probably made it apparent to you that, historically, scientists have tended to focus their attention on the disease-causing microbes. Damage to crops, to raw materials for industry, and even to humans, meant that more funds were available to sponsor research into the pathogens rather than the mutualists. However, recent fears of overpopulation, pollution and unsustainability of agriculture have redirected attention to the role of the mutualists in community productivity and dynamics. The result has been some quite remarkable findings that should revolutionize the way we think about the role of microbes, especially fungi, in ecosystem function.

6.8.1 VARIATIONS ALONG THE PARASITIC–MUTUALISTIC AXIS

Mycorrhizas are considered to be classic mutualisms, in that there is a reciprocal exchange of mineral and organic resources. However, this interpretation is not always correct; there is evidence that some mycorrhizal associations behave more like parasitisms, in that the fungus is a net drain on the host plant's resources. The majority of mycorrhizal fungi are obligate biotrophs, deriving obvious benefits from the association, but what factors may affect the balance of advantage to the host plant?

Mycorrhizal associations are complex hierarchical systems (Figure 6.24).

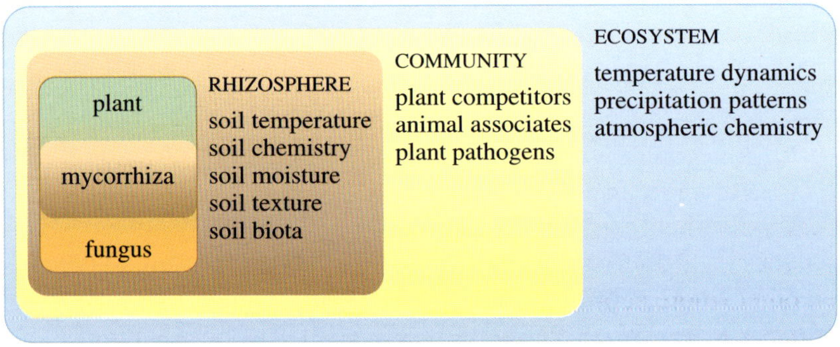

Figure 6.24 The functioning of mycorrhizal systems is mediated by a hierarchy of abiotic and biotic factors.

- ❍ Which levels of influence (plant, fungus, rhizosphere, community, ecosytem) do the following types of change affect?
  (a) A coal burning power station is shut down.
  (b) The host trees suffer a heavy infestation of caterpillars.

- ● (a) This change would produce a drop in emissions that lead to acid precipitation, so it would affect the ecosystem (atmospheric chemistry) and the rhizosphere (soil chemistry).
  (b) This change would affect the community (plant pathogens/herbivores), which would in turn affect the plant (health of the host).

At the core are a fungus and plant living symbiotically. But the dual organism does not function in isolation; the mycorrhiza is subjected to direct and indirect effects from biotic and abiotic factors in the surrounding rhizosphere, community and ecosystem. Furthermore, the larger the scale of interest, the greater the potential for mycorrhizal responses to be influenced by indirect interactions. Mycorrhizas can be grown from plant and fungus propagules inoculated into sterile media in a growth chamber that is isolated from biotic and abiotic factors in the environment.

❍ Could data obtained from this sort of laboratory set-up be used to answer questions concerning, (a) the physiology of the association, and (b) the ecology of mycorrhizas?

● Such an arrangement can answer physiological questions (a), but not ecological ones (b).

Thus, some reports of 'parasitic effects' of mycorrhizal fungi may have been generated by oversimplified experimental systems, or over too short a time period, all of which serves to emphasize the dangers inherent in extrapolating laboratory findings to predict outcomes in natural or agricultural environments. When attempting to find explanations for certain phenomena, it is important to address the appropriate level of the hierarchy.

Mycorrhizal associations are beneficial (mutualistic) to plants when net costs are less than net benefits, and detrimental (parasitic) when costs exceed benefits (Figure 6.25). But whether an association is judged to be parasitic may depend on how costs and benefits are measured; they need to be measured in terms that are appropriate to the question of interest. Clearly, nutrient limitation is a key component of cost–benefit analysis of mycorrhizal effects on plant fitness. However, other (more subtle) fungus-induced changes might be more important to plant fitness; mycorrhizas affect many aspects of plant development and contribute to plant fitness by protecting plants from pathogens (Section 6.7.2) and toxic levels of metals in the soil (Chapter 4, Section 4.6.1).

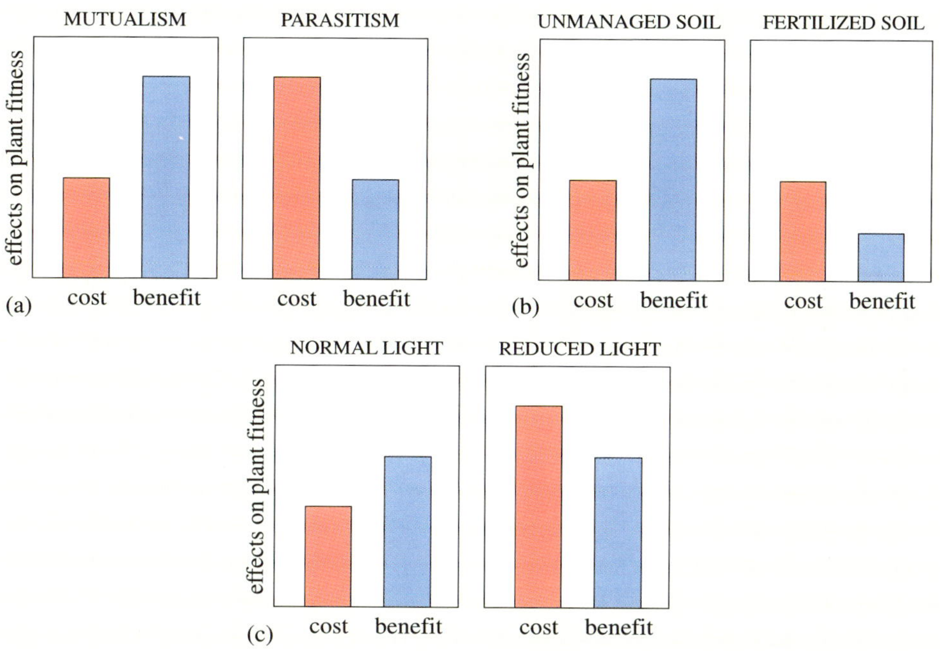

Figure 6.25 (a) Mycorrhizal associations are mutualistic to plants when benefits exceed costs, and parasitic when costs exceed benefits. (b) Use of fertilizers diminishes benefits, and can generate parasitic associations. (c) Factors that limit photosynthesis, such as reduced light, can generate parasitic associations by increasing relative costs.

❍ Recall how mycorrhizal fungi can protect plants from pathogens.

● Infection by mycorrhizal fungi can induce systemic acquired resistance, which increases the plant's resistance to infection by a wide range of potential pathogens.

These considerations are of more than semantic interest. There is potential for mycorrhizas to be used to boost productivity while reducing the application of fertilizers and possibly pesticides. But can we hope to understand these systems well enough to anticipate the consequences of anthropogenic changes and to manage them sustainably, in restoration, forestry and agriculture?

From Figure 6.24, fungal parasitism can be hypothesized to result from:

1 Developmental factors (temporal relationships of the plant–mycorrhiza–fungus)

Short-term losses (by the plant) are often compensated by long-term gains. (Look back at Figure 4.27 for an example.) The balance between net costs and net benefits is remarkably dynamic through the development of a mycorrhizal association, and it is dependent on interactions with the environment.

2 Environmental factors (outside the plant–mycorrhiza–fungus)

Fertilizing a system can eliminate resource limitations so that mycorrhizas become superfluous to host plants (Figure 6.25b). Humans might be inadvertently altering the relationships between plants and mycorrhizal fungi, and so might be affecting the cost–benefit balances. The human factors include:

- increased use of fertilizers over the years;
- deposition of nitrogen emitted (as ammonia) from livestock production;
- generation of oxides of nitrogen (which can be converted to $NO_3{}^{\bullet-}$ in the atmosphere) from internal combustion engines, which now exceeds natural inputs of fixed nitrogen in many ecosystems.

The alarming disappearance of mushroom-forming fungi, including a disproportionate number of ectomycorrhizal taxa, might be linked to anthropogenic inputs of nitrogen. Nitrogen fertilization can change the species composition of AM fungal communities.

Anthropogenic pollution can alter radiation levels and the photosynthetic potential of host plants. If these are limiting, allocation of the products of photosynthesis to a fungal partner may reduce plant allocation to functions related to its fitness (Figure 6.25c). Herbivores consume photosynthetic organs, so high numbers of herbivores could deplete plant carbon reserves to the extent that the cost of maintaining a mycorrhizal association outweighs its benefits. Positive mycorrhizal growth responses decrease as the density of plants increases, apparently as a result of competition between neighbouring mycorrhizal roots. Hence growth of all the individual adjacent plants is reduced compared with that of plants spaced well apart.

❍ What are the possible implications of these observations for farmers?

● Mycorrhizas are likely to be least effective in boosting plant productivity where agriculture is most intensive.

It is not uncommon to find little benefit in improved growth from AM associations in the field.

3 GENOTYPIC FACTORS (INSIDE THE PLANT–MYCORRHIZA–FUNGUS)

Mycorrhizal dependency varies greatly among taxa and varieties of plants. However, the great majority of plants are **mycotrophic** (obtain nourishment via fungi) to some degree. Fungal taxa and isolates vary in mycorrhizal effectiveness, and some isolates of AM fungi can be beneficial on some crop species but parasitic on others. We don't know if there are genotypes of fungi that are universally bad for plants, but logically, the evolution of fungal genotypes that 'cheat' (i.e. act as parasites) is highly likely, as there are massive short-term gains to be made by such fungi.

- ❍ Why should the short-term gains mean that the evolution of 'cheating' fungal genotypes is very probable?

- ● Because mutants that 'cheat' gain relatively more net benefit from the association with plants, than true mutualists. Therefore the 'cheats' can leave more progeny than the mutualists, and so the alleles for 'cheating' will spread in the population.

Native plant populations have diverse gene pools that are continually modified through selection pressures exerted by their environment, which includes local mycorrhizal fungi. Over time, plant genotypes that maximize mycorrhizal benefits would be at a selective advantage, and come to predominate in the population. However, crop plants and plantation stock have no mechanisms to link their gene pool with mycorrhizal functioning. Fertilization and ploughing might further uncouple the link between plants and mycorrhizal fungal evolution. Thus, management practices might actually select for mycorrhizal fungi that are 'cheaters'.

In conclusion, mutualism and parasitism are extremes of a dynamic continuum of interspecific interactions. Mycorrhizal associations are generally at the mutualistic end of the continuum, but they can be parasitic when the genotypes of the symbionts do not form suitably compatible combinations, or when the stage of plant development or environmental conditions make costs greater than benefits (Figure 6.26).

- ❍ Towards which end of the mutualism/parasitism continuum would the mycorrhizal phenotype move if the nutrient status of the soil increased?

- ● The mycorrhizal phenotype would move towards the parasitism end of the continuum. (The plant genotype would become less dependent on mycorrhizas to acquire adequate soil resources. There would also be less potential for the fungus to deliver limiting resources to the plant.)

Usually, by living together, plants and mycorrhizal fungi improve each other's probability of survival and reproductive success, but sometimes their 'interests' are in conflict.

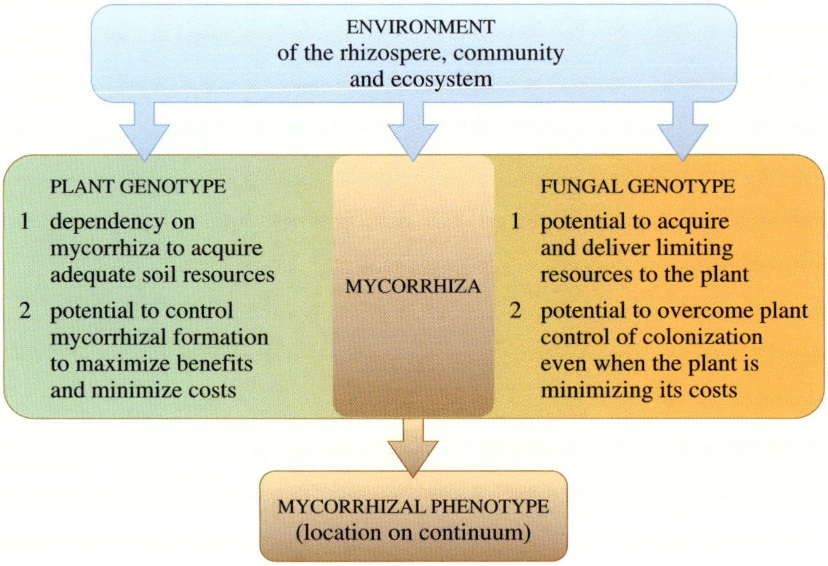

Figure 6.26 Mycorrhizal phenotypes are manifestations of the interaction between plant and fungal genotypes and environmental conditions. These factors determine the functioning of mycorrhizas along the mutualism–parasitism continuum. 1 denotes mutualistic tendencies, and 2 denotes parasitic tendencies.

- Under what circumstances is such a conflict of interests likely to arise?

- It is most likely to arise in highly managed agricultural systems, where fertilization eliminates shortages of soil nutrients, grazing reduces plant photosynthesis and plant genotypes are selected by humans and not by millennia of natural selection.

6.8.2 Multiorganism networks: the 'wood-wide web'

The previous section has emphasized the importance of thinking about mycorrhizal plants within their environmental context, which should include neighbouring mycorrhizal plants. However, recent field research has now revealed a possible, startling new role for mycorrhizal fungi in forming a web of interplant connections, which has an important influence on resource allocation and community composition.

In the nutrient-impoverished conditions that prevail in forests, at least 90% of the 'feeding' roots of the tree are colonized by ectomycorrhizal fungi, but, because most mycorrhizal fungi are catholic in their choice of host species, a single fungus may infect the roots of numerous trees. The roots of trees such as the Douglas fir (*Pseudotsuga menziesii)* or birch (*Betula* spp.), can be colonized by many fungal species, the mycelia of which extend from tree to tree, providing linkages between them (Figure 6.27). In an undisturbed forest ecosystem, almost all of the trees, irrespective of their taxonomic affinities, are interconnected by a diverse population of mycelial systems.

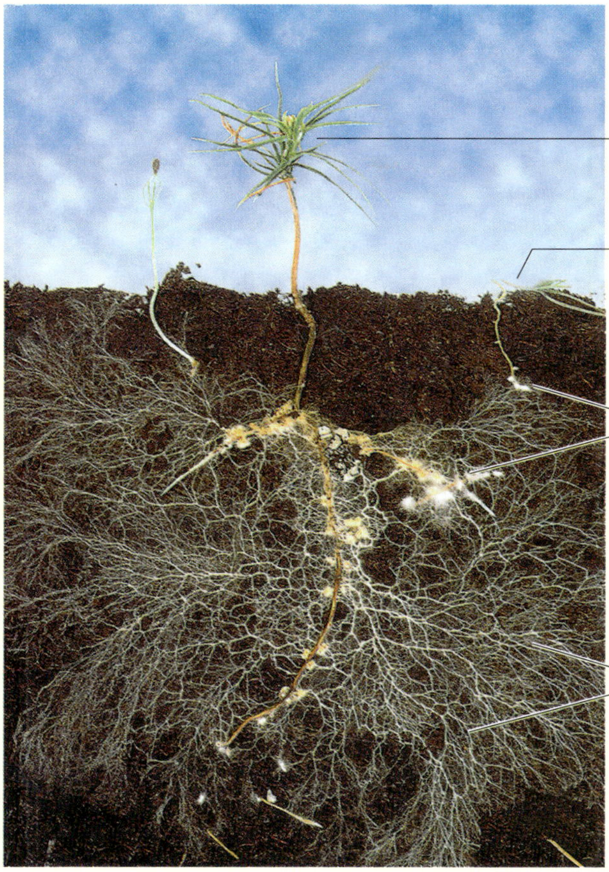

Figure 6.27 Ectomycorrhizal fungus linking two conifer plants. The younger seedling forms a mycorrhiza with the pre-existing mycorrhiza associated with the older plant.

In a recent field-based study, it has been shown that net transfer of *carbon* can occur between neighbouring ectomycorrhizal tree species, both of which share up to ten mutually compatible fungal symbionts. It is important to note that many scientists remain unconvinced by the current evidence.

THE 'WOOD-WIDE WEB' AND CARBON TRANSFER

There have been a number of recent reports claiming that, in the laboratory at least, carbon can be transported from plant to plant via a common mycorrhizal network. A recent paper by Simard *et al.* (1997) presents evidence that such carbon transfer can occur in the field. The study involved establishing seedlings of three naturally occurring, woodland tree species, in small groups. These included two ectomycorrhizal species (a birch, *Betula papyrifera*, and Douglas fir, *Pseudotsuga menziesii*), and an endomycorrhizal cedar (*Thuja plicata*).

- ❍ Why do you suppose the endomycorrhizal cedar was included in the experiment?
- ● To act as a control. Because this species is endomycorrhizal, it should not form fungal linkages with the other two species. Therefore it should be possible to detect transfer of carbon between trees by routes other than the linkages formed by ectomycorrhizal fungi.

Two low natural-abundance isotopes of carbon, ^{13}C and ^{14}C, were used to examine carbon transfer between the trees. Birch and Douglas fir trees in each group were labelled with gaseous $^{13}CO_2$ or $^{14}CO_2$. (This approach enabled the carbon isotope that was received by one seedling to be distinguished from that applied to the other.) The movement of the two isotopes of carbon was then traced. In addition, the fir seedlings were exposed to three light treatments: deep shade, partial shade or full ambient sunlight.

When the seedlings were subsequently harvested and the *roots* were analysed for the presence of the two isotopes of carbon, it was found that carbon transfer between the birch and the Douglas fir occurred in both directions By the end of the second year, there was a net gain in carbon by the Douglas fir in all three light intensities (Figure 6.28).

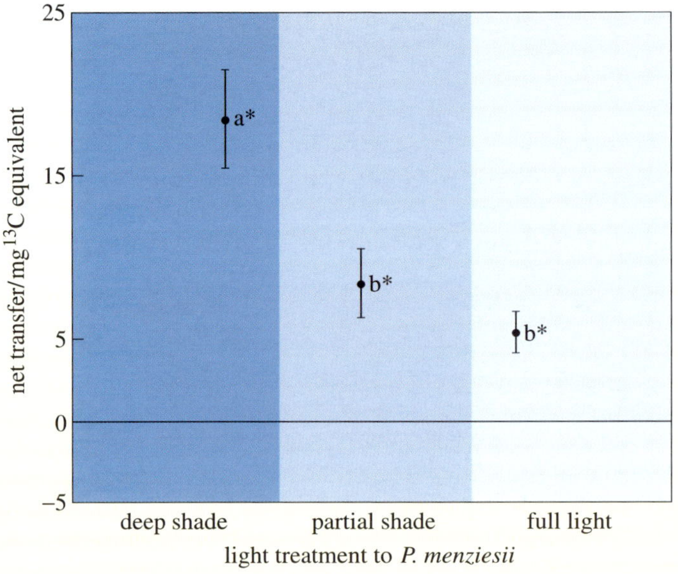

Figure 6.28 Mean (± standard error) *net* transfer of carbon from *B. papyrifera* to *P. menziesii* in deep shade, partial shade and full sunlight after the second year of the experiment. Means denoted by the same letter do not differ significantly ($P < 0.05$). Asterisks indicate treatments in which net transfer was greater than zero ($P < 0.05$). (The *y*-axis is labelled in terms of ^{13}C equivalent to take account of the slightly differing relative atomic masses of ^{13}C and ^{14}C.) Data from Simard *et al.*, 1997.

- ❍ From Figure 6.28, in which light treatment was net transfer to the Douglas fir greatest?
- ● The deep shade treatment.

The greater transfer of carbon to Douglas fir in shaded rather than lighter conditions is a function of the lower photosynthetic rates in the more shaded firs, which suggests that carbon was transferred from species with relatively high levels of photosynthetic products to species with lower levels of photosynthetic products. Moreover, no such transfer occurred between the ectomycorrhizal species and the endomycorrhizal cedar.

- ❍ What does this finding suggest about the importance of interplant hyphal links in nutrient transfer?
- ● The implication is that most carbon transfer between the ectomycorrhizal tree species occurred through hyphal connections and not via respired CO_2, exudates or sloughed root or fungal cells.

This study apparently demonstrated that the direction of net carbon transfer may be determined by the amount of pre-existing carbon in the recipient. If these findings can be extrapolated to the natural population, they could have very important consequences for forest population dynamics. Most forest trees spend the early part of their lives as seedlings in the gloom of the forest floor. The fungi of the 'wood-wide web' are maintained by supplies of carbon from the canopy trees, so a seedling that forms mycorrhizas with these fungi may well obtain 'free' mineral nutrients from them. But it *may* be that the shaded understorey also obtains carbohydrates from the fully illuminated overstorey plants, through pathways provided by their fungal symbionts; this might well make the difference between survival or death for the seedlings. Some plants, such as the Bird's-nest family Monotropaceae, totally lack chlorophyll, so they receive all their carbon from photosynthesizing trees through mycorrhizal connections. If mycorrhizal colonization results in an equalization of resource availability, as suggested by this study, it might be expected to reduce competition between plants and thereby limit the dominance of aggressive species, so promoting coexistence and greater biodiversity.

However, before we get carried away with this Utopian scenario, what about the dissenting voices? A number of objections have been raised to the quality of the evidence for plant-to-plant carbon movement through **common mycorrhizal networks (CMNs)** (Robinson and Fitter, 1999).

❍ Cite any weaknesses in the data presented, or other things you would want to know before you were convinced.

● Robinson and Fitter raised the following objections: (i) the amounts of carbon transferred via CMNs have not been quantified, and so it is not known if the amounts are physiologically or ecologically significant; (ii) the presence of transferred carbon in the shoots of recipient plants has not been demonstrated, so there is no proof that transferred carbon ever leaves the fungal tissues of the mycorrhizal roots.

❍ Do these objections mean that we must reject the hypothesis that it is possible for plants to obtain biologically meaningful carbon supplies from other plants via a CMN?

● No, they only imply that there is insufficient evidence to categorically accept the hypothesis.

So sceptics and enthusiasts alike await further evidence to clarify the situation.

The 'web' and plant diversity

The mechanisms that control plant biodiversity are still being debated, but, so far, little attention has been paid to the effects of plant–microbe interactions, particularly the influence of mycorrhizal symbiosis. However, another recent study has shown that the floristic diversity of two characteristically species-rich grasslands, one representative of calcareous grassland habitats in Europe and the other of abandoned fields in North America, depends on the presence of a species-rich assemblage of fungal symbionts in the soil.

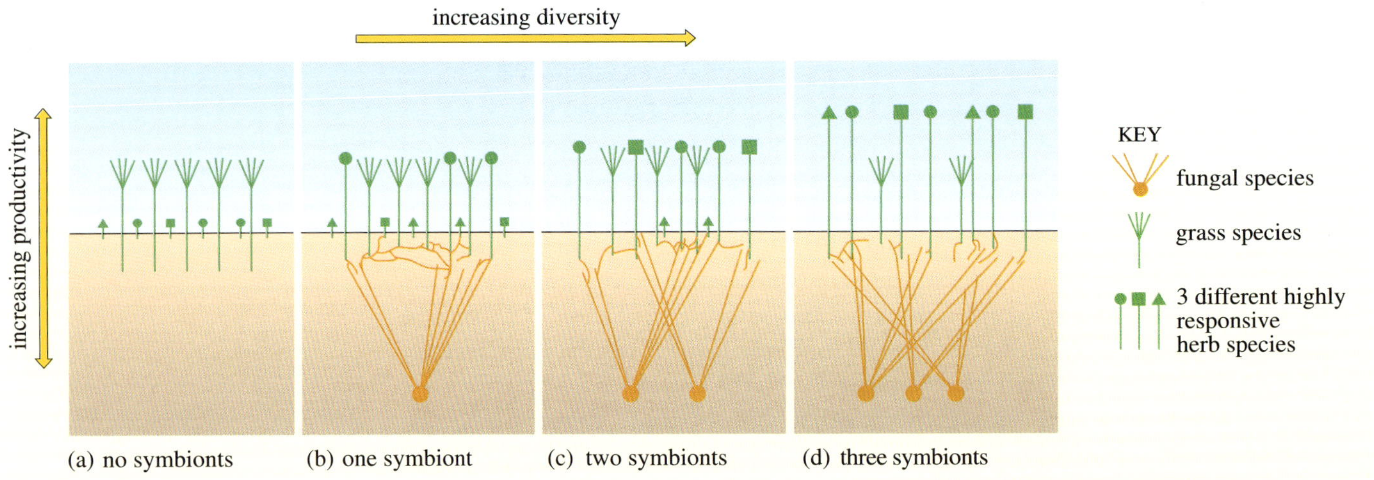

Figure 6.29 Possible basis for the effects of fungal species richness on plant biodiversity and production. In the absence of symbionts (a), species that are relatively unresponsive to mycorrhizal fungi (e.g. grasses) dominate. Addition of a fungal species, and then increase in their number (b–d) enables progressively more of the highly responsive herb species to develop, at the expense of the grasses. Courtesy of Read, 1998.

In the first experiment, four different species of AM fungi were added, either individually or in combination, to calcareous grassland communities, reconstructed in propagators in a greenhouse, and it was found that different host plants were promoted by different fungal species. In other words, changes to the combination of fungal taxa altered the structure and composition of the plant community significantly. These findings imply that plant biodiversity will increase as the number of fungal symbionts increases, because of the additive beneficial effect of each single fungal species. This concept is illustrated diagrammatically in Figure 6.29 (Read, 1998).

This hypothesis was tested in a second experiment using abandoned-field communities (van der Heijden *et al.*,1998). In this case, 0 to 14 fungal species were added per treatment. As the number of fungal species per system was increased, the collective species diversity of the plant community rose, as did the biomass of shoots and roots (Figure 6.30 a-c).

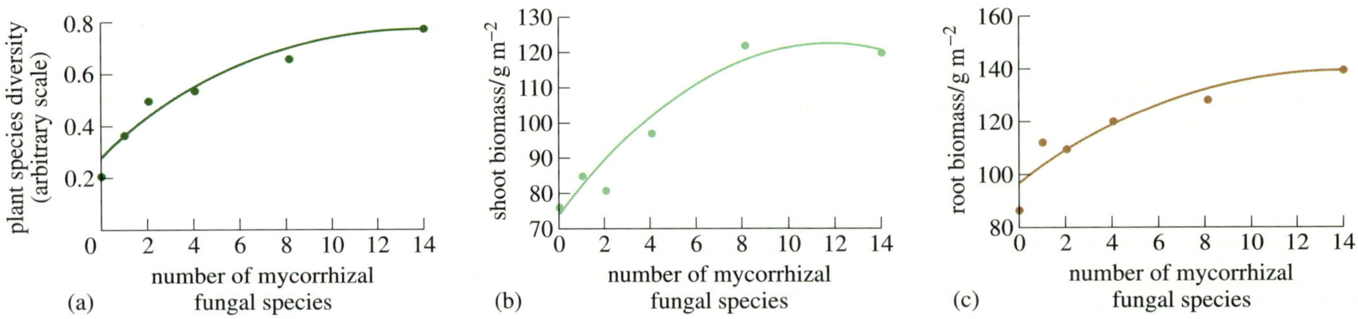

Figure 6.30 The effect of AM fungal species richness on different parameters. Effects on (a) plant community diversity, (b) shoot biomass, (c) root biomass. Data from van der Heijden *et al.*, 1998.

❍ What do these results imply about the relationship between biodiversity and productivity?

● That productivity rises as biodiversity rises (b and c indicate productivity).

Differences in functional compatibility can explain both the stimulatory effect on individual plant species and the influence of fungal species diversity on the overall structure of the plant community. Greater functional compatibility could arise when one fungus, among a group occupying a root system, enables one particular plant species to perform better than the others.

Empirical studies support the view that floristically rich systems are more productive, show greater stability under stress and are more likely to provide amelioration of global problems posed by increased atmospheric CO_2 levels. The implication of the findings presented above, is that a diverse fungal community will be a prerequisite for floristic diversity not only in grasslands, but also in temperate forests. We know that the mycorrhizal community is sensitive to environmental perturbations, especially those associated with cultivation and nutrient enrichment. So these findings are important to those working in the fields of conservation, land restoration, agriculture or forestry who seek to optimize floristic diversity and/or promote high productivity.

In the 1980s many mycorrhizal researchers optimistically predicted that mycorrhizal associations could be successfully managed to reduce reliance on chemical fertilizers, but so far few of the promises concerning the applied value of mycorrhizal fungi in agriculture, forestry and horticulture have been fulfilled. One of the problems may be that commercial production favours intensive **monoculture** (large areas densely sown with a single crop species). These findings suggest that mycorrhizas may be actively unhelpful in these conditions.

❍ Why might mycorrhizas be unhelpful to commercial growers?

● Mycorrhizas promote growth least well where the soil is fertile, competition between crop plants is intense, and host plants are not adapted to the local environment. The experimental results reported here also imply that CMNs may actually reduce crop yields by encouraging the growth of crop competitors — that is, weeds.

Certainly, the ecological complexity of mycorrhizal systems has been underestimated. Knowledge of the full spectrum of plant responses to mycorrhiza formation, and the factors generating these responses in complex systems would enable us to develop a predictive model of mycorrhizal functioning so that appropriate fungi for management or inoculation can be selected. Only then may the full potential of mycorrhizas be realized.

SUMMARY OF SECTION 6.8

1 Recent research has revealed that mycorrhizas may have important influences on plant community composition and function.

2 Normally mutualistic, mycorrhizal fungi can be parasitic under certain conditions, which include developmental factors, environmental factors such as nutrient availability, disturbance and population density, and genotypic factors that affect compatibility between the symbionts.

3 In natural woodland communities, individual trees are interconnected by a range of different mycorrhizal fungi to form a 'wood-wide web'.

4 Experiments have shown that carbon can move from plant to plant via the mycelium of the mycorrhizal fungi.

5 Seedlings and other ground dwelling plant species may obtain mineral and even carbohydrate nutriment from the mycorrhizal fungi, a process that is subsidized by the canopy trees.

6 Experiments have also shown that the diversity of the mycorrhizal fungal community can be directly proportional to the diversity and productivity of the associated plant community.

7 It is possible that increasing diversity in mycorrhizal fungal communities may help overcome problems such as pollution, and promote greater sustainability in agriculture and forestry.

References

Clements, M., and Saffrey, J. (2001) Cell communication. In J. Saffrey (ed.), *The Core of Life* Volume II, The Open University, Milton Keynes.

Davey, B., and Gillman, M. (2001) Defence. In M. Gillman (ed.), *Generating Diversity*, The Open University, Milton Keynes, pp. 151–200.

De Wit, P. J. G. M. (1997) Pathogen avirulence and plant resistance: a key role for recognition, *Trends in Plant Science*, **2**, pp. 453–8.

Heidstra, R., and Bisseling, T. (1996) Nod factor induced host responses and mechanisms of Nod factor perception, *New Phytol*ogy **133**, pp. 25–43.

Johnson, N. C., Graham, J. J., and Smith, F. A. (1997), Functioning of mycorrhizal associations along the mutualism–parasitism continuum, *New Phytol*ogy, **135**, pp. 575–85.

MacQueen, H., Burnett, J., and Cann, A. (2001) The study of microbes. In H. MacQueen (ed.), *Microbes*, The Open University, Milton Keynes, pp.1–64.

Pond, C. (2001) Dealing with food. In M. Gillman (ed.), *Generating Diversity*, The Open University, Milton Keynes, pp. 37–88.

Read, D. (1998) Plants on the web, *Nature*, **396**, pp. 22–3.

Robinson, D., and Fitter, A. (1999) The magnitude and control of carbon transfer between plants linked by a common mycorrhizal network', *Journal of Experimental Botany*, **50**, pp. 9–13.

Simard, S. W., Perry, D. A., Jones, M. D., Mynold, D. D., Durall, D. M., and Molina, R. (1997) Net transfer of carbon between ectomycorrhizal tree species in the field, *Nature*, **388**, pp. 579–82

van der Heijden, M. G. A., Klironomos, J. N., Ursic, M., Moutoglis, P., Streitwolf-Engel, R., Boller, T., Wiemken, A., and Sanders, I. R. (1998) Mycorrhizal fungal diversity determines plant biodiversity, ecosystem variability and productivity, *Nature*, **396**, pp. 69–72.

VanEtten, J. D., and Tegtmeier, K. J. (1982), *Phytopathology*, **72**, p. 609.

Walker, C. (2001) Microbes in the environment. In H. MacQueen (ed.), *Microbes*, The Open University, Milton Keynes, pp. 99–162.

Further Reading

Dickinson, C. J., and Lucas, J. A. (1992) *Plant Pathology and Plant Pathogens* (3rd edn), Blackwell. [Classic textbook on plant pathology.]

Read, D. J., Lewis, D. H., Fitter, A. H., and Alexander, I. J. (1992) *Mycorrhizas in Ecosystems*, CAB International. [Collection of papers by many current researchers in the field, giving a thorough overview of the ecological importance of mycorrhizas.]

Smith, F. A., and Read, D. J. (1997) *Mycorrhizal Symbiosis* (2nd edn), Academic Press. [Standard textbook on mycorrhizal structure and function.]

Postgate, J. (1992) *Microbes and Man* (3rd edn), Penguin.

Postgate, J. (1989) *Nitrogen Fixation* (2nd edn), Edward Arnold [A useful paperback, although now somewhat out of date.].

ACKNOWLEDGEMENTS

Grateful acknowledgement is made to the following sources for permission to reproduce material in this book:

CHAPTER 1

FIGURES

Figures 1.7a–f, 1.11a–c, 1.41: Phillips, R. (1980) *Grasses, Ferns, Mosses & Lichens of Great Britain and Ireland*, Macmillan Publishers Ltd, copyright © Roger Phillips 1980; *Figures 1.9a, 1.43, 1.46*: Raven, P. H., Evert, R. F. and Eichhorn, S. E. (1999) *Biology of Plants*, 6th edn, W. H. Freeman and Company, copyright © 1999 by W. H. Freeman and Company/Worth Publishers; *Figure 1.9b*: Copyright © G. Shih and R. Kessel/Visuals Unlimited, Inc.; *Figure 1.11e*: Courtesy of Sharon Bartholomew-Began, Georgia Southwestern University; *Figure 1.12*: Mauseth, J. D. (1998) *Botany: An Introduction to Plant Biology*, Jones & Bartlett Publishers, Sudbury, Ma. www.jbpub.com., reprinted with permission; *Figures 1.13, 1.15 and 1.18a*: Rose, R. (1989) *Colour Identification Guide to the Grasses, Sedges, Rushes and Ferns of the British Isles and North-Western Europe*, copyright © Francis Rose, 1989, line drawings by Laura Mason and Sophie Allington, reproduced with permission of Penguin Books Ltd; *Figures 1.16 and 1.19e*: Bell, P. R. and Woodcock, C. L. F. (1968) *The Diversity of Green Plants*, Edward Arnold, copyright © Peter R. Bell and Christopher L. F. Woodcock, 1968; *Figures 1.18b, 1.27d and 1.31a*: Perry, J. W., and Morton, D. (1998) *Photo Atlas For Botany*, Wadsworth Publishing Company, copyright © 1998 by Wadsworth Publishing Company, a division of International Thomson Publishing Inc.; *Figure 1.21*: Goldstein, M., Simonetti, G. and Watschinger, M. (1984) *Complete Guide to Trees and their Identification*, Macdonald Illustrated; *Figure 1.28*: Lowson, J. M., revised and rewritten by Howarth, W. O. and Warne, L. G. G., *Textbook of Botany*, 10th edn, 1953, University Tutorial Press Ltd; *Figure 1.32*: from Gunning, B. E. S. and Steer, M. W., *Plant Cell Biology: An Ultrastructural Approach*, Edward Arnold; *Figure 1.34d*: Courtesy of Dr D. E. Juniper, Botany School, Oxford University; *Figure 1.38c*: from Cutter, E. G. (1978) *Plant Anatomy*, Edward Arnold Publishers.

CHAPTER 2

FIGURES

Figures 2.6, 2.10, 2.17 and 2.26: Taiz, L. and Zeiger, E. (1998) *Plant Physiology*, 2nd edn, Sinauer Associates Inc; *Figure 2.3*: Courtesy of J. Barber, Imperial College, London; *Figures 2.4, 2.8 and 2.11a*: Hall, D. O. and Rao, K. K. (1999) *Photosynthesis*, 2nd edn, Cambridge University Press; *Figure 2.5*: D. J. Simpson; *Figure 2.7*: Courtesy of T. Vogelmann; *Figure 2.9*: Demmig-Adams, B. and Adams III, W. W. (1992) 'Photoprotection and other responses of plants to high light stress', with permission, from the *Annual Review of Plant Physiology and*

Plant Molecular Biology, **43** © 1992 by Annual Reviews www.AnnualReviews.org; *Figure 2.13b*: Bassham, T. A. (1965) 'Photosynthesis: The path of carbon' in *Plant Biochemistry*, 2nd edn, Academic Press; *Figure 2.11*: Dr Kari Lounatoa/ Science Photo Library; *Figure 2.14*: Reprinted from *Biochim. Biophys. Acta*, **1015**, Gutteridge, S. (1990) pp. 1–14, Copyright © 1990, with permission from Elsevier Science; *Figure 2.19*: Badger, M. R. and Dean Price, G. (1994) 'The role of carbonic anhydrase in photosynthesis', with permission, from the *Annual Review of Plant Physiology and Plant Molecular Biology,* **45**, © 1994 by Annual Reviews www.AnnualReviews.org; *Figure 2.22*: reproduced, with permission, from the *Annual Review of Plant Physiology,* **29**, © 1978 by Annual Reviews www.AnnualReviews.org; *Figure 2.25*: Courtesy of P. W. Rundel; *Figure 2.28b*: reproduced, with permission, from the *Annual Review of Plant Physiology,* **28**, © 1977 by Annual Reviews www.AnnualReviews.org; *Figure 2.31*: Dennis, D. T., Layzell, D. B. Lefebvre, D. D. and Turpin, D. H. (eds) (1997) *Plant Metabolism,* Longman, by permission of Pearson Education Inc; *Figure 2.32*: reproduced, with permission, from the *Annual Review of Plant Physiology,* **31**, © 1980 by Annual Reviews www.AnnualReviews.org.

CHAPTER 3

FIGURES

Figure 3.2b: O'Brien T. P. and McCully, M. E. (1969) *Plant Structure and Development,* Macmillan Publishers; *Figure 3.3*: Jackson, M. B. (1983), in Jackson, M. B. and Stead, A. D. (eds) *Growth Regulators in Root Development,* Monograph 10, British Plant Growth Regulator Group, Wantage; *Figure 3.5*: Steudle, E. and Peterson, C. A. (1997) 'How does water get through roots?', *Journal of Experimental Botany,* **49**, No. 322, pp. 775–788, reproduced by permission of Oxford University Press; *Figures 3.9 and 3.49*: Taiz, L. and Zeiger, E. (1998) *Plant Physiology,* Sinauer Associates Inc; *Figure 3.11*: Deri Tomos, A. and Leigh, R. A. (1999) 'The pressure probe: A versatile tool in plant cell physiology', with permission, from the *Annual Review of Plant Physiology and Plant Molecular Biology,* **50**, © 1999 by Annual Reviews www.AnnualReviews.org; *Figure 3.13*: Milburn, J. A. (1979) *Water Flow in Plants,* Longman Group, by permission of Pearson Education Ltd; *Figure 3.14*: Syracuse University Press; *Figure 3.21*: Humble, G. D. and Raschke, K. (1971) *Plant Physiology*, **48**, pp. 447–453, American Society of Plant Physiologists; *Figure 3.23*: Talbott, L. D. and Zeiger, E. (1997) 'The role of sucrose in guard cell osmoregulation', *Journal of Experimental Botany*, **49**, Special Issue, pp. 329–337, March 1998, by permission of Oxford University Press; *Figure 3.24a*: Woodward, F. I. (1997) 'Do plants really need stomata?', *Journal of Experimental Botany*, **49**, Special Issue, pp. 471–480, March 1998, by permission of Oxford University Press; *Figure 3.24b*: Oxford University Press; *Figure 3.25*: Adapted from Srivastava, A. and Zeiger, E. (1995) Guard cell zeaxanthin tracks photosynthetic active radiation and stomatal apertures in *Vicia faba* leaves, *Plant Cell and Environment*, **18**, pp. 813–817; *Figure 3.26*: Zeiger, E. and Jianxin Zhu (1997) 'Role of zeaxanthin in blue light photoreception and the modulation of light–CO_2 interactions in guard cells' *Journal of Experimental Botany*, **49**, Special

Issue, pp. 433–442, March 1998, by permission of Oxford University Press; *Figure 3.27*: from *Plant Physiology*, 3rd edn, by Frank B. Salisbury and Cleon W. Ross © 1985 by Wadsworth Inc., reprinted by permission of the publisher; *Figures 3.29 and 3.30*: Tardieu, F. and Simonneau, T. (1997) 'Variability among species of stomatal control under fluctuating soil water status and evaporative demand: modelling isohydric and anisohydric behaviours', *Journal of Experimental Botany*, **49**, Special Issue, pp. 419–432, March 1998, by permission of Oxford University Press; *Figure 3.31*: Woodell, S. R. J. (1973) *Xerophytes*, Oxford University Press; *Figure 3.35*: Rundel, P. W. (1982) 'Water uptake by organs other than roots', *Encyclopedia of Plant Physiology*, **12B**, pp. 111–134, Springer Verlag; *Figure 3.37*: Smith, S. D., Monson, R. K. and Anderson, J. E. (1997) *Physiological Ecology of North American Desert Plants*, Springer Verlag; *Figure 3.38*: Weier, T. E., Stocking, R. C. and Barbour, M. G. (1974) *Botany: An Introduction to Plant Biology*, reproduced by permission of John Wiley and Sons Inc.; *Figure 3.39*: Mike Jones; *Figure 3.41*: Rabideau and Burr (1945) *American Journal of Botany*, No. 32, Botanical Society of America; *Figure 3.42*: Reproduced by permission of the American Society of Plant Physiology; *Figure 3.43*: Zimmermann, M. H. and Milburn, J. A. (1975) *Encyclopedia of Plant Physiology*, Vol. 1, Part 1, reproduced by permission of Springer-Verlag; *Figures 3.46 and 3.48*: Johnson, R. P. C. (1978) 'The microscopy of P-protein filaments in freeze-etched sieve pores', *Planta*, **143**, 1978, reproduced by permission of Springer-Verlag.

Chapter 4

Figures

Figure 4.7: Adapted from Novacky, A. *et al.* (1980) 'pH and membrane potential changes during glucose uptake in *Lemna gibba* G1 and their response to light', *Planta,* **149**, Springer-Verlag GMBH & Co. KG; *Figure 4.14*: Adapted from Marschner, H., *Mineral Nutrition of Higher Plants,* 2nd edn, p. 53, © 1995, by permission of the publisher Academic Press, London; *Figure 4.15*: Redrawn from Clarkson, D. T. and Saker, L. R. (1989) 'Sulphate influx in wheat and barley roots becomes more sensitive to specific protein-binding reagents when plants are sulphate sufficient', *Planta,* **178**, Springer-Verlag GMBH & Co. KG Springer-Verlag GMBH & Co. KG; *Figure 4.16*: Courtesy of D. Clarkson; *Figure 4.18*: Originally from Tarafdar and Jungk (1987), reprinted from Marschner, H., *Mineral Nutrition of Higher Plants*, p. 560, © 1995 Academic Press Ltd. *Figure 4.19*: With permission from the *Annual Review of Plant Physiology,* **36**, © 1985 by Annual Reviews, www.AnnualReviews.org; *Figure 4.22*: From Jackson, M. B. and Stead, A. D. (1983), *Growth Regulators in Root Development,* Monograph No. 10, British Society for Plant Growth Regulation; *Figure 4.23*: O'Brien T. P. and McCully M.E. (1969), *Plant Structure and Development*, Macmillan Publishers; *Figure 4.24*: From Bonfante-Fasolo, P. 'Plant–fungal interface in VA mycorrhizas: a structural point of view' in Read *et al.*, (1992) *Mycorrhizas in Ecosystems,* CAB International; *Figure 4.25a*: Courtesy of H. J. Denny; *Figure 4.27*: From Le Tacon *et al.*,'Variations in field response of forest trees to nursery ectomycorrhizal inoculation in Europe' in Read *et al.*

(1992) *Mycorrhizas in Ecosystems,* CAB International; *Figure 4.28a*: Professor R. J. P. Williams, *The biological role of molybdenum*, Climax Molybdenum Company Limited (1978); *Figure 4.30*: Permission originally granted by John Wiley & Sons, Inc. for reproduction in Chandler, J. A., *X-ray Microanalysis in the Electron Microscope,* Elsevier Science; *Figures 4.32, 4.33 and 4.34*: Denny, H. J. and Wilkins, D. A. (1987) 'Zinc tolerance in *Betula* spp. IV', *The New Phytologist,* **106**, © The New Phytologist; *Figures 4.35, 4.36a, 4.37 and 4.40*: Courtesy of H. Denny; *Figure 4.38*: Gucci *et al.* (1996), 'Salinity tolerance in *Phillyrea* species', *The New Phytologist,* **135**, © The New Phytologist; *Figure 4.39*: Reprinted from Chandler, J. A., *X-ray Microanalysis in the Electron Microscope,* © 1997, p. 332, with permission from Elsevier Science; *Figure 4.41*: Huang, J. W. *et al.* (1996)'Aluminium interactions with voltage-dependent calcium transport in plasma membrane vesicles isolated from roots of aluminium-sensitive and -resistant wheat cultivars', *Plant Physiology,* **110**, American Society of Plant Physiologists; *Figures 4.42, 4.43 and 4.44*: Pellet, D. M. *et al.* (1996) 'Multiple aluminium-resistance mechanisms in wheat', *Plant Physiology,* **112**, 1996, American Society of Plant Physiologists; *Figure 4.45*: Rorison, I. H. (1968) 'The response to phosphorus of some ecologically distinct plant species. I. Growth rates and phosphorus absorption', *The New Phytologist,* **67**, © The New Phytologist.

TABLES

Table 4.3: Hoffland, E., Findenegg, G. R. and Nelemans, J. A. (1989) 'Solubilization of rock phosphate by rape. II. Local root exudation of organic acids as a response to P-starvation', *Plant Soil,* **113**, Kluwer Academic Publishers.

CHAPTER 5

FIGURES

Figure 5.1: Howell, S. H.(1988) *Molecular Genetics of Plant Development,* Cambridge University Press; *Figure 5.2*: Based on Neuffer, M. G. (1994) 'Mutagenesis', in Freeling, M., and Walbot, V. (eds) *The Maize Handbook,* p. 214, Springer-Verlag GmbH & Co. KG, New York; *Figure 5.3*: Reproduced with permission from Nature, Mayer U. *et al.* (1991), 'Mutations affecting body organization in the *Arabidopsis* embryo', *Nature*, **353**, Macmillan Magazines Ltd; *Figure 5.4*: Reprinted with permission from Goldberg, R. B. *et al.* (1994), *Science,* **266**, copyright © 1994, American Association for the Advancement of Science; *Figure 5.5*: From McCarty, D. R. *et al.* (1991) 'The *viviparous*-1 developmental gene of maize encodes a novel transcriptional activator', *Cell*, **66**, p. 896, reprinted by permission of the author and Cell Press; *Figure 5.9*: Data courtesy of Dr J. Roberts, Company of Biologists, on behalf of the Society for Experimental Biology; *Figure 5.10*: From Guzman, P. and Ecker, J. R. (1990) 'Exploiting the triple response of *Arabidopsis* to identify ethylene-related mutants', *Plant Cell*, **2**, p. 515, reprinted by permission of the American Society of Plant Physiologists; *Figure 5.13*: Courtesy of Patrick Mason; *Figure 5.14*: Ranson J. S. and Moore R. (1983), *American Journal of Botany*, **70**, pp. 1048–

1056; *Figure 5.16*: Reprinted with permission from Goldberg *et al.* (1994) *Science,* **266**, 1994, copyright © 1994 American Association for the Advancement of Science; *Figure 5.18*: With permission from the *Annual Review of Plant Physiology and Plant Molecular Biology*, **33**, © 1982 by Annual Reviews www.AnnualReviews.org; *Figures 5.19–5.23*: From Waring, P. F. and Phillips, I. D. J., *Control of Growth and Differentiation in Plants*, Reprinted by permission of Butterworth–Heinemann; *Figure 5.27*: Courtesy of Dr R. Firn; *Figures 5.31 and 5.34*: Hart, J. W. (1988), *Light and Plant Growth,* Kluwer Academic Press; *Figure 5.39a, b*: Gustafson Brown C., Savidge B. and Yanofsky M. F. (1994) Regulation of the *Arabidopsis* floral homeotic gene APETALAI, *Cell,* **76**, p. 132, reprinted by permission of the author and Cell Press; *Figure 5.39c, d*: Bowman J. L., Smyth, D. R. and Meyerowitz, E. M. (1989) 'Genes directing flower development in *Arabidopsis*' *Plant Cell*, **1**, p. 39, reprinted by permission of the American Society of Plant Physiologists; *Figure 5.40*: Reproduced with permission from *Nature*, Theissen, G. and Saedler, H. (2001) 'Floral quartets', *Nature,* **409**, Macmillan Magazines Ltd; *Figure 5.41*: Reproduced with permission from *Nature*, Smith, C. J. S. *et al.* (1988) 'Antisense RNA inhibition of polygalacturonase gene expression in transgenic tomatoes', *Nature,* **334**, Macmillan Magazines Ltd; *Figure 5.42*: Raven, P. H., Evert, R. F. and Eichhorn, S. E., *Biology of Plants* © 1971, 1976, 1981, 1986, 1992, 1999 by W. H. Freeman and Company/Worth Publishers. Used with permission; *Figure 5.43*: Gray, J. and Johal, G. S. 'Programmed cell death in plants' in Anderson, M. and Roberts, J. (eds) *Arabidopsis,* Sheffield Academic Press.

CHAPTER 6

FIGURES

Figure 6.1: Johnson, N. C. *et al.* (1997) *The New Phytologist,* **135**, The New Phytologist; *Figure 6.2*: Udvardi, M. K. and Day, D. A. (1997) *Annual Review of Plant Physiology and Plant Molecular Biology*, **48**; *Figure 6.3*: Fisher, F. *et al.* (1992) *Nature,* **357**, No. 6373, Macmillan Magazines Limited, reprinted with permission from *Nature*, copyright © 1992; *Figures 6.4a, 6.8a and 6.12*: Carlile, M. J. and Watkinson, S. C. (1994) *The Fungi*, Academic Press Limited; *Figures 6.5a, b and 6.27*: Smith, F. A. and Read, D. J. (1977) *Mycorrhizal Symbiosis* (2nd edn), Academic Press Limited; *Figures 6.6, 6.8b and 6.9*: Webster, J. (1970) *Introduction to Fungi*, Cambridge University Press, © John Webster; *Figure 6.7*: Courtesy of C. Grabski and R. Guggenheim, SEM Laboratory, University of Basel, in cooperation with SANDOZ AGRO AG, Basel, Switzerland; *Figure 6.10*: Kellock, N. D. *et al.* (1992) *Perspectives in Plant Cell Recognition*, Cambridge University Press; *Figure 6.13*: Van Etten, H. D. and Tegtmeier, K. J. (1982) *Phytopathology*, **72**, American Phytopathological Society; *Figure 6.14*: Biophoto Associates; *Figure 6.16*: Lamb, C. and Dixon, R. A. (1997) *Annual Review of Plant Physiology and Plant Molecular Biology*, **48**, Annual Reviews, Inc.; *Figure 6.20*: De Wit, P. J. G. M. (1997) *Trends in Plant Science,* **2**, No.12, December 1977, Elsevier Science Publishers Ltd; *Figure 6.22*: Heidstra, R. and Bisseling, T. (1996) *The New Phytologist*, The New Phytologist; *Figures 6.24, 6.25, 6.26 and 6.28*: Johnson, N. C. *et al.* (1997) 'The functioning of mycorrhizal systems is mediated by a hierarchy of abiotic and biotic factors', *The New Phytologist,* **133**, The New Phytologist; *Figure 6.29*: Read, D. J. (1998) 'Possible basis for the effects of fungal species richness on plant biodiversity and production'. Reprinted with permission from *Nature,* **396**, November 1998, copyright © 1998 Macmillan Magazines Limited; *Figure 6.30*: van der Heijden *et al*. (1998), reprinted with permission from *Nature,* **396**, November 1998, copyright © 1998 Macmillan Magazines Limited.

TABLES

Table 6.1: Jasper, D.A. *et al*. (1991) *The New Phytologist,* **118**, The New Phytologist.

Every effort has been made to trace all the copyright owners, but if any has been inadvertently overlooked, the publishers will be pleased to make the necessary arrangements at the first opportunity.

INDEX

Note: Entries in **bold** are key terms. Page numbers referring to information that is given only in a figure or caption are printed in *italics*.

D

E

O

P

S